ZURICH

BUSINESS TAX
AND LAW
HANDBOOK

4th edition

David Bertram

CLAYFIELD PROFESSIONAL GUIDANCE LTD

Richard Lawson

PEARSON EDUCATION LIMITED

Head Office:
Edinburgh Gate
Harlow CM20 2JE
Tel: +44 (0)1279 623623
Fax: +44 (0)1279 431059

London Office:
128 Long Acre, London WC2E 9AN
Tel: +44 (0)20 7447 2000
Fax: +44 (0)20 7447 2170
Websites: www.business-minds.com
www.pearsoned-ema.com

This edition first published in Great Britain in 2003 by Pearson Education

ISBN 0 273 66216 3

British Library Cataloguing in Publication Data
A CIP catalogue record for this book can be obtained
from the British Library

10 9 8 7 6 5 4 3 2 1

Typeset by M Rules
Printed and bound in Great Britain by Biddles Ltd, Guildford and King's Lynn

*The Publishers' policy is to use paper manufactured
from sustainable forests.*

CONTENTS

Preface   xiii

Abbreviations   xiv

1   INTRODUCTION   1

    1.1   Scope of income tax   1
    1.2   How are taxable profits computed?   1
    1.3   Capital gains tax   2
    1.4   Value added tax (VAT)   2
    1.5   Stamp duty   2
    1.6   Contract law   3
    1.7   Sale of goods   3
    1.8   Business tenancies   3
    1.9   Employment law   3
    1.10   Employee compensation   3
    1.11   Life assurance, pensions and permanent health insurance   4
    1.12   Health and safety at work   4
    1.13   Partnership law   4
    1.14   Taxation of unincorporated businesses   5
    1.15   Company law   5
    1.16   How companies are taxed   5
    1.17   Tax and the company proprietor   6
    1.18   Inheritance tax and business property   6
    1.19   Connected persons   6

2   SCOPE OF INCOME TAX   12

    2.1   Scope of taxes on property, profits or gains   12
    2.2   Income tax charge on 'property, profits or gains'   13
    2.3   Schedule D: Annual profits or gains   13
    2.4   Schedule D Cases I and II   16
    2.5   Schedule D Case III   26
    2.6   Schedule D Cases IV and V   27
    2.7   Schedule D Case VI   28
    2.8   Schedule E   28

3	**COMPUTING TRADING PROFITS FOR TAX PURPOSES**	**29**
3.1	How taxable profits are arrived at	29
3.2	Period in which receipt assessable or deduction allowable	36
3.3	Adjustment on change of basis	42
3.4	Expenditure	48
3.5	Receipts	69
3.6	Capital or revenue?	71
3.7	Transfer pricing	73
3.8	Charge or expense?	74
3.9	Research and development (R&D)	74
3.10	Intellectual property	84

4	**CAPITAL ALLOWANCES: BASIC PRINCIPLES**	**94**
4.1	Capital allowances generally	94

PLANT AND MACHINERY ALLOWANCES

4.2	What is plant or machinery?	102
4.3	Availability of plant and machinery allowances	105
4.4	Qualifying activities	106
4.5	Qualifying expenditure	107
4.6	First-year qualifying expenditure	112
4.7	Allowances and charges	121
4.8	Hire-purchase etc and plant or machinery provided by lessee	128
4.9	Computer software	130
4.10	Expensive cars	131
4.11	Short-life assets	134
4.12	Long-life assets	136
4.13	Overseas leasing	139
4.14	Ships	139
4.15	Provisions affecting mineral and oil industries	140
4.16	Fixtures	140
4.17	Asset provided or used only partly for qualifying activity	154
4.18	Partial depreciation subsidies	155
4.19	Anti-avoidance	156
4.20	Supplementary provisions	156

OTHER ALLOWANCES

4.21	Industrial buildings allowance	157
4.22	Agricultural buildings allowances	183
4.23	Flat conversion allowance	192
4.24	Mineral extraction allowances	199
4.25	Research and development allowances	199
4.26	Know-how allowances	203

4.27	Patent allowances	206
4.28	Dredging allowances	209
4.29	Dwelling houses let on assured tenancies	209
4.30	Contributions	210
4.31	Renewals basis	214

5 MAIN PRINCIPLES OF CAPITAL GAINS TAX 215

5.1	Basic outline of capital gains tax	215
5.2	Who is subject to capital gains tax?	216
5.3	What assets are chargeable assets?	217
5.4	Which types of transaction may produce a chargeable gain?	219
5.5	Computation of capital gains	224
5.6	Taper relief	229
5.7	Some special problem areas	242

6 CAPITAL GAINS TAX AND BUSINESS TRANSACTIONS 248

6.1	Loans to private businesses	248
6.2	Losses on unquoted shares	249
6.3	Roll-over relief	251
6.4	Hold-over relief: gifts of business property	255
6.5	Partners and capital gains	258
6.6	Limited liability partnerships (LLPs)	260
6.7	Retirement relief – general provisions	261
6.8	Retirement relief and unincorporated traders	264
6.9	Retirement relief: full-time directors and employees	266

7 OUTLINE OF VAT 268

7.1	Introduction	268
7.2	Legal authorities	269
7.3	Basic principles	270
7.4	Taxable persons	270
7.5	Business	284
7.6	Acquisition of goods from member states	285
7.7	Importation of goods from outside the member states	285
7.8	Goods subject to a fiscal warehouse regime	285
7.9	Determination of value	285
7.10	Payment of VAT by taxable persons	286
7.11	Reliefs, exemptions and repayments	290
7.12	Application of VATA 1994 in certain cases	296
7.13	Supplementary provisions	314

7.14	Accounting for VAT	317
7.15	Imports, exports and single market	321
7.16	Special schemes	323
7.17	Enforcement procedures	324
7.18	Fraud	328
7.19	Appeals	328

8 STAMP DUTY AND BUSINESS TRANSACTIONS — **330**

8.1	Documents liable to duty	330
8.2	Sanctions where duty not paid	336
8.3	Avoiding or reducing duty	338
8.4	Explanatory leaflets	345
8.5	Development of stamp duty	345

9 CONTRACT LAW — **346**

9.1	Offer	346
9.2	Acceptance	349
9.3	Consideration	352
9.4	Mistake	354
9.5	Misrepresentation	358
9.6	Duress and undue influence	361
9.7	Terms of contract	366
9.8	Exemption and exclusion clauses	372
9.9	Breach of contract	380
9.10	Frustration	382
9.11	Privity of contract	384
9.12	Damages	388

10 SALE OF GOODS AND CONSUMER PROTECTION — **389**

10.1	Terms implied into a sale of goods contract	389
10.2	Description	390
10.3	Fitness for purpose and quality	390
10.4	Sale by sample	392
10.5	Exclusion of implied terms	392
10.6	Breach of an implied term	392
10.7	Stipulations of time	393
10.8	Contracts similar to contracts of sale	393
10.9	Passing of property and risk	393
10.10	Delivery and acceptance	395
10.11	Sales by a non-owner	397
10.12	Remedies of the seller	398

| | 10.13 | Remedies of the buyer | 399 |
| | 10.14 | Consumer protection | 401 |

11 BUSINESS PREMISES 408

NICHOLAS MARSHALL

	11.1	Introduction	408
	11.2	What is a protected business tenancy?	408
	11.3	Privity and continuing liability	412
	11.4	Covenant strength	414
	11.5	Rent reviews	416
	11.6	During the lease	419
	11.7	Expiry of the lease	423

12 EMPLOYMENT LAW 431

	12.1	The impact of EU law	431
	12.2	Employment: the worker's status	432
	12.3	The employee	436
	12.4	The contract of employment	437
	12.5	The doctrine of restraint of trade	440
	12.6	Written particulars of employment	442
	12.7	Work permits and immigration matters	445
	12.8	Continuity of employment	448
	12.9	Working time	451
	12.10	Unfair dismissal	454
	12.11	Redundancy	472
	12.12	Termination of employment	477
	12.13	Maternity rights	483
	12.14	Parental leave	490
	12.15	Statutory sick pay (SSP)	494
	12.16	Further statutory payments to employees	496
	12.17	Itemised pay statements	498
	12.18	Wages: payment and deductions	498
	12.19	The minimum wage	500
	12.20	Sex and race discrimination	501
	12.21	Discrimination on grounds of disability	510
	12.22	Equal pay	514
	12.23	Insolvency of employer	518
	12.24	Transfer of Undertakings (Protection of Employment) Regs 1981 (TUPE)	520
	12.25	Data subjects' rights	527
	12.26	Access to medical reports	528

13 TAX AND EMPLOYEE COMPENSATION   531

13.1	Schedule E	531
13.2	PAYE	533
13.3	Benefits in kind	541
13.4	Travelling, subsistence and entertaining	550
13.5	Company cars	553
13.6	Beneficial loans	560
13.7	Living accommodation	561
13.8	Miscellaneous benefits	563
13.9	End of year returns	566
13.10	Personal service companies	566
13.11	Gifts of shares	574
13.12	Non-approved share options	575
13.13	Profit-sharing schemes	577
13.14	Share option schemes	578
13.15	Executive share option schemes	578
13.16	Special employee shares	580
13.17	National insurance contributions (NICs)	580
13.18	Enterprise management incentives	587
13.19	Termination payments	589
13.20	How the Inland Revenue ensures compliance	591

14 LIFE ASSURANCE, PENSIONS AND PERMANENT HEALTH INSURANCE   594

VINCE JERRARD

14.1	Introduction	594

PART I – THE BASICS

14.2	Life assurance	595
14.3	Pensions	600
14.4	Permanent health insurance	607

PART II – THE USES

14.5	Introduction	608
14.6	Sole traders	609
14.7	Partners	612
14.8	Companies	614

15 HEALTH AND SAFETY   618

JEREMY STRANKS

15.1	Introduction	618
15.2	Health and Safety at Work etc Act 1974 (HSWA)	619

15.3 Current trends in health and safety legislation 624
15.4 Management of Health and Safety at Work Regs 1999 625
15.5 Criminal and civil liability 632
15.6 Workplace (Health, Safety and Welfare) Regs 1992 635
15.7 Provision and Use of Work Equipment Regs 1998 636
15.8 Personal Protective Equipment at Work Regs 1992 638
15.9 Manual Handling Operations Regulations 1992 639
15.10 Health and Safety (Display Screen Equipment) Regs 1992 639
15.11 Fire Precautions (Workplace) Regs 1997 641
15.12 Lifting Operations and Lifting Equipment Regs 1998 643
15.13 Control of Substances Hazardous To Health (COSHH) Regs 1999 644
15.14 Health and Safety (Information for Employees) Regs 1999 646
15.15 Reporting injuries, diseases and dangerous occurrences 647
15.16 Compulsory insurance 649
15.17 Consultation with employees 649
15.18 Conclusion 652

16 PARTNERSHIP LAW **654**

KEITH HATCHICK
16.1 What is a partnership? 654
16.2 Limited partnership 655
16.3 Limited Liability Partnership Act 2000 655
16.4 Is there an agreement? 657
16.5 The salaried partner 657
16.6 Partnership and third parties 658
16.7 Liability of partners 659
16.8 Partnership agreement 660
16.9 Dissolution and winding-up 664
16.10 EEIGs 667

17 HOW AN UNINCORPORATED BUSINESS IS TAXED ON ITS PROFITS **668**

SELF-EMPLOYED INDIVIDUALS
17.1 Current year basis 668
17.2 Capital allowance basis periods 672

PARTNERSHIPS
17.3 Assessment of firm's profits: special rules 673
17.4 Treatment of other income 674
17.5 Qualifying loans 674

MISCELLANEOUS

17.6	Relief for trading losses	676
17.7	Post-cessation receipts and expenses	683

PRACTICAL ASPECTS AND INTRODUCTION OF SELF-ASSESSMENT AND HOW IT AFFECTS SELF-EMPLOYED INDIVIDUALS

17.8	Outline of new regime	684
17.9	Penalties and interest charges	688
17.10	Achieving finality	691

ANNUAL PAYMENTS, NICS ETC

17.11	Miscellaneous practical aspects	692
17.12	Limited liability partnerships (LLPs)	693

OPERATING AS AN UNINCORPORATED BUSINESS

17.13	Bringing in a partner (and becoming a partner)	697
17.14	Buying out a partner	699

OPERATING AS A LIMITED COMPANY

17.15	General tax considerations	701
17.16	Possible disadvantages	703
17.17	Other tax aspects	705
17.18	Transferring a business to a company	706

SALE OF THE BUSINESS AND CESSATION

17.19	Sale	711
17.20	Cessation	712

18 COMPANY LAW — **714**

KEITH HATCHICK

18.1	What is a company?	714
18.2	Memorandum of association	716
18.3	Re-registration	718
18.4	After incorporation	720
18.5	Directors	726
18.6	Meetings	733
18.7	Share capital	743
18.8	Dividends	749
18.9	*Ultra vires*	750
18.10	Auditors	751
18.11	Selection of administrative documents to be filed at Companies House	753

19 HOW COMPANIES ARE TAXED   756

19.1 Liability for corporation tax and how 'profits' are defined   756
19.2 Accounting periods, rates and payment of tax   758
19.3 Companies' capital gains   761
19.4 Interest and other charges   762
19.5 Taxation of company distributions   764
19.6 Losses   766
19.7 Groups of companies   768
19.8 Close and investment companies   771
19.9 Double taxation relief on foreign income   773
19.10 Controlled foreign companies and anti-avoidance legislation   774
19.11 Forex transactions   777
19.12 Claims and elections   781

20 ENVIRONMENTAL TAXES   783

20.1 Landfill tax (LFT)   783
20.2 Climate change levy (CCL)   787
20.3 Aggregates levy (AL)   790

21 TAX AND THE COMPANY PROPRIETOR   794

21.1 Buying a company   794
21.2 Corporation tax planning   796
21.3 Treatment of remuneration for PAYE and NICs purposes   798
21.4 Benefits-in-kind   799
21.5 Dividends   800
21.6 Loans to the company   800
21.7 Loans by the company   801
21.8 Sale and purchase of assets by the company   802
21.9 Self-administered pension schemes   805
21.10 Raising business finance   807
21.11 Purchase of own shares   811
21.12 Demergers   813
21.13 Longer term capital gains tax planning   815
21.14 Anti-avoidance legislation   817
21.15 Sale of the company   819

22 INHERITANCE TAX AND BUSINESS PROPERTY   822

22.1 Persons subject to IHT   822
22.2 When a charge arises   822
22.3 Transfers of value   823

22.4   Gifts which are not transfers of value   824
22.5   Exempt transfers   827
22.6   Potentially exempt transfers   830
22.7   Reservation of benefit   831
22.8   Business property   833
22.9   Agricultural property   835
22.10 Computation of tax on lifetime transfers   836
22.11 Computation of tax payable on death   837
22.12 Handing on the family business/company without attracting IHT   839

Index   **845**

NI	national insurance
NICs	national insurance contributions
NRE	net relevant earnings
OFT	Office of Fair Trading
PAYE	Pay As You Earn
PET	potentially exempt transfer
PHI	permanent health insurance
PPE	personal protective equipment
PPP	Personal Pension Plan
PSO	Pension Schemes Office
PY basis	preceding year basis
QCB	qualifying corporate bond
QHP	qualifying holding period
R&D	research and development
RPO	relevant period of ownership
RRA	Race Relations Act 1976
SDA	Sex Discrimination Act 1975
SERPS	State Earnings Related Pensions Scheme
SDRT	stamp duty reserve tax
SME	small or medium-sized enterprise
SMP	statutory maternity pay
SP	Inland Revenue Statement of Practice
SSAP	Statement of Standard Accounting Practice (issued by the Institute of Chartered Accountants)
SSP	statutory sick pay
TA 1988	Income and Corporation Taxes Act 1988
TCGA 1992	Taxation of Chargeable Gains Act 1992
TMA 1970	Taxes Management Act 1970
TULR(C)A	Trade Union and Labour Relations (Consolidation) Act 1992
TURERA	Trade Union Reform and Employment Rights Act 1978
VAT	value added tax
VATA 1994	Value Added Tax Act 1994
WFTC	working families' tax credit

ZURICH

Other titles in the Zurich Handbook series

TAX HANDBOOK 2002/2003

Long established as one of the UK's leading tax guides, the *Tax Handbook* is an invaluable, comprehensive reference source on all aspects of taxation. Written by experienced tax experts to meet the needs of both the professional and non-professional alike, it provides all the information you need to effectively manage any issues relating to tax.

ZURICH INVESTMENT & SAVINGS HANDBOOK 2002/2003

The *Investment & Savings Handbook 2002/2003* guides you through the complexities surrounding the abundance of financial products available, so that you can make informed choices for your investment strategy. Completely up to date with the latest legislation, it highlights the significant changes in the law and how they will impact on your investments and savings.

ZURICH EXPATRIATE TAX & INVESTMENT (8th edition)

For British citizens living abroad this book offers essential guidance on how to manage their financial affairs to their greatest possible advantage. It provides comprehensive coverage of every aspect of expatriate tax and investment from the effect of the single currency to advice on working abroad.

PENSIONS HANDBOOK (8th edition)

This is the complete guide to pension planning, whether you are a business owner, company director, self-employed or a professional pension planner. It examines the different pension choices available and how they work, explains the Inland Revenue requirements that must be followed and shows how individual pensions operate.

RETIREMENT PLANNING HANDBOOK (8th edition)

The *Retirement Planning Handbook* focuses on the financial mechanics of planning a stress-free retirement with no financial worries. It enables you to implement a retirement plan successfully and ensures that you are fully aware of the long- and short-term investment opportunities.

ESTATE PLANNING & TAXATION OF CAPITAL HANDBOOK (3rd edition)

This is an invaluable guide to estate planning, whether you are an individual wishing to control who benefits from your estate, or a professional advisor. It enables you to grasp the implications of capital taxation on personal business and family wealth and how, by careful planning, its impact can be legally mitigated.

**For further information contact your local bookseller,
telephone Pearson Education Ltd on 01279 623333,
e-mail at customer.orders@pearsoned-ema.com
or visit our website www.business-minds.com/zurich**

1

INTRODUCTION

Being in business is not easy and there is a multitude of legal obligations and reporting requirements. A businessman cannot hope to become an expert overnight but he should not just muddle along; if he does so he is bound to come unstuck.

A detailed study of the subject is beyond the scope of this book. Instead, the authors' intention is to describe the basic principles of business tax and law, and to give examples of how these principles work in practice and highlight those areas where the businessman should take professional advice. The following are key aspects to bear in mind.

1.1 SCOPE OF INCOME TAX

UK taxation is based on a schedular system under which various types of income are categorised. Historically there were five Schedules from A to E, with a Schedule F added later. Schedules B and C have been repealed and no longer concern us. Broadly, Schedule A deals with income arising from land; Schedule D covers, exhaustively, annual income and gains; and Schedule E is concerned with income from offices or employments. Schedule F deals with the assessment of income from dividends and other distributions. Capital gains tax (CGT) is levied on chargeable gains realised by individuals, trusts, personal representatives etc on the disposal of capital assets. Corporation tax is charged on the 'profits of companies', which includes both income and chargeable gains.

1.2 HOW ARE TAXABLE PROFITS COMPUTED?

It is important to appreciate that accounts that have been drawn up according to commercial principles may need to be adjusted for tax purposes. For example, there is no tax relief for depreciation charged in accounts, but relief may be due via the capital allowances system.

Accounts should be drawn up on the earnings basis, ie a trader's stock or work in progress at his year end should be brought into account in arriving at his profit. Certain expenses are not allowable for tax purposes, eg entertaining or gifts to customers. A provision for a bad debt can be allowable for tax purposes, but only if it is a specific provision. Bonus payments to employees can be a tax deductible expense even though they are paid after the end of the year. However, they have to be paid within nine months if tax relief is to be obtained for the year to which the bonuses relate. Pension contributions are tax deductible only if they are actually paid during the accounting period.

1.3 CAPITAL GAINS TAX

Chapters 5 and 6 cover CGT as it relates to a businessman. Chapter 5 covers general principles such as what assets are chargeable assets and how a gain is computed for CGT purposes. Particular types of assets such as land and buildings, unquoted shares and foreign property are then discussed. Chapter 6 focuses on various business transactions such as tax relief for a person who has lent money to a businessman where that loan has to be written off, and looks at the circumstances in which income tax relief may be available for a person who has subscribed for shares in an unquoted trading company.

Roll-over relief enables a person who reinvests a capital gain to defer tax. It applies to disposals of land and buildings, goodwill and other similar assets. The relief introduced more recently for reinvestment in unquoted shares is also covered.

Retirement relief is being withdrawn progressively. In its place is a new form of relief, 'taper relief' (see 5.6). Indexation is, in effect, frozen at 5 April 1998. Indexation still applies for companies.

1.4 VALUE ADDED TAX (VAT)

VAT affects almost every businessman. Chapter 7 covers the basic rules as well as those that apply to import and export transactions and special schemes available to traders in certain industries. A trader normally needs to account for VAT on a quarterly basis and it is therefore important to understand the procedures properly. The legislation provides certain 'incentives' for traders to comply since interest and penalties may be levied for failure to render returns and pay VAT promptly.

1.5 STAMP DUTY

This tax, established in 1694, is the oldest form of tax in force in the UK. The general principles are covered in Chap 8. Professional advice should be sought, as liability for stamp duty tends to arise only on certain exceptional (but usually larger) transactions such as the purchase, or taking a lease, of premises.

1.6 CONTRACT LAW

In this increasingly litigious age, it is important to understand the basics of the law of contract. Chapter 9 describes the main principles and deals with the situation where things go wrong, eg one party makes a mistake or suffers loss through misrepresentation. The chapter also covers the Unfair Terms in Consumer Contracts Regulations.

1.7 SALE OF GOODS

Sale of goods law is really part of contract law, but it merits a chapter in its own right. The Sale of Goods Act provides that certain terms are taken as being implied when parties enter into a contract. Chapter 10 also covers matters such as product liability and liability under the Consumer Protection Act.

1.8 BUSINESS TENANCIES

For most businessmen, taking a lease of business premises is their largest single commitment. A lease can be a short- or long-term contract and rent may continue to be payable if the business comes to an end and the premises are no longer needed. Most modern leases contain an obligation on the tenant to return the premises in a fit condition at the end of the lease. It is very important for the tenant to be aware of what he may be letting himself in for. Chapter 11 also takes into account the Landlord and Tenant (Covenants) Act 1995.

1.9 EMPLOYMENT LAW

This is an area of the law where the influence of EU legislation is particularly apparent. Even temporary and part-time employees may acquire significant statutory employment protection rights. It is very important to follow the proper procedures where an employee's work is less than satisfactory or where an employer may need to make the employee redundant. Note that the forthcoming provisions of the Employment Act 2002 will have a bearing on the contents of this chapter.

1.10 EMPLOYEE COMPENSATION

In Chap 13, the rules that require an employer to deduct tax and withhold national insurance contributions (NICs) are set out. The chapter covers matters such as Pay As You Earn – how it works and payments from which

PAYE must be withheld. It then goes on to look at benefits-in-kind, the way in which they are taxed and the returns that must be completed at the end of the year by the employer.

An important element of employee remuneration may consist of special share schemes and these are covered in some detail. Also discussed are the treatment of redundancy payments and compensation for loss of office, and the way in which the Inland Revenue ensures that the proper procedures are observed. A businessman may encounter the Collector's Audit Division and he may also undergo an investigation by one of the Schedule E Compliance Units – it is important to be prepared.

1.11 LIFE ASSURANCE, PENSIONS AND PERMANENT HEALTH INSURANCE

Chapter 14 covers the basics of life assurance, pensions and permanent health insurance (PHI). It details the different types of policy and sets out the legislation governing them. The second part of the chapter considers the uses of life assurance, pensions and PHI, with particular emphasis on the business needs of sole traders, partners and small companies.

1.12 HEALTH AND SAFETY AT WORK

There is a mass of legislation and European and Government regulation covering health and safety. In some situations, an employer who has transgressed could be exposed to criminal liability. Even in cases where only civil penalties are involved, it is not a matter to be taken lightly as the Health and Safety Executive or the local authority may have the power to compel a person to cease trading until certain work is carried out to ensure that adequate standards are in operation. Chapter 15 offers a basic introduction to this complex area.

1.13 PARTNERSHIP LAW

The Partnership Act was passed in 1890 and has been supplemented by a number of cases that have come before the courts over the last 100 years. Entering into a partnership requires careful consideration, as a partner may be jointly and severally liable for all the firm's debts. The position on tax liabilities has changed with the introduction of self-assessment, but this is merely an exception to the general rule. It is therefore crucially important carefully to regulate certain aspects of the firm's financial affairs to ensure that partners who leave it do not avoid their proper share of any problems and liabilities.

PREFACE

This book has been written because we perceived a need for a practical guide for businessmen and their professional advisers. Business taxation and law are key subjects for any proprietor, director of a private company and for specialists responsible for particular functions such as personnel managers, company secretaries and finance directors. Such business people are typical clients of accountants and solicitors and we know from long experience that they need to be guided through the complex maze of legislation regulation and common law. Very often professional advisers are asked specific questions and we believe that it is essential to put advice into a broader context – half the battle in practice is to identify all pertinent questions and matters to be addressed. We have therefore endeavoured to produce a handbook which describes and explains the main principles that lie behind topics such as employment law, contracts, health and safety at work and taxation. We have sought to identify problem areas and matters on which specific advice should be taken from a professional adviser who specialises in that particular field.

Business taxation and law have changed beyond recognition over the past 25 years. Indeed, much tax law has changed substantially in the last five years, following the 1997 and 2001 General Elections and New Labour's two victories. There will always be a need for a professional adviser who gives general advice, helps clients to identify key questions and then interprets the input from specialists and explains to the client what it means in practice.

The law is stated as at 31 July 2002.

David Bertram
Richard Lawson

ABBREVIATIONS

ACAS	Advisory Conciliation and Arbitration Service
ACT	advance corporation tax
ADRs	American Depositary Receipts
AIM	Alternative Investment Market
APPP	Appropriate Personal Pension Plan
ASB	Accounting Standards Board
CA 1985	Companies Act 1985
CAA 2001	Capital Allowances Act 2001
CFC	controlled foreign company
CGT	capital gains tax
CY basis	current year basis
DDA	Disability Discrimination Act 1995
DG	Director General
DPTC	disabled person's tax credit
ECJ	European Court of Justice
EDT	effective date of termination
EIS	Enterprise Investment Scheme
ERA	Employee Rights Act 1996
ESC	extra statutory concession
ETO reason	economic, technical or organisational reason
EU	European Union
EWC	expected week of childbirth
FA	Finance Act
FRS	Financial Reporting Standards
FRSSE	Financial Reporting Standards for Smaller Entities
FSAVC	Free Standing Additional Voluntary Contributions
GAAP	Generally Accepted Accountancy Practice
HP	hire purchase
HSE	Health & Safety Executive
HSWA 1974	Health and Safety at Work Act 1974
IBA	industrial buildings allowance
IHT	inheritance tax
IHTA 1984	Inheritance Tax Act 1984
LAPR	Life Assurance Premium Relief
LLP	limited liability partnership
LTA	Landlord and Tenant Act

1.14 TAXATION OF UNINCORPORATED BUSINESSES

Not only are there special rules that govern the way in which taxable profits are arrived at, there are also special rules covering the way in which self-employed individuals are taxed.

There are additional complications for partners, over and above the rules that apply to individuals who carry on business on their own account as sole traders.

Chapter 17 covers some of the key issues for self-employed businessmen such as the tax implications of bringing in or buying out a partner. The chapter looks at questions such as whether there are tax benefits in transferring a business to a company and the most tax efficient way in which to achieve such a transfer, and some of the tax aspects that need to be considered where an unincorporated business is sold or closed down.

1.15 COMPANY LAW

It is all too easy for individuals to acquire a company 'off the shelf' from formation agents and to commence trading with little or no understanding of the proper legal procedures. Companies House and the Revenue are increasingly taking a tough line and the well advised businessman needs to understand the basic reporting requirements.

It is also important to make provision in case things start to go wrong or to develop in an unexpected way. Situations are often encountered where a 50% shareholder wishes to disengage from a company and the other shareholder has quite different views on how this should be dealt with. There may be deadlock from a legal viewpoint, which is hardly conducive to achieving an orderly and efficient parting of the ways. Similarly, problems may arise if a director is exceeding his authority and committing the company in ways that are not acceptable to his fellow directors. The position is often made worse because proper procedures were not followed in the past (eg there are no formal minutes of directors' meetings at which policy matters were discussed). As in so many areas, legal disputes may arise simply because a situation has arisen that was not envisaged at the outset; we have therefore endeavoured to provide an overview of relevant aspects of company law that need to be borne in mind by individuals who are directors and/or shareholders in private companies.

1.16 HOW COMPANIES ARE TAXED

If a company is formed to carry on a business, it is important to understand how the company will be treated for tax purposes. A return may be required on a quarterly basis for interest and other annual payments paid by the company. Mainstream corporation tax has to be paid nine months after the year end, although large companies now make their payments by instalments.

Companies are now on the self-assessment system for companies. Automatic penalties and interest charges may apply where accounts are filed late with the Revenue.

There are a number of important claims and elections which may need to be made, usually within a set period of either two or six years. The Revenue normally resists late claims unless there are good reasons why the claim was not made in time.

1.17 TAX AND THE COMPANY PROPRIETOR

Tax is an important consideration for shareholder directors. Chapter 21 looks at points to bear in mind when buying a company, the treatment of shareholder directors, the way in which they are assessed on benefits received by them (or by members of their family) and the tax implications of various transactions with the company. Many shareholder directors tend to use their company as a 'money box' and draw cash during the year in anticipation of bonuses that will be declared at the company's AGM – all very well in theory, but doing this may infringe company law and give rise to a tax charge for the company and a separate tax charge for the director.

Matters are considered such as the purchase of assets from the company (or sales of assets to the company), the rules affecting self-administered pension schemes, possible ways in which a shareholder may be bought out (purchase of own shares and demergers) and more technical issues such as CGT planning and anti-avoidance legislation.

1.18 INHERITANCE TAX AND BUSINESS PROPERTY

Inheritance tax (IHT) may take 40% of an individual's assets on his death after various exemptions and a nil rate band. But there are special reliefs available for businesses and in particular 100% business property relief for unincorporated businesses and substantial shareholders in private trading companies. However, business relief may not always be available as once again there are a number of stringent conditions that need to be satisfied.

1.19 CONNECTED PERSONS

Because it would otherwise be possible to manipulate transactions between connected persons to gain tax advantage, the taxing statutes contain a number of provisions aimed at preventing this. As a general rule, transactions between connected persons are deemed to take place at their market value, and not, if different, some other price attributed thereto by the connected parties. The key pieces of legislation are for income and corporation taxes (TA 1988, s 839), for CGT (TCGA 1992, s 286), and for IHT. The definitions found in TA 1988, s 839 and TCGA 1992, s 286 are, for all practical purposes, identical.

1.19.1 Income and corporation taxes and CGT
(TA 1988, s 839; TCGA 1992, s 286)

Individuals

A person (Y) is connected with an individual (Z) if Y is Z's wife or husband, or is a relative, or the wife or husband of a relative, of Z or of Z's wife or husband. A 'relative' means brother, sister, ancestor or lineal descendant.

Trustees

A person, in his capacity as trustee of a settlement, is connected with:

(1) any individual who in relation to the settlement is a settlor;
(2) any person who is connected with such an individual; and
(3) any body corporate that is connected with that settlement.

A body corporate is connected with a settlement if it is:

(a) a close company (or only not a close company because it is not resident in the UK) and the participators include the settlement trustees; or
(b) controlled (under TA 1988, s 840) by a company falling within (a) above.

Partnerships

Except in relation to acquisitions or disposals of partnership assets pursuant to bona fide commercial arrangements, a person is connected with any person with whom he is in partnership, and with the spouse or relative of any individual with whom he is in partnership.

Companies

A company is connected with another company if:

(1) the same person has control of both, or a person has control of one and persons connected with him, or he and persons connected with him, have control of the other; or

(2) a group of two or more persons has control of each company, and the groups either consist of or could be regarded as consisting of the same persons by treating (in one or more cases) a member of either group as replaced by a person with whom he is connected.

A company is connected with another person if that person has control of it or if that person and persons connected with him together have control of it.

Any two or more persons acting together to secure or exercise control of a company are treated in relation to that company as connected with one another and with any person acting on the directions of any of them to secure or exercise control of the company.

A 'company' includes any body corporate or unincorporated association, but does not include a partnership, and applies to a unit trust scheme as if the scheme were a company and as if the rights of the unit holders were shares in the company.

Control

Two definitions of 'control' are offered. The first, which is of general application, is that found in TA 1988, s 840, namely that in relation to a body corporate (eg 'X Corp') 'control' means the power of a person to secure:

(1) by means of holding shares or possessing voting power in or in relation to X Corp or any other body corporate, or

(2) by virtue of any powers conferred by the articles of association or other document regulating X Corp or any other body corporate

that the affairs of X Corp are conducted in accordance with the wishes of that person, and, in relation to a partnership, means the right to a share of more than one-half of the assets, or of more than one-half of the income, of the partnership.

The second definition is that found in TA 1988, s 416. Strictly, it is a definition for close company purposes. However, it is frequently brought into other legislation. Under s 416, a person is said to have 'control' of a company if he exercises, or is able to exercise or is entitled to acquire, direct or indirect control over the company's affairs, and in particular, but without prejudice to the generality of the preceding words, if he possesses or is entitled to acquire:

(a) the greater part of the share capital or issued share capital of the company or of the voting power in it; or

(b) such part of the issued share capital of the company as would, if the whole of its income were in fact distributed among the participators (without regard to any rights that he or any other person has as a loan creditor), entitle him to receive the greater part of the amount so distributed; or

(c) such rights as would, in the event of the winding-up of the company or in any other circumstances, entitle him to receive the greater part of its assets which would then be available for distribution among the participators.

Where two or more persons together satisfy any of the above conditions, they are taken to have control of the company.

A person is treated as entitled to acquire anything that he is entitled to acquire at a future date, or will at a future date be entitled to acquire.

There is attributed to any person any rights or powers of a nominee for him, ie any rights or powers that another person possesses on his behalf or may be required to exercise on his direction or behalf.

Associates

The rights held by a person's associates may also be attributed to him. Rights which he or his associates control are also attributed to him. Such attributions are made as will result in the company being treated as under the control of five or fewer participators if it can be so treated.

By ESC C9, companies are not associated merely because they are treated as controlled by the same loan creditor if apart from the common creditor there is no other connection between the companies. Also, companies are not associated by reason of taking into account fixed-rate preference shares if certain conditions exist. Further, it depends on the facts whether companies are associated because a person can exercise the rights and powers of his associates. Trustee companies that hold rights and powers and thereby exercise control are not to be treated as associates where the rights are held in trust and there is no other connection between the companies.

For the purposes of 'small companies marginal relief' (TA 1988, s 13), the Revenue will, by concession, not treat companies in certain circumstances as associated, and 'relative' includes only a husband, wife or minor child where there is no substantial commercial interdependence.

The Revenue has announced that two associated companies are under the control of the same person(s) only if an irreducible group of persons having control of one company is identical with an irreducible group of persons having control of the second company. An irreducible group of persons is one which has control but which would not have control if any one of them were excluded.

1.19.2 Inheritance tax

Control of company
(IHTA 1984, ss 269 and 270)

A person has control of a company at any time if he then has the control of powers of voting on all questions affecting the company as a whole which, if exercised, would yield a majority of the votes capable of being exercised on them.

Shares or securities are deemed to give a person control of a company if, together with any shares or securities which are related property (under IHTA 1984, s 161), they would be sufficient to give him control of the company (as defined in 1.19.1).

Where shares or securities are comprised in a settlement, any powers of voting that they give to the trustees of the settlement are for the above purpose deemed to be given to the person beneficially entitled in possession to the shares or securities (except in a case where no individual is so entitled). Where a company has shares or securities of any class giving powers of voting limited to either or both of:

(1) the question of winding up the company, and
(2) any question primarily affecting shares or securities of that class,

the reference above to all questions affecting the company as a whole has effect as a reference to all such questions except any in relation to which those powers are capable of being exercised.

Any question of whether a person is connected with another is determined as it falls to be determined under TCGA 1992, s 286, but as if 'relative' included uncle, aunt, nephew and niece.

IHT also introduces two further concepts: associated operations and related property.

Associated operations
(IHTA 1984, s 268)

'Associated operations' means any two or more operations of any kind, being:

(1) operations that affect the same property, whether directly or indirectly, or income arising from that property, or any property representing accumulations of any such income, or
(2) operations which are effected with reference to others, or to enabling the other to be effected. The operations may be effected by the same person or different persons, and whether or not they are simultaneous; 'operation' includes an omission.

The granting of a lease for full consideration in money or money's worth is not taken to be associated with any operation effected more than three years after the grant.

Where a transfer of value is made by associated operations carried out at different times, it is treated as made at the time of the last of them. However, where any one or more of the earlier operations also constitute a transfer of value made by the same transferor, the value transferred by the earlier operations is treated as reducing the value transferred by all the operations taken together, except to the extent that the transfer constituted by the earlier operations but not that made by all the operations taken together is exempt under IHTA 1984, s 18.

Related property
(IHTA 1984, s 161)

Where the value of any property comprised in a person's estate would be less than the appropriate portion of the value of the aggregate of that and any related property, it shall be the appropriate portion of the value of that aggregate. Property is related to the property comprised in a person's estate if:

(1) it is comprised in the estate of his spouse; or
(2) it is or has within the preceding five years been the property of:
    (a) a charity, or held on trust for charitable purposes only, or
    (b) a political party (IHTA 1984, s 24), a housing association (s 24A) or national purposes body (s 25),
    and became so on a transfer of value which was made by him or his spouse and was exempt to the extent that the value transferred was attributable to the property.

The appropriate portion of the value of the aggregate of that and any related property is such portion as would be attributable to the value of the first-mentioned property if the value of that aggregate were equal to the sums of the values of that and any related property, the value of each property being determined as if it did not form part of that aggregate.

The proportion that the value of a smaller number of shares of any class bears to the value of a greater number is taken to be that which the smaller number bears to the greater; and similarly with stock, debentures and units of any other description of property.

Shares are not treated as being of the same class unless they are so treated by the practice of a recognised stock exchange or would be so treated if dealt with on such a stock exchange.

2

SCOPE OF INCOME TAX

2.1 SCOPE OF TAXES ON PROPERTY, PROFITS OR GAINS

TA 1988, s 1 provides that income tax, which applies primarily to individuals, but also to partnerships, trusts, personal representatives etc, is a tax on all 'property, profits or gains' as described in Schedules A, D, E and F (see TA 1988, ss 15–20).

Capital gains tax (CGT) is levied on chargeable gains realised by individuals, trusts, personal representatives etc on assets disposed of in tax years for which they are classed as UK resident or ordinarily resident. Non-UK resident and non-UK ordinarily resident individuals may, on the disposal of assets UK situated used in or for the purposes of a trade, profession or vocation carried on through a branch or agency in the UK, be chargeable to CGT on chargeable gains arising in a tax year in which such trade is carried on. This does not apply if double taxation relief is available. See further Chap 5 regarding taxation of chargeable gains.

Corporation tax is charged on the 'profits of companies' (TA 1988, s 6), which means both income and chargeable gains (TA 1988, s 8; TCGA 1992, ss 1 and 8). A non-resident UK company is not subject to corporation tax unless it carries on a trade in the UK through a branch or agency (TA 1988, s 11; TCGA 1992, s 10); again, this does not apply if double taxation relief is available.

Note that a non-resident company that does not carry on a trade through a UK branch or agency is chargeable to income tax (at basic rate only) on any income arising in the UK, unless double taxation relief is available.

If a company receives any payment on which it bears income tax by deduction, and the payment is taken into account in computing the company's income chargeable to corporation tax, the income tax is set off against any corporation tax assessable on that income.

See further Chap 19 with regard to taxation of company profits.

2.2 INCOME TAX CHARGE ON 'PROPERTY, PROFITS OR GAINS'

The rules prescribed for the measurement of income, profits or gains vary according to the type of income, etc (ie the source from which the income, etc arises). The various categories of income, etc are divided, for assessment purposes, into Schedules A, D, E and F (Schedules B and C were repealed). Schedule E is concerned with income from offices or employments (see Chap 13), while Schedule F (see Chap 21) deals with the assessment of income from dividends and other distributions. Schedule A is charged on the annual profits from rents or other receipts arising from any estate, interest, or rights in or over land in the UK (TA 1988, s 15).

If income is within the scope of Schedule A, E or F, it cannot be charged under Schedule D (among a number of cases, see in particular *Fry v Salisbury House Estate Ltd* (1920) 15 TC 266). These cases concerned the allocation of profits to Schedule A or D. There are other cases concerned with allocation of profits to Schedule D or E (eg *Mitchell and Edon v Ross* (1961) 40 TC 11; *Fall v Hitchin* (1972) 49 TC 433; *Edwards v Clinch* (1981) 56 TC 367; and *Hall v Lorimer* (1993) 66 TC 349). The problem of allocation between Schedules D and E and related matters is ongoing.

For example, if a receipt is to be charged under Schedule D Case I, it must be an annual profit or gain from the trade which is the 'source' of the receipt. The source doctrine prevents any receipt from being chargeable under Case I unless that is clearly the source that gives rise to it. If it is to be chargeable to income tax, another Schedule or Case must be found. Casual or occasional payments may, in some circumstances, be liable under Schedule D Case VI. However, a payment that is genuinely unsolicited (eg a gift) is unlikely to be from any source and is almost certainly outside income taxation altogether.

2.3 SCHEDULE D: ANNUAL PROFITS OR GAINS

In broad terms (see TA 1988, s 18(1)), tax under Schedule D is charged on 'the annual profits or gains arising or accruing' to any person:

(1) residing in the UK from property of any kind, whether situated in the UK or elsewhere, and
(2) residing in the UK from any trade, profession or vocation, whether carried on in the UK or elsewhere, and
(3) although not resident in the UK, from any property in, or from any trade, profession or vocation exercised within, the UK.

Tax is also charged under Schedule D on all interest of money, annuities and other annual profits or gains not charged under Schedule A or E, and not specially exempted from tax.

Although, as noted above, Schedule D taxes *annual* profits or gains arising or accruing, 'annual' here is not restricted to mean profits or gains recurring year by year, nor lasting for a year, nor to be calculated with reference to a year. However, the emphasis here is that it is annual *profits* that are chargeable, not *capital*. In many cases the test in distinguishing between capital receipts and income receipts has been between a sum that is received for the use of an asset (ie income) and a sum received on disposing of an interest in an asset (ie capital). The simile often used is that of the tree, which is capital, and its fruit, which is income.

There are, inevitably, cases where the treatment of revenue capital items is dictated by specific statutory provisions that override the general principles which would otherwise apply (eg certain gains of a capital nature obtained from the disposal of land – see TA 1988, s 776, an anti-avoidance provision).

'Property' in this context is not limited to real property (land and buildings), and means anything that is capable of being owned (eg intangible intellectual property rights such as copyrights and patents).

For income tax, Schedule D is divided into six Cases, each of which has its own specific rules:

Case I: Any trade carried on in the UK or elsewhere but not contained in Schedule A.

Case II: Any profession or vocation not contained in any other Schedule.

Case III: (a) Any interest of money (whether yearly or otherwise) or any annuity or other annual payment, whether payable within or outside of the UK, either as a charge on any property of the person paying it under any deed or will or otherwise, or as a reservation out of it, or as a personal debt or obligation under any contract, or whether it is received and payable half-yearly or at any shorter or more distant periods (but *not* including payment chargeable under Schedule A).

            (b) All discounts.

            (c) Income from securities which is payable out of the UK or Northern Ireland public revenue.

Case IV: Income arising from securities out of the UK.

Case V: Income arising from possessions out of the UK not being income consisting of emoluments of any office or employment.

Case VI: Any annual profits or gains not falling under any other Schedule D case and not charged under Schedule A or E.

For corporation tax the Cases are:

Case I: Any trade carried on in the UK or elsewhere but not contained in Schedule A.

Case II: Any profession or vocation not contained in any other Schedule.

Case III: (a) Profits and gains arising from loan relationships, treated as chargeable under Case III (non-trading loan relationships) by FA 1996, ss 80–105.

    (b)   Any annuity or other annual payment which:

        (i)   is payable (whether inside or outside the UK and whether annually or at shorter or longer intervals) in respect of anything other than a loan relationship; and

        (ii)   is not a payment chargeable under Schedule A.

    (c)   Any discount arising otherwise than in respect of a loan relationship.

Case V: Income arising from possessions out of the UK not being income consisting of emoluments of any office or employment, but not including any income falling within Case III(a) above.

Case VI: Any annual profits or gains not falling under any other Schedule D case and not charged under Schedule A or E.

Although the Revenue has no right to choose under which Schedule it will charge tax, there is greater opportunity for choice between the Schedule D cases.

Schedule D, as outlined above, is not exhaustive, and there are other tax rules which direct that tax be charged under Schedule D, even if it would not normally fit within the charge, eg:

(1) TA 1988, s 1A (income from savings and distributions chargeable under Cases III-V taxed at lower rate).

(2) TA 1988, s 314 (income from employment as a diver concerned with exploration or exploitation of the seabed chargeable under Case I).

(3) TA 1988, s 347A (exclusion from tax of annual payments that would otherwise fall within Case III, subject to specified exceptions).

(4) TA 1988, s 503 (profits from commercially let furnished holiday accommodation in the UK chargeable under Case I).

(5) TA 1988, s 580A (exclusion from tax of annual payments under a long-term disability insurance policy providing insurance against risk of illness, unemployment, etc, provided no relief was claimed for payment of the premium (sometimes referred to as 'permanent health insurance')).

(6) F(No 2)A 1992, Sch 10 (calculation of Case I profits under the 'Rent-a-Room' scheme).

Any annual profits or gains not falling under any other Schedule D case and not charged under Schedule A or E can be charged under Schedule D Case VI, which is the residual case. Case VI is also used to charge tax on some surpluses, which on general principles would not otherwise be liable under Case VI (eg gains of a capital nature obtained from the disposal of land – see TA 1988, s 776, an anti-avoidance provision).

Unlike the Schedules, the first five (four for corporation tax) Schedule D cases, which define specific classes of income, are not exclusive. Thus, if income can fall within more than one case, the Revenue has the right to choose the case under which the charge is made. For example, interest income can be charged under:

(1) Case I as trading income including, for companies, as a credit under the FA 1996 loan relationships regime;
(2) Case III as interest; or
(3) if the source is foreign, Case IV as income from foreign securities or Case V as income from foreign possessions.

For companies, non-trading credits under the FA 1996 loan relationships regime are charged under Case III.

Under self-assessment, the Revenue's right to choose applies (see TMA 1970, s 28A(7A)) where, in a return:

(1) alternative methods are allowed by the income tax rules for bringing amounts into account in that return,
(2) the return is made, or amended, using one of those methods,
(3) the return could have been made using an alternative method, and
(4) the Revenue determines which of the alternative methods is to be used in relation to the taxpayer for that period (there is no right of appeal against such a determination).

In this event, any enquiry into that return or into an amendment of it is conducted as if the only method allowed were the one determined by the Revenue. There are two cases where the tax rules allow alternative methods for bringing amounts into account in a return – in making a computation for the purposes either of Schedule D Case I or II, or of Cases III-V. Similar rules apply for corporation tax (FA 1998, Sch 18, para 84).

The Revenue option does not apply to Case VI, which is exclusive and does not come into play until all other cases have been considered. However, in some circumstances assessments can be made as alternatives to Cases I or II.

2.4 SCHEDULE D CASES I AND II

As explained in 2.2, all taxable income must be derived from a source specified in one or other of the Schedules. The following concerns income assessable under Schedule D Cases I and II.

Following the 'source' doctrine, income can only be charged to tax under Cases I and II if it is shown that the taxpayer carries on, and the income is derived from, a trade (Case I) or a profession or vocation (Case II).

When considering eg whether Case I applies, the general requirements for assessment under Schedule D must be considered along with the specific requirements of the particular case. Thus, Case I applies to the annual profits or gains arising to a UK resident from any trade, whether carried on in the UK or abroad, and to the annual profits or gains arising to a non-UK resident person from a trade carried on in the UK. A similar analysis applies to annual profits or gains arising from a profession or vocation under Case II. A UK resident who carries on a trade wholly abroad might thus appear to be chargeable under Case I. However, such profits are instead liable under Case V as income from a foreign possession, a principle established by *Colquhoun v Brooks* (1889) 2 TC 490. In this case, a UK resident was a sleeping partner in an Australian firm carrying on a business in Australia. Under the law that applied at the time, he was assessed under Case I on the full amount of his share of the business profits. The House of Lords held that his partnership interest was a possession within Case V.

It could be argued that some activities that produce income from the use of land, or that arise out of land, fall within Schedule A as 'annual profits arising from a business carried on for the exploitation, as a source of rents or other receipts, of any estate, interest or rights in or over land in the UK', and that such activities amount to carrying on a trade. However, Schedule A states that it does not apply to profits arising from the occupation of land. More specifically, it excludes farming and market gardening (TA 1988, s 53) and mines, quarries and other concerns (s 55), the profits of which are chargeable under Case I. Here, the cultivation of short rotation coppice and stud farming are regarded as farming under FA 1995, s 154; woodlands and land being prepared for forestry purposes are not regarded as 'farming'.

2.4.1 Profession or vocation

There are no definitions within the legislation for 'profession' and 'vocation'; indeed, there are no reported tax cases in which the point at issue was the distinction between the two. There was, however, an exemption for 'any profession the profits of which are dependent mainly on the personal qualifications' of the person carrying on the profession and 'in which no capital expenditure is required, or only capital expenditure of a comparatively small amount' which applied under the Excess Profits Duty, with similar relief available under National Defence Contribution and Excess Profits Tax, which can be regarded as precedents.

CIR v Maxse (1919) 12 TC 41 concerned the owner of a monthly political magazine who wrote much of it himself. It was held that, for Excess Profits Duty purposes, he carried on a separate profession of journalist and editor. It followed that, in arriving at the profits of his publishing business, an allowance should be made for his services. This decision was followed in *Salt v Fernandez* [1997] SSCD 271, in which a lecturer wrote and published a book in 1983. Later, in 1994, he also published in booklet form a lecture that had been given more than 80 years previously. The Revenue issued Schedule D assessments on the basis that he was acting as a professional author. On appeal, the Special Commissioner accepted his contention that, in addition to being a professional author, he had begun a separate trade of publishing when he published the lecture. However, subsequently, as reported in *Salt v Fernandez (No 2)* [1998] SSCD 176, the Revenue had issued Case I assessments. As a result, the publishing trade's profits in 1993–94 were assessed for both that year and for 1994–95 the following year (under the opening years rule that applied for the preceding year basis of assessment then in force). The author's contention was that the profits should not be assessed again, as they were included in the 1994–95 Case II assessment on him as an author. The Special Commissioner, in rejecting this contention, held that TMA 1970, s 32 (relief for double assessment) required that the amount should be taken out of the Case II assessment and assessed under Case I, even though this might result in the amount 'being assessed more than once under the rules applicable to new trades'.

In *Webster v CIR* [1942] 2 All ER 517, it was held that an ophthalmic optician was not carrying on a profession, but was carrying on the business of selling spectacles, to which eye-testing was ancillary and the receipts from which could not be severed (distinguishing *CIR v Maxse*). However, in *Carr v CIR* [1944] 2 All ER 163, the Commissioners held that an optician was carrying on a profession, which was upheld by the Court of Appeal, holding that whether a trade is a 'profession' turns on the facts of the individual case, and not solely on the trader's 'special skill or ability, or some special qualifications derived from training or experience'.

In the context of corporation tax, in *CIR v Peter McIntyre Ltd* (1926) 12 TC 1006 the Court of Session held that a company that carried on business as auctioneers was not carrying on a profession, on the grounds that a company cannot have the 'personal qualifications' necessary to bring it within the exemption.

Billam v Griffith (1941) 23 TC 757 concerned the meaning of 'vocation'. A former barrister had written and sold a successful play. He had also previously written several plays in his spare time without selling them. It was held that he had been carrying on the vocation of dramatist, and that his receipts from the successful play were receipts of that vocation.

Historically, a 'profession' meant the three learned professions of the Church, Medicine and the Law, but today the term is much wider and normally involves some substantial exercise of either purely intellectual skill, or of any manual skill controlled, as in painting and sculpture or surgery, by the operator's intellectual skill, as distinguished from an occupation that is substantially the production or sale of commodities. Three further tests of a profession have been put forward:

(1) its practice is based on preliminary study, training and, possibly, examination in the general principles of the pursuit;
(2) the profits that may be made from its pursuit do not depend primarily on the provision of great quantities of capital; and
(3) it is a pursuit that is followed not solely as a livelihood but always subject to overriding duties, prescribed by a code of professional honour involving, in an especial degree, the strict observance of confidences, in

which services must be rendered to the client without stint in proportion to the client's need rather than in proportion to the reward that is received.

'Vocation' has a wide meaning related to the way a person passes his life and indicates a calling. This is not necessarily one related to religion, caring or high-minded service to others. Authors, bookmakers, dramatists, jockeys and professional singers have all been dealt with by the courts on the basis that they carried on vocations.

There is generally little difference between the basis of assessment under Cases I and II, so that the distinction between a 'trade' on the one hand and a 'profession' or 'vocation' on the other is now of very limited importance. This all the more so, now that FA 1998, s 42 effectively has brought to an end the cash basis and bills issued basis of accounting for professional practices by providing that the accounting basis for computing the profits of a trade, profession or vocation must give a true and fair view of the profit or loss. This rule applies to periods of account beginning on or after 6 April 1999.

2.4.2 Trade

'Trade', defined in TA 1988, s 832(1), 'includes every trade, manufacture, adventure or concern in the nature of trade'. Regrettably, this is not a model of clarity, and this lack of an exhaustive definition has given rise to much litigation. On the face of it, 'trade' must take its ordinary meaning – thus, to follow a dictionary definition, 'The practice of some . . . business . . . habitually carried on, especially when practised as a means of livelihood or gain . . . now usually applied to a mercantile occupation and to a skilled handicraft, as distinct from a profession'. In *National Association of Local Government Officers v Bolton Corp* [1942] 2 All ER 425, it was held that '"trade" refers to the various activities of commerce – the winning and using the products of the earth and selling them, or manufacturing and selling them, the purchase and sale of commodities, or the offering of services for a reward, such as conveyance and the like'.

In many, perhaps most, cases it is self-evident that a trade is being carried on. There are inevitably a large number of marginal cases that require further consideration. As the statutory definition in s 832(1) provides little guidance on what amounts to trading, it is necessary to consider the large volume of tax cases dealing with this issue. In summary, the message from case-law is that trade cannot be defined precisely, but there are certain characteristics that are normally those of trade, and others that would normally prevent a profit from being derived from a trade.

The definition of 'trade' also includes 'manufacture', which should cause few difficulties. The words 'adventure or concern in the nature of trade' are more problematic. Using ordinary, rather than statutory, meanings, it would appear that such activities, while not amounting to full-blown trades, can nevertheless be taxable under Case I, and bring in transactions that, although less than full trading operations, are within its broader meaning for tax purposes. It is sometimes suggested that it is only the word 'concern' that is qualified by the words 'in the nature of trade'. If this were to be the case, the word 'adventure' stands alone. In fact, the courts frequently use the words 'adventure in the nature of trade' to describe the test for activities within Case I (eg 'To say that a transaction is or is not an adventure in the nature of trade is to say that it has or has not the characteristics which distinguish such an adventure': *Edwards v Bairstow and Harrison* (1955) 36 TC 207). The definition has been held to be wide enough to bring into Case I isolated transactions or speculative adventures that yield unexpected profits (*Martin v Lowry* (1926) 11 TC 297 (purchase and resale of war surplus linen); *CIR v Livingstone & Others* (1926) 11 TC 538 (purchase, conversion and resale of a ship); *Cape Brandy Syndicate v CIR* (1921) 12 TC 358 (speculative purchase and resale of brandy); *Pickford v Quirke* (1927) 13 TC 251 (purchase and resale of cotton mills); *Edwards v Bairstow and Harrison* (above) (purchase and resale of cotton-spinning plant); *Rutledge v CIR* (1929) 14 TC 490 (single purchase and multiple sales of large quantity of toilet paper); *CIR v Fraser* (1942) 24 TC 498 (isolated purchase and resale of whisky in bond); *Wisdom v Chamberlain* (1968) 45 TC 692 (purchase and sale of silver bullion held as a hedge against devaluation)).

However, it does not follow from these cases that every isolated transaction or speculative adventure giving rise to a profit should be within Case I. In *Leeming v Jones* (1930) 15 TC 333 (acquisitions of options to rubber estates; assignment of rights to a public company), it was found that the transaction was not a concern in the nature of trade. It was stated that: 'in the case of an isolated transaction . . . there is really no middle course open. It is either an adventure in the nature of trade, or else it is simply a case of sale and resale of property.' To be assessable under Case I, a profit must be of an income nature and not a capital accretion.

There is no fixed rule to apply to the question of whether a trade exists, and every case must be decided on its own facts and circumstances. However, the courts tend to review transactions to establish whether they bear any of the six 'badges of trade' identified and summarised in 1955 in the Final Report of the Royal Commission on the Taxation of Profits and Income. Over the years, as circumstances have required it, the courts have added further 'badges'.

Each of these badges is described below, together with a summary of what are regarded as the major relevant criteria that have a bearing on whether a trade exists.

A profit-seeking motive

If it is shown that the sole object of acquiring an asset was to sell it on at a profit, and with no intention of holding it as an investment, the natural conclusion would be that a trade is being carried on. However, while an intention to make a profit is a relevant factor in deciding whether there is a trade, it is not of itself decisive. Indeed, for tax purposes a trade may be carried on even though there is no intention to make a profit. The reverse is also true and the realisation and accumulation of a surplus of receipts over outgoings from carrying on an activity does not necessarily amount to a trade. Important decisions in determining whether a trade is being carried on include *Salt v Chamberlain* (1979) 53 TC 143 (speculative stock exchange transactions by an individual did not constitute a trade – he was seeking to establish a trade loss to set against other income). In *Halefield Securities Ltd v Thorpe* (1967) 44 TC 154, an investment company sought, unsuccessfully, to establish that a substantial loss on disposal of a shareholding should qualify for loss relief from a trade of dealing in securities. However, the taxpayer companies in *Lewis Emanuel & Sons Ltd v White* (1965) 42 TC 369 and *Cooper v C & J Clark Ltd* (1982) 54 TC 570 claimed successfully that losses on investments gave rise to trading losses available for relief.

In general, as shown by *Paddington Burial Board v CIR* (1884) 2 TC 46 (surplus income assessable although applicable in aid of poor rates), the destination of a surplus is irrelevant. Similar decisions were arrived at in *Dublin Corp v M'Adam* (1887) 2 TC 387 (surplus of water undertaking assessable although applicable to reduce indebtedness); *Webber v Glasgow Corp* (1893) 3 TC 202 (local authority profits assessable although applicable for public purposes); and *Brighton College v Marriott* (1925) 10 TC 213 (profits of a school assessable although applicable for charitable purposes).

It is also important to note that a trade may be carried on for tax purposes even though there is no intention to make a profit. If a trade is found to be carried on, there is liability to tax on any resulting profits whether or not the trading activities are directed to the making of a profit. In *Carnoustie Golf Course Committee v CIR* (1929) 14 TC 498 and *CIR v Stonehaven Recreation Ground Trustees* (1929) 15 TC 419, where a committee in the first case and trustees in the latter managed public recreation facilities, this was held to be trading. In the latter case it was held that although the trustees' object was never intentionally commercial, it was what they did, and not what they intended to do, that decided whether they were carrying on a trade.

The realisation's subject-matter

While almost any form of property can be acquired to be dealt in, those forms of property, such as commodities or manufactured articles, that are normally the subject of trading are only very exceptionally the subject of investment. Problems may be encountered with assets that are generally bought

(a) as an investment that usually, but not necessarily, yields income (eg shares), or

(b) for personal use or enjoyment (eg works of art), or

(c) as a fixed asset of an admitted trade (eg machinery and plant).

It is the nature of such assets that leads to an initial presumption that they are not acquired as a subject of trade.

Property that does not provide its owner with an income or personal enjoyment merely by virtue of its ownership is more likely to have been acquired with the object of a deal than property that does not (see eg *CIR v Fraser*, *Rutledge v CIR*, *Edwards v Bairstow and Harrison* and *Wisdom v Chamberlain* above). Yet the fact that an asset does not produce income before realisation is no more than a pointer to the possibility that it is held as a trading asset. In most cases the benefit to the holder comes as an enhancement in the asset's capital value (see *Marson v Morton (and related appeals)* (1986) 59 TC 381).

Transactions involving financial assets such as shares, options and futures do not normally amount to trading for tax purposes. In particular, shares are usually held for investment with a view to providing income or capital growth. Yet there are many short-term transactions that cannot be classed as investments, but fall short of trading. There is now a range of provisions which ensures that surpluses from transactions involving various financial instruments are brought into the scope of taxation in income form.

There are also assets that do not produce income, but are acquired for the pleasure that ownership brings (eg antiques or works of art). The owner may well hope for an increase in value in due course, but this does not bring the transaction within the ambit of trading unless there are other significant indications of a trading intention.

If the subject of the transaction is normally used for investment – land, houses, stocks and shares – the inference that the venture was a trading one is not so readily to be drawn from an admitted intention to sell on the arrival of a suitable, preselected time or circumstance (see *CIR v Reinhold* (1953) 34 TC 389).

The quantity purchased can also be a factor. In *CIR v Fraser* and *Rutledge v CIR*, the commodities in question, whisky and one million toilet rolls respectively, had been bought in quantities that were far in excess of anything that could be used by the taxpayer personally.

Transactions involving land are among the most difficult to categorise, as land is capable of functioning both as an investment and trading stock.

Number or frequency of similar transactions by same person

If realisations of the same sort of property occur in succession over a period of years, or there are several such realisations at about the same date, there is a presumption that there has been dealing in relation to each (eg *St Aubyn Estates Ltd v Strike* (1932) 17 TC 412 (breaking up an estate via a company formed for the purpose); *Martin v Lowry* (above) (disposal in small lots of a large quantity of government surplus aeroplane linen)). A large number of similar transactions is also indicative of a trade (eg *Pickford v Quirke* (above); *Leach v Pogson* (1962) 40 TC 585 (setting up and selling driving schools); and transactions in shares in *Lewis Emanuel & Sons Ltd v White* (above), although this was not thought to be conclusive in *Salt v Chamberlain* (above)).

Addition of value to asset(s)

What (if anything) is done to an asset pending resale is a relevant factor. If modifications are carried out to the asset by way of processing or manufacture, or some kind of adaptation to make it more readily marketable, or if any special exertions are made to find or attract purchasers, such as opening an office or large-scale advertising, these are actions typical of trading activities. Similarly, breaking down assets into smaller lots to facilitate a sale may be a pointer to a trading motive as in *Edwards v Bairstow & Harrison* (above). Likewise, in *Cape Brandy Syndicate v CIR*, the work related to a large quantity of Cape brandy which was shipped to the UK, blended expertly with French brandy, re-casked and sold in numerous lots, and was all part of the evidence leading to a conclusion that a trade was carried on. In *CIR v Livingstone* (above), work was undertaken to convert and refit a ship for subsequent sale, and in *St Aubyn Estates Ltd v Strike* (above) roads were laid on an estate in preparation for its break up and sale.

When there is an organised effort to obtain profit, there is a source of taxable income. However, expenditure on an asset after purchase and before resale is not always strong evidence of a trading motive. It will depend on the nature and scale of the expenditure (eg insurance against loss, normal maintenance to prevent deterioration, or to maintain the asset in working condition, would add little weight in favour of trading). However, if an asset did not need any modification or other work then absence of any modification, etc is neutral.

Manner of acquisition

It is less likely that the sale of an asset acquired in some way other than by purchase will be classified as a sale by way of trade than one which was acquired by a purchase. Thus, land acquired by reclamation under an agreement rather than by purchase was held not to be a trade when the land was subsequently sold in *Hudson's Bay Co Ltd v Stevens* (1909) 5 TC 424, but the formation of a company between the inheritor of an estate and its development and sale led to the opposite conclusion in *St Aubyn Estates Ltd v Strike* (above).

If an asset is acquired by gift or inheritance, it is probable, although not inevitable, that a subsequent sale is not by way of trade. However, the sale may give rise to a trading profit if at some point before the sale the asset became trading stock of a trade or an adventure in the nature of trade.

Circumstances of the disposal

The way in which a disposal is carried out is of considerable significance. Thus, the conclusion that a trade is being carried on is likely if the transactions were undertaken in the same manner that an undisputed trader would carry them through. The test that must be used to determine whether a venture is 'in the nature of trade' is whether the operations involved in it are of the same kind, and carried on in the same way, as those that are characteristic of ordinary trading in the line of business in which the venture was made (see *CIR v Livingstone*). In *CIR v Fraser* and *Rutledge v CIR*, it was important that the commodities concerned were sold in much the same way as would apply in the course of an ordinary trade in that commodity. Any organised activity intended to promote sale is evidence of trading (eg a sales campaign by advertisement or canvass or the organisation or employment of a selling agency or sales staff: see *Martin v Lowry*). The formation of a syndicate or company solely or mainly for the purpose of the particular transaction is evidence of trading (see *St Aubyn Estates Ltd v Strike* (above) and *California Copper Syndicate Ltd v Harris* (1904) 5 TC 159).

The 1955 Final Report suggested that the circumstances responsible for the realisation should be considered. There may be some explanation, such as a sudden emergency or opportunity calling for ready money, that negatives the idea that any plan of dealing prompted the original purchase. Such a conclusion might be drawn where a sale of a property, intended to be held as an investment, is a forced sale brought about by pressure from bankers to repay a loan at short notice.

Substantial advertising and the creation of an organisation to deal with sales enquiries, etc indicated trading in *Martin v Lowry* and *Cape Brandy Syndicate v CIR*. The absence of an organisation, because none was necessary, was held to be irrelevant in *Edwards v Bairstow and Harrison*. There may be some explanation, such as a sudden emergency or opportunity calling for ready money, that negates the idea that any plan of dealing prompted the original purchase.

Period between purchase and sale

Generally speaking, purchase and sale transactions carried out over a short period indicate trading (eg *Martin v Lowry*, *Wisdom v Chamberlain*, *Pickford v Quirke*, *Leach v Pogson* and *Lewis Emanuel & Sons Ltd v White*, but not *Salt v Chamberlain* (above), nor *Johnston v Heath* (1970) 46 TC 463, where an agreement to sell a plot of land was made *before* the land was purchased). At the other extreme is *Orchard Parks Ltd v Pogson* (1964) 42 TC 442, where the period between the purchase of land for development (although the project had to be abandoned) and when the land itself was ultimately sold was 25 years!

Association of disposal with seller's other interests

It is likely that a transaction that is related to a trade already carried on by the seller will be looked upon as itself being a trading transaction (*Cape Brandy Syndicate v CIR*; *Pickford v Quirke*; and *Gloucester Railway Carriage & Wagon Co Ltd v CIR* (1925) 12 TC 720).

If there is an admitted trade, then a similarity to the transaction under consideration may be a pointer to that transaction having a trading character.

However, in *Harvey v Caulcott* (1952) 33 TC 159, where a builder claimed successfully that certain properties that he had built and then sold many years later were investments and not part of his trading stock, it was held that the fact the man was a builder put the onus on him to show that the profit was from an investment and not from trading stock.

Other relevant cases include *CIR v Fraser*, where it was held that where there is 'a single transaction entered into by an individual in the line of his own trade (although not part and parcel of his ordinary business)', it is easier to hold that it is an adventure in the nature of trade than 'a transaction entered into by an individual outside the line of his own trade or occupation'. In *Lynch v Edmondson* 1998 SSCD 185, the purchase by a bricklayer of a plot of land and the building thereon of two flats was held to be 'a typical trading transaction'. This case was distinguished from *Marson v Morton* (above), where the question was posed: 'Is the transaction in question in some way related to the trade which the taxpayer otherwise carries on?'

Method of finance

If a transaction is financed by means of borrowing, and it is clear that the borrowing is in due course to be repaid in the short term from the proceeds of sale from the asset concerned, it is likely that trading will be inferred. This conclusion was also drawn in a case where there was an agreement to sell land before it had been purchased in *Johnston v Heath*.

In *Tebrau (Johore) Rubber Syndicate Ltd v Farmer* (1910) 5 TC 658, a company had acquired rubber estates in Malaya, planted them, but then before any rubber was produced sold the estates. In this case the profit was held to be a capital profit. A purchase of eg silver bullion futures was undertaken in the expectation that it would be paid for out of the proceeds of the sale in *Wisdom v Chamberlain*. Furthermore, in this case such activity was entirely outside the taxpayer's normal show business occupation.

The sale by a builder of shops he had built and subsequently let, and a house in which his foreman had lived, was held in *Harvey v Caulcott* to be the realisation of investments. This was despite the fact that the purchase was made out of the resources of an admitted trade that the taxpayer was already carrying on. The court did not consider that the payment of the sale proceeds into the existing business was significant. It could not offset a finding that the asset had been an investment from the beginning.

If an asset provides an income (eg rent, interest or dividends), it is more likely to be an investment than if it produced none. But the income has to be considered alongside any expenses associated with the transaction. Suppose the purchase of an asset is financed by borrowings on which interest is payable: if the interest matches or exceeds the income, the asset's income-bearing nature is of less importance. The conclusion is that any benefit can only come from the actual disposal of the asset, allowing the loan to be repaid, the income being merely set against the outgoings until that surplus is available (see *Cooke v Haddock* (1960) 39 TC 64).

Miscellaneous matters

The Revenue takes the view that transactions undertaken solely for fiscal purposes are not trading, even if the outward characteristics of trading are present, because they lack an underlying commercial purpose. In some cases, the real purpose behind transactions is to obtain a tax advantage by eg establishing a loss to obtain repayment of tax paid at source, or to set against other profits. This view is supported in such cases as *Lupton v FA & AB Ltd* (1971) 47 TC 580; *Coates v Arndale Properties Ltd* (1984) 36 TC 275; *Reed v Nova Securities Ltd* (1988) 59 TC 516; *Overseas Containers (Finance) Ltd v Stoker* (1989) 61 TC 473; and *Ensign Tankers (Leasing) Ltd v Stokes* (1992) 64 TC 617.

Revenue extra-statutory concessions, statements of practice, interpretations, etc deal with a number of marginal situations and should always be consulted.

Two matters arise:

(1) If it is shown that profitable transactions do not amount to a trade, there can be no Case I charge.

(2) If it is shown that loss-making transactions do amount to a trade, such losses can be offset against other income and, in certain circumstances, against chargeable gains.

2.5 SCHEDULE D CASE III

(TA 1988, s 64)

Income under Case III broadly comprises interest, but does not include any payment chargeable under Schedule A, discounts, and income from securities that is payable out of the UK or Northern Ireland public revenue (see 2.3).

Case III charges income tax on the full amount of the income arising within the tax year, and is paid on the actual amount of that income without any deduction. Different rules apply for corporation tax, and most interest, discounts, etc are dealt with under the FA 1996 loan relationships regime.

2.6 SCHEDULE D CASES IV AND V
(TA 1988, ss 65–68)

Income under Cases IV and V comprises income arising from securities out of the UK, and income arising from possessions out of the UK not being income consisting of emoluments of any office or employment respectively.

Cases IV and V charge income tax on the full amount of the income arising in a tax year, whether or not the income has been or will be received in the UK. This is subject in the case of income not received in the UK to:

(1) the same deductions and allowances as if it had been so received, and
(2) a deduction on account of any annuity or other annual payment (not being interest) payable out of the income to a person not resident in the UK.

Income chargeable to tax under Case IV or V from carrying on any trade, profession or vocation either solely or in partnership is computed following the normal Cases I and II rules.

The rules described above do not apply to any person who is not UK-domiciled or, being a Commonwealth or a Republic of Ireland citizen, is not UK-ordinarily resident. In such event tax is computed under:

(1) Case IV on the full amount, so far as it can be computed, of the sums received in the UK in the year of assessment, without any deduction or abatement; and
(2) Case V on the full amount of the actual sums received in the UK in the tax year without any deduction or abatement other than is allowed under Case I.

The meaning of 'received in the UK' in this context is widely drawn, and includes sums received from remittances payable in the UK, or from property imported, or from money or value arising from property not imported, or from money or value so received on credit or on account of any such remittances, property, money or value brought or to be brought into the UK.

There are extensive rules for looking through 'back-to-back' loan transactions designed to receive benefit in the UK without bringing the income back to the UK.

Relief is available (under TA 1988, s 585) if a person can show that he could not transfer income to the UK owing to the laws of the territory where the income arose, or to executive action of its government, or to the impossibility of obtaining foreign currency in that territory; and that the inability was not because of any want of reasonable endeavours on his part.

A special rule applies where a person is chargeable to income tax under Case V on income that arises from rents or other receipts from a business carried on for the exploitation of any estate, interest or rights in or over land outside the UK, and is not income derived from carrying on a trade, profession or vocation. All such businesses and transactions carried on or entered into by a particular person or partnership, so far as they are so chargeable under Case V, are treated as, or as entered into in the course of carrying on, a single 'overseas property business'. The income from an overseas property business is computed under Schedule A rules. It is important to note that an overseas property business is dealt with entirely separately from any actual Schedule A business.

The special treatment under TA 1988, ss 503 and 504, CAA 1990, s 29 and TCGA 1992, s 241 (furnished holiday accommodation) does not apply to the profits or losses of an overseas property business.

Income chargeable to tax under Case IV or V is, in the case of property situated and profits arising in the Republic of Ireland, computed on the full amount of the income arising in the tax year, whether or not the income has been or will be received in the UK. This is subject, in the case of income not received in the UK, to:

(1) the same deductions and allowances as if it had been so received, and
(2) a deduction on account of any annuity or other annual payment (not being interest) payable out of the income to a non-UK resident person.

This does not apply to any income derived by a person from the carrying on by him of any trade, profession or vocation, either solely or in partnership. Tax on any such income arising in the Republic of Ireland is computed either on the full amount thereof arising in the tax year on broadly the same basis as if it had arisen in the UK.

2.7 SCHEDULE D CASE VI

Income tax under Case VI is computed on the full amount of the profits or gains arising in the tax year.

2.8 SCHEDULE E

For a discussion of the income assessable under Schedule E, see Chap 13.

3

COMPUTING TRADING PROFITS FOR TAX PURPOSES

This chapter covers the way in which a business's taxable profits are ascertained, and deals with some of the more common adjustments to business accounts that are required for business purposes.

3.1 HOW TAXABLE PROFITS ARE ARRIVED AT

3.1.1 Introduction

The tax legislation provides no firm rule for what expenditure is deductible in computing, for tax purposes, the profits of a trade, etc. The charge to tax under Schedule D Case I is on 'the full amount of the profits of the year of assessment' (TA 1988, s 60(1)). For income tax, this is generally the profits of a 12-month period ending within a tax year (s 60(3)), although there are special rules that apply on commencement and discontinuance (ss 61–63A). For corporation tax purposes, income under Case I for an accounting period is computed on 'the full amount of the profits or gains arising in the period' (s 70(1)).

As there is no specific definition, 'profits' must be taken to have its natural and ordinary meaning in a commercial context. It can thus be arrived at by taking the receipts of the trade and deducting from them the expenditure necessary to earn those receipts (*Gresham Life Assurance Society v Styles* (1890) 3 TC 185).

An item of expenditure should be deductible in computing the profits of a trade if the expenditure can be justified on commercial accounting principles (*Usher's Wiltshire Brewery v Bruce* (1915) 6 TC 399; *Lothian Chemical Co v Rogers* (1926) 11 TC 508). Where there is a specific statutory prohibition, that expenditure cannot be deducted even if, as a matter of accounting principle, it would be proper to deduct it.

3.1.2 Accounting practice

The measure of profits for tax purposes is, first and foremost, a question of law. However, the courts consider evidence on how accounts are drawn up in practice.

The Accounting Standards Board (ASB), set up under CA 1985, is responsible for setting Accounting Standards. The ASB adopted the existing Statements of Standard Accounting Practice (SSAPs) and has also issued its own Financial Reporting Standards (FRSs). These are, initially, issued for discussion and comment as Financial Reporting Exposure Drafts (FREDs). Additionally, for particular industries, Statements of Recommended Practice (SORPs) are issued. Particular issues are dealt with by the Urgent Issues Task Force (UITF).

A company's balance sheet must give a true and fair view of its affairs at the end of its financial year and its profit and loss account must give a true and fair view of its result for the year. For those companies for which an auditor's report is required, such report must state whether, in the auditor's opinion, the balance sheet and profit and loss account give a true and fair view of the companies' affairs and of its profit or loss. The auditor must qualify his report if the accounts do not represent such view.

SSAP 2 (Disclosure of accounting policies) distinguishes between:

(1) *Fundamental accounting concepts* – SSAP 2 sets out the fundamental accounting concepts that underlie the periodic financial accounts of business enterprises.
(2) *Accounting bases* – These are the methods for expressing or applying the fundamental accounting concepts to financial transactions and items.
(3) *Accounting policies* – These are the specific accounting bases judged by a business to be the most appropriate to its circumstances and adopted for the preparation of its financial accounts.

SSAP 2 identifies four fundamental accounting concepts:

- going concern
- accruals
- consistency, and
- prudence.

The going concern concept makes the assumption, where it is appropriate to do so, that the business will continue to operate for the foreseeable future. The profit and loss account and the balance sheet are prepared on the basis that it is neither intended nor necessary to liquidate the business or to reduce its operations significantly.

Under the accruals concept, income and costs are accrued. This means that they are recognised as they are earned or incurred rather than according to when money is received or paid. In general, income (or 'revenue') and costs should be matched so that revenues are set against associated costs and expenses, so far as a relationship can be established or reasonably assumed. They should be dealt with in the profit and loss account for the period to which they relate. However, if the accruals concept is inconsistent with the prudence concept, the prudence concept prevails.

The consistency concept requires that the same accounting treatment is applied to like items within each account and from one period to the next. The need for consistency has been recognised by the courts. For instance, its importance in relation to the valuation of stocks was stressed in *Ostime v Duple Motor Bodies* (1961) 39 TC 537. Yet it is important to take account of changing facts. For example, a fixed percentage addition for overheads in a stock valuation may lead to inconsistency if there are marked variations in the ratio of overheads to direct charges. The principle of consistency, however, also means that there must be a good reason for a change from one existing valid basis to another (eg a company is taken over and adapts its basis to that of its new owners, or there is some alteration in the nature of a business's trade). If an invalid basis has hitherto been followed in the accounts, together with an adjustment in the tax computation (so that the profits are computed on a valid basis), a business may want to change its accounts to a valid basis other than the one adopted in the tax computations. The Revenue generally accepts this change unless the existing taxation basis has been applied for so long as to raise the question of consistency.

The prudence concept requires that revenue and profits should not be anticipated but rather should be recognised only when realised. Moreover, provision should be made for all known liabilities. If necessary, a provision should be made for costs or expenses for which liability has arisen, with the provision being made on an estimated basis in the light of the information available.

SSAP 9 deals with the valuation of stocks and long-term contracts. As noted above, SSAP 2 recognises the 'consistency concept' and requires the matching of costs with related revenues. The cost of unsold goods or unconsumed materials will have been incurred in the expectation of future receipts. Accordingly, such costs are carried forward and matched with the revenue when it arises. If eg stocks have deteriorated or become obsolescent and there is no reasonable expectation that sufficient revenue will arise to cover the costs that have been incurred, the irrecoverable costs are charged to revenue in the accounts under review. This means that, as a general rule, stocks are stated at the lower of cost or net realisable value. For long-term contracts it may be appropriate to release profit to the profit and loss account as various stages in the contract are reached.

FRS 12 sets out the principles of accounting for provisions, contingent liabilities and contingent assets. Its purpose is to ensure that appropriate recognition criteria and measurement bases are applied thereto.

A provision is a liability that is of uncertain timing or amount, to be settled by a transfer of economic benefit. A contingent liability is either

(1) a possible obligation arising from past events the existence of which will be confirmed only by the occurrence of one or more uncertain future events not wholly within the business's control; or

(2) a present obligation that arises from past events but is not recognised because it is not probable that a transfer of economic benefits will be required to settle the obligation or because the amount of the obligation cannot be measured with sufficient reliability.

A contingent asset is a possible asset arising from past events, the existence of which will be confirmed only by the occurrence of one or more uncertain future events not wholly within the business's control.

Most small companies can now dispense with an audit. Their directors must ensure that the accounts show a true and fair view, and that other Companies Act accounting, reporting and record-keeping requirements are satisfied. This applies to companies with a turnover of:

(a) £90,000 or less, which are entitled to dispense with the audit without any replacement independent check; and

(b) above £90,000, but not more than £100,000 (for financial years ending after 26 July 2000, or £250,000 for charitable companies), which may replace the audit with a 'compilation report' signed by the 'Reporting Accountant'. This is broadly similar to the certificate normally given to the accounts of an unincorporated business prepared by an independent qualified accountant.

There are a number of circumstances where, even though they fall within the above turnover limit, the companies concerned may not dispense with an audit. These apply where the company is a plc, or has a balance sheet gross asset value exceeding £1.4m, or is regulated under the Financial Services Act or the Financial Services and Markets Act 2000, or is a member of a group, or if sufficient shareholders object.

It is a recommendation of the accountancy bodies that the accounts of unincorporated businesses should generally comply with SSAPs and FRSs even though there is no mandatory requirement to do so.

Financial Reporting Standards for Smaller Entities (FRSSE) is a simplified version of the requirements for larger entities. It should be used by those businesses that fall within its scope and have chosen to adopt it. Two points are worthy of note:

(i) 'the treatment prescribed by the standard or requirement is compatible with that already used, or expected to be used, by the Inland Revenue in computing taxable profits'; and

(ii) the FRSSE represents 'a pragmatic relaxation of disclosure rules rather than any new form of financial reporting tailored to the needs of small businesses'.

The current size limits are (under CA 1985, s 247(3)) a turnover of not more than £2.8m, a balance sheet gross asset value not exceeding £1.4m, and not more than 50 employees. However, the FRSSE does not apply to large or medium-sized companies, groups, etc; plcs; banks, building societies or insurance companies; authorised persons under the Financial Services Act; or members of groups containing companies within the last three categories.

Under FRSSE, a provision is defined as 'a liability of uncertain timing or amount'. A liability is 'an entity's obligation to transfer economic benefits as a result of past transactions or events'. An obligation is 'either a legal obligation (derived eg from a contract or legislation) or a constructive obligation, where the entity has indicated to other parties that it will accept certain responsibilities and has created valid expectations in those other parties that it will discharge those responsibilities'. In summary it states that

'A provision should be recognised when, and only when, it is probable (i.e. more likely than not) that a present obligation exists, as a result of a past event, and that it will require a transfer of economic benefits in settlement that can be estimated reliably. The amount recognised as a provision should be the best estimate of the expenditure required to settle the obligation at the balance sheet date.'

So far as concerns individuals and partnerships, there is, under self-assessment, no statutory requirement to prepare a profit and loss account. Unless the business is large or complex (eg partnerships with a turnover in excess of £15m), the Revenue does not require businesses to send in accounts rather than completing the standardised accounts information. However, a business must keep certain records of its dealings, as follows:

(a) details of the amount and description of all receipts and expenses in the course of the trade;
(b) where the trade involves dealing in goods, details of all purchases and sales of goods in the course of the trade; and
(c) supporting documents to the above including accounts, books, deeds, contracts, vouchers and receipts.

A sole trader or partnership whose gross annual turnover is below £15,000 need not submit accounts. The return must, however, show turnover, total business purchases and expenses and net profit. The trader should keep records to substantiate the figures in the return if necessary.

The amount shown as profit by the profit and loss account is not usually the amount of profit to be assessed, for in nearly every case it is necessary to make the adjustments required by the Taxes Acts. For example, accounts prepared for commercial reasons may include a provision for the wear and tear to a building. Such a provision must be 'added back' (ie it is disallowed as a deduction in computing the profit of a business). Although no relief is available for wear and tear or for depreciation in value as such, a form of relief may be given, for appropriate expenditure, through the capital allowances system.

Although, for sole traders and partnerships, there is no statutory authority for the form that accounts are to take, the profit figure must be computed on an accounting basis that provides a true and fair view, subject to any adjustments required by tax law. A profit and loss account is usually accompanied by a balance sheet drawn up as at the date on which the accounting period ends. The purpose of the balance sheet is to show a 'snapshot' of the business's assets and liabilities at that date, along with details of any provisions and reserves and the interests of the proprietors.

There are statutory requirements relating to the allowability of provisions as follows. First, under FA 1989, s 43 a deduction is allowed for emoluments provided they are actually paid (or made available eg by transfer to a directors' current account having been subjected to PAYE and NICs) within nine months of the period of account to which they relate. This could cause problems in relation to long-term contracts. If a provision for losses on a long-term contract include amounts related to employees' remuneration, it would have to be disallowed for tax, notwithstanding that the requirements of FRS 12 are satisfied. This should be borne in mind when periodically releasing profit on a long-term contract into the profit and loss account.

Secondly, any sum paid by an employer as contribution under an approved occupational pension scheme is allowed (under TA 1988, s 592(4)) to be deducted as an expense incurred in the chargeable period in which the sum is paid, but no other sum is allowed to be deducted as an expense relating to making, or any provision for making, any such contributions. The amount of an employer's deductible contributions must not exceed the amount contributed by him under the scheme for employees in a trade or undertaking the profits of which are assessable to UK income or corporation tax. However, a sum not paid by way of ordinary annual contribution may be treated, as the Revenue may direct, either as an expense incurred in the chargeable period in which the sum is paid, or as an expense to be spread over such period of years as the Revenue thinks proper. The Pension Schemes Office determines the period of spread. For chargeable periods ending after 31 May 1996, the period of spread is as follows:

Amount of special contribution	No of years
£500,000–£999,999	2
£1,000,000–£2,000,000	3
£2,000,000+	4

The Revenue's discretion cannot be reviewed by Commissioners (see *Kelsall v Investment Chartwork* (1993) 65 TC 750).

Pension contributions for an unincorporated business proprietor are not an allowable deduction in computing profits, although relief is available as a deduction from taxable profits (see Chap 14 for details of proprietors' personal pension contributions).

Relief is available, under FA 1989, s 76, for contributions to UK pension schemes solely for overseas employees, and to overseas pension schemes that correspond to UK approved pension schemes if the payments are for employees who receive foreign emoluments or are non-resident and working wholly abroad.

However, expenses relating to an unapproved retirement benefit scheme are precluded from relief in computing business profits, if no-one is chargeable to income tax on the sum paid or on the benefits provided or to be provided (see *Tax Bulletin* 17 (June 1995), p 225).

Thirdly, FA 1996, Sch 9, para 2 deals with late payment of interest under the loan relationships rules. Specifically, it applies for the purpose of bringing debits into account in respect of a debtor relationship of a company where an authorised accruals basis of accounting is used for that relationship. If interest payable under that relationship is not paid within 12 months following the end of the accounting period in which it would otherwise be treated as accruing, and credits representing the full amount of the interest are not brought into account for any accounting period in respect of the corresponding creditor relationship, then debits relating to that interest are brought into account on the assumption that the interest does not accrue until it is paid.

Fourthly, FA 1996, Sch 9, para 5 allows a departure from the assumption in the case of creditor relationships that every amount payable under those relationships will be paid in full as it becomes due. This is allowed to the extent only that:

(a) a debt is a bad debt;
(b) a doubtful debt is estimated to be bad; or
(c) a liability to pay any amount is released.

Such a departure is allowed only where there is an appropriate adjustment if any part of an amount taken or estimated to represent an amount of bad debt is paid or otherwise ceases to be an amount in respect of which such a departure is allowed. Where a liability to pay any amount under a debtor relationship of a company is released, and the release occurs in an accounting period for which an authorised accruals basis of accounting is used in that relationship, no credit in respect of the release is required to be brought into account if the release is part of a relevant arrangement or compromise (voluntary arrangements under the Insolvency Act 1986, or a compromise or arrangement under CA 1985, s 425), or the relationship is one as respects which FA 1996, s 87 requires the use of an authorised accruals basis of accounting.

If a company makes a provision for a bad debt due from a connected party, the assumption that every amount payable under the relationship will be paid in full is applied. There is one exception to this rule where:

(a) in consideration of, or of any entitlement to, any shares forming part of the ordinary share capital of the company on whom the liability would otherwise have fallen, the creditor company treats the liability as discharged; and

(b) there would be no connection between the two companies for the accounting period in which that consideration is given if the question whether there is such a connection for that period was determined by reference only to times before the creditor company acquired possession of, or any entitlement to, the shares in question.

Bad debt relief is also denied even if the parties cease to be connected. ESC C28 alleviates potential obstacles to the provision of venture capital and to company rescues.

3.2 PERIOD IN WHICH RECEIPT ASSESSABLE OR DEDUCTION ALLOWABLE

3.2.1 Introduction

The profit or loss of a trade from the sale of goods for a given period depends on four factors:

(1) the sales made in the period;
(2) the cost of acquiring or manufacturing goods for resale;
(3) overhead or establishment expenditure or other expenditure of a revenue nature incurred in carrying on the business; and
(4) the valuation of stock of unsold goods, materials or work in progress.

In the trader's accounts, these matters should be dealt with following accepted accountancy principles applicable to the trade. For tax, this treatment is followed subject to specific statutory provisions and case-law. Although it might be thought that such considerations merely allocate income between one period of account and the next, there are cases where the effect can be of great significance. The inclusion of general reserves or the undervaluation of trading stock may postpone tax liabilities for many years.

BSC Footwear v Ridgeway (1972) 47 TC 495 upheld the Revenue's right to challenge a method of stock valuation that had been adopted for more than 50 years, saying that while the basis used by the company may have given a true picture of the trading results 'over the years', it did not produce 'the profits for 1959 taken in isolation, as was required for tax purposes'. The questions to be asked are thus:

(1) Have all the sources of profit relating to a particular accounting period been reflected in the profit and loss account on which an assessment is based?
(2) Has all allowable expenditure been charged in the appropriate period?
(3) Have trading stock and work in progress been valued on an acceptable basis?

In *Gardner, Mountain and D'Ambrumenil v CIR* (1947) 29 TC 69 it was held that for completely rendered services or supplied goods, where payment is not made until a subsequent tax year, the absence of payment in the tax year of supply cannot be treated as a loss; nor can the later payment be treated as pure profit in the subsequent tax year. Instead, in calculating the taxable profit under Schedule D, the net profit must be accounted for in the year of supply, even though payment has not yet been received.

3.2.2 Timing

The timing of receipts and expenses is governed by the general requirement that persons carrying on a trade or profession are assessable on 'the full amount of the profits or gains' (TA 1988, ss 60(1) (income tax) and 70(1) (corporation tax)) of the relevant period. The starting point is the business profits as shown by the accounts drawn up in accordance with the ordinary principles of commercial accounting. In *Gallagher v Jones* (1993) 66 TC 77, the Master of Rolls held that subject to express or implied statutory rules, accepted commercial accountancy principles, as modified over time, should be applied in ascertaining business profits and losses. Over many years, the courts have held that the principles of commercial accounting are of assistance in determining the period in which costs and receipts are recognised for tax purposes.

In *Southern Railway of Peru v Owen* (1956) 36 TC 602, the company operated a railway in Peru, and at the time, under Peruvian law, an employee was entitled to statutory compensation on the termination of his services. The amount an employee would receive was calculated by reference to the length of service and the rate of salary for each month of service. The company argued that on proper commercial accountancy principles it became liable year by year to pay a specific amount of 'deferred remuneration' when the employee's services terminated, and that the amount thereof accrued due to each employee from year to year and should be allowed as a deduction in computing the company's profits for each year.

The case is interesting because, although it went against the company, it was held that the company was not prevented by any rule of law from making a deduction for the deferred remuneration, and that a provision in its accounts for its prospective liability is permissible if capable of sufficiently accurate calculation. Unfortunately, its calculations were not sufficiently accurate.

Certain types of expenditure are disallowed for tax purposes even though it may be sound accounting practice to deduct such costs in a trader's accounts. However, in *Johnston v Britannia Airways* (1994) 67 TC 99, the High Court upheld the company's appeal to allow provisions made in its accounts for the future overhaul of jet aircraft. This was done by taking the average cost of the ten most recent overhauls. This was then converted to an average cost per flying hour, taking account of the history of the engine concerned. The provision in the accounts was arrived at by taking the average cost multiplied by the actual hours flown by each engine in the accounting period. The Special Commissioners had held that the provision gave a 'true and fair view' of the company's trading position. This case establishes an important precedent.

In a Privy Council case, *Bombay IT Commr v Ahmedabad New Cotton Mills* (1929) 9 ATC 574, stock was found to be grossly undervalued, and it was held that an assessment to rectify the closing undervaluation had to be reduced by the opening undervaluation to bring out the true profits. But in *Pearce v Woodall-Duckham* (1978) 51 TC 271 it was held that, distinguishing *Ahmedabad*, where a company altered its method of dealing with accrued profits on long-term contracts, and the closing work in progress in the first year accounts on the old basis was substantially below the opening figure in the second year accounts on the new basis, the difference must be included in the second year profits.

In *Pearce*, there was a change in the valuation of work in progress from an on-cost method to an accrued profit method. The change in method had increased significantly the opening value, which was brought into the company's accounts as a separate item 'surplus arising on change in valuation of contract work in progress at 31 December 1968'. It was held that this surplus, representing anticipated profits for work carried out prior to 1969, ought to be taxed in 1969 when it was first revealed and brought into account. If, however, those profits were not all received in 1969, that sum could be apportioned between 1969 and subsequent years. The decision was confirmed in the Court of Appeal, where it was stated: 'The company was entitled to produce accounts based on its on-cost method prior to 1969. The company was entitled, but not bound, to produce accounts for 1969 and subsequent years by the accrued profit method. The change was made for sound commercial reasons.' Equally, the Revenue's view is that where a basis that is valid for tax purposes has been adopted in a taxpayer's accounts, the taxpayer does not have the right to adopt a different basis in computing the profits figure to be entered on his tax return.

Pearce applies for accounting periods ending up to 5 April 1999. For changes of accounting basis taking effect after that date, the case-law rule is made statutory by FA 1998, s 44 and Sch 6. This itself is replaced by FA 2002, s 63 and Sch 22 (see 3.3).

3.2.3 Period in which receipts are to be included

The general principle is that an item becomes a trade receipt on the day on which it becomes a debt receivable, even though the date of receipt is postponed: this is the 'accruals' concept. Thus, when a sale is made in an accounting period, the sale price should normally be brought into account for tax purposes in that period even if the proceeds are not received until after the end of the period, although this may be subject to a possible provision for bad debts. Inevitably there are exceptions to this general rule.

In *JP Hall & Co v CIR* (1921) 12 TC 382, it was held that the date at which a transaction becomes a sale depends on the terms of the contract: it may be the date of delivery of the goods.

In *Symons v Weeks* (1983) 56 TC 360, a proportion of progress payments received by an architect that related to future work were excluded from the profit for a period, as they represented work to be done in future periods. Held, the amount to be included is the value of the work in progress estimated in accordance with the correct accountancy principles. Progress payments are only taken into account in the period in which they fall due to the extent that they represent the value of work done in that period.

In *Rownson, Drew and Clydesdale v CIR* (1931) 16 TC 595, a company varied the terms of an existing agreement under which it would receive additional sums, calculated with reference to sales results. The additional sums cannot be apportioned over the whole period of the agreement. The payment was to be made at the conclusion of the contract, dependent on results, and arose as a profit at the date when it became ascertainable.

In *Eckel v Board of Inland Revenue (Trinidad and Tobago)* (1989) 62 TC 331, consideration for a sale cannot be treated as a trade receipt until the trader has fulfilled all the conditions necessary for him to be entitled to the payment.

In *Morley v Tattersall* (1938) 22 TC 51, unclaimed balances of purchase money in the hands of a firm of auctioneers did not, on being subsequently distributed among the partners, become trading receipts. But in *Jay's The Jewellers v CIR* (1947) 29 TC 274, a pawnbroker came into possession of unclaimed surplus money on the sale of unredeemed pledges. It was held that the surpluses were not receipts of the company's trade when they were received, but became receipts of the trade when the company's right to retain the sale proceeds became absolute on the borrowers' failure to claim the surpluses within the statutory time limit.

In *Elson v Prices Tailors* (1962) 40 TC 671, unclaimed deposits left by customers who had failed to collect their made-to-measure suits or claim their deposits were true deposits and not sums in part payment. Thus they were to be included in the computation of profits and gains on the dates when they were received.

3.2.4 Period in which expenses are to be included

The normal accountancy practice is to deduct as an expense in the profit and loss account a sum actually accrued during the accounting period; such deductions are usually allowed in computing that period's taxable profit. In some circumstances, a deduction may also be made in the accounts for a liability that has not yet accrued but for which there is an expectation that it will arise in the future. The tax treatment of such a deduction depends on the facts of a particular case, the nature of the business concerned and, particularly, the degree of contingency. Deductions of this kind are often referred to as 'provisions' or 'reserves'.

Where a provision relates to specific expenditure that has already accrued or that the trader knows will arise and the amount of which can be calculated with a reasonable degree of accuracy, it is known as a 'specific provision' and is allowed for tax purposes. By contrast, a trader may create a general reserve (eg for repairs to property) against which expenditure is charged as and when it arises. This 'general provision' is not usually allowed for tax purposes.

A provision to meet contingent liabilities is only allowed as a deduction if it can be shown that it is an essential charge against the receipts of the accounting period concerned for the true profit to be stated.

In *Peter Merchant v Stedeford* (1948) 30 TC 496, it was held that a distinction must be drawn between an actual liability already accrued, which is deductible, and a liability which is future or contingent and for which no deduction can at present be made.

Insurance agents often receive a commission on selling a policy, subject to the liability to repay part of it if the policy lapses at an early date. If the commission is recognised as income at the outset, the Revenue accepts that the agent is entitled to make a provision for the contingent liability to repay it. However, in calculating the amount of the provision, the agent must make a proper valuation, taking into account factors such as the lapse rate among customers and the proportion of commission usually repayable on the relevant policy (see RI 30).

In *Naval Colliery Co v CIR* (1928) 12 TC 1017, a company was forced to close its mines owing to a strike. The complete work stoppage resulted in severe damage to the mine, and heavy expenditure had to be incurred for pumping and restoring pit props. The expenditure amount was charged in the account in the period before reconditioning work began. It was held that the cost of reconditioning was not a proper deduction in that accounting period. It is only when liability for expenditure is incurred that it becomes a proper charge for tax purposes; the fact that circumstances exist in a given period necessitating the expenditure is not the test to be applied. See also *Johnston v Britannia Airways* at 3.2.2, in which the company successfully made provision for the cost of major overhauls of each of its aircraft.

The Revenue has indicated that it considers provisions for future redundancy payments to be deductible provided:

(1) the provision is made in accordance with generally accepted accounting principles, including FRS 3.18;
(2) a decision is made during the period to proceed with a redundancy programme;
(3) an accurate calculation (usually including the identification of individual employees) is made in line with SSAP 17; and
(4) payment is made within nine months of the end of the period of account as required by FA 1989, s 43.

3.2.5 Anticipated losses

In *H Ford & Co v CIR* (1926) 12 TC 997, a company entered into contracts for the sale of grain from Argentina and undertook liability for detention of the ships. Labour troubles ensued and the ships were delayed. The company never admitted liability for a claim, and ultimately never paid it, but deducted the amount of the claim in its accounts. This amount was an anticipated liability only and therefore was inadmissible for tax purposes.

More recently, following the decision in *Herbert Smith (a firm) v Honour* (1999) STC 173, which concerned a provision for future rent payable on surplus business premises, the Revenue now accepts that there is no tax rule that denies a deduction for provisions made for 'anticipated losses'. Accurate provisions for foreseen losses on long-term contracts made in line with correct accounting practice are deductible.

3.2.6 Delivery and passing of ownership of goods

The strict position is that before goods are treated as sold or purchased for tax purposes, the property in the goods should have passed from the seller to the purchaser. For this purpose it is not essential that the goods should have been physically delivered. The time when the property in the goods has passed depends on the parties' intention, as evidenced by the contract terms and, in the absence of such evidence, is governed by the provisions of the Sale of Goods Act 1979, ss 17–19. In practice, and where considerable sums are not involved, the Revenue may be prepared to accept other methods of valuation of stock in trade at a particular date, so long as the particular method is followed consistently.

Certain traders sell goods on special terms whereby they retain (or reserve) the title to the goods until payment is made. This should be distinguished from the supply of goods as consignment stocks (eg on a sale or return basis), which are normally to be treated as stock in the hands of the supplier until disposed of by the consignee. For accountancy purposes, if the circumstances indicate that the reservation of title is regarded by the parties as having no practical relevance except in the event of the buyer's insolvency, the goods are, notwithstanding the strict legal position, treated as purchases in the buyer's accounts and sales in the supplier's accounts. The Revenue has agreed (in ESC B6) that for sales subject to reservation of title, the above recommended accountancy treatment is accepted for tax purposes provided both parties to the contract follow it.

3.2.7 Pre-trading expenditure
(TA 1988, s 401)

Relief is available for costs incurred within seven years before start of trade. If the normal tests for deductibility are applied, such expenditure is not allowed in computing profits, because at the time none exists. However, if the expenses are such that they would have been allowable if they were incurred at a time when a trade did exist, the expenditure is treated as if it were incurred on the day on which, and taken into the calculations of the profit or loss for the first period in which, the trade is first carried on. Examples of the types of expenditure to which this relief applies include:

- Rent for business premises
- Rates, insurance, heating and lighting
- Bank charges and interest
- Incidental costs of obtaining qualifying loan finance
- Wages or other payments to employees
- Lease rentals on machinery and plant and office equipment
- Accountancy fees
- Advertising costs.

Expenditure on the formation of a company or other capital expenditure is not allowable. The cost of an advance purchase of trading stock does not qualify for relief in this way because it will be deductible in arriving at profits when trading begins.

Where expenditure is incurred on the appraisal of the trade, its viability and its markets, outlets, suppliers or customers, there may be difficulty obtaining relief on the basis that such appraisal expenditure would only be incurred in the period leading up to the commencement of trade because it is incurred with a view to deciding whether to trade at all. Thus, it is expenditure that would not be incurred after the trade has been commenced and does not meet the special deductibility test.

Capital allowances are due in the same way as allowances given for expenditure incurred in the first period of trading, except that there is no seven-year time limit on expenditure.

If a company pays interest (thus giving rise to a non-trading debit under the FA 1996 loan relationship rules), it may make an election to carry forward the debit so that it can be relieved in the first accounting period in which it trades. The election must be made within two years from the end of the period in which it arose (FA 1996, s 82).

3.3 ADJUSTMENT ON CHANGE OF BASIS

3.3.1 Introduction

FA 1988, s 44 and Sch 6 put into legislation the case-law principle established by *Woodall-Duckham* and to provide a relieving provision for the move from a cash basis to an accruals basis. FA 2002, s 63 and Sch 22 extend that principle and provide further relieving measures. FA 1988, s 44 and Sch 6 applied where there was a change in accounting basis, but not where there is a change in the basis of accounting for something for tax purposes.

Accounts prepared under UK GAAP for companies and other taxable persons often necessarily have changes in their accounting policies to comply with new accounting standards, or if they consider that a different policy would be more appropriate for their current circumstances. Note that tax adjustments described below may change to a better understanding, driven by case-law. However, the new rules make very clear the adjustments needed to get from one method of computing taxable profits or losses to another. It does not apply where a method used was not a valid method because it did not comply with UK GAAP or paid insufficient regard to the facts.

3.3.2 Adjustment on change of basis
(FA 2002, s 63)

Specifically, the new rules apply where there is a change of basis of computing profits as between one period of account and another, and where the old basis accorded with either the law or a practice applicable at the time, and the new basis accords with both the law and any practice applicable at that time. The main difference between the new and old rules is that the new rules apply to changes of tax basis *and* of accounting basis. Under the present rules, the old basis may be in accordance with either law or practice but it does not have to be both. The change covers the situation where the courts show that an existing practice is wrong in law.

A 'change of basis' is either:

(1) a relevant change in accounting approach, which is a change in accordance with GAAP (Generally Accepted Accountancy Practice – see TA 1988, s 836A), that gives rise to a prior period adjustment; or

(2) a change in the 'tax adjustments' applied in the accounts. 'Tax adjustments' are the adjustments required or authorised by the existing legislation. A 'change in the tax adjustments applied' includes any change made as a result of a change of view of the law, but it excludes changes made by specific legislation.

Although it was implicit in the old rules, it is made clear that the new rules do not apply to those prior period adjustments that arise because of a fundamental error in previous periods of account (see FRS 3, para 63). This is because such accounts would have been neither in accordance with the law nor with practice.

3.3.3 The general rules
(FA 2002, Sch 22, paras 2–5)

There are two steps in the calculation of the required adjustment.

First step

This requires adding together any amounts representing the extent to which, comparing the two bases, profits were understated (or losses overstated) on the old basis:

(1) Receipts which on the new basis would have been brought into account in computing the profits of a period of account before the change of basis, to the extent that they were not so brought into account; *plus*

(2) Expenses which on the new basis fall to be brought into account in computing the profits of a period, of account after the change, to the extent that they were brought into account in computing the profits of a period of account before the change of basis; *plus*

(3) Deductions for opening trading stock or opening work in the first period of account on the new basis, to the extent that they are:
    (a) not matched by credits for closing trading stock or closing work in progress in the last period of account before the change, or
    (b) calculated on a different basis that if used to calculate those credits would have given a higher figure; *plus*

(4) Amounts recognised for accounting purposes for depreciation in the last period of account before the change to the extent that they were not the subject of an adjustment for tax purposes, where such an adjustment would be required on the new basis.

Second step

The second step establishes the amounts which would, otherwise, result in an overstatement of profits (or understatement of losses). These amounts are deducted to the extent to which they resulted in profits being overstated. They may be receipts that were brought in on the old basis, and will be brought in again on the new, or expenses that were not deducted before the change and would not be deducted after it. Thus any amounts representing the extent to which, comparing the two bases, profits were overstated (or losses understated) on the old basis should be deducted, as follows:

(1) Receipts which were brought into account in a period of account before the change, to the extent that they would not have been so brought into account if the profits had been computed on the new basis.

(2) Expenses which were not brought into account in computing the profits of a period of account before the change to the extent that they would have been brought into account for a period of account
    (a) before the change if the profits had been computed on the new basis, and
    (b) after the change if the profits had continued to be computed on the old basis.

(3) Credits for closing trading stock or closing work in progress in the last period of account before the change of basis, to the extent that they are:

(a) not matched by deductions for opening trading stock or opening work in progress in the first period of account on the new basis, or

(b) calculated on a different basis that if used to calculate those deductions would have given a lower figure.

An amount so deducted may not be deducted again in computing the profits of a period of account.

The references above to items being brought into account in a period of account before the change of basis are to their being brought into account:

(1) in computing the profits of the same trade, profession or vocation (for this purpose a trade, profession or vocation is not regarded as the same if TA 1988, s 113(1) or 337(1) applies (deemed discontinuance on change of persons carrying on trade, profession or vocation)); and

(2) in accordance with the law or practice then applicable (for this purpose the 'practice applicable' means the accepted practice in cases of that description for how profits should be computed under Schedule D Case I or II).

If the amount of the adjustment is positive, it is chargeable to tax. An amount thus chargeable to income tax:

(a) is treated as income arising on the last day of the first period of account for which the new basis is adopted;

(b) is chargeable under Schedule D Case VI;

(c) in the case of an individual whose income from the trade, profession or vocation in question is:

(i) relevant earnings for retirement annuity or personal pension contracts (see TA 1988, s 623(2)(c) or 644(2)(c)), or

(ii) earned income (see TA 1988, s 833(4)(c)),

is similarly relevant earnings or earned income for the tax year in which it is charged to tax; and

(d) is treated for loss relief purposes (see TA 1988, ss 380–391 (income tax) or ss 393–395 (corporation tax)) as profits of the trade, profession or vocation for the chargeable period for which it is charged to tax.

An amount so chargeable to corporation tax is treated as a receipt of the trade, profession or vocation arising on the last day of the first period of account for which the new basis is adopted.

If the amount of the adjustment is negative, it is allowed as an expense of the trade, profession or vocation arising on the last day of the first period of account for which the new basis is adopted.

3.3.4 **Special rules for certain cases**

Where, as a result of a change of basis, expenses brought into account before the change on the old basis would on the new basis be brought into account over more than one period of account after the change, no adjustment is made and the expenses cannot be deducted in computing the profits of the trade, profession or vocation for any period of account after the change.

Where there is a change of basis resulting from a tax adjustment affecting the calculation of any amount brought into account for closing trading stock or work in progress in the last period of account before the change, or for opening trading stock or work in progress in the first period of account on the new basis, or any amount brought into account in respect of depreciation, the adjustment required under the general rule is brought into account only when the asset to which it relates is realised or written off.

A special rule applies where there is a change of basis from not recognising a profit or loss on an asset until the asset is realised, to bringing assets into account in each account at a fair value. To the extent that in such a case a receipt within item (1) of the first step represents the fair value of an asset that is trading stock (see TA 1988, s 100), or an expense within item (2) of that step relates to such an asset, any resulting adjustment is not given effect until the period of account in which the value of the asset in question is realised.

In such a case, the person who is chargeable to tax on any adjustment charge may elect that the adjustment charge be spread over six periods of account. The election must be made by notice in writing, to the Revenue, within the time allowed. The time allowed is, for income tax, up to 31 January following the tax year in which the change of basis occurs, and, for corporation tax purposes, within 12 months of the end of the first accounting period to which the new basis applies. If an election is made, then, in each of the six periods of account beginning with the first period to which the new basis applies, an amount equal to one-sixth of the amount of the adjustment charge is treated as arising and chargeable to tax. If before the whole of the adjustment charge has been charged to tax the trade, profession or vocation is permanently discontinued, the whole of the amount so far as not previously brought into charge to tax is treated as arising and chargeable to tax immediately before the discontinuance.

A special rule applies where an individual makes a change of basis on ceasing to take advantage of the exemption for barristers and advocates in early years of practice (see FA 1998, s 43) or on that exemption coming to an end. Where this rule applies, any adjustment charge is spread over ten tax years, as follows:

(1) In each of the nine tax years beginning with that in which the whole amount would otherwise be chargeable to tax, an amount equal to whichever is the lesser of:

(a) one-tenth of the amount of the adjustment charge leaving out any allowance or charge under CAA 2001, and

(b) 10% of the profits of the profession for that tax year,

is treated as arising and chargeable to tax.

(2) In the tenth tax year, the balance of the adjustment charge is treated as arising and chargeable to tax.

(3) If before the whole of the adjustment charge has been charged to tax the profession is permanently discontinued, the preceding provisions apply, but without the alternative 10% limit.

This rule is subject to any election to accelerate payment of adjustment charge. A person who is chargeable to tax for a tax year on an amount representing part of an adjustment charge may elect that the amount treated as income arising in that tax year should be increased. This election must be made, by notice in writing, to the Revenue, on or before 31 January following the tax year in question. The election must specify the amount to be treated as income arising in the tax year, which may be any amount up to the whole of the adjustment charge so far as not previously charged to tax. Where an election has been made, the amount charged in any subsequent tax year is calculated as if the original amount of the adjustment charge were reduced by the additional amount treated as arising in the year for which the election was made.

3.3.5 Supplementary provisions

Where a trade, profession or vocation is carried on in partnership, the amount of any adjustment is computed for income tax as if the partnership were an individual resident in the UK, and for corporation tax as if it were a company resident in the UK. Each partner's share of any amount chargeable to tax is determined according to the profit-sharing arrangements for the 12 months ending immediately before the date on which the new basis was adopted. Any election must be made jointly by all the persons who have been members of the partnership in that 12-month period.

If spreading of the adjustment charge applies, then each partner's share of the amount chargeable in any tax year is determined for the first tax year, according to the profit-sharing arrangements for the 12 months ending immediately before the date on which the new basis was adopted, and for any subsequent tax year, according to the profit-sharing arrangements for the 12 months immediately preceding the anniversary in that year of that date.

If before the whole of the adjustment charge has been charged to tax the profession is permanently discontinued so the 10% alternative limit does not apply, then each partner's share of any amount chargeable on or after the discontinuance is determined as follows:

(1) if the discontinuance occurs on the date on which the new basis was adopted, according to the profit-sharing arrangements for the 12 months ending immediately before that date;

(2) if the discontinuance occurs after that date but before the first anniversary of that date, according to the profit-sharing arrangements for the period between that date and the date of discontinuance;

(3) if the discontinuance occurs after the first anniversary of the date on which the new basis was adopted, according to the profit-sharing arrangements for the period between the immediately preceding anniversary of that date and the date of discontinuance; and

(4) any election after the discontinuance must be made by each former partner separately.

In the case of the death of a person who, if he had not died, would have been chargeable to tax on an adjustment charge, the tax that would have been so chargeable is assessed and charged on his personal representatives and is a debt due from and payable out of his estate, and his personal representative may make any election that he might have made.

These rules apply to a change of basis taking effect in a period of account ending after 31 July 2001.

3.4 EXPENDITURE

3.4.1 General rules

The guiding principle in computing business profits for income or corporation tax purposes is that expenditure cannot be deducted if:

(1) it falls within the scope of any of the specific prohibitions in the income or corporation tax rule; or

(2) it violates the rule of tax law under TA 1988 that profits or income are computed on:
    (a) the full amount of the tax year's profits (Schedule D Cases I and II: TA 1988, s 60(1));
    (b) the actual amount of income arising in the tax year (Schedule D Case III: TA 1988, s 64(1));
    (c) the full amount of income arising in the tax year (Schedule D Cases IV and V: TA 1988, s 65(1));
    (d) the full amount of profits or gains arising in the tax year (Schedule D Case VI: TA 1988, s 69);
    (e) the full amount of profits, gains or income arising in the accounting period (corporation tax: TA 1988, s 70(1)).

For an item of revenue expenditure to be a proper deduction in computing a trade's taxable profits, it must be properly deductible in the trade's accounts following ordinary commercial accounting principles provided there is no specific statutory prohibition on such deduction. The principal statutory authority under which a deduction may be denied is TA 1988, s 74, which sets out restrictions on the items that may be deducted in computing profits under Schedule D Case I or II. In particular, it prohibits deduction in respect of the following.

Disbursements or expenses not wholly and exclusively laid out or expended

The legislation requires the expenditure to be incurred 'wholly and exclusively for the purposes of the trade'. Consequently, expenses incurred partly for trade purposes and partly for personal reasons are not allowable. For example, the Revenue invoked TA 1988, s 74(1)(a) to disallow the cost of clothing in *Mallalieu v Drummond* (1983) 57 TC 330 and of meals incurred by a self-employed carpenter working away from home in *Caillebotte v Quinn* (1975) 50 TC 222.

Where an expense is incurred for mixed purposes, the whole amount is disallowed. However, where it can be shown that an *additional* cost was incurred wholly for business reasons, a deduction may be due. Consequently, if a trader pays his wife a salary that exceeds the real value of her services as an employee, it is normally only the excess that is disallowed.

Note that the requirement is that the expenditure is incurred wholly for the *purposes* of the trade. This implies that the test to be satisfied is a subjective, rather than an objective, one. There is support for this in *Bentleys, Stokes & Lawless v Beeson* (1952) 33 TC 491, where it was held that if the activity is undertaken to both promote business and, say, entertain a friend, the requirement is not satisfied. If, however, the activity is solely to promote business, the requirement is met and the expenditure allowed. Note, however, that there is now a statutory disallowance for entertaining expenditure (see 3.4.2).

Unfortunately, more recent decisions by the courts have suggested that the proper test may be an objective one. In *Mallalieu v Drummond*, in which a barrister claimed clothing expenses, it was held that she needed clothes to travel to work and to wear at work, and that the fact she had to wear a certain type of clothing (ie black dresses) did not amount to expenditure made wholly for trade purposes.

A similar interpretation lies behind the decision in *Mackinlay v Arthur Young McClelland Moores & Co* (1989) 62 TC 704, which concerned removal expenses borne by the firm for two partners who were relocated within the UK. The problem lies in whether it can be said a partner's removal costs are laid out only partly for partnership purposes, or exclusively. The answer must be ascertained by the motive for the move. Thus here it was held that as the partners had moved to be nearer the partnership business *and* to establish a private residence for themselves and their families, the expenditure could not be treated as exclusively for the partnership's purposes.

Prima facie, terminal payments to employees on the cessation of a business cannot, on the authority of *CIR v Anglo Brewing Co* (1925) 12 TC 803, be deducted. Such payments relate to not carrying on the business!

However, TA 1988, ss 579 and 580 allow the deduction of statutory redundancy payments. Furthermore, TA 1988, s 90 enables payments in addition to statutory redundancy payments to be relieved to the extent that outgoings do not exceed three times the statutory sums. Section 90 also applies to partial discontinuances if the discontinued part of the business can be identified and the s 74(1)(a) test is otherwise satisfied.

Disbursements or expenses for domestic or private, as distinct from trade, purposes

Even if it were not disallowed under s 74(1)(a) as being not wholly and exclusively for business purposes, expenditure for domestic and private purposes is explicitly disallowable under s 74(1)(b).

Often such expenditure has a 'dual purpose'. The cost of nursing home treatment was disallowed even though the reason for the expenditure was the need for a private room from which to conduct business (*Murgatroyd v Evans-Jackson* (1966) 43 TC 581). Expenditure on ordinary clothing is not normally allowable (*Mallalieu*, above). The costs of meals at regular partners' lunchtime meetings was disallowed, but expenditure on accommodation, food and drink at the annual weekend conference was allowed (*Watkis v Ashford, Sparkes and Harward* (1985) 58 TC 468). In *McKnight v Sheppard* (1999) 71 TC 419, legal expenses in defending charges brought by a professional regulatory body were allowed – despite the fact that the taxpayer's 'personal reputation was inevitably involved'. But contributions towards the removal expenses of a partner moved in the interests of the firm were not allowed in *Arthur Young McClelland Moores*, above.

ESC A32 concerns goods taken by traders for personal consumption. *Sharkey v Wernher* (1955) 36 TC 275 established the principle that such a transfer should be treated as if it were a sale at market value. The Revenue takes a reasonably broad view in applying this principle. However, the case is not considered to apply to

(1) services rendered to the trader personally or to his household, the cost of which should be disallowed under s 74(1)(b);
(2) the value of meals provided for proprietors of hotels, boarding houses, restaurants, etc and members of their families, also disallowed under s 74(1)(b);
(3) expenditure incurred by a trader on constructing an asset which is to be used as a fixed asset in the trade.

If an item of trading stock is disposed of otherwise than in due course of the trade, the amount to be brought into account as a trade receipt is that representing the item's market value at the date of its disposal, and not its cost (*Sharkey*, above). This applies where a trader takes goods from trading stock for his personal use or consumption, or disposes of them otherwise than by sale in the course of trade, but it does not apply to services rendered to the trader personally or to expenditure incurred on the construction of a fixed asset for use in the trade.

Example

A is a grocer. Before adjusting for the items noted below, A's accounts for the year ended 30 June 2000 show a profit of £30,800. It is ascertained that

(a) A has withdrawn from his trading stock goods which cost him £1,000, and which he would normally sell for £1,250 for consumption by himself and his family;

(b) an assistant has employed his spare time in:

(i)   constructing shop fittings estimated to be worth £2,450;

(ii) repainting the shop front (value of work done estimated to be £500); and

(iii) decorating a bedroom (value of work done estimated to be £450).

It is estimated that the cost of the assistant's services was (1) £1,100, (2) £200, and (3) £150. The materials involved have already been treated correctly in the accounts.

A's Schedule D Case I computation for the tax year to 30 June 2000 is as follows:

	£	£
Profit shown by accounts		30,800
Add: Market value of goods consumed	1,250	
Cost of assistant's time		
(i) capital – constructing shop fittings	1,100	
(ii) not trading – decorating bedroom	150	2,500
Adjusted profit		33,300

It is useful to bear in mind that the disposal of an asset by a taxpayer after he has withdrawn it from his trading stock may give rise to a chargeable gain or allowable loss, and that for this purpose a trader is treated as having acquired the asset for 'a consideration equal to the amount brought into the accounts of the trade in respect of it for tax purposes' (TCGA 1992, s 161).

Rent for whole or part of dwelling house or domestic offices

If premises are partly used privately (eg a farmhouse, a shop with residential accommodation above), an allowance of not more than two-thirds of the rent is allowed unless the circumstances justify a higher proportion. In practice, council tax and day-to-day repairs are similarly apportioned. In *Thomas v Ingram* (1979) 52 TC 428, a freelance draughtsman's private earnings were minimal, and a claim for an allowance of 25% of the rates, heating and lighting expenses against income of £125 and £136 was reduced to £10. In *Mason v Tyson* (1980) 53 TC 333, the expenses of a flat used occasionally to enable a professional man to work late were not allowed.

Repair of premises; repairs/alterations of implements, utensils or articles

TA 1988, s 74(1)(d) prohibits any deduction 'beyond the sum actually expended' for repairs of premises, and the Revenue's contention that this debarred any allowance for such was rejected by the Special Commissioners in *Jenners Princes Street Edinburgh v CIR* 1998 Sp C 166. The Revenue now accepts that provisions properly made under FRS 12 are tax deductible unless there is an express rule to the contrary (eg provisions for capital expenditure).

Expenditure on repairs to plant, buildings, tools, utensils, office machinery, fixtures and fittings, etc may be deducted, but not expenditure upon the reconstruction of buildings even if undertaken in lieu of repairs, there being no provision for the allowance of a notional amount for repairs not done.

A sum set aside to meet the cost of renewals under a contractual obligation is not allowed if they are not actually carried out (*Peter Merchant v Stedeford* (1948) 30 TC 496).

Disputes arise frequently with the Revenue with regard to repairs to business premises, and while the principle involved is relatively simple, its practical application may be more difficult. If expenses are incurred in erecting a new structure in its entirety so that a new capital asset is created, the expenses are clearly of a capital nature and are therefore not allowable deductions in arriving at trading profits. The replacement of an entirety (ie a distinguishable separate structure having no physical connection with any other part of an industrial plant) is a capital expenditure (*O'Grady v Bullcroft Main Collieries* (1932) 17 TC 93), but the renewal of a part of an existing structure is not (*Samuel Jones & Co (Devondale) v CIR* (1951) 32 TC 513). Expenses incurred in the maintenance or reconstruction of an existing asset are generally allowed as a revenue expense. However, there are borderline cases that depend on their own circumstances.

If repairs and improvements are mixed, there is no provision for an apportionment of the total expenditure between repairs and improvements.

Repairs accumulated before use in the business are not allowable if the expenditure is necessary to bring the asset up to standard. Such expenditure is capital and therefore is disallowed as a charge on the trade profits (*Law Shipping Co v CIR* (1923) 12 TC 621). Where the asset is capable of use before the expenditure is incurred, it is likely to be treated as a repair (*Odeon Associated Theatres v Jones* (1971) 48 TC 257). In this case, some importance was placed on the accounting treatment of the expenditure as a repair. This importance was clarified in *Heather v PE Consulting Group* (1972) 42 TC 293, in which the Court of Appeal made clear that whether expenditure is capital or revenue is a matter of fact for the court to decide.

Loss not connected with or arising out of trade, profession or vocation

In *Strong & Co of Romsey v Woodifield* (1906) 5 TC 215, damages recovered by a guest injured by a falling chimney while staying at an inn were not allowed, on the grounds that the loss fell on the taxpayers in their capacity of 'householder' and not that of 'trader'.

Where a person holds an office and also carries on a profession, the expenses of the office not allowed for Schedule E purposes cannot be deducted from the Schedule D assessment in respect of profits of his profession, as these Schedules are mutually exclusive.

The writing-off of a bad debt cannot be disallowed under TA 1988, s 74(1)(a) because it is not a disbursement or expense. An alternative disallowance would be under s 74(1)(e) as loss not arising out of a trade. In *Sycamore plc and Maple v Fir* 1996 Sp C 104, the company had claimed a deduction for a bad debt for goods that it had supplied to a subsidiary. It had also made a loan to the subsidiary. The point at issue was whether payments made by the subsidiary should be credited to the loan account or should reduce the trade debt. The Special Commissioner held that the value of goods originally supplied to the subsidiary, and subsequently recovered, should be credited to the trade account and not to the loan account. The balance of the trade debt that was written off was allowable under s 74(1)(j). The loss on goods supplied while the subsidiary was making loan repayments was a loss 'connected with or arising out of the trade' and thus was not disallowed by s 74(1)(e).

Capital withdrawn from, or employed or intended to be employed in, the trade

Sums spent on assets of circulating capital may be capital within TA 1988, s 74(1)(f), equally with sums spent on assets that are fixed capital. In *European Investment Trust Co v Jackson* (1932) 18 TC 1, a finance company was financed, in part, by fluctuating advances from its parent company. Interest was paid on daily balances. It was held that the advances were of moneys employed or intended to be employed as capital in the company's trade. Accordingly, the interest was disallowed.

Capital expenditure is not a cost that may be deducted in arriving at profits for tax purposes. The generally accepted definition of capital expenditure was given in *Atherton v British Insulated and Helsby Cables* (1925) 10 TC 155, where it was held that:

'when an expenditure is made with a view to bringing into existence an asset or an advantage for the enduring benefit of a trade . . . there is very good reason (in the absence of special circumstances leading to an opposite conclusion) for treating such an expenditure as properly attributable not to revenue but to capital.'

The definition in *Atherton* is most general; for example, the fact that expenditure is recurring expenditure rather than a 'once and for all' outlay does not mean that it is revenue expenditure. Thus, 'if the sum payable is not a revenue payment it cannot be made so by permitting it to be paid by annual instalments' (*Henriksen v Grafton Hotel* [(1942) 24 TC 453]). It was also held in that case that an enduring benefit need not be a long-term benefit; expenditure incurred in obtaining a liquor licence for three years was held to provide an enduring benefit which was capital in nature.

Money spent on acquiring an asset to be used for the trade is a capital outlay, whether the asset is a building or something liable to be worn out, such as a machine. The purchase of goodwill is capital expenditure, even though there is no tangible asset. Similarly, extensive repairs that had to be carried out before a ship could be used for a company's trade are regarded as capital expenditure (*Law Shipping Co v CIR* (1923) 12 TC 621). However, in *Odeon Associated Theatres* (above), the company had acquired several theatres that, because of wartime restrictions, needed repair and redecoration. This had not affected the purchase price and did not restrict their use for public performances. *Law Shipping* was distinguished because the theatres could still be used, whereas the ship required a refit to make it seaworthy. A lump sum payment to secure release from an onerous liability, such as a lease at a high rent or a fixed rate loan, is also regarded as capital expenditure.

The Revenue can take this to extremes. In the November 1991 issue of *Tax Bulletin*, it stated that expenditure on a course attended by a proprietor is regarded as capital expenditure if he attends to acquire new expertise, knowledge or skills. In contrast, where the individual attends merely to update expertise that he already possesses, the expenditure is normally regarded as revenue expenditure.

Capital employed in improvements of premises occupied for trade purposes

No deduction is allowed for any capital employed in the improvement of premises occupied for trade purposes. It follows that a deduction can be allowed only for the sum actually expended on repairing the business premises. There have been many cases on the question whether what was done was repair work or amounted to rebuilding.

In *Margrett v Lowestoft Water and Gas Co* (1935) 19 TC 481, the company built a water tower and constructed a new reservoir. However, the new reservoir was on a different site from and replaced an old reservoir that was considered to be not worth repairing. It was twice the size of the old one and technically it was an improvement on the old reservoir. It was held that no part of the expenditure on the new reservoir was expenditure for repairs and that the whole of it was capital expenditure.

In *Samuel Jones & Co* (above), the cost of replacing an old factory chimney by a new one, which was not a significant improvement over the old one, was allowed, together with the cost of removing the old chimney. In *O'Grady v Bullcroft Main Collieries* (above), the cost of replacing a chimney by another of an improved type, and on a different site, was disallowed as being capital expenditure. The distinction being made here is that in the latter case the replacement was regarded as being of the 'entirety', while in the former the chimney was merely an inseparable part of an 'entirety', ie the factory.

In *Thomas Wilson (Keighley) v Emmerson* (1960) 39 TC 360, the roof of a three-storey building fell into disrepair and reconstruction became necessary. The building acquired a new top floor and roof which was much higher than the old roof. It was held that the expenditure on this work was capital expenditure and therefore not an allowable deduction in computing the company's profits.

In the context of *Lurcott v Wakely and Wheeler* [1911] 1 KB 905, it was held that:

> 'Repair is restoration by renewal or replacement of subsidiary parts of a whole. Renewal, as distinguished from repair, is reconstruction of the entirety, meaning by the entirety not necessarily the whole but substantially the whole subject matter under discussion.'

Interest that might have been made

No allowance can be given on interest on any of the amounts disallowed in the foregoing commentary.

Debts

A general provision against bad debts is not allowable, but provisions against specific debts are a proper deduction for tax purposes provided it can be shown that the amount is a reasonable provision. The exceptions are as follows:

(a) a bad debt;
(b) a debt or part of a debt released by the creditor wholly and exclusively for the purposes of his trade, profession or vocation as part of a relevant arrangement or compromise (Insolvency Act 1986 (voluntary arrangements); CA 1985, s 425 (compromise or arrangement)); and
(c) a doubtful debt estimated to be bad, ie in the case of the debtor's bankruptcy or insolvency, except to the extent that any amount may reasonably be expected to be received on the debt.

A provision may be allowable even though the debt is subsequently collected: the key question is whether the provision was reasonable at the time the accounts were drawn up. If this test is satisfied, the provision is allowable and the amounts subsequently collected are brought into account as receipts for the year in which they are received.

The Revenue has explained its approach to provisions for bad or doubtful debts in *Tax Bulletin*, August 1994. Its interpretation is that a trader may be entitled to a deduction provided the following circumstances are satisfied:

(1) the debt existed at the balance sheet date; or
(2) before the accounts were finalised the trader or the company's directors discovered that the debtor's financial position at the balance sheet date was such that the debt was unlikely to be paid.

The Revenue states that a common example of this is where a debtor goes into administration or liquidation shortly after the balance sheet date and before the date on which the financial statements are approved by the trader. Its occurrence before the accounts were finalised normally sheds light on the debtor's financial position at the balance sheet date. If the period between that date and approval of the accounts is short, it is unlikely that a debtor would have gone from financial good health to insolvency in that period. In these circumstances it is normally reasonable for the trader to regard the debt as doubtful. The acceptable amount of provision depends on the information available.

The Revenue contrasts this with a situation where a debtor is an habitually slow payer and there are no grounds to believe his financial position has changed. Here the Revenue argues that the length of time that a debt has been outstanding is not in itself a sufficient reason to regard the debt as doubtful.

A general bad debt provision to cover contingent bad debts is not allowed. A provision for discounts on debtors' accounts may be allowed, if it is reasonable and on a consistent basis from year to year.

Average loss beyond actual amount of loss after adjustment

The prohibition of the deduction of any sum in respect of 'any average loss beyond the actual amount of loss after adjustment' applies to cases of marine and aviation risk where either there is no insurance, or the insurance is for less than the full value, or is 'free from average'. If the loss is fully covered by insurance, the question does not arise. A 'general average loss' occurs where any damage or loss has been properly and voluntarily incurred in relation to a ship or its cargo for its safety. This would apply eg if cargo was thrown overboard to lighten the ship during a storm. The rule allows those who do not suffer any loss in such circumstances to deduct as an expense adjusted average contributions paid, and those who do suffer loss to deduct only the amount reduced by the average contribution received.

Sums recoverable under insurance or contract of indemnity

Where a business can get back from an insurance company the money that it has paid out, there is no deduction due for the expenditure. The same treatment applies where a trader has been indemnified against particular cost.

Premiums for business purposes are normally allowable, including insurance of assets, against accidents to employees and against loss of profits, and premiums under mutual insurance schemes. Any corresponding recoveries are trading receipts (or set off against trading expenses – see TA 1988, s 74(1)(l)) or capital, according to the nature of the policy.

Premiums on policies in favour of the employer insuring against death or critical illness of key employees are generally allowable, and the proceeds of any such policies are treated as trading receipts.

Annuity or other annual payment (other than interest) payable out of profits

The combined effect of subss (m) and (p) (and, before 6 April 1997, subs (q), now repealed) of TA 1988, s 74(1) is to prohibit the deduction in computing profits of annuities, annual payments (other than interest), patent royalties, etc payable under deduction of tax at source. Subsection (m) applies only to amounts 'payable out of the profits'. Payments made before the profits can be ascertained are not payable out of the profits and therefore not within the s 74(1)(m) prohibition (see *Gresham Life Assurance v Styles* (1890) 3 TC 185). A company can deduct the amounts paid as an annual charge.

Interest paid to non-UK resident person at more than reasonable commercial rate

Interest payable to non-UK residents is deductible only to the extent that it is payable at a reasonable commercial rate and either:

(1) is paid under deduction of tax (TA 1988, s 349) – in this event the gross amount of the interest is deductible from profits (TA 1988, s 82(5)), or
(2) is contractually payable abroad (and is in fact so paid) by a UK-resident sole trader or partnership either on a liability incurred for purposes of the foreign activities of the trade, etc or in a currency other than sterling.

There can be no deduction of interest if the recipient is a partner in the trade, or both payer and recipient are under common control.

Note that this does not apply for corporation tax. Also, there are anti-avoidance provisions for interest paid to a connected non-resident.

Royalties or other similar payments
(See also comments above with regard to TA 1988, s 74(1)(m)).

Certain annual payments (eg patent royalties) generally need to be paid net of income tax at the basic rate. The payments are not deductible in arriving at an unincorporated trader's profits which are assessable under Schedule D Case I or II, although they are allowed as a deduction for higher rate purposes. A company can deduct the amounts paid as an annual charge.

Note that s 74(1)(p) does not cover royalties paid to a non-UK resident for the user of a patent abroad.

3.4.2 Expenditure specifically disallowed

Entertaining and gifts to customers
(TA 1988, s 577)

Any expenses for entertaining customers or suppliers are disallowed. There used to be an exception for the cost of entertaining overseas customers, but this no longer applies. There is an exception that may apply where the entertaining is provided by an hotelier, restaurateur or by someone else who provides entertainment in the ordinary course of his trade. Staff entertainment is also an allowable expense, but the individual employee may be assessed on a benefit-in-kind.

The cost of gifts to customers, potential customers and potential introducers is also disallowed unless the gift carries a conspicuous advertisement and is neither food, drink, tobacco or a voucher exchangeable for such goods, nor an item that costs more than £50 per recipient per year.

Illegal payments and fines
(TA 1988, s 577A)

There is a specific provision disallowing illegal payments such as bribes. This also covers payments made in response to threats, menaces, blackmail and other forms of extortion.

Fines and penalties for breach of the law have been disallowed since *CIR v Alexander von Glehn & Co* (1920) 12 TC 232, in which a company was refused a deduction for the costs of settling an action for breach of World War I regulations. The Revenue often invokes this case to disallow parking fines.

Expenditure on car hire
(TA 1988, ss 578A and 578B)

There is a reduction in the amounts allowable as deductions in computing profits chargeable to tax under Schedule D Case I or II, or which can be included as expenses of management of an investment company (see TA 1988, s 130) for expenditure on the hiring of a car to which this rule applies. This applies to the hiring of a car which is not a qualifying hire car, and the retail price of which when new exceeds (for 2002–03) £12,000.

'Car' means a mechanically propelled road vehicle other than one of a construction primarily suited for the conveyance of goods or burden of any description, or of a type not commonly used as a private vehicle and unsuitable for such use (references to a car accordingly include a motorcycle). A car is a qualifying hire car if it is hired under a hire-purchase agreement (per TA 1988, s 784(6)) under which there is an option to purchase exercisable on the payment of a sum equal to not more than 1% of the retail price of the car when new, or it is a qualifying hire car under the plant or machinery allowances rules (CAA 2001, s 82). 'New' means unused and not second-hand.

For expenditure incurred on the hiring of a car that was first registered in the period beginning on 17 April 2002 and ending on 31 March 2008, the restriction *does not* apply to the hiring during that period of a car, other than a motorcycle, if it is an electrically propelled car, or it is a car with low CO_2 emissions (see CAA 2001, s 45D).

Where the restriction applies, the amount that would otherwise be allowable or capable of being included must be reduced by multiplying it by the fraction:

$$\frac{£12,000 + P}{2P}$$

where P = the retail price of the car when new. If an amount has been thus reduced and subsequently there is a rebate (however described) of the rentals, or there occurs in connection with the rentals a transaction within TA 1988, s 94 (debts deducted and subsequently released), the amount of the rebate or transaction otherwise taxable must be reduced by multiplying it by the fraction as above.

War risk premiums
(TA 1988, ss 586 and 587)

War damage insurance premiums are not allowed for tax purposes except for ships, aircraft or goods in transit. Premiums relating to the risk of war injuries to employees are disallowed, as are payments to employees in respect of war injuries.

3.4.3 Expenditure specifically allowed

Cost of raising business finance
(TA 1988, s 77)

There are often certain costs in raising long-term finance. For many years these costs were regarded as capital expenditure by the Revenue. A statutory deduction is now available provided certain conditions are satisfied, ie the costs must:

(1) be wholly and exclusively incurred in obtaining loan finance, providing security or repaying a loan; and

(2) represent expenditure on professional fees, commissions, advertising, printing or other incidental expenses in relation to raising finance.

In some cases a deduction is available even though the attempt to raise business finance failed.

The Revenue's view is that premiums paid on an insurance policy do not qualify, even though the policy may have been taken out at the lender's insistence.

Contributions to local enterprise agencies
(TA 1988, s 79)

Contributions made to an approved local enterprise agency are deductible.

Contributions to training and enterprise councils and local enterprise companies
(TA 1988, s 79A)

Contributions made to a training and enterprise council (in England and Wales) or a local enterprise company (in Scotland) are deductible.

Expenses connected with foreign trades, etc
(TA 1988, ss 80 and 81)

Travelling expenses incurred by a UK resident and domiciled taxpayer from his home to a place of work carried on entirely overseas, where he carries on a trade, profession or vocation, are allowable for tax purposes. The section parallels broadly TA 1988, s 193. This means that board and lodging overseas is allowed. If the taxpayer is working overseas for a continuous period of 60 days or more, up to two visits per tax year by his spouse and by his children aged 18 or under at the beginning of the outward journey are also deductible.

Where such a person has more than one trade carried on overseas and at least one is carried on wholly overseas, the expenses of business travel between those trades are deductible for tax purposes (apportioned between the respective trades).

Expenditure on research and development (R&D)
(TA 1988 s 82A)

Where a person carrying on a trade incurs revenue expenditure on R&D related to that trade, and which is undertaken directly by him or on his behalf, the expenditure incurred may be deducted as an expense in computing the trade's profits for tax purposes.

For a description of the R&D tax credit scheme see 3.9.

Payments to research associations, universities, etc
(CAA 1990, s 82B)

Expenditure falling into either of the following categories may be deducted as an expense in computing a trade's profits for tax purposes. These are the payment of any sum to:

(1) an approved association the object of which is to undertake scientific research related to the class of trade to which the trade belongs, or
(2) be used for such scientific research to any approved university, college, research institute or other similar institution.

Patent fees, etc and expenses
(TA 1988, s 83)

In computing a trade's profits, there may be deducted any fees paid or expenses incurred in obtaining the grant of a patent, an extension of the term of a patent, the registration of a design or trademark, an extension of the period for which the right in a registered design subsists or the renewal of registration of a trademark, or in connection with a rejected or abandoned application for a patent made for the purposes of the trade.

Gifts in kind to charities
(TA 1988, s 83A)

Relief applies to gifts to charities by a trader of machinery or plant which he manufactures or sells, or has used in his trade, and claimed capital allowances therefor. This is achieved by providing that no amount is required to be brought into the Schedule D Case I computation as trading receipts or into the capital allowances computation as disposal consideration.

Gifts of medical supplies and equipment
(FA 2002, s 54)

Relief applies where for humanitarian purposes a company makes a gift from trading stock of medical supplies, or medical equipment for human use. This includes the related costs of transportation, delivery and distribution. Nothing has to be brought into account as a trading receipt of the company as would normally apply to gifts.

Gifts to educational establishments
(TA 1988, s 84)

Relief applies to gifts by a trader of machinery or plant which he manufactures or sells, or has used in his trade, and claimed capital allowances. The relief is achieved by not requiring any credit, either as a trading receipt or in the capital allowances computations.

Costs of establishing share option or profit-sharing schemes: relief
(TA 1988, s 84A)

Relief is available for the cost of establishing an approved share option scheme or a profit-sharing scheme.

Payments to trustees of approved profit-sharing schemes
(TA 1988, s 85)

Payments by a company to trustees of an approved profit-sharing scheme are allowable deductions for computing the company's trading profits.

Costs of establishing employee share ownership trusts
(TA 1988, s 85A)

Relief is available for the cost of establishing a qualifying employee share ownership trust.

Employees seconded to charities and educational establishments
(TA 1988, s 86)

An employer can obtain a deduction for the salary costs of staff seconded to charities and educational establishments.

Payroll giving schemes: contributions to agent's expenses
(TA 1988, s 86A)

If an employer operates an approved payroll giving scheme (under TA 1988, s 202), any voluntary contributions to the agent for the expenses of a running scheme are deductible.

Taxable lease premiums
(TA 1988, s 87)

Where the payer of an amount treated as a premium paid under a lease (under TA 1988, ss 34 and 35) uses the property acquired for the purposes of his trade, he is given relief in addition to any rent paid under the lease terms. Relief is given each year on the fraction of the chargeable amount that year. Note, however, that the relief is not granted for a premium paid for the assignment of a lease, but an assignee takes over the unexpired relief of the assignor.

Example

> B acquired on 30 September 1987 a leasehold interest in factory premises to be used for his trade. The term of the lease was 30 years, and B paid a premium of £40,000. Accounts are made up annually to 31 December. For each accounting year B can deduct £560 from his chargeable profits in respect of the premium, computed as follows:
>
> | | £ |
> |---|---|
> | Premium paid | 40,000 |
> | Less: $\dfrac{30-1}{50} \times 40,000$ | 23,200 |
> | Chargeable amount | 16,800 |
> | | |
> | Period of lease (30 years) | |
> | $\dfrac{16,800}{30}$ = Annual deduction | £560 |

Improvement to lease

Where the cost of work carried out by a tenant is deemed to be a payment of a premium, it shall be disregarded for the above relief if a claim for capital allowances may be made for it. Otherwise, the lease premium is increased by the amount of the cost of the work.

Alteration of lease premium

Where an alteration is made to the amount of any lease premium, the original deduction must be recalculated.

Payments to Export Credits Guarantee Department
(TA 1988, s 88)

Payments to the Export Credits Guarantee Department can be deducted as a trading expense under Schedule D Case I or II.

Debts proving irrecoverable after event treated as discontinuance
(TA 1988, s 89)

If a trade is treated as discontinued under TA 1988, s 113 on a change in partners or if a company ceases to trade within TA 1988, s 337, future profits of the trade are reduced by any additional bad debts not previously provided for.

Additional payments to redundant employees
(TA 1988, s 90)

Redundancy or similar payments made to employees which would have been allowable had the business continued to trade are deemed to be paid as allowable expenses on the last day of business, so long as it does not exceed three times the redundancy or other payments as defined by TA 1988, s 580.

Under general Schedule D Case I and II rules, redundancy payments are normally an allowable deduction provided they are laid out wholly and exclusively for business purposes and the payments are not of a capital nature.

Where such payments are made in the course of the discontinuance of a trade, they are not admissible as a deduction (*CIR v Anglo Brewing Co* (1925) 12 TC 803). However, TA 1988, s 579 provides a deduction for statutory redundancy payments, and s 90 gives relief for additional payments, inadmissible on the *Anglo Brewing* principle, up to three times the statutory payment made. See further 3.2.4(1)-(4).

Where the right to a tax deduction is dependent on s 90 or 579, relief is due for the period of account in which the payment is made. If the payment is made after the discontinuance of the business, it is regarded for tax relief purposes as if it was made on the last day on which the business was carried on.

Cemeteries
(TA 1988, s 91)

The cost of land used for graves is allowed as a trading expense when sold. The amounts expended on land and buildings are written off progressively, as they are likely to be of little use when the cemetery is full. This is achieved by applying to such costs the fraction:

$$\frac{\text{number of graves sold}}{\text{number of graves sold} + \text{number of spaces remaining at period end}}$$

The same principle is applied to crematoria with the computation based on 'memorial garden plots' instead of grave spaces.

Waste disposal: restoration payments
(TA 1988, s 91A)

Where, as a condition of planning permission, expenditure is incurred to restore a waste disposal site, such expenditure is an allowable expense of the trade.

Waste disposal: preparation expenditure
(TA 1988, ss 91B and 91BA)

If a trader incurs expenditure to prepare a site for waste disposal, tax relief is given for appropriate expenditure. This includes the cost of obtaining the licence; it does not include site acquisition costs nor expenditure qualifying for capital allowances. Pre-trading expenditure is allowed as if incurred on the first day of trading.

Where the whole of a site is transferred to a new operator and he holds the necessary licence, he will become entitled to allowances on the same basis as they were given to the original operator.

Mineral exploration and access
(TA 1988, s 91C)

Businesses that incur expenditure on mineral exploration and access are not entitled to an immediate 100% deduction for the intangible cost of drilling oil production wells. The expenditure does, however, qualify for mineral extraction capital allowances at 25% a year on the reducing balance basis.

Expenditure on remediation of contaminated land
(FA 2001 s 70 and Sch 22)

If the company concerned so elects, a deduction is available for capital expenditure on remediation of contaminated land.

Rents payable for electric line, etc wayleaves
(TA 1988, s 120)

Rents for any easement in connection with electric, telegraphic or telephonic wires or cables are now made without deduction of tax and are therefore allowed as Schedule D Case I deductions in the normal way.

Schemes for rationalising industry
(TA 1988, ss 568–572)

Contributions made to certified schemes for rationalising industry and to statutory redundancy schemes are deductible.

Statutory redundancy payments
(TA 1988, s 579)

The net cost of statutory redundancy payments is an allowable cost and is treated as paid on the last day of business. Additional payments to redundant employees of up to three times the statutory amount are also deductible (TA 1988, s 90).

Relief for unremittable overseas income
(TA 1988, ss 584 and 585)

If a UK resident is due to receive foreign income, but is prevented by the foreign government from bringing it directly or indirectly into the UK, the UK tax liability is not collected until the income becomes remittable and account is taken of any change in value. For corporation tax, when the income becomes remittable it is treated as income arising then, and is not related back to when it originally arose.

The foreign income of a non-domiciled UK resident is taxable on a remittance basis under Schedule D Case IV or V or under Schedule E Case III and a claim for relief is available for delayed remittances, if it is shown that remittance was delayed because of government or monetary restrictions in the foreign country. In this event the income may be deemed to have been remitted in the basis year for the tax year in which it arises and not in the year in which it is actually remitted.

Training courses for employees
(TA 1988, ss 588 and 589)

Expenditure on a qualifying course undertaken by a current or former employee for retraining him for future employment elsewhere is allowable. If the retraining conditions are not fulfilled (eg because the employee is retained in employment), the relief is withdrawn and PAYE recovered on the benefits. A course is a 'qualifying course' if:

(1) it provides training designed to impart or improve skills or knowledge relevant to, and intended to be used in the course of, gainful employment (including self-employment) of any description; and
(2) it is devoted entirely to the teaching and/or practical application of the skills or knowledge; and
(3) its duration does not exceed one year; and
(4) all teaching and practical application forming part of it takes place within the UK.

It is not regarded as a 'qualifying course' in relation to a particular employee unless:

(a) he attends the course on a full-time or substantially full-time basis; and
(b) he is employed by the employer full time throughout the period of two years ending when he begins to undertake the course or, if it is earlier, when he ceases to be employed by that employer; and
(c) the opportunity to undertake the course, on similar terms as to payment or reimbursement of relevant expenses, is available either generally to holders or past holders of offices or employment under the employer or to a particular class or classes of such holders or past holders.

An employee must

(i) begin to undertake the course of training while he is employed by the employer or within one year after he ceases to be so employed; and

(ii) cease to be employed by the employer not later than the end of two years beginning at the end of the qualifying course of training.

Where an employee undertakes a qualifying course, the relevant expenses consist of:

- fees for attendance;
- fees for any examination taken during or at the conclusion of the course;
- the cost of books which are essential for a person attending the course; and
- travelling expenses incurred wholly, exclusively and necessarily in attending the course.

Counselling services for employees
(TA 1988, ss 589A and 589B)

Expenditure on qualifying counselling services for redundant employees is allowable. Services are 'qualifying counselling' services if:

(1) their purpose is to enable the employee to adjust to the loss of job and/or to find a new job (including self-employment);

(2) they consist of advice and guidance, imparting or improving skills, or providing the use of office equipment or similar facilities (but financial counselling is not covered);

(3) the employee has been employed full time for two years;

(4) the services are available either generally or to that class of employees; and

(5) the services are provided in the UK; if provided partly abroad, the expense can be apportioned.

Related travelling expenses incurred wholly, exclusively and necessarily in obtaining the counselling services are also deductible.

Pools payments for football ground improvements
(FA 1990, s 126)

Football pools promoters can, in computing their trading profits, deduct payments made to the trustees of the Football Trust 1990. The trustees spend the money on capital works to improve spectators' safety and comfort at football grounds in accordance with the recommendations in Taylor LJ's report on the Hillsborough disaster. Football clubs can claim capital allowances on their gross qualifying capital expenditure and do not have to deduct the contribution received from the trustees.

Expenditure on films
(F(No 2)A 1997, ss 41–43 and 48)

Preliminary expenditure on planning on a qualifying film up to the first day of shooting is deductible. However, this must not exceed 20% of the film's total budget. Abortive expenditure is allowed if the film would have been a qualifying film.

Expenditure on producing or acquiring a qualifying film may be written off as to one third in the period in which it is completed or acquired and one third in each of the following two years. For expenditure between 1 July 1997 and 2 July 2002, a 100% write off is available. Extensive guidance on the treatment of such expenditure is given in SPs 1/93 and 1/98.

Consideration for certain restrictive undertakings
(FA 1988, s 73)

Payments to past, present or future employees for restrictive undertakings, where the employee is assessable on the payment as an emolument of the employment (TA 1988, s 313), are deductible in calculating the employer's taxable profits.

Contributions to qualifying employee share ownership trust
(FA 1989, s 67)

Corporation tax relief is given where a UK-resident company makes a payment to the trustees of a trust that is a qualifying employee share ownership trust, the purpose of which is to acquire and distribute shares in the founding company to employees.

Expenditure on security assets and services
(TA 1988, ss 112 and 113)

Where a special threat to an individual's personal physical security (or that of any member of his family or household) arises directly from his trade, profession or vocation (carried on by him alone, or in partnership), then the cost of certain assets and services of improving physical security is deductible. Security assets include equipment and structures (eg a wall), but exclude cars, ships, aircraft and dwellings (including associated grounds). The Revenue's view is that only those persons who are at a special risk from terrorists, extremists and other similar groups qualify for relief.

Loan relationships
(FA 1996, ss 82 and 84)

Deficits on a company's trading loan relationships are deductible. Charges and expenses in connection with a loan relationship are also allowed.

3.5 RECEIPTS

3.5.1 Introduction

The initial assumption is that most receipts coming into the hands of a person carrying on a trade, etc 'arise' from the trade (TA 1988, s 18(1)), insofar as they relate to the disposal of trading stock or from the provision of services, etc. So far as concerns such receipts, the only open question may be one of timing (ie the period of account in which they should be recognised). However, receipts may arise otherwise than as consideration for the provision of goods and services. There are two main points at issue: Does the sum concerned arise from the trade at all? If it does, is it a capital or revenue item?

Although receipts may be excluded because they are not trading receipts of the particular business under review, it is possible that they arise from another, separate business or are otherwise assessable under Schedule D. If a receipt is of a capital nature, or arises out of an asset or rights of some description, it is possible that there may be a disposal giving rise to a chargeable gain or allowable loss (see Chap 5).

There is a distinction to make between money received by a trader in that capacity (receipts arising from the trade) and that received in a personal capacity. Sums received in a personal capacity include an unsolicited sum in the nature of a testimonial or a solatium, albeit with compensatory elements (which would make it a voluntary payment and not taxable), or where the recipient has suffered personal injury (which would be compensation for personal injury and not taxable). Compensation for personal injuries should not be included in the Schedule D Case I or II computation, even if the sum is calculated by reference to the loss of income already sustained, or the loss of future earning power. Indeed, the courts, in calculating amounts referable to the loss of earnings, treat the compensation as if paid net of the tax liabilities that would have arisen had the individual not suffered injury and the consequent income loss (following *British Transport Commission v Gourley* [1955] 3 All ER 796). This treatment applies only to compensation for injuries suffered by the proprietor of a business. Compensation received to compensate a trader for an injury to an employee is taxable, as are payments to companies.

3.5.2 Items included as trading receipts

The adjustment of accounts for tax purposes may involve the addition of sums that are assessable as trading income, or are dealt with in some special way, but that have not been credited in the trading/profit and loss accounts. Among the items that may be involved are the following:

(1) Sums recovered under insurance policies on items that are current assets (eg amounts recovered from the insurer of stock destroyed by fire must be included as a trading receipt).

(2) Compensation, in so far as it fills 'a hole in the profits' rather than a 'hole in the capital' (eg compensation received upon the cancellation of an agency agreement (*Anglo-Persian Oil Co v Dale* (1931) 16 TC 253)).

(3) Sums recovered under insurance policies on the lives of employees where the premiums were allowed against profits.

(4) Agricultural and similar subsidies, but not those on capital account (see Chap 4 for effect on capital allowances).

(5) If a trade is treated as discontinued under TA 1988, s 113 on a change in partners or if a company ceases to trade within s 337, future profits of the trade may be reduced by any additional bad debts not previously provided for (s 89).

(6) Trade debts previously allowed as a deduction for tax purposes are assessed if they are released otherwise than as part of a relevant arrangement or compromise (s 94).

(7) Rents received by the landlord of tied premises (eg public houses owned by brewers) which are let in the course of a trade are treated as trading receipts (and expenses relating to the premises are treated as trading expenses) (s 98).

3.5.3 Receipts excluded from trading profits

There are also items that should be excluded from trading profits:

(1) Dividends and interest received under deduction of tax should be excluded from the adjusted profit as they have already suffered tax. Such interest as is received gross is strictly assessable under Schedule D Case III, and should similarly be deducted.

(2) The letting of property is not an operation of trade so any rent received should normally be excluded and taken in under Schedule A in the normal way. Where property is leased for the purposes of the trade and then sublet, it is common practice to include small amounts of rent receivable as a trading receipt, and deduct the rent payable.

(3) Capital profits on the sale of fixed assets should be excluded as such a surplus is not assessable in the normal way, but should be taken into account in the capital allowances computation or in the computation of a chargeable gain or allowable loss.

(4) Where insurance moneys are quantified with reference to a capital asset's diminished value, and not with reference to loss of trading profits, they are not a revenue receipt.

(5) Any re-transfer from a reserve or provision that was disallowed at the time it was made would also not be taxable.

(6) Enterprise allowance payments (business start-up allowances) are taxable under Schedule D Case VI (TA 1988, s 127).

3.6 CAPITAL OR REVENUE?

There is no statutory definition of 'capital' or 'revenue'. It can, however, be stated as a general rule that a receipt which is connected with the fixed capital (ie property acquired for retention and employment in a business with a view to profit) of a trade is not a trading receipt. But an item connected with the circulating capital (ie property acquired or produced with a view to sale at a profit) should be included in trading profits.

Normally, this is not a difficult distinction to make. For example, in a manufacturing business the factory and machinery and plant are fixed capital that the trader uses long term for generating profits. Any disposal proceeds from the sale of such an asset would be a capital receipt. Stock in trade, debtors and cash, on the other hand, are the trade's circulating capital. There are cases where it is not immediately clear whether a receipt is of a revenue (income) nature or of a capital nature. Here, it is necessary to look not only at the nature of the asset concerned, but also at transactions involving that asset in the context of the particular trade. Thus, in a manufacturing business, an item of plant or machinery would usually be regarded as a capital asset and a sum received on the disposal thereof would be a capital receipt. But if the plant and machinery was itself manufactured by the trader and sold by him, that sale would be a trading receipt. A capital asset need not be tangible (eg a building or plant and machinery): it can be intangible (eg a lease or goodwill).

A receipt in a lump sum does not necessarily mean that the item is a capital one. The lump sum has to be treated for its capital or revenue character in just the same way as if it were a series of sums. But an isolated lump sum, which is unlikely to recur, is a pointer towards its being a capital item, although of itself this test is not conclusive. A surer test is whether the lump sum was received as consideration of the trader surrendering an asset that was wholly or mainly the foundation of his source of income. The following have been held to be capital receipts:

(1) compensation received by a fireclay company from a railway company for leaving part of the fireclay unworked (*Glenboig Union Fireclay Co v CIR* (1922) 12 TC 427);

(2) sum received on cancellation of the company's future rights under comprehensive agreements for sharing profits (*Van den Berghs v Clark* (1935) 19 TC 390);

(3) sums received from traders for the installation of plant for carrying out the company's patented process for renovating motor tyres, the company agreeing not to introduce another plant, nor canvass for orders, within the trader's territory (*Margerison v Tyresoles* (1942) 25 TC 59);

(4) compensation for the loss of an agency by a ship-managing company, which derived almost all of its receipts from this agency (*Barr, Crombie & Co v CIR* (1945) 26 TC 406);

(5) lump sums received by the owners of vessels, for reconditioning and refitting the vessels when derequisitioned, in place of the Ministry's original undertaking to return the ships in good order (*CIR v West* (1950) 31 TC 402);

(6) a lump sum paid to a company as compensation for a change in the continuity clause in an annually renewed contract (*Sabine v Lookers* (1958) 38 TC 120); and

(7) a payment to an actor not to engage in any film for any other person for a period of 18 months (*Higgs v Olivier* (1952) 33 TC 136). However, such a payment will only be a capital receipt under this rule if the trading activities are greatly restricted (*White v G & M Davis (a firm)* (1979) 52 TC 597).

The following have been held to be revenue receipts:

(a) a lump sum received on making a new agreement for hiring out the company's track (*Greyhound Racing Association (Liverpool) v Cooper* (1936) 20 TC 373);

(b) a lump sum received for the cancellation of an agreement to pay commission (*Shove v Dura Manufacturing Co* (1941) 23 TC 779);

(c) compensation on termination of agency agreement received by a company having a number of such agreements (*Kelsall Parsons & Co v CIR* (1938) 21 TC 608);

(d) a lump sum received by a company on a contract for the purchase of certain chemicals being cancelled, which was held to have been received in the ordinary course of the business (*Bush, Beach and Gent v Road* (1939) 22 TC 519);

(e) a lump sum received by a building company from a landowner following the latter withdrawing plots from a building agreement made with the former (*Shadbolt v Salmon Estate (Kingsbury)* (1943) 25 TC 52);

(f) compensation to a colliery company where part of the colliery was requisitioned for opencast working (*Waterloo Main Colliery Co v CIR (No 1)* (1947) 29 TC 235);

(g) compensation under planning legislation received by a building company where consent to the development of some of the company's land had been refused by the local authority (*Johnson v Try (W S)* (1946) 27 TC 167);

(h) a lump sum paid to an author as compensation for the termination of his contract with a film company (*Household v Grimshaw* (1953) 34 TC 366);

(i) a grant under the EC Dairy Herd Conversion Scheme to refrain from marketing milk products for a period of four years (*CIR v Biggar* (1982) 56 TC 254);

(j) compensation for loss of an opportunity to extend a company business (*Creed v H&M Levinson* (1981) 54 TC 479);

(k) compensation for unremunerated work or loss of anticipated profits paid to a diamond broker who solicited the payment (*Rolfe v Nagel* (1981) 55 TC 585);

(l) compensation under the Criminal Injuries to Property (Compensation) Act (Northern Ireland) 1971 paid by the Northern Ireland Office for consequential loss (comprising loss of profits) where the recipient did not recommence trading (*Lang v Rice* (1984) 57 TC 80);

(m) compensation received by a tenant for its agent's negligence in failing to serve a counternotice opposing an excessive rent increase on its leased business premises (*Donald Fisher (Ealing) v Spencer* (1989) 63 TC 168); and

(n) a lump sum received on termination of an agreement between a consultant and a corporation, even though the terms of the termination included restrictive covenants (*Consultant v Insp of Taxes* [1999] STC (SCD) 63).

So, what are the tests for distinguishing between capital and revenue expenditure? Such a test was put forward in *Vallambrosa Rubber Co v Farmer* (1910) 5 TC 529, where the distinction was drawn between expenditure that is made once and for all (capital) and expenditure that will recur year by year (revenue). However, in *Smith v Incorporated Council of Law Reporting for England and Wales* (1914) 6 TC 477, a lump sum paid to a reporter on his retirement was held to be a payment on revenue account. In *Hancock v General Reversionary and Investment Co* (1919) 7 TC 358, a sum paid for purchasing an annuity for the benefit of a retiring employee was also held to be a revenue expense. The test most frequently resorted to is that applied in *British Insulated and Helsby Cables v Atherton* (1926) 10 TC 155:

'The true question is: what does the company get for its expenditure? If the answer be that it is something of an enduring character . . . then the expenditure is a capital expenditure.'

In *Pitt v Castle Hill Warehousing Co* (1974) 49 TC 638, a company constructed a new road to avoid disturbance to local residents and claimed the cost was a revenue expense to protect its trade. The High Court held it to be capital, as an asset with enduring qualities had been acquired:

'But when an expenditure is made, not only once and for all, but with a view to bringing into existence an asset or an advantage for the enduring benefit of a trade, I think that there is very good reason (in the absence of special circumstances leading to an opposite conclusion) for treating such an expenditure as properly attributable, not to revenue, but to capital.'

3.7 TRANSFER PRICING

TA 1988, s 770A and Sch 28AA govern the 'transfer pricing' regime for accounting periods and tax years ending after 30 June 1999. Their purpose is to bring about the result that would have occurred had arm's length pricing been employed, by increasing the taxable profit of one of the parties to the transaction and providing for the other party to claim a corresponding adjustment to its profit. These are complex provisions and outside the scope of this book.

3.8 CHARGE OR EXPENSE?

Interest, whether short or annual, incurred wholly and exclusively for business purposes, may be deducted as an expense in computing the trade's profit or loss for income tax purposes, subject to certain restrictions on the deduction of annual interest paid to a person not resident in the UK (TA 1988, s 82). Annual interest may also qualify as a charge on income under TA 1988, s 353 if it is paid on a loan for one of the purposes specified in ss 354 and 359–365. Where interest qualifies for relief both as a deduction in computing trading profits and as a charge on income, the trader can claim under either head, but not under both (s 368). Where the trader chooses to treat the interest as a charge on income, but it cannot be wholly relieved because of a deficiency of income in the year of assessment in which it is paid, the unallowed part of the interest may be carried forward to succeeding years in the same way as a trading loss (s 390).

For corporation tax purposes, annual interest paid by a company can only be deducted in computing the trading profit for tax purposes if it is paid in accordance with the FA 1996 loan relationship provisions (TA 1988, s 337A).

Charges on income, such as any annuities and other annual payments not in respect of loan relationships, are treated as a deduction from the total company profits.

3.9 RESEARCH AND DEVELOPMENT (R&D)

3.9.1 Meaning of 'R&D'
(TA 1988, ss 837A and 837B; CAA 2001, ss 437–440)

R&D comprises activities that are treated as such following normal accounting practice for the accounts of companies incorporated in a part of the UK. This ensures that normal accounting practice has the same meaning as UK GAAP (see 3.3.1 and 3.3.2 above). Thus, the definition of 'R&D' in SSAP 13 is included in the statutory definition.

However, this can be altered by regulations made by the Treasury to exclude certain activities from the definition, and to include other activities. These regulations are made by reference to guidelines issued by the Secretary of State for Trade and Industry which clarify the definition to be imported into the legislation.

Unless otherwise expressly provided, 'oil and gas exploration and appraisal' is not included within R&D. This is because, although this exploration and appraisal is not within the accounting definition of 'R&D', it has been accepted as qualifying for scientific research allowances in the past. A new definition of such exploration and appraisal is included to allow it to qualify as R&D.

Oil and gas exploration and appraisal activities are those carried out in the search for petroleum in any area, or in ascertaining the extent or characteristics of any petroleum-bearing area, or the reserves of petroleum in such an area, so as to determine whether the petroleum is suitable for commercial exploitation.

References to expenditure incurred on R&D do not include expenditure incurred in the acquisition of rights in, or arising out of, R&D, but include all expenditure incurred for the prosecution, or the provision of facilities for the prosecution, of R&D.

References to R&D related to a trade include any R&D:

(1) that may lead to or facilitate an extension of that trade; or
(2) of a medical nature which has a special relation to the welfare of workers employed in that trade.

The same expenditure cannot be taken into account for any R&D allowance purposes for more than one trade.

3.9.2 Allowances for capital expenditure
(CAA 1990, s 137)

Where a person incurs expenditure (and any additional VAT) of a capital nature on R&D

(1) while carrying on a trade, which is related to that trade and directly undertaken by him or on his behalf, or
(2) directly undertaken by him or on his behalf, and thereafter sets up and commences a trade connected with that R&D,

a deduction equal to the whole of the expenditure is allowed in taxing the trade for the relevant chargeable period. No allowance is made for expenditure on the acquisition of, or of rights in or over, any land except in so far as, on a just apportionment, that expenditure is referable to the acquisition of, or of rights in or over, or of machinery or plant which forms part of, a building or other structure already constructed on that land.

Expenditure on the provision of a dwelling is not R&D expenditure; but where part of a building is used for R&D and part consists of a dwelling and, disregarding any additional VAT liability or rebate, the just apportionment of capital expenditure on the construction or acquisition of the dwelling is not more than one-quarter of that of the whole building, the whole building is treated as used for R&D.

The relevant chargeable period is the chargeable period in which the expenditure was incurred. If it was incurred before the trade was set up and commenced, it is the chargeable period beginning with that setting-up and commencement.

3.9.3 Assets ceasing to belong to traders
(CAA 1990, s 138)

The following rules apply where an asset representing allowable R&D expenditure of a capital nature incurred by the person carrying on a trade ceases to belong to him ('the relevant event'). If the relevant event occurs in or after the chargeable period for which an allowance for the expenditure (and any additional VAT) is made, then

(1) the sum by which the aggregate of the asset's disposal value and the amount of the allowance exceeds the expenditure amount, or
(2) the amount of the allowance if it is less than that sum

are treated as a trading receipt of the trade accruing at the time of the relevant event or, if such event occurs on or after the date on which the trade is permanently discontinued, accruing immediately before the discontinuance.

If the relevant event occurs before the chargeable period for which an allowance for expenditure would be so made, that allowance is not made, but, if the asset's disposal value is less than the expenditure, a deduction equal to the difference is allowed in taxing the trade for the chargeable period in which the relevant event occurs.

In any case where:

(a) a person carrying on a trade has incurred allowable R&D expenditure of a capital nature, and
(b) an additional VAT rebate relating to that expenditure is made to him at any time before the relevant event occurs in relation to the asset in question,

then, unless that rebate is brought into account to make allowances and charges under the industrial buildings or the plant or machinery allowance rules, an amount equal to the rebate is treated as a trading receipt of the trade accruing for the chargeable period related to making the rebate or, if the rebate is made on or after the date on which the trade is permanently discontinued, accruing immediately before the discontinuance.

An asset's disposal value depends on the nature of the relevant event, and

(1) if that event is the actual sale of the asset at a price not lower than that which it would have fetched in the open market, equals the proceeds of that sale;
(2) if that event is the deemed sale of the asset, equals the deemed proceeds of sale; and
(3) in any other event, equals the price the asset would have fetched if sold in the open market.

Where an asset is destroyed, it is treated as if it had been sold immediately before its destruction. Any insurance moneys or other compensation of any description received by the person carrying on the trade in respect of the destruction, and any moneys received by him for the remains of the asset, are treated as if they were proceeds of that sale. Where this rule applies on the demolition of an asset:

(a) the cost of demolition to the person carrying on the trade is added to the expenditure represented by the asset, and
(b) if, by reason of that addition, the aggregate of the asset's disposal value and the amount of the allowance is less than the amount of the expenditure represented by the asset, then, unless prior to its demolition the asset had begun to be used for purposes other than R&D related to the trade, a deduction equal to the difference is allowed in taxing the trade for the chargeable period in which the asset is treated as having been sold or for the last chargeable period before discontinuance.

No amount can be charged under this rule on any relevant event if that event gives rise to a balancing charge under the industrial buildings or the plant or machinery allowance rules.

3.9.4 Entitlement to R&D relief
(FA 2000, Sch 20, paras 1–12)

Small and medium-sized companies can deduct 150% of their qualifying R&D expenditure when computing their profits. Companies in profit reduce the cash cost of their qualifying R&D by 30% if they are taxed at the current small companies rate. Companies not in profit can take the relief up front as a cash payment by surrendering their R&D losses in return for payment of an R&D tax credit equal to 24% of the cash cost of the qualifying R&D. Companies that are carrying on R&D, but have not yet started trading for tax purposes, are also able to benefit from this measure.

There is an overriding rule that, to qualify for the relief, the company must be a small or medium-sized enterprise for the accounting period and its annualised qualifying R&D expenditure deductible in that period must not be less than £25,000.

In this context, a 'small or medium-sized enterprise' is defined in European Commission Recommendation 96/280/EC of 3 April 1996 as enterprises that:

(1) have fewer than 250 employees, and
(2) have either:
    (a) an annual turnover not exceeding Euro 40m (about £25m), or
    (b) an annual balance sheet total not exceeding Euro 27m (about £17m), and

(3) are not owned as to 25% or more of the capital or the voting rights by one or more enterprises falling outside the definition in (1) and (2). This threshold may be exceeded if:
  (a) the enterprise is held by public investment corporations, venture capital companies or institutional investors, provided no control is exercised either individually or jointly, or
  (b) the capital is spread in such a way that it is not possible to determine who holds it and if the enterprise declares that it can legitimately presume that it is not owned as to 25% or more by one enterprise or jointly by several enterprises falling outside the definition in (1) and (2).

There is an overriding requirement that all of the following conditions must be satisfied for expenditure to qualify as R&D expenditure on which a company may claim R&D tax relief:

(i) the expenditure must not be of a capital nature;
(ii) the expenditure must be attributable to relevant R&D undertaken directly by the company or on its behalf;
(iii) the expenditure must be incurred on staffing costs, or on consumable stores, or be qualifying expenditure on subcontracted R&D;
(iv) any intellectual property created as a result of the R&D to which the expenditure is attributable is, or will be, vested in the company (whether alone or with other persons);
(v) the expenditure must not be incurred by the company in carrying on activities contracted out to the company by any person; and
(vi) the expenditure must not be subsidised.

'Relevant R&D', in relation to a company, means R&D related to a trade carried on by the company, or from which it is intended that a trade to be carried on by it will be derived. R&D that is 'related to a trade carried on by the company' includes R&D that may lead to or facilitate an extension of that trade, and R&D of a medical nature that has a special relation to the welfare of workers employed in that trade.

The 'staffing costs' that can qualify for R&D tax reliefs comprise the following:

(1) the emoluments paid by the company to company directors or employees, including all salaries, wages, perquisites and profits (excluding benefits-in-kind);
(2) the secondary Class 1 NICs paid by the company (excluding NICs on excluded benefits-in-kind); and
(3) the contributions paid by the company to any pension fund (TA 1988, s 231A(4)) operated for the benefit of company directors or employees.

A company's staffing costs attributable to relevant R&D are those paid to or for directors or employees directly and actively engaged in such R&D. Persons who provide purely 'support' services are not treated as directly and actively engaged in R&D. Therefore, staff peripheral to or remote from the R&D activity (eg central payroll, clerical, secretarial and administrative services) are excluded; however, staff directly engaged in carrying on the R&D, including ancillary staff employed in a dedicated R&D facility such as technicians and maintenance, clerical and security staff, are included.

Where a director or employee is partly engaged directly and actively in relevant R&D, the following rules apply:

(i) if the time he spends so engaged is less than 20% of his total working time, none of the staffing costs relating to him are treated as attributable to relevant R&D;

(ii) if the time he spends so engaged is more than 80% of his total working time, the whole of the staffing costs relating to him are treated as attributable to relevant R&D;

(iii) in any other case, an appropriate proportion of the staffing costs relating to him is treated as attributable to relevant R&D.

Expenditure on consumable stores is expenditure that would be treated as such following normal accounting practice. Such expenditure is attributable to relevant R&D if the stores are employed directly in that R&D.

'Intellectual property' means:

(a) any industrial information or techniques likely to assist in:
   (I) the manufacture or processing of goods or materials, or
   (II) the working of a mine, oil well or other source of mineral deposits or the winning of access to it, or
   (III) the carrying out of any agricultural, forestry or fishing operations; and

(b) any patent, trademark, registered design, copyright, design right or plant breeder's right, and any corresponding or similar rights under the law of a country outside the UK.

A company's expenditure is treated as subsidised in the following circumstances:

(1) if a notified state aid is or has been obtained for the whole or part of the expenditure, or any other expenditure (whenever incurred) attributable to the same R&D project, no expenditure on the R&D project can qualify for tax relief;

(2) to the extent that a grant or subsidy (other than a notified state aid) is obtained for the expenditure;

(3) to the extent that it is otherwise met directly or indirectly by any person other than the company.

Here, 'notified state aid' is a state aid (other than R&D tax reliefs or R&D tax credit) notified to and approved by the European Commission. Any grant towards an R&D project out of government or public funds, or from the Commission itself, would normally fall into this category. A notified state aid, grant, subsidy or payment that is not allocated purely for R&D expenditure is apportioned accordingly.

Subcontracted R&D

A company incurs expenditure on subcontracted R&D if it makes a 'sub-contractor payment' to a subcontractor for relevant R&D contracted out by the company to that subcontractor. Whether R&D tax reliefs can be claimed in such circumstances depends on whether the parties are connected under TA 1988, s 839, and whether the actual expenditure is incurred by the sub-contractor in carrying out the subcontracted R&D.

The subcontractor must have brought the whole of the subcontractor payment and all of its relevant expenditure into account in its profit or loss for a relevant period, in accordance with normal accounting principles. The amount of the company's qualifying expenditure on subcontracted R&D is the lower of the amount of the particular subcontractor payment and the subcontractor's relevant expenditure. 'Relevant expenditure' is defined here as revenue expenditure (ie not expenditure of a capital nature) that is not subsidised expenditure incurred by the subcontractor on staffing costs and consumable stores in carrying out the subcontracted work represented by the company's subcontractor payment.

A 'relevant period' is defined as a period for which the subcontractor draws up accounts ending not more than 12 months after the end of the accounting period of the company in which the company recognises the sub-contractor payment as a deduction brought into account in accordance with normal accounting principles. Any necessary apportionment of expenditure of the company or the subcontractor is made on a just and reasonable basis.

A company and a subcontractor who are not connected may elect jointly for the connected persons' treatment to be applied to subcontractor pay-ments. This election, which once made is irrevocable, must be made for all subcontractor payments paid under the same contract or other arrangement.

Where the company and subcontractor are not connected, and no election for connected persons treatment has been made, and a company makes a subcontractor payment, 65% of the subcontractor payment amount is treated as qualifying expenditure on subcontracted R&D.

3.9.5 Manner of giving effect to relief
(FA 2000, Sch 20, paras 13–20)

Where a company is entitled to R&D tax reliefs for an accounting period, is carrying on a trade in that period, and has qualifying R&D expenditure that is allowable as a deduction in computing for tax purposes the trade's profits for that period, it may (on making a claim) treat that qualifying R&D expenditure as if it were an amount equal to 150% of the actual amount.

The rule described here applies to pre-trading qualifying R&D expenditure. It has effect where a company is entitled to R&D tax reliefs for an accounting period, and has incurred qualifying R&D expenditure in that accounting period which meets the following test. It must be shown that it is not allowable as a deduction in computing, for tax purposes, the profits of a trade that was carried on by it at the time the expenditure was incurred, but that it would have been so allowable had the company, at that time, been carrying on a trade consisting of the activities in relation to which the expenditure was incurred.

Companies carrying on R&D, but not as part of a taxable trade, can gain the immediate benefit of R&D tax reliefs by electing to treat 150% of the deductible qualifying R&D expenditure as if it were a trading loss of the period. The loss can then be used under the normal provisions for trading losses (eg by offset against investment income that the company may be earning on its capital). Where such an election is made for an accounting period, TA 1988, s 401 (relief for pre-trading expenditure) cannot also apply to that qualifying R&D expenditure.

A company can claim an R&D tax credit for an accounting period in which it has a 'surrenderable loss'. In this context, a company has a surrenderable loss in an accounting period in two circumstances:

(1) if it is entitled to R&D tax reliefs for that accounting period, is carrying on a trade in that accounting period, has qualifying R&D expenditure that is allowable in computing, for tax purposes, the profits of the trade for that period and has made a claim to treat the expenditure as increased to 150% of the actual amount of the expenditure, and has made a trading loss in that trade and for that period; or

(2) if it is entitled to R&D tax reliefs for an accounting period, has incurred qualifying R&D expenditure which, being incurred before the trade commenced, the company has elected to be treated as if it had incurred a trading loss in that accounting period equal to 150% of the actual amount of the expenditure.

The surrenderable loss amount for claiming an R&D tax credit is equal to the lower of so much of that trading loss as is unrelieved, or 150% of the related qualifying R&D expenditure.

The amount of a trading loss that is 'unrelieved' is the amount of that loss reduced by the following amounts:

(a) any relief that was or could have been obtained by the company making a claim under TA 1988, s 393A(1)(a) to set the loss against profits of whatever description of the same accounting period;

(b) any other relief obtained by the company for the loss, including relief under s 393A(1)(b) to set the losses against profits of an earlier accounting period;

(c) any loss surrendered under s 403(1) to group or consortium members; and

(d) amounts surrendered as group relief are also excluded.

No account is taken of any losses brought forward from earlier accounting periods under s 393(1), or carried back from later accounting periods under s 393A(1)(b), being taken into account when computing the surrenderable amount.

The amount of the R&D tax credit payable in relation to a surrenderable loss is 16% of qualifying R&D expenditure which corresponds to 24% of the corresponding R&D expenditure. It is, however, subject to a 'cap' and cannot exceed the 'total amount of the companies' PAYE and NICs liabilities' for payment periods within the accounting period. The effect of this rule is to allow companies that are carrying out R&D, but which are not in profit, to receive the benefit of R&D tax reliefs earlier than would otherwise be the case.

For the above purpose the amount of the company's PAYE liabilities for a payment period is the total income tax for which the company is required to account to the Revenue for that period under the PAYE regulations, disregarding any deduction the company is authorised to make in relation to the working families' and disabled person's tax credits (WFTC and DPTC, respectively).

The amount of the company's Class 1 NICs is the total amount for which the company is required to account to the Revenue for that period, disregarding any deduction the company is authorised to make in relation to payments of statutory sick pay, statutory maternity pay, and WFTC and DPTC.

The amounts of PAYE and NICs taken into account are for the whole company, and are not limited to the liabilities in relation to staff directly carrying on the R&D.

The amount of loss that can be carried forward where a claim is made under TA 1988, s 393 for trading losses to be relieved against future trading profits is restricted where there is a claim for an R&D tax credit. In such a case, the company's trading loss for a period for which it claims an R&D tax credit is treated as reduced by the amount of the loss surrendered.

The amount of the loss surrendered is defined. Where the maximum amount of R&D tax credit was claimed, it is the whole of the surrenderable loss for that period. Where less than the maximum amount was claimed, it is a corresponding proportion of the surrenderable loss for that period. The 'maximum amount' is (at the time of writing) 16% of the amount of the surrenderable loss for the period.

A payment of the R&D tax credit is not treated as income of the company for any tax purpose and is exempt from tax.

The rules providing relief for R&D expenditure do not apply to expenditure incurred before 1 April 2000. Furthermore, the pre-trading rules in TA 1988, s 401 are prevented from treating expenditure made before 1 April 2000 as qualifying R&D expenditure if the trade in relation to which the R&D is carried out commences after that date.

3.9.6 Extension of R&D tax credit to all companies
(FA 2002, ss 52 and 54 and Schs 12 and 15)

From 1 April 2002, the R&D tax credit is extended to all companies. Also, the amount a company can deduct for qualifying R&D expenditure when computing its profits is increased from 100% to 125%.

Large companies (defined as companies that are not SMEs (small or medium-sized enterprises)) receive R&D tax credit for the first time. SMEs receive the new credit in some circumstances where they would not, at present, be able to claim the existing SME R&D tax credit (introduced in FA 2000). In particular, they can claim the new credit where work is subcontracted to them by a large company.

Companies in profit will, under the enhanced R&D relief, reduce the cash cost of their qualifying R&D by 7.5% if they are taxed at the current main corporation tax rate of 30%.

Minor amendments are made to the existing R&D tax credit scheme for SMEs. In particular there are changes to the rules for determining whether the minimum expenditure of £25,000 required for a company to receive R&D tax credit has been made. Also an SME may be doing work in its own right *and* as a subcontractor for a large company, in which case it can claim both the SME credit and the new credit. Both schemes require a minimum expenditure of £25,000 for credit to be received. Spending under both schemes counts towards this limit, making it slightly easier for an SME to qualify.

3.9.7 Tax relief for expenditure on vaccine research
(FA 2002, s 53 and Schs 13 and 14)

There is an additional relief for spending on research and development into vaccines and medicines for the prevention and treatment of tuberculosis and malaria, vaccines for the prevention of infection by the human immunodeficiency virus (HIV) and for vaccines and medicines for the prevention of the onset of, and the treatment of, acquired immune deficiency syndrome (AIDS) arising from particular strains of HIV found mostly in countries in the developing world. From a date to be announced by the Treasury, companies can deduct from their corporation tax profits an additional 50% of qualifying expenditure for R&D that they either carry out themselves or subcontract to other companies. They are also entitled to relief on the same basis for any contribution made to independent research and development. Companies not in profit can surrender losses arising from the relief in return for payment of a vaccines tax credit equal to 24% of the cash cost of the qualifying R&D.

3.10 INTELLECTUAL PROPERTY

3.10.1 Patents and know-how

Interpretation
(TA 1988, s 533)

'Income from patents' includes any royalty or other sum paid for the user of a patent; and any amount on which tax is payable for any chargeable period under TA 1988, s 524 or 525 and CAA 2001, s 472(5) or Sch 3, para 100. 'Patent rights' comprise the right to do or authorise the doing of anything that would, but for that right, be an infringement of a patent. 'UK patent' means a patent granted under UK laws.

Any reference to the sale of part of patent rights includes the grant of a licence for the patent in question, and any reference to the purchase of patent rights includes the acquisition of a licence for a patent. If a licence granted by a person entitled to any patent rights is a licence to exercise those rights to the exclusion of the grantor and all other persons for the whole of the remainder of the term for which the right subsists, the grantor is treated as thereby selling the whole of the rights.

Where, under the Patents Act 1949, ss 46–49, the Patents Act 1977, ss 55–59 or any corresponding provisions of the law of any country outside the UK, an invention that is the subject of a patent is made, used, or exercised or vended by or for the service of the Crown or the government of the country concerned, the rules for dealing with receipts from the sale of patent rights (TA 1988, ss 524–529) apply as if the making, use, exercise or vending of the invention had taken place under a licence, and any sums paid therefore are treated accordingly.

Expenditure incurred in obtaining a right to acquire in the future patent rights for any invention for which the patent has not yet been granted is deemed to be expenditure on the purchase of patent rights; if the patent rights are subsequently acquired, the expenditure is deemed to have been expenditure on the purchase of those rights. Any such sum received from a person which is deemed to be expenditure incurred by him on the purchase of patent rights is deemed to be proceeds of a sale of patent rights.

'Know-how' means any industrial information and techniques likely to assist in the manufacture or processing of goods or materials, or in the working of a mine, oil well or other source of mineral deposits (including the searching for, discovery or testing of deposits or the winning of access thereto), or in the carrying out of any agricultural, forestry or fishing operations.

Taxation of receipts from sale of patent rights
(CAA 1988, s 524)

Where a UK-resident person sells all or any part of any patent rights and the net proceeds of the sale consist wholly or partly of a capital sum, he is charged to tax under Schedule D Case VI for the chargeable period in which the sum is received by him and successive chargeable periods, being charged in each period on the same fraction of the sum as the period is of six years (or such less fraction as has not already been charged).

A person can, by notice served on the Revenue, elect that the whole of the sum be charged to tax for the chargeable period in which it was received. The election must, for income tax, be lodged within the period ending with the first anniversary of the 31 January next following the tax year in which the sum was received. For corporation tax, the period is two years beginning at the end of the accounting period in which the sum was received.

Where a non-UK resident person sells all or any part of any patent rights and the net proceeds of the sale consist wholly or partly of a capital sum, and the patent is a UK patent, then

(1) he is chargeable to tax on that sum under Schedule D Case VI; and
(2) TA 1988, s 349(1) applies to that sum as if it was an annual sum payable otherwise than out of profits or gains charged to income tax; and
(3) all other provisions of the Tax Acts, unless otherwise provided, have effect accordingly.

If, on or before the first anniversary of 31 January next following the tax year in which the sum is paid, the person to whom it is paid, by notice to the Revenue, elects that the sum be treated for income tax for that year and each of the five succeeding years as if one-sixth thereof, and no more, were included in his income chargeable to tax for all those years respectively. For corporation tax the period is two years after the end of the accounting period in which the sum is paid.

Where the person selling all or any part of any patent rights acquired the rights sold, or the rights out of which they were granted, by purchase and the price paid by him consisted wholly or partly of a capital sum, the above applies as if any capital sum received by him when he sells the rights were reduced by the amount of that sum. Where between the purchase and the sale the seller has sold part of the rights acquired by him and the net proceeds of that sale consist wholly or partly of a capital sum, the amount received on the subsequent sale is itself reduced by the amount of that sum.

Capital sums: death, winding up or partnership change
(TA 1988, s 525)

Where a person on whom, by receiving a capital sum, a charge falls or would otherwise fall to be made under TA 1988, s 524 dies or, being a company, commences to be wound up:

(1) no sums are charged on that person for any chargeable period subsequent to that in which the death takes place or the winding-up commences; and
(2) the amount falling to be charged for the chargeable period in which the death occurs or the winding-up commences is increased by the total amounts which, but for the death or winding-up, would have fallen to be charged for subsequent chargeable periods.

Where sums arise on a death, a form of top-slicing relief is available.

Where, under CAA 2001, s 559 (effect of successions), a charge is made on two or more persons jointly as being the persons carrying on a trade in partnership, and that trade is discontinued, the above is applied on the discontinuance as if it were a company commencing to be wound up. Where this applies:

(1) the additional sum which, as above, falls to be charged for the chargeable period in which the discontinuance occurs is apportioned among the members of the partnership immediately before the discontinuance, according to their respective interests in the partnership profits, and each partner (or, if he is dead, his personal representatives) is charged separately for his proportion; and
(2) each partner (or, if he is dead, his personal representatives) has the same right to require a reduction of the total income tax payable by him or out of his estate by reason of the increase as would have been exercisable by the personal representatives in the case of a death.

Relief for expenses
(TA 1988, s 526)

Where

(1) a person, otherwise than for the purposes of a trade carried on by him, pays any fees or incurs any expenses in connection with the grant or maintenance of a patent, or the obtaining of an extension of a term of a patent, or a rejected or abandoned application for a patent, and
(2) those fees or expenses would, if they had been paid or incurred for the purposes of a trade, have been allowable as a deduction in estimating the profits of that trade,

there is made to him, for the chargeable period in which the expenses were paid or incurred, an allowance equal to the amount thereof.

Where a patent is granted for any invention, an allowance equal to so much of the net amount of any expenses incurred by an individual who, whether alone or in conjunction with any other person, actually devised the invention as is properly ascribable to the devising thereof (not being expenses for which, or of assets representing which, an allowance could be made under any other provision) is made to that individual for the tax year in which the expenses were incurred.

Spreading of royalties over several years
(TA 1988, s 527)

Where a royalty or other sum is paid for the use of a patent, and that use extended over a period of six complete years or more, the person receiving the payment may on making a claim require that the income or corporation tax payable by him on receipt of that sum be reduced so as not to exceed the total amount of income or corporation tax that would have been payable by him if that royalty or sum had been paid in six equal instalments at yearly intervals, the last of which was paid on the date on which the payment was in fact made.

This applies to a royalty or other sum where the period of use is two complete years or more but less than six complete years as it applies to the royalties and sums mentioned above, but by reference to so many equal instalments as there are complete years comprised in that period.

Manner of making allowances and charges
(TA 1988, s 528)

Where an allowance is made to a person for any tax year for expenses for income tax, and the allowance is not to be made in taxing a trade:

(1) the amount of the allowance is deducted from or set off against his income from patents for that tax year, and
(2) if the amount to be allowed is greater than that of his income from patents for that tax year, the balance is deducted from or set off against his income from patents for the next tax year, and so on for subsequent tax years.

Where an allowance falls to be made to a company for any accounting period for corporation tax, and is not to be made in taxing a trade:

(a) the allowance is, as far as may be, given effect by deducting the amount of the allowance from the company's income from patents of the accounting period;
(b) where the allowance cannot be given in full in that period by reason of a deficiency of income from patents, then (so long as the company remains within the charge to corporation tax) the amount disallowed is carried forward to the succeeding accounting period, and treated as the

amount of a corresponding allowance for that period, and so on for subsequent accounting periods.

Here, references to a person's or a company's income from patents are to that income after any allowance has been deducted from or set off against it under CAA 2001, s 479 or 480.

Patent income to be earned income in certain cases
(TA 1988, s 529)

Any income from patent rights arising to an individual where the patent was granted for an invention actually devised by him, whether alone or jointly with any other person, is treated as earned income. Where any part of the rights in question or of any rights out of which they were granted has at any time belonged to any other person, so much only of that income is treated as earned income as is not properly attributable to the rights that have belonged to that other person.

Disposal of know-how
(TA 1988, s 531)

Where a person disposes of know-how that has been used in a trade carried on by him, and he continues to carry on the trade after the disposal, the amount or value of any consideration received by him for the disposal is, so far as it is not brought into account as a disposal value under CAA 2001, s 462, and is not otherwise chargeable to tax as a revenue or income receipt, treated for all purposes as a trading receipt.

Where a person disposes of a trade or part of a trade and, together with that trade or part, of know-how used in it, any consideration received by him for the know-how is dealt with both to him and to the person acquiring it, if that person provided the consideration, and for the purposes of corporation tax, income tax and CGT, as a payment for goodwill. This does not apply to either of the persons concerned if they so elect within two years of the disposal, or to the person acquiring the know-how if the trade in question was, before the acquisition, carried on wholly outside the UK.

Any consideration received by a person for the disposal of know-how is, if it is

(1) received on the disposal of know-how and is not brought into account as a disposal value under CAA 2001, s 462, or
(2) neither chargeable to tax as above or otherwise as a revenue or income receipt, nor dealt with in relation to him as a payment for goodwill above,

treated as a profit or gain chargeable to tax under Schedule D Case VI.

Where the person concerned has incurred expenditure wholly and exclusively in the acquisition or disposal of the know-how, the amount that would otherwise be treated as a profit or gain chargeable to tax under Schedule D Case VI is reduced by the amount of that expenditure; but a deduction cannot be twice made for the same expenditure.

Where in connection with any disposal of know-how a person gives an undertaking (whether absolute or qualified, and whether legally valid or not) the tenor or effect of which is to restrict his or another's activities in any way, any consideration received for the giving of the undertaking or its total or partial fulfilment is treated as consideration received for the disposal of the know-how.

3.10.2 Creative artists: relief for fluctuating profits
(TA 1988, s 95A and Sch 4A)

The provisions enable an individual to make an 'averaging claim' if his profits from a qualifying trade, profession or vocation fluctuate from one tax year to the next. These rules apply or 2000–01 and subsequent tax years. This means that the first years which may be the subject to averaging are 2000–01 and 2001–02.

The previous relief for copyright payments (TA 1988, s 534), relief where copyright sold after ten years (TA 1988, s 535), relief for payments for designs (TA 1988, s 537A), and relief for painters, sculptors and other artists (TA 1988, s 538) ceased with effect for payments actually receivable after 5 April 2001.

A trade, profession or vocation is a 'qualifying trade, profession or voca-tion' if an individual's profits from it are derived wholly or mainly from qualifying creative works, and are chargeable to tax under Schedule D Case I or II. 'Qualifying creative works' are literary, dramatic, musical or artis-tic works, or designs, created by the taxpayer personally or, where the trade, profession or vocation is carried on by the taxpayer in partnership, by one or more of the partners personally.

Averaging claims

An averaging claim may be made if the taxpayer has been carrying on the qualifying trade, profession or vocation in two consecutive tax years and either his relevant profits for one of the tax years are less than 75% of his relevant profits for the other, or his relevant profits for one (but not both) of the tax years are nil. An averaging claim relates to both of the years involved.

An averaging claim cannot be made for a tax year if an averaging claim for the same qualifying trade, profession or vocation has already been made for a later tax year. Nor can an averaging claim be made for a tax year in which an individual starts, or permanently ceases, to carry on the trade, pro-fession or vocation, or the trade, etc begins or ceases to be a qualifying one. An averaging claim may, however, be made for a tax year which was the later year on a previous averaging claim.

An averaging claim must be made not later than 12 months after 31 January next following the end of the later of the tax years to which it relates. This is subject an extended time limit where profits are adjusted for some other reason.

Where an individual is entitled to make, and makes, an averaging claim, the amount taken as his profits from the qualifying trade, profession or vocation for each of the tax years to which the claim relates is adjusted as follows:

(1) If his relevant profits for one of the years amount to 70% or less of his relevant profits for the other year, or his relevant profits for one (but not both) of the years are nil, the amount of the adjusted profits for each of the years to which the claim relates is the average of the relevant profits for the two years.

(2) If the taxpayer's relevant profits for one of the years amount to more than 70%, but less than 75%, of his relevant profits for the other year, the amount of the profits in each of the years is calculated as follows, so as to reduce the variation between them.

Step 1 The amount of the adjustment is given by the formula:
$$\left(\tfrac{D}{3}\right) - \left(\tfrac{P}{6.75}\right)$$
where:

D = the difference between the taxpayer's relevant profits for the two tax years, and

P = the relevant profits for the year in which those profits are higher.

Step 2 Add the amount of the adjustment to the relevant profits for the year in which those profits are lower. The result is the amount of the adjusted profits for that year.

Step 3 Subtract the amount of the adjustment from the taxpayer's relevant profits for the year in which those profits are higher. The result is the amount of the adjusted profits for that year.

Subject as follows, the adjusted profits are taken as the relevant profits for the years to which the claim relates for all income tax purposes, including the further application of this rule.

An averaging claim relating to two tax years is given effect in the later year. In so far as the claim involves an adjustment to the profits for the earlier year, it is treated as a claim for the amount of the difference between the amount in which the taxpayer is chargeable to tax for the earlier year (amount A), and the amount in which he would be so chargeable if effect were given to the adjustment in that year (amount B).

That claim is given effect in the later year by increasing the aggregate amount of payments on account made by the taxpayer or, as the case may require, by increasing the amount of tax payable. Where effect falls to be given to two or more associated claims, amounts A and B are each determined on the assumption that effect could have been, and had been, given to the other claim(s) in relation to the earlier year.

Where this rule applies twice for the same tax year, the increase or reduction in tax payable for that year as a result of the earlier application is disregarded in determining amounts A and B for the later application.

A claim by an individual for relief under any other income tax provision for either of the years to which an averaging claim relates is not out of time if made on or before the last date on which the averaging claim could have been made and, if already made, may be amended or revoked on or before that date. If the other claim is made by being included in a return, the amending or revoking claim is read as a reference to amending the return by amending or omitting the claim.

Modification

A modification applies where the individual makes or amends a claim for relief under any other income tax provision for either of the years to which an averaging claim relates, and the making or amendment of the claim would otherwise be out of time. The claim or amendment is given effect in the later year. In so far as the claim or amendment relates to income of the earlier year, the amount claimed, or (as the case may be) the increase or reduction in the amount claimed, is equal to the difference between the amount in which the taxpayer is chargeable to tax for the earlier year (amount A), and the amount in which he would be so chargeable on the assumption that effect could be, and was, given to the claim or amendment for that year (amount B).

That claim or amendment is given effect in the later year by increasing the aggregate amount of payments on account made by the taxpayer or, as the case may require, by increasing the amount of tax payable. Where effect falls to be given to two or more associated claims, amounts A and B are each determined on the assumption that effect could have been, and had been, given to the other claim or claims in relation to the earlier year.

Other matters in relation to averaging/modification

If, after the individual has made an averaging claim, his relevant profits in either or both of the tax years to which the claim relates are adjusted for some other reason, the averaging claim is disregarded, and a further averaging claim may be made in relation to the taxpayer's relevant profits as adjusted.

A further averaging claim is not out of time provided it is made not later than 12 months after 31 January next following the tax year in which the adjustment for the other reason is made.

References here to an individual's profits from a qualifying trade, profession or vocation are to profits before making deductions for losses sustained in any tax year. If the taxpayer sustains a loss in the qualifying trade, profession or vocation in any tax year, the profits of that year are taken to be nil. This does not prevent an individual from obtaining relief for a loss sustained by him in that or any other tax year.

Any reference in these rules to the amount in which a person is chargeable to tax is a reference to the amount in which he is so chargeable after taking into account any relief or allowance for which a claim is made.

3.10.3 Taxation of royalties where owner is abroad
(TA 1988, s 536)

Where the usual place of abode of the owner of a copyright is not within the UK, TA 1988, s 349(1) applies to any payment of any royalties or sums paid periodically for that copyright as it applies to annual payments not payable out of profits or gains brought into charge to income tax. Here,

(1) 'copyright' does not include copyright in a cinematograph film or video recording, or the soundtrack of such a film or recording, so far as it is not separately exploited; and

(2) 'owner of a copyright' includes a person who, notwithstanding that he has assigned a copyright to some other person, is entitled to receive periodical payments in respect of that copyright.

The reference to royalties or sums paid periodically for or in respect of a copyright does not include royalties or sums paid for copies of works that have been exported from the UK for distribution outside the UK.

Where any payment to which the above applies is made through an agent resident in the UK and that agent is entitled as against the copyright owner to deduct any sum by way of commission for services rendered, the amount of the payment is taken to be diminished by the sum that the agent is so entitled to deduct.

Where the person by or through whom the payment is made does not know that any such commission is payable nor the amount of any such commission, any income tax deducted by or assessed and charged on him is computed in the first instance on, and the account to be delivered of the payment is an account of, the total amount of the payment without regard being had to any diminution thereof.

The time of making such payment is, for all tax purposes, taken to be the time when it is made by the person by whom it is first made and not the time when it is made by or through any other person.

Any agreement for making any such payment applies in full and without deduction of income tax.

This also applies where royalties or sums paid periodically for a right in a design as it applies to annual payments not payable out of profits or gains are brought into charge to income tax. Here:

(1) 'right in a design' means design right or the right in a registered design;

(2) the reference to the owner of a right includes a person who, notwithstanding that he has assigned the right to some other person, is entitled to receive periodical payments in respect of the right; and

(3) the reference to royalties or other sums paid periodically for or in respect of a right does not include royalties or sums paid for articles that have been exported from the UK for distribution outside the UK.

4

CAPITAL ALLOWANCES: BASIC PRINCIPLES

The Capital Allowances Act (CAA) 2001 contains the rules for capital allowances (ie deductions on account of 'depreciation') in connection with:

(1) Plant or machinery (ss 11–270)
(2) Industrial buildings and structures (ss 271–360)
(3) Agricultural land and buildings (ss 361–393)
(4) Flat conversion (ss 393A–393W)
(5) Mineral extraction (ss 394–436)
(6) R&D (ss 437–451)
(7) Know-how (ss 452–463)
(8) Patents (ss 464–483)
(9) Dredging (ss 484–489)
(10) Dwelling houses let on assured tenancies (ss 490–531)
(11) Contributions (ss 532–543).

All statutory references in this chapter are to the CAA 2001 unless otherwise stated.

4.1 CAPITAL ALLOWANCES GENERALLY

Capital allowances are given for capital expenditure which is excluded in arriving at the amount of profits for Cases I and II purposes. Once it is established that capital expenditure has been incurred, the nature of the expenditure must be identified and the rules followed for the type of expenditure concerned. If the expenditure does not fit into any category for which capital allowances are given, no relief is due.

4.1.1 Manner of granting relief
(CAA 2001, s 2)

In general, capital allowances and charges are given, for income tax, in calculating income, and for corporation tax, in calculating profits (see TA

1988, s 6), for a chargeable period. Additionally, there are rules directly relating to the particular allowance which must also be taken into account:

4.1.2 Chargeable period
(CAA 2001, s 6)

The general rule, for income tax, is that the chargeable period is a period of account, ie a period for which accounts are drawn up for the trade, etc, and for any other person entitled to an allowance or liable to a charge, the chargeable period is a tax year. If two periods of account overlap, or one period of account includes another, the part that is common to both is treated as part of the first period of account only. If there is a gap between two periods of account, the gap is also treated as part of the first period of account. If a period of account would, otherwise, be longer than 18 months, it is divided into separate periods of account, the first beginning with the start date of the original period, and each subsequent one beginning with an anniversary of that date, for a period of longer than 12 months.

For corporation tax, in general, a chargeable period is an accounting period of a company.

4.1.3 Claims for allowances
(CAA 2001, s 3)

Capital allowances must be claimed in, for income tax, a self-assessment tax return (per TMA 1970), or for corporation tax, a company tax return (per FA 1998, Sch 18). This does not apply, for income tax, for claims for allowances for special leasing of plant or machinery (CAA 2001, s 258) or claims for patent allowance for non-trading expenditure (CAA 2001, s 479). Instead these are dealt with under the special procedure for making claims not included in returns.

There are also special provisions for partnerships (TMA 1970, s 42(6) and (7)) as the partnership makes the claim and not the individual partners.

4.1.4 Meaning of expenditure
(CAA 2001, s 4)

'Capital expenditure' and 'capital sums' are defined negatively by what these expressions do not include. Thus, they do not include, for a person incurring expenditure or paying the sums, any expenditure that can be deducted in arriving at the profits of a trade, etc or of a property business carried on by him, or any expenditure or sum that may be deducted in calculating the emoluments of an employment or office held by him. Similarly, for the recipient of such expenditure, any amounts that are added in calculating the profits of a trade, etc or property business carried on by him, or any amounts that are emoluments of an employment or office held by him. Nor do they include, for the person incurring the expenditure, or a recipient of the expenditure, any expenditure for which an income tax deduction should be made under TA 1988, ss 348 or 349(1) (annual payments). However, this does not apply to any expenditure for which an income tax deduction should be made under TA 1988, s 524(3)(b) (receipts from sale of patent rights by a person not resident in the UK).

4.1.5 When capital expenditure is incurred
(CAA 2001, s 5)

In most cases an amount of capital expenditure is treated as incurred as soon as there is an unconditional obligation to pay it. This general rule applies even if all or a part of the expenditure is not required to be paid until a later date. There are however, a number of exceptions to the general rule so that expenditure is treated as incurred immediately before the end of a chargeable period if the following conditions are met. The requirements are that, under an agreement, the capital expenditure is expenditure on the provision of an asset, an unconditional obligation to pay an amount comes into being as a result of the giving of a certificate or some other event. The giving of a certificate, or other event, is within one month after the end of a chargeable period, and prior to the end of that chargeable period, the asset has become the property of the person subject to the unconditional obligation to pay.

There is an overriding rule that if, under an agreement an amount of capital expenditure is not required to be paid until a date more than 4 months after the unconditional obligation to pay has come into being, the amount is treated as incurred on that date. However, there is also an anti-avoidance rule which applies where there is an unconditional obligation to pay an amount on a date earlier than normal in commercial usage, and the sole or main benefit obtained thereby is that the amount would be treated, under the general rule, as incurred in an earlier chargeable period. In this event, the amount is treated as incurred on the date on or before which it is required to be paid.

This rule is subject to any overriding provision by which expenditure is treated as incurred on a date later than would apply under the general rule. Furthermore, the general rule does not apply to expenditure treated as incurred as a result of a person incurring an additional VAT liability.

4.1.6 Exclusion of double relief
(CAA 2001, ss 7–9)

If an allowance for capital expenditure is given under one category of allowance , no allowance can then be made to him under any other category for that expenditure. Note, however, that this restriction does not apply to know-how (see 4.26) and patent allowances (see 4.27). Where expenditure qualifies for more than one type of allowance the taxpayer may choose which claim to make; other claims are then precluded.

If a person's expenditure is allocated to a plant or machinery pool an allowance cannot also be given under any other category of allowance. The reverse is also true. Again this restriction does not apply to know-how and patent allowances.

The making of a fixtures claim for capital expenditure is prohibited if an allowance has previously been claimed under another category of allowance and the claim was for an allowance for capital expenditure relating, in whole or part, to the asset. This does not prevent a person making a fixtures claim (under ss 172–204) for capital expenditure if the only previous claim was under the industrial buildings or R&D allowances, and the limit on the amount of expenditure that may be taken into account applies to that expenditure.

Here, 'capital expenditure' includes any contribution to capital expenditure. 'Expenditure' includes the construction or acquisition of an asset (s 10).

4.1.7 Additional VAT liabilities and rebates
(CAA 2001, ss 546–551)

There are general rules which supplement and interpret the rules dealing with additional VAT liabilities and rebates under the plant or machinery allowances rules (ss 234–246), the industrial buildings allowances rules (ss 345–351), and under the rules for R&D allowances under ss 446–449 (s 546). 'Additional VAT liability' is an amount which a person becomes liable to pay by way of adjustment under the VAT capital items scheme for input tax. Likewise, 'additional VAT rebate' means an amount which a person becomes entitled to deduct by way of adjustment under the VAT capital items legislation (s 548).

The VAT rules concerned are VATA 1994, s 34 and VAT Regulations 1995, regs 112, which provide for the proportion of input tax on an asset of a specified description which may be deducted by a person from his output tax to be adjusted from time to time as a result of an increase, or a decrease, in the extent to which the asset is used by him for making taxable supplies (or taxable supplies of a specified class or description) during a specified period.

4.1.8 Partnerships, successions and transfers
(CAA 2001, ss 557–561))

There are special rules which deal with partnership changes and successions. These apply for all of the capital allowances rules except for the plant and machinery allowances, the R&D allowances and the assured tenancy allowances.

If a relevant activity has been set up and is at any time carried on in partnership, and there is a change in the persons engaged in carrying it on, but the change does not result in the relevant activity being treated as permanently discontinued (per TA 1988, ss 113(1) or 337(1)), then, in such event, any allowance or charge is made to, or on, the present partners. The amount of any allowance or charge thus arising is calculated as if the present partners had always been carrying on the relevant activity, and everything done to or by their predecessors in carrying on the relevant activity had been done to or by the present partners.

On the other hand, if a person succeeds to a relevant activity, which previously was carried on by another person, and the relevant activity is treated as discontinued (per TA 1988, s 113(1) or 337(1)) the property in question is treated as if it had been sold to the successor when the succession takes place, and as if the net proceeds of the sale were the market value of the property. It is important to note that this does not give rise to any initial allowance to the successor.

4.1.9 Apportionment of sales proceeds
(CAA 2001, s 562)

All property sold as a result of one bargain is treated as sold together even though separate prices are, or purport to be, agreed for separate items of that property, or there are, or purport to be, separate sales of separate items of that property.

If an item of property is sold together with other property, then, for all capital allowances purposes the net proceeds of the sale of that item are treated as being so much of the net proceeds of sale of all the property as, on a just and reasonable apportionment, is attributable to that item. The Revenue do not challenge an amount apportioned to qualifying assets as too low unless they consider that something else is overvalued, assuming arm's length transaction.

4.1.10 Procedure for determining certain questions affecting two or more persons
(CAA 2001, ss 563 and 564)

Arrangements are made to deal with questions that are material to the tax liabilities of two or more persons.

There are also provisions dealing with the determination of the market value of property for the plant or machinery allowances (ss 11–270) as well as where there is a succession (s 559), sales treated as being for alternative amount (ss 568 or 569), or where transfers treated as sales (s 573). These rules also apply to any determination of the amount of any sums paid or proceeds received under the industrial buildings allowances rules, where there are arrangements which have an artificial effect on pricing (s 357).

Finally, there are arrangements to decide whether the Special Commissioners or the General Commissioners are to rule on the case, and if the General Commissioners, to which body of Commissioners. The Commissioners must determine the question in the same way as an appeal, but all the persons concerned are entitled to appear before and be heard by the Commissioners, or to make representations to them in writing.

4.1.11 Tax agreements for income tax purposes
(CAA 2001, s 565)

A 'tax agreement' is an agreement in writing as to the extent to which the allowance in question is given effect for the tax year in question. Where this rule applies, the allowance is treated as if it had been given effect under an assessment for the tax year for which the tax agreement is made, and to the extent set out in the tax agreement.

4.1.12 Sales treated as being for alternative amount
(CAA 2001, ss 567–570)

A sale of property that is not at market value is treated as being at market value if either the control test or the tax advantage test is met. However, the application of this rule is subject to any election made under s 569.

The rules described in ss 568–570 apply for industrial buildings allowances (ss 271–360), agricultural buildings allowances (ss 361–393), flat conversion allowances (ss 393A–393W), R&D allowances (ss 437–451) and assured tenancy allowances (ss 490–531).

In these rules, the control test is met if the buyer is a body of persons over whom the seller has control, the seller is a body of persons over whom the buyer has control, both the seller and the buyer are bodies of persons and another person has control over both of them, or the seller and the buyer are connected persons. A 'body of persons' includes a partnership.

Also, under these rules, the tax advantage test is met if it appears that the sole or main benefit which might be expected to accrue from the sale, or transactions of which the sale is one, is the obtaining of a tax advantage by all or any of the parties under the plant or machinery allowances rules (see ss 11–270).

The parties to a sale of property may elect that the sale be treated as being for an alternative amount if the control test is met or the rules for transfers to be treated as sales (s 573) apply, but the tax advantage test is not met. Note that this does not apply to a sale that is relevant for agricultural buildings allowances (ss 361–393) or flat conversion allowances (ss 393A–393W).

The following situations may arise:

(1) if the sale is relevant for industrial buildings allowances (ss 271–360) or assured tenancy allowances (ss 490–531), the alternative amount is the lower of market value and the residue of the qualifying expenditure immediately before the sale;

(2) if the sale is relevant for R&D allowances (s 437–451)
- (a) in a case where an R&D allowance is given for the expenditure represented by the asset sold, the alternative amount is the lower of market value and nil;
- (b) in any other case, the alternative amount is the lower of market value and the qualifying expenditure represented by the asset sold.

If the sale is relevant for industrial buildings allowances (ss 271–360) or assured tenancy allowances (ss 490–531), and is treated as being for the residue of the qualifying expenditure immediately before the sale, no balancing adjustment is made as a result of the sale of a building which is not an industrial building, etc throughout (under s 319) or a building which is not a qualifying dwelling-house throughout (s 517).

If, following the date of the sale, an event occurs such that a balancing charge would have been made on the seller if he had continued to own the property, and had done all the things, and been allowed all the allowances, as were done by, or allowed to, the buyer, that balancing charge is made on the buyer.

This election cannot be made if the circumstances of the sale, or the parties to it, mean that a relevant allowance or charge cannot be made, or the buyer is a dual resident investing company.

Here, the 'relevant allowance or charge' means an allowance or charge under the rules for industrial buildings allowances (ss 271–360), R&D allowances (ss 437–451) or assured tenancy allowances (ss 490–531) which would otherwise be made.

If the sale is relevant for assured tenancy allowances (ss 490–531), no election under s 569 can be made unless, at the time of the sale or any earlier time, both the seller and the buyer are or have been approved bodies (see s 492).

4.1.13 Application to parts of assets
(CAA 2001, s 571)

Under the capital allowance rules, references to an asset of any kind (including a building or structure, plant or machinery or works) include a part of an asset, unless the context otherwise requires.

4.1.14 References to sale of property and time of sale
(CAA 2001, s 572)

References in the capital allowance rules to the sale of property include exchanges of property, and the surrender, for valuable consideration of a leasehold interest (or Scottish equivalent). Any provision of CAA 2001 referring to a sale applies with the necessary modifications, including, in particular, references to:

(1) the net proceeds of sale and to the price include the consideration for the exchange or surrender, and

(2) capital sums included in the net proceeds of sale or paid on a sale include so much of the consideration for the exchange or surrender as would have been a capital sum if it had been a money payment.

Any reference, except in the R&D allowances rules (ss 437–451), to the time of any sale is to whichever is the earlier of the time of completion, and the time when possession is given.

4.1.15 Transfers treated as sales
(CAA 2001, s 573)

The rule described here applies under the rules for industrial buildings allowances (ss 271–360), agricultural buildings allowances (ss 361–393) flat conversion allowances (ss 393A–393W) and assured tenancy allowances (ss 490–531) and other situations where there is a transfer of the relevant interest under the rules in question, and the transfer is not a sale. Where the rule applies, the transfer is treated as a sale of the relevant interest made at market value, subject to any election to treat sale as being for alternative amount (s 569).

4.1.16 Definitions of general application

Meaning of 'control'
(CAA 2001, s 574)

In relation to a company, 'control' means the power of a person to secure:

(1) by means of holding shares, or possessing voting power in, that or any other company, or

(2) as a result of any powers conferred by the articles of association or other document regulating that or any other company,

that the affairs of the company are conducted in accordance with that person's wishes.

For a partnership, 'control' means the right to a share of more than half of the assets, or of more than one half of the income, of the partnership.

Connected persons
(CAA 2001, s 575)

TA 1988 s 839 which explains how to tell whether persons are 'connected' applies, generally, throughout the capital allowances rules. However, this is subject to an extended meaning in the following cases:

(1) under the anti-avoidance rules in ss 213–233 (s 232),
(2) where additional VAT liability is incurred in anti-avoidance cases (s 246(2)), and
(3) elections where predecessor and successor are connected persons (s 266(5)).

PLANT AND MACHINERY ALLOWANCES

4.2 WHAT IS PLANT OR MACHINERY?

As there is no general definition of 'plant or machinery' in the legislation, and it has been left to the courts to decide what is and is not plant or machinery, the identification of 'machinery' causes few problems. Machinery includes machines and their working parts (eg motor vehicles, lathes and computers), as the long line of cases about the meaning of 'plant' proves.

In *Yarmouth v France* (1887) 19 QBD 647, 'plant', in its ordinary sense was held to include:

> 'whatever apparatus is used by a businessman for carrying on his business – not his stock-in-trade which he buys or makes for sale; but all goods and chattels, fixed or moveable, live or dead, which he keeps for permanent employment in his business.'

This case makes it clear that something which is not used for carrying on the business cannot be plant; furthermore, 'plant' excludes stock-in-trade. The case also shows that business premises are not plant.

This question of whether an item is 'apparatus used in carrying on a business' is sometimes called the 'functional test', which in *Benson v The Yard Arm Club* (1979) 53 TC 67, was held to provide the criteria to be applied. Thus apparatus used in carrying on the business activities is plant. By contrast, an asset which functions as the business premises is not plant. Examples are as follows.

J Lyons and Co v A-G [1944] 1 All ER 477 was a war damage compensation case. The War Damage Act distinguished between buildings and plant. Here lamps destroyed by enemy action were held not be plant and thus did not qualify for compensation. They were part of the general setting in which, and not apparatus with which, the business was carried on.

Moveable partitions that possess mobility and flexibility were classified as being part of the apparatus with which the trade was carried on in *Jarrold v John Good & Sons* (1962) 40 TC 681. However, this does not mean that all moveable partitions are plant and the Revenue is likely to check whether they need to possess mobility as a matter of commercial necessity and that they have in fact been moved. In *Leeds Permanent Building Society v*

Proctor (1982) 56 TC 293 it was found that decorative screens used for window displays were plant, as their purpose was to attract attention and thus bring business to the Society.

In *CIR v Scottish & Newcastle Breweries* (1982) 55 TC 252, light fittings and decorative items such as wall plaques, tapestries, murals, prints and sculptures, were held to be plant on the basis that they created an 'ambience' – an important function in running a public house – and thus met the functional test. The electric wiring was merely part of the fabric of the building.

Note, however, rare instances where, for example, a dry dock in *CIR v Barclay Curle* (1969) 45 TC 221 and a grain silo in *Schofield v Hall* (1974) 49 TC 538, despite being part of the fabric of the building, were held to be plant because they both passed the functional test.

Wimpy International v Warland (1988) 61 TC 51 set out the boundaries of the 'setting' test. Wimpy had claimed machinery or plant allowances on replacement shop fronts. Following *Scottish & Newcastle*, the Special Commissioners allowed as plant such items as murals, decorative brickwork and wall panels, but disallowed floor and wall tiles, murals, lighting, water tanks, staircases and raised floors. The House of Lords allowed the light fittings. The case sets three tests, all of which fall within the category of 'functional', to be considered in deciding whether an item is plant:

(1) Is the item stock-in-trade?
(2) Is the item the business premises or part of them (the premises test)? An item used for carrying on the business is not plant if the business use is at the premises or the place on which the business is conducted.
(3) Is the item used for carrying on the business (the business use test)? An item may pass this test, but that is not sufficient to make it plant (eg if the business use is as stock-in-trade). The asset must be employed in carrying on the business. In *Wimpy*, as in *Scottish & Newcastle*, the lighting was to create atmosphere and to attract customers.

Thus, through various cases 'plant' has been held to include:

- A brewery dray-horse (*Yarmouth v France* (1887) 19 QBD 647 (as above)), but not stallions kept at stud (*Earl of Derby v Aylmer* (1915) 6 TC 665)
- Loose tools, knives and lasts used by a shoe manufacturer (*Hinton v Maden & Ireland* (1959) 38 TC 391)
- Moveable (and frequently moved) office partitioning (*Jarrold v John Good & Sons*, above)
- A dry dock (*CIR v Barclay, Curle & Co*, above)
- A swimming pool (*Cooke v Beach Station Caravans* (1974) 45 TC 221)
- Grain silos holding grain and from which the grain could conveniently be delivered (*Schofield v R & H Hall*, above)

- Law books as 'chattels of a barrister's profession' (*Munby v Furlong* (1977) 50 TC 491)
- Light fittings and murals in a hotel (*Scottish & Newcastle Breweries*, above)
- Decorative screens in windows (*Leeds Permanent Building Society*, above).
- Associated payments ie:
  - Finance charges for an oil rig (*Ben-Odeco v Powlson* (1978) 52 TC 460)
  - Option cancellation payments (*International Drilling Co v Bolton* (1982) 56 TC 449)
  - The extra sterling cost of a foreign currency instalment purchase (*Van Arkadie v Sterling Coated Materials* (1982) 56 TC 479).

Assets held not to be plant include:

- Electric lighting in teashop part of the 'general setting' (*J Lyons and Co*, above)
- Prefabricated buildings (*St John's School v Ward* (1974) 49 TC 524; note, however, that plant in the buildings did not qualify because there were no records apportioning the cost between plant and buildings)
- A filling station canopy (*Dixon v Fitch's Garage* (1975) 50 TC 509; compare a later Irish case where the canopy played an essential role in advertising the station's presence in *O'Culachain v McMullan Brothers* (1990) 1 IR 363)
- A ship used as a floating restaurant (*Benson v Yard Arm Club* (1979) 53 TC 67)
- A football spectators' stand (*Brown v Burnley Football & Athletic Club* (1980) 53 TC 357)
- Suspended ceilings covering service piping etc (*Hampton v Forte Autogrill* (1980) 53 TC 691)
- An inflatable tennis court cover (*Thomas v Reynolds & Broomhead* (1987) 59 TC 502)
- Glasshouses at a garden centre (*Gray v Seymour's Garden Centre (Horticulture)* (1995) 67 TC 401; see also *Tax Bulletin* 5 (November 1992), p 46)
- Newly constructed putting greens on a golf course (*Family Golf Centres v Thorne* 1998 SpC 150).

An apportionment has been made in some cases where there are allowable and non-allowable assets:

- Wallpaper pattern books (*Rose & Co (Wallpapers & Paints) v Campbell* (1967) 44 TC 500)
- Certain electrical installations in a department store, but not all (*Cole Brothers v Phillips* (1982) 55 TC 188)
- Restaurant improvements to premises and light fittings for general

illumination (not specific to the trade) (*Wimpy International*, above; compare the earlier decision in *J Lyons and Co*)

- Mezzanine storage platforms in warehouses (*Hunt v Henry Quick; King v Bridisco* (1992) 65 TC 108)
- The structure of an underground electricity substation to contain plant (*Bradley v London Electricity* (1996) 70 TC 155)
- A car wash site (*Attwood v Anduff Car Wash* (1997) 69 TC 575).

The underlying principles of these cases are now codified in ss 21–25 (see 4.5.1), so as to restrict the area of dispute, by reference, in particular, to qualifying activities and qualifying expenditure. There are rules which exclude, from the meaning of plant or machinery, expenditure on a building or structure or on the acquisition of an interest in land. These rules also set out general categories of assets which do not qualify as plant, but so as not to disqualify particular items within those categories which the courts have held to be plant, the tables include specific exemptions to cover such items. These rules do not apply to the items for which the plant or machinery allowances are provided by specific legislation.

4.3 AVAILABILITY OF PLANT AND MACHINERY ALLOWANCES
(CAA 2001, ss 11–14)

Plant or machinery allowances are available (per ss 11–270) to a person who carries on a 'qualifying activity' (see ss 15–20) and incurs 'qualifying expenditure' (ss 21–38). These allowances must be calculated separately for each qualifying activity which a person carries on.

The general rule is that expenditure is qualifying expenditure if it is capital expenditure on the provision of plant or machinery for the qualifying activity carried on by the person incurring the expenditure, and that person must own the plant or machinery as a result of incurring it. However, this general rule may be overridden by other provisions.

It is important to note that the Revenue construe 'on the provision of plant or machinery' narrowly. Thus transportation and installation costs are included, but professional fees are included only if directly related to the acquisition and installation. Where assets are provided for directors or employees, capital allowances are not normally restricted unless there is a 'blatant incongruity' between the asset provided and the business requirements.

Under the plant or machinery allowance rules, expenditure incurred for a qualifying activity by a person who is about to carry on the activity is treated as incurred by him on the first day on which he carries on the activity.

A special rule applies if a person brings into use for a qualifying activity carried on by him plant or machinery which he had previously acquired for a non-qualifying activity (eg personal use). In such a case he is treated as having incurred 'notional' capital expenditure on the provision of the plant or machinery for the qualifying activity on the date on which it is brought into qualifying use.

Generally, the amount of the notional expenditure is the market value of the plant or machinery on the date when it is brought into use for the qualifying activity. If the market value is greater than the actual expenditure, the amount of the notional expenditure is under the anti-avoidance provisions of ss 218 and 224.

Some adjustment is required if a person is the owner of plant or machinery following a gift, and then brings the plant or machinery into use for a qualifying activity carried on by him. He is treated as having incurred capital expenditure on the plant or machinery for the qualifying activity on the date on which it is so brought into use, and as owning the plant or machinery as a result of having incurred that expenditure. The amount of that capital expenditure is treated as being the market value of the plant or machinery on the date when it was brought into use.

4.4 QUALIFYING ACTIVITIES
(CAA 2001, ss 15–20)

Each of the following is a qualifying activity for the machinery and plant allowances:

(1) a trade,
(2) an ordinary Schedule A business,
(3) a furnished holiday lettings business (see TA 1988, s 504),
(4) an overseas property business,
(5) a profession or vocation,
(6) any of the following concerns:
    (a) mines and quarries (including gravel pits, sand pits and brickfields);
    (b) ironworks, gasworks, salt springs or works, alum mines or works (not being mines falling within (a) above) and waterworks and streams of water;
    (c) canals, inland navigation, docks and drains or levels;
    (d) fishings;
    (e) rights of markets and fairs, tolls, bridges and ferries;
    (f) railways and other ways;
    (g) other concerns of the like nature as any of the concerns specified in paragraphs (b)-(e) above (see TA 1988, s 55(2)),
(7) the management of an investment company (see TA 1988, s 75),
(8) special leasing of plant or machinery, and
(9) an employment or office (but not employment as a diver in the North Sea etc (see TA 1988, s 314).

4.5 QUALIFYING EXPENDITURE

4.5.1 Buildings, structures and land
(CAA 2001, ss 21–25)

Expenditure on plant or machinery does not include expenditure on buildings. The provision of a building includes its construction or acquisition. Here, 'building' includes an asset which:

(a) is incorporated in the building,
(b) although not incorporated in the building (whether because the asset is moveable or for any other reason), is in the building and is of a kind normally incorporated in a building, or
(c) is in, or connected with, the building and is in list A.

The assets under list A are:

- Walls, floors, ceilings, doors, gates, shutters, windows and stairs.
- Mains services, and systems, for water, electricity and gas.
- Waste disposal systems.
- Sewerage and drainage systems.
- Shafts or other structures in which lifts, hoists, escalators and moving walkways are installed.
- Fire safety systems.

Expenditure on the provision of plant or machinery does not include expenditure on:

(a) the provision of a structure or other asset in list B, or
(b) any works involving the alteration of land.

Excluded structures and other assets under list B are:

- A tunnel, bridge, viaduct, aqueduct, embankment or cutting.
- A way, hard standing (such as a pavement), road, railway, tramway, a park for vehicles or containers, or an airstrip or runway.
- An inland navigation, including a canal or basin or a navigable river.
- A dam, reservoir or barrage, including any sluices, gates, generators and other equipment associated with the dam, reservoir or barrage.
- A dock, harbour, wharf, pier, marina or jetty or any other structure in or at which vessels may be kept, or merchandise or passengers may be shipped or unshipped.
- A dike, sea wall, weir or drainage ditch.
- Any structure not within the above items other than
  (a) a structure (but not an industrial building),
  (b) structure in use for an undertaking for the extraction, production, processing or distribution of gas, and
  (c) a structure in use for a trade which consists in the provision of telecommunication, television or radio services.

The provision of a structure or other asset includes its construction or acquisition. Here:

(a) 'structure' means a fixed structure of any kind, other than a building in list A, and
(b) 'land' does not include buildings or other structures, but otherwise includes land covered with water, any estate, interest, easement, servitude or right in or over land.

Lists A and B do not apply to any expenditure on:

(1) thermal insulation of industrial buildings (s 28);
(2) fire safety (s 29);
(3) safety at designated sports grounds (s 30);
(4) safety at regulated stands at sports grounds (s 31);
(5) safety at other sports grounds (s 32);
(6) personal security (s 33);
(7) software and rights to software (s 71);
(8) election relating to tax treatment of films expenditure (F(No2)A 1992, s 40D).

List A and List B also do not affect the question whether expenditure on any item described in List C is expenditure on the provision of plant or machinery. But List C items (1)-(16) do not include any asset whose principal purpose is to insulate or enclose the interior of a building or to provide an interior wall, floor or ceiling which (in each case) is intended to remain permanently in place. The List C items are:

(1) Machinery (including devices for providing motive power) not within any other item in this list.
(2) Electrical systems (including lighting systems) and cold water, gas and sewerage systems provided mainly:
    (a) to meet the particular requirements of the qualifying activity, or
    (b) to serve particular plant or machinery used for the qualifying activity.
(3) Space or water heating systems; powered systems of ventilation, air cooling or air purification; and any floor or ceiling comprised in such systems.
(4) Manufacturing or processing equipment; storage equipment (including cold rooms); display equipment; and counters, checkouts and similar equipment.
(5) Cookers, washing machines, dishwashers, refrigerators and similar equipment; washbasins, sinks, baths, showers, sanitary ware and similar equipment; and furniture and furnishings.
(6) Lifts, hoists, escalators and moving walkways.
(7) Sound insulation provided mainly to meet the particular requirements of the qualifying activity.
(8) Computer, telecommunication and surveillance systems (including their wiring or other links). Refrigeration or cooling equipment. Fire

alarm systems; sprinkler and other equipment for extinguishing or containing fires.

(9) Burglar alarm systems. Strong rooms in bank or building society premises; safes.

(10) Partition walls, where moveable and intended to be moved in the course of the qualifying activity. Decorative assets provided for the enjoyment of the public in hotel, restaurant or similar trades.

(11) Advertising hoardings; signs, displays and similar assets.

(12) Swimming pools (including diving boards, slides and structures on which such boards or slides are mounted).

(13) Any glasshouse constructed so that the required environment (namely, air, heat, light, irrigation and temperature) for the growing of plants is provided automatically by means of devices forming an integral part of its structure.

(14) Cold stores.

(15) Caravans provided mainly for holiday lettings. 'Caravan' includes, in relation to a holiday caravan site, anything that is treated as a caravan under the Caravan Sites and Control of Development Act 1960 or the Caravans Act (Northern Ireland) 1963.

(16) Buildings provided for testing aircraft engines run within the buildings.

(17) Moveable buildings intended to be moved in the course of the qualifying activity.

(18) The alteration of land for the purpose only of installing plant or machinery.

(19) The provision of dry docks.

(20) The provision of any jetty or similar structure provided mainly to carry plant or machinery.

(21) The provision of pipelines or underground ducts or tunnels with a primary purpose of carrying utility conduits.

(22) The provision of towers to support floodlights.

(23) The provision of:
   (a) any reservoir incorporated into a water treatment works, or
   (b) any service reservoir of treated water for supply within any housing estate or other particular locality.

(24) The provision of:
   (a) silos provided for temporary storage, or
   (b) storage tanks. The provision of slurry pits or silage clamps. The provision of fish tanks or fish ponds.

(25) The provision of rails, sleepers and ballast for a railway or tramway. The provision of structures and other assets for providing the setting for any ride at an amusement park or exhibition.

(26) The provision of fixed zoo cages.

It is important to note that the items in List C must qualify as plant under normal rules in order to qualify for capital allowances. Expenditure on the

provision of plant or machinery does not include expenditure on the acquisition of an interest in land. Here, 'land' does not include buildings or other
structures, or any asset which is so installed or otherwise fixed to any
description of land as to become, in law, part of the land, but otherwise
includes land covered with water, any estate, interest, easement, servitude or
right in or over land. Subject to this 'interest in land' means:

(1) the fee simple estate in the land or an agreement to acquire such an
    estate,
(2) in relation to Scotland, the interest of the owner or an agreement to
    acquire such an interest,
(3) a lease,
(4) an easement or servitude or an agreement to acquire an easement or
    servitude, and
(5) a licence to occupy land.

If a person carrying on a qualifying activity incurs capital expenditure on
alterations to an existing building which are incidental to the installation of
plant or machinery for qualifying activity, the plant or machinery allowance
rules apply as if the expenditure were expenditure on the provision of the
plant or machinery, and the works representing the expenditure formed
part of the plant or machinery.

4.5.2 Demolition costs
(CAA 2001, s 26)

Special treatment applies if plant or machinery is demolished, and the last
use of the plant or machinery was for a qualifying activity. If the person carrying on the qualifying activity replaces the plant or machinery with other
plant or machinery then the net cost of the demolition to that person is
treated as expenditure incurred on the provision of the other plant or
machinery.

If the person carrying on the qualifying activity does not replace the
plant or machinery, the net cost of the demolition to that person is allocated
to the pool to which the expenditure on the demolished plant or machinery
has been or would be allocated under the plant or machinery allowance
rules.

The 'the net cost of the demolition' is the amount, if any, by which the
cost of the demolition exceeds any money received for the remains of the
plant or machinery.

4.5.3 Expenditure on thermal insulation, safety measures, etc
(CAA 2001, s 27)

Special rules deal with expenditure on thermal insulation of industrial buildings (s 28), fire safety (s 29), safety at designated sports grounds (s 30),

safety at regulated sports grounds (s 31) and safety at other sports grounds (s 32) , and a plant or machinery allowance for the expenditure could not, otherwise, be made in calculating the income from the qualifying activity in question.

The general rules for plant or machinery expenditure are applied as if such expenditure for the qualifying activity carried on by the person incurring the expenditure, and as if the person incurring the expenditure owns the plant or machinery as a result of incurring it.

4.5.4 Personal security
(CAA 2001, s 33)

Expenditure incurred by an individual or partnership carrying on a relevant qualifying activity on any asset used for personal safety is eligible for an allowance if it meets the criteria for the special threat conditions. These are that:

(1) the asset is provided or used to protect an individual in carrying out a qualifying activity, and
(2) the expense is incurred with the sole object of improving that personal physical security.

If in relation to (2) above there happens to be an incidental use for the asset arising from the motive for sole security use, that incidental use is ignored. The same applies if the item happens to protect the individual's family as well. If the asset is not intended to be used solely to improve personal physical security, but the expenditure incurred on it would otherwise be qualifying expenditure, the relief applies only to the proportion of the expenditure attributable thereto.

A car, ship, aircraft, or a dwelling or grounds appurtenant to a dwelling are specifically excluded. However, IT equipment, a structure (such as a wall) and an asset which becomes fixed to land are included. The extended meaning of 'car' (see s 81) does not apply.

4.5.5 Exclusion of certain types of expenditure
(CAA 2001, ss 34–38)

Certain types of expenditure are excluded, such as:

(1) expenditure relating to residential or overnight accommodation incurred by Members of Parliament and of the regional assemblies.
(2) in the case of a property business, costs incurred in providing plant or machinery for use in a dwelling-house.

   A flat used as a residence is a dwelling-house, but a block of flats is not a single dwelling-house. If such plant or machinery serves a whole of a block of flats, the cost is allowed. For non-residential buildings, rent is not apportioned between building and plant but capital allowances are given against rents for the building.

(3) where the qualifying activity consists of an employment or office, expenditure incurred in providing a car, or a motorcycle (see the Road Traffic Act 1988, s 192), is not qualifying expenditure – although other expenditure incurred in providing for use in the performance of the duties of the employment or office is allowed.

(4) where payments are made to an individual to cover the whole of the asset's depreciation during its use for the qualifying activity (but note that this does not apply if the sums are taken into account as part of his income, or in calculating the profits of that activity carried on by him).

4.6 FIRST-YEAR QUALIFYING EXPENDITURE

4.6.1 General
(CAA 2001, s 39)

A first-year allowance is not available unless the qualifying expenditure is first-year qualifying expenditure ie expenditure incurred for Northern Ireland purposes by small or medium-sized enterprises (see s 40), expenditure incurred by small or medium-sized enterprises (s 44), ICT expenditure incurred by small enterprises (s 45), expenditure on energy-saving plant or machinery (s 45A), expenditure on cars with low CO_2 emissions (s 45D), expenditure on plant or machinery for a gas refuelling station (s 45E) or expenditure on plant or machinery for use wholly in a ring fence trade (s 45F).

4.6.2 Northern Ireland (NI)
(CAA 2001, ss 40–43)

Separate provisions apply in NI for first-year qualifying expenditure incurred before 12 May 2002, by small or medium-sized enterprises for plant or machinery for use primarily in NI, and it is not excluded as a miscellaneous exclusion (see s 41), as plant or machinery partly for use outside NI (s 42), or under the general exclusions (see s 46). This is subject to special rules setting out the effect of plant or machinery subsequently being primarily for use outside NI (s 43).

Such expenditure does not qualify if:

(1) it is on long-life assets (see ss 90–104), on an aircraft or hovercraft, or on a goods vehicle for a trade which consists primarily of goods conveyance.

(2) it is on plant or machinery for use primarily in agriculture, fishing or fish farming, or any relevant activity unless it is authorised by the NI Department of Agriculture and Rural Development.

(3) when it is incurred, the plant or machinery is intended to be used partly outside NI, and the main benefit reasonably expected to arise from the arrangements is to obtain a first-year allowance, or greater first-year allowance, for the expenditure that is attributable to use outside NI.

If the expenditure concerned exceeds £3.5m and the asset is primarily used or held outside NI within five years from when the expenditure was incurred, it cannot be treated as first-year qualifying expenditure. In any other case the period is two years.

4.6.3 Expenditure incurred by small or medium-sized enterprises
(CAA 2001, s 44)

Expenditure incurred by a small or medium-sized enterprise is first-year qualifying expenditure if it is not covered by any of the general exclusions (see s 46). Long-life asset expenditure is not first-year qualifying expenditure in this context.

4.6.4 ICT expenditure incurred by small enterprises
(CAA 2001, s 45)

Expenditure is first-year qualifying expenditure if it is incurred before 1 April 2003 by a small enterprise, is expenditure on information and communications technology, and is not within the general exclusions (see s 46). 'Expenditure on information and communications technology' is expenditure on items within any of the following classes.

Class A. Computers and associated equipment

1   computers,
2   peripheral devices designed to be used by being connected to or inserted in a computer,
3   equipment (including cabling) for use primarily to provide a data connection between one computer and another, or between a computer and a data communications network, and
4   dedicated electrical systems for computers.

For this purpose a 'computer' does not include computerised control or management systems etc that are part of a larger system whose principal function is not processing or storing information.

Class B. Other qualifying equipment

1   wireless application protocol telephones,
2   third generation mobile telephones,
3   devices designed to be used by being connected to a television set and capable of receiving and transmitting information from and to data networks, and
4   other devices substantially similar to those within paragraphs 1, 2 and 3, and which are capable of receiving and transmitting information from and to data networks.

Class C. Software

The right to use or otherwise deal with software for any equipment within Class A or B.

4.6.5 Expenditure on energy-saving plant or machinery
(CAA 2001, ss 45A to 45C)

The first-year qualifying expenditure rules apply to energy-saving plant or machinery bought as new (and not second-hand) after 31 March 2001 and not subject to the general exclusions in s 46 (see 4.6.8). They apply when the cost is incurred or when the contract for its provision is entered into. The plant or machinery must meet the specified energy-saving criteria (see eg Capital Allowances (Energy-saving Plant or Machinery) Order 2000, art 3).

A certificate of energy efficiency (ie one issued or authorised by the Secretary of State DETR, or by the regional assemblies) may be required for certain plant or machinery to qualify. If a certificate is revoked, it is treated as never having been issued.

Where components in plant or machinery are a mixture of energy and non-energy efficient parts, the expenditure can be apportioned (subject to an aggregate or maximum amount). Payments made by instalments must be apportioned in the same way as payment in full would be. The apportionment rules do not apply where the plant or machinery is sold with other property.

4.6.6 Expenditure on cars with low carbon dioxide emissions
(CAA 2001, s 45D)

Expenditure is first-year qualifying expenditure if:

(1) it is incurred in the period beginning on 17 April 2002 and ending on 31 March 2008,

(2) it is expenditure on a car which is first registered after 16 April 2002 and which is unused and not second-hand,

(3) the car is an electrically-propelled car, or is a car with low CO_2 emissions, and

(4) the expenditure is not excluded by s 46 (general exclusions).

Here, a car with low CO_2 emissions is a car which satisfies the conditions set out below.

The first condition is that, when the car is first registered, it is so registered on the basis of an EC certificate of conformity, or a UK approval certificate, that specifies:

(a) in the case of a car other than a bi-fuel car, a CO_2 emissions figure in terms of grams per kilometre driven, or

(b) in the case of a bi-fuel car, separate CO_2 emissions figures in terms of grams per kilometre driven for different fuels.

The second condition is that the applicable CO_2 emissions figure in the case of the car does not exceed 120 grams per kilometre driven. For this purpose the applicable CO_2 emissions figure in the case of a car other than a bi-fuel car is:

(1) where the EC certificate of conformity or UK approval certificate specifies only one CO_2 emissions figure, that figure, and

(2) where the certificate specifies more than one CO_2 emissions figure, the figure specified as the CO_2 emissions (combined) figure.

The applicable CO_2 emissions figure in the case of a bi-fuel car is:

(1) where the EC certificate of conformity or UK approval certificate specifies more than one CO_2 emissions figure in relation to each fuel, the lowest CO_2 emissions (combined) figure specified, and

(2) in any other case, the lowest CO_2 figure specified by the certificate.

Here any reference to a car:

(1) includes a reference to a mechanically propelled road vehicle of a type commonly used as a hackney carriage, but

(2) does not include a reference to a motorcycle.

For the above purposes, a car is an electrically-propelled car only if:

(1) it is propelled solely by electrical power, and

(2) that power is derived from:
    (a) a source external to the vehicle, or
    (b) an electrical storage battery which is not connected to any source of power when the vehicle is in motion.

Here 'bi-fuel car' means a car which is capable of being propelled by petrol and road fuel gas, or diesel and road fuel gas; and 'car' has the extended meaning of 'car' given by s 81.

4.6.7 Expenditure on plant or machinery for gas refuelling station
(CA 2001 s 45E)

Expenditure is first-year qualifying expenditure if:

(1) it is incurred in the period beginning on 17 April 2002 and ending on 31 March 2008,

(2) it is expenditure on plant or machinery for a gas refuelling station where the plant or machinery is unused and not second-hand, and

(3) it is not excluded by s 46 (general exclusions).

Here expenditure on plant or machinery for a gas refuelling station is expenditure on plant or machinery installed at a gas refuelling station for use solely for or in connection with refuelling vehicles with natural gas or

115

hydrogen fuel. For this purpose the plant or machinery which is for use for or in connection with refuelling vehicles with natural gas or hydrogen fuel includes:

(1) any storage tank for natural gas or hydrogen fuel,
(2) any compressor, pump, control or meter used for or in connection with refuelling vehicles with natural gas or hydrogen fuel, and
(3) any equipment for dispensing natural gas or hydrogen fuel to the fuel tank of a vehicle.

A 'gas refuelling station' means any premises, or that part of any premises, where vehicles are refuelled with natural gas or hydrogen fuel. 'Hydrogen fuel' means a fuel consisting of gaseous or cryogenic liquid hydrogen which is used for propelling vehicles; and 'vehicle' means a mechanically propelled road vehicle.

4.6.8 General exclusions
(CAA 2001, s 46)

Expenditure within any of the general exclusions is not first-year qualifying expenditure under the rules for expenditure incurred for NI purposes by small or medium-sized enterprises (see s 40), expenditure incurred by small or medium-sized enterprises (see s 44), ICT expenditure incurred by small enterprises (see s 45), expenditure on energy-saving plant or machinery (see s 45A), expenditure on cars with low CO_2 emissions (s 45D), or expenditure on plant or machinery for a gas refuelling station (s 45E).

The general exclusions are:

General exclusion 1

Expenditure incurred in the chargeable period in which the qualifying activity is permanently discontinued.

General exclusion 2

Expenditure incurred on the provision of a car (as defined by s 81). This does not prevent expenditure being first-year qualifying expenditure under s 45D.

General exclusion 3

Expenditure on ships (as described in s 94) (outside the scope of this book).

General exclusion 4

Expenditure on railway assets (as described in s 95).

General exclusion 5

Expenditure which would be long-life asset expenditure but for transitional provisions (see Sch 3, para 20).

General exclusion 6

Expenditure is on the provision of plant or machinery for leasing (whether in the course of a trade or otherwise). Here, the letting of a ship on charter, or of any other asset on hire, is regarded as leasing (whether or not it would otherwise be so regarded).

General exclusion 7

Expenditure incurred in circumstances such that:

(1) the provision of the plant or machinery on which the expenditure is incurred is connected with a change in the nature or conduct of a trade or business carried on by a person other than the person incurring the expenditure, and
(2) the obtaining of a first-year allowance is the main benefit, or one of the main benefits, which could reasonably be expected to arise from the making of the change.

General exclusion 8

Either of the following conditions applies:

(1) use for qualifying activity of plant or machinery provided for other purposes (s 13);
(2) use for qualifying activity of plant or machinery which is a gift (s 14).

4.6.9 Expenditure of small or medium-sized enterprises
(CAA 2001, ss 47–49)

An important matter to be decided is whether expenditure incurred by a company is, for the first-year allowances rules, incurred by a small or medium-sized enterprise, or a small enterprise.

The expenditure is incurred by a small or medium-sized enterprise if the company qualifies (or is treated as qualifying) as small or medium-sized under the relevant companies legislation for the financial year of the company in which the expenditure is incurred, and is not a member of a large group at the time when the expenditure is incurred.

The expenditure is incurred by a small enterprise if the company qualifies (or is treated as qualifying) as small under the relevant companies legislation for the financial year of the company in which the expenditure is incurred, and is not a member of a large or medium-sized group at the time when the expenditure is incurred.

'The relevant companies legislation' is the Companies Act (CA) 1985, s 247 (see below), and 'financial year' has the same meaning as the CA 1985, s 223, or equivalent legislation in Northern Ireland. A 'company' is a company (per CA 1985, s 735), or an overseas company (per the CA 1985, s 744), or equivalent legislation in NI.

Qualification of company as small or medium-sized
(CA 1985 s 247)

The qualifying conditions are met by a company in a year in which it satisfies two or more of the following requirements:

Small company

1. Turnover   Not more than £2.8m
2. Balance sheet total   Not more than £1.4m
3. Number of employees   Not more than 50

Medium-sized company

1. Turnover   Not more than £11.2m
2. Balance sheet total   Not more than £5.6m
3. Number of employees   Not more than 250.

For a period which is less than a year the maximum figures for turnover are proportionately adjusted.

The 'balance sheet' total means:

(1) where in the company's accounts, Format 1 is adopted, the aggregate of the amounts shown in the balance sheet under the headings corresponding to items A-D in that Format, and

(2) where Format 2 is adopted, the aggregate of the amounts shown under the general heading 'Assets'.

The number of employees means the average number of persons employed by the company in the year, determined on a monthly basis by applying the method of calculation prescribed by CA 1985, Sch 4, para 56(2) and (3) for determining the corresponding number required to be stated in a note to the company's accounts.

Likewise, it is important whether expenditure incurred by a business is incurred by a small or medium-sized enterprise, or a small enterprise.

Here 'business' means an individual, a partnership of individuals, or a registered friendly society (see TA 1988, ss 460–466), or a body corporate which is not a company but is within the charge to corporation tax.

The expenditure is incurred by a small or medium-sized enterprise if the expenditure is incurred for a qualifying activity carried on by the business, and the business passes the hypothetical company test, in relation to that expenditure, as a small or medium-sized company.

The expenditure is incurred by a small enterprise if the expenditure is incurred for a qualifying activity carried on by the business, and the business passes the hypothetical company test, in relation to that expenditure, as a small company.

To apply the hypothetical company test, it has to be assumed that:

(1) the qualifying activity is carried on by 'the hypothetical company',

(2) every trade, etc carried on by the business is carried on by it as part of that activity,

(3) the financial years of the hypothetical company coincide with the chargeable periods of the business, and

(4) accounts of the hypothetical company for any relevant chargeable period have been duly drawn up as if that period were a financial year of the company.

The business passes the hypothetical company test as a small or medium-sized company if, on the above assumptions, a company would qualify as small or medium-sized under the relevant companies legislation for the financial year in which the expenditure is assumed to be incurred.

The business passes the hypothetical company test as a small company if, on the above assumptions, the company would qualify as small under the relevant companies legislation for the financial year in which the expenditure is assumed to be incurred.

It also has to be decided whether a company is a member of a large group, or a member of a large or medium-sized group.

Subject as below, a company is a member of a large group at the time when any expenditure is incurred if it is at that time the parent undertaking of a group which does not qualify as small or medium-sized for the financial year of the parent undertaking in which that time falls, or is at that time a subsidiary undertaking in relation to the parent undertaking of such a group.

Subject also as below, a company is a member of a large or medium-sized group at the time when any expenditure is incurred if it is at that time the parent undertaking of a group which does not qualify as small in relation to the financial year of the parent undertaking in which that time falls, or it is at that time a subsidiary undertaking in relation to the parent undertaking of such a group.

It must be ascertained whether, at the time when any expenditure is incurred by a company, any arrangements exist which are such that, had effect been given to them immediately before that time, the company or a successor of the company would, at that time, have been a member of a large group, or would, at that time, have been a member of a large or medium-sized group. In such event, the company incurring the expenditure is treated as a member of a large group or (as the case may be) a large or medium-sized group at that time.

The question whether a group qualifies as small or medium-sized, or a group qualifies as small, is decided by reference to the relevant companies legislation (CA 1985, s 249), but reading references in that legislation to a parent company as references to a parent undertaking.

A company is the successor of another if it carries on a trade which the predecessor company has ceased to carry on, and the circumstances are such that TA 1988, s 343 (company reconstructions without a change of ownership) applies to the two companies and 'arrangements' means arrangements of any kind (whether or not in writing or legally enforceable).

The following expressions are defined in CA 1985 (or equivalent NI legislation): 'financial year' (CA 1985, s 223), 'group' (CA 1985, s 262), 'parent undertaking' (CA 1985, s 258) and 'subsidiary undertaking' (CA 1985, s 258).

Qualification of group as small or medium-sized
(CA 1985 s 249)

A group qualifies as small or medium-sized for a financial year if the qualifying conditions are met in the parent company's first financial year, in that year, and any subsequent financial year, in that year and the preceding year.

A group is treated as qualifying as small or medium-sized for a financial year if it so qualified in relation to the previous financial year as above or was treated as so qualifying in relation to the previous year as above and the qualifying conditions are met in the year in question.

The qualifying conditions are met by a group in a year in which it satisfies two or more of the following requirements:

Small group

1. Aggregate turnover	Not more than £2.8m net (or £3.36m gross)
2. Aggregate balance sheet total	Not more than £1.4m net (or £1.68m gross)
3. Aggregate number of employees	Not more than 50

Medium-sized group

1. Aggregate turnover	Not more than £11.2m net (or £13.44m gross)
2. Aggregate balance sheet total	Not more than £5.6m net (or £6.72m gross)
3. Aggregate number of employees	Not more than 250.

The aggregate figures are ascertained by aggregating the relevant figures determined under CA 1985, s 247 for each member of the group.

In relation to the aggregate figures for turnover and balance sheet total, 'net' means with the set-offs and other adjustments in the case of group accounts and 'gross' means without those set-offs and other adjustments; and a company may satisfy the relevant requirements on the basis of either the net or the gross figure.

The figures for each subsidiary undertaking are those included in its accounts for the relevant financial year, ie if its financial year ends with that of the parent company, that financial year, and if not, its financial year ending last before the end of the financial year of the parent company.

If those figures cannot be obtained without disproportionate expense or undue delay, the latest available figures are taken.

4.6.10 Time when expenditure is incurred
(CAA 2001, s 50)

In determining whether expenditure is first-year allowances qualifying expenditure, any effect of the general rules as to treatment of expenditure incurred before qualifying activity carried on (s 12) on the time at which it is to be treated as incurred is disregarded.

4.6.11 Disclosure of information between UK tax authorities
(CAA 2001, s 51)

The obligation as to secrecy does not prevent

(1) the Revenue from disclosing information, for the purpose mentioned below, to the Department of Agriculture and Rural Development in NI, or vice versa;
(2) disclosing information, for the purpose mentioned below, to the Revenue.

The purpose referred to is assisting the Revenue, in carrying out its functions relating to allowances for expenditure incurred for NI purposes by small or medium-sized enterprises (see s 40), or the Department, in carrying out its functions.

4.7 ALLOWANCES AND CHARGES

4.7.1 First-year allowances
(CAA 2001, s 52)

A person is entitled to a first-year allowance for his first-year qualifying expenditure if the expenditure is incurred in a chargeable period, and he owns the plant or machinery at some time during that chargeable period.

This must be read in conjunction with the rules for first-year allowances for additional VAT liabilities (see s 236 and 4.1.7) and is subject to reduction of first-year allowance if plant or machinery is provided partly otherwise than for the qualifying activity (see s 205), if it appears that a partial depreciation subsidy is payable (see s 210), or if, under anti-avoidance provisions no first-year allowance is available (see ss 217, 223 and 241). Any first-year allowance is made for the chargeable period in which the first-year qualifying expenditure is incurred.

The amount of the allowance is a percentage of the first-year qualifying expenditure for which the allowance is made, as shown in Table 4.1.

Table 4.1 – Amount of first-year allowances

Type of first-year qualifying expenditure	Amount (%)
Expenditure incurred for Northern Ireland purposes by small or medium-sized enterprises (s 40)	100
Expenditure incurred by small or medium-sized enterprises (s 44)	40
ICT expenditure incurred by small enterprises (s 45)	100
Expenditure on energy-saving plant or machinery (s 45A)	100
Expenditure on cars with low CO_2 emissions (s 45D)	100
Expenditure on plant or machinery for gas refuelling stations (s 45E)	100

A person who is entitled to a first-year allowance may claim the allowance for the whole or a part of the first-year qualifying expenditure.

4.7.2 Pooling of qualifying expenditure
(CAA 2001, ss 53 and 54)

Qualifying expenditure has to be pooled to determine a person's entitlement to writing-down allowances and balancing allowances, and liability to balancing charges. If he carries on more than one qualifying activity, expenditure relating to the different activities is allocated to separate pools. In addition to the main pool, there are single asset pools and class pools.

A single asset pool cannot contain expenditure relating to more than one asset. The following provide for qualifying expenditure to be allocated to a single asset pool:

(1) s 74 (expensive cars);
(2) s 86 (short-life assets);
(3) s 206 (plant or machinery provided or used partly otherwise than for the qualifying activity);
(4) s 211 (payment of partial depreciation subsidy);
(5) s 538 (contribution allowances).

A class pool is a pool which may contain expenditure relating to more than one asset. Qualifying expenditure on long-life assets (s 101), and in relation to overseas leasing (s 107) are allocated to class pools.

Qualifying expenditure can be allocated to the main pool only if it does not have to be allocated to a single asset pool or a class pool.

4.7.3 Writing-down and balancing allowances and balancing charges
(CAA 2001, ss 55 and 56)

Whether a person is entitled to a writing-down allowance or a balancing allowance, or liable to a balancing charge, for a chargeable period is determined separately for each pool of qualifying expenditure and depends on:

(1) the Available Qualifying Expenditure in that pool for that period ('AQE'), and
(2) the Total of Disposal Receipts brought into account in that pool for that period ('TDR').

If AQE exceeds TDR, the person is entitled to a writing-down allowance or a balancing allowance for the period. If TDR exceeds AQE, the person is liable to a balancing charge for the period. The entitlement is to a writing-down allowance if AQE exceeds TDR except for the final chargeable period (see s 65) when it is to a balancing allowance.

In general, the amount of the writing-down allowance to which a person is entitled for a chargeable period is 25% of the amount by which AQE exceeds TDR. However, only a restricted allowance is available for long-life asset expenditure for which the allowance is 6% (see s 102).

If the chargeable period is more or less than a year, the amount of the allowance is increased or reduced pro rata. If the qualifying activity has been carried on for part only of the chargeable period, the amount is proportionately reduced. A person claiming a writing-down allowance may require that the allowance be reduced to a specified amount.

The balancing charge to which a person is liable for a chargeable period is the amount by which TDR exceeds AQE, whereas the balancing allowance to which a person is entitled for the final chargeable period is the amount by which AQE exceeds TDR.

4.7.4 Available qualifying expenditure (AQE)
(CAA 2001, ss 57–59).

The general rule is that a person's AQE in a pool for a chargeable period consists of any qualifying expenditure allocated to the pool for that period (per s 58), and any unrelieved qualifying expenditure carried forward in the pool from the previous chargeable period (per s 59).

A person's AQE in a pool for a chargeable period may also include any amount allocated to the pool for that period under:

(1) s 26(3) (net costs of demolition);
(2) ss 86(2) or 87(2) (allocation of expenditure in short-life asset pools);
(3) s 206(3) (plant or machinery used partly otherwise than for the qualifying activity); and
(4) s 211(4) (partial depreciation subsidy paid).

A person's AQE in a pool does not include any expenditure excluded by:

(1) ss 8(4) or 9(1) (rules against double relief);
(2) ss 185(2), 186(2) or 187(2) (restrictions where other claims are made for fixtures);
(3) ss 218(1), 224(1), 228(2), 242(2), or 243(2) (general anti-avoidance provisions).

The following rules apply in the allocation of a person's qualifying expenditure to the appropriate pool.

An amount of qualifying expenditure cannot be allocated to a pool for a chargeable period if that amount has already been taken into account in determining the AQE for an earlier chargeable period. Qualifying expenditure cannot be allocated to a pool for a chargeable period before that in which the expenditure is incurred. Qualifying expenditure cannot be allocated to a pool for a chargeable period unless the person owns the plant or machinery at some time in that period.

If a first-year allowance is made for an amount of first-year qualifying expenditure then, in general, none of that amount can be allocated to a pool for the chargeable period in which the expenditure is incurred, and the amount that may be allocated to a pool for any chargeable period is limited to the balance left after deducting the first-year allowance. Also, if a first-year allowance is made for of an amount of first-year qualifying expenditure, a disposal event occurs for the plant or machinery in any chargeable period, and none of the balance left after deducting the first-year allowance has been allocated to a pool for an earlier chargeable period, the following applies. The balance (or some of it) must be allocated to a pool for the chargeable period in which the disposal event occurs. This applies even if the balance is nil (because of a 100% first-year allowance). The appropriate pool here is whichever pool is otherwise applicable under the plant or machinery allowance rules.

A person has unrelieved qualifying expenditure to carry forward from a chargeable period if for that period AQE exceeds TDR. The amount of the unrelieved qualifying expenditure is the excess less the writing-down allowance made for the period, or if no writing-down allowance is claimed for the period, the excess. Nothing can be carried forward as unrelieved qualifying expenditure from the final chargeable period.

4.7.5 Disposal events and disposal values: general
(CAA 2001, ss 60–64 and 66)

In the plant or machinery allowance rules a 'disposal receipt' is the disposal value that a person is required to bring into account under:

(1) ss 61, 62 and 63 (disposal events, disposal values and the general limit on the amount of a disposal value),
(2) any of the following
  (a) s 68 (hire-purchase etc: disposal value on cessation of notional ownership),
  (b) s 72 and 73 (grant of new software right: disposal value),
  (c) s 79 (cars: disposal value in avoidance cases)
  (d) s 88 and 89 (short-life assets: disposal at under-value or to connected person),
  (e) s 104 (long-life assets: avoidance cases),

(f)   ss 196 and 197 (fixtures: disposal values on cessation of notional ownership and in avoidance cases),

(g)   s 208 (effect of significant reduction in use of plant or machinery for a qualifying activity),

(h)   s 211 (effect of payment of partial depreciation subsidy),

(i)   s 222 (anti-avoidance: limit on disposal value), and

(j)   ss 238 and 239 (additional VAT rebates)

when read with ss 64 and 264(3) (cases in which no disposal value need be brought into account).

In the plant or machinery allowances rules 'disposal event' means any event of a kind that requires a disposal value to be brought into account under those rules (whether under s 61 or otherwise). If qualifying expenditure has been allocated to a pool, and more than one disposal event occurs in to the plant or machinery, a disposal value is required to be brought into account in the pool for the first event only. Here, 'disposal event' does not include a disposal event arising under the rules for:

(1)   s 72 (computer software), or

(2)   s 238(2) (additional VAT rebates).

A person who has incurred qualifying expenditure must bring the disposal value of plant or machinery into account for the chargeable period in which:

(1)   he ceases to own the plant or machinery;

(2)   he loses possession of the plant or machinery in circumstances where it is reasonable to assume that the loss is permanent;

(3)   the plant or machinery ceases to exist as such (as a result of destruction, dismantling or otherwise);

The disposal value to be brought into account depends on the disposal event, as shown in Table 4.2:

Table 4.2 – Disposal values: general

Item No	1. Disposal event	2. Disposal value to be brought into account
1	Sale of the plant or machinery, except in a case where item 2 applies.	The net proceeds of the sale, together with: (a) any insurance money received for the plant or machinery following an event affecting the price obtainable on the sale, and (b) any other compensation so received, so far as it consists of a capital sum.

Table 4.2   *Cont.*

Item No	1. Disposal event	2. Disposal value to be brought into account
2	Sale of the plant or machinery where: (a) the sale is at less than market value, (b) there is no charge to tax under Schedule E, and (c) the condition set out aside* is met by the buyer.	The market value of the plant or machinery at the time of the sale
3	Demolition or destruction of the plant or machinery.	The net amount received for the remains of the plant or machinery, together with: (a) any insurance money received following the demolition or destruction, and (b) any other compensation so received, so far as it consists of capital sums.
4	Permanent loss of the plant or machinery otherwise than by its demolition or destruction.	Any insurance money following the loss and, so far as it consists of capital sums, any other compensation so received.
5	Mineral exploration (outside the scope of this book).	
6	Permanent discontinuance of the qualifying activity followed by an event within any of items 1–5.	The disposal value for the item in question.
7	Any event not falling within any of items 1–6.	The market value of the plant or machinery at the time of the event.

* This condition is met by the buyer if his expenditure on the acquisition of the plant or machinery cannot be qualifying expenditure under the plant or machinery allowance rules or under the R&D allowance rules.

The amount of any disposal value to be brought into account by a person for any plant or machinery is limited to the qualifying expenditure incurred by him on its provision.

A special rule applies if a person who is required to bring a disposal value into account acquired the plant or machinery as a result of a transaction which is, or a series of transactions each of which are, between connected persons. The amount of the disposal value brought into account is limited to the amount of the qualifying expenditure on the plant or machinery incurred by whichever party to the transaction, or to any of the transactions, incurred the greatest such expenditure. This rule is subject to the limit on disposal value where an additional VAT rebate, or rebates, has or have been made in relation to the original expenditure.

If a person disposes of plant or machinery by way of gift in circumstances such that there is a charge to tax under Schedule E, the disposal value of the plant or machinery is nil.

The disposal value of plant or machinery is nil if a person carrying on a relevant qualifying activity makes a gift of plant or machinery used in that activity to a charity (see TA 1988, s 506), to various heritage bodies and museums (listed in TA 1988, 507(1)), or for a designated educational establishment (see TA 1988, s 84).

Here, 'relevant qualifying activity' means a qualifying activity consisting of a trade, an ordinary Schedule A business, a furnished holiday lettings business, an overseas property business, or a profession or vocation.

TA 1988, ss 83A(4) and 84(4) provide for a tax charge if the donor or a connected person receives a benefit attributable to the gift.

If expenditure on thermal insulation, fire safety, safety measures at sports grounds or personal security, is treated (see s 27(2)) as having been incurred on plant or machinery, the disposal value of the plant or machinery is nil.

Under a general rule, a person is not required to bring a disposal value into account in a pool for a chargeable period for plant or machinery if none of the qualifying expenditure is or has been taken into account in a claim in determining the person's AQE in the pool for that or any previous chargeable period.

The modification set out below applies if:

(1) a person has incurred qualifying expenditure on plant or machinery,
(2) that person acquired the plant or machinery as a result of a transaction which was, or a series of transactions each of which was, between connected persons,
(3) any other connected person who was a party to the transaction, or one of the series of transactions, is or has been required to bring a disposal value into account as a result of the transaction,
(4) a relevant disposal event occurs in respect of the plant or machinery at a time when it is owned by that person, and
(5) none of that person's qualifying expenditure is or has been taken into account in a claim in determining his AQE for the chargeable period in which the relevant disposal event occurs or any previous chargeable period.

Where this modification applies the general rule described above does not apply to the relevant disposal event, and that person's qualifying expenditure is treated as allocated to the appropriate pool for the chargeable period in which the relevant disposal event occurs.

Here, 'qualifying expenditure' means, if a first-year allowance has been made to that person, the amount (including a nil amount) remaining after deducting the allowance, and 'the appropriate pool' means whichever pool is applicable in relation to that person under the plant or machinery allowances rules.

4.7.6 The final chargeable period
(CAA 2001, s 65)

The final chargeable period for the main pool, or a long-life asset pool, is the chargeable period in which the qualifying activity is permanently discontinued.

The final chargeable period for a single asset pool is the first chargeable period in which any of the following disposal events occurs.

(1) the person ceases to own the plant or machinery;
(2) the person loses possession of the plant or machinery in circumstances where it is reasonable to assume that the loss is permanent;
(3) the plant or machinery has been in use for mineral exploration and access and the person abandons it at the site where it was in use for that purpose;
(4) the plant or machinery ceases to exist as such, as a result of destruction, dismantling or otherwise.

This is subject to:

(a) there being no final chargeable period merely because plant or machinery begins to be used partly otherwise than for a qualifying activity (see ss 77(1) and 206(4));
(b) the ending of short-life asset pool at the four-year cut-off without a final chargeable period (see ss 86(2) and 87(2));

4.8 HIRE-PURCHASE ETC AND PLANT OR MACHINERY PROVIDED BY LESSEE

4.8.1 Hire-purchase and similar contracts
(CAA 2001, ss 67–69)

Provision is made to deal with the case where a person carrying on a qualifying activity trade incurs capital expenditure on machinery or plant for that activity under a hire-purchase or similar contract whereby he will or may become the owner of the machinery or plant at the end of the contract. The machinery or plant is treated as owned by him at any time when he is entitled to the benefit of the contract so that he is entitled to writing-down allowances, etc under those rules.

When the plant or machinery is brought into use for the qualifying activity, the person is treated as having incurred all capital expenditure for the plant or machinery to be incurred by him under the contract after that time. This is subject to anti-avoidance provisions (see s 229).

If a person is treated under the above rule as owning plant or machinery, but ceases to be entitled to the benefit of the contract in question, and does not then in fact become the owner of the plant or machinery, he is treated as ceasing to own the plant or machinery at that time.

The treatment of plant or machinery as owned by the person entitled to the benefit of a hire-purchase type contract does not apply to expenditure incurred on plant or machinery which is a fixture, but nor does it prevent the special rules for fixtures from applying to expenditure on plant or machinery incurred under such a contract (ss 172–204).

If a person is treated as owning plant or machinery, the plant or machinery becomes a fixture, and the person is not treated under ss 172–204 (fixtures) as being the owner of the plant or machinery, the person is to be treated under the plant or machinery allowance rules as ceasing to own the plant or machinery at the time when it becomes a fixture.

This rule deals with the disposal value on the cessation of notional ownership. Thus it applies if a person is treated, as above, as ceasing to own plant or machinery, and as a result he is required to bring a disposal value into account as a result. If the plant or machinery has been brought into use for the qualifying activity before he ceases to own the plant or machinery, the disposal value is the total of any relevant capital sums, and any capital expenditure treated, as above, as having been incurred when the plant or machinery was brought into use but which has not in fact been incurred. If the plant or machinery has not been brought into use for the qualifying activity before he ceases to own the plant or machinery, the disposal value is the total of any relevant capital sums (ie capital sums that he receives or is entitled to receive by way of consideration, compensation, damages or insurance money for his rights under the contract, or the plant or machinery. This is also subject to anti-avoidance rules in s 229.

4.8.2 Plant or machinery provided by lessee
(CAA 2001, s 70)

The rule described below applies where:

(1) under the terms of a lease, a lessee is required to provide plant or machinery,
(2) the lessee incurs capital expenditure on that plant or machinery for a qualifying activity which he carries on,

(3) the plant or machinery is not so installed, or otherwise fixed in or to a building or any other description of land, as to become, in law, part of that building or other land, and

(4) he does not own the plant or machinery.

In this event the lessee is treated as being the owner of the plant or machinery, as a result of incurring the capital expenditure, for so long as it continues to be used for the qualifying activity, but is not required to bring a disposal value into account because the lease ends.

The lessor must bring a disposal value into account in the appropriate pool for the chargeable period in which the disposal event occurs if:

(1) the plant or machinery continues to be used for the lessee's qualifying activity until the lease ends,

(2) the lessor holds the lease in the course of a qualifying activity, and

(3) on or after the ending of the lease, a disposal event occurs in respect of the plant or machinery at a time when the lessor owns the plant or machinery as a result of the requirement under the terms of the lease.

Here, 'the appropriate pool' means the pool which would be applicable under the plant or machinery allowance rules in relation to the lessor's qualifying activity if the expenditure incurred by the lessee had been qualifying expenditure incurred by him, and that qualifying expenditure were being allocated to a pool for the chargeable period in which the disposal event occurs.

'Lease' includes an agreement for a lease if the term to be covered by the lease has begun, and any tenancy, but does not include a mortgage.

4.9 COMPUTER SOFTWARE
(CAA 2001, ss 71–73)

Computer software is to be treated as plant. Thus, capital expenditure incurred on computer software means that the right to use or otherwise deal with it is to be treated as plant for so long as he is entitled to that right.

The person incurring the expenditure in this way needs to determine a disposal value if he grants the right to use or otherwise deal with the software to another person for a monetary capital sum. The disposal value needs to be brought into account unless, while he owned the right to use etc, but before the grant of such right, there is a disposal event arising on use otherwise than for the qualifying activity (s 61(1)(e)) or a permanent discontinuance of the qualifying activity (s 61(1)(f)).

The disposal value to be brought into account depends on the circumstances of the grant of the right, as shown in Table 4.3.

Table 4.3 – Disposal values: grant of software right

Item no	1. Circumstances of grant	2. Disposal value
1	The grant is for a consideration not consisting entirely of money.	The market value of the right granted at the time of the grant.
2	The grant is made where: (a) it is for no consideration or at less than market value, (b) there is no charge to tax under Schedule E, and (c) the condition set out aside* is met by the grantee.	The market value of the right granted at the time of the grant
3	The grant is made in circumstances other than those given in item 1 or 2.	The net consideration in money received in respect of the grant, together with: (a) any insurance money received in respect of the computer software as a result of an event affecting the consideration obtainable on the grant, and (b) any other compensation of any description so received, so far as it consists of capital sums.

*The condition referred to aside is met by the grantee if the grantee's expenditure on the acquisition of the plant cannot be qualifying expenditure under the plant or machinery allowance rules or under the rules for R&D allowances.

The amounts referred to in Table 4.3 are those received by the person required to bring the disposal value into account.

Some adjustment may be necessary if a person is required to bring into account a disposal value for computer software, or the right to use or otherwise deal with computer software. For the purpose only of determining whether the general limit on disposal value (see s 62) is exceeded, and reducing the amount of that disposal value so that the limit is not exceeded, the disposal value is taken to be increased by the total of any disposal values which, for that person and that plant, must be brought into account (see Table 4.3).

4.10 EXPENSIVE CARS
(CAA 2001, ss 74–82)

For 2002–03, the writing-down allowance for an expensive car (ie costing £12,000+) is restricted to £3,000. Qualifying expenditure incurred on an expensive car must be allocated to a single asset pool; this does not apply to qualifying hire cars or qualifying first-year expenditure on cars with low CO_2 emissions (as to which, see 4.6.6 above).

'Car' in this instance does not include a vehicle used to carry or convey goods, nor one not commonly used or is unsuitable for use as a private vehicle.

A 'qualifying hire car' is one provided wholly or mainly for hire to, or for the carriage of, members of the public in the ordinary course of a trade, and applies only to a vehicle if it falls into any of the following three categories:

(1) the hire to or carriage of the same person is normally for less than 30 consecutive days, and the total number of days in any 12-month period is normally less than 90;
(2) it is provided for hire to a person who himself hires it to or carries members of the public in the ordinary course of a trade and for the same periods as under (1) above; and
(3) it is provided wholly or mainly for persons receiving disability living allowance who are entitled to the mobility component, a mobility supplement or similar payment.

A number of cases have been decided on the issue of whether a car can be classed as 'private':

(a) Dual-control driving school cars are not private cars (*Bourne v Auto School of Motoring* (1964) 42 TC 217).
(b) Vans and minivans of a type commonly used privately held as private vehicles (*Tapper v Eyre* (1967) 43 TC 720; *Laing v CIR* (1967) 44 TC 681).
(c) Vans and minivans licensed as goods vehicles held not to be commonly used as private vehicles (*Roberts v Granada TV Rental* (1970) 46 TC 295).

Furthermore, Land Rovers are regarded not to be commonly used as private vehicles, but Range Rovers, other four-wheel drive vehicles and estate cars are.

The £3,000 writing-down allowance limit mentioned above is increased or reduced *pro rata* if the chargeable period is more or less than one year. The allowance may be further limited if expenditure is met by another person (s 76), if the car is used partly for other purposes (s 77) or if a partial depreciation subsidy is received (s 78). In separating the expenditure of £12,000+ for trade purposes into a single asset pool, the writing-down allowance is restricted to £3,000 for a full 12-month period (*pro rata* for shorter periods).

If only part of the capital expenditure incurred on an expensive car is treated as incurred by a person, the amount of the writing down allowance to be made to that person for a chargeable period for the qualifying period must not exceed:

$$£3,000 \times \frac{E - X}{E}$$

where   E = the amount of capital expenditure incurred on the provision of
         the car, and
       X = the amount of the expenditure excluded as above.

Where the £12,000+ capital expenditure is incurred and a contributor is entitled to writing-down allowances for his contribution towards the cost of the
car, the limits are increased or reduced *pro rata* where necessary, as above.
Here, the contributor's writing-down allowance for a chargeable period for
his contribution must not exceed:

$$£3,000 \times \quad \frac{C}{E}$$

where   E = the amount of capital expenditure incurred on the provision of
         the car, and
       C = the amount of the contribution.

In any situation where the car begins to be used partly otherwise than for the
qualifying activity, the writing-down or balancing allowance must be
reduced to a just and reasonable amount. There is no final chargeable period
or disposal event merely because of that other use. In calculating the amount
of unrelieved qualifying expenditure carried forward (see s 59), any such
reduction is disregarded. In applying this rule, the general rules for part
other use of plant or machinery under ss 205–208 do not apply.

At times the Revenue has argued for an additional disallowance on the
personal choice of more expensive cars, based on *GH Chambers (Northiam
Farms) v Watmough* (1956) 36 TC 711 (part allowance due on Bentley disallowed). But this depends on the facts of the case, and this restriction will
only be followed if there is a 'blatant incongruity' between the type of car
and its use for the business's requirements.

An adjustment is also required where payments are made on account to
the person using the car to cover part of the depreciation resulting from that
use. This applies for the chargeable period in which such payment is first
paid and any subsequent chargeable period. Any reduced adjustment to a
writing-down or balancing allowance, or balancing charge, must be just and
reasonable. Such reduction cannot be taken into account in calculating unrelieved qualifying expenditure under s 59. Further, the general provisions
regarding partial depreciation subsidies under ss 209–212 do not apply.

When the car is sold or the contract of ownership ends, adjustment must
be made where the disposal value must be brought into account to comply
with the anti-avoidance provisions under ss 213–223. The disposal value is
the car's market value at the time of disposal or, if less, the capital expenditure incurred or treated as incurred on the provision of the car by the
person disposing of it. The person acquiring it is treated as having incurred
capital expenditure on its provision of an amount equal to the disposal
value that must be brought into account.

4.11 SHORT-LIFE ASSETS
(CAA 2001, ss 83–89)

Treatment of plant or machinery as a short-life asset is ruled out in any of the cases listed in col 1 of Table 4.4, unless an exception (if any) listed in col 2 applies.

Table 4.4 – Short-life asset treatment

Item No	1. Short-life asset treatment ruled out	2. Exception (if any)
1.	The expenditure is treated as incurred for the purposes of a qualifying activity under: (a) use for qualifying activity of plant or machinery provided for other purposes (s 3), or (b) s 14 (use for qualifying activity of plant or machinery which is a gift).	
2.	Outside the scope of this book	
3.	The plant or machinery is a car (s 81).	The car is hired out to persons receiving disability allowances etc (s 82(4)).
4.	The expenditure is long-life asset expenditure (ss 90–104).	
5.	The plant or machinery is provided for leasing.	The plant or machinery is a car which is hired out to persons receiving disability allowances etc (s 82(4)). The plant or machinery will be used within a period of 10 years (s 106) for a various leasing purpose (ss 122–125).
6.	Section 109 (leasing) provides only a 10% writing-down allowance for expenditure on the plant or machinery.	
7.	The plant or machinery is leased to two or more persons jointly in circumstances such that s 116 (mitigation) applies.	
8.	Outside the scope of this book.	

Table 4.4 *Cont.*

Item No	1. Short-life asset treatment ruled out	2. Exception (if any)
9.	The expenditure was incurred partly for the purposes of a qualifying activity and partly for other purposes (ss 205–208).	
10.	The expenditure is required to be allocated to a single asset pool having received a partial depreciation subsidy (s 211).	

An accelerated form of plant or machinery allowance is available for short-life assets provided that its treatment as a short-life asset is not ruled out, and the person incurring the expenditure elects for it to be treated as a short-life asset.

An election (which is irrevocable) for short life asset treatment must specify the plant or machinery which is the subject of the election, the qualifying expenditure incurred on it, and the date on which the expenditure was incurred.

In short-life asset rules there is a four-year cut-off. This is the fourth anniversary of the end of the chargeable period in which the qualifying expenditure was incurred on the provision of the short-life asset, or if the qualifying expenditure was incurred in different chargeable periods, the first chargeable period in which any of the qualifying expenditure was incurred.

Qualifying expenditure on a short-life asset must be allocated to a single 'short-life asset pool'. If the final chargeable period for the short-life asset pool has not occurred before the four-year cut-off date the pool ends at the four-year cut-off without a final chargeable period, the available qualifying expenditure in the pool is allocated to the main pool for the first chargeable period ending after the four-year cut-off, and the asset ceases to be a short-life asset.

A special rule applies if plant or machinery is a short-life asset on the basis that it has been provided for leasing but will be used within the designated period for a qualifying purpose (see Table 4.4, item 5), in a chargeable period ending on or before the four-year cut-off, the short-life asset begins to be used otherwise than for a qualifying purpose, and where that time falls within the first 4 years of the designated period.

In this event the short-life asset pool ends without a final chargeable period, the available qualifying expenditure in the pool is allocated to the main pool for the chargeable period in which the asset begins to be used otherwise than for a qualifying purpose, and the asset ceases to be a short-life asset.

The disposal value to be brought into account under the general rules for allowances and charges (see ss 52–66) is the market value of the asset if a short-life asset is disposed of at less than market value, the disposal is not one for which a connected persons election is made (see below), and there is no Schedule E tax charge.

Where, at any time before the four-year cut-off, 'the transferor' disposes of a short-life asset to a connected person the transferor is treated as having sold the short-life asset to the connected person for an amount equal to the available qualifying expenditure in the short-life asset pool for the chargeable period in which the disposal occurs, and the connected person is to be treated as having incurred qualifying expenditure of the same amount in buying the short-life asset.

Neither the restrictions on first-year and other allowances in the case of certain transactions between connected persons, to obtain a tax advantage etc (see ss 217 and 218), nor the further restrictions in the case of sale and finance leaseback (see ss 222–225), apply to the disposal. This treatment only applies to a disposal only if the transferor, and the connected person, elect that they should apply.

Immediately after the disposal of the short-life asset, the connected person is taken to have made an election under s 83 so that the plant or machinery is a short-life asset in his hands. In relation to the connected person, 'the four-year cut-off' means the date that would have been the four-year cut-off in relation to the transferor.

4.12 LONG-LIFE ASSETS

4.12.1 Long-life asset expenditure
(CAA 2001, ss 90–92)

'Long-life asset expenditure' is qualifying expenditure incurred on a long-life asset for a qualifying activity, and not within any of the exclusions (see ss 93–100). A 'long-life asset' means plant or machinery which:

(1) if new (ie unused and not second-hand), can reasonably be expected to have a useful economic life of at least 25 years, and
(2) if not new, could reasonably have been expected when new to have a useful economic life of at least 25 years.

The useful economic life of plant or machinery is the period beginning when it is first brought into use by any person for any purpose, and ending when it is no longer used or likely to be used by anyone for any purpose as a fixed asset of a business. If any of the long-life asset rules are applied to part only of the capital expenditure on plant or machinery, the part to which they apply, and the part to which they do not, are treated as expenditure on separate items of plant or machinery. All such apportionments are to be made as are just and reasonable.

4.12.2 Expenditure excluded from being long-life assets
(CAA 2001, ss 93–100)

Expenditure is not long-life asset expenditure if it is incurred on plant or machinery which is a fixture (see s 173(1)) in, or is provided for use in, any building used wholly or mainly as a dwelling-house, hotel, office, retail shop or showroom, or for purposes ancillary to such use. A 'retail shop' includes any premises of a similar character where a retail trade or business, including repair work, is carried on.

Expenditure on an expensive car (see s 81) is not a long-life asset.

4.12.3 Monetary limit
(CAA 2001, ss 97–100)

Expenditure is not long-life asset expenditure if it is expenditure which falls below the monetary limits, and is incurred in a chargeable period for which the relevant monetary limit is not exceeded. The monetary limits apply to expenditure incurred by an individual for a chargeable period if the expenditure was incurred by him for the purposes of a qualifying activity carried on by him, the whole of his time is substantially devoted in that period to the carrying on of that qualifying activity, and the expenditure is not on the excluded list.

The monetary limits apply to expenditure incurred by a partnership for a chargeable period if all of the members of the partnership are individuals, the expenditure was incurred by the partnership for the purposes of a qualifying activity carried on by it, at all times throughout that period at least half the partners for the time being devote the whole or a substantial part of their time to the carrying on of that qualifying activity, and the expenditure is not on the excluded list.

The monetary limits apply for corporation tax to any expenditure incurred by a company for a chargeable period other than expenditure on the excluded list.

Expenditure is on the excluded list if it is incurred for a share in plant or machinery, is a contribution (see s 538) treated as incurred on plant or machinery, or is incurred on plant or machinery for leasing (whether or not in the course of a trade).

The general rule is that the monetary limit for a chargeable period of 12 months is £100,000. If, for an individual or partnership, the chargeable period is longer or shorter than 12 months, the monetary limit is increased or reduced pro rata. Also, if a company has a chargeable period which is shorter than 12 months, the monetary limit is reduced pro rata. Furthermore, if, in a chargeable period, a company has one or more associated companies (see TA 1988, s 13), the monetary limit for that period is divided by the number of associated companies plus one.

The monetary limit for a chargeable period is exceeded if the total expenditure in that period that meets the conditions exceeds that limit. The conditions are that the expenditure is long-life asset expenditure, or would be long-life asset expenditure were it not for exclusion of expenditure which falls below the monetary limit (see s 97), and is expenditure to which the monetary limits apply.

There are rules dealing with contracts for the provision of plant or machinery where the capital expenditure for which is (or is to be) incurred under the contract is (or may fall to be) treated as incurred in different chargeable periods. In this event, all of the expenditure to be incurred under the contract is to be treated as incurred in the first chargeable period in which any of the expenditure is incurred.

4.12.4 Rules applying to long-life asset expenditure
(CAA 2001, ss 101 and 102)

Long-life asset expenditure must be allocated to a 'long-life asset class pool'. This applies to long-life asset expenditure which is incurred on long-life assets wholly and exclusively for the purposes of a qualifying activity, and is not expenditure which is required to be allocated to a single asset pool.

The writing-down allowance to which a person is entitled for a chargeable period on long-life asset expenditure is 6% of the amount by which AQE exceeds TDR. This applies even if the long-life asset expenditure is in a single asset pool. For expenditure which is for overseas leasing which is not protected leasing (see s 107(2)(a) and (b)), this is subject to the prohibition allowances in certain cases etc (see ss 110, 114 and 115).

If the chargeable period is more or less than a year, the amount of the allowance is increased or reduced pro rata. If the qualifying activity has been carried on for part only of the chargeable period, the amount is proportionately reduced.

4.12.5 Anti-avoidance provisions
(CAA 2001, s 103 and 104)

A special rule applies if a person has made a claim for allowances on expenditure incurred on plant or machinery, and it becomes apparent that the expenditure could be treated as long-life asset expenditure. A problem arises if, at any time after making the plant or machinery allowances claim, that claimant or another person makes a plant or machinery allowances claim for any qualifying expenditure incurred at any time (including a time before the incurring of the expenditure to which the earlier claim relates) on the provision of the same plant or machinery. If the expenditure to which the later claim relates would not otherwise be treated as long-life asset expenditure, and is not prevented from being long-life asset expenditure (eg fixtures or expensive cars (see ss 93–96)), the plant and machinery allowance rules apply to the later claim as if the expenditure to which it relates were long-life asset expenditure.

A special rule also applies if the 6% writing-down allowances (see s 102) has applied to any long-life asset expenditure incurred by a taxpayer, any disposal event occurs in relation to the long-life asset, the disposal value to be brought into account would otherwise be less than the notional written-down value of the long-life asset, and the disposal event is part of, or occurs as a result of, a scheme or arrangement the main purpose or one of the main purposes of which is the obtaining by the taxpayer of a tax advantage under the plant and machinery allowances.

The disposal value that the taxpayer must bring into account is the notional written-down value of the long-life asset which is

$$QE - A$$

where QE = the taxpayer's expenditure on the plant or machinery that is qualifying expenditure, and

   A = the total of all allowances which could have been made to the taxpayer for that expenditure if:

 (a) that expenditure had been the only expenditure that had ever been taken into account in determining his available qualifying expenditure,

 (b) that expenditure had not been prevented by the application of a monetary limit from being long-life asset expenditure, and

 (c) all allowances had been made in full.

4.13 OVERSEAS LEASING
(CAA 2001, ss 105–126)

Rules of considerable complexity govern the availability of plant or machinery allowances for expenditure on assets for overseas leasing and are outside the scope of this book.

4.14 SHIPS

The treatment of ships is an exception to the normal plant or machinery allowances rules. A trader who incurs qualifying expenditure on a ship can elect for postponement of the whole or part of the first-year allowance. The amount withheld can then be claimed in any subsequent chargeable period without time limit. Thus, a ship owner can claim the allowances as and when it best suits his tax position.

The term 'ship' is not defined in the legislation. However, it is generally understood to include 'every description of vessel used in navigation' (Merchant Shipping Act 1995, s 313(1)). More specifically, a 'qualifying ship' is a ship of a seagoing kind, registered in any jurisdiction, with a gross tonnage of at least 100 tons (s 151).

A detailed account thereof is beyond the scope of this book. Readers are advised to seek specialist advice on this subject.

4.15 PROVISIONS AFFECTING MINERAL AND OIL INDUSTRIES

There are detailed provisions dealing with expenditure connected with mineral extraction trades. A detailed account thereof is beyond the scope of this book. Readers are advised to seek specialist advice on this subject.

4.16 FIXTURES

4.16.1 Introduction
(CAA 2001, s 172–175A)

Sections 172–204 provide relief for expenditure on plant or machinery which becomes a fixture in a building. This legislation reverses *Stokes v Costain Property Investment* (1984) 57 TC 688, where it was held that the lessee was not entitled to capital allowances on fixtures which become part of the building, since they belonged to the landlord. Thus, for expenditure incurred on building fixtures where a lease applies, an allowance is given to the lessee incurring the expenditure, even though in law the asset belongs to the landlord.

The special rules for fixtures apply to determine entitlement to allowances for expenditure on plant or machinery that is, or becomes, a fixture. The fixture allowances rules determine ownership of plant or machinery that is, or becomes, a fixture. The provisions of the fixtures allowance rules that treat a person as being the owner of a fixture (see ss 176–184 and 193–195B) are subject to provisions of those rules which treat a person as ceasing to be the owner of a fixture (see ss 188–192A).

References to a person being treated as the owner of plant or machinery, or as ceasing to be the owner of plant or machinery, are read as references to the person being so treated. These rules do not affect any entitlement a person has to an allowance as a result of contribution allowances for plant and machinery (see s 538).

In the fixtures allowances rules, 'fixture' means plant or machinery that is so installed or otherwise fixed in or to a building or other description of land as to become, in law, part of that building or other land, and includes any boiler or water-filled radiator installed in a building as part of a space or water heating system.

'Relevant land' in relation to a fixture means the building or other description of land of which the fixture becomes part, or in the case of a boiler or water-filled radiator which is a fixture, the building in which it is installed as part of a space or water heating system. An 'equipment lease' means an agreement entered into in the circumstances set out below, or a lease entered into under or as a result of such an agreement. The circumstances are that a person incurs capital expenditure on the provision of plant or machinery for leasing, an agreement is entered into for the lease, directly or indirectly from that person, of the plant or machinery to another person, the plant or machinery becomes a fixture, and the agreement is not an agreement for the plant or machinery to be leased as part of the relevant land.

An 'equipment lessor' means the person from whom (directly or indirectly) the equipment lease provides for the plant or machinery to be leased, and 'equipment lessee' means the person to whom the equipment lease provides for the plant or machinery to be leased.

Except in the context of leasing plant or machinery, any reference to a lease is to any leasehold estate in the land (whether in the nature of a head-lease, sub-lease or under-lease), or any agreement to acquire such an estate and, in relation to such an agreement, 'grant' is read accordingly. There are equivalent rules in Scotland.

An 'interest in land' means the fee simple estate in the land or an agreement to acquire such an estate, a lease, an easement or servitude or an agreement to acquire an easement or servitude, and a licence to occupy land. There are equivalent rules in Scotland.

If an interest in land is conveyed or assigned by way of security, and subject to a right of redemption, the person with the right of redemption is treated as having that interest, and not the creditor.

An 'energy services agreement' is an agreement entered into by an energy services provider and his client that makes provision, with a view to saving energy or using energy more efficiently. This includes provision for the design of plant or machinery, or one or more systems incorporating plant or machinery, obtaining and installing the plant or machinery, the operation of the plant or machinery, the maintenance of the plant or machinery, and the amount of any payments for the operation of the plant or machinery to be linked (wholly or in part) to energy savings or increases in energy efficiency resulting from the provision or operation of the plant or machinery. An 'energy services provider' is a person carrying on a qualifying activity consisting wholly or mainly in the provision of energy management services.

4.16.2 Persons who are treated as owners of fixtures
(CAA 2001, ss 176–184)

If a person incurs capital expenditure on plant or machinery for a qualifying activity carried on by him, the plant or machinery becomes a fixture, and that person has an interest in the relevant land at the time the plant or machinery becomes a fixture, he is treated, on and after that time, as the owner of the fixture as a result of incurring the expenditure.

If there are two or more persons with different interests in the relevant land who would, following the above rule, be treated as the owner of the same fixture, only one interest is taken into account. Which one is taken into account is given by the following rules:

Rule 1

If one of the interests is an easement or servitude or any agreement to acquire an easement or servitude, that interest is the interest to be taken into account.

Rule 2

If Rule 1 does not apply, but one of the interests is a licence to occupy land, that interest is the interest to be taken into account.

Rule 3

In any other case the interest to be taken into account is the interest which is not in reversion (at law or in equity and whether directly or indirectly) on any other interest in the relevant land which is held by any of the persons referred to above. There are equivalent rules in Scotland.

If the conditions that an equipment lessee has a qualifying activity etc (see s 178), an equipment lessor has right to sever a fixture that is not part of a building (see s 179), or an equipment lease is part of an affordable warmth programme (s 180), are met in relation to an equipment lease,

(1) the equipment lessor and the equipment lessee are not connected persons, and
(2) they elect to apply the rule set out below,

the equipment lessor is treated, on and after the relevant time, as the owner of the fixture as a result of incurring the capital expenditure on the provision of the plant or machinery that is the subject of the equipment lease.

The relevant time here is the time when the equipment lessor incurs the expenditure. However, this is overridden if the conditions in s 178 are met in relation to an equipment lease (but the conditions in ss 179 and 180 are not), and the equipment lessor incurs the capital expenditure before the equipment lessee begins to carry on the qualifying activity. In such a case the relevant time is the time when the equipment lessee begins to carry on the qualifying activity.

If an election is made hereunder, the equipment lessee is not treated under s 176 as the owner of the fixture.

The first set of conditions referred to above are that:

(1) the equipment lease is for the lease of the plant or machinery for a qualifying activity which is, or is to be, carried on by the equipment lessee,
(2) if the equipment lessee had incurred the capital expenditure incurred by the equipment lessor on the plant or machinery that is the subject of the equipment lease, he would, as a result of s 176, have been entitled to an allowance in respect of it, and
(3) the equipment lease is not for the lease of the plant or machinery for use in a dwelling-house.

The second set of conditions referred to in s 177 are that—

(1) the plant or machinery becomes a fixture by being fixed to land that is neither a building nor part of a building,

(2) the equipment lessee has an interest in the land when taking possession of the plant or machinery under the equipment lease,

(3) under the terms of the equipment lease, the equipment lessor is entitled to sever the plant or machinery, at the end of the period for which it is leased, from the land to which it is fixed at that time,

(4) under the terms of the equipment lease, the equipment lessor will own the plant or machinery on its severance in accordance with the equipment lease,

(5) the nature of the plant or machinery and the way in which it is fixed to land are such that its use on one set of premises does not, to any material extent, prevent it from being used, once severed, for the same purposes on a different set of premises,

(6) the equipment lease is one which under normal accountancy practice falls (or would fall) to be treated in the accounts of the equipment lessor as an operating lease, and

(7) the equipment lease is not for the lease of the plant or machinery for use in a dwelling-house.

Note that in (6) above, the equipment lessor is to be treated as being a company incorporated in a part of the UK.

The third set of conditions referred to in s 177 are that:

(1) the plant or machinery which is the subject of the equipment lease consists of a boiler, heat exchanger, radiator or heating control that is installed in a building as part of a space or water heating system,

(2) the expenditure of the equipment lessor is incurred before 1 January 2008, and

(3) the equipment lease is approved, by the Treasury, by the DETR Secretary of State or by ministers in the regional assemblies, as entered into as part of the affordable warmth programme.

If an approval is withdrawn, it is treated as never having had effect.

An energy services provider is treated, on and after the time at which he incurs the expenditure, as the owner of the fixture as a result of incurring the expenditure, if:

(1) an energy services agreement is entered into,

(2) the energy services provider incurs capital expenditure under the agreement on the provision of plant or machinery,

(3) the plant or machinery becomes a fixture,

(4) at the time the plant or machinery becomes a fixture the client has an interest in the relevant land, and the energy services provider does not,

(5) the plant or machinery is not provided for leasing, and is not provided for use in a dwelling-house,
(6) the operation of the plant or machinery is carried out wholly or substantially by the energy services provider or a person connected with him,
(7) the energy services provider and the client are not connected persons, and
(8) they so elect.

But if the client would not have been entitled to an allowance (under s 176) for the expenditure if he had incurred it, the above does not apply unless the plant or machinery belongs to a class of plant or machinery specified by Treasury order.

If an election is made hereunder, the client is treated under s 176 as the owner of the fixture.

The 'relevant chargeable period' means the chargeable period in which the capital expenditure was incurred.

A purchaser is treated, after the acquisition, as the owner of the fixture as a result of incurring that expenditure, if after any plant or machinery has become a fixture, a purchaser acquires an interest in the relevant land, that interest was in existence before the purchaser's acquisition of it, and the consideration which the purchaser gives for the interest is or includes a capital sum that, in whole or in part, falls to be treated as expenditure on the provision of the fixture,

If, after any plant or machinery has become a fixture, a purchaser acquires an interest in the relevant land, that interest was in existence before the purchaser's acquisition of it, before that acquisition, the plant or machinery was let under an equipment lease, and in connection with that acquisition, the purchaser pays a capital sum to discharge the obligations of the equipment lessee under the equipment lease, he is treated, on and after the time of the acquisition, as the owner of the fixture as a result of incurring expenditure, consisting of that capital sum, on the provision of the fixture.

If, after any plant or machinery has become a fixture, a purchaser acquires an interest in the relevant land, that interest was in existence before the purchaser's acquisition of it, before that acquisition, the plant or machinery was provided under an energy services agreement, and in connection with that acquisition, the purchaser pays a capital sum to discharge the obligations of the client under the energy services agreement, the purchaser is treated, on and after the time of the acquisition, as the owner of the fixture as a result of incurring expenditure, consisting of that capital sum, on the provision of the fixture.

None of the above paragraphs apply, and are treated as never having applied, if, immediately after the time of the acquisition, a person has a prior right in relation to the fixture. A person has a prior right in relation to the fixture if he is treated as the owner of the fixture immediately before the time referred to above as a result of incurring expenditure on the provision of the fixture, is not so treated as a result of contribution allowances for plant and machinery (s 538), is entitled to an allowance in respect of that expenditure, and makes or has made a claim in respect of that expenditure.

If:

(1) after any plant or machinery has become a fixture, a lessor who has an interest in the relevant land grants a lease,

(2) the lessor is entitled to an allowance in respect of the fixture for the chargeable period in which the lease is granted or would be if he were within the charge to tax,

(3) the consideration which the lessee gives for the lease is or includes a capital sum that, in whole or in part, falls to be treated as expenditure on the fixture,

(4) the lessor and the lessee are not connected persons, and

(5) the lessor and the lessee so elect,

the lessee is treated, on and after the time when the lease is granted, as the owner of the fixture as a result of incurring that expenditure.

If:

(1) after any plant or machinery has become a fixture, a lessor who has an interest in the relevant land grants a lease,

(2) the lessor is not entitled to an allowance in respect of the fixture for the chargeable period in which the lease is granted or would be if he were within the charge to tax,

(3) before the lease is granted, the fixture has not been used for the purposes of a qualifying activity carried on by the lessor or any person connected with the lessor, and

(4) the consideration which the lessee gives for the lease is or includes a capital sum that, in whole or in part, falls to be treated as expenditure on the fixture,

the lessee is to be treated, on and after the time when the lease is granted, as the owner of the fixture as a result of incurring that expenditure.

This does not apply, and is to be treated as never having applied, if, immediately after the time when the lease is granted, a person has a prior right in relation to the fixture (as above).

4.16.3 Restrictions on amount of qualifying expenditure
(CAA 2001, ss 185–187)

This rule applies if

(1) the current owner is treated as the owner of a fixture as a result of incurring new capital expenditure on its provision,

(2) the plant or machinery is treated as having been owned at a relevant earlier time by the past owner as a result of incurring other expenditure,

(3) the plant or machinery meets the test in (2) otherwise than as a result of contribution allowances for plant and machinery (see s 538), and

(4) the past owner is or has been required to bring the disposal value of the plant or machinery into account (as a result of having made a claim in respect of that other expenditure).

In (2) above the 'relevant earlier time' means any time before the earliest time when the current owner is treated as owning the plant or machinery as a result of incurring the new expenditure. If, before the earliest time when the current owner is treated as owning the plant or machinery as a result of incurring the new expenditure any person has ceased to own the plant or machinery as a result of a sale, the sale was not a sale of the plant or machinery as a fixture, and the buyer and seller were not connected persons at the time of the sale, the relevant earlier time does not include any time before the seller ceased to own the plant or machinery.

If the new expenditure exceeds the maximum allowable amount, the excess is left out of account in determining the current owner's qualifying expenditure, or if the new expenditure has already been taken into account, is treated as expenditure that should never have been taken into account.

The maximum allowable amount is:

$$D + I$$

where D = the disposal value of the plant or machinery which the past owner has been or is required to bring into account, and

I = any of the new expenditure that is treated (by s 25 (building alterations in connection with installation)) as expenditure on the provision of the plant or machinery.

If more than one disposal event has occurred requiring the past owner to bring the disposal value of the plant or machinery into account, the maximum allowable amount is calculated by reference only to the most recent of those events.

The current owner and the past owner may be the same person.

This rule applies if the past owner has at any time claimed an industrial buildings allowance (see ss 271–360) for expenditure which was or included expenditure on the provision of plant or machinery, the past owner has transferred the interest which is the relevant interest for industrial allowances, and the current owner of the plant or machinery makes a claim in respect of new expenditure incurred on the provision of the plant or machinery, and at a time when it is a fixture in the building.

If the new expenditure exceeds the maximum allowable amount, the excess is left out of account in determining the current owner's qualifying expenditure.

The maximum allowable amount is:

$$\frac{F}{T} \times R$$

where F = the part of the consideration for the transfer by the past owner
             that is attributable to the fixture,

       T = is the total consideration for that transfer, and

       R = the residue of qualifying expenditure attributable to the rele-
             vant interest immediately after that transfer, calculated on the
             assumption that the transfer was a sale of the relevant interest.

Here the current owner of the plant or machinery is the person to whom the past owner transferred the relevant interest, or any person who is subsequently treated as the owner of the plant or machinery.

Here also, 'building' and 'residue of qualifying expenditure' have the same meaning as in the industrial buildings allowance (see ss 271–360).

This rule applies if:

(1) a person has at any time claimed an R&D allowance (see ss 437–451) for qualifying expenditure under the R&D allowances rules,

(2) an asset representing the whole or part of the R&D expenditure has ceased to be owned by the past owner,

(3) the R&D expenditure was or included plant or machinery, and

(4) the current owner makes a fixtures claim for new expenditure incurred on the provision of the plant or machinery, and at a time when it is a fixture.

If the new expenditure exceeds the maximum allowable amount, the excess is left out of account in determining the current owner's qualifying expenditure.

The maximum allowable amount is:

$$\frac{F}{T} \times A$$

where F = the part of the consideration for the disposal of R&D asset by
             the past owner that is attributable to the fixture,

       T = the total consideration for that disposal, and

       A = an amount equal to whichever is the smaller of:

           (a) the disposal value of the R&D asset when the past owner
             ceased to own it, and

           (b) so much of the R&D expenditure as related to the provi-
             sion of the R&D asset.

The current owner of the plant or machinery is the person who acquired the R&D asset from the past owner, or any person who is subsequently treated as the owner of the plant or machinery.

4.16.4 Cessation of ownership of fixtures

This rule applies if a person is treated as the owner of a fixture under

(1) s 176 (person with interest in land having fixture for purposes of qualifying activity),

(2) s 181 (purchaser of land giving consideration for fixture),

(3) s 182 (purchaser of land discharging obligations of equipment lessee),

(4) s 182A (purchaser of land discharging obligations of client under energy services agreement),

(5) s 183 (incoming lessee where lessor entitled to allowances), or

(6) s 184 (incoming lessee where lessor not entitled to allowances).

If the person concerned ceases at any time to have the qualifying interest, he is treated as ceasing to be the owner of the fixture at that time.

Here 'the qualifying interest' means, if any of ss 176, 181, 182 or 182A applies, the interest in the relevant land referred to in any of those provisions, and if ss 183 or 184 applies, the lease referred to in either of those sections.

If a person's qualifying interest is an agreement to acquire an interest in land, and that interest is subsequently transferred or granted to that person, the interest transferred or granted is to be treated as the qualifying interest.

If a person's qualifying interest ceases to exist as a result of its being merged in another interest acquired by that person, that other interest is treated as the qualifying interest.

If the qualifying interest is a lease, and on its termination, a new lease of the relevant land (with or without other land) is granted to the lessee, the new lease is to be treated as the qualifying interest.

If the qualifying interest is a licence, and on its termination, a new licence to occupy the relevant land (with or without other land) is granted to the licensee, the new licence is to be treated as the qualifying interest.

If the qualifying interest is a lease, and with the consent of the lessor, the lessee remains in possession of the relevant land after the termination of the lease without a new lease being granted to him, the qualifying interest is treated as continuing so long as the lessee remains in possession of the relevant land.

This rule applies if a lessee is treated under s 183 (incoming lessee where lessor entitled to allowances) as the owner of a fixture. The lessor is to be treated as ceasing to be the owner of the fixture when the lessee begins to be treated as the owner.

If a person is treated as the owner of the fixture as a result of any provision relating to fixtures, the fixture is permanently severed from the relevant land (so that it ceases to be a fixture), and once it is severed, it is not in fact owned by that person, that person is treated as ceasing to be the owner of the fixture when it is severed.

This rule applies if an equipment lessor is treated under s 177 as the owner of a fixture. If the equipment lessor at any time assigns his rights under the equipment lease, or the financial obligations of the equipment lessee under an equipment lease are at any time discharged (on the payment of a capital sum or otherwise), the equipment lessor is to be treated as ceasing to be the owner of the fixture at that time (or, as the case may be, at the earliest of those times). The reference here to the equipment lessee is, in a case where the financial obligations of the equipment lessee have become vested in another person (by assignment, operation of law or otherwise), a reference to the person in whom the obligations are vested when the capital sum is paid.

This rule applies if an energy services provider is treated under s 180A as the owner of a fixture. If the energy services provider at any time assigns his rights under the energy services agreement, or the financial obligations of the client in respect of the fixture under an energy services agreement are at any time discharged (on the payment of a capital sum or otherwise), the energy services provider is treated as ceasing to be the owner of the fixture at that time (or, as the case may be, the earliest of those times). The reference here to the client is, in a case where the financial obligations of the client have become vested in another person (by assignment, operation of law or otherwise), a reference to the person in whom the obligations are vested when the capital sum is paid.

4.16.5 Acquisition of ownership of fixture when another ceases to own it
(CAA 2001, s 193–195B)

If, on the termination of a lease or licence, the outgoing lessee or licensee is treated under s 188 as ceasing to be the owner of a fixture, the lessor or licensor is treated, on and after the termination of the lease or licence, as the owner of the fixture.

If s 192(2)(a) (cessation of ownership of equipment lessor as a result of assignment) applies, the assignee is treated, on and after the assignment as having incurred expenditure, consisting of the consideration given by him for the assignment, on the provision of the fixture, and as being the owner of the fixture.

For the purposes of ss 192 and 195(1) the assignee is treated as being an equipment lessor who owns the fixture under s 177.

If s 192(2)(b) (discharge of obligations of equipment lessee) applies because the equipment lessee has paid a capital sum, the equipment lessee is treated as having incurred expenditure, consisting of the capital sum, on the provision of the fixture, and as being, on and after the time of payment, the owner of the fixture. The reference here to the equipment lessee is, in a case where the financial obligations of the equipment lessee have become vested in another person (by assignment, operation of law or otherwise), a reference to the person in whom the obligations are vested when the capital sum is paid.

If s 192A(2)(a) applies (cessation of ownership of energy services provider as a result of assignment), the assignee is treated, on and after the assignment as having incurred expenditure, consisting of the consideration given by him for the assignment, on the provision of the fixture, and as being the owner of the fixture. For the purposes of ss 192 and 195(1) the assignee is treated as being an energy services provider who owns the fixture under s 180A.

If s 192A(2)(b) (discharge of obligations of client) applies because the client has paid a capital sum, the client is treated as having incurred expenditure, consisting of the capital sum, on the provision of the fixture, and as being, on and after the time of payment, the owner of the fixture.

The reference here to the client is, in a case where the financial obligations of the client have become vested in another person (by assignment, operation of law or otherwise), a reference to the person in whom the obligations are vested when the capital sum is paid.

4.16.6 Disposal values
(CAA 2001, ss 196 and 197)

The disposal value brought into account in relation to a fixture depends on the nature of the disposal event, as shown in Table 4.5.

Table 4.5 – Disposal values: fixtures

Item No	1. Disposal event	2. Disposal value
1.	Cessation of ownership of the fixture under s188 because of a sale of the qualifying interest except where item 2 applies.	The part of the sale price that: (a) falls to be treated for the purposes of the plant or machinery allowances rules as expenditure incurred by the purchaser on the provision of the fixture, or (b) would be so treated if the purchaser were entitled to an allowance.
2.	Cessation of ownership of the fixture under s 188 because of a sale of the qualifying interest where: (a) the sale is at less than market value, and (b) the condition set out below is met by the purchaser.*	The part of the price that would be treated for the plant or machinery allowance rules as expenditure by the purchaser on the provision of the fixture if: (a) the qualifying interest were sold at market value, (b) the sale took place immediately before the event which causes the former owner to be treated as ceasing to be the owner of the fixture, and (c) that event were disregarded in determining that market value.
3.	Cessation of ownership of the fixture under s 188 where: (a) neither item 1 nor 2 applies, but	The disposal value given for item 2.

Table 4.5   *Cont.*

Item No	1. Disposal event	2. Disposal value
	(b) the qualifying interest continues in existence after that time or would so continue but for its becoming merged in another interest.	
4.	Cessation of ownership of the fixture under s 188 because of the expiry of the qualifying interest.	If the person receives a capital sum, by way of compensation or otherwise, by reference to the fixture, the amount of the capital sum. In any other case, nil.
5.	Cessation of ownership of the fixture under s 190 because the lessee has become the owner under s 183.	The part of the capital sum given by the lessee for the lease referred to in s 183 that is treated for the purposes of the plant or machinery rules as the lessee's expenditure on the provision of the fixture.
6.	Cessation of ownership of the fixture under s 191 (severance).	The market value of the fixture at the time of the severance.
7.	Cessation of ownership of the fixture because s 192(2)(a) (assignment of rights) applies.	The consideration given by the assignee for the assignment.
8.	Cessation of ownership of the fixture because s 192(2)(b) (discharge of equipment lessee's obligations) applies on the payment of a capital sum.	The capital sum paid to discharge the financial obligations of the equipment lessee.
8A.	Cessation of ownership of the fixture because s 192A(2)(a) (assignment of rights) applies.	The consideration given by the assignee for the assignment. ˙
8B.	Cessation of ownership of the fixture because s 192A(2)(b) (discharge of client's obligations) applies on the payment of a capital sum.	The capital sum paid to discharge the financial obligations of the client.
9.	Permanent discontinuance of the qualifying activity followed by the sale of the qualifying interest.	The part of the sale price that: (a) falls to be treated as expenditure incurred by the purchaser on the provision of the fixture, or (b) would fall to be so treated if the purchaser were entitled to an allowance.

Table 4.5 *Cont.*

Item No	1. Disposal event	2. Disposal value
10.	Permanent discontinuance of the qualifying activity followed by the demolition or destruction of the fixture	The net amount received for the remains of the fixture, together with: (a) any insurance money received in respect of the demolition or destruction, and (b) any other compensation of any description so received, so far as it consists of capital sums.
11.	Permanent discontinuance of the qualifying activity followed by the permanent loss of the fixture otherwise than as a result of its demolition or destruction.	Any insurance money received in respect of the loss and, so far as it consists of capital sums, any other compensation of any description so received.
12.	The fixture begins to be used wholly or partly for purposes other than those of the qualifying activity.	The part of the price that would fall to be treated under the plant or machinery allowances rules as expenditure incurred by the purchaser on the provision of the fixture if the qualifying interest were sold at market value.

*The condition referred to is met by the purchaser if his expenditure on the provision of the fixture cannot be qualifying expenditure under the plant or machinery allowances rules nor under the R&D allowances rules.

Items 1 and 5 of Table 4.5 are subject to ss 198 and 199 (election to fix apportionment on sale of qualifying interest or grant of lease).

The reference in item 8 to the equipment lessee is, in a case where the financial obligations of the equipment lessee have become vested in another person (by assignment, operation of law or otherwise), a reference to the person in whom the obligations are vested when the capital sum is paid.

The reference in item 8B of the table to the client is, in a case where the financial obligations of the client have become vested in another person (by assignment, operation of law or otherwise), a reference to the person in whom the obligations are vested when the capital sum is paid. Section 192A(3) (assignee of client) applies to item 8B of the Table.

Nothing in ss 188–192A or 196 prevents a disposal value having to be brought into account under the general rules for allowances and charges (ss 52–66) because of a disposal event not dealt with in those sections.

The above is subject to s 197 (disposal value in avoidance cases), which applies if:

(1) a taxpayer is treated under the fixtures allowance rules as the owner of any plant or machinery as a result of incurring any expenditure,

(2) any disposal event occurs in relation to the plant or machinery,

(3) the disposal value to be brought into account by the taxpayer would (otherwise) be less than the notional written-down value of the plant or machinery, and

(4) the disposal event is part of, or occurs as a result of, a scheme or arrangement the main purpose or one of the main purposes of which is the obtaining by the taxpayer of a tax advantage under the plant or machinery allowances rules.

The disposal value that the taxpayer must bring into account is the notional written-down value of the plant or machinery, which is calculated as:

$$QE - A$$

where   QE   =   the taxpayer's expenditure on the plant or machinery that is qualifying expenditure,

        A   =   the total of all allowances which could have been made to the taxpayer in respect of that expenditure if:

(a) that expenditure had been the only expenditure that had ever been taken into account in determining his available qualifying expenditure, and

(b) all allowances had been made in full.

4.16.7 Election to fix apportionment
(CAA 2001, s 198–201)

If the disposal value of a fixture is required to be brought into account by item 1 of Table 4.5 in s 196 (sale of qualifying interest at not less than market value, etc), the seller and the purchaser may jointly, by an election, fix the amount that is treated for item 1 of Table 4.5, and for other purposes of the plant or machinery allowances rules, as the part of the sale price that is expenditure incurred by the purchaser on the fixture.

The amount fixed by the election must not exceed the amount of the capital expenditure treated as incurred by the seller on the fixture or of the plant or machinery which became the fixture, or the actual sale price.

If an election fixes the amount treated as the part of the sale price:

(1) the remaining amount (if any) of the sale price is to be treated as expenditure attributable to the acquisition of the property which is not the fixture but is acquired for that amount, and

(2) if there is no remaining amount, the expenditure so attributable is to be treated as nil.

A special rule applies if the disposal value of a fixture is required to be brought into account under item 5 of the Table in s 196 (on acquisition of ownership by incoming lessee under s 183). The persons who are the lessor and the lessee under s 183 may jointly, by an election, fix the amount that is to be treated for item 5, and for the other purposes of the plant or machinery allowances rules, as the part of the capital sum that is expenditure incurred by the lessee on the provision of the fixture.

The amount fixed by the election must not exceed the amount of the capital expenditure which was treated as incurred by the lessor on the provision of the fixture or of the plant or machinery which became the fixture, or the actual capital sum.

If an election fixes the amount treated as the part of the capital sum, the remaining amount (if any) of the capital sum is treated as expenditure attributable to the acquisition of the property which is not the fixture but is acquired for that amount, and if there is no remaining amount, the expenditure so attributable is nil.

The above rules are subject to:

(1) ss 186 and 187 (fixtures on which industrial buildings allowance or R&D allowance has been made),
(2) s 197 (disposal values in avoidance cases), and
(3) ss 200 and 201 (further provisions about elections).

4.17 ASSET PROVIDED OR USED ONLY PARTLY FOR QUALIFYING ACTIVITY
(CAA 2001, ss 205–208)

If a person carrying on a qualifying activity has incurred expenditure on plant or machinery partly for the qualifying activity, and partly for other purposes, any first-year allowance claimed must be reduced to an amount which is just and reasonable having regard to the relevant circumstances. The relevant circumstances include, in particular, the extent to which the plant or machinery is likely to be used for purposes other than those of the qualifying activity in question. However, in calculating (under s 58) the balance left after deducting a first-year allowance, the full amount of the first-year allowances is deducted and the reduction in the amount claimed is disregarded.

Qualifying expenditure to which this rule applies, if allocated to a pool, must be allocated to a single asset pool.

If a person is required to bring a disposal value into account in a pool for a chargeable period because the plant or machinery begins to be used partly for purposes other than those of the qualifying activity, an amount equal to that disposal value is allocated (as expenditure on the plant or machinery) to a single asset pool for that chargeable period.

In the case of first mentioned single asset pool, there is no final chargeable period or disposal event merely because the plant or machinery begins to be used partly for purposes other than those of the qualifying activity.

A similar rule apples for writing-down allowances or balancing allowances.

4.18 PARTIAL DEPRECIATION SUBSIDIES
(CAA 2001, ss 209–212)

A 'partial depreciation subsidy' is a sum which:

(1) is payable directly or indirectly to a person who has incurred qualifying expenditure for the qualifying activity,
(2) is for, or takes account of, part of the depreciation of the plant or machinery resulting from its use in that activity, and
(3) does not fall to be taken into account as income of that person or in calculating the profits of any qualifying activity carried on by him.

If a person has incurred qualifying expenditure for a qualifying activity carried on by him, and it appears that a partial depreciation subsidy is, or will be, payable to him in the period during which the plant or machinery will be used for the purposes of that qualifying activity, the amount of any first-year allowance in respect of that expenditure must be reduced to an amount which is just and reasonable having regard to the relevant circumstances. In calculating the balance left after deducting a first-year allowance under s 58, a reduction as above is disregarded.

A special rule applies to qualifying expenditure if a partial depreciation subsidy relating to the plant or machinery has been paid to the person who incurred the expenditure. Qualifying expenditure within this rule, if allocated to a pool, must be allocated to a single asset pool. The rule applies if:

(1) qualifying expenditure has been allocated to a pool, and
(2) a partial depreciation subsidy relating to the plant or machinery is paid to that person.

For the chargeable period in which the partial depreciation subsidy is paid the person is required to bring a disposal value into account in the pool referred to above, and an amount equal to the disposal value is allocated (as expenditure on the plant or machinery) to a single asset pool.

If qualifying expenditure for any plant or machinery is in a single asset pool under this rule, there is no further allocation of that qualifying expenditure because a further partial depreciation subsidy is paid for that plant or machinery.

A further special rule applies if expenditure is in a single asset pool (under s 211(1) or (4)).

The amount of any writing-down allowance or balancing allowance to which the person is entitled, or any balancing charge to which the person is liable, must be reduced to an amount which is just and reasonable having regard to the relevant circumstances.

In calculating under s 59 the amount of unrelieved qualifying expenditure carried forward, a reduction of a writing-down allowance as above is disregarded.

4.19 ANTI-AVOIDANCE

4.19.1 Relevant transactions

In order to prevent misuse of the plant or machinery allowances rules to obtain tax relief to which, under the scheme of allowances, claimants are not considered to be entitled, various anti-avoidance provisions are built in to the legislation (see ss 213–233). These are considered to be outside the scope of this book.

4.20 SUPPLEMENTARY PROVISIONS

4.20.1 Miscellaneous

If a person carrying on a qualifying activity, or an employee of that person, provides business entertainment in connection with that activity, the use of plant or machinery for providing the entertainment is treated as use for purposes other than those of that activity.

Here 'entertainment' includes hospitality of any kind, and the use of an asset for providing entertainment includes the use of an asset for providing anything incidental to the entertainment.

'Business entertainment' does not include anything provided by a person for employees unless its provision for them is incidental to its provision for others. Nor does it include the use of plant or machinery for the provision of anything by a person if it is a function of that person's qualifying activity to provide it, and it is provided by that person in the ordinary course of that qualifying activity for payment, or free of charge with the object of advertising to the public generally.

For these purposes directors of a company, or persons engaged in the management of a company, are regarded as employed by the company.

4.20.2 Shares in plant or machinery

The plant or machinery allowances rules apply to a share in plant or machinery as they apply (under s 571) to a part of plant or machinery.

For the purposes of the plant and machinery allowance rules, a share in plant or machinery is treated as used for the purposes of a qualifying activity so long as, and only so long as, the plant or machinery is used for the purposes of the qualifying activity.

OTHER ALLOWANCES

4.21 INDUSTRIAL BUILDINGS ALLOWANCE

4.21.1 Introduction
(CAA 2001, s 271–273)

Allowances are given under the industrial buildings allowances rules if expenditure has been incurred on the construction of a 'building or structure' (referred to as a building), the building is (or, is to be) in use for the purposes of a qualifying trade, a qualifying hotel, a qualifying sports pavilion, or a commercial building or structure in a qualifying enterprise zone, and the expenditure incurred on the construction of the building, or other expenditure, is qualifying expenditure.

Allowances under the industrial buildings allowances rules are made to the person who for the time being has the relevant interest in the building (see ss 286–291) in relation to the qualifying expenditure (see ss 292–304).

Expenditure on the construction of a building does not include expenditure on the acquisition of land or rights in or over land.

The industrial buildings allowances rules apply to capital expenditure incurred on repairs to a part of a building as if it were capital expenditure on the construction of that part of the building for the first time. Here, expenditure incurred for a trade on repairs to a building is treated as capital expenditure if it is not expenditure that would be allowed to be deducted in calculating the profits of the trade for tax purposes.

The industrial buildings allowances rules apply to the expenditure as if the purpose of incurring the expenditure were to prepare the land as a site for the construction of a building, and the installed plant or machinery were a building. Thus they apply if capital expenditure is incurred in preparing, cutting, tunnelling or levelling land to prepare land as a site for the installation of plant or machinery, and no allowance could otherwise be made for that expenditure under the industrial buildings allowances rules or the plant and machinery allowances rules.

4.21.2 Meaning of 'industrial buildings'
(CAA 2001, ss 274–285)

Buildings in use for the purposes of a qualifying trade

Trades and undertakings which are 'qualifying trades' are trades of a kind described in Table 4.6, or an undertaking of a kind described in Table 4.7, if the undertaking is carried on by way of trade.

Table 4.6 – Trades which are 'qualifying trades'

1.	*Manufacturing*	A trade consisting of manufacturing goods or materials.
2.	*Processing*	A trade consisting of subjecting goods or materials to a process. This includes (subject to exclusions (s 276(3))) maintaining or repairing goods or materials.
3.	*Storage*	A trade consisting of storing goods or materials: (a) which are to be used in the manufacture of other goods or materials, (b) which are to be subjected, in the course of a trade, to a process, (c) which, having been manufactured or produced or subjected, in the course of a trade, to a process, have not yet been delivered to any purchaser, or (d) on their arrival in the UK from a place outside the UK.
4.	*Agricultural contracting*	A trade consisting of (a) ploughing or cultivating land occupied by another, (b) carrying out any other agricultural operation on land occupied by another, or (c) threshing another's crops. 'Crops' includes vegetable produce.
5.	*Working foreign plantations*	Outside the scope of this book.
6	*Fishing*	A trade consisting of catching or taking fish or shellfish.
7.	*Mineral extraction*	Outside the scope of this book.

Table 4.7 – Undertakings which are 'qualifying trades' if carried on by way of trade

1.	*Electricity*	An undertaking for the generation, transformation, conversion, transmission or distribution of electrical energy.
2.	*Water*	An undertaking for the supply of water for public consumption.
3.	*Hydraulic power*	An undertaking for the supply of hydraulic power.
4.	*Sewerage*	An undertaking for the provision of sewerage services within the meaning of the Water Industry Act 1991.
5.	*Transport*	A transport undertaking.

Table 4.7 *Cont.*

6.	*Highway undertakings*	A highway undertaking, that is, so much of any undertaking relating to the design, building, financing and operation of roads as is carried on: (a) for the purposes of, or (b) in connection with, the exploitation of highway concessions (ss 341–344).
7.	*Tunnels*	A tunnel undertaking.
8.	*Bridges*	A bridge undertaking.
9.	*Inland navigation*	An inland navigation undertaking.
10	*Docks*	A dock undertaking, including: (a) any harbour, and (b) any wharf, pier, jetty or other works in or at which vessels can ship or unship merchandise or passengers, other than a pier or jetty primarily used for recreation.

Despite the specific nature of the definition, there have been several cases concerned with its meaning.

Cases where buildings were held to be industrial include: *Ellerker v Union Cold Storage Co, Thomas Borthwick & Sons v Compton* (1938) 22 TC 195 (cold-storage premises containing ice-making machinery within definition of a mill); *CIR v Leith Harbour & Docks Commissioners* (1941) 24 TC 118 (grain elevators at docks similar premises to a mill); *Lancashire Electric Power Co v Wilkinson* (1947) 28 TC 427 (power house of an electricity generating station a single industrial building (each internal division not to be treated as a separate building, some qualifying and some not)); *CIR v Lambhill Ironworks* (1950) 31 TC 393 (drawing office related to the industrial process); *Kilmarnock Equitable Cooperative Society v CIR* (1966) 42 TC 675 (building in which goods repackaged for retail sale not subjecting good to a process); and *CIR v Saxone, Lilley & Skinner (Holdings)* (1967) 44 TC 122 (warehouse in which were stored finished goods manufactured by the taxpayer (even though bought-in goods were also stored there)).

Cases where buildings were held not to be industrial include: *Dale v Johnson Brothers* (1951) 32 TC 487 (warehouse for imported goods of a trade (not a manufacturer)); *CIR v National Coal Board* (1957) 37 TC 264 (employee's house at a colliery capable of subsequent use by others); *Bourne v Norwich Crematorium* (1967) 44 TC 164 (cremation of human remains not subjecting goods to a process); *Abbott Laboratories v Carmody* (1968) 44 TC 569 (administrative offices within industrial complex, but connected to manufacturing part of site by means of covered walkway not part of industrial site); *Buckingham v Securitas Properties* (1979) 53 TC 292 (secure area for counting wages (by a security company) not subjecting goods to a process); *Vibroplant v Holland* (1981) 54 TC 658 (premises for maintenance of plant where business was plant hire not subjecting goods to a process); *Girobank v Clarke* (1997) 70 TC 387 (building used by bank for processing documents not subjecting goods to a process); *Bestway (Holdings) v Luff* (1998) 70 TC 512 (cash and carry wholesale supermarket warehouse subjecting goods to a process); and *Sarsfield v Dixons Group* [1998] STC 938 (distribution warehouse within retail group not subjecting goods to a process).

The subjection of goods to a process includes repair or maintenance work on any goods or materials provided that the activity does not form part of a retail business, or does not form part of a trade which would itself not qualify premises for industrial buildings allowance (eg plant hire: see *Vibroplant v Holland*, above). Accordingly expenditure on buildings for such purposes qualifies for industrial buildings allowance.

In the light of the decision in *Crusabridge Investments v Casings International* (1979) 54 TC 246, the Revenue practice is to grant allowance for buildings used for warehousing and storage by traders and wholesalers where the goods involved are to be used for an industrial process. The allowance is not extended to premises used for storage for retailing purposes.

'Qualifying trade' includes servicing and maintaining vehicles, but not the sale of cars, parts or vehicle hire. If a garage business carries on a trade of servicing and maintaining vehicles for the public it is carrying on a qualifying trade and the premises used (eg a repair bay or a repair workshop) wholly or mainly for this purpose qualify for industrial buildings allowance. Many garages carry on other trades such as the sale of cars or spare parts. However, these are not qualifying trades and the premises used for these purposes do not qualify. Some garages carry on a trade of hiring vehicles – again, this is not a qualifying trade and any premises used for this purpose (including a repair workshop used to maintain and service the hired vehicles) do not qualify.

A building is in use for a qualifying trade if it is provided by the person carrying it on for the welfare of workers employed in that qualifying trade, and in use for the welfare of such workers.

The above rules also apply to part of a trade or undertaking. However:

(1) if a building is in use for a trade or undertaking, and part only thereof is a qualifying trade, the building is treated as used for the qualifying trade only if it is in use for that part of the trade or undertaking.

(2) maintaining or repairing goods or materials is not a qualifying trade if the goods or materials are employed in a trade or undertaking, the maintenance or repair is carried out by the person employing the goods or materials, and the trade or undertaking is not itself a qualifying trade.

A building is not in use for a qualifying trade if it is used as, or as part of, or for any purpose ancillary to its use as a dwelling-house, a retail shop, or premises of a similar character where a retail trade or business (including repair work) is carried on, a showroom, or a hotel (other than a qualifying hotel (see s 279)), or an office.

If the qualifying expenditure relating to the non-industrial part is no more than 25% of the total qualifying expenditure on the whole building, the whole of the building is an industrial building. Note that this is an expenditure test; the proportion of space occupied is irrelevant.

A building used by more than one licensee of the same person is not in use for the purposes of a qualifying trade unless each licensee uses it, or the part to which the licence relates, for a qualifying trade.

Qualifying hotels and sports pavilions
(CAA 2001, ss 279 and 280)

A hotel is a qualifying hotel if the accommodation in the hotel is in a building of a permanent nature and the hotel is open for at least 4 months during April to October. When the hotel is open during April to October it must have at least 10 letting bedrooms, the sleeping accommodation it offers must consist wholly or mainly of letting bedrooms, and the services provided for guests must normally include breakfast and an evening meal, the making of beds and the cleaning of rooms.

A hotel does not meet the last two conditions at any time in a chargeable period after it has ceased altogether to be used.

Whether a hotel meets these conditions at any time in a chargeable period is determined by looking at the 'reference period'. The tests are whether:

(1) the hotel was in use for the purposes of a trade carried on by the person claiming the allowance, or a lessee occupying the hotel under a lease to which the relevant interest is reversionary throughout the 12-month period ending with the last day of the chargeable period, the reference period is that 12-month period.
(2) the hotel was first used for a trade carried on as described above after the beginning of the 12-month period referred to there, the reference period is the 12-month period beginning with the date on which it was first so used.

If a hotel does not qualify as above because it had fewer than 10 letting bedrooms until too late a date, the reference period is the 12-month period beginning with the date when it had 10 or more letting bedrooms.

A building (whether or not on the same site as any other part of the hotel) which is provided for the welfare of workers employed in the hotel, and in use for the welfare of such workers, is treated as part of the hotel.

If a qualifying hotel is carried on by an individual (alone or in partnership), accommodation which, when the hotel is open during April to October, is normally used as a dwelling by that individual, or a member of his family or household, is treated as not being part of the hotel.

Here, a 'building' does not include a structure, and a 'letting bedroom' is a private bedroom available for letting to the public generally and not normally in the same occupation for more than one month.

A building is a qualifying sports pavilion if it is occupied by a person carrying on a trade, and used as a sports pavilion for the welfare of all or any of the workers employed in that trade.

Commercial buildings (enterprise zones)
(CAA 2001, s 281)

For the industrial buildings allowance rules as they apply to qualifying enterprise zone expenditure, 'commercial building' means a building which is used for a trade, etc, or as an office or offices (whether or not for a trade, etc.), and which is not used as, or as part of, a dwelling-house.

Supplementary provisions
(CAA 2001, ss 282–285)

A building outside the UK which is in use for the purposes of a trade is not an industrial building at any time when the profits of the trade are not assessable under Schedule D Case I.

If, otherwise, but bearing in mind that, in general a building includes a part that would be an industrial building, and another non-industrial part, then if the qualifying expenditure relating to the non-industrial part is no more than 25% of the total qualifying expenditure on the whole building, the whole of the building is an industrial building. Note that this is an expenditure test; the proportion of space occupied is irrelevant.

A road on an industrial estate is an industrial building if the estate consists wholly or mainly of buildings that are treated as industrial buildings. So far as concerns qualifying enterprise zone expenditure, 'industrial estate' includes an area (such as a business park) which consists wholly or mainly of commercial buildings.

Under the industrial buildings allowances rules a building is not regarded as ceasing altogether to be used merely because it falls temporarily out of use, and if a building is an industrial building immediately before a period of temporary disuse, it is treated as being an industrial building during the period of temporary disuse.

4.21.3 The relevant interest in the building
(CAA 2001, ss 286–291)

The relevant interest in relation to any qualifying expenditure is the interest in the building to which the person who incurred the expenditure on the construction of the building was entitled when the expenditure was incurred. This is subject to ss 287–291 and to ss 342 (highway undertakings) and 359 (provisions applying on termination of lease).

If the person who incurred the expenditure on the construction of the building was entitled to more than one interest in the building when the expenditure was incurred, and one of those interests was reversionary on all the others, the reversionary interest is the relevant interest.

In determining the relevant interest, a person who incurs expenditure on the construction of a building, and is entitled to an interest in the building on or as a result of the completion of the construction, is treated as having had that interest when the expenditure was incurred.

An interest does not cease to be the relevant interest merely because of the creation of a lease or other interest to which that interest is subject. However, this is subject to any election under s 290.

If the relevant interest is a leasehold interest which is extinguished on being surrendered, or the person entitled to the interest acquiring the interest which is reversionary on it, the interest into which the leasehold interest merges becomes the relevant interest when the leasehold interest is extinguished.

The lessor and the lessee join in an election if expenditure has been incurred on the construction of a building, a lease of the building is granted out of the interest which is the relevant interest in relation to the expenditure, and the duration of the lease exceeds 50 years.

If this election is made, the industrial buildings allowances rules apply as if:

(1) the grant of the lease were a sale of the relevant interest by the lessor to the lessee at the time when the lease takes effect,
(2) any capital sum paid by the lessee in consideration for the grant of the lease were the purchase price on the sale, and
(3) the interest out of which the lease was granted had at that time ceased to be, and the interest granted by the lease had at that time become, the relevant interest.

The election applies to all the expenditure in relation to which the interest out of which the lease is granted is the relevant interest, and which relates to the building (or buildings) that is (or are) the subject of the lease.

This election cannot be made by a lessor and lessee who are connected persons unless the lessor is a body discharging statutory functions, and the lessee is a company of which it has control. Nor can the election be made if it appears that the sole or main benefit which may be expected to accrue to the lessor from the grant of the lease and the making of an election is obtaining a balancing allowance.

Whether the duration of a lease exceeds 50 years is determined under TA 1988, s 38(1)-(4) and (6), and without regard to CAA 2001, s 359(3) (new lease granted as a result of the exercise of an option treated as continuation of old lease).

4.21.4 **Qualifying expenditure**

Introduction
(CAA 2001, ss 292 and 293)

In the industrial buildings allowances rules 'qualifying expenditure' means expenditure which is qualifying expenditure under:

- s 294: capital expenditure on construction of a building
- s 295: purchase of unused building where developer not involved
- s 296: purchase of building which has been sold unused by developer
- ss 301 and 303: qualifying expenditure on sale within two years of first use where all or part of expenditure is qualifying enterprise zone expenditure, respectively

In the provisions about qualifying expenditure a developer is a person who carries on a trade which consists in whole or in part in the construction of buildings with a view to their sale, and an interest in a building is sold by the developer in the course of the development trade if he sells it in the course of the trade or (as the case may be) that part of the trade that consists in the construction of buildings with a view to their sale.

Qualifying expenditure
(CAA 2001, ss 294–297)

If capital expenditure is incurred on the construction of a building, and the relevant interest in the building has not been sold or, if it has been sold, it has been sold only after the first use of the building, the capital expenditure is qualifying expenditure.

A special rule applies if expenditure is incurred on the construction of a building, the relevant interest in the building is sold before the building is first used, a capital sum is paid by the purchaser for the relevant interest, and s 296 (purchase of building which has been sold unused by developer) does not apply. The capital sum paid by the purchaser for the relevant interest, and the expenditure incurred on the construction of the building, is qualifying expenditure. The qualifying expenditure is treated as incurred by the purchaser when the capital sum became payable. If the relevant interest is sold more than once before the building is first used, this applies only to the last of those sales.

The treatment described below applies if expenditure is incurred by a developer on the construction of a building, and the relevant interest in the building is sold by the developer in the course of the development trade before the building is first used. In this event, if the sale of the relevant interest by the developer was the only sale of that interest before the building is used, and a capital sum is paid by the purchaser for the relevant interest, the capital sum is qualifying expenditure.

But if the sale by the developer was not the only sale before the building is used, and a capital sum is paid by the purchaser for the relevant interest on the last sale, the lesser of that capital sum and the price paid for the relevant interest on its sale by the developer is qualifying expenditure.

The qualifying expenditure is to be treated as incurred by the purchaser when the capital sums referred to above become payable.

The treatment set out below applies if expenditure is incurred by a developer on the construction of a building, and the relevant interest is sold by the developer in the course of the development trade after the building has been used. In such a case, the industrial buildings allowances rules have effect for the person to whom the relevant interest is sold as if the expenditure on the construction of the building had been qualifying expenditure, all appropriate writing-down allowances had been made to the developer, and any appropriate balancing adjustment had been made on the occasion of the sale.

This is subject to amendment on the purchase of a building in an enterprise zone within 2 years of first use (ss 301 and 303).

Qualifying enterprise zone expenditure
(CAA 2001, ss 298–301)

The time limit for expenditure on the construction of a building on a site in an enterprise zone (an EZ building) is 10 years after the site was first included in the zone, or if the expenditure is incurred under a contract entered into within those 10 years, 20 years after the site was first included in the zone.

An 'enterprise zone' is an area designated as such by an order made by the DETR Secretary of State or ministers in the regional assemblies

If capital expenditure is incurred on the construction of an EZ building, and the expenditure is incurred within the time limit, the qualifying expenditure is qualifying enterprise zone expenditure.

If expenditure is incurred on the construction of an EZ building, and all the expenditure is incurred within the time limit, any qualifying expenditure in relation to that expenditure is qualifying enterprise zone expenditure.

A special rule applies if:

(1) expenditure is incurred on the construction of an EZ building,
(2) all the expenditure is incurred within the time limit,
(3) the relevant interest in the building is sold after the building has been used, but within the period of 2 years beginning with the date on which the building was first used, and
(4) that sale (referred to here as 'the relevant sale') is the first sale in that period after the building has been used.

Where this rule applies any balancing adjustment which falls to be made on the occasion of the relevant sale is to be made, and the residue of qualifying expenditure immediately after the relevant sale is disregarded under the industrial buildings allowances rules.

If a capital sum is paid by the purchaser for the relevant interest on the relevant sale, the purchaser is treated as having incurred qualifying expenditure that is qualifying enterprise zone expenditure of an amount given in the circumstances described below, and in relation to that qualifying enterprise zone expenditure, the industrial buildings allowances rules apply as if the building had not been used before the date of the relevant sale.

Unless the circumstances apply, the amount of the qualifying enterprise zone expenditure is the lesser of the capital sum paid by the purchaser for the relevant interest on the relevant sale, and the expenditure incurred on the construction of the building.

The circumstances apply if the expenditure incurred on the construction of the EZ building was incurred by a developer, and the relevant interest in the building has been sold by the developer in the course of the development trade.

If the sale by the developer is the relevant sale, the amount of the qualifying enterprise zone expenditure is the capital sum paid by the purchaser for the relevant interest on that sale.

If the sale by the developer is not the relevant sale, the amount of the qualifying enterprise zone expenditure is the lesser of the capital sum paid by the purchaser for the relevant interest on the relevant sale, and the price paid for the relevant interest on its sale by the developer.

The qualifying expenditure is treated as incurred when the capital sum on the relevant sale became payable.

Part of expenditure within time limit for qualifying enterprise zone expenditure
(CAA 2001, ss 302–304)

A special rule applies where expenditure is incurred on the construction of an EZ building, only a part of the expenditure is incurred within the time limit, and the circumstances are as described in:

(1) s 295(1) (purchase of unused building where developer not involved), or
(2) s 296(1) (purchase of building which has been sold unused by developer).

Only a part of the qualifying expenditure is qualifying enterprise zone expenditure.

In this event, the part of the qualifying expenditure that is qualifying enterprise zone expenditure is:

$$QE \times \frac{E}{T}$$

where   QE = the qualifying expenditure,
      E = the part of the expenditure on the construction of the EZ
              building that is incurred within the time limit, and
      T = the total expenditure on the construction of the building.

A further rule applies if:

(1) expenditure is incurred on the construction of an EZ building,
(2) only a part of the expenditure is incurred within the time limit,
(3) the relevant interest in the building is sold after the building has been used, but within the period of two years beginning with the date on which the building was first used, and
(4) that sale (here referred to as 'the relevant sale') is the first sale in that period after the building has been used.

Where this rule applies any balancing adjustment which falls to be made on the relevant sale is made, and the residue of qualifying expenditure immediately after the relevant sale is disregarded under the industrial buildings allowances rules.

If a capital sum is paid by the purchaser for the relevant interest on the relevant sale:

(1) the purchaser is treated as having incurred qualifying expenditure:
    (a) part of which is qualifying enterprise zone expenditure (Z), and
    (b) part of which is not (N), and
(2) in relation to that qualifying expenditure, the industrial buildings allowances rules apply as if the building had not been used before the date of the relevant sale.

Unless a developer is involved the following formulae apply

$$Z - L \times \frac{E}{T}$$

and

$$N = L - Z$$

where   L = the lesser of:
    (a) the capital sum paid for the relevant interest on the relevant sale, and
    (b) the expenditure incurred on the construction of the building,
      E = the part of the expenditure on the construction of the EZ building that is incurred within the time limit, and
      T = the total expenditure on the construction of the building.

Any qualifying expenditure arising is treated as incurred when the capital sum on the relevant sale became payable.

Where a developer is involved and the expenditure on the construction of the building was incurred by him, and the relevant interest in the building has been sold by the developer in the course of the development trade the following formulae apply (and here Z, N, E and T have the same meaning as above).

If the sale by the developer is the relevant sale:

$$Z - C \times \frac{E}{T}$$

and

$$N = L - L \times \frac{E}{T}$$

where   C =   the capital sum paid for the relevant interest by the purchaser, and
       L =   the lesser of
           (1)   the capital sum paid for the relevant interest on the relevant sale, and
           (2)   the expenditure incurred on the construction of the building.

If the sale by the developer is not the relevant sale:

$$Z = D \times \frac{E}{T}$$

and

$$N = D - Z$$

where D is the lesser of:
        (a) the price paid for the relevant interest on its sale by the developer, and
        (b) the capital sum paid for the relevant interest on the relevant sale.

4.21.5 Initial allowances
(CAA 2001, ss 305–308)

A person who has incurred qualifying enterprise zone expenditure is entitled to an initial allowance on that expenditure if the building on which the expenditure is incurred is to be an industrial building occupied by that person or a qualifying lessee, or used by a qualifying licensee.

Here, a 'qualifying lessee' is a lessee under a lease to which the relevant interest is reversionary, and 'qualifying licensee' is a licensee of the person incurring the qualifying expenditure, or a lessee of the person incurring the qualifying expenditure.

The amount of the initial allowance is 100% of the qualifying enterprise zone expenditure although a person claiming an initial allowance may require the allowance to be reduced to a specified amount.

The initial allowance is made for the chargeable period in which the qualifying expenditure is incurred. Here, expenditure incurred for the purposes of a trade, etc. by a person about to carry it on is treated as if it had been incurred on the first day on which the person carries on the trade, profession or vocation.

No initial allowance is given if, when the building is first used, it is not an industrial building. An initial allowance which has been made for a building which is to be an industrial building is withdrawn if, when the building is first used, it is not an industrial building. An initial allowance which has been made for a building which has not been used is withdrawn if the person to whom the allowance was made sells the relevant interest before the building is first used.

No initial allowance is made for expenditure to the extent that it is taken into account for a relevant grant or relevant payment made towards that expenditure. A grant or payment is relevant if it is a grant made under the Transport Act 1968, s 32, 34 or 56(1), a payment made under the Transport Act s 56(2), or a grant made under the Greater London Authority Act 1999, s 101, and which is declared by the Treasury by order to be relevant for the withholding of initial allowances.

If a relevant grant or relevant payment towards the expenditure is made after the making of an initial allowance, the allowance is to be withdrawn to that extent. If the amount of the grant or payment is repaid by the grantee to the grantor, in whole or in part, the grant or payment is treated, to that extent, as never having been made.

4.21.6 Writing down allowances
(CAA 2001, ss 309–313)

A person is entitled to a writing-down allowance (which he may require the allowance to be reduced to a specified amount) for a chargeable period if qualifying expenditure has been incurred on a building, at the end of that chargeable period, the person is entitled to the relevant interest in the building in relation to that expenditure, and at the end of that chargeable period, the building is an industrial building.

The writing-down allowance for a chargeable period is 25% of the expenditure in the case of qualifying enterprise zone expenditure, and 4% in the case of other qualifying expenditure. The allowance is increased or reduced pro rata if the chargeable period is more or less than a year.

If a relevant event occurs, the writing-down allowance for any chargeable period ending after the event is found by the formula:

$$RQE \times \frac{A}{B}$$

where   RQE   =   the amount of the residue of qualifying expenditure immediately after the event,

A   =   the length of the chargeable period, and

B   =   the length of the period from the date of the event to the end of the period of 25 years beginning with the day on which the building was first used.

On any later relevant event, the writing-down allowance is further adjusted.

Here, a 'relevant event' is a sale of the relevant interest in the building which is a balancing event to which ss 314–331 applies, or an event which is a relevant event under the rules for additional VAT liabilities and rebates.

The amount of the writing-down allowance for a chargeable period is limited to the residue of qualifying expenditure. The residue is ascertained immediately before writing off the writing-down allowance at the end of the chargeable period.

The residue of qualifying expenditure is the qualifying expenditure that has not yet been written off.

4.21.7 Balancing adjustments

General
(CAA 2001, ss 314–317)

A balancing adjustment is made if qualifying expenditure has been incurred on a building, and a balancing event occurs while the building is an industrial building or after it has ceased to be an industrial building. A balancing adjustment is either a balancing allowance or a balancing charge and is made for the chargeable period in which the balancing event occurs. A balancing allowance or balancing charge is made to or on the person entitled to the relevant interest in the building immediately before the balancing event. No balancing adjustment is made if the balancing event occurs more than 25 years after the building was first used. If more than one balancing event occurs during a period when the building is not an industrial building, a balancing adjustment is made only on the first of them.

The following are balancing events under the industrial buildings allowances rules:

(1) the relevant interest in the building is sold;

(2) if the relevant interest is a lease, the lease ends otherwise than on the person entitled to it acquiring the interest reversionary on it;

(3) the building is demolished or destroyed;

(4) the building ceases altogether to be used (without being demolished or destroyed);

(5) if the relevant interest depends on the duration of a foreign concession (ie a right or privilege granted by the government of, or any municipality or other authority in, a territory outside the UK), the concession ends.

Other balancing events are provided for by:

(1) s 328 (realisation of capital value where site of building is in enterprise zone);
(2) s 343 (ending of highway concession);
(3) s 350 (additional VAT rebates and balancing adjustments);

and a balancing event may also occur as a result of s 317 (hotel not qualifying hotel for two years).

References in the industrial allowances rules to the proceeds from a balancing event within s 315(1) are to the amounts received or receivable in connection with the event, as shown in Table 4.8.

Table 4.8 – Balancing events and proceeds

1. Balancing event	2. Proceeds from event
The sale of the relevant interest.	The net proceeds of the sale.
The demolition or destruction of the building.	The net amount received for the remains of the building, together with: (a) any insurance money received in respect of the demolition or destruction, and (b) any other compensation of any description so received, so far as it consists of capital sums.
The building ceases altogether to be used.	Any compensation of any description received in respect of the event, so far as it consists of capital sums.
A foreign concession ends.	Any compensation payable in respect of the relevant interest.

The amounts in col 2 of Table 4.8 are those received or receivable by the person whose entitlement to a balancing allowance or liability to a balancing charge is in question.

A special rule applies if:

(1) a building ceases to be a qualifying hotel otherwise than on the occurrence of a balancing event as above, and
(2) after the building ceases to be a qualifying hotel, a period of two years elapses in which it is not qualifying hotel, and without the occurrence of a balancing event.

In this event, the industrial buildings allowances rules apply as if the relevant interest in the building had been sold at the end of the two-year period, and the net proceeds of the sale were equal to the market value of that interest. This does not affect the treatment where a building is deemed to continue to be an industrial building during a period of temporary disuse. But a building is not treated as continuing to be a qualifying hotel for more than two years after the end of the chargeable period in which it falls temporarily out of use.

The above rule does not apply to qualifying enterprise zone expenditure.

Calculation of balancing adjustments
(CAA 2001, ss 318–320)

Balancing adjustments are required where the building was an industrial building, or used for R&D, for the whole of the relevant period of ownership.

A balancing allowance is made if there are no proceeds from the balancing event, or the proceeds from the balancing event are less than the residue of qualifying expenditure immediately before the event. The amount of the balancing allowance is the amount of the residue (if there are no proceeds), or the difference (if the proceeds are less than the residue).

A balancing charge is made if the proceeds from the balancing event are more than the residue, if any, of qualifying expenditure immediately before the event. The amount of the balancing charge is the amount of the difference, or the proceeds (if the residue is nil). A special rule provides for balancing adjustments where the building was not an industrial building, or used for R&D, for a part of the relevant period of ownership. A balancing allowance is made if there are no proceeds from the balancing event or the proceeds are less than the starting expenditure, and the net allowances made are less than the adjusted net cost of the building. The amount of the balancing allowance is the amount of the difference between the adjusted net cost of the building and the net allowances made.

A balancing charge is made if the proceeds from the balancing event are equal to or more than the starting expenditure. The amount of the balancing charge is an amount equal to the net allowances made.

A balancing charge is also made if there are no proceeds from the balancing event or the proceeds are less than the starting expenditure, and the net allowances made are more than the adjusted net cost of the building. The amount of the balancing charge is the amount of the difference between the net allowances made and the adjusted net cost of the building.

The amount of a balancing charge cannot exceed the amount of the net allowances made.

Meaning of 'the relevant period of ownership' etc
(CAA 2001, ss 321–326)

The relevant period of ownership is the period beginning with the day on which the building was first used for any purpose, or if the relevant interest has been sold after that day, with the day following that on which the sale (or the last such sale) occurred, and ending with the day on which the balancing event occurs.

If the person to or on whom the balancing allowance or balancing charge falls to be made is the person who incurred the qualifying expenditure, that expenditure is the starting expenditure. Otherwise, the starting expenditure is the residue of qualifying expenditure at the beginning of the relevant period of ownership. If there are demolition costs, the starting expenditure is increased by an amount equal to the net cost of the demolition.

The amount of the adjusted net cost is:

$$(S - P) \times \frac{I}{R}$$

where   S   =   the starting expenditure,

        P   =   the amount of any proceeds from the balancing event,

        I   =   the number of days in the relevant period of ownership on which the building was an industrial building or used for R&D, and

        R   =   the number of days in the whole of the relevant period of ownership.

The amount of the net allowances made, in relation to any qualifying expenditure, is:

$$(I + WDA + RDA) - B$$

where   I   =   the amount of any initial allowances made to the person in relation to that qualifying expenditure,

        WDA   =   the amount of any writing-down allowances made to the person for chargeable periods ending on or before the date of the balancing event giving rise to the balancing adjustment,

        RDA   =   is the amount of any allowances under Pt 6 (R&D allowances) made to the person for such chargeable periods, and

        B   =   the amount of any balancing charges made on the person for such chargeable periods.

Balancing allowances restricted where sale subject to subordinate interest
(CAA 2001, ss 325–326)

Balancing allowances are restricted where the relevant interest in a building is sold subject to a subordinate interest, the person entitled to the relevant interest immediately before the sale ('the former owner') would, otherwise, be entitled to a balancing allowance under ss 314–331 as a result of the sale, and condition A or B is met.

Condition A is that the former owner, the person who acquires the relevant interest, and the person to whom the subordinate interest was granted, or any two of them, are connected persons.

Condition B is that it appears that the sole or main benefit which might have been expected to accrue to the parties or any of them from the sale or the grant, or transactions including the sale or grant, was the obtaining of an industrial buildings allowance.

In deciding what balancing adjustment is to be made in a case where balancing allowances are restricted where a sale subject to subordinate interest, the net proceeds to the former owner of the sale are increased by an amount equal to any premium receivable by him for the grant of the subordinate interest, and if no rent, or no commercial rent, is payable for the subordinate interest, by the amount by which the proceeds would have been greater if a commercial rent had been payable and the relevant interest had been sold in the open market. But the net proceeds of the sale are not treated as being greater than the amount which secures that no balancing allowance is made.

If the terms on which a subordinate interest is granted are varied before the sale of the relevant interest any capital consideration for the variation is treated as a premium for the grant of the interest, and the question whether any, and if so what, rent is payable in respect of the interest is determined by reference to the terms in force immediately before the sale.

If the above applies, in relation to a sale, to deny or reduce a balancing allowance, the residue of qualifying expenditure immediately after the sale is nevertheless calculated as if the balancing allowance had been made or not reduced.

Qualifying enterprise zone expenditure: effect of realising capital value
(CAA 2001, ss 327–331)

The rules described here apply only if expenditure on the construction of a building has been incurred at a time when the site of the building was wholly or mainly in an enterprise zone, and which was not more than 10 years after the site was first included in the zone, or under a contract entered into at such a time.

There is a balancing event if, while the building is an industrial building or after it has ceased to be one, any capital value is realised. However, no balancing allowance is made because of a balancing event under this rule. The amount of capital value realised is treated as the proceeds from the balancing event.

If a balancing event under this rule occurs, the rule requiring a balancing adjustment where a building is not an industrial building etc throughout (see s 319) applies as if, immediately after the balancing event, the starting expenditure were reduced by the amount of capital value realised, and if the net proceeds of a sale of the relevant interest have to be increased under the rule requiring balancing allowances to be restricted where the sale is subject to subordinate interest (see s 325(4)), those proceeds as so increased are reduced by the amount of any capital value realised before the sale.

Capital value is realised if an amount of capital value is paid which is attributable to an interest in land ('the subordinate interest') to which the relevant interest in the building is or will be subject. The capital value is realised on the making of the payment. The amount of capital value realised is the amount of capital value that is attributable to the subordinate interest.

Capital value is attributable to the subordinate interest if it is paid:

(1) in consideration of the grant of the subordinate interest,
(2) instead of any rent payable by the person entitled to the subordinate interest,
(3) in consideration of the assignment of such rent, or
(4) in consideration of:
    (a) the surrender of the subordinate interest, or
    (b) the variation or waiver of any of the terms on which it was granted.

Capital value is attributable to the subordinate interest if it is paid in consideration of the grant of the subordinate interest as if the commercial premium had been paid on and in consideration of the grant of the subordinate interest, if no premium is given in consideration of the grant of the subordinate interest, or any premium so given is less than the commercial premium and no commercial rent is payable for the subordinate interest.

If any value given instead of any rent payable by the person entitled to the subordinate interest is less than the commercial amount, capital value is attributable to the rent payable by the person entitled to the subordinate interest as if the commercial amount had been paid.

If any rent payable for the subordinate interest is assigned, but no value is given in consideration of the assignment or any value so given is less than the commercial amount, capital value is attributable to the subordinate interest if it is paid in consideration of the assignment of such rent as if the commercial amount had been given on and in consideration of the assignment.

If the subordinate interest is surrendered, or any of the terms on which the subordinate interest was granted are varied or waived, but no value is given in consideration of the surrender, variation or waiver or any value so given is less than the commercial amount, capital value is attributable to the subordinate interest if it is paid in consideration of the surrender of the subordinate interest, or for the variation or waiver of any of the terms on which it was granted as if the commercial amount had been given on and in consideration of the surrender, variation or waiver.

Capital value is not attributable to the subordinate interest if it is paid in consideration of the grant of a lease to which an election treating the grant of lease exceeding 50 years as sale (see s 290) applies.

No capital value is realised in the context of the realisation of a capital sum while a building is an industrial building or after it has ceased to be one (see s 328) if the payment is made more than 7 years after the agreement under which the qualifying expenditure was incurred was entered into, or if that agreement was conditional, the time when the agreement became unconditional.

If an agreement is made to pay, on the happening of any event, an amount of capital value which would be attributable to the subordinate interest, and the agreement is made, or if conditional becomes unconditional, before the end of the period of seven years referred to above, and the event occurs, or any payment in consideration of the event is made, after the end of that period, the event or payment is treated as occurring or made before the end of the seven years.

The treatment described above does not apply if arrangements under which the person entitled to the relevant interest acquired it, or which were made in connection with its acquisition, include provision which requires, or makes substantially more likely, any of the events set out below.

The events referred to are the subsequent sale of the relevant interest, the subsequent grant of an interest in land out of the relevant interest, any other event on which capital value attributable to the subordinate interest would be paid or treated as paid. Here, 'capital value' means any capital sum including what would have been a capital sum if it had been a money payment (and references to payment are to be read accordingly), but excluding so much of any sum as corresponds to an amount of rent or profits treated as rent under TA 1988, s 34.

'Interest in land' means a leasehold estate in the land, whether in the nature of a head lease, sub-lease or under-lease, an easement or servitude or a licence to occupy land. References to granting an interest in land include agreeing to grant any such an interest.

4.21.8 Writing off qualifying expenditure
(CAA 2001, ss 332–340)

For the purposes of the industrial buildings allowances rules qualifying expenditure is written off to the extent and at the times specified therein.

If an initial allowance is made for the qualifying expenditure, the amount of the allowance is written off at the time when the building is first used.

If a writing-down allowance is made for qualifying expenditure, the amount of the allowance is written off at the end of the chargeable period for which the allowance is made. If a balancing event occurs at the end of this chargeable period, the amount written off thereunder is taken into account in calculating the residue of qualifying expenditure immediately before the event to determine what balancing adjustment (if any) is to be made.

If R&D allowances (under ss 437–451) are made for qualifying expenditure, the amount of the allowance is written off at the end of the chargeable period for which the allowance is made. If a balancing event occurs at the end of this chargeable period, the amount written off thereunder is taken into account in calculating the residue of qualifying expenditure immediately before that event to determine what balancing adjustment (if any) is to be made.

Special treatment is required when writing off expenditure when building a non-industrial building. This applies if, for any period or periods between the time when the building was first used for any purpose, and the time when the residue of qualifying expenditure falls to be ascertained, the building was not an industrial building. An amount equal to the notional writing-down allowances for the period or periods is written off at the time when the residue falls to be ascertained. The notional writing-down allowances are the allowances that would have been made for the period or periods in question (if the building had remained an industrial building), at such rate or rates as would have been appropriate having regard to any relevant sale. Here, 'relevant sale' means a sale of the relevant interest as a result of which a balancing adjustment falls to be made (under s 314).

Special treatment is also required when writing off or increasing expenditure where a balancing adjustment is made if the relevant interest in the building is sold. If a balancing allowance is made, the amount by which the residue of qualifying expenditure before the sale exceeds the net proceeds of the sale is written off at the time of the sale. If a balancing charge is made, the amount of the residue of qualifying expenditure is increased at the time of the sale by the amount of the charge.

But if the balancing charge is made where there are no proceeds from the balancing event or the proceeds are less than the starting expenditure and the net allowances are less than the adjusted net cost of the building (see s 319(6)), the residue of qualifying expenditure immediately after the sale is limited to the net proceeds of the sale.

If a balancing adjustment is made on a balancing event where there is a realisation of capital value while a building is an industrial building, or after it has ceased to be one, an amount equal to any capital value realised is written off at the time of the event.

A modification applies if at any time the Crown, or a person who is not within the charge to tax (A) is entitled to the relevant interest in a building. The rules for writing off qualifying expenditure (see ss 333–338) apply as if all writing-down allowances and balancing adjustments had been made as could have been made if a person (B) who is not the Crown, is within the charge to tax, and is not a company, had been entitled to the relevant interest, and the other assumptions below had been made.

The assumptions are that:

(1) while A was entitled to the relevant interest, all things which were done in relation to the building by or to A, or by or to a person using the building under the authority of A, were done by or to B for the purposes of, and in the course of, a trade carried on by B,

(2) any sale of the relevant interest in the building by or on behalf of A was made in connection with the termination of the trade carried on by B, and

(3) B's periods of account for that trade had, in the case of each tax year, ended immediately before the beginning of the next tax year.

The following treatment applies if a building is demolished, and the person to or on whom any balancing allowance or balancing charge is or might be made is the person incurring the cost of the demolition. In this event, the net cost of the demolition is added to the residue of qualifying expenditure immediately before the demolition. Here, 'the net cost of the demolition' means the amount, if any, by which the cost of the demolition exceeds any money received for the remains of the property. Where this treatment applies, neither the cost of the demolition nor the net cost of the demolition is treated (for any purposes other than for the assured tenancy allowances (see ss 490–531)) as expenditure on any other property replacing the property demolished.

4.21.9 Highway undertakings

Under the industrial buildings allowances rules, the carrying on of a highway undertaking is treated as the carrying on of an undertaking by way of trade. A person carrying on a highway undertaking is treated as occupying, for the purposes of the undertaking, any road in relation to which it is carried on. For this purpose a 'highway undertaking' is so much of any undertaking relating to the design, building, financing and operation of roads as is carried on for the purposes of, or in connection with, the exploitation of highway concessions (see s 274, Table B, item 6). 'Highway concession', in relation to a road, means a right to receive sums from the relevant authority because the road is or will be used by the general public, or if the road is a toll road, the right to charge tolls in respect of the road. Here, 'the relevant authority' is the Secretary of State, the Scottish Ministers, the National Assembly for Wales, or the Department for Regional Development in Northern Ireland.

Under the rules defining the relevant interest in the building (see s 286–291) as they apply to expenditure incurred on the construction of a road, a highway concession is not treated as an interest in the road. But if the person who incurred the expenditure on the construction of the road was not entitled to an interest in the road when he incurred the expenditure, but was at that time entitled to a highway concession in respect of the road, the highway concession is treated as the relevant interest in relation to that expenditure.

Any question as to what is the relevant interest is to be determined on the assumption that, if the rule allowing a renewed or new concession to be treated as extension of earlier concession (see s 344) applies, the renewed or new concession is a continuation of the earlier concession.

If the relevant interest is a highway concession, and the concession is brought to, or comes to, an end without being extended (see s 344), the ending of the concession is a balancing event.

The proceeds from such a balancing event are any insurance money received by the person entitled to the highway concession in respect of any qualifying expenditure, and other compensation so received so far as it consists of capital sums.

A highway concession for a road is to be treated as extended if the person entitled to the concession takes up a renewed concession in respect of the whole or a part of the road, or that person, or a person connected with him takes up a new concession for the whole or a part of the road, or a road that includes the whole or a part of the road.

But the concession is treated as extended only to the extent that the concession which has in fact ended, and the renewed or new concession, relate to the same road, and for the period of the renewed or new concession.

A person takes up a renewed or new concession if he is afforded, whether or not under legally enforceable arrangements, an opportunity to be granted the renewed or new concession and takes advantage of the opportunity. It does not matter whether the renewed or new concession is on the same terms as the previous concession or on modified terms.

If a highway concession is treated as extended hereunder, and the period of the extension is different in relation to different parts of the road in relation to which the concession has been granted, such apportionments are to be made (see s 343) as are just and reasonable.

4.21.10 Giving effect to allowances and trades
(CAA 2001, ss 352–355)

An allowance or charge under the industrial buildings allowances rules is given effect in calculating the profits of that person's trade, by treating the allowance as an expense of the trade, and the charge as a receipt of the trade. For a person who is entitled to an allowance or liable to a charge for a commercial building, and occupies the building in the course of a profession or vocation, the references above to a trade are read as references also to the profession or vocation.

A special rule applies if a person is entitled or liable to an allowance or charge for a chargeable period (here referred to as 'the relevant period'), but his interest in the building in question is or was subject to a lease or a licence at the relevant time.

Here, 'the relevant time' means in relation to an initial allowance, the time when the expenditure was incurred or any subsequent time before the building is used for any purpose; in relation to a writing-down allowance, the end of the relevant period; in relation to a balancing allowance or balancing charge, the time immediately before the event giving rise to the allowance or charge.

If a person's interest in the building is an asset of a Schedule A business carried on by him at any time in the relevant period, the allowance or charge is given effect in calculating the profits of that business for the relevant period, by treating the allowance as an expense of that business, and the charge as a receipt of that business.

If a person's interest in the building is an asset of an overseas property business carried on by him at any time in the relevant period, the allowance or charge is to be given effect in calculating the profits of the overseas property business for the relevant period, by treating the allowance as an expense of that business, and the charge as a receipt of that business.

If a person's interest in the building is not an asset of any property business carried on by him at any time in the relevant period, the allowance or charge is given effect by treating him as if he had been carrying on a Schedule A business in that period and as if the allowance were an expense of that business, and the charge were a receipt of that business.

Particular treatment applies if a person is entitled to an allowance or liable to a charge for a chargeable period during which the building is treated as an industrial building despite temporary disuse (see s 285). If, when the building was last in use as an industrial building it was in use for the purposes of a trade which has since been permanently discontinued, or the relevant interest in the building was subject to a lease or a licence which has since come to an end, the treatment of the allowance or charge (see s 353(4)) applies to him as if the relevant interest were subject to a lease or licence at the relevant time.

If a person is liable to a balancing charge, and when the building was last in use as an industrial building, it was in use for the purposes of a trade which was carried on by that person but which has since been permanently discontinued, the same deductions may be made from the balancing charge as may be made under the rules for deductions allowed in case of post-cessation receipts(see TA 1988, s 105). This does not affect the making of any deduction allowed under any other provision of the Tax Acts.

For the purposes of this rule the permanent discontinuance of a trade does not include an event treated as a permanent discontinuance (under TA 1988, s 113(1) or 337(1) on a change in persons carrying on a trade etc and where a company ceases to trade etc).

Here, 'trade', in relation to a commercial building, includes a profession or vocation.

A special rule applies if

(1) a balancing allowance falls to be made under the industrial buildings rules for the last chargeable period in which the trade is carried on, and
(2) full effect cannot be given to the allowance because there are insufficient profits for that chargeable period.

Where this rule applies, the person entitled to the allowance may claim that the balance of the allowance is to be given for the last preceding chargeable period, and so on for other preceding chargeable periods. But allowances are not given for chargeable periods amounting in total to more than five years. However, a proportionately reduced allowance may be given for a chargeable period of which part is required to make up the five years. In counting the five years, any period for which an allowance might be made but cannot be given effect because there are insufficient profits is included.

For a company, no allowance may be given so as to create or increase a loss in any accounting period. Where the rule applies to a company and a claim is made both to carry back balancing allowances and company trading losses (under s 393A(1)), effect is to be given to the claim under s 393A(1) before a claim hereunder to carry-back balancing allowances is applied, and in giving effect to the claim under s 393A(1), the allowance for which the claim to carry-back balancing allowances hereunder is disregarded.

4.21.11 Supplementary provisions
(CAA 2001, s 356–360)

If a sum paid for the sale of the relevant interest in a building is attributable partly to assets representing expenditure for which an allowance can be made under the industrial buildings allowances rules, and partly to assets representing other expenditure, only so much of the sum as on a just and reasonable apportionment is attributable to the assets eligible for industrial buildings allowances is taken into account.

This applies to other proceeds from a balancing event relating to a building as it applies to a sum given for the sale of the relevant interest in the building. It does not affect any other provision of CAA 2001 requiring an apportionment of the proceeds of a balancing event.

Where the relevant interest in a building is sold, related arrangements have been entered into, at or before the time when the sale price is fixed, which had the effect at that time of enhancing the value of the relevant interest, and the arrangements contain a provision which has an artificial effect on pricing (see below), the sum paid on the sale of the relevant interest is treated in arriving at qualifying expenditure as reduced to what it would have been if the arrangements had not contained the provision having that artificial effect.

If qualifying expenditure is equal to a price paid on a sale of the relevant interest in a building, related arrangements have been entered into, at or before the time when the sale price is fixed, which had the effect at that time of enhancing the value of the relevant interest, and the arrangements contain a provision which has an artificial effect on pricing, the proceeds from any balancing event subsequently occurring in relation to the building are treated under the industrial buildings allowances rules as reduced to what they would have been if the arrangements had not contained the provision having that artificial effect.

'Related arrangements' are arrangements between two or more persons which relate to an interest in or right over the building, or to other arrangements made with respect to such an interest or right; and for this purpose it is immaterial whether the interest or right in question is granted by the person entitled to the relevant interest or another person.

Arrangements contain a provision having an artificial effect on pricing to the extent that they go beyond what could reasonably have been regarded as required in comparable commercial transactions by the market conditions prevailing when the arrangements were entered into. 'Comparable commercial transactions' means transactions involving interests in or rights over buildings of the same kind as (or of a similar kind to) the building to which the arrangements relate, and made by persons dealing with each other at arm's length in the open market.

The rule applying to requisitioned land applies for any period of requisition for which compensation is payable, or but for any agreement would be payable, under the Compensation (Defence) Act 1939, s 2(1)(a). The industrial buildings allowances rules apply in relation to the period of requisition as if the Crown had been in possession of the land for that period under a lease. If a person carrying on a trade is authorised by the Crown to occupy the land (or part of it) during the whole or a part of the period of requisition, the industrial buildings allowances rules apply as if the Crown had granted a sub-lease of the land (or that part of it) to the occupier.

If either of the above circumstances applies, references in the industrial buildings allowances rules to the surrender of a leasehold interest, a leasehold interest being extinguished on the person entitled to it acquiring the interest which is reversionary on it, or the merger of a leasehold interest, apply (with the necessary modifications) to the lease or the sub-lease as above

If the person who (subject to the rights of the Crown) is entitled to possession of the land pays any sum to the Crown, or, in the second circumstance, the occupier, for a building constructed on the land during the period of requisition, the sum is to be treated under the industrial buildings allowances rules as paid in consideration of the surrender of the lease or sub-lease (as the case may be).

Where, with the consent of the lessor, the lessee of a building remains in possession of the building after the termination of the lease, without a new lease being granted to him, the lease is treated as continuing so long as the lessee remains in possession.

If on the termination a new lease is granted to the lessee as a result of the exercise of an option available to him under the terms of the first lease, the second lease is treated as a continuation of the first.

If on the termination the lessor pays a sum to the lessee for a building comprised in the lease, the lease is treated as if it had come to an end by surrender in consideration of the payment.

If on the termination another lease is granted to a different lessee, and in connection with the transaction that lessee pays a sum to the person who was the lessee under the first lease, the two leases are treated as if they were the same lease which had been assigned by the lessee under the first lease to the lessee under the second lease in consideration of the payment.

Meaning of 'lease' etc

In the industrial buildings allowances rules 'lease' includes an agreement for a lease if the term to be covered by the lease has begun, and any tenancy, but does not include a mortgage (and 'lessee', 'lessor' and 'leasehold interest' are to be read accordingly). In applying the industrial buildings allowances rules to Scotland, 'leasehold interest' (or 'leasehold estate') means the interest of a tenant in property subject to a lease, and any reference to an interest which is reversionary on a leasehold interest or on a lease is to be read as a reference to the interest of the landlord in the property subject to the leasehold interest or lease.

4.22 AGRICULTURAL BUILDINGS ALLOWANCES

4.22.1 Introduction

(CAA 2001, ss 361–363)

Allowances are available under the agricultural buildings allowance rules if:

(1) capital expenditure has been incurred on the construction of a building (such as a farmhouse, farm building or cottage) or on the construction of fences or other works,

(2) the expenditure was incurred by a person having a freehold or leasehold interest in land in the UK occupied wholly or mainly for the purposes of husbandry, and for the purposes of husbandry on that land, and

(3) the expenditure, or other expenditure, is qualifying expenditure.

In the agricultural buildings allowance rules an 'agricultural building' is a building, fence or other works as above, and 'the related agricultural land' is the land referred to above.

Allowances under the agricultural buildings allowance rules are made to the person who, for the time being, has the relevant interest (see ss 364–368) in relation to the qualifying expenditure (see ss 369–371).

'Husbandry' includes any method of intensive rearing of livestock or fish on a commercial basis for the production of food for human consumption, and the cultivation of short rotation coppice (which comprises tree species planted at high density where stems are harvested at intervals of less than 10 years (see FA 1995, s 154(3)).

Expenditure on the construction of a building does not include expenditure incurred on the acquisition of land or rights in or over land.

4.22.2 The relevant interest

(CAA 2001, ss 364–368)

The relevant interest in relation to any qualifying expenditure is the freehold or leasehold interest in the related agricultural land to which the person who incurred the expenditure on the construction of the agricultural building was entitled when the expenditure was incurred. This is subject to modification as below.

If, when the expenditure was incurred the person was entitled to freehold and leasehold interests or to more than one leasehold interest in the related agricultural land, and one of those interests was reversionary on all the others, the reversionary interest is the relevant interest.

An interest does not cease to be the relevant interest merely because of the creation of a lease or other interest to which that interest is subject.

If an interest in land is conveyed or assigned by way of security, and subject to a right of redemption, the person with the right of redemption is treated under the agricultural buildings allowance rules as having that interest, and not the creditor.

If the relevant interest is a leasehold interest which is extinguished on being surrendered, or the person entitled to it acquired the interest which is reversionary on it, the interest into which the leasehold interest merges becomes the relevant interest when the leasehold interest is extinguished. This does not apply if a new lease of the whole or a part of the related agricultural land is granted to take effect on the extinguishment of the former leasehold interest.

If the person who owns the interest into which the leasehold interest is merged is not the same as the person who owned the leasehold interest, the relevant interest is treated under the agricultural buildings allowance rules as acquired by the owner of the interest into which the leasehold interest is merged.

Provisions applying on ending of lease
(CAA 2001, s 368)

This rule applies if a lease which is the relevant interest comes to an end, and there is no merger of interests (s 367(1)).

If a new lease of the whole or a part of the related agricultural land is granted to the same lessee, the lessee is treated as continuing to have the same relevant interest in the whole of the related agricultural land.

Where a new lease of the whole or a part of the related agricultural land is granted to a different lessee, and the incoming lessee makes a payment to the outgoing lessee for assets representing the qualifying expenditure, the incoming lessee is treated as acquiring the relevant interest in the whole of the related agricultural land.

In any other case, the former lease and the interest of the lessor under it are to be treated as the same interest; and so the relevant interest in the whole of the related agricultural land is to be treated as acquired by the lessor.

4.22.3 Qualifying expenditure
(CAA 2001, s 369–371)

Where capital expenditure has been incurred on the construction of an agricultural building, the expenditure was incurred for the purposes of husbandry (see ss 361 and 362), and the relevant interest has not been sold or, if it has been sold, has been sold only after the first use of the building, the capital expenditure is qualifying expenditure.

If the capital expenditure has been incurred on the construction of a farmhouse and the accommodation and amenities of the farmhouse are proportionate to the nature and extent of the farm, only one third of the capital expenditure is taken into account. If they are disproportionate, only such part of the expenditure as is just and reasonable (and not exceeding one third) is taken into account.

If the capital expenditure is incurred on the construction of any agricultural building other than a farmhouse, and the building is used partly for the purposes of husbandry on the related agricultural land and partly for other purposes, only such part of the expenditure as, on a just and reasonable apportionment, is referable to use for the purposes of husbandry is to be taken into account.

A further rule applies if capital expenditure has been incurred on the construction of an agricultural building, the expenditure was incurred for the purposes of husbandry (see ss 361 and 362), the relevant interest is sold before the building is first used, and a capital sum is paid by the purchaser for the relevant interest.

In this case, the lesser of the capital expenditure incurred on the construction of the agricultural building, and the capital sum paid by the purchaser, is qualifying expenditure.

For the above purposes:

(1) capital expenditure incurred on the construction of the agricultural building does not include any amount on the construction of a farmhouse which is disallowed (see s 369(3)-(5)), and

(2) the capital sum paid by the purchaser for the relevant interest does not include any amount which, on a just and reasonable apportionment, is attributable to assets representing expenditure for which no allowance can be made under the agricultural buildings allowance rules. This does not affect the general rules for apportionment and procedure for determining apportionment (see ss 562, 563 and 564(1)).

The qualifying expenditure is treated as incurred when the capital sum became payable.

If the relevant interest is sold more than once before the building is first used, the limit on qualifying expenditure applies only to the last of those sales.

If a person is entitled to different relevant interests in different parts of the related agricultural land the expenditure is apportioned between those parts on a just and reasonable basis, and the agricultural buildings allowances rules apply as if the person had incurred the expenditure apportioned to each part separately.

4.22.4 Writing down allowances
(CAA 2001, ss 372–379)

A person is entitled to a writing-down allowance for a chargeable period if qualifying expenditure has been incurred, at any time during that chargeable period, he is entitled to the relevant interest in relation to the qualifying expenditure, and that time falls within the writing-down period. The writing-down period, for qualifying expenditure incurred by a person, is 25 years beginning with the first day of the chargeable period of that person in which the qualifying expenditure was incurred. A person claiming a writing-down allowance may require the allowance to be reduced to a specified amount.

The basic rule is that the writing-down allowance for a chargeable period is 4% of the qualifying expenditure. The allowance is increased or reduced pro rata if the chargeable period is more or less than a year.

No writing-down allowance can be made if, when the agricultural building is first used, it is not used for the purposes of husbandry. Any writing-down allowance which has been made for an agricultural building which has not been used is to be withdrawn if when the building is first used, it is not used for the purposes of husbandry, or the person to whom the allowance was made sells the relevant interest before the building is first used.

The treatment described here applies if the former owner would be entitled to an allowance under the agricultural buildings allowances rules for any expenditure if he continued to be the owner of the relevant interest, and the new owner acquires the relevant interest in the whole or a part of the related agricultural land, whether the relevant interest is acquired by transfer, by operation of law or otherwise.

The former owner is not entitled to an allowance for any chargeable period after that in which the acquisition occurs, and if the acquisition occurs during a chargeable period, is entitled only to an appropriate part of any writing-down allowance for that period.

The new owner is entitled to allowances for the chargeable period in which the acquisition occurs and for subsequent chargeable periods falling wholly or partly within the writing-down period, and if the acquisition occurs during a chargeable period, is entitled only to an appropriate part of any writing-down allowance for that period.

If the new owner acquires the relevant interest in part only of the related agricultural land, the above applies to so much only of the allowance as is properly referable to that part of the agricultural land as if it were a separate allowance.

The formula set out below applies if there has been an acquisition of the relevant interest after first use, and the acquisition is a balancing event as a result of an election made as below.

The writing-down allowance for a chargeable period ending after the event is:

$$RQE \times \frac{A}{B}$$

where RQE = the residue of qualifying expenditure immediately after the event,

A = the length of the chargeable period, and

B = the length of the period from the date of the event to the end of the writing-down period.

On any later acquisition that is a balancing event following the making of an election (see below), the writing-down allowance is further adjusted.

The residue of qualifying expenditure immediately after a balancing event is calculated using the formula

$$QE + B - A$$

(see below), taking into account any balancing adjustment falling to be made on the event. For this purpose, any balancing allowance on that or any previous balancing event which is reduced or denied under s 389 (sale subject to subordinate interest) is treated as having been made in full.

The allowance is reduced pro rata if the person entitled to the allowance is not entitled to the relevant interest in relation to the expenditure in question during part of the chargeable period.

A person is not entitled to a writing-down allowance for a chargeable period in which a balancing allowance or balancing charge is made to or on him for the qualifying expenditure.

The amount of a writing-down allowance for a chargeable period is limited to the residue of qualifying expenditure immediately before it is made or would, otherwise, be made. The residue of qualifying expenditure is calculated using the formula

$$QE + B - A$$

(see s 386).

The final writing-down allowance is the writing-down allowance which is made to the person who is entitled to the relevant interest when the writing-down period ends, and for the chargeable period in which it ends.

If the final writing-down allowance would, otherwise, be less than the amount of the residue of qualifying expenditure immediately before it is made, the allowance is increased to that amount.

When determining the residue of qualifying expenditure (see s 386) for the above purposes, it is assumed that all such writing-down allowances have been made to the persons who have been entitled to the relevant interest during the writing-down period as could have been made if each of them had been entitled to allowances, and had claimed allowances in full.

4.22.5 Balancing adjustments

General
(CAA 2001, ss 380–384)

A balancing adjustment is made if qualifying expenditure has been incurred, and a balancing event occurs in a chargeable period for which a person would (otherwise) be entitled to a writing-down allowance. A balancing adjustment is either a balancing allowance or a balancing charge and is made for the chargeable period in which the balancing event occurs. A balancing allowance or balancing charge is made to or on the person entitled to the relevant interest in relation to the qualifying expenditure immediately before the balancing event.

Any event described below is a balancing event, but only if an election is made (under s 382) for it to be treated as such.

The events are the relevant interest is acquired after first use of the building (see s 375), the agricultural building is demolished or destroyed, or the agricultural building ceases altogether to be used (without being demolished or destroyed). An election relating to the acquisition of the relevant interest after first use of the building under s 375 (see s 381(2)(a)) must be made jointly by the former owner and the new owner.

No election relating to such an event can be made if it appears that the sole or main benefit which might have been expected to accrue to the parties, or any of them, from the acquisition, or transactions of which the acquisition is one, is the obtaining of an allowance, or a greater allowance, under the agricultural buildings allowances rules.

In determining for this purpose what benefit might have been expected to accrue, the rules (see ss 568 and 573) which are concerned with sales treated as being for an alternative amount are disregarded.

An election relating to an event whereby the agricultural building is demolished or destroyed, or the agricultural building ceases altogether to be used (without being demolished or destroyed), must be made by the person entitled to the relevant interest immediately before the event.

No election relating to any event may be made if any person by whom the election is to be made is not within the charge to tax.

References in the agricultural buildings allowances rules to the proceeds from a balancing event are to the amounts received or receivable in connection with the event, as shown in Table 4.9.

Table 4.9 – Balancing events and proceeds

1. Balancing event	2. Proceeds from event
The sale of the relevant interest.	The net proceeds of the sale.
The acquisition of the relevant interest under s 368(3) (ending of lease where incoming lessee makes payment to outgoing lessee).	The net amount of the payment to the outgoing lessee.
The demolition or destruction of the agricultural building.	The net amount received for the remains of the building, together with (a) any insurance money received in respect of the demolition or destruction, and (b) any other compensation of any description so received, so far as it consists of capital sums.
The agricultural building ceases altogether to be used.	Any compensation of any description received in respect of the event, so far as it consists of capital sums.

The amounts in col 2 of Table 4.9 are those received or receivable by the person whose entitlement to a balancing allowance or liability to a balancing charge is in question.

The amounts in col 2 (in s 383) do not include any amount which, on a just and reasonable apportionment, is attributable to assets representing expenditure in respect of which an allowance cannot be made under the agricultural buildings allowances rules.

If the qualifying expenditure for which the balancing adjustment is made was restricted as a result of the restrictions on expenditure on farmhouses (see s 369(3) or (4)), or the restriction on expenditure on buildings to be used partly for purposes other than husbandry (see s 369(5)), a corresponding proportion only of the amounts referred to in Table 4.9 (see s 383) is treated as proceeds from the balancing event.

The general rules for apportionment and procedure for determining apportionment (see ss 562, 563 and 564(1)) are unaffected

Calculation of balancing adjustments
(CAA 2001, ss 385–390)

A balancing allowance is made if there are no proceeds from the balancing event, or the proceeds from the balancing event are less than the residue of qualifying expenditure immediately before the event. The amount of the balancing allowance is the amount of the residue (if there are no proceeds) or the difference (if the proceeds are less than the residue).

A balancing charge is made if the proceeds from the balancing event are more than the residue of qualifying expenditure immediately before the event. The amount of the balancing charge is the amount of the difference.

The residue of qualifying expenditure at any time is:

$$QE + B - A$$

where   QE =   the amount of qualifying expenditure,

      •   B =   the total amount of balancing charges previously made under the agricultural buildings allowances rules for the expenditure, and

       A =   the total amount of any allowances (including balancing allowances) previously made under the agricultural buildings allowances rules for that expenditure (whether to the same or to different persons).

The amount of a balancing charge made on a person for any qualifying expenditure must not exceed the total allowances made under the agricultural buildings allowances rules to the person for the expenditure for chargeable periods ending before that in which the balancing event occurs.

This following rule applies if a balancing event relates to the acquisition of the relevant interest in part only of the related agricultural land in which the interest subsisted when the qualifying expenditure was incurred, or only part of the agricultural building.

Entitlement or liability to, and the amount of, the balancing adjustment, are determined by reference to the part of the qualifying expenditure that is properly attributable to the part of the related agricultural land or (as the case may be) the part of the agricultural building.

The rule that no writing-down allowance for qualifying expenditure for the chargeable period in which a balancing adjustment is made applies to the part of the qualifying expenditure referred to above (see s 377).

The procedure described below applies if the relevant interest is sold subject to a subordinate interest, the person entitled to the relevant interest immediately before the sale ('the former owner') would, otherwise, be entitled to a balancing allowance as a result of the sale (see s 380–390), and condition A or B is met.

Condition A is that the former owner, the person who acquires the relevant interest, and the person to whom the subordinate interest was granted, or any two of them, are connected persons.

Condition B is that it appears that the sole or main benefit which might have been expected to accrue to the parties or any of them from the sale or the grant, or transactions including the sale or grant, was the obtaining of an allowance under the agricultural buildings allowances rules.

In deciding what balancing adjustment is to be made in a case to which this rule applies, the net proceeds to the former owner of the sale are to be increased by an amount equal to any premium receivable by him for the grant of the subordinate interest, and if no rent, or no commercial rent, is payable for the subordinate interest, by the amount by which the proceeds would have been greater if a commercial rent had been payable and the relevant interest had been sold in the open market. But the net proceeds of the sale are not treated as being greater than the amount which secures that no balancing allowance is made.

If the terms on which a subordinate interest is granted are varied before the sale of the relevant interest any capital consideration for the variation is to be treated for the purposes of this rule as a premium for the grant of the interest, and the question whether any, and if so what, rent is payable in respect of the interest is determined by reference to the terms in force immediately before the sale.

If this rule applies in relation to a sale to deny or reduce a balancing allowance, the residue of qualifying expenditure immediately after the sale is nevertheless calculated as if the balancing allowance had been made or not reduced.

4.22.6 Supplementary provisions

Giving effect to allowances and charges
(CAA 2001, ss 391–393)

An allowance or charge to which a person is entitled or liable under the agricultural buildings allowances rules is to be given effect in calculating the profits of that person's trade, by treating the allowance as an expense of the trade, and the charge as a receipt of the trade.

If the person was carrying on a Schedule A business at any time in that period, the allowance or charge is to be given effect in calculating the profits of that business, by treating the allowance as an expense of that business, and the charge as a receipt of that business.

If the person was not carrying on a Schedule A business at any time in that period, the allowance or charge is given effect by treating him as if he had been carrying on such a business in that period and as if the allowance were an expense of that business, and the charge were a receipt of that business.

Meaning of 'freehold interest', 'lease' etc
(CAA 2001, s 393)

In the agricultural buildings allowances rules 'freehold interest in land' means the fee simple estate in the land, or in relation to Scotland, the interest of the owner. 'Freehold interest in land' also includes an agreement to acquire the fee simple estate in the land, or in relation to Scotland, an agreement to acquire the interest of the owner. 'Lease' includes an agreement for a lease if the term to be covered by the lease has begun, and any tenancy, but does not include a mortgage (and 'lessee', 'lessor' and 'leasehold interest' are to be read accordingly).

In the application of the agricultural buildings allowances rules to Scotland 'leasehold interest' means the interest of a tenant in property subject to a lease, and any reference to an interest which is reversionary on a leasehold interest or on a lease is to be read as a reference to the interest of the landlord in the property subject to the leasehold interest or lease.

4.23 FLAT CONVERSION ALLOWANCE

4.23.1 Introduction
(CAA 2001, s 393A)

Allowances are available under the flat conversion allowances rules if a person incurs qualifying expenditure on a flat. Allowances under the flat conversion allowances rules are made to the person who incurred the expenditure, and has the relevant interest in the flat.

'Flat' means a dwelling which is a separate set of premises (whether or not on the same floor), forms part of a building, and is divided horizontally from another part of the building. 'Dwelling' means a building or part of a building occupied or intended to be occupied as a separate dwelling.

4.23.2 Qualifying expenditure
(CAA 2001, s 393B)

In the flat conversion allowances rules 'qualifying expenditure' is capital expenditure incurred on, or in connection with the conversion of part of a qualifying building into a qualifying flat, the renovation of a flat in a qualifying building if the flat is, or will be, a qualifying flat, or repairs to a qualifying building, to the extent that the repairs are incidental to such expenditure. Such expenditure is not qualifying expenditure unless the part of the building, or the flat, for which the expenditure is incurred was unused, or was used only for storage, throughout the period of one year ending immediately before the date on which the conversion or renovation work began.

Expenditure is not qualifying expenditure if it is incurred on or in connection with the acquisition of land or rights in or over land, the extension of a qualifying building (except to the extent required for the purpose of providing a means of getting to or from a qualifying flat), the development of land adjoining or adjacent to a qualifying building, or the provision of furnishings or chattels.

Here, expenditure incurred on repairs to a building is treated as capital expenditure if it is not expenditure that would be allowed to be deducted in calculating the profits of a Schedule A business for tax purposes.

Treasury regulations may make further provision as to expenditure which is, or is not, qualifying expenditure.

4.23.3 Qualifying buildings and qualifying flats
(CAA 2001, ss 393C to 393E)

In the flat conversion allowances rules 'qualifying building' means a building in respect of which the following requirements are met:

(1) all or most of the ground floor of the building must be authorised for business use,
(2) it must appear that, when the building was constructed, the storeys above the ground floor were for use primarily as one or more dwellings,
(3) the building must not have more than 4 storeys above the ground floor (the attic storey does not count unless it is or has been in use as a dwelling or part of a dwelling), and
(4) the construction of the building must have been completed before 1 January 1980 (this requirement is met even if the building has been extended after 31 December 1979, provided any extension was completed on or before 31 December 2000).

'Authorised for business use' means:

(1) in the case of a building in England or Wales, authorised for use within class A1, A2, A3, B1 or D1(a) specified in the Schedule to the Town and Country Planning (Use Classes) Order 1987;
(2) in the case of a building in Scotland:
    (a) authorised for use within class 1, 2, 3 or 4 specified in the Schedule to the Town and Country Planning (Use Classes) (Scotland) Order 1997,
    (b) authorised for a use specified in Article 3(5)(j) of that Order, or
    (c) authorised for use for the provision of medical or health services other than from premises attached to the residence of the consultant or practitioner;
(3) in the case of a building in Northern Ireland:
    (a) authorised for use within class 1, 2, 3, 4 or 15(a) specified in the Schedule to the Planning (Use Classes) Order (Northern Ireland) 1989, or
    (b) authorised for a use specified in Article 3(5)(b), (c) or (h) of that Order.

A 'qualifying flat' is a flat meeting the following requirements so that the flat:

(1) is in a qualifying building,
(2) is suitable for letting as a dwelling,
(3) is held for the purpose of short-term letting (letting as a dwelling on a lease for a term (or, in Scotland, period) of not more than 5 years),
(4) is capable of access without using the part of the ground floor of the building that is authorised for business use (see s 393C(2)),
(5) is of not more than 4 rooms (ignoring any kitchen or bathroom, and any closet, cloakroom or hallway not exceeding 5 square metres in area),
(6) is not a high value flat,

(7) is not (or has not been) created or renovated as part of a scheme involving the creation or renovation of one or more high value flats, and

(8) is not let to a person connected with the person who incurred the expenditure on its conversion or renovation.

Under the flat conversion allowances rules, if a flat is a qualifying flat immediately before a period when it is temporarily unsuitable for letting as a dwelling, it is treated as being a qualifying flat during that period.

A flat is a high value flat (see s 392D(1)(f)) if the notional rent exceeds the relevant limit set out in Table 4.10.

The 'notional rent' means the rent that could reasonably be expected for the flat on the relevant date, on the assumption that, on that date the conversion or renovation has been completed, the flat is let furnished, the lease does not require the tenant to pay a premium or make any other payments to the landlord or a person connected with the landlord, the tenant is not connected with the person incurring the expenditure on the conversion or renovation of the flat, and in England or Wales or Scotland, the flat is let on a shorthold tenancy. The 'relevant date' means the date on which expenditure on the conversion of part of the building into the flat, or (as the case may be) the renovation of the flat, is first incurred. 'Shorthold tenancy' means in the case of a flat in England or Wales, an assured shorthold tenancy, in Scotland, a short assured tenancy.

Table 4.10 – Notional rent limits

Number of rooms in flat	Flats in Greater London (pw)	Flats elsewhere (pw)
1 or 2 rooms	£350	£150
3 rooms	£425	£225
4 rooms	£480	£300

The rules set out in s 393D(3) for determining the number of rooms in a flat also apply.

4.23.4 The relevant interest in the flat
(CAA 2001, s 393F and 393G)

The relevant interest in a flat for any qualifying expenditure is the interest in the flat to which the person who incurred the expenditure was entitled when it was incurred. This is subject as below and to provisions applying on the termination of a lease (see s 393V).

If the person who incurred the qualifying expenditure was entitled to more than one interest in the flat when the expenditure was incurred, and one of those interests was reversionary on all the others, the reversionary interest is the relevant interest in the flat.

An interest does not cease to be the relevant interest merely because of the creation of a lease or other interest to which that interest is subject.

If the relevant interest is a leasehold interest, and that interest is extinguished on the person entitled to it acquiring the interest which is reversionary on it, the interest into which the leasehold interest merges becomes the relevant interest when the leasehold interest is extinguished.

In determining the relevant interest in a flat, a person who incurs expenditure on the conversion of part of a building into the flat, and is entitled to an interest in the flat on or as a result of the completion of the conversion, is treated as having had that interest when the expenditure was incurred.

4.23.5 Initial allowances

A person who has incurred qualifying expenditure on a flat is entitled to a 100% initial allowance for the expenditure. A person claiming an initial allowance may require the allowance to be reduced to a specified amount. The initial allowance is made for the chargeable period in which the qualifying expenditure is incurred.

No initial allowance is made if, at the relevant time, the flat is not a qualifying flat. An initial allowance which has been made for a flat which is to be a qualifying flat is withdrawn if the flat is not a qualifying flat at the relevant time, or the person to whom the allowance was made has sold the relevant interest in the flat before the relevant time. Here, 'the relevant time' is the time when the flat is first suitable for letting as a dwelling.

4.23.6 Writing-down allowances
(CAA 2001, ss 393J to 393L)

A person is entitled to a writing-down allowance for a chargeable period if he has incurred qualifying expenditure on a flat and, at the end of the chargeable period:

(1) the person is entitled to the relevant interest in the flat,
(2) the person has not granted a lease in excess of 50 years duration (see TA 1988, s 38(1)-(4) and (6)) of the flat out of the relevant interest in consideration of the payment of a capital sum (but ignoring s 393V(3)) (whereby a new lease granted as a result of the exercise of an option treated as continuation of old lease), and
(3) the flat is a qualifying flat.

A person claiming a writing-down allowance may require the allowance to be reduced to a specified amount.

The writing-down allowance for a chargeable period is 25% of the qualifying expenditure (increased or reduced pro rata) if the chargeable period is more or less than a year. The amount of the writing-down allowance for a chargeable period is limited to the residue of qualifying expenditure. For this purpose the residue is ascertained immediately before writing off the writing-down allowance at the end of the chargeable period.

The residue of qualifying expenditure is the qualifying expenditure that has not yet been written off (see ss 393Q to 393S).

4.23.7 Balancing adjustments
(CAA 2001, ss 393M to 393P)

A balancing adjustment is made if qualifying expenditure is incurred in respect of a flat, and a balancing event occurs. A balancing adjustment is either a balancing allowance or a balancing charge and is made for the chargeable period in which the balancing event occurs. A balancing allowance or balancing charge is made to or on the person who incurred the qualifying expenditure. No balancing adjustment is made if the balancing event occurs more than seven years after the time when the flat was first suitable for letting as a dwelling. If more than one balancing event occurs, a balancing adjustment is made only on the first of them.

The following are balancing events under the flat conversion rules:

(1) the relevant interest in the flat is sold;
(2) a lease in excess of 50 years duration (see TA 1988, s 38(1)-(4) and (6)) of the flat out of the relevant interest in consideration of the payment of a capital sum (but ignoring s 393V(3) (whereby a new lease granted as a result of the exercise of an option treated as continuation of old lease));
(3) if the relevant interest is a lease, the lease ends otherwise than on the person entitled to it acquiring the interest reversionary on it;
(4) the person who incurred the qualifying expenditure dies;
(5) the flat is demolished or destroyed;
(6) the flat ceases to be a qualifying flat (without being demolished or destroyed).

References in the flat conversion allowances rules to the proceeds from a balancing event are to the amounts received or receivable in connection with the event, as shown in Table 4.11.

Table 4.11 – Balancing events and proceeds

1 Balancing event	2 Proceeds from event
The sale of the relevant interest.	The net proceeds of the sale.
The grant of a long lease out of the relevant interest.	If the capital sum paid in consideration of the grant is less than the commercial premium, the commercial premium. In any other case, the capital sum paid in consideration of the grant.

Table 4.11 *Cont.*

1 Balancing event	2 Proceeds from event
The coming to an end of a lease, where a person entitled to the lease and a person entitled to any superior interest are connected persons.	The market value of the relevant interest in the flat at the time of the event.
The death of the person who incurred the qualifying expenditure.	The residue of qualifying expenditure immediately before the death.
The demolition or destruction of the flat.	The net amount received for the remains of the flat, together with: (a) any insurance money received in respect of the demolition or destruction, and (b) any other compensation of any description so received, so far as it consists of capital sums.
The flat ceases to be a qualifying flat.	The market value of the relevant interest in the flat at the time of the event.

The amounts referred to in col 2 are those received or receivable by the person who incurred the qualifying expenditure.

In item 2 of Table 4.11 'the commercial premium' means the premium that would have been given if the transaction had been at arm's length.

A balancing allowance is made if there are no proceeds from the balancing event, or the proceeds from the balancing event are less than the residue of qualifying expenditure immediately before the event. The amount of the balancing allowance is the amount of the residue (if there are no proceeds), or the difference (if the proceeds are less than the residue).

A balancing charge is made if the proceeds from the balancing event are more than the residue, if any, of qualifying expenditure immediately before the event. The amount of the balancing charge is the amount of the difference, or the proceeds (if the residue is nil). The amount of a balancing charge made on a person cannot exceed the total amount of any initial allowances made to the person for the expenditure, and any writing-down allowances made to the person for the expenditure for chargeable periods ending on or before the date of the balancing event giving rise to the balancing adjustment.

4.23.8 Writing off qualifying expenditure
(CAA 2001, ss 393Q to 393S)

Under the flat conversion allowances rules qualifying expenditure is written off to the extent and at the times specified below.

If an initial allowance is made for qualifying expenditure, the amount of the allowance is written off at the time when the flat is first suitable for letting as a dwelling.

If a writing-down allowance is made for the qualifying expenditure, the amount of the allowance is written off at the end of the chargeable period for which the allowance is made.

If a balancing event occurs at the end of the chargeable period referred to above, the amount written off is taken into account in calculating the residue of qualifying expenditure immediately before the event to determine what balancing adjustment (if any) is to be made.

The rule described below applies if a qualifying flat is demolished, and the person who incurred the qualifying expenditure incurs the cost of the demolition.

The net cost of the demolition is added to the residue of qualifying expenditure immediately before the demolition. 'The net cost of the demolition' means the amount, if any, by which the cost of the demolition exceeds any money received for the remains of the flat.

Where this rule applies, neither the cost of the demolition nor the net cost of the demolition is treated for CAA 2001 as expenditure on any other property replacing the flat demolished.

4.23.9 Supplementary provisions
(CAA 2001, ss 393T to 393W)

The procedure that applies if a person is entitled or liable under the flat conversion allowances rules to an allowance or charge for a chargeable period is described below.

If the person's interest in the flat is an asset of a Schedule A business carried on by him at any time in that period, the allowance or charge is given effect in calculating the profits of that business for that period, by treating the allowance as an expense of that business, and the charge as a receipt of that business.

If the person's interest in the flat is not an asset of a Schedule A business carried on by him at any time in that period, the allowance or charge is given effect by treating him as if he had been carrying on a Schedule A business in that period and as if the allowance were an expense of that business, and the charge were a receipt of that business. If the sum paid for the sale of the relevant interest in a flat is attributable partly to assets representing expenditure for which an allowance can be made under the flat conversion allowances rules, and partly to assets representing other expenditure, only so much of the sum as on a just and reasonable apportionment is attributable to assets eligible for the flat conversion allowance is taken into account.

This applies to other proceeds from a balancing event in respect of a flat as it applies to a sum given for the sale of the relevant interest in the flat. However, it does not affect any other provision of CAA 2001 requiring an apportionment of the proceeds of a balancing event.

A special rule applies under the flat conversion allowance rules if a lease is terminated. If, with the consent of the lessor, the lessee of a flat remains in possession of the flat after the termination without a new lease being granted to him the lease is treated as continuing so long as the lessee remains in possession.

If on the termination a new lease is granted to the lessee as a result of the exercise of an option available to him under the terms of the first lease, the second lease is treated as a continuation of the first.

If on the termination the lessor pays a sum to the lessee in respect of a flat comprised in the lease, the lease is treated as if it had come to an end by surrender in consideration of the payment.

If on the termination another lease is granted to a different lessee, and in connection with the transaction that lessee pays a sum to the person who was the lessee under the first lease, the two leases are treated as if they were the same lease which had been assigned by the lessee under the first lease to the lessee under the second lease in consideration of the payment.

In the context of the flat conversion allowances rules 'lease' includes an agreement for a lease if the term to be covered by the lease has begun, and any tenancy, but does not include a mortgage (and 'lessee', 'lessor' and 'leasehold interest' are to be read accordingly). In the application of the flat conversion allowances rules to Scotland 'leasehold interest' or 'leasehold estate' means the interest of a tenant in property subject to a lease, and any reference to an interest which is reversionary on a leasehold interest or on a lease is read as a reference to the interest of the landlord in the property subject to the leasehold interest or lease.

4.24 MINERAL EXTRACTION ALLOWANCES

A detailed account of the capital allowance rules for mineral extraction activities is beyond the scope of this book. Readers should refer to the legislation and/or seek specialist advice for further details on this subject.

4.25 RESEARCH AND DEVELOPMENT ALLOWANCES

4.25.1 Introduction
(CAA 2001, ss 437 and 438)

Research and development (R&D) allowances are available if a person incurs qualifying expenditure on R&D. Here, 'R&D' has the meaning given by TA 1988, s 837A (see below) which identifies activities falling to be treated as R&D under normal accounting practice in relation to the accounts of companies incorporated in a part of the UK, subject to regulations, and includes oil and gas exploration and appraisal. However this is subject to regulations prescribed by The Treasury that such activities as may be prescribed are not 'R&D' and that such other activities as may be prescribed are 'R&D'.

These regulations may be made by reference to guidelines issued by the DTI Secretary of State. Currently, the regulations concerned are R&D (Prescribed Activities) Regulations (prescription of activities for the purposes of this section by reference to the Guidelines on the Meaning of R&D, issued by the DTI on 28 July 2000).

Unless otherwise expressly provided, 'R&D' does not include oil and gas exploration and appraisal.

Expenditure on R&D includes all expenditure incurred for carrying out R&D, or providing facilities for carrying out R&D. But it does not include expenditure incurred in the acquisition of rights in R&D, or rights arising out of R&D. Nor does it include expenditure on the provision of a dwelling. But if part of a building consists of a dwelling and the rest of the building is used for R&D, and no more than 25% of the capital expenditure referable to the construction or acquisition of the whole building is referable to the construction or acquisition of the dwelling, the whole of the building is to be treated as used for R&D.

The expenditure referable to the construction or acquisition of the building is to be apportioned in a just and reasonable manner.

Any additional VAT liability or rebate is disregarded.

4.25.2 Qualifying expenditure
(CAA 2001, ss 439–440)

In the R&D allowances rules 'qualifying expenditure' means capital expenditure incurred by a person on R&D directly undertaken by him or on his behalf if he is carrying on a trade when the expenditure is incurred and the R&D relates to that trade, or after incurring the expenditure he sets up and commences a trade connected with the R&D.

The same expenditure may not be taken into account as qualifying expenditure in relation to more than one trade. The trade by reference to which expenditure is qualifying expenditure is referred to as 'the relevant trade' in relation to that expenditure. If capital expenditure is partly qualifying expenditure and partly not, the expenditure is apportioned in a just and reasonable manner.

References in the R&D allowances rules to R&D related to a trade include R&D which may lead to or facilitate an extension of that trade, and R&D of a medical nature which has a special relation to the welfare of workers employed in that trade. Expenditure on the acquisition of land, or rights in or over land, is not qualifying expenditure. But this does not prevent such expenditure from being qualifying expenditure so far as it is referable to the acquisition of a building or structure already constructed on the land, rights in or over such a building or structure, or plant or machinery which forms part of such a building or structure. Expenditure is apportioned in a just and reasonable manner.

4.25.3 Allowances and charges
(CAA 2001, ss 441–445)

A person who incurs qualifying expenditure is entitled to an allowance for that expenditure for the relevant chargeable period equal to the amount of the qualifying expenditure, or if a disposal value is required to be brought into account for that period for that expenditure, the amount (if any) by which that expenditure exceeds the disposal value.

The relevant chargeable period is the chargeable period in which the expenditure is incurred, or if the expenditure was incurred before the chargeable period in which the relevant trade is set up and commenced, that chargeable period.

A person claiming an allowance hereunder may require the allowance to be reduced to a specified amount.

A special rule applies if an allowance is made to a person for a chargeable period in respect of qualifying expenditure, and the person is required to bring a disposal value into account for a later chargeable period for that expenditure. That person is liable to a balancing charge for the later chargeable period for the qualifying expenditure. The amount of the balancing charge is the amount (if any) by which the disposal value to be brought into account for the period exceeds any unclaimed allowance, or if less, the allowance made for the qualifying expenditure.

'Unclaimed allowance' means any part of the allowance to which the person was entitled for the qualifying expenditure but which has not been claimed.

This rule is read with s 449 (effect on balancing charges of additional VAT rebates in earlier chargeable periods).

A person is required to bring a disposal value into account in respect of qualifying expenditure incurred by him if he ceases to own an asset representing the expenditure, or an asset representing the expenditure is demolished or destroyed at a time when he owns the asset. This is read with s 555 (disposal of oil licence with exploitation value).

But a person is not required to bring a disposal value into account as above if the disposal event gives rise to a balancing charge under the plant or machinery allowances rules (ss 11–270) or under the industrial buildings allowances rules (ss 271–360).

The disposal value to be brought into account depends on the disposal event, as shown in Table 4.12.

Table 4.12 – Disposal values

1. Disposal event	2. Disposal value
1. Sale of the asset at not less than market value.	The net proceeds of the sale.
2. Demolition or destruction of the asset.	The net amount received for the remains of the asset, together with: (a) any insurance money received in respect of the demolition or destruction, and (b) any other compensation of any description so received, so far as it consists of capital sums.
3. Any event not falling within item 1 or 2.	The market value of the asset at the time of the event.

This is subject to costs of demolition (see s 445), nil value in case of disposal of oil licence relating to undeveloped area (see s 553), and disposal of oil licence with exploitation value (see s 555).

A person is also required to bring a disposal value into account where an additional VAT rebate (see s 448) generates disposal value.

Here 'disposal event' means an event of a kind that requires a disposal value to be brought into account as above.

The chargeable period for which a disposal value is to be brought into account as above for qualifying expenditure is given by this rule. The following applies if the disposal event occurs in or after the chargeable period for which the allowance in respect of the expenditure is made.

The disposal value is brought into account for the chargeable period in which the event occurs, or if the event occurs after the chargeable period in which the relevant trade is permanently discontinued, that chargeable period. If the disposal event occurs before the chargeable period for which the allowance for the expenditure is made, the disposal value is brought into account for that chargeable period.

Where an asset representing qualifying expenditure incurred by a person is demolished at a time when he owns the asset, and he incurred costs of demolition, the disposal value which he is required to bring into account in respect of the qualifying expenditure is reduced by the cost to the person of the demolition.

If the amount of the disposal value is reduced to nil (or less than nil), the person is not required to bring a disposal value into account.

Where the cost to the person of the demolition exceeds the disposal value, and before its demolition the asset had not begun to be used for purposes other than R&D related to the relevant trade, he is treated as incurring qualifying expenditure equal to the excess. That qualifying expenditure is treated as incurred when the demolition occurs, or if that is on or after the date on which the relevant trade is permanently discontinued, immediately before the discontinuance.

Where this applies, the cost to the person of the demolition is not treated for the purposes of CAA 2001 as expenditure on any property that replaces the demolished asset.

4.25.4 Supplementary provisions
(CAA 2001, ss 450 and 451)

An allowance or charge to which a person is entitled or liable under the R&D allowances rules for a chargeable period is given effect in calculating the profits of the relevant trade, by treating the allowance as an expense of the trade, and the charge as a receipt of the trade.

Any reference in the R&D allowances rules to the time when a person ceases to own an asset is to be read, in the case of a sale, as a reference to whichever is the earlier of the time of completion, and the time when possession is given.

4.26 KNOW-HOW ALLOWANCES

4.26.1 Introduction
(CAA 2001, ss 452 and 453)

Allowances are available under the know-how allowances rules if a person incurs qualifying expenditure on the acquisition of know-how. Here, 'know-how' means any industrial information or techniques likely to assist in manufacturing or processing goods or materials, working a source of mineral deposits (including searching for, discovering or testing mineral deposits or obtaining access to them), or carrying out any agricultural, forestry or fishing operations.

'Mineral deposits' includes any natural deposits capable of being lifted or extracted from the earth and geothermal energy is to be treated as a natural deposit, and a 'source of mineral deposits' includes a mine, an oil well and a source of geothermal energy. Know-how is treated as property for the purposes of CAA 2001 and reference to the purchase or sale of property include the acquisition or disposal of know-how.

4.26.2 Qualifying expenditure
(CAA 2001, ss 454 and 455)

'Qualifying expenditure' means capital expenditure incurred on the acquisition of know-how by a person if he:

(1) is carrying on a trade at the time of the acquisition and the know-how is acquired for use in that trade,

(2) acquires the know-how and subsequently sets up and commences a trade in which it is used,

(3) acquires the know-how together with the trade or part of a trade in which it was used and the parties to the acquisition make an election under s 531(3)(a) such that consideration for know-how on disposal of trade is treated as payment for goodwill unless parties otherwise elect, or

(4) acquires the know-how together with the trade or part of a trade in which it was used and the trade in question was, before the acquisition, carried on wholly outside the UK.

The same expenditure cannot be taken into account as qualifying expenditure in relation to more than one trade.

Qualifying expenditure incurred before the setting up and commencement of the relevant trade is to be treated under the know-how allowances rules as incurred when the trade is set up and commenced.

Expenditure on the acquisition of know-how not qualifying expenditure to the extent that it is otherwise deducted for tax purposes. Nor is expenditure on the acquisition of know-how not qualifying expenditure if the buyer is a body of persons over whom the seller has control, the seller is a body of persons over whom the buyer has control, or the buyer and the seller are both bodies of persons and another person has control over both of them. A 'body of persons' includes a partnership.

Expenditure on the acquisition of know-how is not qualifying expenditure if it is treated as a payment for goodwill under TA 1988, s 531(2) (consideration for know-how on disposal of trade to be treated as payment for goodwill, unless parties otherwise elect etc).

4.26.3 Allowances and charges
(CAA 2001, ss 456–463)

Qualifying expenditure has to be pooled for determining a person's entitlement to writing-down allowances and balancing allowances and liability to balancing charges. There is a separate pool for each trade for which the person has qualifying expenditure.

Whether a person is entitled to a writing-down allowance or a balancing allowance, or liable to a balancing charge, for a chargeable period is determined separately for each pool of qualifying expenditure and depends on:

(1) the Available Qualifying Expenditure in that pool for that period ('AQE'), and

(2) the Total of any Disposal Values to be brought into account in that pool for that period ('TDV').

If AQE exceeds TDV, the person is entitled to a writing-down allowance or a balancing allowance for the period. The entitlement is to a writing-down allowance except for the final chargeable period when it is to a balancing allowance. The final chargeable period is the chargeable period in which the trade is permanently discontinued.

If TDV exceeds AQE, the person is liable to a balancing charge for the period.

The amount of the writing-down allowance to which a person is entitled for a chargeable period is 25% of the amount by which AQE exceeds TDV. If the chargeable period is more or less than a year, the amount is proportionately increased or reduced. If the trade has been carried on for part only of the chargeable period, the amount is proportionately reduced. A person claiming a writing-down allowance may require the allowance to be reduced to a specified amount.

The amount of the balancing charge to which a person is liable for a chargeable period is the amount by which TDV exceeds AQE. The amount of the balancing allowance to which a person is entitled for the final chargeable period is the amount by which AQE exceeds TDV.

A person's available qualifying expenditure in a pool for a chargeable period consists of any qualifying expenditure allocated to the pool for that period in accordance under s 460, and any unrelieved qualifying expenditure carried forward in the pool from the previous chargeable period under s 461.

An amount of qualifying expenditure cannot be allocated to the pool for a chargeable period if that amount has been taken into account in determining the person's available qualifying expenditure for an earlier chargeable period. Qualifying expenditure cannot be allocated to the pool for a chargeable period before that in which the expenditure is incurred.

A person has unrelieved qualifying expenditure to carry forward from a chargeable period if for that period AQE exceeds TDV. The amount of the unrelieved qualifying expenditure is the excess less the writing-down allowance made for the period, or if no writing-down allowance is claimed for the period, the excess. No amount may be carried forward as unrelieved qualifying expenditure from the final chargeable period.

A person is required to bring a disposal value into account for the chargeable period in which he sells know-how on which he has incurred qualifying expenditure. The disposal value to be brought into account is the net proceeds of the sale, so far as they consist of capital sums. But no disposal value need be brought into account if the consideration received for the sale is treated as a payment for goodwill under TA 1988, s 531(2) (consideration for know-how on disposal of trade to be treated as payment for goodwill, unless parties otherwise elect).

An allowance or charge to which a person is entitled or liable under the know-how allowances rules for a chargeable period is given effect in calculating the profits of the trade, by treating the allowance as an expense of the trade, and the charge as a receipt of the trade.

4.27 PATENT ALLOWANCES

4.27.1 Introduction
(CAA 2001, ss 464–466)

Allowances are available under the patent allowances rules if a person incurs qualifying expenditure on the purchase of patent rights. Here, 'patent rights' means the right to do or authorise the doing of anything which would, but for that right, be an infringement of a patent.

References in the patent allowances rules to expenditure incurred on the purchase of patent rights include expenditure incurred on obtaining a right to acquire future patent rights.

If a person incurs expenditure on obtaining a right to acquire future patent rights, and subsequently acquires those rights, the expenditure is treated as having been expenditure on the purchase of those rights.

'A right to acquire future patent rights' means a right to acquire in the future patent rights relating to an invention in respect of which the patent has not yet been granted.

References in the patent allowances rules to the proceeds of a sale of patent rights include a sum received from a person which is treated under this section as expenditure incurred by him on the purchase of patent rights.

The acquisition of a licence in respect of a patent is treated as the purchase of patent rights. The grant of a licence in respect of a patent is treated as a sale of part of patent rights. But the grant by a person entitled to patent rights of an exclusive licence is treated as a sale of the whole of those rights. 'Exclusive licence' means a licence to exercise those rights to the exclusion of the grantor and all other persons for the period remaining until the rights come to an end.

4.27.2 Qualifying expenditure
(CAA 2001, ss 467–469)

Expenditure is qualifying expenditure only if it is qualifying trade expenditure, or qualifying non-trade expenditure.

'Qualifying trade expenditure' means capital expenditure incurred by a person on the purchase of patent rights for the purposes of a trade within the charge to tax carried on by the person. The same expenditure may not be taken into account as qualifying trade expenditure in relation to more than one trade. Expenditure incurred for the purposes of a trade by a person about to carry on the trade is treated as if it had been incurred by him on the first day on which he carries on the trade. But this does not apply if the person has before that day sold all the rights on the purchase of which the expenditure was incurred.

'Qualifying non-trade expenditure' means capital expenditure incurred by a person on the purchase of patent rights if any income receivable by the person for the rights would be liable to tax, and the expenditure is not qualifying trade expenditure.

4.27.3 Allowances and charges
(CAA 2001, ss 470–477)

Qualifying expenditure has to be pooled to determine a person's entitlement to writing-down allowances and balancing allowances and liability to balancing charges. There is a separate pool for each trade for which the person has qualifying trade expenditure, and for all of his qualifying non-trade expenditure.

Whether a person is entitled to a writing-down allowance or a balancing allowance, or liable to a balancing charge, for a chargeable period is determined separately for each pool of qualifying expenditure and depends on the Available Qualifying Expenditure in that pool for that period ('AQE'), and the Total of any Disposal Receipts to be brought into account in that pool for that period ('TDR').

If AQE exceeds TDR, the person is entitled to a writing-down allowance or a balancing allowance for the period.

If TDR exceeds AQE, the person is liable to a balancing charge for the period.

The entitlement above is to a writing-down allowance except for the final chargeable period when it is to a balancing allowance. The final chargeable period for a pool to which qualifying trade expenditure has been allocated is the chargeable period in which the trade is permanently discontinued. The final chargeable period for a pool to which qualifying non-trade expenditure has been allocated is the chargeable period in which the last of the patent rights on which the person has incurred qualifying non-trade expenditure comes to an end without any of those rights being revived, or is wholly disposed of.

The amount of the writing-down allowance to which a person is entitled for a chargeable period is 25% of the amount by which AQE exceeds TDR. If the chargeable period is more or less than a year, the amount is increased or reduced pro rata. If in the case of qualifying trade expenditure the trade has been carried on for part only of the chargeable period, the amount is proportionately reduced. A person claiming a writing-down allowance may require the allowance to be reduced to a specified amount.

The amount of the balancing charge to which a person is liable for a chargeable period is the amount by which TDR exceeds AQE.

The amount of the balancing allowance to which a person is entitled for the final chargeable period is the amount by which AQE exceeds TDR.

A person's available qualifying expenditure in a pool for a chargeable period consists of any qualifying expenditure allocated to the pool for that period under s 474, and any unrelieved qualifying expenditure carried forward in the pool from the previous chargeable period under s 475.

The following rules apply to the allocation of a person's qualifying expenditure to a pool.

An amount of qualifying expenditure is not allocated to the pool for a chargeable period if that amount has been taken into account in determining the person's available qualifying expenditure for an earlier chargeable period.

Qualifying expenditure is not allocated to the pool for a chargeable period before that in which the expenditure is incurred. Qualifying expenditure incurred on patent rights is not allocated to the pool for a chargeable period if in any earlier period those rights have come to an end without any of them having been revived, or have been wholly disposed of.

A person has unrelieved qualifying expenditure to carry forward from a chargeable period if for that period AQE exceeds TDR. The amount of the unrelieved qualifying expenditure is the excess less the writing-down allowance made for the period, or if no writing-down allowance is claimed for the period, the excess.

No amount may be carried forward as unrelieved qualifying expenditure from the final chargeable period.

In ss 470–477 'disposal receipt' means a disposal value that a person is required to bring into account in accordance with s 476, or FA 1997, Sch 12, para 11 (finance lease or loan: receipt of major lump sum) or any other enactment.

A person is required to bring a disposal value into account for the chargeable period in which he sells the whole or a part of any patent rights on which he has incurred qualifying expenditure. Subject to s 477, the disposal value to be brought into account is the net proceeds of the sale, so far as they consist of capital sums.

The amount of any disposal value, or the total amount of any disposal values, required to be brought into account by a person on the sale of the whole of any patent rights, or on one or more sales of part of any patent rights, is limited to the capital expenditure incurred by the person on purchasing the rights.

This is modified if the person acquired the rights as a result of a transaction which was between connected persons, or a series of transactions each of which was between connected persons. In this event, that amount, or total amount, is limited to the capital expenditure on purchasing the rights incurred by whichever party to the transaction, or to any of the transactions, incurred the greatest such expenditure.

4.27.4 Supplementary provisions
(CAA 2001, ss 481–483)

In the two cases given below, the amount (if any) by which the capital expenditure incurred by a person ('the buyer') on the purchase of patent rights exceeds the relevant limit is to be left out of account in determining the buyer's qualifying expenditure.

The first case is where the buyer and the seller are connected with each other.

The second case is where it appears that the sole or main benefit which (but for this section) might have been expected to accrue to the parties from the sale, or transactions of which the sale is one, was obtaining an allowance under the patent allowances rules.

If the seller is required to bring a disposal value into account under the patent allowances rules because of the sale, the relevant limit is that disposal value.

If this does not apply but the seller receives a capital sum on the sale, and is chargeable to tax on that sum under TA 1988, s 524 (taxation of receipts from sale of patent rights) the relevant limit is that sum.

If neither of the above applies, the relevant limit is whichever of the following is the smallest; the market value of the rights: if the seller incurred capital expenditure on acquiring the rights, the amount of that expenditure; if a person connected with the seller incurred capital expenditure on acquiring the rights, the amount of that expenditure.

If an invention which is the subject of a patent is used by or for the services of the Crown under the Patents Act 1977, ss 55–59, or the government of a country outside the UK under corresponding provisions of the law of that country, the use is treated as having taken place under a licence. Sums paid for the use are to be treated as having been paid under a licence.

For the purposes of the patent allowances rules a person's 'income from patents' means royalties or other sums paid in respect of the use of a patent, balancing charges to which the person is liable under the patent allowances rules, and amounts on which tax is payable under TA 1988, s 524 or 525 (taxation of receipts from sale of patent rights).

4.28 DREDGING ALLOWANCES

These are considered to be outside the scope of this book.

4.29 DWELLING HOUSES LET ON ASSURED TENANCIES
(CAA 2001, ss 490–531)

A form of capital allowances was available for expenditure incurred before 1 April 1992 on the construction of dwelling houses let under the assured tenancy scheme. A writing-down allowance of 4% (straight line) is available. The allowance, the rules of which were similar to those for industrial buildings, was only available to companies.

4.30 CONTRIBUTIONS

4.30.1 Rules excluding contributions
(CAA 2001, ss 532 and 533)

The general rule is that a person (R) is regarded as not having incurred expenditure to the extent that it has been, or is to be, met (directly or indirectly) by a public body, or a person other than R. Here 'public body' means the Crown or any government or public or local authority (whether in the UK or elsewhere).

This general rule does not apply to dredging allowances (see s 484–489).

Under the dredging allowance rules, a person (D) who has incurred expenditure is regarded as not having incurred it for the purposes of a trade carried on or to be carried on by D to the extent that it has been, or is to be, met (directly or indirectly) by a public body, or capital sums contributed by another person for purposes other than those of D's trade.

4.30.2 Exceptions to the general rule excluding contributions
(CAA 2001, s 534–536)

A person is regarded as having incurred expenditure (notwithstanding the general rule in s 532) to the extent that it is met (directly or indirectly) by a grant made under Northern Ireland legislation, and declared by the Treasury by order to correspond to a grant under the Industrial Development Act 1982, Pt II.

A grant is treated as not falling within the above exception if, by Oil Taxation Act 1975, Sch 3, para 8, expenditure which has been or is to be met by the grant is not regarded as having been incurred by any person. If only a proportion of the expenditure which has been or is to be met by the grant is expenditure which, if it were not so met, would be allowable under OTA 1975, ss 3 or 4, only a corresponding proportion of the grant is treated as not falling within the above exception.

A person is regarded as having incurred expenditure (notwithstanding the general rule in s 532) to the extent that it is met (directly or indirectly) by insurance money, or other compensation money, payable in respect of an asset which has been destroyed, demolished or put out of use.

A person (R) is regarded as having incurred expenditure (notwithstanding the general rule in s 532) to the extent that the requirements set out below are satisfied in relation to the expenditure.

The first requirement is that the person meeting R's expenditure (C) is not a public body.

The second requirement is that no allowance can be made for C's expenditure, and the expenditure is not allowed to be deducted in calculating the profits of a trade or relevant activity carried on by C. When determining whether an allowance can be made, it is assumed that C is within the charge to tax.

Here 'relevant activity' means:

(1) for the purposes of the plant or machinery allowances (ss 11–270):
   (a) an ordinary Schedule A business;
   (b) a furnished holiday lettings business;
   (c) an overseas property business;
   (d) a profession or vocation;
   (e) any of the following concerns:
      (i) mines and quarries (including gravel pits, sand pits and brick-fields);
      (ii) ironworks, gasworks, salt springs or works, alum mines or works (not being mines falling within (i) above) and water-works and streams of water;
      (iii) canals, inland navigation, docks and drains or levels;
      (iv) fishings;
      (v) rights of markets and fairs, tolls, bridges and ferries;
      (vi) railways and other ways;
      (vii) other concerns of the like nature as any of the concerns specified in paras (ii)-(vi) above (see TA 1988, s 55(2)).
   (f) the management of an investment company,
(2) for other purposes, a profession or vocation.

4.30.3 Contribution allowances under certain rules
(CAA 2001, ss 537–541)

This rule sets out general conditions for making contribution allowances under rules for plant or machinery allowances, industrial buildings allowances, agricultural buildings allowances and mineral extraction allowances. The general conditions are that:

(1) a person (C) has contributed a capital sum to expenditure on the provision of an asset,
(2) the expenditure would (notwithstanding the general rule in s 532) have been regarded as wholly incurred by another person (R), and if R is not a public body, have entitled R to allowances under the above categories or to allocate the expenditure to a pool under the plant or machinery allowances rules, and
(3) C and R are not connected persons.

Here a 'public body' means the Crown or any public or local authority in the UK.

A special rule applies to contribution allowances under the plant or machinery allowances rules and applies if the general conditions for contribution allowances are met, and C's contribution is made for the purposes of a trade or relevant activity carried on, or to be carried on, by C.

C is to be treated for the purposes of the plant or machinery allowances as if:

(1) the contribution were expenditure incurred by *C* on the provision, for the purposes of *C*'s trade or relevant activity, of the asset provided by means of *C*'s contribution (such expenditure, if allocated to any pool, must be allocated to a single asset pool).

(2) *C* owned the asset as a result of incurring that expenditure at any time when *R* owns it or is treated under the plant or machinery allowances as owning it, and

(3) the asset were at all material times in use for the purposes of *C*'s trade or relevant activity.

The following provisions apply for contribution allowances under the plant or machinery rules if the whole or a part of the trade or relevant activity for the purposes of which *C*'s contribution was made is transferred.

(1) If the whole of the trade or relevant activity is transferred, writing-down allowances for chargeable periods ending after the date of the transfer are made to the transferee instead of to the transferor.

(2) If a part of the trade or relevant activity is transferred, writing-down allowances for chargeable periods ending after the date of the transfer are made to the transferee instead of to the transferor to the extent that they are properly referable to the part transferred.

A further rule is concerned with contribution allowances under the industrial buildings allowances rules and applies if the general conditions for contribution allowances are met, and *C*'s contribution is made for the purposes of a trade or relevant activity carried on, or to be carried on by *C*, or by a tenant of land in which *C* has an interest.

C is treated for the purposes of allowances under the industrial buildings allowances rules as if the contribution were expenditure incurred by *C* on the provision, for the purposes of the trade or relevant activity, of an asset similar to that provided by means of *C*'s contribution, and the asset were at all material times in use for the purposes of the trade or relevant activity.

The following applies if *C*'s contribution was made for the purposes of a trade or relevant activity carried on, or to be carried on, by a tenant of land in which *C* had an interest, and *C* was entitled to allowances as above.

A person is entitled to a writing-down allowance for a chargeable period if at the end of the period the person is entitled to the interest held by *C* when the contribution was made. For these purposes the industrial buildings allowances rules relating to the relevant interest apply (with any necessary modifications) to the contribution made for the purposes of the trade or relevant activity carried on, or to be carried on, by the tenant as they apply in relation to expenditure incurred on the construction of an industrial building.

The general rule for the calculation of writing-down allowance after sale of relevant interest (see s 311) does not apply in relation to writing-down allowances to be made in respect of contributions.

The rule about contribution allowances under the agricultural buildings allowances applies if the general conditions for contribution allowances are met, and C's contribution is made for the purposes of a trade or relevant activity carried on, or to be carried on by C, or by a tenant of land in which C has an interest.

C is treated for the purposes of agricultural buildings allowances as if the contribution were expenditure incurred by C on the provision, for the purposes of the trade or relevant activity, of an asset similar to that provided by means of C's contribution, and the asset were at all material times in use for the purposes of the trade or relevant activity.

The following applies if C's contribution was made for the purposes of a trade or relevant activity carried on, or to be carried on, by a tenant of land in which C had an interest, and C was entitled to agricultural buildings allowances as above.

A person is entitled to a writing-down allowance for a chargeable period if at the end of the period the person is entitled to the interest held by C when the contribution was made. For this purpose, the agricultural buildings allowances rules relating to the relevant interest apply (with any necessary modifications) in relation to the contribution made for the purposes of the trade or relevant activity carried on, or to be carried on, by the tenant as they apply in relation to expenditure incurred on the construction of an agricultural building.

The treatment of contribution allowances under the mineral extraction allowances rules applies if the general conditions for contribution allowances are met, and C's contribution is made for the purposes of a trade carried on, or to be carried on, by C.

C is treated for the purposes of mineral extraction allowances as if the contribution were expenditure incurred by C on the provision, for the purposes of C's trade, of an asset similar to that provided by means of C's contribution, and the asset were at all material times in use for the purposes of C's trade.

Contribution allowances under the rules: industrial buildings allowances, agricultural buildings allowances and mineral extraction allowances

(CAA 2001, s 542)

The following apply for the purposes of contribution allowances under rules for industrial buildings allowances, agricultural buildings allowances and mineral extraction allowances if C's contribution was made for the purposes of C's trade or relevant activity, and the whole or a part of the trade or relevant activity is subsequently transferred.

If the whole of the trade or relevant activity is transferred, writing-down allowances for chargeable periods ending after the date of the transfer are to be made to the transferee instead of to the transferor. If a part of the trade or relevant activity is transferred, writing-down allowances for chargeable periods ending after the date of the transfer are to be made to the transferee instead of to the transferor to the extent that they are properly referable to the part transferred.

4.30.4 Contribution allowances under the dredging allowances rules
(CAA 2001, s 543)

A person who contributes a capital sum to expenditure incurred by another person on dredging is regarded as incurring capital expenditure on that dredging.

4.31 RENEWALS BASIS

As an alternative to claiming capital allowances, it is possible to claim the cost of replacements on the renewals basis (*Caledonian Railway v Banks* (1880) 1 TC 487). The cost of replacing implements, utensils and articles employed for trade purposes can be deducted in computing that trade's profits (TA 1988, s 74(1)(d)); this is taken to include loose tools. If expenditure on such items is claimed as a revenue deduction, they do not qualify for capital allowances. By ESC B1, a trader may claim a revenue deduction for the cost of replacing larger items of plant or machinery instead of claiming capital allowances (known as the 'renewals basis'). No allowance is given for the cost of the original asset, and when a replacement is acquired the allowance is restricted by excluding any part of the cost representing addition or improvement. No capital allowances can be given on any part of the replacement cost, even if some of it has been excluded from the renewals allowance. Expenditure on any improvement of the original assets is not allowed to be charged, although it may be claimed as a capital allowance. The renewals basis is now very rarely used in practice.

5

MAIN PRINCIPLES OF CAPITAL GAINS TAX

5.1 BASIC OUTLINE OF CAPITAL GAINS TAX
(TA 1988, s 6; TCGA 1992, s 1)

An individual's capital gains are assessed for a tax year. The due date for payment of tax is 31 January following the tax year concerned (ie for 2002–03 payment is due on 31 January 2004). A company's capital gains are included in its 'profits' and corporation tax is charged thereon for the accounting period concerned.

All legislative references are to the Taxation of Chargeable Gains Act 1992 unless otherwise stated.

5.1.1 Annual exemption
(TCGA 1992, s 3)

An individual is entitled to an annual exemption, as follows:

	£		£
2002–03	7,700	1999–00	7,100
2001–02	7,500	1998–99	6,800
2000–01	7,200	1997–98	6,500

A company is not entitled to an annual exemption.

5.1.2 No gain/loss on spouse transactions
(TCGA 1992, s 58)

There is no chargeable gain on any assets transferred from one spouse to the other, whether by gift or sale. The asset is treated as passing across on a no gain/no loss basis, with the recipient acquiring it at the spouse's cost plus indexation up to 5 April 1998 (see 5.5.5 on indexation relief). The only exception to this rule is where the couple is separated on a permanent basis.

5.1.3 Losses
(TCGA 1992, ss 16 and 18)

Capital losses are, broadly, computed in the same way as capital gains. The normal rule is that capital losses cannot be off-set against a person's income but may be carried forward against capital gains of future years. However, losses arising from transactions involving connected persons may only be set against gains arising from transactions with the same person. Brought forward losses do not need to be set against gains that are covered by the annual exemption. Current year losses must be set against capital gains before using the annual exemption.

Save that companies are not entitled to an annual exemption, losses suffered by them are dealt with in a similar way.

An individual can obtain relief for trading losses, insofar as not relieved against other income sources for the tax year, against capital gains of that tax year or against income and capital gains of the previous tax year.

5.1.4 Rate of tax for individuals
(TCGA 1992, s 4)

Once an individual's gains for a tax year have been computed (net of any losses), the annual exemption is deducted. The balance is then added to the individual's taxable income and the CGT is normally ascertained by working out the additional income tax that would be payable if the capital gains had been taxable income.

5.1.5 Rate of tax for companies
(TCGA 1992, ss 6, 8, 13 and 13AA)

A company's chargeable gains are taxed as part of its overall profits, with no differentiation from its income. The full rate of corporation tax on its gains for the financial year 2002–03 is 30% (full rate) or 19% (small companies rate). See further at 19.2.

5.2 WHO IS SUBJECT TO CAPITAL GAINS TAX?
(TCGA 1992, ss 2, 10, 10A and 12)

An individual's residence and domicile status may have a crucial bearing on his liability to CGT. He can be liable only if he is resident or ordinarily resident for the year in which relevant disposals take place. Residence and ordinary residence are determined in the same way as for income tax. Where a non-resident and non-ordinarily resident person has been carrying on a trade or profession through a branch or agency in the UK, CGT may be charged on a disposal of assets used in that branch despite the fact that the person would normally be outside the charge on capital gains.

An individual who is resident (or ordinarily resident) and domiciled in the UK is subject to CGT on gains realised both in this country and abroad. By contrast an individual who is not domiciled in the UK is charged tax on gains from foreign assets only if the proceeds are brought into this country (or, as the legislation puts it, the gains are 'remitted' to the UK).

For a fuller discussion of residence and domicile, see *Zurich Tax Handbook 2002–03*, Chapters 21 and 22.

A company is subject to tax on its capital gains if it is UK resident or if the gains arise from disposals of assets used in a UK branch or agency (see 19.1.1).

5.3 WHAT ASSETS ARE CHARGEABLE ASSETS?

5.3.1 Assets within scope of CGT
(TCGA 1992, s 21)

Gains on virtually all types of assets are potentially subject to CGT, subject to certain stated exceptions under s 21(1) including:

(a) options, debts and incorporeal property generally,

(b) any currency other than sterling, and

(c) any form of property created by the person disposing of it, or otherwise coming to be owned without being acquired.

Examples of 'assets' in this context include:

(1) An employer's rights under a contract of service with an employee (*O'Brien v Benson's Hosiery (Holdings)* (1979) 53 TC 241 (payment made by employee to employer to secure release from employment contract)).

(2) Compensation received by a UK resident for property confiscated in 1940 when Latvia was annexed by the USSR. Property that she had held in her own right was categorised under s 22(1)(a) (capital sums received by way of compensation for damage or injury to, or for the loss, destruction or dissipation of, or for depreciation or risk of depreciation of, an asset). Property that had been held by her late mother was categorised under s 21(1)(a) (options, debts and incorporeal property generally) (see *Davenport v Chilver* (1983) 57 TC 661).

(3) A payment for an unfettered right to pursue trading activities was, in effect, a capital sum derived from an asset, namely goodwill (*Kirby v Thorn EMI* (1987) 60 TC 519).

(4) An arrangement for the future allotment of shares against an advance payment was held to be a disposal of incorporeal rights in *Cleveley's Investment Trust Co v CIR (No 1)* (1971) 47 TC 300.

(5) A right to receive deferred consideration on an earlier sale (*Marren v Ingles* (1980) 54 TC 76; *Marson v Marriage* (1980) 54 TC 54).

In some circumstances, transactions have been held to comprise the disposal of two or more assets:

(a) On the disposal of a business, a lease of a shop and the goodwill of the business were separate assets (*Butler v Evans* (1980) 53 TC 558).

(b) The disposal of a milk quota under EU regulations is separate from the land to which it relates (*Cottle v Coldicott* (1995) SpC 40, following *R v Ministry of Agriculture Fisheries and Food, ex p Bostock* (1994) 1 ECR 955).

(c) The sale of land and the grant of a mortgage, where part of the purchase consideration was left outstanding by way of loan from the vendor to the purchaser, were separate transactions so that the disposal proceeds for the sale of the land was the gross consideration passing (ie the cash paid plus the amount left on loan) and a set-off producing a lower (net) figure was not possible (*Coren v Keithley* (1972) 48 TC 370).

(d) The sale of shares and the accompanying waiver of a debt were separate transactions (*EV Booth (Holdings) v Buckwell* (1980) 53 TC 425).

In some cases, consideration between various elements in a transaction must be apportioned (*Neely v Rourke* [1988] STC 216).

The asset does not have to be transferable or capable of being assigned. The term 'any form of property' is all embracing. For example, the courts have held that CGT was due on an employer's right to compensation from an employee who wished to be released from his service agreement. In another case, the right to compensation in respect of property expropriated by the USSR in 1940 was held to be a form of property and therefore an asset for CGT purposes. Similarly, the High Court held in *Zim Properties v Procter* [1985] STC 90 that the right to bring an action before the courts constitutes an asset that can be turned to account by the potential litigant negotiating a compromise and receiving a lump sum.

Thus the conclusion is that virtually all forms of property that can yield a capital sum are subject to CGT unless they are specifically exempt.

5.3.2 What assets are specifically exempt?

The main categories of exempt assets relevant in the context of this book are:

(1) Chattels which are wasting assets (s 44).

(2) Chattels where the sale consideration is less than £6,000 (s 262). There may be some marginal relief where more than £6,000 is received.

(3) Foreign currency acquired for personal expenditure outside the UK (s 269). This includes money spent on the purchase or maintenance of any property situated outside the UK.

(4) Compensation or damages for wrong or injury suffered in a profession or vocation (s 51).

(5) Debts (s 251).

(6) Gilt-edged securities and qualifying corporate bonds (QCBs) and any options to acquire or dispose of such investments (s 115). A QCB is a loan stock that is not convertible and is not a deep discount or a deep gain security.

(7) Shares held by an individual in ISAs and PEPs (s 151).

(8) Shares issued under the Enterprise Investment Scheme provided the EIS relief has not been withdrawn (FA 1994, s 135 and Sch 14).

(9) Shares held by an individual in a Venture Capital Trust (TA 1988, s 842 and Sch 28).

(10) Sale by an individual of his principal private residence.

(11) Motor cars (unless not suitable or commonly used for the carriage of passengers) (s 263). Also veteran and vintage cars.

(12) Woodlands (s 250).

(13) Gifts to charities (s 257).

(References are to the TCGA 1992 unless otherwise stated.) No gain is assessable where an asset is exempt. Unfortunately, it follows that no relief is normally given for losses (losses on a disposal of shares in an EIS are an exception to this general rule).

5.4 WHICH TYPES OF TRANSACTION MAY PRODUCE A CHARGEABLE GAIN?

The most obvious type of disposal is an outright sale with immediate settlement, but there are many other transactions that count as a disposal for CGT purposes, as discussed in 5.4.1–5.4.8 below. The liability to CGT is determined by the tax year or accounting period in which the date of disposal falls.

5.4.1 Outright sale
(TCGA 1992, s 28)

The date of disposal is the day on which the unconditional contract is entered into, which may, of course, be different from the date the property is conveyed or transferred, or when the vendor receives payment (s 28(1)). Where payment is made by instalments, it may be possible to pay CGT over a period of up to eight years if the Revenue is satisfied that hardship would otherwise result (s 280).

The Revenue operates a concession where a purchaser defaults and the vendor takes back the asset in satisfaction of the sums due to him (see ESC D18). The disposal is effectively treated as if it has never happened.

5.4.2 **Conditional sale**

A conditional sale is a contract that does not take effect until a stated condition is satisfied or an option is exercised (s 28(2)).

Example – Conditional sale

A agrees to purchase *B*'s shares in XYZ Ltd provided the local authority grants planning permission over land owned by XYZ Ltd by April 2002. Under this type of agreement, *B* remains the legal owner of his shares until the condition is satisfied. If the local authority does not in fact grant planning permission, *A* is under no obligation to buy *B*'s shares.

The date of disposal under such contracts is the day the condition is satisfied and the contract becomes unconditional, eg here, the date planning permission is granted.

5.4.3 **Exercise of an option**
(TCGA 1992, s 144)

A 'call' option is a legally binding agreement between the owner of an asset and a third party under which the owner agrees to sell the asset if the other party decides to exercise his option. The purchase price payable upon the exercise of the option is normally fixed at the outset; this constitutes one of the terms of the option. A 'put' option is one where the other party agrees to buy the asset if the owner decides to exercise an option requiring him to do so.

The grant of either type of option does not constitute a disposal of the asset concerned. This happens only when the option is exercised; the day on which this happens is the date of disposal. In some cases, payment is made for the option to be granted. This is treated as a disposal of a separate asset unless the option is subsequently exercised.

5.4.4 **Exchange of property**

An agreement to exchange an asset for another is a disposal of the old asset and an acquisition of the new one. If there is any cash adjustment, this must also be brought into account. For example, if *A* exchanges his holding in EF plc for *B*'s shareholding in GH plc, *A* is treated as if he has disposed of the EF plc shares for the market value of the GH plc shares at the time of the exchange. This type of transaction commonly occurs where an individual transfers portfolio investments to a unit trust in return for units.

Exception for certain share exchanges
(TCGA 1992, s 135–138)

There is an important exception to the rule, in s 135, that an exchange constitutes a disposal that may apply where a shareholder takes securities offered to him on a company takeover. Provided the conditions set out below are satisfied, the exchange does not count as a disposal and the securities issued by the acquiring company are deemed to have been derived from the original shares, with the shareholder carrying forward his original acquisition value.

The conditions to be satisfied are that the share exchange is a bona fide commercial transaction and not part of a tax avoidance scheme and either:

(a) the acquiring company secures 25% or more of the target company's ordinary share capital; or

(b) the offer that is made, if accepted, would result in the offeror obtaining control of the target company.

It is possible to obtain advance clearance from the Revenue that s 136 requirements are satisfied. A written application should be sent to the Revenue's specialist division and the Revenue has 30 days in which to give clearance or come back for further information. The Revenue, once clearance has been given, cannot subsequently go back on this unless it can show that the information supplied by the taxpayer was incorrect or incomplete.

A recent High Court case, *Fallon and Kersley v Fellows*, has established that some types of corporate restructuring, which were previously accepted by the Revenue as meeting the conditions for this 'no disposal' treatment, do not in law satisfy them. From 1 April 1992, TCGA 1992 new ss 135 and 136 and new Sch 5A reverse the effect of the High Court decision, and also put other forms of corporate restructuring on a firm statutory footing. These changes allow share and debenture holders to continue to benefit from the no disposal treatment in all circumstances that were previously accepted as qualifying for it.

The new provisions also extend the no disposal treatment to certain circumstances where it was not previously available, because the relevant company did not have a share capital, or because the transactions were in units in a unit trust.

Example – Exchange of shares on company takeover

B holds 1,000 shares in XYZ plc which he acquired in 1985 for £9,000. Another company, ABC plc, makes a takeover bid and offers all XYZ shareholders a share exchange whereby they receive one ABC share (worth £30 each) for every two XYZ shares they own. The offer document confirms that agreement has been obtained from the Revenue that s 136 applies.

If *B* accepts, he will receive 500 ABC shares worth £15,000. However, he will be deemed to have acquired them in 1985 for £9,000. No disposal is deemed to have occurred on the share exchange.

Professional advice should be taken if the securities offered by way of the share exchange include QCBs (see 5.3.2).

5.4.5 Compulsory acquisition of assets
(TCGA 1992, ss 22 and 246)

The transfer of land to eg a local authority exercising its compulsory purchase powers is a disposal for CGT purposes. In some cases, once the compulsory purchase order (CPO) has been served, contracts are drawn up and the land is transferred under the contract. In such a case, the rules in relation to outright sales and conditional sales apply.

Where the CPO is disputed, the date of disposal is that on which compensation for the acquisition is agreed or otherwise determined. Variations on appeal are disregarded for this purpose.

5.4.6 Sums payable as compensation or proceeds under insurance policy
(TCGA 1992, s 22)

Where a capital sum is received as compensation for a destroyed or damaged asset (eg a building), the asset is deemed to have been disposed of at the date such sum is received. Similarly, where a capital sum is received from an insurance policy following such damage, the receipt of that money constitutes a disposal.

5.4.7 Gifts
(TCGA 1992, ss 17, 165 and 260)

A gift is treated as a disposal at market value (except where it is from one spouse to the other). It was once possible for assets to be transferred at cost, but FA 1989 abolished this general form of hold-over relief. In some cases the capital gains may still be held over, such as where the gift involves business property or is a chargeable transfer for IHT purposes (see 22.10 on lifetime gifts to discretionary trusts).

A gift is normally a 'bargain not at arm's length' which is treated in the same way as a transaction between connected persons.

5.4.8 Asset destroyed or becoming of negligible value
(TCGA 1992, s 24)

The total destruction or entire loss of an asset constitutes a disposal. This could be physical destruction (eg by fire) or legal/financial destruction (eg bankruptcy or winding-up). The legislation also permits a person to elect to be treated as having disposed of an asset that has become of negligible value. Normally, a capital loss arises on such an occasion.

'Negligible value' is interpreted by the Revenue as meaning considerably less than small. For example, the Revenue will only agree that shares, loan stock and other securities are of negligible value on being satisfied that the owner is unlikely to recover anything other than a nominal amount on the company's liquidation. The mere fact that shares have been suspended or de-listed by The Stock Exchange is not sufficient.

The legislation provides that a disposal is deemed to take place in the year during which the inspector agrees that the asset has become of negligible value. A claim takes effect up to two tax years prior to the claim provided the asset was of negligible value in the prior year.

5.4.9 Disposals by companies with substantial shareholdings
(TCGA 1992 s 192 and Sch 7AC)

For disposals on or after 1 April 2002, an exemption regime for substantial shareholdings is introduced to enable UK-based companies and groups to restructure flexibly and rapidly in response to emerging global opportunities without facing the prospect of a large tax charge.

The exemption regime for gains and losses on disposals by companies of substantial shareholdings applies to most disposals by trading companies of shareholdings of 10% or more in other trading companies. Schedule 7AC contains the main provisions, and introduces three exemptions for companies disposing of shares, an interest in shares or an asset related to shares.

The main exemption applies to disposals by trading companies or members of trading groups of all or part of a substantial shareholding in another trading company or the holding company of a trading group or subgroup. To have a substantial shareholding a company must have owned at least 10% of the ordinary shares in another company for a 12-month continuous period during the two years before the disposal. The effect of the exemption is that any gain on the disposal is not chargeable to tax and any loss is not available to be set off against gains.

A subsidiary exemption applies where the requirements for the main exemption are met and a company disposes of an asset related to shares in the company in which the substantial shareholding is owned. Broadly speaking, assets are related to shares in a company if they are options over, or securities convertible into or exchangeable for, shares in that company.

The second subsidiary exemption applies where the conditions for the other exemptions are not met at the time of the disposal, but a disposal within the previous two years would have qualified for the main exemption and certain conditions are satisfied.

There are special rules to cover groups of companies, where more than one member may hold shares in the same company. There are also detailed rules for establishing whether companies or groups are trading.

5.5 COMPUTATION OF CAPITAL GAINS

5.5.1 Amount to be brought in as disposal value

Market value
(TGCA 1992, s 17)

The general rule is that market value must be used unless the transaction is a bargain at arm's length. In the straightforward situation where a contract is entered into with a third party on a commercial basis, the disposal proceeds are the actual sale proceeds. An individual is not penalised because he has made a bad bargain and sold an asset for less than it is really worth. However, if the bargain is not at arm's length and he deliberately sells the asset for an amount that is less than its true value, the legislation requires market value to be substituted. If the disposal is to a connected person such as a relative or the trustee of a family settlement or a family company, there is an automatic assumption that the bargain is not at arm's length and market value will always be substituted for the actual sale proceeds if the two amounts are different.

The two main exceptions to this are transactions between spouses and gifts to charities and similar bodies. In both of these circumstances, the person making the disposal is deemed to sell at a figure that produces a no gain/no loss situation.

Contingent liabilities
(TCGA 1992, s 49)

There may be occasions where the contract requires part of the proceeds to be returned at some time in the future. This is known as a sale with 'contingent liabilities'. For example, suppose a vendor receives £150,000 for the disposal of a plot of land, but is under an obligation to return £60,000 in certain circumstances. Is the capital gain charged on sale proceeds of £150,000 or £90,000? In fact, s 49 provides that the capital gain must be computed in the first instance without any deduction for the contingent liability. However, if and when the vendor is required to refund part of the sale proceeds because the contingent liability has become an actual liability, the CGT assessment is adjusted accordingly.

Contingent consideration
(TCGA 1992, s 48)

In a similar way, it is possible the contract may provide that additional sums may be payable if certain conditions are satisfied in the future. If it is possible to put a value on the further amount of consideration which is 'contingent' (ie payable only if certain conditions are satisfied), the full amount which may be received is brought into account at the date of disposal without any discount. If the conditions are not in fact satisfied, so that the further amounts are never received, an adjustment is made when that becomes clear.

The position is different where the contingent consideration cannot be ascertained at the date of disposal (this is normally the situation where the contingent consideration may vary and is not a fixed amount). Basically, the legislation requires that the market value of the right to receive the future consideration should be regarded as the disposal proceeds (*Marren v Ingles* (1980) 54 TC 76). The difference between this amount and that eventually received forms a *separate* CGT computation for the year in which the final amount of the actual contingent consideration is determined. The treatment of contingent consideration, especially variable contingent consideration, is complex. It normally arises in relation either to land or shares in private companies. This is an area where it is essential to take professional advice.

Adjustment for amounts charged as income or deducted from income
(TCGA 1992, ss 37 and 39)

In some cases the disposal of an asset by an individual may give rise to an income tax charge. Where this happens, the amount charged as income is deducted from the sale proceeds and only the balance is brought into account for CGT purposes. This commonly arises where a private company buys back its own shares from an individual or trustee shareholders and the transaction is treated as a distribution (see 19.5). Unfortunately, the Revenue does not accept that this applies where a corporate shareholder has shares bought back by the company in which it has invested.

Amounts deducted in arriving at amounts chargeable to income tax cannot also be taken into account in the computation of capital gains.

5.5.2 What costs are allowable?
(TCGA 1992, s 38)

Certain specific types of expenditure

The legislation permits a limited range of expenses to be deducted in computing capital gains and losses. Section 38(1) states:

'. . . the sums allowable as a deduction from the consideration in the computation of the gain accruing to a person on the disposal of an asset shall be restricted to –

(a) the amount or value of the consideration, in money or money's worth, given by him or on his behalf wholly and exclusively for the acquisition of the asset, together with the incidental costs to him of the acquisition or, if the asset was not acquired by him, any expenditure wholly and exclusively incurred by him in providing the asset,

(b) the amount of any expenditure wholly and exclusively incurred on the asset by him or on his behalf for the purpose of enhancing the value of the asset, being expenditure reflected in the state or nature of the asset at the time of the disposal, and any expenditure wholly and exclusively incurred by him in establishing, preserving or defending his title to, or to a right over, the asset,

(c) the incidental costs to him of making the disposal.'

Incidental costs of acquisition

These are limited to:

(1) fees, commission or remuneration paid to a surveyor, valuer, auctioneer, accountant, agent or legal adviser;

(2) transfer/conveyancing charges (including stamp duty); and

(3) advertising to find a seller.

Enhancement expenditure

The legislation permits a deduction to be claimed for expenditure incurred to enhance the asset's value provided such expenditure is reflected in the asset's state or nature at time of disposal. The latter condition excludes relief for improvements that have worn out by the time of disposal. Certain grey areas are worth mentioning:

(a) Initial expenditure by way of repairs to newly acquired property which is let may be allowable if no relief has been given in computing Schedule A income.

(b) Expenditure means money or money's worth. It does not include the value of personal labour or skill.

Incidental costs of disposals

The same fees, charges and advertising costs as apply to incidental costs of acquisition (see (1)-(3) above) may be deductible, as well as any other costs reasonably incurred in making any valuation or apportionment for CGT purposes, including in particular expenses reasonably incurred in ascertaining market value where this is required. Professional costs incurred in getting a valuation agreed with the Revenue are not allowable.

Part disposals
(TCGA 1992, s 42)

Where a person disposes of part of an asset, the cost is apportioned between the part disposed of and that retained according to the formula $[A \div (A + B)]$ where A is the consideration received or deemed to have been received and B is the market value of the part retained.

Example – Part disposals

B holds 1,000 shares in XYZ Ltd which cost him £10,000. The company is taken over and he receives cash of £5,000 and convertible loan stock issued by the acquiring company worth £15,000 (assume in this particular case that no capital gain arises in respect of the loan stock because it is issued on the occasion of a takeover and the necessary Revenue clearances have been obtained). B's acquisition value is apportioned as follows:

$$£10,000 \times \frac{5,000}{5,000 + 15,000} = £2,500$$

ie the proportion of acquisition value that relates to the part sold.

£7,500 is treated as the acquisition value of the part retained, ie it is taken into account in computing any gain or loss as and when the loan stock is sold.

Special rules may apply where shares are sold out of a shareholding that includes shares held on 31 March 1982 and shares acquired after that date.

Small capital receipts
(TCGA 1992, s 122)

There are occasions where the formula $[A \div (A + B)]$ does not have to be used, and the amount received is simply deducted from the owner's acquisition value. The most common situation is where a shareholder sells his entitlement under a rights issue, normally on a nil paid basis. Provided the amount received is small as compared with the asset's value, the receipt can be deducted from the owner's acquisition value. 'Small' in this context is interpreted by the Revenue as an amount not exceeding 5% of the market value or £3,000, whichever is less.

Capital sums applied in restoring assets
(TCGA 1992, s 23)

Under normal circumstances, an asset is regarded as having been disposed of for CGT purposes if it is lost or destroyed. However, where a capital sum is received from such an asset (eg the proceeds of an insurance policy), the owner may claim that the asset is not treated as disposed of if at least 95% of the capital sum is spent in restoring it.

5.5.3 Assets held at 31 March 1982
(TCGA 1992, s 35 & Scheds 2–3)

This applies only to companies, and to individuals to establish 'frozen' indexation up to 5 April 1998.

The general rule is that where assets were held at 31 March 1982, it is to be assumed that the assets were sold on that date and immediately re-acquired at their market value at that time. This is known as 'rebasing'.

The original cost still applies in certain circumstances as the rebasing rule is subject to the following qualifications:

(1) Where the gain since March 1982 is smaller than that measured by reference to original cost (or vice versa), the chargeable gain is confined to that figure.

(2) Where a loss has arisen, the allowable loss is the smaller of the loss measured by reference to original cost and the loss measured by reference to the 31 March 1982 value.

(3) Where a gain arises when one has regard to original cost, but a loss arises when one takes the 31 March 1982 value (or vice versa), the position is regarded as no gain/no loss.

However, even these qualifications are ignored if a universal rebasing election has been made.

5.5.4 Other acquisition values

Assets acquired via inheritance or from family trust
(TCGA 1992, ss 62 and 71)

Where a person inherits an asset, he is generally deemed to have acquired it for its market value at the date of the testator's death (ie probate value). There is one exception to this. It is possible to claim a form of relief from IHT where quoted securities have gone down in value after the person has died. Where such relief has been claimed, a corresponding adjustment is made so that the person taking the assets concerned is deemed to have acquired them not at probate value, but at the value actually brought into account for IHT purposes after taking account of the fall in value.

Where assets have been acquired from a trust, the beneficiary's acquisition value is normally the market value at the time the asset is transferred to him. However, the acquisition value may be lower than this where the trustees have claimed hold-over relief either under the general hold-over relief provisions that prevailed up to 5 April 1989, or under the more restrictive provisions that have applied subsequently.

5.5.5 Indexation
(TA 1992, ss 53–57)

This now only applies to companies, and to individuals to establish 'frozen' indexation up to 5 April 1998.

A company that makes a capital gain is allowed to deduct not only its actual acquisition value, but also a proportion representing the increase in the RPI between the month of acquisition and the month of disposal. The formula used is $[(RD - RI) \div RI]$ where:

RD = retail prices index in month of disposal

RI = retail prices index for March 1982 or month in which expenditure incurred, whichever is the later.

Example – Indexation

A acquired shares in X plc on 1 June 1991 for £20,000. He sells them in January 1997 for £30,000. The gain before indexation is £10,000. Indexation relief is as follows:

$$\text{Cost } £20,000 \times \frac{\text{RPI for January 1997} - \text{RPI for June 1991}}{\text{RPI for June 1991}}$$

$$\text{That is} \quad £20,000 \times \frac{157.5 - 134.1}{134.1} \quad \text{or } £20,000 \times 0.174 = £3,480$$

The chargeable gain is £6,520.

Restriction to indexation relief
(TCGA 1992, s 55(2A))

Indexation relief may only reduce or extinguish a gain; it cannot convert a gain into a loss or increase a loss.

5.6 TAPER RELIEF

5.6.1 Overview

The effect of taper relief (s 2A) is that the amount on which CGT is levied, on non-corporate taxpayers, is reduced by a percentage that varies according to the length of time (up to ten years) an asset is held. A different scale of percentages applies to gains on the disposal of business assets and non-business assets. Also for business assets, there is an extension to the general definition applying for assets acquired before 17 March 1998. The period for which the asset has been held after 5 April 1998 is, for disposals in 1998–99 and 1999–2000, notionally extended by a 'bonus' year.

For disposals of business assets made after 5 April 2000, the maximum relief is obtained after four complete years. However, the 'bonus' year given for business assets held on 17 March 1998 is not available for disposals of business assets made after 5 April 2000.

Indexation allowance (s 53) is frozen as at April 1998 for expenditure prior to that date, and does not apply at all for later expenditure. Indexation remains available for disposals by companies, to whom taper relief does not apply.

5.6.2 **How taper relief is given**
(TCGA 1992, s 2A)

Taper relief is given as an adjustment to the amount otherwise chargeable to CGT for the tax year concerned. This is the amount by which a person's chargeable gains for a tax year exceeds the aggregate of any allowable losses arising in that tax year and any unrelieved allowable losses brought forward from earlier tax years (s 2(2)). Where there is such an excess, taper relief is available if the excess is, or includes the whole or a part of any chargeable gain that is, eligible for taper relief. CGT is then chargeable only on a reduced amount which is found by taking the amount otherwise chargeable to CGT and recomputing the reduced amount as follows:

(1) taper relief is applied to so much of every chargeable gain as is eligible for the relief which is represented within the excess;
(2) the reduced amounts of each such gain are then aggregated;
(3) to this aggregate is then added the full amount of any gain, represented in the excess, but not eligible for taper relief.

It is necessary to establish whether the asset on which a chargeable gain has arisen is a non-business or a business asset. For a disposal of a business asset a chargeable gain is eligible for taper relief after a qualifying holding period (QHP) of at least one year. If the gain arises on disposal of a non-business asset the QHP must be of at least three years.

Taper relief is then calculated by reference to a table appropriate to non-business or business assets, as the case may be, and is applied on the basis of a percentage of the gain given by the relevant table for the number of whole years in the QHP of that asset.

The QHP for an asset is, broadly, the period for which it had been held at the time of its disposal. More specifically, the QHP starts on 6 April 1998, or on the actual date of acquisition, whichever is later, and ends with the disposal of the asset concerned.

Where taper relief applies to the whole or any part of a gain on the disposal of a non-business or business asset, that relief is given by multiplying the amount of the gain or part of a gain by the percentage given by Table 5.1 for the number of whole years in the QHP of that asset (s 2A(4) and (5), as amended by FA 2000, s 66(2)).

The extent to which the whole or any part of a gain on the disposal of a non-business or business asset is treated as represented in the excess referred to above is found by taking the deductions made to give effect to taper relief as set against chargeable gains in such order as results in the largest reduction of the amount otherwise chargeable to CGT. The first step is to identify the extent to which the chargeable gains for the year exceed the current and brought forward losses. The rules allow the individual concerned to allocate the particular gains of the year to the excess (as contrasted with being covered by allowable losses) on the basis that

Table 5.1

Gains on disposals of non-business assets		Gains on disposals of business assets after 5 April 2002	
Number of whole years in qualifying holding period	Percentage of gain chargeable	Number of whole years in qualifying holding period	Percentage of gain chargeable
–	–	1	50
–	–	2 or more	25
3	95		
4	90		
5	85		
6	80		
7	75		
8	70		
9	65		
10 or more	60		

produces the result most favourable to him. Losses carried back, from the year of an individual's death, for up to three years are treated in the same way as brought forward losses for the purposes of taper relief. They are deducted before taper relief so that the relief only applies to reduce the net gains after allowing the losses brought back.

The QHP of an asset depends on whether it is a non-business or a business asset. There are several possibilities (under s 2A(8), as inserted by FA 2000, s 66(3)):

(1) For a business asset, the QHP is the period after 5 April 1998 for which the asset had been held at the time of its disposal.
(2) For a non-business asset, where:
    (a) the time (under Sch A1, para 2) when the asset is taken to have been acquired by the person making the disposal is a time before 17 March 1998, and
    (b) there is no period which (under Sch A1, para 11 (change of activity by the company) or 12 (share subject to value shifting)) does not count for the purposes of taper relief,
    the QHP is the period after 5 April 1998 for which the asset has been held at the time of its disposal plus a 'bonus' year.
(3) For any other non-business asset, the QHP is the period after 5 April 1998 for which the asset had been held at the time of its disposal.

Note that where Sch A1, para 11 or 12 applies to deny taper relief for some part of the period of ownership of a non-business asset (ie where the asset is a holding of shares in a non-trading company where there has been either a relevant change in that company's activities or a relevant shift of value involving those shares), there is a double penalty. In addition to a reduction in the QHP being reduced (Sch A1, para 2(4)), the 'bonus year' is also withdrawn. Schedule A1, para 10 (periods of limited exposure to fluctuations in value) can also reduce the QHP, but in that case the bonus year is not forfeited.

Where the period after 5 April 1998 for which an asset had been held at the time of its disposal includes any period which, under Sch A1, para 10 or 12, is a period that does not count for taper relief purposes (Sch A1, para 2(4)):

(a) the asset's QHP is reduced by the length of any period that does not count; and
(b) any period that does not count:
    (i) is left out of account in computing the ten-year period ending with the time of disposal; and
    (ii) is assumed not to be comprised in the asset's relevant period of ownership.

In the context of the EIS, the QHP of the original shares for taper relief purposes is the period beginning with the date of issue of the original shares and ending with the date of the relevant disposal (Sch 5BA, para 3). This is subject to adjustment if there are periods that do not count for taper relief purposes.

Schedule A1 provides more detailed rules for applying taper relief.

The following points are worth noting:

(1) Except in relation to companies, indexation ceased to run on 6 April 1998. The new scheme is advantageous to persons whose assets have a comparatively low acquisition cost (eg shares in newly formed companies). In their case the taper relief reduces the amount chargeable to a percentage of the gain. Under indexation, the gain was reduced only by a percentage of the acquisition cost.

(2) For acquisitions after 6 April 1998 the QHP runs from when the asset is first acquired. This is of considerable importance if the asset's value is disproportionately enhanced by subsequent allowable expenditure. No adjustment to taper relief is made for subsequent expenditure.

(3) Losses are not tapered. Care is needed to ensure that sufficient untapered gains or gains qualifying only for a smaller amount of taper relief are realised in a tax year where the taxpayer has allowable losses.

(4) Taper relief does not apply to gains realised by companies (because s 2(2) only applies to CGT, and s 2A applies only where there are net gains chargeable to CGT).

(5) Indexation continues to apply to companies. Furthermore, indexation continues to apply to the gains of non-resident close companies apportioned to participators under s 13.

(6) Changes in the rules for shares and other assets to qualify as business assets took effect for periods of ownership from 6 April 2000. As a result, some shares and other assets might be treated as non-business assets for periods of ownership up to 5 April 2000 but as business assets after 5 April 2000. The gain on disposal is apportioned between a gain on a business asset and a gain on a non-business asset.

5.6.3 Definitions of general application to taper relief rules

Period for which asset held and relevant period of ownership
(TCGA 1992, Sch A1, para 2)

When an asset is disposed of after 5 April 1998, the period of ownership is taken as measured down to the time of its disposal. It is taken as the period for which the asset had been held at time of disposal which:

- begins with whichever is the later of 6 April 1998 and the time when the asset concerned was acquired by the person making the disposal; and
- ends with the time of the disposal on which the gain accrued.

This rule applies equally to non-business and business assets. Taper relief is, however, given only for the 'relevant period of ownership'. This is whichever is the shorter of:

- the period after 5 April 1998 for which the asset had been held at time of disposal; and
- the period of ten years then ending.

Certain matters are disregarded in determining whether a person is treated for this purpose as having acquired an asset. The matters concerned are:

(1) the death of a person entitled to an interest in settled property (as against trustees) insofar as it treats the asset concerned as acquired at a date before 6 April 1965 (s 73(1)(b));
(2) employee trusts (s 239(2)(b));
(3) gifts to charities (s 257(2)(b)); and
(4) gifts to housing associations (s 259(2)(b)).

Where the period after 5 April 1998 for which an asset had been held at time of disposal includes any period that does not count for taper relief purposes, certain adjustments are required. The periods concerned are those of:

(a) limited exposure to fluctuations in value (Sch A1, para 10);
(b) share ownership where there has been a change of activity by a company (para 11); and
(c) ownership affected by value shifting (para 12).

The adjustments required are:

(1) reduce the asset's QHP by the length of the period, or by the aggregate of the lengths of such periods;

(2) leave such period(s) concerned out of account in computing the ten-year period ending at the time of the asset's disposal; and

(3) assume that such periods are not comprised in the asset's relevant period of ownership.

These rules are modified in the following circumstances (Sch A1, para 5):

- Options (Sch A1, para 13)
- Assets derived from other assets (para 14)
- Assets transferred between spouses (para 15)
- Postponed gains (para 16)
- Property settled by a company (para 17)
- Assets acquired in the reconstruction of mutual businesses, etc (para 18)
- Ancillary trust funds (para 19).

Relevant period of ownership
(TCGA 1992, Sch A1, para 2)

The 'relevant period of ownership' (RPO) is a period, within the period of ownership, being whichever is the shorter of the period after 5 April 1998 for which the asset had been held at the time of its disposal and the ten-year period then ending.

5.6.4 Business or non-business assets

Basic rule
(TCGA 1992, Sch A1, para 3)

The basic rule is that a chargeable gain accruing to any person on the disposal of any asset is a gain on its disposal if it was a business asset throughout its RPO. This is subject to a number of modifications to deal with particular circumstances.

Suppose eg that a person realises a chargeable gain on the disposal of an asset that has not been a business asset throughout its RPO, but *has* been a business asset for periods comprising *part* of its RPO. In such event, a proportional part of that gain is treated as a gain on the disposal of a business asset, with the remainder treated as a gain on the disposal of a non-business asset.

A slightly different treatment is applied where, under the above rules, there are gains on a joint disposal of both a non-business asset *and* a business asset. The two gains are treated for taper relief as separate gains on separate disposals of separate assets. However, the periods after 5 April 1998 for which each of the assets is treated as having been held at the time of their disposal is the same and is determined without reference to the length of the RPO and the periods throughout which an asset is taken to have been a business asset.

5.6.5 Conditions for shares to qualify as business assets
(TCGA 1992, Sch A1, para 4(1)-(5))

There is a number of rules which apply in particular circumstances, and set out how to determine, in those particular circumstances, whether a disposal of shares or of an interest in shares in a company (here referred to as the 'relevant company') can be treated as a disposal of the underlying business assets.

Disposal by an individual

The asset is treated as a business asset if, at time of disposal, the relevant company is a qualifying company by reference to that individual.

Disposal by the trustees of a settlement

The asset is treated as a business asset if, at time of disposal, the relevant company is a qualifying company by reference to those trustees.

Disposal by an individual's personal representatives

The asset is treated as a business asset if, at time of disposal,

(1) the relevant company is a trading company or the holding company of a trading group; and
(2) not less than 25% of the voting rights in that company are exercisable by the deceased's personal representatives.

Disposal by a legatee

A special rule applies where the disposal is made by an individual who acquired the asset as a legatee (under s 64) at which time the asset was represented by shares in a company which would, at that time, have been a qualifying company by reference to him. In such a case the asset is treated as a business asset at that time if, at that time, it was held by the deceased's personal representatives.

5.6.6 Conditions for other assets to qualify as business assets
(TCGA 1992, Sch A1, para 5(1)-(5))

The following rules apply to determine whether, prior to its disposal, an asset other than shares, or an interest in shares, is a business asset.

Disposals by individuals

For disposals by an individual, the asset is treated as a business asset if, at time of disposal, it was being used, wholly or partly, for any one or more of the following purposes:

(1) a trade carried on at that time by him or a partnership of which he was at that time a member;

(2) any trade carried on by a company which at that time was
   (a) a qualifying company by reference to him; or
   (b) a member of a trading group the holding company of which was a qualifying company by reference to him;

(3) any qualifying office or employment to which he was at that time required to devote substantially the whole of his time; and/or

(4) any other office or employment provided that it was with a trading company in relation to which he was, at that time, a full-time working officer or employee.

Disposal by trustees of a settlement

The asset is treated as a business asset if, at time of disposal, it was being used, wholly or partly, for any one or more of the following purposes:

(1) a trade carried on at the time by the settlement trustees;

(2) a trade carried on at that time by an eligible beneficiary or by a partnership of which an eligible beneficiary was at that time a member;

(3) any trade carried on by a company which at that time was
   (a) a qualifying company by reference to the settlement trustees or an eligible beneficiary; or
   (b) a member of a trading group the holding company of which was at that time a qualifying company by reference to the settlement trustees or an eligible beneficiary;

(4) any qualifying office or employment to which an eligible beneficiary was at that time required to devote substantially the whole of his time; and/or

(5) any office or employment provided that it was with a trading company in relation to which an eligible beneficiary was, at that time, a full-time working officer or employee.

Disposal by an individual's personal representatives

The asset is treated as a business asset if, at time of disposal, it was being used, wholly or partly, for any one or more of the following purposes:

(1) a trade carried on by the deceased's personal representatives; and/or

(2) any trade carried on by a company which at that time was
   (a) a qualifying company by reference to the deceased's personal representatives; or

(b) a member of a trading group the holding company of which was at that time a qualifying company by reference to the deceased's personal representatives.

Disposal by a legatee

A special rule applies where the disposal is made by an individual who acquired the asset as a legatee (under s 64) at which time the asset does not qualify as a business asset under the rules applying for individuals but, being held by the deceased's personal representatives, is being used wholly or partly for a purpose within the rules for personal representatives. In such a case the asset is treated as a business asset at that time if, at that time, it was so held and used by the personal representatives.

5.6.7 Companies that are qualifying companies
(TCGA 1992, Sch A1, para 6(1)-(3))

The following rules are applied to determine whether a company is a qualifying company.

By reference to an individual

A company is a qualifying company by reference to an individual at any time when the following conditions are satisfied:

(1) it is a trading company or the holding company of a trading group, and
(2) one or more of the following conditions is met:
    (a) it is unlisted;
    (b) the individual is an officer or employee of the company, or of a company having a relevant connection with it; and/or
    (c) the voting rights in the company are exercisable, as to not less than 5%, by him.

By reference to the trustees of a settlement

A company is a qualifying company by reference to the trustees of a settlement at any time when:

(1) it was a trading company or the holding company of a trading group, and
(2) one or more of the following conditions is met:
    (a) it is unlisted;
    (b) an eligible beneficiary is an officer or employee of the company, or of a company having a relevant connection with it; or
    (c) the voting rights in the company are exercisable, as to not less than 5%, by the trustees.

By reference to an individual's personal representatives

A company is taken to have been a qualifying company by reference to an individual's personal representatives at any time when:

(1) the company was a trading company or the holding company of a trading group, and
(2) one or more of the following conditions was met:
    (a) the company was unlisted; or
    (b) the voting rights in the company were exercisable, as to not less than 5%, by the personal representatives.

In the above cases, prior to 6 April 2000, the voting rights test was applied as to not less than 25%.

5.6.8 Persons who are eligible beneficiaries
(TCGA 1992, Sch A1, para 7)

An eligible beneficiary, in relation to an asset comprised in a settlement and a time, is any individual having at that time *a relevant interest in possession* under the settlement in either:

- the whole of the settled property; or
- a part of the settled property that is or includes that asset.

For this purpose 'relevant interest in possession', in relation to property comprised in a settlement, means any interest in possession under that settlement other than:

- a right under that settlement to receive an annuity; or
- a fixed-term entitlement.

Here, 'fixed-term entitlement', in relation to property comprised in a settlement, means any interest under that settlement which is limited to a term that is fixed and is not a term at the end of which the person with that interest will become entitled to the property.

5.6.9 Cases where there are non-qualifying beneficiaries
(TCGA 1992, Sch A1, para 8)

A further rule applies to a disposal of an asset by the trustees of a settlement where the asset's RPO is or includes a period throughout which:

- the asset was a business asset by reference to one or more eligible beneficiaries;
- the asset would not otherwise have been a business asset; and
- there is a non-qualifying part of the relevant income, or there would be if there were any relevant income for that period.

This is referred to as a 'sharing period'.

The period throughout which the asset disposed of is to be taken to have been a business asset is determined as if the relevant fraction of every sharing period were a period throughout which the asset was not a business asset. Here, 'the relevant fraction', in relation to any sharing period, is that representing the proportion of relevant income for that period which is, or (if there were such income) would be, a non-qualifying part of that income. Where a sharing period is a period in which such proportion has been different at various times, a separate relevant fraction has to be determined for, and applied to, each part of that period for which there is a different proportion. The non-qualifying part of any relevant income for any period is so much of that income for that period as is or, as the case may be, would be income to which:

- no eligible beneficiary has any entitlement; or
- a non-qualifying eligible beneficiary has an entitlement.

A 'non-qualifying eligible beneficiary', in relation to a period, means an eligible beneficiary who is not a beneficiary by reference to whom (if he were the only beneficiary) the asset disposed of would be a business asset throughout that period. 'Relevant income' is income from the part of the settled property comprising the asset disposed of.

5.6.10 Cases where asset used at same time for different purposes
(TCGA 1992, Sch A1, para 9)

A special rule applies to a disposal by any person of an asset where the asset's RPO is or includes a 'mixed-use period' throughout which the asset was:

- a business asset by reference to the conditions for other assets to qualify as business assets (Sch A1, para 5(2)-(5)); but
- at the same time, being put to a non-qualifying use.

The period throughout which the asset disposed of is to be taken to have been a business asset is determined as if the relevant fraction of every mixed-use period were a period throughout which the asset was not a business asset. Here, 'the relevant fraction', in relation to any mixed-use period, means the fraction that represents the proportion of the asset's use during that period that was a non-qualifying use.

A special rule applies in circumstances where both of the rules for cases where there are non-qualifying beneficiaries (Sch A1, para 8) apply to cases where an asset is used at the same time for different purposes. In such event, the rules for cases where there are non-qualifying beneficiaries take precedence. Further reductions in the period for which the asset disposed of is taken to have been a business asset are made only in respect of the relevant part of any non-qualifying use. In this context, the relevant part of any non-qualifying use is the proportion of that use which is not a use to which a non-qualifying part of any relevant income is attributable.

The following rule applies where a mixed-use period is a period in which:

(1) the proportion of the asset's use during that period that was a non-qualifying use has been different at various times, or

(2) different attributions have to be made for different parts of the period because both of the rules for cases where there are non-qualifying beneficiaries apply to cases where an asset is used at the same time for different purposes.

In such cases, a separate relevant fraction has to be determined for, and applied to, each part of the period for which there is a different proportion or attribution.

Under these rules, 'non-qualifying use', in relation to an asset, means any use of the asset for purposes that are not purposes for which the asset would fall to be treated as a business asset at the time of its use.

The non-qualifying part of any relevant income for any period is so much of that income for that period as is or, as the case may be, would be income to which:

- no eligible beneficiary has any entitlement; or
- a non-qualifying eligible beneficiary has an entitlement.

'Relevant income' is income from the part of the settled property comprising the asset disposed of.

5.6.11 Anti-avoidance measures

In order to prevent manipulation of the taper relief rules so as to gain a tax advantage, or to mitigate the effect of the rules, a number of anti-avoidance measures are built into the legislation. The areas concerned are:

- Periods of limited exposure to fluctuations (Sch A1, para 10)
- Periods of share ownership where there is a change of activity by the company (para 11)
- Periods of share ownership where there is value shifting (para 12)
- Special rules where property is settled by a company (para 17).

5.6.12 Miscellaneous special rules

There are rules to deal with a number of special situations:

- Options (Sch A1, para 13)
- Further rules for assets derived from other assets (para 14)
- Assets transferred between spouses (para 15)
- Postponed gains (para 16)
- Assets acquired in the reconstruction of mutual businesses (para 18)

- Ancillary trust funds (para 19)
- General rule for settlements (para 20)
- General rule for apportionments (para 21).

5.6.13 Disposals of business assets after 5 April 2002
(FA 2002, s 45)

Taper relief progressively reduces the amount of a gain that is charged to CGT on the disposal of an asset the longer that asset is held after 5 April 1998. Taper relief applies to the capital gains of individuals, trusts and the personal representatives of deceased persons, but not to the chargeable gains of companies.

Different taper rates apply to non-business and business assets. Business assets include those used in an individual's own trade, and certain shareholdings in trading companies.

From 6 April 2002, the effective rate of tax for higher rate taxpayers on chargeable gains on assets that have always been business assets is reduced to 20% after a holding period of one year, and 10% after only two years.

The existing and new effective rates for disposals of business assets by higher rate taxpayers are set out in the following table.

Table 15.2

Whole years held from 6 April 1998	Existing rates		New rates (disposals from 6 April 2002)	
	Percentage of gain charged to tax	Effective rate of tax for higher rate taxpayer (%)	Percentage of gain charged to tax	Effective rate of tax for higher rate taxpayer (%)
<1	100	40	100	40
1	87.5	35	50	20
2	75	30	25	10
3	50	20	25	10
4 or more	25	10	25	10

This change applies to all relevant disposals made on or after 6 April 2002, and not just to disposals of business assets held for more than two years after that date.

Example

An asset is acquired on 5 June 2000 and sold on 10 July 2002. It was a business asset throughout the period of ownership. Because it had been held for more than two whole years at the time of disposal, 25% of the gain is chargeable to tax.

There is no change to the non-business assets taper, nor is there any change to the definition of a business asset. If an asset has been both a non-business asset and a business asset, the gain on disposal is apportioned to reflect the time that the asset was a business asset and the time that it was a non-business asset. The apportioned gain on the business asset benefits from business assets taper relief at the new rates proposed by this clause, as the example below shows.

Example

An asset was acquired on 6 July 1999 and disposed of on 6 July 2002. It was a non-business asset from 6 July 1999 to 5 July 2000, and a business asset from 6 July 2000 to 6 July 2002. Thus the total holding period was three years, one year as a non-business asset, and two years as a business asset. The total gain on disposal was £18,000.

The gain is apportioned to reflect the proportions of time that the asset was a non-business and a business asset. So, one third of the gain is treated as a gain on a non-business asset, ie

$$\text{⅓ of £18,000 = £6,000.}$$

Two thirds of the gain is treated as a gain on a business asset, ie

$$\text{⅔ of £18,000 = £12,000}$$

Each gain receives three years' worth of taper relief at the appropriate rate. Therefore 95% of the gain on the non-business asset and 25% of the buiness asset is charged to tax, ie

$$\text{95\% of £6,000 = £5,700}$$
$$\text{25\% of £12,000 = £3,000}$$

The total gain charged to tax is £5,750 + £3,000 = £8,750.

5.7 SOME SPECIAL PROBLEM AREAS

5.7.1 Land and buildings

The basic principles apply in computing gains on land and buildings as they do for other assets. However, there are certain complications that arise regularly in practice.

Expenditure on improvements

Where a property is disposed of, bear in mind that the acquisition cost includes allowable enhancement expenditure only if the expenditure is reflected in the state of the property at date of disposal. Thus, beware of a situation where property has a high cost but much of the enhancement expenditure relates to additions or improvements that have been worn out, or have themselves been replaced.

Disallowed initial repairs

The reverse situation often applies where a property is acquired in a very poor state of repair. Expenditure incurred in bringing it into a fit condition is often disallowed. Such repairs are treated as capital expenditure. Where this has happened, the amount disallowed in computing trading profits or Schedule A income can be treated as enhancement expenditure for CGT purposes.

Past expenditure qualified for capital allowances

A trader's expenditure on a building may include sums that have qualified for capital allowances, eg expenditure on installing a lift or carrying out structural work so that a computer can be installed. Such expenditure can be allowed for CGT purposes provided it does not mean there is a loss.

Leases with less than 50 years to run
(TCGA 1992, s 240 & Sch 8)

Another aspect to bear in mind is that the interest in the property being disposed of may be a lease that has less than 50 years to run and is therefore regarded as a wasting asset. Where a person disposes of such an asset, his acquisition value is restricted according to specific rules that effectively write off the cost of a wasting asset over the period of its life.

Example – Disposal of short lease

A Ltd purchased a 20-year lease in 1985 for £100,000. In 1995 it disposes of the lease for £100,000. However, this is not a no gain/no loss situation as the proper calculation is as follows:

	£	£
Disposal proceeds		100,000
Original cost of lease	100,000	
Reduced by $\dfrac{72.770 - 46.695}{72.770}$ =	(35,832)	
		(64,168)
Gain before indexation		35,832

The figures of 72.770 and 46.695 for 20- and ten-year leases are contained in the table in Sch 8.

Time apportionment and land held before 6 April 1965
(TCGA 1992, s 35 & Sch 2)

Where a person has owned land or buildings since a date prior to 6 April 1965, it may be possible for any capital gain to be computed on the time apportionment basis. This is not possible if the person has made a universal rebasing election (see 5.5.3) or if the land or buildings have development value when they are sold.

The time apportionment basis operates on the assumption that appreciation has occurred at an even rate over the total period of ownership. Because CGT was first introduced on 6 April 1965, the chargeable gain is computed as follows:

$$\text{Overall gain} \times \frac{\text{Period since 6 April 1965} - \text{date of disposal}}{\text{Total period of ownership}}$$

Example – Where time apportionment basis is beneficial

B Ltd sells an agricultural property in March 2001 for £510,000. It was originally acquired in April 1945 for £10,000. Its value at 31 March 1982 was £150,000. Ignoring indexation, the time apportionment basis produces the following result:

$$£500,000 \times \frac{\text{6 April 1965} - \text{March 2001 (36 years)}}{\text{6 April 1945} - \text{March 2001 (56 years)}} = £321,429$$

This compares with a gain of £350,000 before indexation if the gain is measured by reference to the 31 March 1982 value.

5.7.2 Unquoted shares

A valuation may be required where a shareholder makes a gift or there is some other disposal that is not a bargain at arm's length and the transaction is treated as a disposal at market value (see 5.5.1). A valuation may also be required at 31 March 1982 where this value may be deducted instead of original cost in computing the person's capital gain (see 5.5.3). In both these situations, it is generally necessary to negotiate with the Revenue's Shares Valuation Division. This division operates according to long established rules that have been upheld by court decisions.

Valuation of minority shareholdings

It must not be assumed that the value of a 10% shareholding is the same as 10% of the value of the company as a whole. A firm distinction is drawn between a 51% or greater shareholding which carries control and a minority shareholding. The Revenue's normal view is that the underlying assets are irrelevant when valuing a small minority shareholding and what matters is the dividend history and the extent to which an investor could reasonably expect the past level of dividends to be maintained in the future.

General principles

One aspect to be borne in mind is that the definition of market value for capital gains purposes is the value for the person who acquires the asset. In this regard, the valuation may differ from that used for IHT purposes (see 22.3.3). Thus, if an individual makes a gift out of his 51% shareholding of shares which add up to 17% of the company's share capital, the disposal is normally deemed to take place at a consideration equal to the market value of a 17% shareholding.

Special rules where series of connected disposals made
(TCGA 1992, ss 19 and 20)

There are anti-avoidance provisions designed to prevent a person achieving an advantage by making several separate disposals to connected persons. Basically, the anti-avoidance provisions apply where a person makes several gifts or other disposals to connected persons within a six-year period and the value of the property given away in stages is more, when valued at a totality, than the combined value of the separate gifts.

Example – How a series of gifts may be dealt with

A made five separate gifts of shares in B Ltd to his son. Assume that an 11% shareholding in B Ltd is worth only £20,000 whereas a 55% controlling shareholding has a value of £300,000.

Where the Revenue is able to apply the anti-avoidance legislation, the transactions are linked and the individual is assessed as if he had made a disposal on each occasion on a part of the overall value. Thus, A would be deemed to have made five separate disposals on the basis that the deemed disposal proceeds on each occasion amounted to £60,000 (ie ⅕ of the value of a 55% shareholding).

Valuing shareholdings at 31 March 1982

When valuing shares it is not normally appropriate to have regard to shares held by a connected person. Thus, if a husband and wife each held 30% of the shares in a company at 31 March 1982, each shareholding should be valued on the basis of a 30% minority shareholding, even though when taken together the husband and wife would have control. However, the Revenue operates an extra statutory concession so that if a husband and wife held 30% each at 31 March 1982, but one spouse later transferred all his or her shares to the other, the 31 March 1982 value may then be based on the rights etc attaching to a 60% shareholding.

The Revenue also has a concession which deals with the converse situation. Suppose that an individual had 51% of the shares in his private company at 31 March 1982, and his wife had 9%. If he gave 21% of his shareholding to his wife with a view to equalising their shareholdings, there could be a disadvantage in that the combined value of the two 30% share-holdings might not equate to the value of a 51% and a 9% shareholding. In these circumstances, the Revenue allows the individual's wife to claim that the 21% shareholding given to her by her husband should have a 31 March 1982 value based on it being part of a 51% controlling shareholding.

Time apportionment basis

The time apportionment method of computing gains (mentioned in 5.7.1) also applies to shares in an unquoted company.

5.7.3 Foreign property

Gains should be computed in sterling

Where a foreign property or shares in a foreign company are disposed of, it is not correct to calculate the gain or loss in foreign currency terms and then convert that into sterling at the time of disposal. Instead, the following for-mula should be used:

> Disposal proceeds converted into sterling at the rates prevailing at the time of the disposal
> *Less* acquisition cost of 31 March 1982 value converted into sterling at the exchange rate prevailing at that time
> *Equals* gain before indexation.

Borrowings in foreign currency

Often an individual or partnership has financed the acquisition of a foreign property with a foreign currency loan and the foreign currency appreciates against sterling. When a disposal of the property takes place, and the loan is redeemed, the extra cost of repaying the loan is not allowable in computing the capital gain on the disposal of the asset.

Example – Gain on foreign property

A financed the purchase of a warehouse in Germany by borrowing the full pur-chase price of DM 4m. At that time, the sterling equivalent was £1m (DM 4 = £1). When *A* sells the warehouse for DM 6m, the exchange rate is DM 2.50 = £1.

Overall, *A*'s profit after repaying his loan is DM 2m ie £800,000 when one looks at the exchange rate at the time of disposal. However, for tax purposes, the transaction is broken down as follows:

	£
Sale proceeds (DM 6m converted at DM 2.50 = £1)	2,400,000
Cost (DM 4m converted at DM 4 = £1)	1,000,000
Capital gain before indexation	1,400,000
Extra cost in sterling terms of repaying loan	(600,000)

A will be taxed on his gain of £1.4m (less indexation relief) with no relief for the currency loss on repaying his borrowings.

A currency loss of this nature is also not normally allowable in computing an unincorporated trader's profits although special rules now apply for companies (see 19.11 on Forex).

5.7.4 Foreign currency
(TCGA 1992, s 252)

This is regarded as a chargeable asset and a gain (or loss) may arise when the currency is disposed of. Such a disposal may take the form of the foreign currency being spent, or being converted into another foreign currency, or converted into sterling. In each of these situations, the sterling equivalent of the foreign currency at the date of disposal is compared with the sterling equivalent at the date of acquisition.

The one circumstance where foreign currency is an exempt asset is where it was acquired for an individual's personal expenditure abroad.

6

CAPITAL GAINS TAX AND BUSINESS TRANSACTIONS

This chapter focuses on the CGT aspects of various business transactions. All legislative references are to the TCGA 1992 unless stated otherwise.

6.1 LOANS TO PRIVATE BUSINESSES

A person may make a loan to a sole trader or partnership (an 'unincorporated business') or to a private company, or may give a guarantee to a bank etc that makes a loan to a business. CGT loss relief may be available if a loan has to be written off or a person is required to make a payment under a bank guarantee given by him.

6.1.1 Loans to unincorporated businesses
(TCGA 1992, s 253)

A CGT loss may be deemed to arise if the Revenue is satisfied that a loan has become irrecoverable. There are various conditions that must be fulfilled, in that the borrower must:

(1) not be the lender's spouse;
(2) be UK-resident; and
(3) have used the loan wholly for the purposes of a trade carried on by him (though not one that consists of (or includes) lending money).

When a claim is submitted, the inspector of taxes must satisfy himself that any outstanding amount of the loan is irrecoverable and that the lender has not assigned his right to recover the loan. Strictly speaking, relief is due only when a claim is made and admitted but, in practice, the Revenue permits claims to be made within two years of a tax year provided the other conditions were satisfied at the end of that year of assessment (ESC D36).

6.1.2 Loans to companies
(TCGA 1992, s 253)

Similar provisions apply where a person has made a loan to a company which proves to be irrecoverable. The principal conditions to be satisfied are that the company must be UK-resident and must be a trading company. No relief is due where a company makes a loss on a loan to another company in the same group unless the loan is a debt on security (ie a debenture that is capable of being transferred).

6.1.3 Payments under loan guarantees
(TCGA 1992, s 253(4))

Instead of lending money to a relative or friend or his private company, an individual may have given a guarantee to a bank etc. Similarly, a director of a company may have had to give personal guarantees for bank loans to his company.

Where the borrower cannot repay the loan, the bank calls on the guarantor to pay the amount due. In such a case, the guarantor may be able to claim a CGT loss under s 253 as if he had made a loan that was irrecoverable. The conditions to be satisfied to claim such relief are that:

(1) payment has been made under a guarantee;
(2) the payment should arise from a formal calling in of the guarantee – a voluntary payment attracts no relief;
(3) the original loan met the requirements listed in 6.1.1;
(4) the amount paid under the guarantee cannot be recovered either from the borrower or from a co-guarantor.

Where a company has guaranteed another UK company's borrowings and the money has been used for the borrower's trade, a payment under the guarantee may qualify under TA 1988, s 253. This still applies even if the guarantor and borrower are members of the same group of companies.

6.2 LOSSES ON UNQUOTED SHARES
(TA 1988, s 574)

6.2.1 Special relief for subscribers

From time to time, an individual may invest in a private company, either as a working director/shareholder or perhaps as a 'passive' investor with a minority shareholding. Investments may also be made in companies which, while they are public companies as defined by the Companies Act 1985, are not quoted companies.

A loss may arise on a disposal of shares in such a company. If the investor acquired existing shares by purchasing them, the loss is a normal

CGT loss and the only way in which it can be relieved is by its being set against capital gains. However, if the individual acquired his shares by *subscribing* for new ones, it may be possible to obtain income tax relief for the loss. Subject to certain conditions, the capital loss may be off-set against his income for the year in which the loss is realised. The following conditions must be satisfied:

(1) The loss must arise from one of the following:
    (a) a sale made at arm's length for full consideration (this rules out a sale to a connected person); or
    (b) a disposal that takes place when the company is wound up; or
    (c) a deemed disposal where the shares have become of negligible value.

(2) There are conditions that relate to the company itself, in particular:
    (a) It must have been UK-resident throughout the period from its incorporation until the date of the individual's disposal of shares.
    (b) It must not have been a quoted company at any time during his period of ownership. The fact that any class of shares has had a Stock Exchange quote rules out relief under TA 1988, s 574 even though the loss may have arisen on a class of share that did not have a quote.
    (c) It must be a trading company, or the holding company of a trading group, at the date of disposal or it must have ceased to have been a trading company not more than three years prior to the date of disposal and it must not have been an investment company since that date.
    (d) Its trade must not have consisted wholly or mainly of dealing in shares, securities, land, trades or commodity futures.
    (e) Its trade must have been carried on on a commercial basis.

6.2.2 Relief also available for subscriber's spouse

The spouse of a person who subscribed for shares may also claim relief under TA 1988, s 574 where he has acquired them through an *inter vivos* transfer from his spouse. However, shares acquired on a spouse's death do not entitle the widow(er) to s 574 relief on a subsequent disposal.

6.2.3 Nature of relief

The loss is calculated according to normal CGT principles. If it is eligible for relief under TA 1988, s 574, the individual may elect within two years for the loss to be set against his taxable income. It may be set against his taxable income either for the year of the loss or for the preceding year. Either claim may be made independently of the other. Where he has losses which are available for s 574 relief and he is also entitled to relief for trading losses (see 17.6), he can choose which losses should be relieved in priority to the other.

Any part of the capital loss that cannot be relieved under s 574 can be carried forward for set-off against capital gains in the normal way.

6.2.4 Similar relief for companies
(TA 1988, s 573)

There is a similar relief for investment companies (see 19.8.5) that realise capital losses. Once again, the shares must have been acquired by subscription. The shares must not be in a subsidiary company or in an associated company (see 19.2.6).

Once again, the investment company's capital loss must be computed on ordinary CGT principles. If relief is required under TA 1988, s 573, an election must be submitted to the Revenue within two years of the end of the company's accounting period in which the loss is realised. The loss may then be set against the company's income and other profits for that year. If the loss exceeds the company's profits for that period, the excess is carried back and set against profits of the preceding accounting period. Any balance can then be carried forward and set against the investment company's capital gains.

6.3 ROLL-OVER RELIEF

6.3.1 Basic principles
(TCGA 1992, s 152(1) and (2))

Relief may be available where a person disposes of an asset used by him in a trade (or, in certain circumstances, by his family company) and reinvests in replacement assets used for business purposes. This relief is termed 'roll-over' relief. The gain is said to be rolled over in that it is not charged to tax, but is deducted from the person's acquisition cost of the new assets.

Example – Roll-over relief

A sells a farm for £450,000; his capital gain is £200,000. He starts up a new business and invests £500,000 in a warehouse.

By claiming roll-over relief, A avoids having to pay tax on the £200,000 gain. The acquisition cost of his warehouse is reduced as follows:

	£
Actual cost	500,000
Less rolled-over gain	(200,000)
Deemed acquisition cost	300,000

The relief is really a form of deferment since a larger gain will arise on the replacement asset's subsequent disposal.

6.3.2 Conditions that need to be satisfied
(TCGA 1992, s 155)

There must be a relevant disposal, although this need not be a sale and could eg be a gift or an exchange of assets. The asset disposed of must have been used in a business and have fallen into one of the following categories:

Class 1   Head A: Land and buildings
            Head B: Fixed plant and machinery
Class 2   Ships, aircraft and hovercraft
Class 3   Satellites, space-stations and spacecraft
Class 4   Goodwill
Class 5   Milk and potato quotas
Class 6   Ewe and suckler cow premium quotas
Class 7   Fish quotas
Class 8   Lloyd's syndicate rights ('capacity').

The replacement assets must also fall into one of these categories, but not necessarily the same category as the one that has been sold. Moreover, the asset can be used for a completely different trade. It is not possible to claim roll-over relief on the disposal of shares in a family company, nor is it possible to claim it for expenditure on such shares on the basis that this is replacement expenditure.

The replacement assets must normally be acquired within a period starting one year before the date of the original asset's disposal and ending three years after that date. The time limit can be extended (at the Revenue's discretion) if the acquisition of replacement assets within three years was not possible because of circumstances outside the person's control.

Example – Full relief available only where all sale proceeds reinvested
(TCGA 1992, ss 152(3)-(11) and 154)

> Using the same figures as above, *A* starts up a new business but invests only £400,000 in the new warehouse. The part of the £450,000 disposal consideration for the farm which is not applied in acquiring the warehouse is £50,000. This is less than the gain that arose on the disposal of the farm and the balance of the gain may be rolled over. The warehouse's acquisition value is reduced by £150,000.

6.3.3 Old assets not used for business throughout ownership

In such a case, s 152(7) applies as if a part of the asset used for the purposes of the trade was a separate asset to that which had not been wholly used for those purposes.

Example – Old assets

In April 2000, *B* sells a hotel for a gain, after indexation has been calculated, of £50,000. It had originally been bought in April 1992 but was at first let out as an investment. *B* used it for a trade carried on by him only from April 1994. The amount of gain that can be rolled over into the purchase of a new asset is calculated as follows:

$$\text{Chargeable gain £50,000} \times \frac{\text{period of trading use of old asset}}{\text{period of ownership}}$$

This equals £50,000 × ¾ = £37,500. The balance of £12,500 (£50,000 – £37,500) is a chargeable gain.

6.3.4 Treatment where replacement assets are wasting assets
(TCGA 1992, s 154)

The roll-over relief is modified where the replacement expenditure consists of the purchase of a wasting asset (ie with an expected useful life of less than 50 years) or an asset that will become a wasting asset within ten years. Plant and machinery is always considered to have a useful life of less than 50 years. Furthermore, a lease acquired with less than 60 years to run also constitutes a wasting asset, but, rather paradoxically, the goodwill of a business is not.

The capital gain in these circumstances is not deferred indefinitely, but becomes chargeable on the first of the following occasions:

(1) the disposal of the replacement asset; or
(2) the asset ceasing to be used in the business; or
(3) the expiry of ten years.

Examples – Roll-over relief on wasting assets

(1) *C* sells a factory and reinvests in a 59-year lease of a warehouse which he uses in his business. In the sixth year the warehouse is let as an investment property. The rolled-over gain would become chargeable in Year 6.
(2) *D* also rolls over into a 59-year lease. He is still using the property after ten years, but because it has become a wasting asset within that period, the rolled-over gain becomes chargeable in Year 10.

6.3.5 Reinvestment in non-wasting assets
(TCGA 1992, s 154(5))

If a person acquires new non-wasting replacement assets during the ten years, the capital gain that was originally rolled over into the purchase of the wasting assets can be transferred to the replacement assets. Assume in example (1) above that *C* had bought the goodwill of a business in Year 5. He could transfer his roll-over relief claim to the new asset. No gain would then become chargeable in Year 6 when he lets the warehouse.

6.3.6 Replacement asset must be brought into use

Temperley v Visibell [1974] STC 64 concerned a company that purchased land to build a factory. In the event, planning permission was refused and the factory never built. It was held that the intention to use an asset for the trade was not sufficient and the expenditure on the land did not qualify for roll-over relief.

However, where the replacement asset is not brought into use right away, roll-over relief may still be available if the following conditions are satisfied:

(a) the trader proposes to incur capital expenditure for the purpose of enhancing its value;
(b) any work arising from such expenditure begins as soon as possible after acquisition, and is completed within a reasonable time;
(c) on completion of the work the asset is taken into use solely for the purpose of the trade; and
(d) the asset is not let or used for any non-trading purpose in the period between acquisition and the time it is taken into use for the purpose of the trade.

6.3.7 Acquisition of freehold

The Revenue used to deny roll-over relief where a trader acquired a further interest in an asset already used by him for his trade, eg where a tenant farmer bought the freehold. ESC D25 now provides relief as if the expenditure were on a new asset.

6.3.8 Roll-over relief for partners

Where a partnership owned the asset disposed, part of the gain belongs to each partner (see 6.5) and it is up to him to claim roll-over relief. Because the replacement asset need not be used by the disponor in the same trade, an individual partner may roll over by incurring expenditure on his own account, whereas other partners may choose not to do so.

Roll-over relief can be secured where the replacement assets are used by a partnership in which the owner is a partner (SP D11).

6.3.9 Use by individual's personal trading company
(TCGA 1992, s 157)

Relief can also be obtained where an individual disposes of a property etc used by his 'personal trading company', but only if the replacement asset is acquired by him and is used by the same company. A personal trading company is one in which the individual personally owns at least 5% of the voting shares. He need not be a director – indeed he need not even be employed by it. Nor is roll-over relief lost because he has charged the company rent.

6.3.10 Assets owned by employee or office-holder
(TCGA 1992, s 158)

An employee or office-holder may claim roll-over relief where he disposes of an asset used in the employment. This condition may apply eg to a sub-postmaster who has an 'office' for tax purposes, but generally owns the sub-post office premises. For further details, see SP5/86.

There are circumstances where these provisions mean that a director of a family company who has sold an asset used by one company, and bought new assets used by another family company, is entitled to roll-over relief. However, this is a difficult area where professional advice is essential.

6.4 HOLD-OVER RELIEF: GIFTS OF BUSINESS PROPERTY
(TCGA 1992, s 165)

Under the legislation that applied up to 5 April 1989, a UK-resident individual could transfer any asset to another UK-resident person on a no gain/no loss basis by claiming hold-over relief.

Example – Hold-over relief

> *E* transferred shares in X plc to her brother *F* in 1988. They were both UK-resident. *E*'s shares were worth £29,000 and her capital gain would normally have been £13,000. By claiming hold-over relief, *E* could avoid having a chargeable gain of £13,000. *F*'s acquisition value was then taken as:
>
> | | £ |
> |---|---|
> | Market value at acquisition | 29,000 |
> | *Less* held-over capital gain | (13,000) |
> | | 16,000 |
>
> In 1989, the Chancellor abolished the hold-over relief for gifts in general. However, the same type of relief can still be claimed on gifts of business property and shares in unquoted trading companies.

6.4.1 Definition of 'business property'
(TCGA 1992, s 165(2))

'Business property' is defined for these purposes as:

(1) an asset used by the transferor in a trade, profession or vocation;
(2) an asset used by the transferor's personal company in a trade;
(3) an asset used for a trade by a subsidiary of the transferor's family company;
(4) agricultural land that qualifies for IHT agricultural property relief (see 22.9).

Where an asset has been used for non-qualifying purposes for part of the person's period of ownership, only a corresponding part of any capital gain may be held over.

Example – Restriction on hold-over relief

A Ltd acquired a property in March 1985 for £190,000; in 2000 it is worth £480,000. Take indexation as 84%.

To begin with, A Ltd rented it out as an investment and occupied it for its business only for the period from April 1993 to March 2000. If it transfers the property by way of a gift, its capital gain will be:

	£	£
Market value		480,000
Less cost	190,000	
Indexation	160,000	
		(350,000)
		130,000

The maximum part of the gain that may be held over is as follows:

$$\frac{\text{April 1993 to March 2000}}{\text{March 1985 to March 2000}} = \frac{7}{15}$$

Thus only £50,000 of the gain may be held over.

6.4.2 Relief on shares

The definition of 'business property' also includes:

(1) unquoted shares in a trading company; and
(2) quoted shares if the company concerned is the transferor's personal company (a condition rarely satisfied).

A similar restriction to that illustrated in the example in 6.4.1 may apply on a transfer of shares in an unquoted trading company if that company holds investments or other chargeable assets which are not business assets. The restriction is based on the following formula:

$$\frac{\text{Chargeable assets used in the business}}{\text{Total chargeable assets}}$$

Example – Restriction on hold-over relief

G gives his son his shares in X Ltd. The balance sheet of X Ltd shows assets as follows:	
	£
Stock	100,000
Factory	500,000
Investments	500,000
Cash	200,000
Only half of G's capital gain may be held over, ie	$\dfrac{\text{Value of factory}}{\text{Factory and investments}}$

6.4.3 Relief not available on certain gifts

The legislation provides that hold-over relief is available only if the recipient of the transfer is either UK-resident or ordinarily resident. Moreover, it is not available if he is dual resident, and the relevant double taxation agreement has the effect of treating him as if he were non-UK resident.

Hold-over relief is also precluded where an individual etc transfers an asset to a UK-resident company controlled by persons who are neither UK-resident nor ordinarily resident.

6.4.4 Relief for chargeable transfers for IHT purposes
(TCGA 1992, s 260)

There is a completely separate provision that provides hold-over relief where the disposal is a chargeable transfer for IHT purposes and the recipient is UK-resident or ordinarily resident. The main circumstance where this may apply is where assets are transferred by way of gift etc to a discretionary trust (see 22.10).

Where a transfer of assets comes within both ss 165 and 260, s 260 takes priority. Note that where hold-over relief is available under s 260 on a disposal that is a chargeable transfer for IHT purposes, there is no restriction as in 6.4.1 or 6.4.2 because the asset has not been used for business for the whole of the person's period of ownership, or the property includes non-business assets.

6.4.5 Clawback
(TCGA 1992, s 168)

Hold-over relief is clawed back if the recipient of the gift etc ceases to be resident within six years. The held-over gain is deemed to arise immediately before he ceases to be resident and, if he fails to pay the resultant CGT, the transferor can be held liable.

There is one circumstance where the recipient's emigration does not give rise to a chargeable gain. If he is required to work abroad because of his employment, and he returns to the UK within three years still owning the asset, the temporary 'emigration' does not count.

6.4.6 Practical aspects

In strictness, an individual's capital gain should formally be agreed even though it is held over. However, if both the transferor and transferee agree, it can be left in abeyance, to be ascertained only as and when the transferee makes a chargeable disposal. See SP8/92.

6.5 PARTNERS AND CAPITAL GAINS

The way in which CGT affects partnership transactions can be complex at times. The Revenue's practice is set out in SP D12, but this is extremely technical and professional advice should be sought to understand its implications. The following describes some key aspects.

6.5.1 Partnership's acquisition value

Although individual partners' entitlement to profits may vary from time to time, the partnership's acquisition value for the firm's chargeable assets is not affected unless there are cash payments from one partner to another to acquire a greater interest in the firm or unless assets are revalued as part of the arrangements for changes in profit sharing.

6.5.2 Assets held by firm at 31 March 1982

The partnership may make a universal rebasing election for the values at 31 March 1982 to be used instead of cost. This is quite separate from the individual partners' position in relation to their personal assets when disposal of an asset takes place. There may be partners who were not in the partnership at that date, but this does not affect the computation of the gain.

6.5.3 Partnership gains divisible among partners

Where a partnership asset is sold at a capital gain (or loss), the gain/loss is divided among the partners in accordance with their profit-sharing ratios. Each partner is personally assessable on his share of the gain. The partner's actual CGT liability depends on his own situation, ie whether he has other gains for the year, has available losses, can claim roll-over relief or is entitled to retirement relief (see 6.7).

6.5.4 Revaluations

Problems may arise where a partnership has substantial, chargeable assets that are worth more than their book value (ie the value at which they are shown in the firm's accounts). A revaluation to bring their book value into line with their market value can produce a liability for individual partners if there is a reduction in their profit-sharing ratios. This commonly happens when existing partners retire or new partners are introduced.

There is no such problem where partners leave or come in and there is no revaluation of assets. In such a case, the remaining or incoming partners normally take over the outgoing partners' acquisition values for the firm's asset.

Example – Retirement of partner

H is a partner in a five-partner firm and is entitled to 20% of the profits. He retires and his colleagues then share profits on the basis of 25% each. As part of the arrangements for his retirement, the book value of the firm's office block is increased from £150,000 to its current value of £750,000. The surplus is credited to each partner's account so that *H* is credited with £120,000.

H is treated as if he has realised a gain on the disposal of a one-fifth share of the building. This would be based on the £120,000. The remaining four partners are not treated as having made a disposal. Indeed, they each have made an acquisition of a 5% interest in the building for an outlay of £30,000.

Example – Introduction of new partner

J and *K* are partners. Their premises are included in their firm's balance sheet at £200,000 (original cost), but are actually worth £500,000. They agree to admit *L* as an equal partner in return for his paying in new capital into the firm of £700,000. They revalue the premises before admitting *L* as a partner, and the surplus of £300,000 is credited to their accounts. In this case, *J* and *K* are each regarded as having made a disposal of a one-sixth interest in the premises. This is because *L*'s new capital goes into the firm as a whole. After coming in, he effectively owns one third of all the assets (and is responsible for one third of the liabilities). The former partners' ownership of the premises has been reduced from 50% to a one-third interest.

Example – Change of partners with no assets revaluation

M and *N* are in partnership. They own premises with a book value of £94,000 (equal to cost in 1980). *M* retires and is replaced by *O*. The premises are not revalued. Later the premises are sold for £244,000. *M* and *O* are assessed on their share of the gain.

The gain is computed by reference to the original cost (£94,000) or the premises' market value at 31 March 1982, *not* their value at the time *O* became a partner.

This does *not* apply where the partners are connected persons (eg they are relatives), or where cash payments are made to acquire an interest in the firm. In either of these categories you should seek specialist advice.

6.5.5 Partner leaves after roll-over relief secured on purchase of new asset by firm

A capital gain may arise for a partner on his leaving the firm, even though he receives no consideration from his former partners in return for giving up his interest in the firm beyond being paid out his capital account. Take a situation where there are five partners sharing profits and losses equally. One partner leaves and the remaining four continue. The balance sheet shows the partnership premises as having a cost of £500,000. However, on closer examination, it transpires that some years ago the former partnership premises were disposed of, realising a capital gain of £280,000. Roll-over relief was obtained against this capital gain by reference to the purchase of the current partnership premises.

The Revenue takes the view that the outgoing partner is deemed to have realised a capital gain as follows:

	£
⅕ share in partnership premises (deemed proceeds)	100,000
Less: cost (⅕ of cost as adjusted for roll-over relief)	(44,000)
Gain before indexation	56,000

The four continuing partners' base value for CGT purposes is increased by £25,000 each.

6.6 LIMITED LIABILITY PARTNERSHIPS (LLPS)
(TCGA 1992, s 59A)

Where an LLP carries on a trade or business with a view to profit:

(1) assets held by it are treated for CGT purposes as held by its members as partners, and

(2) any dealings by the LLP are treated for those purposes as being by its members in partnership (and not by the LLP as such);

and tax on chargeable gains accruing to the LLP's members on the disposal of any of its assets are assessed and charged on them separately.

For all purposes, except as otherwise provided, in TCGA 1992 references:

(a) to a partnership include an LLP as above,
(b) to members of a partnership include members of such an LLP,
(c) to a company do not include such an LLP, and
(d) to members of a company do not include members of such an LLP.

The above continues to apply in relation to an LLP that no longer carries on any trade or business with a view to profit:

(1) if the cessation is only temporary, or
(2) during a period of winding-up following a permanent cessation, provided:
    (a) the winding-up is not for reasons connected in whole or in part with tax avoidance, and
    (b) the period of winding-up is not unreasonably prolonged.

The LLP CGT treatment ceases to apply in relation to an LLP on:

(i) the appointment of a liquidator or (if earlier) the making of a winding-up order by the court, or
(ii) the occurrence of any event under the law of a country or territory outside the UK corresponding to an event specified in (i) above.

Where the LLP CGT treatment ceases to apply in relation to an LLP with the effect that tax is assessed and charged on:

(a) the LLP (as a company) on chargeable gains accruing on the disposal of any of its assets, and
(b) the members in respect of chargeable gains accruing on the disposal of any of their capital interests in the LLP,

it is assessed and charged on the LLP as if the LLP CGT treatment had never applied to it.

Neither the commencement of the application of the LLP CGT rules nor the cessation of its application to an LLP is taken as giving rise to the disposal of any assets by it or any of its members.

6.7 RETIREMENT RELIEF – GENERAL PROVISIONS
(TCGA 1992, s 163)

Where an individual is aged at least 50 and satisfies the necessary conditions for a ten-year period, he may be entitled to total exemption for the gain up to a lower threshold, plus one-half of the gain up to a higher threshold.

6.7.1 Amount available for relief
(TCGA 1992, Sch 6, para 13)

Retirement relief is being phased out over the tax years 1999–2000 to 2002–03. The thresholds are being reduced progressively over those tax years as set out below (FA 1998, s 140).

Year	Full relief (£)	Partial relief (£)
1998–99	250,000	1,000,000
1999–00	200,000	800,000
2000–01	150,000	600,000
2001–02	100,000	400,000
2002–03	50,000	200,000

On a qualifying disposal by an individual the amount available for relief is

- so much of the gains qualifying for relief as do not exceed the appropriate percentage of £250,000; and
- one half of so much of those gains as exceed the appropriate percentage of, for 1988–99, £250,000 but do not exceed that percentage of £1,000,000 (or the appropriate limits for later years).

'The appropriate percentage' is one tapered according to the length of the qualifying period which is appropriate to the disposal on a scale rising arithmetically from 10% where that period is precisely one year to 100% where it is ten years. Full retirement relief is thus available only where the individual has been in business for a period of at least ten years ending with the disposal. The relief is not determined by the period of ownership of particular assets.

Example

P, who has been a sole trader manufacturing widgets since 1994, acquired factory premises in 1996 for £100,000. If P sold his business in September 2000, at which time the factory premises are worth £800,000, and all of the capital gains realised relate to the premises, he will qualify for retirement relief as follows:

		£	£
Capital gains on premises			800,000
Indexation (say)			(80,000)
			720,000
Retirement relief:	% × 150,000	90,000	(90,000)
	% × 600,000	360,000	
	Less: relief at full rate	(150,000)	
		300,000	
		× 50%	(150,000)
Chargeable gain			480,000

If *B* had started the business in 1987 the relief would be:

Capital gains on premises			800,000
Indexation (say)			(80,000)
			720,000
Retirement relief			(150,000)
		600,000	
	Less: relief at full rate	(150,000)	
		450,000	
		× 50%	(225,000)
Chargeable gain			345,000

Trustees' disposals are treated as being by the qualifying beneficiary. If, on the same day, there is both a trustees' disposal and a material disposal of business assets by the qualifying beneficiary, the amount available for relief is applied to the beneficiary's own disposal in priority to the trustees' disposal.

6.7.2 Date of disposal for retirement relief

Although the date of disposal for CGT purposes is generally that on which contracts are exchanged, or the point in time that a conditional contract becomes unconditional, the Revenue operates a concession for retirement relief purposes. The key date here is that on which the contract is completed.

Example – Retirement relief by reference to completion date

Q is aged 49 and 10 months when he enters into a contract to sell his hotel business. However, the sale is actually completed three months later, just after he has attained age 50. Because of ESC D31, *Q* will normally be given retirement relief.

6.7.3 Retirement through ill health
(TCGA 1992, s 164(1)(b))

The legislation provides that retirement relief is also available to an individual who is below age 50 but needs to dispose of his business because of ill health. In practice, the Revenue requires claimants to provide a medical certificate, signed by a qualified medical practitioner (whether or not the claimant's own GP). The Board itself takes advice from the Regional Medical Service of the Department of Health, and in some cases a further medical examination by the regional medical officer is required.

The Revenue has made it clear that retirement relief will *not* be given to someone aged below 50 where he has ceased work because of someone else's ill health (eg his spouse).

6.7.4 Conditions to be satisfied for ten years if full relief to be available
(TCGA 1992, s 163(4))

The full relief is given only if the individual has satisfied various requirements for a ten-year period, but some relief is due provided the qualifying period is at least 12 months. A period is 'qualifying' if he was in business as a sole trader or partner or was a full-time officer (eg a director) or employee of a personal trading company (ie as to 5% voting rights: see 6.3.9). Separate periods during which he satisfied one of these requirements can normally be aggregated provided there is not an interval between them of more than two years.

For specific requirements in relation to disposals by sole traders, partners and full-time directors and employees of personal trading companies, see 6.8 and 6.9 respectively.

6.7.5 Retirement relief for trustees
(TCGA 1992, s 164(3))

There are certain circumstances where the sale by trustees of family settlements of business property or shares can attract retirement relief. This is an area where professional advice should be taken, but in essence the trustees may be able to utilise unused relief available to a beneficiary (normally a life tenant) who uses land etc owned by the trustees for a trade carried on by him. Similarly retirement relief may be due to trustees who hold shares in a company where the beneficiary is a full-time director or employee.

6.8 RETIREMENT RELIEF AND UNINCORPORATED TRADERS

The sale of a business may be broken down for tax purposes into the disposal of distinct assets (ie goodwill and buildings, plant and equipment, stock debtors and cash). The CGT position must be looked at separately for each asset.

6.8.1 Retirement relief for sole traders

The legislation requires that a capital gain should arise on the disposal of a business or part of a business. There have been several cases concerning farmers where the individual disposed of part of his land. In each of these cases, the courts held that retirement relief was not due since the asset disposed of was used in the business rather than part of the business itself. A similar point arises if a sole trader sells a warehouse or office block, but continues in business.

In practice, the Revenue resists relief for farmers unless the disposal concerns at least 50% or more of the total area being farmed.

6.8.2 Retirement relief for partners

A gain may attract retirement relief where it arises on a disposal that takes place on the introduction of a new partner or on some other change in profit-sharing ratios combined with a revaluation of partnership assets (see 6.5.4). In some cases, a partner may own an asset used by his firm. Retirement relief is available to cover a gain arising from its disposal provided the following conditions are satisfied:

(1) The disposal must take place as part of his withdrawal from participation in the partnership business.
(2) Immediately before the disposal (or the cessation of the business) the asset must have been used for the purposes of the partnership business.
(3) During the whole or part of the period in which it has been in his ownership, the asset must have been used for the purposes of:
    (a) the business; or
    (b) another business carried on by him or by a partnership of which he was a member.

The amount of retirement relief on the disposal may be restricted where the partner has charged his firm a commercial rent for use of the property.

Example – Restriction on retirement relief where partner has charged rent

R is a partner in a four-partner firm, and takes a 25% share of profits. He owns the offices used by the firm and charges a market rent of £10,000 pa.

The Revenue ignores the rent that R effectively bears himself, but in this situation only 25% of any capital gain realised on the sale of the offices would qualify for retirement relief. If R had charged only £5,000 (ie less than the market rent of £10,000), the proportion of the gain eligible for retirement relief would be

$$\frac{10,000 - 3750}{10,000} \quad \text{ie} \quad \frac{5}{8}$$

6.9 RETIREMENT RELIEF: FULL-TIME DIRECTORS AND EMPLOYEES
(TCGA 1992, ss 163–164)

This section focuses on the way in which the capital gain on the sale of shares in a personal trading company (see 6.3.9) and assets owned privately by the shareholder may qualify for retirement relief.

6.9.1 Full-time working directors and managers

To qualify for retirement relief, it is sufficient for an individual to work for the company on a full-time basis in a managerial or technical capacity.

There is no statutory definition of what 'full-time' means in this context. In practice, the Revenue is understood to accept that a director whose normal working week is 30 hours (excluding meal breaks) qualifies for relief. A person is required to devote more or less the whole of his time if that is what his job and service contract involve. Absence through illness does not normally prejudice entitlement to the relief.

In some cases, the individual will be working full-time for a group of related companies. Relief is available where he is required to devote more or less the whole of his time to the service of a commercial association of companies that carry on businesses and are of a nature that the business of a company and the associated companies taken together may reasonably be considered to make up a single composite undertaking. This is an area where professional advice may be required.

A director who has retired from full-time employment, but who continues to spend an average of at least ten hours per week in the conduct and management of the company's business, may qualify for relief. However, his entitlement is based on the period of full-time service that he had up to his retirement date.

6.9.2 Possible restriction of retirement relief

Where a company has investments as well as business interests, the gain that may attract retirement relief is restricted to the proportion of the gain determined by the following fraction:

$$\frac{\text{Chargeable assets used for business purposes}}{\text{Total chargeable assets}}$$

Where a company has disposed of business assets within six months of a disposal of shares, the individual may elect for the restriction to be computed by reference to the position if the company had not sold those assets.

Example of restriction

S holds all the shares in X Ltd. X Ltd's balance sheet shows the following assets:

	£
Cash at bank	100,000
Gilts	400,000
Quoted shares	500,000
Factory	1,000,000
	2,000,000

The normal approach would be to treat only a proportion of any gain as qualifying for retirement relief. The proportion would be:

$$\frac{1,000,000}{1,500,000} \quad \text{ie} \quad \frac{\text{(Business assets)}}{\text{(chargeable assets)}}$$

The cash and gilts are not chargeable assets and are left out of the equation altogether.

However, it may be that the company has a chargeable asset that does not feature in the balance sheet (eg goodwill) and its inclusion at market value may increase the proportion of the gain that qualifies for retirement relief.

6.9.3 Sale of premises etc used by company

An individual who has been a full-time director or employee may own property or some other assets used by his personal trading company. Retirement relief may be claimed in respect of a disposal of such assets provided the following conditions are satisfied:

(1) the disposal must take place as part of his withdrawal from participation in the company's business;

(2) the asset must be in use for the purposes of the company's business at the time of disposal or must have been so used at the time the company's business ceased; and

(3) the asset must have been used in the whole or part of the period in which he owned it for the purposes of:

   (a) the business carried on by the company; or

   (b) another business carried on by him or by a partnership of which he was a member; or

   (c) another business carried on by his personal trading company.

Relief is restricted where he has charged rent. If a full market rent has been charged, no retirement relief is due whatsoever. If the rent is half the market rent, half the gain on disposal of the property may be eligible for retirement relief.

7

OUTLINE OF VAT

7.1 INTRODUCTION

In concept VAT is a simple tax, although various exclusions from a VAT charge and the EU influence have resulted in a simple concept becoming one of the most complicated taxes of all time.

The harmonisation of VAT has been the subject of much discussion by the EU Commission, which has resulted in the introduction of transitional rules with effect from 1 January 1993, commonly referred to as the Single Market Legislation. These implement a degree of harmonisation on the VAT accounting requirements of the movement of goods between member states. The ultimate legal authority for VAT is a number of EU VAT directives, which must be reflected in each member state's national legislation. To that extent, directives have direct effect. For example, if the national law is not in accordance with a directive and thereby disadvantages the taxpayer, he can argue his case in the national court, which must recognise the directive. The ultimate right of appeal lies to the European Court of Justice.

In principle, for the majority of businesses VAT is not a tax on profits: it is a tax on the consumer collected in stages throughout the business chain and, eventually, by the business person supplying the consumer (ie an individual or business that is not VAT registered). If a business fails to charge and account for VAT correctly, it must account for both the VAT and any penalties from its own resources and thereby, by default, VAT becomes a charge on profits. Put simply, the business person is a tax collector.

Example – How the VAT system works

A retailer sells goods for £1,000 excluding VAT and therefore adds £175 (at a UK VAT rate of 17.5%). The retailer pays his supplier £750 plus VAT of £131.25. He has to pay VAT charged on the sale to Customs but is entitled to deduct the VAT paid to his suppliers. Hence the net payment to Customs is £43.75.

7.2 LEGAL AUTHORITIES

7.2.1 The Value Added Tax Act 1994 (VATA 1994)

VATA 1994 provides the broad shape of VAT and deals with the administration of the tax. It also provides for certain aspects to be dealt with by delegated legislation. All references in this chapter are to the VATA 1994 unless otherwise stated.

7.2.2 Statutory instruments (SIs)

There are various SIs that deal with particular aspects of VAT administration. The most wide-ranging are the Value Added Tax Regulations (VAT Regs) 1995, which deal with a wide range of administrative procedures that must be complied with

7.2.3 Treasury orders

Certain Treasury orders describe, among other things, what is or is not chargeable to VAT and also give legal authority to certain organisations able to recover VAT that would otherwise be irrecoverable.

7.2.4 Customs notices and leaflets

The general principle is that VAT public notices are not part of the law. Certain notices, however, are published under VATA 1994 and SIs and, thereby, *are* part of the law. As such they have the same status as an Act of Parliament and are legally binding on the taxpayer. For example, Notice 700 (General Guide) is principally Customs' interpretation of the law, but the section dealing with the maintenance of accounting records is part of the law, as is the Public Notice on the special VAT Retail Schemes (Notice 727).

Customs' leaflets are not strictly part of the law but certain leaflets, which explain Customs' requirements for particular types of transactions, are, in practical terms, legally binding. This applies to relatively few of the leaflets, the vast majority being simply Customs' interpretation of the law.

7.2.5 EC directives

All VAT law stems from the EC Sixth VAT Directive, which has direct effect in all member states through respective national laws. Other directives deal with specific aspects such as that which, on 1 January 1993, introduced VAT harmonisation in the single market and others which provide the right to recover VAT incurred in other countries.

7.3 BASIC PRINCIPLES
(VATA 1994, ss 1 and 2)

The basic rule is that VAT is charged on the supply of goods or services in the UK, on goods acquired in the UK from other member states, and on goods imported from places outside the member states. VAT on any supply of goods or services is a liability of the person who makes the supply, due at the time of supply (subject to provisions about accounting and payment), acquires the goods from another member state due at the time of acquisition (subject to provisions about accounting and payment), or imports the goods from a place outside the member states, in which case it is charged as if it were a duty of customs.

The standard rate of VAT is 17.5% of the value (see s 19) of the supply of goods or services, and on the value (see s 20) of goods acquired from another member state, or imported from outside the member states following special rules to determine the value thereof (see s 21). A reduced 5% rate is applied to supplies under s 29A and Sch 7A.

The Treasury can, by order, increase or decrease the rate of VAT by up to 25% of the previous rate.

In appropriate circumstances, VAT is charged, not on the value of the supply, but on the profit margin on a transaction (s 50A). The profit margin scheme applies to supplies such as supplies of works of art, motor vehicles, second-hand goods and supplies by agents. The detailed rules are set out in VATA 1994 and VAT (Special Provisions) Order 1995.

7.4 TAXABLE PERSONS
(VATA 1994, s 3 and Schs 1–3A; VAT Regs 1995, regs 5–7)

7.4.1 Introduction

A 'taxable person' is one who is or is liable to be registered for VAT. In other words, it is not possible to avoid VAT by failing to register.

'Taxable person' is also defined by art 4 of the EC Sixth Directive as 'any person who independently carries out in any place any economic activity'. 'Economic activity' includes all activities of producers, traders and persons supplying services (including mining and agricultural activities) and professionals' activities. It also includes the exploitation of tangible or intangible property to obtain income therefrom on a continuing basis.

Further details relating to registration are set out in Schs 1–3A. Persons registered under any of those schedules are registered in a single register kept by Customs. There are four categories, all under FA 1994, under which a person may be registered:

(1) taxable supplies (FA 1994, Sch 1);
(2) supplies from other member states (Sch 2);

(3) acquisitions from other member states (Sch 3);

(4) disposals of assets for which a VAT repayment is claimed (Sch 3A).

7.4.2 Registration

Registration for taxable supplies
(VATA 1994, Sch 1)

An unregistered person who makes taxable supplies becomes liable to be registered at the end of any month if his taxable supplies, in the one-year period then ending, exceeds (from 25 April 2002) £55,000 in value; or at any time, if there are reasonable grounds for believing that such value in the 30-day period then beginning will exceed (from 25 April 2002) £55,000.

If a business is transferred as a going concern from a taxable person to a non-taxable transferee, the transferee becomes liable to register for VAT, subject to the £55,000 limit (Sch 1, para 1(2)).

If Customs are satisfied that the value of taxable supplies will not exceed £53,000 over the one-year period, there is no requirement to be registered (para 1(3)).

In determining the value of taxable supplies, supplies of goods or services that are capital assets of the business in the course or furtherance of which they are supplied are disregarded (unless they fall to be zero-rated) (para 1(7)). Furthermore, the relief for acquisitions or supplies of goods before removal from fiscal warehousing (see s 18B(4)) applies and self-supplies of services on removal of goods from warehousing (see s 18C(3)) are disregarded (para 1(8)). There are a number of other supplies that are disregarded for registration purposes:

(1) supplies by a person who does not belong in the UK, where the recipient of the supply is liable to VAT on a 'reverse charge' (s 8);

(2) overseas supplies (s 14);

(3) companies within a 'VAT group' (s 43).

The maintenance or creation of any artificial separation of business activities carried on by two or more persons from resulting in an avoidance of VAT is prevented (para 1A). In determining whether any separation of business activities is artificial, regard is had to the extent to which the different persons carrying on those activities are closely bound to one another by financial, economic and organisational links (para 2). If Customs make a direction, the persons named in it are treated as a single taxable person carrying on the business activities described in the direction and that taxable person is liable to be registered with effect from the date of the direction or from such later date as may be specified therein.

A person who has become liable to be registered ceases to be so liable at any time if Customs are satisfied in relation to that time that he has ceased to make taxable supplies, or is not at that time a person who meets the above conditions for registration (para 3). A person who has become liable to be registered ceases to be so liable at any time after being registered if Customs are satisfied that the value of his taxable supplies in the period of one year then beginning will not exceed (from 25 April 2002) £53,000 (para 4). A person does not cease to be liable to be registered if Customs are satisfied that the reason the value of his taxable supplies will not exceed (from 25 April 2002) £53,000 is that in the period in question he will cease making taxable supplies, or will suspend making them for a period of 30 days or more. In determining the value of a person's supplies for this purpose, supplies of goods or services that are capital assets of the business in the course or furtherance of which they are supplied, and the other supplies referred to above are disregarded.

In general, a person who becomes liable to be registered must notify Customs of the liability within 30 days of the end of the relevant month (para 5). Customs register any such person (whether or not he so notifies them) with effect from the end of the month following the relevant month or from such earlier date as may be agreed between them and him (paras 6–8).

Where a person who is not liable to be registered and is not already registered satisfies Customs that he makes taxable supplies, or is carrying on a business and intends to make such supplies in the course or furtherance of that business, then, if he so requests, they will register him with effect from the day on which the request is made or from such earlier date as may be agreed between them and him (para 9).

A person who is registered as above who ceases to make or have the intention of making taxable supplies must notify Customs of that fact within 30 days of the day on which he does so (para 11). This does not apply if he would, when he so ceases, be otherwise liable or entitled to be registered if his registration, and any enactment preventing him from being liable to be registered under different provisions at the same time were disregarded.

Where a person who is not liable to be registered and is not already so registered satisfies Customs that he makes supplies as described below, or is carrying on a business and intends to make such supplies in the course or furtherance of that business, and (in either case) meets the condition set out below, they will, if he so requests, register him with effect from the day on which the request is made or from such earlier date as may be agreed between them and him (para 10). The condition referred to here is that a person has a business establishment in the UK or his usual place of residence is in the UK, and that he does not make and does not intend to make taxable supplies. A person carrying on a business through a branch or agency in the UK is treated as having a business establishment in the UK. 'Usual place of residence', in relation to a body corporate, means the place where it is legally constituted. Again if he ceases to make such supplies he must similarly notify Customs (para 12).

Where a registered person satisfies Customs that he is not liable to be registered they will cancel his registration with effect from the day on which the request is made or from such later date as may be agreed between them and him. Where Customs are satisfied that on the day on which a registered person was registered he was not registrable, they may cancel his registration with effect from that day (para 13).

Where a person who makes or intends to make taxable supplies satisfies Customs that any such supply is zero-rated or would be zero-rated if he were a taxable person, they may, if he so requests and they think fit, exempt him from registration (para 14). However, if there is a material change in the nature of the supplies made by him, he must notify Customs of the change within 30 days of the date on which it occurred; or if no particular day is identifiable as the day on which it occurred, within 30 days of the end of the quarter in which it occurred.

Registration in respect of supplies from other member states
(VATA 1994, Sch 2)

A person who is not registered and is not liable to be registered as a person making taxable supplies under Sch 1 becomes liable under Sch 2 on supplies from other member states on any day if, in the period beginning with 1 January of the year in which that day falls, he has made relevant supplies whose value exceeds £70,000.

Registration in respect of acquisitions from other member states
(VATA 1994, Sch 3)

A person who is not registered, and is not liable to be registered by reference to his taxable supplies under Sch 1 or in respect of supplies from other member states (Sch 2), becomes liable to be registered by reference to acquisitions from other member states at the end of any month if, in the period beginning with 1 January of the year in which that month falls, that person had made relevant acquisitions whose value exceeds (from 24 April 2002) £55,000.

Registration in respect of disposals of assets for which a VAT repayment is claimed
(VATA 1994, Sch 3A)

A person who is not registered, and is not liable to be registered by reference to his taxable supplies (under Sch 1), in respect of supplies from other member states (Sch 2) or in respect of acquisitions from other member states (Sch 3), becomes liable to be registered by reference to disposals of assets for which a VAT repayment is claimed, becomes liable to be registered under this Schedule at any time if he makes relevant supplies, or if there are reasonable grounds for believing that he will make such supplies in the period of 30 days then beginning.

7.4.3 Supplies of goods or services in the UK
(VATA 1994 ss 4 and 5, and Sch 4)

The application of VAT differs depending on whether there is a supply of goods or of services.

VAT is charged on any taxable supply of goods or services made in the UK, made by a taxable person in the course or furtherance of his business. A 'taxable supply' is one of goods or services made in the UK other than an exempt supply. Subject to any provision in Sch 4 and to Treasury orders as below:

(1) 'supply' includes all forms of supply unless done otherwise than for a consideration;
(2) anything that is not a supply of goods but is done for a consideration (including, if so done, granting, assigning or surrendering any right) is a supply of services

Schedule 4 sets out matters which are to be treated as the supply of goods, or as the case may be, of services:

(1) a transfer of the whole property in goods is a supply of goods. However, the transfer of an undivided share in property, or of possession (but not ownership) is a supply of services; But, if the transfer of possession is under an agreement for the sale of goods, or an agreement whereby the ownership of the property will pass at some future time, that is a supply of goods (para 1);
(2) the supply of any form of power, heat, refrigeration or ventilation (para 2);
(3) the transfer of title in land by means of a freehold sale or a lease exceeding 21 years is a supply of goods (para 3);
(4) Assets formerly used for business purposes that are transferred or disposed of so that they are no longer used for that business constitute a supply of goods (para 1). This does not apply where:
    (a) goods made in the course or furtherance of the business are given by way of a one-off gift not exceeding £50 in acquisition or production cost value; and
    (b) samples of goods given to any person.

A number of conditions are attached to this provision under para 5. These encompass putting business assets into private use (supply of services: see above).

Schedule 4, para 6 applies to transfers and disposals of business assets between member states, which are regarded as supplies of goods, with some exceptions (ie supplies within and outside of a member state).

Goods sold by a person liable to VAT in satisfaction of a debt are deemed to be supplied in the course or furtherance of the business (para 7).

If a person ceases to be a taxable person, and goods are transferred or disposed of with a VAT charge of over £1,000, they are deemed to have been supplied immediately before he ceased to be liable (para 8). This provision does not apply where the business:

(a) is transferred as a going concern to another taxable person; or
(b) in the case of cessation of liability because of death, bankruptcy etc (see s 46(4)), is carried on by another person who is liable to VAT.
(c) was certified under the flat-rate scheme for farmers and is no longer VAT liable, is excluded from this provision (s 54).

Note that business assets as referred to above include land used for business purposes (para 9).

The Treasury may by order state that a particular supply is to be treated as one of goods, or one of services, or neither one of goods nor services. For example, an order may prescribe that any goods held or used for the business that are put to eg private use or use otherwise than for relevant business purposes, whether or not for a consideration, may be classed as a supply of services in certain circumstances. Or it may prescribe that anything done in relation to a business that is not a supply of services, but if it was done for a consideration *would* be such a supply, is treated as a supply in the course or furtherance of the business.

A full account of the content of current orders and their effect on the nature of supplies of goods and services is outside the scope of this book. The orders in operation at the time of writing are:

- VAT (Treatment of Transactions) (No 1) Order 1973
- VAT (Treatment of Transactions) Order 1986
- VAT (Tour Operators) Order 1987
- VAT (Self-supply of Construction Services) Order 1989
- VAT (Water) Order 1989
- VAT (Treatment of Transactions) Order 1992
- VAT (Removal of Goods) Order 1992
- VAT (Cars) Order 1992
- VAT (Supply of Temporarily Imported Goods) Order 1992
- VAT (Supply of Services) Order 1993
- VAT (Treatment of Transactions) Order 1995
- VAT (Special Provisions) Order 1995
- VAT (Fiscal Warehousing) (Treatment of Transactions) Order 1996.

A supply is subject to VAT at the standard rate unless the VAT legislation provides for specific relief. VATA 1994 provides for three forms of relief:

(1) Reduced rate of VAT under s 30 and specified in Sch 7A.
(2) Zero rating under s 30 and specified in Sch 8.
(3) Exemption under s 31 and specified in Sch 9.

Reduced rate of VAT

A reduced rate of 5% is applied to the following groups of supplies under Sch 7A:

Group 1   Domestic fuel or power
Group 2   Energy-saving materials: installation
Group 3   Heating equipment, security goods and gas supplies: grant-funded installation or connection
Group 4   Women's sanitary products
Group 5   Children's car seats
Group 6   Residential conversions
Group 7   Renovation and alteration of dwellings.

Zero-rated supplies
(VATA 1994, s 30 and Sch 8; VAT Regs 1995, regs 127–135; SI 1987 No 1806)

The zero-rated supplies are exports of goods to places outside the EU (s 30) and the groups listed in Sch 8.

Where a taxable person supplies goods or services and the supply is zero-rated, then, whether or not VAT would otherwise be chargeable on the supply, no VAT is so charged; but the VAT rate charged is nil.

The groups listed in Sch 8 are

Group 1   Food for human consumption
Group 2   Sewerage services and water (but not bottled water)
Group 3   Books, etc
Group 4   Talking books for the blind and handicapped, and wireless sets for the blind
Group 5   Construction and sales of new dwellings
Group 6   Approved alterations to protected buildings
Group 7   International services
Group 8   Transport
Group 9   Caravans and houseboats
Group 10 Gold
Group 11 Bank notes
Group 12 Drugs, medicines, aids for the handicapped etc
Group 13 Imports, exports etc
Group 14 Tax-free shops (spent)
Group 15 Charities (certain supplies to or by charities)
Group 16 Protective and young children's clothing and footwear.

Generally, a supply of goods and services falls under the Sch 8 zero-rating list under the following circumstances:

(a) a treatment or process applied to another person's goods to produce a final product that is a zero-rated supply;

(b) zero-rated goods acquired in the UK from another member state or outside of the EU;

(c) goods exported by charities to countries outside of the EU;

(d) goods supplied to or destined for countries outside the EU;

(e) retail merchandise sold to the public on ships and aircraft;

(f) transfer of goods warehoused in one member state to be warehoused in another member state;

(g) goods let or hired outside the UK.

Forfeiture of zero-rated status may occur if goods for export are found to be still in the UK after they were alleged to have been exported, or if any conditions imposed by Customs in relation to such goods have been breached, and hence the goods no longer fall to be zero rated. A VAT charge arises and must be paid immediately; Customs may, if they think fit, waive payment of the whole or part of that VAT.

Exempt supplies
(VATA 1994, s 31 and Sch 9)

Schedule 9 lists exempt supplies of goods or services. Furthermore, if these goods are acquired from another member state, the acquisition is treated as exempt.

Exemption and zero-rating must not be confused because the overall effect on a business is totally different. Zero-rating gives entitlement to recover VAT on underlying costs whereas exemption does not. The main headings under Sch 9 are:

Group 1   Land (with some exceptions)
Group 2   Insurance
Group 3   Postal services (by the Post Office)
Group 4   Betting, gaming and lotteries
Group 5   Finance
Group 6   Education (when provided by eligible bodies); this heading also includes supplies by youth clubs
Group 7   Health and welfare
Group 8   Burial and cremation
Group 9   Subscriptions to trade unions, professional and other public interest bodies
Group 10 Sports competitions and physical education
Group 11 Works of art etc (in limited circumstances)
Group 12 Fund-raising events by charities and other qualifying bodies
Group 13 Cultural services
Group 14 Supplies of goods where input tax cannot be recovered
Group 15 Investment gold.

Outside the scope

Certain supplies or business activities are 'outside the scope' of VAT. This includes an employee's services to an employer but can also include what, on the face of it, are the organisation's normal trading activities. For example, the supply of goods situated outside the UK, although part of the UK business activities, are outside the scope of UK VAT. Similarly, with effect from 1 January 1993, certain services that are either physically performed or are to be received outside the UK are deemed to have been supplied outside the UK and, therefore, outside the scope of UK VAT.

Generally speaking, an organisation's 'outside the scope' activities do not permit recovery of VAT on related costs, except where a VAT-registered person supplies goods or services outside the UK that would be subject to VAT if made in the UK. There are also special arrangements for certain services that are exempt in the UK but the recipient belongs outside the EU.

7.4.4 Time of supply
(VATA 1994, s 6)

The output tax on a supply of goods or services becomes chargeable at a definite time, called the time of supply. The rate of tax charged is the rate in force at the time of supply, and the supply must be accounted for on the VAT return which covers the prescribed accounting period in which the time of supply occurs. The time of supply is also important for recovery of VAT because it determines when a claim for VAT may be made. Particular rules are laid down which determine the time of supply in a wide variety of circumstances. Many of the rules are, in principle, common to both supplies of goods and services. The rules explained here apply, subject to ss 18, 18B and 18C (fiscal warehousing), for determining the time when a supply of goods or services is treated as taking place for the purposes of the charge to VAT (s 14A).

The basic time of supply is when VAT becomes due and chargeable and is generally determined at the time:

(1) goods are removed by or, or if not removed, when they are made available to the customer;
(2) services are performed (ie completed).

A supply of services is, generally, treated as taking place when the services are performed (VATA 1994 s 6(3)).

The basic time of supply for both goods and services may be overridden by the issue of a tax invoice or the receipt of payment in either of the following circumstances:

(a) Where a tax invoice is issued or payment is received before the time of supply, this earlier date is taken as the tax point.

(b) Where a tax invoice is issued within 14 days after the time of supply, the date of the invoice is taken as the tax point. Customs has discretion to allow a longer period than 14 days if requested.

Where a supply of goods involves their removal from the UK, and their acquisition in another member state by a taxable person under the laws of that State, the supply is treated as taking place on the earlier of the 15th day of the month following that in which the removal occurred and the day on which a VAT invoice (or equivalent) is issued for the supply in question.

Customs may, at the request of a taxable person, by direction alter the time at which supplies made by him (or such supplies made by him as may be specified in the direction) are to be treated as taking place, either:

(1) by directing those supplies to be treated as taking place:
   (a) at times or on dates determined by or by reference to the occurrence of some event described in the direction; or
   (b) at times or on dates determined by or by reference to the time when some event so described would in the ordinary course of events occur, the resulting times or dates being in every case earlier than would otherwise apply; or
(2) by directing that those supplies will (to the extent that they are not treated as taking place at the above time be treated as taking place:
   (a) at the beginning of the relevant working period (as defined in his case in and for the purposes of the direction); or
   (b) at the end of the relevant working period (as so defined).

Where goods are treated as supplied by an order (per s 5(5)), the supply is treated as taking place when they are appropriated to use. Where there is a supply of goods whereby goods no longer form part of the assets of the business (Sch 4, para 5(1)), the supply is treated as taking place when the goods are transferred or disposed to himself. Where there is a supply of services allowing goods to be used privately (see para 5(4)), the supply is treated as taking place when the goods are appropriated to such use.

Note that there are special arrangements which apply to the supply of continuous or periodic services. Customs may by regulations make provision with respect to the time at which (notwithstanding the above, or s 55(4) (supplies of gold)) a supply is treated as taking place in cases where:

(1) it is a supply of goods or services for a consideration the whole or part of which is determined or payable periodically, or from time to time, or at the end of any period, or
(2) it is a supply of goods for a consideration the whole or part of which is determined at the time when the goods are appropriated for any purpose, or
(3) there is a supply of gold (see s 55), or
(4) there is a supply of services on private use of business assets (see Sch 4, para 5(4)) or a transfer of business assets to him (see s 5(4));

and for any such case the regulations may provide for goods or services to be treated as separately and successively supplied at prescribed times or intervals.

A 'VAT invoice' is such an invoice as is required under Sch 11 para 2(1) (accounting requirements), or would be so required if the person to whom the supply is made were a person to whom such an invoice should be issued.

The relevant regulations are the VAT Regs 1995, regs 81, 84–86 and 88–95.

In relation to any services of a description specified in an order (under s 7(11)) varying where a supply of goods or services is made, the rules relating to time of supply and any regulations thereunder or the time of supply of a reverse charge on supplies received from abroad (under s 8(4)) are subject to the transitional provisions relating to place of supply orders (per s 97A).

7.4.5 Place of supply
(VATA 1994, s 7)

The rules relating to the place of supply have effect (subject to ss 14 (acquisition from persons belonging in other member states), 18 and 18B (fiscal warehousing)) for determining whether goods or services are supplied in the UK.

The general rule is that, if the supply of any goods does not involve their removal from or to the UK they are treated as supplied in the UK, and otherwise they are treated as supplied outside the UK.

Goods are treated as supplied in the UK where their supply involves their installation or assembly at a place in the UK to which they are removed; and as supplied outside the UK where their supply involves their installation or assembly at a place outside the UK to which they are removed.

Goods whose place of supply is not determined as above are treated as supplied in the UK where:

(1) the supply involves the removal of the goods to the UK by or under the directions of the person who supplies them;

(2) the supply is a transaction under which the goods are acquired in the UK from another member state by a person who is not a taxable person;

(3) the supplier:
   (a) is liable to be registered in respect of supplies from other member states (see Sch 2); or
   (b) would be so liable if he were not already registered or liable to be registered by reference to the value of his taxable supplies (see Sch 1); and

(4) the supply is neither a supply of goods consisting in a new means of transport nor anything which is treated as a supply only because it is a deemed supply of goods or services:

(a) where goods forming part of the assets of a business are transferred or disposed of so that they no longer form part of the assets of the business (Sch 4, para 5(1)); or

(b) where goods forming part of the assets of any business are removed from any member state by the person carrying on the business, in the course or furtherance of that business for the purpose of being taken to a place in a member state other than that from which they are removed (Sch 4, para 6)

Goods whose place of supply is not determined under any of above provisions and which do not consist in a new means of transport are treated as supplied outside the UK where:

(a) the supply involves the removal of the goods, by or under the directions of the person who supplies them, to another member state;

(b) the person who makes the supply is taxable in another member state; and

(c) provisions of the law of that member state corresponding, in relation to that member state, to the provisions made above make that person liable to VAT on the supply. This does not apply to any supply in a case where the liability mentioned in (3) above depends on the exercise by any person of an option in the UK corresponding to such an option (see Sch 2, para 1(2)) unless that person has given, and has not withdrawn, a notification to Customs that he wishes his supplies to be treated as taking place outside the UK where they are supplies in relation to which the other requirements set out here are satisfied. Customs may by regulations provide that a notification for these is not to be given or withdrawn except in such circumstances, and in such form and manner, as may be prescribed.

Goods whose place of supply is not determined under any of the preceding provisions are treated as supplied in the UK where:

(1) their supply involves their being imported from a place outside the member states; and

(2) the person who supplies them is the person by whom, or under whose directions, they are so imported.

Goods whose place of supply is not determined under any of the preceding provisions but whose supply involves their removal to or from the UK are treated:

(1) as supplied in the UK where their supply involves their removal from the UK without also involving their previous removal to the UK; and

(2) as supplied outside the UK in any other case.

In the preceding provisions, where goods, in the course of their removal from a place in the UK to another place in the UK, leave and re-enter the UK the removal is not treated as a removal from or to the UK.

A supply of services is treated as made in the UK if the supplier belongs in the UK; and in another country (and not in the UK) if the supplier belongs in that other country.

These rules, in relation to goods or services generally, or to particular goods or services, can be varied for determining where a supply of goods or services is made.

The relevant regulations are the VAT Regs 1995, reg 98. Currently, the following orders are in operation:

- VAT (Tour Operators) Order 1987
- VAT (Place of Supply of Services) Order 1992
- VAT (Place of Supply of Goods) Order 1992.

7.4.6 Reverse charge on supplies received from abroad
(VATA 1994, s 8 and Sch 5)

Where relevant services are supplied by a person who belongs in a country other than the UK, and are received by a person who belongs in the UK for the purposes of any business carried on by him, then all the same consequences follow under VATA 1994 (and particularly so much as charges VAT on a supply and entitles a taxable person to credit for input tax) as if the recipient had himself supplied the services in the UK in the course or furtherance of his business, and that supply were a taxable supply. Here, 'relevant services' are services of any of the descriptions specified in Sch 5, not being services within any of the descriptions specified as exempt supplies in Sch 9.

Supplies which are treated as made by the recipient as above are not taken into account as supplies giving rise to input tax (per s 26(1)). In applying this treatment, the supply of services treated as made by the recipient are assumed to have been made at a time determined by regulations. The relevant regulations are the VAT Regs 1995, reg 82 and the VAT (Reverse Charges) (Anti-avoidance) Order 1997.

The following services are treated as supplied where received:

(1) Transfers and assignments of copyright, patents, licences, trademarks and similar rights.
(2) Advertising services.
(3) Services of consultants, engineers, consultancy bureaux, lawyers, accountants and other similar services; data processing and provision of information (but excluding from this head any services relating to land).
(4) Acceptance of any obligation to refrain from pursuing or exercising, in whole or part, any business activity or any such rights as are referred to in (1) above.
(5) Banking, financial and insurance services (including reinsurance, but not including the provision of safe deposit facilities).

(6) The supply of staff.

(7) The letting on hire of goods other than means of transport

(8) Telecommunications services, that is to say services relating to the transmission, emission or reception of signals, writing, images and sounds or information of any nature by wire, radio, optical or other electromagnetic systems, including the transfer or assignment of the right to use capacity for such transmission, emission or reception.

(9) The services rendered by one person to another in procuring for the other any of the services mentioned in (1)-(8) above. This applies to any service in (10) below and whose place of supply is determined under place of supply regulations (ie those listed under 7.4.5) as if the recipient belonged in the UK for the reverse charge (per s 8(1)(b));

(10) Any services not of a description in (1)-(7) and (9) above when supplied to a recipient who is registered under for VAT.

7.4.7 Place where supplier or recipient of services belongs
(VATA 1994, s 9)

The rule described below applies for determining, for any supply of services, whether the supplier belongs in one country or another and whether the recipient belongs in one country or another.

The supplier of services is treated as belonging in a country if:

(1) he has there a business establishment or some other fixed establishment and no such establishment elsewhere; or

(2) he has no such establishment (there or elsewhere) but his usual place of residence is there; or

(3) he has such establishments both in that country and elsewhere and the establishment of his which is most directly concerned with the supply is there.

If the supply of services is made to an individual and received by him otherwise than for the purposes of any business carried on by him, he is treated as belonging in whatever country he has his usual place of residence. Where this does not apply, the person to whom the supply is made is treated as belonging in a country if:

(a) either of the conditions mentioned in (1) and (2) above is satisfied; or

(b) he has a business establishment or some other fixed establishment both in that country and elsewhere and the establishment of his at which, or for the purposes of which, the services are most directly used or to be used is in that country.

Here, but not for any other purposes:

(1) a person carrying on a business through a branch or agency in any country is treated as having a business establishment there; and

(2) 'usual place of residence', in relation to a body corporate, means the place where it is legally constituted.

7.5 BUSINESS
(VATA 1994, s 94)

A supply, for VAT purposes, must be made in the course or furtherance of any business. Although 'business' is not defined in the legislation, it has been interpreted to have a very wide meaning and covers all organisations that carry on activities in a businesslike way. There are directions in the legislation of what the term encompasses and excludes, eg:

(1) Business includes any trade, profession or vocation.
(2) Any act done in the furtherance of a business's termination or disposition, whether or not in connection with its reorganisation or winding-up, is regarded as a supply in the course or furtherance of a business.
(3) A body is *not* treated as carrying on a business if its objects are in the public domain and are of a political, religious, philanthropic, philosophical or patriotic nature, and a subscription by members only entitles the member to participate in the management or receive reports on its activities.

In *C & E Commissioners v Apple and Pear Development Council* [1984] STC 296 the decision included the following definition of business:

> 'a business for the purpose of VAT requires the carrying on of an occupation, function or activity which includes the making of some supplies recognised for VAT purposes.'

A number of organisations that do not consider themselves to be carrying on a business (eg clubs and associations, charities etc) must conform with the VAT legislation and, where appropriate, register and account for VAT on their business income.

If it can be demonstrated that the activity is purely and simply a hobby, there is no requirement to charge VAT on any resulting income. An employee's services to an employer in return for a salary meets the 'supply of services' definition but the law specifically provides that such services are not in the course or furtherance of a business and, therefore, are outside the scope of VAT.

The admission, for payment, of persons to any premises is a business activity. Any person carrying on such an activity is required to register and account for VAT if such income exceeds the registration threshold. To avoid the risk of penalties, all clubs, associations, charities and similar organisations should review their activities to ensure they meet their VAT obligations at the correct time.

7.6 ACQUISITION OF GOODS FROM MEMBER STATES
(VATA 1994, ss 10–14)

Broadly, parallel rules apply to the acquisition of goods from member states.

7.7 IMPORTATION OF GOODS FROM OUTSIDE THE MEMBER STATES
(VATA 1994, ss 15–17)

Broadly, parallel rules apply to the importation of goods from outside the member states

7.8 GOODS SUBJECT TO A FISCAL WAREHOUSE REGIME
(VATA 1994, ss 18–18F and Sch 5A))

The scheme of VAT for goods subject to the 'fiscal warehousing regime' applies where:

(1) any goods have been removed from a place outside the member states and have entered the territory of the Community;
(2) the material time for any acquisition of those goods from another member state or for any supply of those goods is while they are subject to a warehousing regime and before the duty point; and
(3) those goods are not mixed with any dutiable goods which were produced or manufactured in the UK or acquired from another member state.

In this event the acquisition in (2) above is treated as taking place outside the UK.

7.9 DETERMINATION OF VALUE

7.9.1 Value of supply of goods or services
(VATA 1994, s 19)

The value of any supply of goods or services is, except as otherwise provided, determined as set out here and in Sch 6 (which deals with special cases). If the supply is for a consideration in money its value is such amount as, with the addition of the VAT chargeable, is equal to the consideration. If the supply is for a consideration not consisting or not wholly consisting of money, its value is such amount in money as, with the addition of the VAT chargeable, is equivalent to the consideration. Where a supply of any goods or services is not the only matter to which a consideration in money relates, the supply is deemed to be for such part of the consideration as is properly attributable to it. The open market value of a supply of goods or services is the amount that would be taken as its value if the supply were for such consideration in money as would be payable by a person standing in no such relationship with any person as would affect that consideration.

7.9.2 Valuation of acquisitions from other member states
(VATA 1994, s 20)

The rules for valuation of acquisitions from other member states are set out in s 20.

7.9.3 Value of imported goods
(VATA 1994, s 21)

The rules for valuation of goods imported from outside the member states are set out in s 22.

7.9.4 Gaming machines
(VATA 1994, s 23)

Where a person plays a game of chance (see the Gaming Act 1968) by means of a gaming machine, then the amount paid by him to play is treated as the consideration for a supply of services to him. There are special rules set out in s 23 by which supplies are valued.

7.10 PAYMENT OF VAT BY TAXABLE PERSONS

7.10.1 Input tax and output tax
(VATA 1994, s 24)

'Input tax', in relation to a taxable person, means the following tax:

(1) VAT on the supply to him of any goods or services;
(2) VAT on the acquisition by him from another member state of any goods; and
(3) VAT paid or payable by him on the importation of any goods from a place outside the member states,

being (in each case) goods or services used or to be used for the purpose of any business carried on or to be carried on by him.

'Output tax', in relation to a taxable person, means VAT on supplies which he makes or on the acquisition by him from another member state of goods (including VAT which is also to be counted as input tax on the acquisition by him from another member state of any goods).

Where goods or services are supplied to a company, goods are acquired by a company from another member state or goods are imported by a company from a place outside the member states and the goods or services which are so supplied, acquired or imported are used in connection with the provision of accommodation by the company, they are not treated as used for the purposes of any business carried on by the company to the extent that the accommodation is used for domestic purposes by a director of the company, or a person connected with a director of the company.

The Treasury may provide for any description of goods or services that, where such goods or services are supplied to a person who is not a taxable person, they are as supplied to such other person as may be determined under the order.

Where goods or services supplied to a taxable person, goods acquired by a taxable person from another member state or goods imported by a taxable person from a place outside the member states are used or used partly for the purposes of a business carried on by him and partly for other purposes, VAT on supplies, acquisitions and importations is apportioned so that only so much as is referable to his business purposes is counted as his input tax.

7.10.2 Payment by reference to accounting periods and credit for input tax against output tax

(VATA 1994, ss 25 and 26; VAT (Input Tax) Order 1992; VAT (Input Tax) (Specified Supplies) Order 1991)

A taxable person must:

(1) for supplies made by him, and
(2) for the acquisition by him from other member states of any goods,

account for and pay VAT by reference to such 'prescribed accounting periods' at such time and in such manner as may be determined by or under regulations and regulations may make different provision for different circumstances (VAT Regs 1995, regs 99–111).

A taxable person is entitled at the end of each prescribed accounting period to credit for so much of his input tax as is allowable under s 26, and then to deduct that amount from any output tax that is due from him.

If either no output tax is due at the end of the period, or the amount of the credit exceeds that of the output tax then the amount of the credit or, as the case may be, the amount of the excess is paid to the taxable person by Customs; and this is referred to as a 'VAT credit'.

The whole or any part of such credit may, subject to regulations, be held over to be credited in a subsequent period.

Where at the end of any period a VAT credit is due to a taxable person who has failed to submit returns for any earlier period, Customs may withhold payment of the credit until he has complied with that requirement.

The amount of input tax for which a taxable person is entitled to credit at the end of any period is so much of the input tax for the period (that is input tax on supplies, acquisitions and importations in the period) as is allowable under regulations as being attributable to the supplies described below. Supplies made or to be made by the taxable person in the course or furtherance of his business are:

(1) taxable supplies;
(2) supplies outside the UK which would be taxable supplies if made in the UK;
(3) such other supplies outside the UK and such exempt supplies as the Treasury may by order specify.

Customs will make regulations to provide for securing a fair and reasonable attribution of input tax to supplies. In particular the regulations provide for:

(1) determining a proportion by reference to which input tax for any prescribed accounting period is to be provisionally attributed to those supplies;
(2) adjusting, in accordance with a proportion determined in like manner for any longer period comprising two or more prescribed accounting periods or parts thereof, the provisional attribution for any of those periods;
(3) the making of payments in respect of input tax, by Customs to a taxable person (or a person who has been a taxable person) or by a taxable person (or a person who has been a taxable person) to Customs, in cases where events prove inaccurate an estimate on the basis of which an attribution was made; and
(4) preventing input tax on a supply which a person makes to himself from being allowable as attributable to that supply.

7.10.3 Disallowance of input tax where consideration not paid
(VATA 1994, s 26A)

It has been proposed (by FA 2002, s 22) that, if a person has become entitled to credit for any input tax, but the consideration for the supply to which it relates remains unpaid at the end of six months following the relevant date, he is to be taken, as from the end of that period, not to have been entitled to credit for input tax for VAT relating to the unpaid consideration. these arrangements apply from a day to be appointed.

7.10.4 Flat-rate scheme
(VATA 1994, s 26B)

There is an optional flat rate scheme which is intended to simplify the way small businesses account for VAT. Businesses with a taxable turnover of up to £100,000 and total turnover, including the value of exempt supplies and other non-taxable income of up to £125,000 are eligible to join the scheme. Businesses which join the scheme are not required to account internally for VAT on all their purchases and sales. Instead, in most cases, they are able to calculate the net VAT due by simply applying a flat rate percentage to their total turnover for the period.

7.10.5 Goods imported for private purposes
(VATA 1994, s 27)

Where goods are imported by a taxable person from a place outside the member states and

(1) at the time of importation they belong wholly or partly to another person and
(2) the purposes for which they are to be used include private purposes (ie not business purposes) either of himself or of the other,

VAT paid or payable by the taxable person on the importation of the goods is not regarded as input tax to be deducted or credited (see s 25); but he may make a separate claim to Customs for it to be repaid. Customs will allow the claim if they are satisfied that to disallow it would result, in effect, in a double charge to VAT; and where they allow it they will do so only to the extent necessary to avoid the double charge. In considering such a claim, Customs must have regard to the circumstances of the importation and, so far as appearing to them to be relevant, things done with, or occurring in relation to, the goods at any subsequent time.

7.10.6 Payments on account of VAT
(VATA 1994 s 28; VAT Regs 1995, Pt VI)

Certain taxable persons may be required to make payments on account of tax for any prescribed accounting period which they may become liable to pay (s 28(2) and VAT (Payments on Account) Order 1993). There is an appeal procedure (ss 28(2AA) and 83). Customs may give directions to a trader specifying the manner in which he is to make payments on account (s 28(2A)).

7.10.7 Invoices provided by recipients of goods or services ('self-billing')
(VATA 1994, s 29)

Where:

(1) a taxable person provides a document to himself which purports to be an invoice in respect of a taxable supply of goods or services to him by another taxable person and

(2) that document understates the VAT chargeable on the supply,

Customs may elect to treat the amount of VAT understated as VAT due from the recipient and not from the supplier.

7.11 RELIEFS, EXEMPTIONS AND REPAYMENTS

7.11.1 Refunds of VAT in certain cases
(VATA 1994, s 33; VAT (Refund of Tax) Orders 2001 *et seq*)

Where:

(1) VAT is chargeable on the supply of goods or services to certain public bodies on the acquisition of any goods by such a body from another member state, or on the importation of any goods by such a body from a place outside the member states, and
(2) the supply, acquisition or importation is not for the purpose of any business carried on by the body,

Customs will, on a claim made by the body concerned, refund to it the amount of the VAT so chargeable.

Where goods or services so supplied to or acquired or imported by the body cannot be conveniently distinguished from goods or services supplied to or acquired or imported by it for a business carried on by it, the amount to be refunded is such amount as remains after deducting from the whole of the VAT chargeable on any supply to or acquisition or importation by the body such proportion thereof as appears to Customs to be attributable to the carrying on of the business. Where, however,

(1) the VAT so attributable is or includes VAT attributable, in accordance with regulations under s 26, to exempt supplies by the body, and
(2) the VAT attributable to the exempt supplies is an insignificant proportion of the VAT so chargeable,

they may include it in the VAT refunded under this section. References here to VAT chargeable do not include any VAT which, by any order under s 25(7), is excluded from credit.

7.11.2 Refunds of VAT to museums and galleries
(VATA 1994, s 33A; VAT (Refund of tax to Museums and Galleries) Order 2001)

Following the adoption of free right of admission to certain museums and galleries, arrangements have been put in force to repay input tax on supplies of goods and services to such bodies, on the acquisition of goods by such bodies from another member state and the importation by any such body of any goods from a place outside the member states.

7.11.3 Capital goods
(VATA 1994, s 34)

The Treasury may make provision for giving relief, in such cases, to such extent and subject to such exceptions as may be specified in an order, from VAT paid on the supply, acquisition or importation for the purpose of a business carried on by any person of machinery or plant, or any specified description of machinery or plant, in cases where that VAT or part of that VAT cannot be credited under s 25 and such other conditions are satisfied as may be specified in the order.

Such an order may provide for relief to be given by deduction or refunding of VAT and for aggregating or excluding the aggregation of value where goods of the same description are supplied, acquired or imported together.

7.11.4 Refund of VAT to persons constructing certain buildings
(VATA 1994, s 35)

Where:

(1) a person carries out works to which this rule applies,
(2) his carrying out of the works is lawful and otherwise than in the course or furtherance of any business, and
(3) VAT is chargeable on the supply, acquisition or importation of any goods used by him for the purposes of the works,

Customs will refund to that person the amount of VAT so chargeable. The works to which this rule applies are:

(a) the construction of a building designed as a dwelling or number of dwellings;
(b) the construction of a building for use solely for a relevant residential purpose or relevant charitable purpose; and
(c) a residential conversion.

Goods are treated as used for the purposes of works to which this rule applies by the person carrying out the works in so far only as they are building materials which, in the course of the works, are incorporated in the building in question or its site.

Where:

(1) a person carries out a residential conversion by arranging for any of the work of the conversion to be done by a contractor,
(2) the relevant person's carrying out of the conversion is lawful and otherwise than in the course or furtherance of any business,
(3) the contractor is not acting as an architect, surveyor or consultant or in a supervisory capacity, and

(4) VAT is chargeable on services consisting in the work done by the contractor,

Customs will refund to the relevant person the amount of VAT so chargeable.

Works constitute a residential conversion to the extent that they consist in the conversion of a non-residential building, or a non-residential part of a building, into:

(1) a building designed as a dwelling or a number of dwellings;
(2) a building intended for use solely for a relevant residential purpose; or
(3) anything which would fall within (1) or (2) above if different parts of a building were treated as separate buildings.

Customs are not required to entertain a claim for a refund of VAT under this section unless the claim:

(1) is made within such time and in such form and manner, and
(2) contains such information, and
(3) is accompanied by such documents, whether by way of evidence or otherwise,

as Customs may by regulations prescribe or, in the case of documents, as Customs may determine in accordance with the regulations (s 35(2) and VAT Regs 1995, regs 200 and 201). This rule applies:

(1) as if the reference above to the VAT chargeable on the supply of any goods included a reference to VAT chargeable on the supply in accordance with the law of another member state; and
(2) in relation to VAT chargeable in accordance with the law of another member state, as if references to refunding VAT to any person were references to paying that person an amount equal to the VAT chargeable in accordance with the law of that member state;

and the provisions of VATA 1994 and of any other enactment or subordinate legislation (whenever passed or made) so far as they relate to a refund hereunder are construed accordingly.

7.11.5 Bad debts
(VATA 1994, s 36; VAT Regs 1995, regs 156–172)

The rule described below applies where:

(a) a person has supplied goods or services and has accounted for and paid VAT on the supply,
(b) the whole or any part of the consideration for the supply has been written off in his accounts as a bad debt, and
(c) a six-month period (beginning with the date of the supply) has elapsed.

Subject as below and to regulations made under this rule the person is entitled, on making a claim to Customs, to a refund of the amount of VAT chargeable by reference to the outstanding amount. 'The outstanding amount' means:

(1) if at the time of the claim no part of the consideration written off in the claimant's accounts as a bad debt has been received, an amount equal to the amount of the consideration so written off;

(2) if at that time any part of the consideration so written off has been received, an amount by which that part is exceeded by the amount of the consideration written off;

and 'received' means received either by the claimant or by a person to whom has been assigned a right to receive the whole or any part of the consideration written off.

Where the whole or any part of the consideration for the supply does not consist of money, the amount in money taken to represent any non-monetary part of the consideration is so much of the amount made up of:

(1) the value of the supply, and
(2) the VAT charged on the supply,

as is attributable to the non-monetary consideration in question.

A person is entitled to a refund as above unless the value of the supply is equal to or less than its open market value.

Where

(1) a person is entitled as above to be refunded an amount of VAT, and
(2) that VAT has at any time been included in the input tax of another person,

that other person is taken, as from the time when the claim for the refund is made, not to have been entitled to any credit for input tax in respect of the VAT that has to be refunded on that claim. Note that this ceases to apply, from an appointed day, when s 26A comes into effect.

7.11.6 From VAT on acquisition if importation would attract relief
(VATA 1994, s 36A)

The Treasury may provide that no VAT is payable on an acquisition of goods in the UK from another member state where VAT would be relieved on the importation of the same goods into the UK from outside the European Union.

7.11.7 Imports, overseas businesses etc

Relief from VAT on importation of goods
(VATA 1994, s 37; VAT Regs 1995, regs 123–126; VAT (Imported Goods) Relief Order 1984; VAT (Small Non-commercial Consignments) Relief Order 1986; VAT (Imported Gold) Relief Order 1992)

The Treasury may make provision for giving relief from the whole or part of the VAT chargeable on the importation of goods from places outside the member states, subject to such conditions (including conditions prohibiting or restricting the disposal of or dealing with the goods) as may be imposed by the order, if and so far as the relief appears to the Treasury to be necessary or expedient, having regard to any international agreement or arrangements.

In any case where:

(1) it is proposed that goods which have been imported from a place outside the member states by any person with the benefit of relief as above is transferred to another person, and

(2) on an application made by the transferee, Customs direct that this rule applies,

VATA 1994 has effect as if, on the date of the transfer of the goods (and in place of the transfer), the goods were exported by the original importer and imported by the transferee and, accordingly, where appropriate, provision made above has effect in relation to the VAT chargeable on the importation of the goods by the transferee.

Customs may by regulations make provision for remitting or repaying, if they think fit, the whole or part of the VAT chargeable on the importation of any goods from places outside the member states which are shown to their satisfaction to have been previously exported from the UK or removed from any member state.

Customs may by regulations make provision for remitting or repaying the whole or part of the VAT chargeable on the importation of any goods from places outside the member states if they are satisfied that the goods have been or are to be re-exported or otherwise removed from the UK and they think fit to do so in all the circumstances and having regard to:

(1) the VAT chargeable on the supply of like goods in the UK;

(2) any VAT which may have become chargeable in another member state in respect of the goods

Importation of goods by taxable persons
(VATA 1994, s 38; VAT Regs 1995, reg 122)

Customs may by regulations make provision for enabling goods imported from a place outside the member states by a taxable person in the course or furtherance of any business carried on by him to be delivered or removed, subject to such conditions or restrictions as Customs may impose for the protection of the revenue, without payment of the VAT chargeable on the importation, and for that VAT to be accounted for together with the VAT chargeable on the supply of goods or services by him or on the acquisition of goods by him from other member states.

Repayment of VAT to those in business overseas
(VATA 1994, s 39; VAT Regs 1995, regs 173–197)

Customs may, by means of a scheme embodied in regulations, provide for the repayment, to persons to whom this rule applies, of VAT on supplies to them in the UK or on the importation of goods by them from places outside the member states which would be input tax of theirs if they were taxable persons in the UK. This rule applies to persons carrying on business in

(1) another member state, and
(2) other countries if, under any Community Directive, rules are adopted by the Council of the Communities about refunds of VAT to persons established elsewhere than in the member states,

but does not apply to persons carrying on business in the UK.

Repayment is made in such cases only, and subject to such conditions, as the scheme may prescribe (being conditions specified in the regulations or imposed by Customs either generally or in particular cases); and the scheme may provide:

(1) for claims and repayments to be made only through agents in the UK;
(2) either generally or for specified purposes:
    (a) for the agents to be treated as if they were taxable persons; and
    (b) for treating claims as if they were returns under VATA 1994 and repayments as if they were repayments of input tax; and
(3) for generally regulating the methods by which the amount of any repayment is to be determined and the repayment is to be made.

Refunds in relation to new means of transport supplied to other member states
(VATA 1994, s 40; VAT Regs 1995, regs 146, 149–154)

Subject as below, where a person who is not a taxable person makes such a supply of goods consisting in a new means of transport as involves the removal of the goods to another member state, Customs will, on a claim, refund to that person, as the case may be:

(1) the amount of any VAT on the supply of that means of transport to that person, or
(2) the amount of any VAT paid by that person on the acquisition of that means of transport from another member state or on its importation from a place outside the member states.

The amount of VAT refunded cannot exceed the amount that would have been payable on the supply involving the removal if it had been a taxable supply by a taxable person and had not been zero-rated.

Customs are not entitled to entertain a claim for refund of VAT unless the claim:

(1) is made within such time and in such form and manner;
(2) contains such information; and
(3) is accompanied by such documents, whether by way of evidence or otherwise, as they may by regulations prescribe.

7.12 APPLICATION OF VATA 1994 IN CERTAIN CASES

7.12.1 Application to the Crown
(VATA 1994, s 41)

VATA 1994 applies to taxable supplies by the Crown as it applies in relation to taxable supplies by taxable persons.

Where the supply by a Government department of any goods or services does not amount to the carrying on of a business but it appears to the Treasury that similar goods or services are or might be supplied by taxable persons in the course or furtherance of any business, then, if and to the extent that the Treasury so direct, the supply of those goods or services by that department are treated as a supply in the course or furtherance of any business carried on by it.

Where VAT is chargeable on the supply of goods or services to a Government department, on the acquisition of any goods by a Government department from another member state or on the importation of any goods by a Government department from a place outside the member states and the supply, acquisition or importation is not for the purpose of:

(1) any business carried on by the department, or
(2) a supply by the department which, under a direction as above, is treated as a supply in the course or furtherance of a business,

then, if and to the extent that the Treasury so direct and as below, Customs will, on a claim made by the department at such time and in such form and manner as Customs may determine, refund to it the amount of the VAT so chargeable.

Customs may make the refunding of any amount due as above conditional upon compliance by the claimant with requirements with respect to the keeping, preservation and production of records relating to the supply, acquisition or importation in question.

Goods or services obtained by one Government department from another Government department are treated, if and to the extent that the Treasury so direct, as supplied by that other department and similarly as regards goods or services obtained by or from the Crown Estate Commissioners.

As to the meaning of 'Government department', see s 41(6)-(8).

7.12.2 Local authorities
(VATA 1994, s 42)

A local authority which makes taxable supplies is liable to be registered, whatever the value of the supplies.

7.12.3 Groups of companies

General
(VATA 1994, s 43; VAT (Self-supply of Construction Services) Order 1989; VAT (Cars) Order 1992; VAT (Special Provisions) Order 1995)

Where any bodies corporate are treated as members of a group, any business carried on by a member of the group is treated as carried on by the representative member, and:

(1) any supply of goods or services by a member of the group to another member of the group is disregarded; and

(2) any other supply which is a supply of goods or services by or to a member of the group is treated as a supply by or to the representative member; and

(3) any VAT paid or payable by a member of the group on the acquisition of goods from another member state or on the importation of goods from a place outside the member states is treated as paid or payable by the representative member and the goods are treated:

    (a) in the case of goods acquired from another member state, for the purposes of s 73(7); and

    (b) in the case of goods imported from a place outside the member states, for those purposes and the purposes of s 38 (importation of goods by a taxable person),

as acquired or, as the case may be, imported by the representative member;

and all members of the group are liable jointly and severally for any VAT due from the representative member.

Where:

(a) it is material, for the purposes of any provision made by or under VATA 1994, whether the person by or to whom a supply is made, or the person by whom goods are acquired or imported, is a person of a particular description,

(b) paras (2) or (3) above applies to any supply, acquisition or importation, and

(c) there is a difference that would be material for the purposes of the relevant provision between:

    (i) the description applicable to the representative member, and

    (ii) the description applicable to the body which (otherwise) would be regarded as making the supply, acquisition or importation or, as the case may be, as being the person to whom the supply is made,

the relevant provision has effect in relation to that supply, acquisition or importation as if the only description applicable to the representative member were the description in fact applicable to that body.

This does not apply to the extent that what is material for the purposes of the relevant provision is whether a person is a taxable person.

An order under s 5(5) or (6) (meaning of supplies of goods or services) may make provision for securing that any goods or services which, if all the members of the group were one person, would fall to be treated as supplied to and by that person, are treated as supplied to and by the representative member and may provide that the representative member is treated as a person of such description as may be determined under the order.

A supply made by a member of a group to another UK member of the group is not disregarded as above if:

(1) it would (if there were no group) be a supply of services falling within Sch 5 (services supplied where received) to a person belonging in the UK;

(2) those services are not within any of the descriptions specified in Sch 9 (exempt supplies);

(3) the supplier has been supplied (whether or not by a person belonging in the UK) with any services falling within Sch 5, paras 1–8 (services supplied where received) which do not fall within any of the exempt supplies specified in Sch 9;

(4) the supplier belonged outside the UK when it was supplied with the services mentioned in (3) above; and

(5) the services so mentioned have been used by the supplier for making the supply to the UK member.

For this purpose, where:

(1) there has been a supply of the assets of a business of a person to a person to whom the whole or any part of that business was transferred as a going concern,

(2) that supply is either:

    (a) a supply falling to be treated, by an order under s 5(3) (meaning of supply), as being neither a supply of goods nor a supply of services, or

    (b) a supply that would have fallen to be so treated if it had taken place in the UK, and

(3) the transferor was supplied with services falling within Sch 5, para 1–8 (services supplied where received) at a time before the transfer when the transferor belonged outside the UK,

those services, so far as they are used by the transferee for making any such supply, is deemed to have been supplied to the transferee at a time when the transferee belonged outside the UK.

Where, in the case of a supply of assets falling within paras (1) and (2) above:

(1) the transferor himself acquired any of the assets in question by way of a previous transfer of a going concern, and

(2) there are services falling within Sch 5, paras 1–8 (services supplied where received) which, if used by the transferor for making such supplies, would be deemed to have been supplied to the transferor at a time when he belonged outside the UK,

notwithstanding that the services have not been so used by the transferor, as if the transferor were a person to whom those services were supplied and as if he were a person belonging outside the UK at the time of their deemed supply to him; and this applies through any number of successive transfers as a going concern.

Where a supply is excluded as above from the supplies that are disregarded all the same consequences follow as if that supply:

(1) were a taxable supply in the UK by the representative member to itself, and

(2) without prejudice to that, were made by the representative member in the course or furtherance of its business.

Except in so far as Customs may by regulations otherwise provide a supply which is deemed to be a supply by the representative member to itself is:

(1) not taken into account as a supply made by the representative member when determining any allowance of input tax (under s 26(1)) for the representative member;

(2) deemed for the purposes of Sch 6, para 1 (valuation) to be a supply in which the person making the supply and the person supplied are connected (per TA 1988, s 839); and

(3) subject to (2) above, a supply the value and time of which are determined as if it were a supply of services which is treated by s 8 (reverse charges on supplies received from abroad) as made by the person by whom the services are received.

Sch 9A contains detailed provisions ensuring that the group treatment is not used for tax avoidance.

Eligibility
(VATA 1994, s 43A)

Two or more companies are eligible to be treated as members of a group if each is established or has a fixed establishment in the UK and:

(1) one of them controls each of the others,

(2) one person (whether a company or an individual) controls all of them, or

(3) two or more individuals carrying on a business in partnership control all of them.

Here, a company is taken to control another company if it is empowered by statute to control that company's activities or if it is that company's holding company (per CA 1985, s 736).

An individual or individuals are taken to control a company if he or they, were he or they a company, would be that company's holding company.

Applications
(VATA 1994, s 43B)

The procedure described here applies where an application is made to Customs for two or more companies, which are eligible under s 43A(1), to be treated as members of a group. It also applies where two or more companies are treated as members of a group and an application is made to Customs:

(1) for another company, which is eligible under s 43A(1) to be treated as a member of the group, to be so treated,
(2) for a company to cease to be treated as a member of the group,
(3) for a member to be substituted as the group's representative member, or
(4) for the company no longer to be treated as members of a group.

An application with respect to any companies:

(1) must be made by one of them or by the person controlling them, and
(2) in the case of an application for the companies to be treated as a group, must appoint one of them as the representative member.

Termination of membership
(VATA 1994, s 43C)

Customs may, by notice given to a company, terminate its treatment as a member of a group from a date:

(1) which is specified in the notice, and
(2) which is, or falls after, the date on which the notice is given.

Customs may give such a notice only if it appears to them to be necessary for the protection of the revenue.
Where:

(1) a company is treated as a member of a group, and
(2) it appears to Customs that the company is not, or is no longer, eligible under s 43A(1) to be treated as a member of the group,

Customs will, by notice given to the company, terminate its treatment as a member of the group from a date specified in the notice.

Supplies to groups
(VATA 1994, s 44)

The treatment described below applies where:

(1) a business, or part of a business, carried on by a taxable person is transferred as a going concern to a body corporate treated as a member of a group under s 43;
(2) on the transfer of the business or part, chargeable assets of the business are transferred to the body corporate; and
(3) the transfer of the assets is treated by s 5(3)(c) (meaning of supply) as neither a supply of goods nor a supply of services.

The treatment does not apply if the representative member of the group is entitled to credit for the whole of the input tax on supplies to it and acquisitions and importations by it:

(1) during the prescribed accounting period in which the assets are transferred, and
(2) during any longer period to which regulations under s 26(3)(b) (input tax allowable) relate and in which the assets are transferred.

Nor does the treatment apply if Customs are satisfied that the assets were assets of the taxable person transferring them more than 3 years before the day on which they are transferred.

The treatment does not apply to the extent that the chargeable assets consist of capital items (for which regulations made under s 26(3) and (4) (input tax allowable) are in force when the assets are transferred, provide for adjustment to the deduction of input tax.

The chargeable assets are treated as being, on the day on which they are transferred, both supplied to the representative member of the group for the purpose of its business and supplied by that member in the course or furtherance of its business. Such supply treated as made by a representative member cannot be taken into account as a supply made by him when determining the allowance of input tax (under s 26) in his case. The value of a supply is taken to be the open market value of the chargeable assets. The open market value of any chargeable assets is taken to be the price that would be paid on a sale (on which no VAT is payable) between a buyer and a seller who are not in such a relationship as to affect the price.

Customs may reduce the VAT chargeable in a case where they are satisfied that the person by whom the chargeable assets are transferred has not received credit for the full amount of input tax arising on the supply to or acquisition or importation by him of the chargeable assets. Assets are chargeable assets if their supply in the UK by a taxable person in the course or furtherance of his business would be a taxable supply (and not a zero-rated supply).

7.12.4 **Partnerships**
(VATA 1994, s 45)

The registration of persons carrying on:

(1) a business in partnership, or
(2) in partnership any other activities in the course or furtherance of which they acquire goods from other member states,

may be in the name of the firm; and no account is taken, in determining whether goods or services are supplied to or by such persons or are acquired by such persons from another member state, of any change in the partnership.

Without prejudice the Partnership Act 1890, s 36 (rights of persons dealing with firm against apparent members of firm), until the date on which a change in the partnership is notified to Customs a person who has ceased to be a member of a partnership is regarded as continuing to be a partner and, in particular, for the purpose of any liability for VAT on the supply of goods or services by the partnership or on the acquisition of goods by the partnership from another member state.

Where a person ceases to be a member of a partnership during a prescribed accounting period (or is treated as so doing as above) any notice, whether of assessment or otherwise, which is served on the partnership and relates to, or to any matter arising in, that period or any earlier period during the whole or part of which he was a member of the partnership is treated as served also on him.

Without prejudice to the Partnership Act 1890, s 16 (notice to acting partner to be notice to the firm) any notice, whether of assessment or otherwise, which is addressed to a partnership by the name in which it is registered is treated as served on the partnership and, accordingly, as served also on the former partner.

This does not affect the extent to which, under the 1890 Act, s 9, a partner is liable for VAT owed by the firm; but where a person is a partner in a firm during part only of a prescribed accounting period, his liability for VAT on the supply by the firm of goods or services during that accounting period or on the acquisition during that period by the firm of any goods from another member state is such proportion of the firm's liability as may be just.

7.12.5 **Business carried on in divisions or by unincorporated bodies, personal representatives etc**
(VATA 1994, s 46; VAT Regs 1995, regs 8 and 9)

The registration of a company carrying on a business in several divisions may, if the company so requests and Customs see fit, be in the names of those divisions.

Customs may by regulations make provision for determining by what persons anything required to be done by a person carrying on a business is to be done where a business is carried on in partnership or by a club, association or organisation the affairs of which are managed by its members or a committee or committees of its members. The registration of any such club, association or organisation may be in the name of the club, association or organisation; and in determining whether goods or services are supplied to or by such a club, association or organisation or whether goods are acquired by such a club, association or organisation from another member state, no account is taken of any change in its members.

Customs may by regulations make provision for persons who carry on a business of a taxable person who has died or become bankrupt or has had his estate sequestrated or has become incapacitated to be treated for a limited time as taxable persons, and for securing continuity in cases where persons are so treated. In relation to a company which is a taxable person, the reference to the taxable person having become bankrupt or having had his estate sequestrated or having become incapacitated is construed as a reference to its being in liquidation or receivership or to an administration order being in force in relation to it.

References here to a business include references to any other activities in the course or furtherance of which any body corporate or any club, association, organisation or other unincorporated body acquires goods from another member state.

7.12.6 Agents etc
(VATA 1994, s 47)

Where:

(1) goods are acquired from another member state by a person who is not a taxable person and a taxable person acts in relation to the acquisition, and then supplies the goods as agent for the person by whom they are so acquired; or
(2) goods are imported from a place outside the member states by a taxable person who supplies them as agent for a person who is not a taxable person,

then, if the taxable person acts in relation to the supply in his own name, the goods are treated as acquired and supplied or, as the case may be, imported and supplied by the taxable person as principal.

A person who is not resident in the UK and whose place or principal place of business is outside the UK may be treated as not being a taxable person if as a result he is not required to be registered.

Where, in the case of any supply of goods to which the above does not apply, goods are supplied through an agent who acts in his own name, the supply is treated both as a supply to the agent and as a supply by the agent.

Where services are supplied through an agent who acts in his own name Customs may, if they think fit, treat the supply both as a supply to the agent and as a supply by the agent.

7.12.7 VAT representatives
(VATA 1994, s 48; VAT Regs 1995, reg 10)

Where any person

(1) is a taxable person or, without being a taxable person, is a person who makes taxable supplies or who acquires goods in the UK from one or more other member states;
(2) is not established, and does not have any fixed establishment, in the UK;
(3) is established in a country or territory in respect of which it appears to Customs that the condition specified below is satisfied; and
(4) in the case of an individual, does not have his usual place of residence in the UK, Customs may direct that person to appoint a 'VAT representative' to act on his behalf in relation to VAT. The condition mentioned above is that:
   (a) the country or territory is neither a member state nor a part of a member state, and
   (b) there is no provision for mutual assistance between the UK and the country or territory similar in scope to the assistance provided for between the UK and each other member state by the mutual assistance provisions.

'The mutual assistance provisions' are:

(1) FA 1977, s 11 (recovery of duty due etc in other member states),
(2) FA 1978, s 77 (disclosure of tax information to tax authorities in other member states), and
(3) Council Regulation (EEC) No 218/92.

A person who has not been required to appoint another person to act on his behalf in relation to VAT, and in relation to whom the conditions specified above are satisfied, may nonetheless appoint another person to act on his behalf in relation to VAT.

Where any person is appointed to be the VAT representative of another person, then the VAT representative:

(1) is entitled to act on his principal's behalf;
(2) must secure (where appropriate by acting on his principal's behalf) his principal's compliance with and discharge of the obligations and liabilities to which his principal is subject; and
(3) is personally liable for:
   (a) any failure to secure his principal's compliance with or discharge of any such obligation or liability; and

(b) anything done for purposes connected with acting on his principal's behalf,

as if the obligations and liabilities imposed on his principal were imposed jointly and severally on the VAT representative and his principal.

A VAT representative is not liable himself to be registered, but regulations made by Customs may:

(1) require the registration of the names of VAT representatives against the names of their principals in any register kept for the purposes of this Act; and
(2) make it the duty of a VAT representative, for the purposes of registration, to notify Customs, within such period as may be prescribed, that his appointment has taken effect or has ceased to have effect.

A VAT representative is not guilty of any offence except in so far as:

(1) the VAT representative has consented to, or connived in, the commission of the offence by his principal;
(2) the commission of the offence by his principal is attributable to any neglect on the part of the VAT representative; or
(3) the offence consists in a contravention by the VAT representative of an obligation which is imposed both on the VAT representative and on his principal.

Customs may by regulations make provision as to the manner and circumstances in which a person is to be appointed, or is to be treated as having ceased to be, another's VAT representative; and regulations may include such provision as Customs think fit for with respect to the making or deletion of entries in any register.

If a person fails to appoint a VAT representative in accordance with any direction, Customs may require him to provide such security, or further security, as they may think appropriate for the payment of any VAT which is or may become due from him. A sum required by way of security is deemed for the purposes of:

(1) FA 1997, s 51 (enforcement by distress) and any regulations thereunder, and
(2) FA 1997, s 52 of that Act (enforcement by diligence),

to be recoverable as if it were VAT due from the person who is required to provide it.

A person is not treated as having been directed to appoint a VAT representative, or as having been required to provide security as above, unless Customs have either:

(1) served notice of the direction or requirement on him; or
(2) taken all such other steps as appear to them to be reasonable for bringing the direction or requirement to his attention.

305

7.12.8 Transfers of going concerns
(VATA 1994, s 49; VAT Regs 1995, reg 6)

Where a business carried on by a taxable person is transferred to another person as a going concern, then:

(1) in determining whether the transferee is liable to be registered he is treated as having carried on the business before as well as after the transfer and supplies by the transferor is treated accordingly; and

(2) any records relating to the business which are required to be preserved for any period after the transfer must be preserved by the transferee instead of by the transferor, unless Customs, at the request of the transferor, otherwise direct.

Customs may by regulations make provision for securing continuity where a business carried on by a taxable person is transferred to another person as a going concern and the transferee is registered in substitution for the transferor. Such regulations may, in particular, provide for:

(1) liabilities and duties (excluding ss 59–70 (default surcharge)) of the transferor to become, to such extent as may be provided by the regulations, liabilities and duties of the transferee; and

(2) any right of either of them to repayment or credit in respect of VAT to be satisfied by making a repayment or allowing a credit to the other;

but ss 59–70 (default surcharge) do not apply to any transferor and transferee unless an application in that behalf has been made by them under the regulations.

7.12.9 Terminal markets
(VATA 1994, s 50; VAT (Terminal Markets) Order 1973)

The Treasury may make provision for modifying the provisions of VATA 1994 in their application to dealings on terminal markets and such persons ordinarily engaged in such dealings as may be specified in the order, subject to such conditions as may be so specified. Such an order may include provision for:

(1) zero-rating the supply of any goods or services or for treating the supply of any goods or services as exempt;

(2) the registration of any body of persons representing persons ordinarily engaged in dealing on a terminal market and for disregarding such dealings by persons so represented in determining liability to be registered, and for disregarding such dealings between persons so represented;

(3) refunding, to such persons as may be specified by or under the order, input tax attributable to such dealings on a terminal market as may be so specified,

OUTLINE OF VAT

and may contain such incidental and supplementary provisions as appear to the Treasury to be necessary or expedient.

7.12.10 Margin schemes
(VATA 1994, s 50A; VAT (Special Provisions) Order 1995)

The Treasury may provide, in relation to any such description of supplies as may be specified in the order, for a taxable person to be entitled to opt that, where he makes supplies of that description, VAT is charged by reference to the profit margin on the supplies, instead of by reference to their value. This applies to the following supplies:

- works of art, antiques or collectors' items;
- motor vehicles;
- second-hand goods; and
- goods through a person who acts as an agent, but in his own name, in relation to the supply.

An option for the purposes of an order is exercisable, and may be withdrawn, in such manner as may be required by such an order.

The profit margin on a supply is taken, for the purposes of an order hereunder, to be equal to the amount (if any) by which the price at which the person making the supply obtained the goods in question is exceeded by the price at which he supplies them. The price at which a person has obtained any goods and the price at which he supplies them are each calculated in accordance with the provisions contained in an order hereunder. Such an order may, in particular, make provision stipulating the extent to which any VAT charged on a supply, acquisition or importation of any goods is to be treated as included in the price at which those goods have been obtained or are supplied. An order may provide that the consideration for any services supplied in connection with a supply of goods by a person who acts as an agent, but in his own name, in relation to the supply of the goods is to be treated for the purposes of any such order as an amount to be taken into account in computing the profit margin on the supply of the goods, instead of being separately chargeable to VAT as comprised in the value of the services supplied.

Furthermore, an order hereunder may provide for the total profit margin on all the goods of a particular description supplied by a person in any prescribed accounting period to be calculated by:

(1) aggregating all the prices at which that person obtained goods of that description in that period together with any amount carried forward to that period as below;
(2) aggregating all the prices at which he supplies goods of that description in that period;
(3) treating the total profit margin on goods supplied in that period as being equal to the amount (if any) by which, for that period, the aggregate

307

calculated under (1) above is exceeded by the aggregate calculated under (2) above; and

(4) treating any amount by which, for that period, the aggregate calculated under (2) above is exceeded by the aggregate calculated under (1) above as an amount to be carried forward to the following prescribed accounting period so as to be included, for the period to which it is carried forward, in any aggregate falling to be calculated under (1) above.

7.12.11 Buildings and land
(VATA 1994, s 51)

Schedule 10 applies to transactions concerned with buildings and land. In particular, the so-called 'election to waive exemption' under which transactions which would otherwise be exempt may instead be made subject to VAT. The effect of this treatment is to allow the recovery of input tax that would not otherwise be available.

7.12.12 Co-owners etc of buildings and land
(VATA 1994, s 51A)

This rule applies to a supply consisting in the grant, assignment or surrender of any interest in or right over land in a case where there is more than one person by whom the grant, assignment or surrender is made or treated as made; and for this purpose:

(1) a licence to occupy land, and
(2) in relation to land in Scotland, a personal right to call for or be granted any interest or right in or over land,

is taken to be a right over land. 'The grantors' are treated, in relation to that supply and in relation to any other such supply with respect to which the grantors are the same, as a single person (here referred to as 'the property-owner') who is distinct from each of the grantors individually.

Registration of the property-owner is in the name of the grantors acting together as a property-owner. The grantors are jointly and severally liable in respect of the obligations falling on the property-owner.

Any notice, whether of assessment or otherwise, which is addressed to the property-owner by the name in which the property-owner is registered and is served on any of the grantors is treated as served on the property-owner.

Where there is any change in some, but not all, of the persons who are for the time being to be treated as the grantors in relation to any supply:

(1) that change is disregarded in relation to any prescribed accounting period beginning before the change is notified in the prescribed manner to Customs; and
(2) any notice (whether of assessment or otherwise) which is served, at any time after such a notification, on the property-owner for the time being

is so far as it relates to, or to any matter arising in, such a period, be treated as served on whoever was the property-owner in that period.

7.12.13 Trading stamp schemes
(VATA 1994, s 52; VAT Regs 1995, regs 76–80)

Customs may modify s 19 and Sch 6 (value of supply of goods or services) and s 20 and Sch 7 (value of acquisitions from other member states for the purpose of providing in place of the provision for the time being contained therein) for the manner of determining the value of

(1) a supply of goods, or
(2) a transaction in pursuance of which goods are acquired from another member state,

in a case where the goods are supplied or acquired under a trading stamp scheme (within the meaning of the Trading Stamps Act 1964 or the Trading Stamps Act (Northern Ireland) 1965) or under any scheme of an equivalent description which is in operation in another member state.

7.12.14 Tour operators
(VATA 1994, s 53; VAT (Tour Operators) Order 1987)

The Treasury may by order modify the application of VATA 1994 in relation to supplies of goods or services by tour operators or in relation to such of those supplies as may be determined by or under the order. Here 'tour operator' includes a travel agent acting as principal and any other person providing for the benefit of travellers services of any kind commonly provided by tour operators or travel agents. Such an order may make provision:

(1) for two or more supplies of goods or services by a tour operator to be treated as a single supply of services;
(2) for the value of that supply to be ascertained, in such manner as may be determined by or under the order, by reference to the difference between sums paid or payable to and sums paid or payable by the tour operator;
(3) for account to be taken, in determining the VAT chargeable on that supply, of the different rates of VAT that would otherwise have been applicable;
(4) excluding any body corporate from treatment as a member of a group (see VATA 1992, s 43);
(5) as to the time when a supply is to be treated as taking place.

7.12.15 Farmers etc
(VATA 1994, s 54; VAT Regs 1995, regs 202–211)

Customs may, under regulations made by them, certify any person who satisfies them:

(1) that he is carrying on a business involving one or more designated activities (ie farming – see below);
(2) that he is of such a description and has complied with such requirements as may be prescribed; and
(3) where an earlier certification of that person has been cancelled, that more than the prescribed period has elapsed since the cancellation or that such other conditions as may be prescribed are satisfied.

Where a person is for the time being certified hereunder, then (whether or not that person is a taxable person) so much of any supply by him of any goods or services as, in accordance with provision contained in regulations, is allocated to the relevant part of his business is disregarded in determining whether he is, has become or has ceased to be liable or entitled to be registered as a taxable person under Sch 1.

Customs may by regulations provide for an amount included in the consideration for any taxable supply which is made:

(1) in the course or furtherance of the relevant part of his business by a person who is for the time being certified hereunder;
(2) at a time when that person is not a taxable person; and
(3) to a taxable person,

to be treated, for the purpose of determining the entitlement of the person supplied to credit under ss 25 and 26 (input tax credit), as VAT on a supply to that person.

The amount which may be included in the consideration for any supply is an amount equal to such percentage as the Treasury may by order specify of the sum which, with the addition of that amount, is equal to the consideration for the supply.

Customs' power by regulations under s 39 (repayment of VAT to those in business overseas) to provide for the repayment to such persons to whom VAT which would be input tax of theirs if they were taxable persons in the UK includes power to provide for the payment to such persons of sums equal to the amounts which, if they were taxable persons in the UK, would be input tax of theirs by regulations hereunder; and references in s 39, or in any other enactment, to a repayment of VAT is construed accordingly.

The regulations may provide for:

(1) the form and manner in which an application for certification, or for the cancellation of any such certification, is to be made;
(2) the cases and manner in which Customs may cancel a person's certification;
(3) entitlement to a credit such as above to depend on the issue of an invoice containing such particulars as may be prescribed, or as may be notified by Customs in accordance with provisions contained in regulations; and
(4) the imposition on certified persons of obligations with respect to the

keeping, preservation and production of such records as may be prescribed and of obligations to comply with such requirements with
respect to any of those matters as may be so notified;

and regulations made under (2) above may confer on Customs power, if
they think fit, to refuse to cancel a person's certification, and to refuse to
give effect to any entitlement of that person to be registered, until the end
of such period after the grant of certification as may be prescribed.
References here, in relation to any person, to the relevant part of his business are references:

(1) where the whole of his business relates to the carrying on of one or
more designated activities, to that business; and
(2) in any other case, to so much of his business as does so relate.

Here 'designated activities' means such activities, being activities carried on
by a person who, by carrying them on, falls to be treated as a farmer for the
purposes of the EC Council Directive 77/388/EEC, Art 25 (common flat-
rate scheme for farmers), as the Treasury may by order designate. Currently,
the orders in operation are the VAT (Flat-rate Scheme for Farmers)
(Designated Activities) Order 1992 and the VAT (Flat-rate Scheme for
Farmers) (Percentage Addition) Order 1992.

7.12.16 Customers to account for tax on supplies of gold
(VATA 1994 s 55)

Where a person makes a supply of gold to another person and that supply is
a taxable supply (but not a zero-rated supply), that supply is treated (per
Sch 1) as a taxable supply by that other person, as well as one by the person
who makes it. The supply is also treated, insofar as that other person is supplied in connection with the carrying on of any business by him, as a supply
made by him in the course or furtherance of that business. However, this
does not require that any supply be disregarded (for VATA 1994 Sch 1) on
the grounds that it is a capital asset of that other person's business.

Where a taxable person makes a supply of gold to a person who is himself a taxable person, and is supplied in connection with the carrying on by
him of any business, it is the person supplied who must, on the supplier's
behalf, account for and pay VAT and not the supplier. The general rules for
determining when a supply of gold is to be treated as taking place (see s 6)
are modified for the purposes of the supply. Section 6(4)–(10) is disregarded, so that the time of supply is therefore determined under ss 6(1)-(3),
(11)-(15), 18(4) and VAT Regs 1995, Pt XI.

A supply of gold for the above purposes comprises any:

(a) supply of fine gold, gold grain of any purity, or gold coins of any purity;
(b) supply of goods containing gold sold for a price equivalent to the open
market value of the gold content;

(c) treatment or process applied to another person's goods which produces gold, gold grain or gold coins within (a) above.

7.12.17 Fuel for private use
(VATA 1994, ss 56 and 57)

The rules described below apply where, in any prescribed accounting period, fuel which is or has previously been supplied to or imported or manufactured by a taxable person in the course of his business:

(1) is provided or to be provided by the taxable person to an individual for private use in his own vehicle or a vehicle allocated to him and is so provided by reason of that individual's employment; or
(2) where the taxable person is an individual, is appropriated or to be appropriated by him for private use in his own vehicle; or
(3) where the taxable person is a partnership, is provided or to be provided to any of the individual partners for private use in his own vehicle.

Fuel is not regarded as provided to any person for his private use if it is supplied at a price which:

(1) in the case of fuel supplied to or imported by the taxable person, is not less than the price at which it was so supplied or imported; and
(2) in the case of fuel manufactured by the taxable person, is not less than the aggregate of the cost of the raw material and of manufacturing together with any excise duty thereon.

Here:

(1) 'fuel for private use' means fuel which, having been supplied to or imported or manufactured by a taxable person in the course of his business, is or is to be provided or appropriated for private use as above;
(2) any reference to fuel supplied to a taxable person includes fuel acquired by a taxable person from another member state and any reference to fuel imported by a taxable person is confined to a reference to fuel imported by that person from a place outside the member states;
(3) any reference to an individual's own vehicle is construed as including any vehicle of which for the time being he has the use, other than a vehicle allocated to him;
(4) a vehicle is at any time taken to be allocated to an individual if at that time it is made available (without any transfer of the property in it) either to the individual himself or to any other person, and is so made available by reason of the individual's employment and for private use; and
(5) fuel provided by an employer to an employee and fuel provided to any person for private use in a vehicle which, under (4) above, is for the time being taken to be allocated to the employee is taken to be provided to the employee by reason of his employment.

Where under s 43 (group treatment) any bodies corporate are treated as members of a group, any provision of fuel by a member of the group to an individual is treated as provision by the representative member.

In relation to the taxable person, tax on the supply, acquisition or importation of fuel for private use is treated as input tax, notwithstanding that the fuel is not used or to be used for the purposes of a business carried on by the taxable person (and, accordingly, no apportionment of VAT is made under s 24(5) by reference to fuel for private use).

At the time at which fuel for private use is put into the fuel tank of an individual's own vehicle or of a vehicle allocated to him, the fuel is treated as supplied to him by the taxable person in the course or furtherance of his business for a consideration determined as below (and, accordingly, where the fuel is appropriated by the taxable person to his own private use, he is treated as supplying it to himself in his private capacity).

In any prescribed accounting period of the taxable person in which, as above, he is treated as supplying fuel for private use to an individual, the consideration for all the supplies made to that individual in that period for any one vehicle is that which is appropriate to a vehicle of that description, and that consideration is taken to be inclusive of VAT.

In any case where:

(1) in any prescribed accounting period, fuel for private use is, as above, treated as supplied to an individual for one vehicle for a part of the period and for another vehicle for another part of the period; and

(2) at the end of that period one of those vehicles neither belongs to him nor is allocated to him,

the above has effect as if the supplies made to the individual during those parts of the period were in respect of only one vehicle.

In any prescribed accounting period a vehicle is not regarded as allocated to an individual by reason of his employment if:

(1) in that period it was made available to, and actually used by, more than one of the employees of one or more employers and, in the case of each of them, it was made available to him by reason of his employment but was not in that period ordinarily used by any one of them to the exclusion of the others; and

(2) in the case of each of the employees, any private use of the vehicle made by him in that period was merely incidental to his other use of it in that period; and

(3) it was in that period not normally kept overnight on or in the vicinity of any residential premises where any of the employees was residing, except while being kept overnight on premises occupied by the person making the vehicle available to them.

Here, 'employment' includes any office; and related expressions are construed accordingly, and 'vehicle' means a mechanically propelled road vehicle other than:

(a) a motor cycle as defined in the Road Traffic Act 1988, s 185(1) or, for Northern Ireland, the Road Traffic (Northern Ireland) Order 1981, art 37(1)(f), or

(b) an invalid carriage as defined in s 185(1) of the 1988 Act or, for Northern Ireland, art 37(1)(g) of the 1981 Order.

Where the prescribed accounting period is a period of 12, three or one month(s), the consideration appropriate to any vehicle is that specified in relation to a vehicle of the appropriate description in the second column of Table 7.1.

Table 7.1

Description of vehicle (type of engine and cylinder capacity in cubic centimetres)	12-month period (£)	3-month period (£)	1-month period (£)
Diesel engine:			
2000 or less	850	212	70
More than 2000	1075	268	89
Any other type of engine			
1400 or less	905	226	75
More than 1400 but not			
more than 2000	1145	286	95
More than 2000	1690	422	140

Where, as above, supplies of fuel for private use made for two or more vehicles were made for only one vehicle, the consideration is allocated between them. The rules are set out in s 57(5) and (6).

7.13 SUPPLEMENTARY PROVISIONS

7.13.1 Supplies spanning change of rate etc
(VATA 1994, s 88)

The following procedure applies where there is a change in the rate of VAT in force or in the descriptions of exempt, zero-rated or reduced-rate supplies acquisitions.

Where:

(1) a supply affected by the change would be treated as made wholly or partly at a time when it would not have been affected by the change; or

(2) a supply not so affected would be treated as made wholly or partly at a time when it would have been so affected,

the rate at which VAT is chargeable on the supply, or any question whether it is zero-rated or exempt or a reduced-rate supply, is if the person making it so elects determined without regard to s 6(4), (5), (6) or (10) (special rules relating to time of supply).

Any power to make regulations with respect to the time when a supply is treated as taking place includes power to provide for this rule to apply as if the references above to s 6(4), (5), (6) or (10) included references to specified provisions of the regulations.

Where:

(1) any acquisition of goods from another member state which is affected by the change would not have been affected (in whole or in part) if it had been treated as taking place at the time of the event which, in relation to that acquisition, is the first relevant event for the purposes of taxing the acquisition; or

(2) any acquisition of goods from another member state which is not so affected would have been affected (in whole or in part) if it had been treated as taking place at the time of that event,

the rate at which VAT is chargeable on the acquisition, or any question whether it is zero-rated or exempt or a reduced-rate acquisition, is, if the person making the acquisition so elects, determined as at the time of that event.

The VAT Regs 1995, reg 95 make provision for the replacement or correction of any VAT invoice which:

(1) relates to a supply in respect of which an election is made under this rule, but

(2) was issued before the election was made.

No election may be made hereunder in respect of a supply to which s 6(9) (self-billing) or Sch 4, para 7 (sale under a power) applies.

References here to an acquisition being zero-rated are references to an acquisition of goods from another member state being one in relation to which s 30(3) (imports) provides for no VAT to be chargeable. References here to:

(1) a supply being a reduced-rate supply, or

(2) an acquisition being a reduced-rate acquisition,

are references to a supply, or (as the case may be) an acquisition, being one on which VAT is charged at the reduced rate in force under s 29A and Sch 7A (s 88(8)).

7.13.2 Adjustments of contracts on changes in VAT
(VATA 1994, s 89)

Where, after the making of a contract for the supply of goods or services and before the goods or services are supplied, there is a change in the VAT charged on the supply, then, unless the contract otherwise provided, there is added to or deducted from the consideration for the supply an amount equal to the change.

This applies in relation to a tenancy or lease as it applies to a contract except that a term of a tenancy or lease is not taken to provide that this rule is not to apply in the case of the tenancy or lease if the term does not refer specifically to VAT or this rule.

References here to a change in the VAT charged on a supply include references to a change to or from no VAT being charged on the supply (including a change attributable to the making of an election under Sch 10, para 2 (election to waive exemption)).

7.13.3 Meaning of 'new means of transport'
(VATA 1994, s 95; VAT Regs 1995, reg 147)

'Means of transport' in the expression 'new means of transport' means any of the following:

(1) any ship exceeding 7.5 m in length;
(2) any aircraft the take-off weight of which exceeds 1550 kg;
(3) any motorised land vehicle which:
   (a) has an engine with a displacement or cylinder capacity exceeding 48 cm^3; or
   (b) is constructed or adapted to be electrically propelled using more than 7.2 kw.

A ship, aircraft or motorised land vehicle does not fall within the above unless it is intended for the transport of persons or goods.

A means of transport is treated as new, in relation to any supply or any acquisition from another member state, at any time unless at that time:

(1) the period that has elapsed since its first entry into service is in the case of:
   (a) a ship or aircraft, a period of more than 3 months; and
   (b) a land vehicle, a period of more than 6 months; and
(2) it has, since its first entry into service, travelled under its own power in the case of:
   (a) a ship, for more than 100 hours;
   (b) an aircraft, for more than 40 hours; and
   (c) a land vehicle, for more than 6000 km.

The Treasury may amend the above:

(1) by adding or deleting any ship, aircraft or vehicle of a description specified in the order to or from those which are for the time being specified above; and
(2) by altering, omitting or adding to the provisions for determining whether a means of transport is new.

Customs may by regulations make provision specifying the circumstances in which a means of transport is to be treated as having first entered into service.

A ship includes a hovercraft.

7.14 ACCOUNTING FOR VAT

It is a requirement for all taxpayers to maintain a VAT account. The VAT Regs 1995, regs 31–39 set down specifically what is to be included in the account. Separate accounts should be maintained for each tax period, known as prescribed accounting periods, and each account should be split into two portions – tax payable and tax allowable. The tax payable portion should include a total of output tax due for that prescribed accounting period, a total of output tax due on acquisitions from other member states, and corrections and adjustments to the tax payable. The tax allowable portion should include a total of the input tax allowable to the taxable person for that prescribed accounting period including the total allowable for acquisitions from other member states and corrections and adjustments.

VAT returns have to be submitted on a regular basis. Each VAT-registered person is normally allocated a three-monthly VAT accounting period, but it is possible to request a particular VAT period (for example to coincide with the business's financial year). It is also possible to request monthly returns if the business regularly recovers VAT from Customs. There is also a scheme whereby it is possible to make annual returns.

The largest VAT-registered businesses (ie those which normally pay more than £2m annually to Customs) are required to make monthly payments on account with a balancing payment when the three-monthly VAT return is submitted. The actual monthly payments are calculated by reference to the VAT liability of a reference year.

Returns must be submitted with full payment by the end of the month following the end of the VAT accounting period (the due date). A failure to submit returns and make full payment by the due date is subject to penalties. Taxpayers who make regular payments can apply to use the Credit Transfer Scheme which allows a further seven days for payment.

Where a registered person has failed to make a return for a period or where the return appears to be incomplete or incorrect, Customs is empowered to make an assessment of the amount due and notify it to the registered person. The assessment is usually produced automatically by the VAT Central Unit and estimates the amount based on the taxpayer's previous VAT return history. Where the assessed amount is lower than the actual liability, a further assessment is issued when this fact is discovered, usually by the local VAT control officer.

7.14.1 Output VAT

The VAT chargeable on supplies (known as output tax) made during a period must be declared on the return which is provided automatically each period by Customs. Output VAT is due on all supplies made (normally invoices issued during the period), irrespective of whether the invoices have been paid for. There are special schemes available to ease this particular requirement for certain business classes as explained below. In addition, VAT is due on all money received for supplies made during the period and for which a tax invoice has not been issued (eg scrap sales, vending machine income, emptying telephone boxes, staff canteen sales, and certain deductions from salaries for supplies to staff).

For businesses which do not issue tax invoices, such as retailers, VAT is due on the gross taxable income received during the VAT period.

7.14.2 Tax invoices

A registered taxable person making a standard-rated taxable supply to another taxable person must provide him with a tax invoice. The issue of invoices for zero-rated supplies and for supplies to customers who are not taxable persons is optional. A tax invoice must, unless Customs agrees otherwise, be issued within 30 days after the basic tax point (see below), the time the VAT is due.

The invoices are often addressed to the person who is going to pay them and not to whom the goods and services are supplied. It is important to be aware that this may cause problems as only the person receiving goods or services can recover VAT on the invoice.

The details to be shown on a tax invoice are the:

- identifying number
- date of supply (ie tax point)
- date of issue
- supplier's name, address and registration number
- name and address of the person to whom the goods or services are supplied
- type of supply
- description
- for each description, quantity or extent of services, rate of tax and amount payable excluding tax
- gross amount payable
- rate of any cash discount offered
- amount of tax chargeable at each rate
- total amount of tax chargeable.

7.14.3 **VAT recovery**

VAT-registered businesses may offset any VAT paid to suppliers (known as input tax) against the output tax declared, subject to the following conditions:

(1) Goods or services have been *supplied to* and have been, or will be, used by the business to make taxable supplies.

(2) Documentary evidence of the supply received (ie a tax invoice to the business by the supplier) is retained. If there is no tax invoice or other documentary evidence, the VAT officer may refuse claims for input tax, although Customs has discretion to accept alternative evidence.

Supplies of zero-rated goods or services are taxable supplies with an entitlement to recover VAT on related costs; there is no such entitlement for exempt supplies. In addition VAT is not recoverable as input tax on goods or services received by the VAT-registered person which are used for a non-business activity or for private use, or are certainly outside the scope of transactions. Many people believe that because a VAT-registered business pays an invoice, there is an entitlement to recover the VAT shown on the invoice. This is not correct and to do so may give rise to penalties.

Subject to certain exceptions, VAT on the purchase of a motor car or on business entertainment expenses is not recoverable as input tax (VAT (Cars) Order 1992 and VAT (Input Tax) Order 1992). Note that a question has been raised of whether the UK is correct in blocking VAT recovery on cars, and the law may be altered.

7.14.4 **Motor cars**

'Motor car' is defined as a vehicle usually used on public roads with three or more wheels which either:

(1) is constructed solely for the carriage of passengers; or

(2) has roofed accommodation fitted with, or constructed or adapted for the fitting of, windows to the rear of the driver.

The definition is wide and a number of semi-commercial vehicles fall within the definition, eg Land Rovers.

VAT is normally recoverable on the acquisition of a motor car where it is:

(1) leased or hired (not a lease purchase);

(2) acquired unused specifically to be sold;

(3) acquired to convert it into a vehicle which is not a motor car;

(4) unused and supplied to a person whose only taxable supply is the hire of motor cars to other taxable persons whose business is predominately the provision of motor cars to disabled persons in respect of a mobility allowance.

In addition, VAT is recoverable on the purchase of motor cars by the following businesses:

(1) self-drive hire companies providing the hiring is to the same person (which may be a company) and is less than 30 consecutive days on any one occasion and 90 days total pa;
(2) driving schools;
(3) taxi firms;
(4) companies leasing cars to any of the above businesses.

Recovery of VAT is allowed on cars purchased wholly for business use. If a car is made available for private use, recovery of input tax remains blocked. The relief generally applies to car leasing companies. Taxpayers leasing cars where there is an element of private use are restricted to a 50% recovery of VAT on the leasing charges. The UK has applied for a derogation from the European Commission to restrict recovery.

7.14.5 Business entertainment

Business entertainment is not regarded as including staff entertainment, but problems may arise where costs of staff entertainment arise incidentally from the provision of entertainment for clients. Staff entertainment does not include entertainment of self-employed representatives and therefore the VAT is non-recoverable.

There are a number of occasions where VAT on promotional activities is classified as business entertaining and the VAT non-recoverable. It includes for example the cost of a box at a racecourse, entertainment at trade fairs, exhibitions etc, subscriptions to squash clubs etc, entertaining shareholders, and entertainment by market research companies who invite people for group discussions.

There are two conflicting court decisions on business entertainment. In each case the issue was whether, where the supply in question was used partly for business entertainment and partly for normal use, the whole of the input tax should be excluded from credit, or whether an apportionment was permissible. In *C&E Commrs v Plant Repair and Services (South Wales)* [1994] STC 232 it was decided that once it was shown that goods or services were used or to be used for business entertainment purposes, the input tax on the entire supply was non-recoverable. In *Thorn EMI v C&E Commrs* [1994] STC 469 the opposite conclusion was reached. It was held that a system of proportional deduction was in order where goods and services were used in part for business use and in part for business entertainment. This decision was upheld in the High Court where the previous ruling in *Plant Repair and Services,* above, was also overturned.

7.14.6 Partial exemption

A business that makes both exempt and taxable supplies is known as partially exempt and is generally unable to recover all VAT paid to its suppliers. However, if the VAT on costs relating, directly and indirectly, to the exempt activities (known as exempt input tax) is below prescribed limits, all the VAT is recoverable in full. The current limits for VAT years commencing on or after 1 December 1994 are that exempt input tax must not exceed £625 pm on average in the VAT year (which ends 31 March, 30 April or 31 May depending on the business's VAT return period). In addition, this exempt input tax must also represent less than 50% of the total input tax incurred by a business on all its purchases and expenses for the period. If these limits should be exceeded in any VAT year, *all* the relevant VAT is irrecoverable.

There are other minor limits that apply in particular circumstances and certain exempt supplies may be ignored. The rules are complex and it is advisable to obtain professional advice. Full details may be found in the VAT Regs 1995, regs 99–109 and Customs VAT Notice 706.

Input tax which can be directly attributable to taxable supplies can be recovered in full. Input tax wholly attributable to exempt supplies is not recoverable. The purpose of a partial exemption method is to allocate such input tax as cannot be directly related in either taxable or exempt supplies, in a fair and reasonable proportion. The method, known as the standard method, allocates input tax on the basis of a ratio of the value of taxable supplies to the value of total supplies, rounded up to the nearest whole number. This method can be used without obtaining permission from Customs.

The use of any other method requires Customs' agreement. Customs normally approves any method which produces a fair and reasonable result. Other methods available include using a ratio of exempt input tax to total input tax, a ratio of staff generating taxable income to staff generating exempt income, or a ratio of the number of taxable transactions to exempt transactions.

7.15 IMPORTS, EXPORTS AND SINGLE MARKET

The term imports and exports refers only to goods entering or leaving the UK from or to a place outside the EU.

7.15.1 Imports of goods from outside EU

VAT is due upon the importation of all goods into the UK which would bear VAT if supplied within the UK. The VAT may be paid on importation in one of three ways:

(1) via a deferment facility arranged with Customs;

(2) by arrangement with the clearing/shipping agent;

(3) payment in cash or a banker's draft.

The recovery of VAT paid is determined by the same considerations as would apply to any purchase made in the UK. The evidence required to support input tax deduction on importation is form C79. This is issued by Customs as a certificate detailing the amounts of VAT paid or deferred on importations within the previous calendar month.

7.15.2 Export of goods outside EU

In general, the export of goods from the UK is zero rated. However, to satisfy Customs that zero rating is appropriate it is necessary to hold some evidence that the goods have been exported. An overseas address on a sales invoice is insufficient.

Customs requires supporting evidence in the form of commercial documentation. If this is not available within three months of the date of zero rating the supply, Customs states that the supply is to be treated as standard rated, and VAT accounted for on the relevant VAT return.

7.15.3 Transactions within the single market

With effect from 1 January 1993, supplies to and from EU member states are not regarded as imports (known as acquisitions) or exports (known as supplies). Businesses must maintain records of all movements of goods and make returns for statistical and control purposes.

No VAT is charged on goods arriving from other EU countries where the UK business's VAT registration number is quoted on the invoice. The recipient of the goods must account for VAT on his next VAT return as if he had supplied them. He must calculate the VAT which would have been payable and include the amount with his normal output tax. The same amount may also be recovered as input tax, subject to the normal rules and restrictions on recovery. If the UK VAT number is not quoted, the supplier charges VAT at source.

Supplies of goods to other EU countries are zero rated, provided that the customer's VAT registration number is shown on the sales invoice. If the customer's number is not shown, VAT must be charged at the rate which would be applicable if the goods had been supplied in the UK. Persons selling goods to other EU member states must submit an aggregate sales list within 42 days of the end of each period. This must show, for each quarter, the value of goods supplied to each EU customer together with each customer's VAT registration number.

There is a requirement to furnish more detailed information, known as 'intrastat' returns, for acquisitions (known as arrivals) and supplies (known as despatches). The returns must be furnished when the threshold for arrivals or despatches is exceeded. Currently the threshold for both is

£150,000. Returns are required monthly and should be lodged within ten working days following the end of the month. The information required on the intrastat is extensive, and reference should be made to Customs Notice 60. Note that intrastat relates only to goods, not services.

7.16 SPECIAL SCHEMES

7.16.1 Retail schemes

These schemes are used by retailers, ie those in trade classification Groups 24 (Retail Division) and 28 (Miscellaneous Services). Generally, this means those who deal direct with the public on a cash basis and who do not normally issue tax invoices.

7.16.2 Second-hand schemes

There are a number of special second-hand schemes that provide for VAT to be charged on the profit, if any, as opposed to the full selling price. Schemes are available for:

- cars
- motor cycles
- caravans/motor caravans
- works of art, antiques and collector's items
- boats and outboard motors
- electronic organs
- aircraft
- firearms
- horses and ponies.

Special stock recording and detailed records including invoices are required. The scheme was extended from June 1995 to cover virtually all second-hand goods, works of art, antiques and collectors' items except precious metals and gemstones. It is recognised that dealers in low value, high volume goods will have difficulty maintaining the detailed records required. A simplified method of VAT accounts has therefore been introduced, known as 'global accounting'. Under the system 'eligible businesses' (those who cannot maintain the detailed records) are able to account for VAT on the difference between the total of purchases and sales in each tax period rather than on individual items. This scheme can only be used for eligible second-hand goods which have a purchase price of less than £500 per item.

7.16.3 Cash accounting

The general principle is that VAT must be accounted for on all tax invoices issued whether or not the customer/client has paid for the supply.

Businesses that cannot use the retail scheme, and whose annual turnover is less than £350,000 (excluding VAT), may use the cash accounting scheme, provided certain conditions are satisfied. The conditions are laid down in regulations as described in Customs Notice 731, which in this respect has the force of law. Output VAT is not due until payment has been received but, similarly, input tax on purchases/expenses cannot be recovered until the supplier has been paid and a receipt obtained.

7.16.4 Annual accounting

To avoid having to submit returns quarterly, businesses with an annual turnover not exceeding £300,000 (excluding VAT) may be authorised, in writing, by Customs to use the annual accounting scheme. Nine payments, based on the previous year's VAT liability, are made by direct debit and a final, balancing payment is made with the VAT return at the end of the second month following the allocated VAT year.

7.17 ENFORCEMENT PROCEDURES

7.17.1 VAT visits

Customs regularly visits VAT-registered businesses to verify the returns submitted. Its powers are extensive and include the rights to see any documents, accounts, etc relating to the business activities and to inspect (but not search) the business premises. The frequency of visit depends upon a number of factors such as the business's size, types of business activity and compliance history. Visits can range from half a day every few years for smaller businesses to several weeks a year for multinationals.

Where errors are discovered, the visiting officer raises an assessment for VAT previously under-declared and, where appropriate, imposes a penalty and interest charges. It is advisable, therefore, to have all assessments independently reviewed. Customs collects over £1,000m by way of additional assessments from approximately 450,000 visits each year, but most visits do not result in assessments being issued. If the accounting records are well kept and independently reviewed regularly no problem should arise at the visit.

7.17.2 Penalties

There are a number of penalty provisions which Customs may impose automatically, and arbitrarily, for a failure to comply with the many complex VAT regulations. These were introduced with the view to improving compliance and reducing the amount of VAT outstanding at any one time.

7.17.3 Late registration
(VATA 1994, s 67(1))

Failure to notify a liability to register at the correct time (see 7.4.1) results in Customs imposing a financial penalty. From 1 January 1995 the penalty is a percentage of the net tax due between the date notification was required and the actual date of notification, as follows:

- Belatedness not exceeding nine months: 5%.
- Belatedness exceeding nine months but not exceeding 18 months: 10%.
- Belatedness exceeding 18 months: 15%.

A penalty is not imposed (or is withdrawn) where there is a reasonable excuse for the late notification. What amounts to a reasonable excuse is constantly explored by VAT tribunals. In *G Davies* (LON/86/174 (2126)) it was held that an understandable error in determining the liability of supplies was a reasonable excuse.

Ignorance (see *Neal v C&E Commrs* [1988] STC 131), overwork or the reliance on another person are not normally reasonable excuses. Appeals have succeeded where, on the facts of a particular case, an appellant took reasonable steps to notify (*S Zoweni* (*t/a The Paper Shop*) (1986) VATTR 133).

7.17.4 Late returns
(FA 1994, s 59)

If one payment is submitted late in any 12-month period, Customs notifies the VAT-registered person that payments submitted late during the following 12 months are subject to a default surcharge. If a payment is submitted late during the 12-month surcharge period, a 2% penalty is imposed and the surcharge period extended for a further 12 months. The surcharge rises for each successive late payment to 5% and by increments of 5% to a maximum of 15%. If payments are submitted by the due dates for 12 months, the business is removed from the default surcharge regime and the cycle starts again. The surcharge is waived if it is assessable at the lower rates and is below a minimum amount (ie £200).

A default surcharge is not imposed until after Customs has issued a Surcharge Liability Notice (SLN). There have been several tribunal hearings on this subject and where the taxpayer has been able to demonstrate that he never received an SLN, the surcharge has been withdrawn.

A default surcharge does not apply if a taxpayer has a reasonable excuse for late submission or payment. It is difficult to satisfy this requirement. The tribunal has accepted that the last minute breakdown of the computer, the unforeseen sickness of the person preparing the return at the time it was due or other such catastrophes constitute a reasonable excuse. If a taxpayer can demonstrate that the return and payment were posted in reasonably sufficient time to reach Customs by the due date, there is a reasonable excuse and a default surcharge is not imposed. Posting the return on the last day of the month, however, results in a default occurring.

Insufficiency of funds is not a reasonable excuse. However, *C&E Commrs v Steptoe* [1992] STC 727 confirmed that where lack of funds was due to an unforeseeable inescapable misfortune, beyond the taxpayer's control, insufficiency of funds was a reasonable excuse for non-payment of VAT. The taxpayer had one major customer who was persistently slow in paying invoices.

7.17.5 Misdeclaration penalty
(FA 1985, s 14)

If a VAT officer discovers an under-declaration which exceeds specified limits, he assesses a serious misdeclaration penalty of 15% of the additional VAT assessed. The penalty, which is based on each individual period (ie it is not cumulative), is imposed where the additional VAT assessed exceeds the lesser of:

(1) £1m; and
(2) 30% of the gross amount of tax due for the appropriate return period.

The gross amount of tax is the total combined input tax and output tax for the period. Prior to the aforementioned date, the basis applied was the true amount of tax, ie the amount payable or repayable. The old basis continues to apply for failure to render VAT return cases where the taxpayer fails to notify Customs within 30 days that an assessment issued centrally is lower than the true liability.

7.17.6 Reasonable excuse

A penalty is not imposed where a taxpayer can establish a reasonable excuse to the satisfaction of Customs or on appeal to a VAT tribunal. In addition, a penalty can be mitigated down to an amount (including nil) by Customs or, on appeal, a tribunal.

In *Clean Car Co* (90/1381 (5965)) the chairman tried to provide objective guidelines for when an appellant has a reasonable excuse. It was stated that the correct test was whether the taxpayer's actions would have been a reasonable action had it been done by a reasonable trader, conscious of, and intending to comply with, his tax obligations, but having the experience and other relevant attributes of a taxpayer and placed in the taxpayer's actual situation at the relevant time.

7.17.7 Voluntary disclosure

A penalty is not imposed where an error is notified to Customs at a time when a taxpayer has no reason to believe his affairs are being looked into. This condition was imposed very strictly by Customs, but they have since been persuaded that the strict application is creating a disincentive to disclose errors. Under a revised code of practice, errors discovered after a visit date has been arranged, including those disclosed at the start of a visit, and in some cases during and after a visit, are normally accepted as voluntary disclosures.

7.17.8 Tax which would have been lost

This is the amount of understatement of output tax or overstatement of input tax. For prescribed accounting periods beginning prior to 1 June 1994, where for any period there was an understatement of output tax or an overstatement of input tax, allowance for the error could be made in determining the lost tax for the prescribed accounting period concerned. This was as a result of a decision in *C&E Commrs v Peninsular and Oriental Steam Navigation Co C/A 1993* [1994] STC 259.

However, following this case, the VAT legislation was amended to prevent the offsetting against an under-declaration of over-declarations arising in other periods. The change is not retrospective, ie it only has effect for prescribed accounting periods beginning after 1 June 1994. For periods prior to this date, the old legislation remains in force and thus errors discovered in previous periods can be offset.

7.17.9 Interest
(FA 1994, s 74)

An interest charge is imposed on assessments for additional tax issued by VAT visiting officers. The interest rate is the prescribed rate as enacted by Treasury order and is not deductible for income or corporation tax. However, Customs has stated that interest may not be imposed where there is no overall loss of revenue eg where a supplier has failed to charge VAT to a customer who would have been entitled to recover the VAT charge. Customs has indicated that each case is decided on its merits, but that officers have been made aware of the need to consider whether there has been a loss of revenue.

7.17.10 Other penalties

There are a number of other penalty provisions such as failure to maintain or produce records, unauthorised issue of a tax invoice (by non-registered persons), and persistent incorrect returns. There are, in fact, over 60 regulatory offences which could give rise to a penalty.

7.18 FRAUD

7.18.1 Civil
(FA 1994, s 60)

If, after an investigation, Customs is satisfied there has been an element of dishonesty, it may seek to impose a civil fraud penalty of 100% of the tax involved. If there has been full co-operation by the taxpayer, Customs, or (on appeal) a VAT tribunal, may reduce the penalty by whatever percentage is considered reasonable. In a civil fraud investigation, Customs has only to prove on a balance of probabilities that a fraud had been committed to impose a penalty.

7.18.2 Criminal
(VATA 1994, s 72)

The more serious cases are dealt with under criminal law with penalties of up to three times the VAT involved, or imprisonment, or both. In these cases Customs must use the criminal rules of evidence, etc and prove beyond reasonable doubt that a fraud has been committed deliberately.

7.19 APPEALS

7.19.1 VAT tribunals

There is a right of appeal to an independent VAT tribunal on a number of matters including:

(1) assessments which are considered to be incorrect or not issued to Customs' best judgement;
(2) liability rulings by Customs in respect of a specified supply;
(3) penalties, other than the interest charged for errors, if there is a reasonable excuse for the error; the law does not define 'reasonable excuse' but does state the insufficiency of funds or the reliance on another is not one;
(4) the amount of the reduction, if any, of a penalty for a civil fraud where the taxpayer considers he has provided full co-operation with the investigating officers.

The details of appeal procedures are outside the scope of this book. However, the procedure for lodging an appeal to a VAT tribunal (which must be made within 30 days of the appealable event) is straightforward. It is prudent to obtain professional advice before doing so and it is advisable to be represented at the tribunal hearing, which in many ways resembles a court hearing although less formal.

A VAT tribunal decision may be appealed to a higher court on a point of law and, in limited circumstances, an appeal may be referred to the European Court of Justice for a ruling.

7.19.2 Departmental reviews

Many disputes are settled by negotiations with Customs by formally requesting a departmental review of the disputed ruling/assessment within the 30-day time limit. This allows discussions to continue without the loss of the right to appeal to an independent VAT tribunal. Commissioners, if requested, usually review an assessment after the 30-day limit has expired and will, where appropriate, reduce the amount assessed. In certain circumstances it is also possible to make an application to a VAT tribunal to hear a case that is out of time. It is prudent to take professional advice before lodging an appeal.

8

STAMP DUTY AND
BUSINESS TRANSACTIONS

Stamp duty is a tax payable on the processing of documents; it is not paid directly on transactions, unlike most taxes. It is paid when documents are written and signed in connection with transactions. Stamp duty is one of the oldest of UK taxes and is governed broadly by the Stamp Act (SA) 1891. The Act sets out the basis of stamp duty charge and itemises by process of scheduling the various types of document that can attract a stamp duty charge.

It is important to note that UK documents (or indeed non-UK documents that relate to something done inside the UK) cannot be used as evidence in court (except in proceedings of a criminal nature) unless they have been properly stamped in accordance within the terms of the 1891 Act. Similarly, documents that have to be registered in an official register or entered in statutory books must carry a stamp signifying that the appropriate level of duty has been paid.

Stamp duty reserve tax (SDRT) is payable on certain undertakings, 'agreements' or 'deals' effecting the transfer of chargeable securities. Such agreements need not be effected in writing as SDRT is not a documentary tax or duty. Where a transfer is made between the parties to an agreement of this sort, a document is effected to evidence it and the transfer is then duly stamped; the SDRT paid is deducted from the amount then due.

8.1 DOCUMENTS LIABLE TO DUTY

Stamp duty was first introduced in 1694 and the law has not been redrafted since SA 1891. Numerous amendments have however been made (to block loopholes or to grant new reliefs) and the result is legislation that is archaic, exceptionally complex and difficult to follow, and in which the detailed exceptions are more important than the broad general rules. For example, the scheme of the legislation is not to impose duty on documents implementing the sale of certain types of property, but to impose duty on all documents implementing the sale of any type of property and then to provide a series of exceptions.

The practical effect of this legislation is to impose stamp duty on documents implementing the sale of:

(a) shares and other securities;
(b) freehold land and buildings and the grant or assignment of leases;
(c) certain types of business property, such as goodwill and patent rights.

This is not a comprehensive list but it does include all the charges likely to be incurred by a business proprietor.

Stamp duty is charged only on sales and not (since 1985) on gifts. Nor is any duty payable when assets are put into trust. However, a sale is defined to include the exchange of property for shares or securities, or the exchange of one block of shares for another. Stamp duty is either charged at a fixed rate (eg 50p) or as a percentage of the value (ie ad valorem duty)

A document should be presented for stamping within 30 days of execution (ie signature). Late stamping attracts a substantial financial penalty (see 8.2).

Exempt instruments

Some documents are completely exempt from stamp duty, provided an appropriate certificate is signed and endorsed at the time of the execution of the instrument.

The relevant instruments (as far as companies are concerned) are contained in the Stamp Duty (Exempt Instruments) Regulations 1987 as follows:

- Property vesting in a trust where new trustees are being appointed, or where a trustee retires
- Conveyances by a liquidator to a shareholder of the company in satisfaction of the shareholders' rights in a winding-up
- The grant of a service contract for money or money's worth
- The grant of easements over land
- Declarations of trust of life policies executed on or after 1 October 1999 (added by the Stamp Duty (Exempt Instruments) (Amendment) Regulations 1999.

Most of the other exempt instruments are concerned with the death of individuals or the transfer of property by individuals.

The Stamp Office provides a recommended form of words to accompany a document where it is claimed that an exempt instrument is being effected. If such a certificate is effected, there is no requirement to send the documents to the Stamp Office for adjudication.

8.1.1 Sale of shares or other securities

Stamp duty is charged on documents transferring ownership of shares (in both quoted and private companies), debentures, unit trust units and other securities. The rate is 0.5%, rounded up to the next 50p (eg duty on a sale for £325 would be £2). British Government stocks ('gilts') and stocks issued by certain international bodies (eg the EU) are exempt from duty. The stamp duty is borne by the purchaser and is shown as a disbursement on the broker's contract note. It counts as part of the cost of the holding for CGT purposes.

Where one block of shares is exchanged for another, the transaction is treated as two sales, so both participants must pay the usual duty. In certain circumstances it is possible for shares to be sold without a stampable document being created. This most commonly happens where a block of shares, traded on The London Stock Exchange, changes hands several times in the space of a few days. In such circumstances, SDRT is charged on the transaction. The SDRT is equal in amount to the stamp duty that would otherwise have been paid and so, from the purchaser's point of view, it is immaterial which tax is paid.

For some years now, the Government and the Revenue have been intent on the abolition of the charges to stamp duty on trades in stocks and shares as and when The Stock Exchange introduces its so-called 'paperless trading system'. There have been several attempts to introduce such a system over the last 15 years, beginning with TAURUS in 1991 and CREST in 1996. For instruments executed on or after 1 October 1999, under FA 1999, s 112 (see below) the rate of duty is 0.5% of the consideration, rounded up to the nearest multiple of £5.

8.1.2 Sale of freehold land and buildings

From 28 March 2000 the rates of stamp duty are as follows:

Transactions of value over £500,000	4%
Transactions of value between £250,000 and £500,000	3%
Transactions of value between £60,000 and £250,000	1%

Property transactions (except shares and marketable securities) are free of stamp duty if the total consideration is less than £60,000.

Under FA 1999, s 112, for documents executed after 30 September 1999, the old charging provisions under which the amount of duty otherwise due was rounded up to a multiple of between 50p and £12 have been changed. For documents executed after that date, stamp duty is charged in multiples of £5 in all cases.

Stamp duty is payable by reference to the actual consideration that passes and has no relationship to the actual value of the asset that is the subject of the transaction. Although some gifts were taxable at one stage, these are now mainly exempt.

Some contracts for property sales are subjected to ad valorem stamp duty. This occurs where there is no immediate conveyance or transfer by way of sale. Where such properties are later transferred by way of sale or conveyance covered by a document, no additional stamp duty is chargeable on that subsequent document.

If a contract includes stampable and non-stampable property (eg movable goods that normally pass by simple delivery), the purchase price must be apportioned to arrive at the appropriate level of duty.

FA 2000, s 118 introduced an anti-avoidance measure that provides for stamp duty to be charged at the relevant property rate when land or buildings are transferred in exchange for other property. This takes effect for instruments executed on or after 28 March 2000. However, it does not apply if an instrument executed on or after that date gives effect to a contract made on or before 21 March 2000, unless the instrument:

(1) is made in consequence of the exercise after 21 March 2000 of an option, right of pre-emption or similar right; or
(2) transfers the property involved (or vests it in) a person other than the purchaser under the contract, because of an assignment or further contract made after 21 March 2000.

Consideration in the form of securities is taken into account when computing stamp duty. FA 2000, s 126 introduced a charge when the consideration received for a conveyance on sale is the right to future issue of securities. This applies to instruments executed on or after 28 July 2000. FA 2000, s 122 provides for duty to be charged at the shares rate where marketable securities are transferred in exchange for property that is exempt from SDRT (eg gilts). This applies to instruments executed on or after 28 March 2000. However, it does not apply if an instrument executed on or after 28 March 2000 gives effect to a contract made on or before 21 March 2000, unless the rules under (1) and (2) above apply.

8.1.3 Sale and grant of a lease

The stamp duty payable on an assignment of an existing lease is calculated in exactly the same way as for freehold property. It is the capital sum paid for the lease that determines the amount of duty; the amount of rent payable under the lease is irrelevant.

Where a new lease is granted, and a premium is paid, it must carry stamp duty at the appropriate ad valorem rate as if it were a transfer of conveyance on sale. Lease duty is also chargeable on the average rent payable over the length of the lease.

For short leases of up to seven years (or for an indefinite term), the threshold for stamp duty on the granting of a lease is £5,000. This threshold applies to the annual rent charge so if the rent is less than £5,000 pa and there is no premium the lease does not need to be stamped.

Surrendering leases

Prior to the introduction of FA 2000, s 128, when a lease was surrendered for a consideration it was possible to avoid stamp duty by surrendering the lease by operation of law rather than by means of a deed of surrender. In such cases, registration was often achieved by the submission of a statutory declaration to the Land Registry.

Section 128 provides that where a lease has been surrendered, any document evidencing the surrender and any document containing a statutory declaration will be stampable. This means that such a statutory declaration (or other documentary evidence provided to a Land Registry) will in future be subject to stamp duty as if it were a deed of surrender. So a surrender of a lease will be subject to stamp duty even if there is no deed of surrender. This applies to leases surrendered on or after 28 July 2000.

8.1.4 Fixed Stamp Duty

Some documents only carry a fixed pre-set level of stamp duty. The fixed stamp duties have now all been increased to £5 (eg in relation to declarations of trust and transfers to a nominee) in relation to documents executed on or after 1 October 1999 (FA 1999, s 112).

8.1.5 Stamp duty and VAT

Sales and rentals of some commercial property may be subject to VAT. In such cases, stamp duty is charged on the VAT-*inclusive* sale price, premium and/or rent. Moreover, in certain circumstances the landlord may have the right to add VAT to the rent at a later date: again, the VAT-inclusive figure must be taken (see SP11/91).

8.1.6 Sub-sales
(SA 1891, s 58)

Where a person

(a) has entered into a contract to purchase a property, and
(b) enters into a sale contract before the original contract has been completed,

and the property is then conveyed to the new purchaser, only the second contract generally attracts ad valorem duty. The original purchase contract is not subject to stamp duty. Thus, if *A* enters into a contract to buy a property for £1m, and then enters into a sub-sale for £1.5m to *B*, stamp duty is payable by *B* only on the conveyance arising out of the contract for sale for £1.5m.

FA 1984 introduced some restrictions; specialist legal advice should therefore be taken.

8.1.7 Sale of contract

If a purchaser who holds the benefit of a contract that has not been completed sells that benefit to a third party who then completes the purchase, the transaction is treated in a similar way to a sub-sale. Thus if the contract is for the purchase of a property for £1m, and C sells that contract to D for £500,000, D pays ad valorem duty each on the £500,000 purchase price of the contract and on completing the purchase. Overall he pays 4% of £1.5m.

8.1.8 Sale of goodwill and other business assets

Types of property that may be included in arriving at a business's value for stamp duty purposes include book debts, plant and machinery and stock in trade, goodwill, and copyrights, patents and trademarks. The way in which a contract is drafted may have stamp duty consequences and the advice of an experienced solicitor should be sought. Having said this, the normal position is as follows:

(1) The usual arrangement for book debts is for the purchaser to collect them as agent for the vendor as this means ownership remains with the vendor and so no stamp duty is payable on them. Unless documentation is defective, no duty should be payable on the transfer of plant and machinery and stock in trade as legal title can pass by delivery and the purchaser can therefore acquire a good title without a stampable document. The rate of duty on goodwill, copyrights, patents and trademarks is the same as for land and buildings.

(2) Exemption is available where the value of the transaction does not exceed £60,000, but the sale of a business as a going concern counts as a single transaction. Therefore, if a shopkeeper sells his shop premises for £50,000 and his goodwill for £20,000, the transaction value is £70,000 and exemption is not available.

Because the stamp duty definition of a sale includes an exchange of property for shares, the incorporation of a sole trader's or partnership business is treated as a sale of that business in exchange for shares in the new company. Stamp duty is charged according to the value of the shares received by the proprietor or the partners, which will, effectively, be an amount equal to the value of the business as a going concern (discussed in greater detail at 8.3.7).

8.1.9 Partnerships

A partnership deed or agreement is not normally liable for stamp duty but special rules may apply for a limited partnership (see 16.2).

Where a person joins a partnership, ad valorem duty is payable on any document transferring an interest in the firm to him from an existing partner on the basis that the document is a conveyance. However, the contribution of new partnership capital gives rise to no such charge unless an existing partner withdraws capital at the same time (in which case the document for the transaction is regarded as a conveyance that attracts ad valorem duty).

The dissolution of a partnership and the division of the firm's assets do not normally attract ad valorem duty. The exception is if an individual partner takes a greater proportion of certain assets and makes a cash adjustment for this; it is then effectively a type of sale.

8.1.10 Instruments relating to intellectual property (IP)

FA 2000, s 129 abolished stamp duty on transactions (ie sale, transfer or other disposition) in IP (eg patents, trademarks, registered designs, copyrights, plant breeders' rights). This applies to instruments executed on or after 28 March 2000. Transfer documents that relate only to IP no longer need to be stamped. Where property sold under an instrument consists partly of IP and partly of other chargeable property, an apportionment of the sale price will be made to determine the amount chargeable to duty.

Where an instrument is to be certified as not forming part of a larger transaction or series of transactions, the value of any IP involved will now be disregarded.

8.2 SANCTIONS WHERE DUTY NOT PAID

As a general rule, the Revenue cannot enforce payment of stamp duty by taking court proceedings (although it can do so for SDRT). Nevertheless, a number of effective sanctions do exist, which mean that in practice it is usually best to ensure a stampable document is indeed stamped:

(1) Although the Revenue cannot take civil enforcement proceedings as above, it can prosecute a purchaser or lessee who fails to produce for stamping a conveyance of freehold land, or the grant or transfer of a lease for seven years or more. The maximum fine is £1,000.

(2) HM Land Registry will not accept any document that is not duly stamped and it is very unwise not to register a purchase of land or a lease for a term exceeding 21 years at the Registry.

(3) A transfer of shares or debentures cannot be registered unless the transfer document has been properly stamped. (Any purported registration by the company is simply not valid in law.)

(4) An unstamped document will not be accepted in any court proceedings.

8.2.1 Interest and penalties

Stamp duty must be paid within 30 days of a document's execution. Until 1 October 1999, if a document was executed in the UK, the duty had to be paid within 30 days of its execution. If it was executed outside the UK, it had to be stamped within 30 days of being brought into the UK. No interest was chargeable on late payment (apart from interest at 5% pa if the duty exceeded £10 when paying a penalty: see below).

For documents executed on or after 1 October 1999, a new interest regime for late payment has been introduced, with interest incurred on stamp duty not paid within 30 days of execution. It starts to accrue from the date stamp duty was due until the date it is paid. This applies wherever execution has taken place: therefore a document executed overseas on or after 1 October 1999 will be brought within the interest regime immediately if it later has to be brought into the UK and stamped. If it is stamped within 30 days of being brought into the UK, although a penalty will not be charged, it appears that interest will be chargeable from the date of execution.

The amount of interest to be paid depends on the duty and how late the payment is. A standard rate of interest is applied in working out the charge. The amount of interest will be rounded down where necessary to a multiple of £5, but no interest will be payable unless the calculated amount is at least £25.

Interest paid is not allowable against corporation tax and interest added to repayments do not count in computing profits or income for tax purposes.

Interest is also added to repayments of overpaid stamp duty and runs from 30 days after execution of the document, or from the date of payment of the duty if later.

The Taxes (Interest Rate) (Amendment No 3) Regulations 1999 and the Stamp Duty Reserve Tax (Amendment) Regulations 1999 – both of which came into force on 1 October 1999 – provide for the current rates of interest on late paid and overpaid stamp duty and SDRT.

Interest rates are the same as those applying to late paid and overpaid income tax and CGT. The applicable interest rates for underpaid and overpaid stamp duty and SDRT are as follows:

	Underpaid	*Overpaid*
6 November 2001 onwards	6.5%	2.5%
6 May 2001 to 5 November 2001	7.5%	3.5%
6 February 2000 to 5 May 2001	8.5%	4.0%

Penalties for late payment of stamp duty

Until 1 October 1999, late stamping (ie after 30 days from execution) could be effected if a penalty of £10 plus the unpaid stamp duty was paid. If the duty exceeded £10 then interest at 5% p.a. was also to be paid. If the duty was charged ad valorem, then the penalty could be an amount up to or equalling the duty itself. Penalties had to be paid within 14 days after assessment.

For documents executed on or after 1 October 1999, penalties apply to all documents submitted for stamping more than 30 days after the document was executed (or, in the case of documents executed abroad, over 30 days after the document is first brought into the UK).

There will be a maximum penalty of £300 (or the amount of duty if it is less) on documents submitted up to one year late and of £300 (or the amount of duty if it is more) for documents submitted later than that. No penalty will be charged if there is a reasonable excuse for delay, and all penalties will be open to mitigation.

All stamp duty penalties for administrative offences will rise to £300 or, where the case is one of fraud, to £3,000. The Stamp Duty (Collection and Recovery of Penalties) Regulations 1999 provide for the collection and recovery of administrative penalties relating to stamp duty. The regime applies to acts or omissions on or after 1 October 1999.

8.3 AVOIDING OR REDUCING DUTY

8.3.1 Sale of shares or other securities

The opportunities to avoid or mitigate duty are circumscribed by the rule that a company may not register a transfer of shares or debentures unless the transfer document has been duly stamped. Beneficial ownership may, of course, be transferred without any change in the registered owner of the shares (eg where the shares are registered in the name of a nominee company).

8.3.2 Depositary receipts

From 25 August 1999, no SDRT is payable on UK depository receipts in foreign securities. This exemption is made by the Stamp Duty Reserve Tax (UK Depository Interests in Foreign Securities) Regulations 1999 under FA 1999, s 119.

Otherwise, there is a charge to SDRT under FA 1986, s 93 on the issue of a depository receipt for chargeable securities. The rate is the same as that applicable to stamp duty on bearer securities (ie 1.5%). There is no SDRT charge when a depository receipt changes hands (FA 1986, s 99(6)).

A depository receipt is defined by s 99(7) as an instrument acknowledging both:

(a) that a person holds stocks or shares or evidence of the right to receive them; and

(b) that another person is entitled to the rights, whether expressed as units or otherwise, in or in relation to stocks or shares of the same kind, including the right to receive such stocks and shares (or evidence of the right to receive them from the person mentioned above).

There are three occasions of charge under s 93(1):

(1) the chargeable securities are transferred to the nominee of the person whose business is or includes issuing depository receipts (usually a bank);

(2) the chargeable securities are issued to the nominee; and

(3) the securities are appropriated by such a person towards the eventual satisfaction of the entitlement of the holder of the receipts to receive chargeable securities.

Transfers of UK securities within depositary receipt schemes or clearance services are generally exempt from the usual stamp duty and SDRT charges. This is on the basis that a 1.5% 'season ticket' charge applies when shares enter such a system. There is a relief for transfers between depositary receipt schemes and a parallel relief for transfers between clearance services. FA 2000, s 134 extends the reliefs to make them apply comprehensively to all transfers between the two types of systems, with effect from 28 July 2000.

8.3.3 Company reconstructions
(FA 1986, s 75)

There is a limited statutory relief for the stamp duty payable on the documentation arising out of certain company reconstructions and mergers without change of ownership: this is an area in which proper professional advice is essential. The basic conditions for relief are that:

(a) the acquiring company issues shares to all the target company's shareholders;
(b) no other consideration passes other than the assumption or discharge by the acquiring company of liabilities of the target company; and
(c) both companies must be incorporated in the UK.

Furthermore, relief is due only where the following further conditions are satisfied.

(i)   The acquisition is effected for bona fide commercial reasons and does not form part of a scheme or arrangement of which the main purposes, or one of the main purposes, is avoidance of liability to stamp duty, income tax, corporation tax or CGT.
(ii) After the acquisition has been made, each shareholder of the target company will be a shareholder of the acquiring company.
(iii) After the acquisition has been made, the proportion of the acquiring company's shares held by any shareholder is the same as the proportion of shares originally held in the target company.

The Stamp Office has indicated that it will regard the requirement of the reconstruction to be effected for bona fide commercial reasons as being satisfied where clearance has been granted under TCGA 1992, s 138 (see 5.4.4).

The procedure for claiming s 75 relief is set out below.

First, a claim should be made in a letter signed by a responsible officer of the acquiring company (eg the secretary or a director or the company's professional advisers).

Secondly, the letter should include the following information and be accompanied by:

(a) the name, registered number and authorised and issued capital of the acquiring company at the relevant date;

339

(b) the name, registered number and authorised and issued capital of the acquired company at the relevant date;

(c) details of and the reason for the reconstruction;

(d) details of the consideration and how it was satisfied;

(e) whether an application for clearance under TCGA 1992, s 138 or 139 has been made to the Revenue and a copy of any application for clearance together with copies of any correspondence with the Revenue;

(f) confirmation that the shares in the acquiring company have been issued to the acquired company's registered shareholders and that their names have been entered on the acquiring company's register of members;

(g) a copy of the certificate of incorporation of all relevant companies and all changes of names;

(h) particulars of the acquired company's register of members immediately prior to the transaction;

(i) particulars of the acquired company's register of members immediately after the transaction for which relief is claimed;

(j) a copy of the agreement or offer document; and

(k) a copy of the instruments of transfer.

Finally, a completed Adjudication Application Form (ADJ 467) stating any related adjudication references known should be sent with the claim to: The Controller of Stamps (Adjudication Section), West Block, Barrington Road, Worthing, West Sussex BN12 4SF.

FA 2000, s 127 provides for the reorganisation reliefs under FA 1986, ss 75 and 76 to be disapplied if redeemable shares form part of the consideration for acquisition. This applies to instruments executed on or after 28 July 2000.

8.3.4 Loan stock

Where a person takes loan stock as consideration for the sale of an asset, such acquisition does not normally attract duty unless:

(a) the loan capital carries a right of conversion into shares or other securities or to the acquisition of shares or other securities; or

(b) the interest rate exceeds a reasonable commercial return on the capital's nominal amount; or

(c) the amount of interest is determined to any extent by reference to the results of, or any part of, a business or to the value of any property; or

(d) there is a right to be repaid more than the nominal amount of the loan and that amount is not reasonably comparable with what is generally repayable (in respect of a similar capital's nominal amount) under the terms of issue of loan capital in the Official List of The Stock Exchange.

Any transfer of loan capital that does not come within these exemptions is chargeable at 0.5% ad valorem.

8.3.5 **Sale of land and buildings**

One widely used way of mitigating stamp duty was closed by FA 1994. If two owners exchange houses, stamp duty is now payable on the properties' market value as well as on any cash adjustment. Prior to 8 December 1993, stamp duty was payable only on the cash element in the consideration and even this attracted duty only if it exceeded £60,000.

The Stamp Office has agreed that where the documents are correctly drafted, the ad valorem charge can be limited to one property. It appears that if a person transfers property A to another person on the basis that the sale consideration is £x and this is to be satisfied by the other person transferring property B, 1% stamp duty is payable on property A and the transfer of property B attracts only 50p stamp duty. However, very careful drafting is required in cases where there is a cash adjustment rather than a straightforward exchange with no other consideration passing between the parties.

Stamp duty is not charged on that part of the agreed purchase price that is allocated to items such as fixtures and fittings which are left in the property. This is because ownership of such items is transferred by delivery, and not by the conveyance.

To reduce duty, purchasers are sometimes tempted to apportion an unrealistically high percentage of the agreed overall price to the contents – especially where this brings the price allocated to the house itself below the threshold and so avoids duty altogether. The Stamp Office is, of course, alive to this temptation and will refuse to stamp a conveyance if the valuations used cannot be justified.

A suggestion sometimes put forward is that a person can buy the site and then contract separately with the builder for him to carry out the building work. Certainly, if the buyer buys a building plot and then contracts with an unrelated third party for the construction of a house, stamp duty is payable only on the 'site value' price actually paid. *Prudential Assurance Co v IRC* [1993] 1 WLR 211 indicates that this applies even if the buyer buys a plot from the builder and then commissions him to construct a building on that site *provided* the site is conveyed to the purchaser before a substantial start is made on the building work.

Where a long lease at a substantial rent is proposed, it is sometimes possible to save duty by splitting the period between two shorter leases; eg instead of a 50-year lease with stamp duty of 12% of the annual rent (see 8.1.3), at the outset sign two leases, one for 20 years and the second for 30 years (commencing on the expiry of the first), with the duty on each lease then being only 2% of the annual rent. For legal reasons, the first lease must be 21 years or less and so counts as a short lease that cannot be registered at the Land Registry.

8.3.6 **Sale of business assets**

In general, the ownership of buildings and goodwill can only be transferred by a written document and so duty must be paid. There are however three ways of avoiding or reducing duty, though all three are usually only practicable where vendor and purchaser trust each other completely.

(1) Stamp duty is payable on a *conveyance* of freehold land, although the *contract* is sufficient to transfer beneficial ownership to the purchaser. Therefore, if vendor and purchaser sign and exchange contracts, but never 'complete' by conveyance, no duty is payable. The courts upheld this method in 1889 and the Government has never blocked the loophole. The drawback is that, without a stamped conveyance, the purchase cannot be registered at the Land Registry, and this is why this device is only to be recommended where vendor and purchaser trust each other completely (eg on a sale to a connected company or a sale within a family).

(2) The second method is simply not to stamp the documentation. Though failing to stamp a conveyance or the grant or assignment of a lease is a punishable offence (see 8.2), the only sanction against failure to stamp a transfer of goodwill is the double charge if it later needs to be stamped out of time.

(3) Where substantial amounts of money are at stake, advantage may be taken of the rule that a document executed (signed) outside the UK need not be stamped until it is brought into the UK. (The document may be stamped without interest or penalty provided it is presented at a Stamp Office within 30 days of being brought to the UK, as required under SA 1891, s 15.) The usual procedure is to take a day trip to Jersey or Guernsey, sign the documents, and leave them in a local safe deposit or bank vault.

8.3.7 Transfer of a business to a company

Stamp duty is payable where a sole trader's or partnership business is incorporated because the trader or the partnership is treated as having sold the business in exchange for shares in the new company (see 8.1.7). Where the successor company is a limited company, its proprietors must produce to the Registrar of Companies a properly stamped copy of the contract by which the business was sold to the company. It is therefore necessary to pay duty on assets that did not pass by delivery. However, a stamped contract is not required where a business is transferred to an unlimited company (see 18.1.2); it is possible to transfer a business to an unlimited company by means of an unstamped contract (eg one kept outside the UK) and then to re-register that company as limited.

8.3.8 Intra-group transfers

Statutory exemption from stamp duty applies, subject to conditions, where property is transferred from one member of a group of companies to another. For this purpose, a 'group' consists of a holding company and its

75% subsidiaries (ie the parent company owns, directly or indirectly, 75% of the subsidiary's ordinary share capital). The holding company need not be a UK company. Until May 1995, the requirement was that the subsidiary should be a 90% subsidiary, but the test was by reference to the nominal value of issued share capital of all classes, not just ordinary shares.

FA 1967, s 27(3) provides that, to obtain the relief, the transferee company must provide confirmation that the document giving rise to the intra-group transfer was not executed in pursuance of or in connection with an arrangement whereunder:

(a) the consideration, or any part of the consideration, for the conveyance or transfer was to be provided or received, directly or indirectly, by a person other than a body corporate which at the time of the execution of the instrument was associated with either the transferor or the transferee; or

(b) the said interest was previously transferred or conveyed, directly or indirectly, by such a person; or

(c) the transferor and the transferee were to cease to be associated by reason of a change in the percentage of the issued share capital of the transferee in the beneficial ownership of the transferor or a third body corporate.

In order to prevent manipulation of group structures to exploit the inter-company relief, the stamp duty provisions are fully aligned with the membership requirements for corporation tax so that only companies that qualify as a group for corporation tax purposes can benefit from stamp duty relief.

FA 2000, s 119 provides for duty to be charged at the relevant property rate when land or buildings are transferred into a company to which the transferor is connected. This applies to documents executed on or after 28 March 2000. However, it does not apply if an instrument executed on or after 28 March 2000 gives effect to a contract made on or before 21 March 2000, unless the instrument:

(1) is made in consequence of the exercise after 21 March 2000 of an option, right of pre-emption or similar right; or

(2) transfers the property involved (or vests it in) a person other than the purchaser under the contract, because of an assignment or further contract made after 21 March 2000

On 14 July 2000 the Revenue announced a change to this anti-avoidance measure in response to representations. As a result, it is disapplied under FA 2000, s 120 from transfers to or from independent trustees or nominees. It also does not apply generally to distributions of real property on liquidation or transfers of property as a dividend to corporate shareholders.

Section 120 applies to documents stamped after 28 July 2000. Where documents in the disapplied categories are stamped between 28 March 2000 and 28 July 2000, a claim may be made for repayment of any excess duty, but these must be made before 1 April 2001.

8.3.9 Duty exemption for disadvantaged areas

Property transactions in the most disadvantaged areas of the UK will be exempted from stamp duty. This new exemption was announced in the Budget on 7 March 2001 and confirmed in the pre-budget statement of November 2001. The Government hopes that this concession will help to promote regeneration in areas where the property market is depressed. This exemption is one of a package of measures to encourage urban regeneration, including tax relief on the conversion of flats over shops, and tax relief for cleaning up contaminated land.

It is intended that a list of the areas in which the exemption was available will be published on the Revenue website. In the meantime, if you have the postcode you can telephone the Inland Revenue Stamp Taxes Helpline on 0845 603 0135. They will tell you whether your property is in a designated area qualifying for relief.

The areas are selected by using the deprivation indices used by the Government to determine the poorest areas in Britain. The list is organised by postcode. In cases where a new property has no postcode, the Stamp Office will be able to determine whether the exemption is claimable or not by reference to electoral ward.

Since 30 November 2001 property sales with values between £60,000 and £150,000 have been exempted from duty. Assignments of existing leases will be treated the same way as sales of freeholds and will be eligible for the exemption. Premiums on leases may also be exempt.

8.3.10 Exemption for goodwill

An exemption from stamp duty for the transfer of goodwill was introduced in the 2002 Budget Statement. The exemption applies for all documents executed on or after 23 April 2002.

The documents transferring goodwill do not need to be stamped. Form Stamps 22 should be completed and sent to the Stamps Office. If the goodwill is transferred as part of a group of assets, a reasonable apportionment of the value to the goodwill will be acceptable to the Revenue.

8.3.11 Exemption for individual pension plans

Individuals may hold a number of units in unit trusts or may have shares in open-ended investment companies (OEICs) in the Individual Pension Accounts (IPA). From 6 April 2001, these units can be bought and sold within the IPAs and no SDRT will be payable. The investment fund manager needs to be able to identify the units and shares that will qualify for the exemption.

The Revenue has provided guidance on this, outlining what to do for each type of unit trust and OEIC that might be held:

(1) Where all of the units in a given unit trust, or all of the shares in a given OEIC, have to be held in IPAs, then no SDRT return will have to be made.

(2) Some OEICs have a special class of shares that are to be held in IPAs. Transfers in such shares do not have to be used in calculating the SDRT due on share transfers in the OEIC. The number of exempt shares can be disclosed on the SDRT return but there is no requirement to do so.

(3) For unit trusts in which the units can be held in IPAs or by other portfolios, the investment manager can certify to the Revenue that the unit trust's trustee or managers can identify the units that are held in IPAs and that no charge has been made to the IPA holders for stamp duty or any related tax.

8.4 EXPLANATORY LEAFLETS

These can be obtained from the Stamp Office or via the Revenue website at <www.inlandrevenue.gov.uk/so/index>.

8.5 DEVELOPMENT OF STAMP DUTY

Changes to the stamp duty system have been in the pipeline for some time. The Chancellor of the Exchequer, Gordon Brown, first announced his intention to reform the stamp duty system in November 2000.

In the April 2002 Budget Statement it was announced that the regulations governing stamp duty on land and buildings were to be reformed. The main reason for this is to stop the perceived abuse of the existing legislation. It is also hoped that the changes will prepare the stamp duty system for the introduction of electronic conveyancing, following the implementation of the Electronic Communications Act 2000. This is in line with the Government's commitment to getting its services online.

The operation of the SDRT system is not being altered by the proposed changes to the stamp duty system. At present, transfers of shares and securities are subject to SDRT.

The proposed reforms were published in a consultation document, *Modernising Stamp Duty on land and buildings in the UK*. The document can be found in the consultation section of the Revenue website at <www.inlandrevenue.gov.uk>. Further consultation will be carried out on aspects of the proposed reforms before they are introduced.

9

CONTRACT LAW

For the most part, contract law is essentially judge-made. Statute has intervened relatively rarely, but notably in relation to the use of exclusion clauses and, most recently, to give rights to those who are not parties to the contract. This chapter considers the main features of contract law, and deals with important topics such as the essential ingredients of a binding contract, the nature of the terms of a contract, the extent to which mistake or misrepresentation can vitiate an otherwise binding contract, the controls exercised over exclusion clauses, and the remedies available upon breach.

There are three major components in any binding contract:

(a) an offer that is made by one party and accepted by the other;
(b) an intention to be legally bound by both parties; and
(c) consideration.

9.1 OFFER

For an offer to be capable of being accepted, and leading to a binding contract, an intention must be shown, on the part of the party making the offer, to be legally bound if the offer is accepted. It may be made to an individual person or to a group of people. It may be made expressly in words or by conduct. Sometimes a party may be bound by his offer even if he can later show that he did not intend to make it to the person who accepted it; it is the impression given to the person who accepted it that is important and account is taken of whether a reasonable man in the circumstances would also have had the same view.

9.1.1 Invitation to treat

It is not uncommon for parties to enter into preliminary discussions prior to a contract being made which include requests for information. These are known as 'invitations to treat', which generally invite an offer and are sometimes confused with an offer.

In *Harvey v Facey* [1893] AC 552, the plaintiff sent a telegram to the defendant saying 'will you sell us Bumper Hall Pen? Telegraph us lowest cash price'. The court decided that no contract had been formed. This telegram was a request for information that the defendant had supplied in their telegram and not an offer.

Generally speaking, a display of goods on which is indicated the price of those goods for sale, in either a shop window or inside a store, is an invitation to treat. If the customer decides to buy some goods then the action by him to take them to the cash till is the offer to buy which can be accepted by the shop owner or his employee.

9.1.2 Advertisements

A newspaper advertisement may show certain goods for sale at certain prices. This is not an offer capable of acceptance. Furthermore, in *Partridge v Crittenden* [1968] 1 WLR 1204, it was held that circulation of a price list by a wine merchant is merely an invitation to treat. Yet there are some circumstances where the advertisement could only be held to relate to one matter and to a certain individual or party of individuals: then it may be an offer.

In *Carlill v Carbolic Smoke Ball Co* [1893] 1 QB 256, the advertisement stated that anyone who purchased a carbolic smoke ball, used it in accordance with the instructions and then suffered from 'flu would receive £100 from the company. The court held that this was an offer that the defendants had shown themselves to be legally bound by and which was capable of acceptance. Their intention to be bound was confirmed in that they had deposited £1,000 with their bankers to show their sincerity.

In *Wood v Letrik* (1932) *The Times*, 12/13 January, an advertisement for an electric comb said: 'What is your trouble? Is it grey hair? In 10 days not a grey hair left. £500 guarantee'. Mr Wood used the comb without success and claimed the £500. Rowlatt J held that:

> '"guarantee" was about as emphatic a word in a contract as one could well imagine. When people read the word "guarantee" they understand that the person using it was offering to bind himself to be responsible for the happening, continuance or existence of a certain state of facts.'

In *Fordy v Harwood* (unreported, Court of Appeal, 30 March 1999), the phrases 'absolutely mint', with 'all the right bits and does it go!' in an advert for a kit replica car were held by the High Court to be no more than puffs that were not intended to give rise to any legal obligation. As regards the phrase 'absolutely mint', the Court of Appeal noted that the car's appearance was obvious to anyone looking at it: it was not a museum piece and was intended to be driven as a normal car. As regards 'all the right bits', the Court of Appeal disagreed with the High Court and held that, while the words no doubt meant that the car had all the authentic component parts and fittings, they would also mean that the right bits had been installed as such, which, in this case, they had not.

9.1.3 Termination of offer

Generally an offer may be terminated at any time before it is accepted. Revocation must be communicated to the offeree. This need not be done by the offeror himself so long as the offeree knows it has been terminated.

9.1.4 Rejection and counter offers

Where an offer is rejected it is terminated and therefore cannot be accepted. Where an offer is made on new terms that were not contained in the original offer, it may be a rejection accompanied by a counter offer. In *Hyde v Wrench* (1840) 3 Beav 334, *A* offered to sell a farm to *B* for £1,000. *B* replied, offering to buy it for £950. *A* rejected the counter offer so *B* tried to accept *A*'s original offer. It was held that no contract had been made since *B*'s rejection and counter offer terminated *A*'s original offer.

In some cases the communication from the offeree may not be regarded as a counter offer but merely a request for more information. An objective test then has to be applied to determine whether a communication is sufficient to be regarded as a counter offer.

In *Norfolk County Council v Dencora Properties* (unreported, 1996, *The Buyer*, Issue 1), a contract for a lease gave a right to terminate 'before 25 March'. The tenant had asked if this meant that notice could be given at any time, so long as not given before that date. The tenant said that this was a mere request for information, but the court held that it was a counter offer. Its effect was 'to sweep the offer . . . off the negotiating table so that it was no longer there to accept'. The landlord found the terms of the tenant's proposals 'not acceptable' and this in turn meant that the counter offer had been rejected.

In *Society of Lloyd's v Twinn* (unreported, 23 March 2000), the claimant had served bankruptcy petitions, and the registrar made bankruptcy orders, against accepting Names for unpaid sums said to be due from them under the claimant's Reconstruction and Renewal plans. The High Court allowed the Names' appeals on the ground that the registrar had been wrong to hold that they were accepting Names, since their purported acceptance was in fact a counter offer. The Court of Appeal reversed the High Court decision, holding the Names had effected an acceptance by executing acceptance forms. The covering letter that stated they had no means to pay the finality amounts was an attempt to obtain concessions. The Names were accepting even though they could not pay: there was an effective acceptance and not a counter offer.

The issue also arose in *Durabella v J Jarvis & Sons* (unreported, 19 September 2001). D submitted an estimate for building work dated 10 August, saying the work would be on its terms of contract. On 24 August, JJS sent D an order which provided that its own terms would apply, attaching those terms to the letter. On 13 December, JJS sent D a letter of intent which confirmed its intention to enter into a contract with D which would be on JJS's terms. On 14 December, D sent a letter stating that the project file had been entered in their books, and also wrote the following day about JJS's programme and methods. D sent a further letter on 9 January acknowledging receipt of JJS's letter of intent 'which we are pleased to take as an acceptance' of the estimate of 10 August. It was argued that the letter of 9 January was a counter offer because it sought to impose terms differing from D's letter of 13 December. The court, however, ruled that the letter of intent sent on 13 December was an offer and was treated by D in its letters of 14 December and 9 January as having contractual force. The January letter was said to be 'clearly an acceptance' of the offer, and the reference in it to D's estimate was not enough to displace JJS's terms. There had been no reassertion by D of its terms. The court added that, if this conclusion were incorrect, D had in any case accepted the offer by actually performing the works. (See too the battle of the forms, considered in 9.7.2.)

9.1.5 Lapse of time

An offer that expressly states that it will last for a specified period of time cannot be accepted once that time has passed. Where the offer is not limited in time, it only lapses after whatever period of time is considered reasonable in the circumstances.

In *Ramsgate Victoria Hotel v Montefiore* (1866) LR 1 Exch 109, the defendant applied to the company for shares and paid a deposit. Five months later, the company sent him an acceptance by issuing a letter of allotment and requesting the balance due on the shares. He refused to pay, contending that his offer had expired. The court upheld his argument. His offer was for a reasonable time only and five months was deemed unreasonable.

In *Chemco Leasing v Rediffusion* [1987] 1 FTLR 201, an offer was made in January to assume certain liabilities; it was accepted in November. The court held that, since about four months was a reasonable time for the offer to run, it had lapsed by the time of the purported acceptance, which therefore had no effect.

9.2 ACCEPTANCE

Acceptance of an offer must be final and unqualified and must be communicated to the offeror. An acknowledgement of the offer is not acceptance of it. Acceptance may be made by conduct, eg where C offers to send goods, sends them to D and D then uses them, D's conduct can be regarded as acceptance.

Where the parties carry on lengthy negotiations it may be difficult to say when exactly an offer is made and accepted. Parties may in fact not agree that an offer has been made and accepted. In these circumstances, a court considers all negotiations and looks to the parties' intentions to establish whether an agreement exists. There may be correspondence between them after an offer has been made but before acceptance. Careful examination must be made to determine whether such communication can be regarded as an acceptance or whether it is an attempt to vary terms or introduce new ones.

In *Manatee Towing v Oceanbulk Maritime* (unreported, 18 May 1999), the High Court laid down the following principles:

(1) The court's task is to review what the parties said and did, and from the material to infer whether their objective intentions as expressed to each other were to enter into a mutually binding contract.

(2) When a contract by telex or correspondence is alleged, the court will look at the correspondence as a whole and not merely at one or two documents picked out from a connected sequence.

(3) Where the parties have not reached agreement on terms they regard as essential to a binding agreement, it follows that there can be no binding agreement until they do agree on them. At the same time, the parties may, by words and conduct, make it clear that they do intend to be bound, even though there are other terms yet to be agreed, even terms that may often or usually be agreed before a binding contract is made. The more important the term, the less likely the parties will leave it for future decision, but there is no legal obstacle in the way of their agreeing immediately to be bound and leaving important matters for later agreement.

(4) Though the parties might have reached agreement on all the terms of the proposed contract, they might still intend the agreement not to become binding until some further condition is fulfilled. This is the ordinary 'subject to contract' case. Alternatively, the intention may be that the agreement does not become binding until some further term is agreed. Conversely, they may agree to be bound immediately, even though there are further terms to be agreed or some formality to be fulfilled.

(5) The court must always bear in mind the subject-matter with which it is dealing. The relevant principles of the law of contract are of universal application, but the proper inference to draw may differ widely according to the facts of any particular case.

(6) The courts recognise that business terminology and practice may differ from one market to the next. See also *Pagnan v Feed Products* [1987] 2 Lloyd's Rep 601.

The battle of the forms

It is common business practice for one party to wish a contract to be governed by his standard trading conditions. An offer by him may include a statement that both parties should be bound by these terms. The other party's reaction to this determines whether he is bound by these terms. (See further 9.7.2 below.)

This can often give rise to what is sometimes called 'the battle of the forms' when each side presents its own terms and conditions as providing the basis of the contract. The basic rule is that the person who is the last to present his terms and conditions is the one who succeeds in having them incorporated into the contract (*Butler Machine Tool v Ex-Cell-o* [1979] 1 All ER 963; see also *Albright & Wilson UK v Biachem* (unreported, 12 April 2000) (sequence of five contracts sent by fax and the confusion of which company's terms and conditions applied)).

9.2.1 Cross offers

Where each party concerned makes an offer to the other that mirrors the other's offer, there can be no contract even though the offer is identical. What one party must do on receipt of the other's offer is to contact him and confirm acceptance.

9.2.2 Communication of acceptance

This must be made to the offeror, otherwise no contract exists. The communication need not be made by the offeree. However, the third party who communicates the acceptance (eg an agent) must have the authority to do so from the offeree.

An exception to communicating acceptance to the offeror arises where acceptance is by conduct. For example, a tenant may be regarded as accepting an offer of new tenancy by remaining in the property.

9.2.3 Method of acceptance

There is no set method of acceptance, although the offeror may indicate that acceptance can only be made in a certain way; if so, that requirement must be adhered to. Acceptance by an alternative method (eg orally where the offer states that acceptance must be in writing) may not bind the offeror.

The offeror cannot impose acceptance where the offeree is silent, a principle laid down in *Felthouse v Bindley* (1862) 11 CBNS 869. Where, however, the offeree himself indicates that the offer is to be taken as accepted if there is no indication to the contrary, that can amount to acceptance (*Re Selectmove* [1995] 2 All ER 531).

9.2.4 Acceptance by post

This is effective when the letter is posted, not when the letter is received. If it is not received by the offeror it may still be deemed effective acceptance. Nevertheless, the offeree may have difficulty proving that he had posted the acceptance.

If the circumstances of the negotiations make it clear that an acceptance must reach the other party, this is what must happen (*Holwell Securities v Hughes* [1974] 1 All ER 161).

Acceptance by post takes priority over the withdrawal of an offer that may have been posted before the acceptance was, but had not reached the offeree when the acceptance was posted. This is an exception to the general rule that an offer may be withdrawn at any time before the offeror is notified of an acceptance.

9.2.5 Contract to make a contract

In certain cases, the parties may have agreed in principle but might not have sorted out all the details of the contract. Whether a contract exists depends on the terms still left to be agreed. It is, though, possible for the parties to be bound by a contract to make a contract. This differs from an agreement to negotiate, which is too vague to form a binding contract (see *Courtney & Fairbairn v Tolaini Bros (Hotels)* [1975] 1 All ER 716; *Walford v Miles* [1992] 2 AC 128).

9.2.6 Certainty of terms

Where the terms are vague or uncertain, they cannot be binding. This does not necessarily mean that there is no contract since a court may, if it considers appropriate, merely delete the ambiguous words from the contract (see 9.7.4).

9.2.7 Contractual intention

The parties must have intended to create legal relations. It is not necessary generally to produce evidence to show this: it will normally be inferred. However, where one party alleges that this requirement does not exist, then it is for him to show that it does not.

9.3 CONSIDERATION

A contract is not binding unless it is either made as a deed or supported by some consideration. 'Consideration' is the value by which one party suffers a detriment (promisee) or the other gains (promisor). For example, E's payment to F is in consideration of F's promise to deliver the goods to E.

The court does not generally concern itself whether adequate consideration has been given – whether a person has paid too little or too much does not affect the contract's validity but it might give rise to a claim by that person against the other. An exception to this general rule would occur where a party may have exercised undue influence on the other to enter the contract and the contract may therefore be regarded as being one-sided (see 9.6).

Consideration may be nominal; eg a contract in which G agrees to buy a valuable business for only £1 is just as valid as if he were to agree to pay £10,000. However, consideration must be real in that it must have some value in the eyes of the law.

Where a contract is made but the performance of it is utterly impossible, so long as both parties are unaware of that fact the consideration is still likely to be effective.

9.3.1 Past consideration

It is often said that consideration for a promise is given in return for the promise itself. If the act or agreement not to do an act, regarded as a consideration, has already been carried out before the 'promise' is made and independently of it, then it is regarded as being 'past consideration'. In these circumstances the contract is not enforceable.

Where eg an employer promises to make a payment to an ex-employee for his past services, the contract is unenforceable unless, perhaps, the ex-employee agreed not to work for a competitor for a certain period after leaving (ie the consideration is his promise not to work for the competitor).

There is an exception to the general rule for past consideration; there is consideration where an act is performed before a promise made where three conditions are satisfied:

(1) the act must be done at the request of the person making the promise;
(2) it must be understood that the payment would be made; and
(3) the payment must in any event be legally recoverable.

The Limitation Act 1980 qualifies the rules relating to past consideration, providing that where a person acknowledges a debt in writing and signs the acknowledgement, the debt is deemed to accrue on that date and no earlier date. This extends the period of limitation and enables a party to sue at a later date than he would otherwise have been able to on a debt. However, where a debt has become statutorily barred, the right to sue is lost and the later acknowledgement cannot revive it.

9.3.2 Agreement not to sue

Where a creditor *H* agrees not to sue *J* in return for a promise by *J* to pay interest or additional interest on the sum involved, the promise by *H* is valid consideration. The agreement may be for a limited period of time (perhaps to allow *J* time to pay) or it may be final and perhaps incorporated in a settlement.

The agreement or forbearance to sue may be implied from a person's actions (eg where a party does not sue even though he has stated to the other to whom he owes the money that he will). However, the forbearance must be accompanied by a promise from the debtor for it to be a consideration.

9.3.3 Promising to perform existing obligations

Generally, a person cannot provide consideration by promising to do something that he is already legally obliged to do. However, where he promises to do more than he is legally obliged to do (eg a police force providing a greater degree of protection than it thinks reasonably necessary in the circumstances) then this may be good consideration.

Nevertheless, there are situations where one party's legal obligation to perform something for another can be regarded as consideration to a third party. In *Scotson v Pegg* (1861) 6 H&N 295, *B* contracted with *A* to deliver coal to *B* or to *B*'s order. *B* then ordered *A* to deliver the coal to *C* who promised to unload it. *A* sued *C* for failure to unload. It was held that *A*'s delivery was good consideration for *C*'s promise even though he was contractually bound by his contract with *B* to deliver to *C*.

It has been held that the principle that a promise to perform an existing obligation can amount to good consideration where there were practical benefits to the party receiving the performance is confined to cases where the obligation involved a supply of goods or services. The principle cannot be extended to an obligation to make a payment (eg a tax payment: *Re Selectmove* [1995] 2 All ER 531).

9.4 MISTAKE

The traditional way of dealing with the effect of mistake on a contract is to ask whether it is one that falls into any of the categories dealt with below.

9.4.1 Common mistake

If the parties have made the same mistake about a fundamental element of the contract, the court may find it void. For example, if two parties agree to supply and purchase goods but, unknown to them, the goods do not exist when the contract is made, the court may declare it void. In deciding whether the contract should be made void in these circumstances, the court first has to be sure that neither party had accepted responsibility for the goods' existence. That is, could a term be implied into the contract which encompassed that obligation? In the majority of disputes this is usually the case. In *Associated Japanese Bank (International) v Credit du Nord* [1988] 3 All ER 902, the court emphasised that the rules on mistake were for exceptional circumstances, so mistake is not an excuse to exit a bad bargain. Consequently, a mistake regarding the quality of the contract's subject-matter will not affect the contract's validity.

In *Leaf v International Galleries* [1950] 1 All ER 693, *L* bought a painting believed by both parties to be by John Constable from *IG*. Five years later, *L* discovered it was not by Constable. The court held the contract was unaffected: both parties had made the mistake, so the contract remained valid.

Where a common mistake is not sufficiently fundamental to render the contract void at common law, equity may hold that the contract is voidable so as to achieve a fair result. In *Solle v Butcher* [1950] 1 KB 671, both parties to a lease thought that the recently refurbished flat was no longer subject to the Rent Acts and agreed a rent of £250 pa. However, they were mistaken, and the maximum rent under the Acts, at that time, was £140 pa. The tenant claimed repayment of the excess rent; the landlord served notice on the lessee. The Court of Appeal held the mistake was not sufficiently fundamental for the contract to be void, but it was voidable in equity. The tenant had the choice of giving up the lease or accepting a new one at an increased maximum rent under the Rent Acts. Note that *Solle v Butcher* was held not to be good law in *Great Peace Shipping v Tsavliris Salvage (International)* [2002] EWCA CIV 1407.

9.4.2 Mutual mistake

This involves situations where the parties are at cross purposes. For example, *M*, when buying a house, thinks the carpets are included in the sale, but *N*, the seller, believes they are excluded. The sale goes ahead, then the mistake is discovered. Clearly there is no consensus, but rarely is the contract held to be void at common law. Usually, the court resolves the contract in favour of one party by deciding what a reasonable onlooker would understand the terms of the contract to be. In *Smith v Hughes* (1871) LR 6 QB 597, a racehorse owner, after inspecting a sample, bought 'last season's' oats instead of 'this season's', and they were of no use to him. He claimed the contract was void for mistake. The seller had not misrepresented the oats as being last season's; neither was he aware of the buyer's impression. The court held that, taking an objective view, there was a valid contract. The buyer had been careless and merely misled himself as to the type of oats.

If, however, from the reasonable onlooker's standpoint, the parties have clearly failed to reach any agreement, the contract will be void for mistake. This is exemplified in *Raffles v Whichelhaus* (1864) 2 H&C 906. The parties agreed, in London, on a contract of sale for a cargo of cotton 'Ex Peerless from Bombay'. There were, in fact, two ships called Peerless sailing from Bombay with cotton, one departing in October, the other in December. The buyer intended to buy the October shipment, the seller intended to sell the December shipment. It was held there was no agreement, offer and acceptance did not coincide, and the contract was void for mistake.

9.4.3 Unilateral mistake

A unilateral mistake arises when only one party is mistaken and the other is aware of it. This may arise in two situations: a mistake regarding the contract terms or regarding a party's identity. In *Harthog v Colin Shields* [1939] 3 All ER 566, the defendants offered to sell animal skins and negotiated a price per skin, as was the trade custom. Subsequently, the contract was concluded mistakenly at a price per pound, which the plaintiffs accepted. They were prevented from enforcing the deal on the basis that they must have been aware of the defendants' mistake.

For the contract to be void at common law, the unilateral mistake must be fundamental to the nature of the contract and it must induce the innocent party to enter into it. In *Cundy v Lindsay* (1877–78) 3 AC 459, a fraudster called Blenkarn wrote to C ordering goods, giving his address as 37 Wood Street and signing his name so that it appeared to be Blenkiron & Co, a respectable business with whom C had traded on previous occasions and whose offices were at 123 Wood Street. C sent the goods to Blenkiron at No 37 and Blenkarn sold them on to L. C sued L to recover the goods' value, claiming the contract was void for mistake. The court held that the contract was void. C intended only to contract with Blenkiron and no title passed to Blenkarn.

Similarly, in *Ingram v Little* [1961] 1 QB 31, private sellers of a car were visited by a potential buyer who gave them a particular name and address. The sellers checked the 'phone directory and found that there was such a person of such an address, and the deal went ahead. It was held that the sellers had not meant to deal with the person in front of them, but with the person who he claimed to be. Accordingly, there was never any contract at all, and the car could be recovered from the innocent purchaser.

If, however, the parties deal face to face rather than by letter or 'phone, it is more likely that the contract will be voidable for fraudulent misrepresentation. In *Lewis v Avery* [1971] 3 All ER 907, the plaintiff advertised his car for sale. A person falsely claiming to be the actor Richard Green came to buy it. A deal was agreed and the 'actor' signed a cheque, showing a pass for Pinewood Studios as proof of identity. L accepted the cheque, which was dishonoured when presented at the bank. Meantime, the fraudster sold the car to A, who bought it in good faith with no knowledge of the fraud.

If the contract between L and the fake Green was void for mistake, then 'Green' never had title to the car and therefore neither did A. L would get his car back and A would bear the loss. If, on the other hand, the contract between L and 'Green' was voidable for fraudulent misrepresentation, then 'Green' did have good title to the car which he had passed on to A before L avoided the contract. In that case, L would bear the loss. The Court of Appeal found that the contract was not void for mistake because the evidence showed that L intended to sell the car to the person who turned up at his house.

A classic example occurred in *Hudson v Shogun Finance* (unreported, 28 June 2001). A man holding another person's driving licence, and claiming to be that person, made an offer to buy a car on hire purchase (HP). The dealer contacted the finance company, SF, which after checks confirmed that the name on the licence and the address given by the customer were correct, and that his credit record was clean. The customer took the car, failed to make any HP payments and sold the car to an innocent buyer, from whom SF sought to recover the car.

The county court held that SF had meant to deal with the person named in the driving licence and with no one else; accordingly, there had been no contract. There was no unanimity in the Court of Appeal on whether this was a correct ruling. Sedley LJ found the facts far removed from *Ingram v Little*. There is, he said, a presumption that when parties are negotiating face-to-face, there is meant to be a contract between those parties unless there is evidence to rebut that presumption. Here was a case of parties dealing face-to-face, albeit through the agency of the dealers, and nothing rebutted the applicable presumption. There was a contract between these parties and the innocent third party was not protected. His judgement was to allow the appeal.

Dyson LJ regarded the face-to-face principle as no more than an aid to determining the issue arising when an apparent contract has been made orally by parties in the presence of each other. The question then becomes whether, when viewed objectively, the claimants had accepted an offer to contract with the fraudster or with the person he said he was. This in turn raised the question whether this was a face-to-face contract at all. Dyson LJ disagreed. The dealer was not authorised to make a contract, but was no more than an intermediary, simply passing on information to the claimant to help it come to a decision.

Dyson LJ also disagreed over what would have been the position had the parties really been contracting face-to-face. Evidence from SF showed that the precise identity of the contracting party was crucial, and that a thorough check was made on the details given to them. Dyson LJ was also impressed by that part of the evidence that, to comply with the formalities imposed by the Consumer Credit Act 1974, particularly when sending default notices, the identity of the contracting party was of the essence. Given this evidence, he held that the normal face-to-face rule did not apply, and that the appeal should be dismissed.

Brooke LJ agreed with Dyson LJ that the appeal should be dismissed. Rather than tackle the issue of the effect of mistake on the contract, however, he took a relatively short point, also adopted by Dyson LJ, to the effect that the face-to-face rule had no application where the agreement was in writing. In *Hector v Lyons* (1988) 58 P&CR 156, a person had contracted to buy a house in his son's name. The court had ruled in that case that, where a contract is wholly in writing, the face-to-face principles are inapplicable since the parties' identity is established by their names as stated in the contract. Accepting the binding authority of this case, Dyson and Brooke LLJ held that the appeal could be dismissed on the short ground that the fraudulent party in this case was not the hirer named in the written HP agreement with the result that the 1964 Act could not apply to him, and hence could not protect the innocent third party who had bought from him.

9.4.4 *Non est factum*

Where a party has been misled into signing or executing a document that is substantially different to that which he intended to sign or execute, is he bound by it? To be successful in setting a transaction aside, he must be able to show that the document he thought he was signing was markedly different from the one he actually signed. He must have made a fundamental mistake in the character and effect of the document.

Where a person signs a document in blank and hands it to another to complete the blanks and finalise the transaction, he may be able to rely on this doctrine. However, where the completed details are not what the signatory believed they would be, but nevertheless they do not change the transaction's subject, then the contract is unlikely to be set aside.

A person trying to have the contract set aside must show that he acted carefully (eg that he was not negligent in any way). The standard to be applied to his actions would be that of a reasonably prudent person (*Foster v McKinnon* (1869) LR 4 CP 704; *Saunders v Anglia Building Society* [1971] AC 1004).

9.5 MISREPRESENTATION

There are basically three types of misrepresentation: negligent, fraudulent and innocent. Misrepresentation arises from a statement of fact as opposed to one of opinion, intention or law. If a statement of opinion later turns out to be unfounded it is not usually enough to have a transaction set aside. It *is* enough where a statement of opinion is clearly intended to be relied on, the same way the statement of fact would be. For example, in *Smith v Land and House Property* (1884) 28 ChD 7, the vendor, during a sale of property, described a tenant as 'a most desirable tenant' when he knew the tenant was substantially in arrears with the rent. In these circumstances the purchaser was not bound by his contract with the vendor.

It is not always easy to distinguish between statement of fact and statement of the law, although it is important to do so because, whereas the former constitutes representation, the latter does not.

Further light on this point is provided by *BG v Nelson Group Services (Maintenance)* [2002] EWCA 547. BG had contracted out the installation of gas appliances sold in its showrooms. In 1995, N was awarded four regional contracts for installation work. The relationship between the parties terminated in 1997 and N began proceedings claiming to have sustained losses of £1.7m from entering into the contracts which it was induced to do by BG's misrepresentations consisting of the original forecasts that were negligently prepared, false, inaccurate and misleading. N argued that BG had, by implication, represented that it knew all the facts that justified the forecasts and/or that they were based on substantial and reasonable grounds.

The court said that, on occasions, an expression of opinion might carry with it no implication other than that the opinion was genuinely held, but, on other occasions, as in the present case, the circumstances might be such that they give rise to an implied representation that the representor knew of facts that justified the opinion. When an opinion was expressed, the person who expressed it either did or did not know those facts. The existence of those facts, and the representor's state of mind, were themselves capable of being misrepresented by implication by virtue of the expression of opinion.

To successfully claim misrepresentation, a party must be able to show that it was reasonable for him to rely on the other's statements, rather than to rely on his own judgement.

9.5.1 Non-disclosure

This does not generally lead to misrepresentation. Exceptions occur where a certain special relationship exists between the parties.

It is possible to be liable for misrepresentation as a result of a party's conduct. For example, a person who goes into a restaurant and sits down and orders a meal is representing that he has the ability to pay.

If O makes a representation to P which is true at the time he made it but which later becomes untrue, and he does not communicate this to P prior to the contract being entered into, O's failure to tell P of the changes amounts to misrepresentation.

9.5.2 Constructive notice

In *Barclays Bank v O'Brien* [1992] 4 All ER 983, O'B wanted to borrow money from BB, which insisted on security. The security was provided by a charge over property jointly owned by O'B and his wife, and BB required her to enter the charge also. She gave her consent as a result of a misrepresentation made to her by O'B and under undue influence exerted by O'B on her. The court held that in circumstances where a close relationship arises and the wife's position is not as favourable financially as the husband's, then the bank has constructive notice of the misrepresentation unless it has taken reasonable steps to satisfy itself that the wife entered into the transaction freely and with full knowledge of the facts.

A misrepresentation may be made to a group of persons. However, a plaintiff will only be successful if he can show that he is within the group of people who might be regarded as likely to rely on the misrepresentation.

The misrepresentation must have induced a person to enter the contract. Where an estate agent's particulars misrepresented the size of a garage and the buyer had himself examined the property on two occasions, the misrepresentation was held not to have induced the plaintiff to enter the contract.

The person who makes a misrepresentation does not have to intend that the other party will rely on the misrepresentation; it is usually sufficient to show that he should have realised that the other party would be likely to.

9.5.3 Damages for misrepresentation

Damages can be recovered as a result of misrepresentation. The extent of damages claimed depends largely on the type of misrepresentation.

Fraudulent misrepresentation

A wronged person may rescind the contract, claim damages or do both. Fraud has been described as being a false representation which 'has been made (1) knowingly or (2) without belief in its truth or (3) recklessly as to whether or not this is true or false' (*Hartelid v Sawyer & McCockin Real Estate* [1977] WLR 481). The damages will compensate for all the actual loss resulting from the fraud *(Smith New Court Securities v Scrimegour Vickers* [1996] 4 All ER 769).

It is sufficient if the maker of the statement suspects that it is inaccurate without actually knowing it to be false. It is not necessary to show that his motive is dishonest.

Negligent misrepresentation

Negligent misrepresentation is a statement made in the belief that it is true, but with no reasonable grounds for that belief. There are two paths open to a party misled by a negligent statement to gain compensation. First, since the decision in *Hedley Byrne and Co v Heller and Partners* [1964] AC 465, it is possible to take action in tort for negligent misstatement, and provided the claimant can prove a special relationship with the defendant and therefore reliance on the defendant's skill, compensatory damages will be payable. Secondly, the innocent party may rescind the contract and claim damages under the Misrepresentation Act 1967. Under the Act, it is the defendant who must prove that he had reasonable grounds for making the statement, whereas in tort it is the claimant who must prove that the defendant was negligent.

In *Howard Marine and Dredging v A Ogden & Sons (Excavations)* [1978] QB 574, the plaintiffs hired two barges from the defendants. Their carrying capacity was crucial and the defendants misrepresented the sizes, basing their information on facts from Lloyd's Register, which were wrong; however, they could have checked with the barge owners. The court was not sure whether there was a duty of care in negligence, but under the Misrepresentation Act the defendants failed to prove they had not been negligent.

Innocent misrepresentation

A statement made in the belief that it is true, and with reasonable grounds for that belief, is an innocent misrepresentation. The remedy is rescission of the contract, but under s 2(2) of the 1967 Act the court may instead award damages. In *Government of Zanzibar v British Aerospace (Lancaster House)* (unreported, 26 January 2000), it was held that, under s 2(2), if the claimant had lost the right to rescind, he also lost the right to damages.

9.5.4 Other matters

Where a party after discovering a misrepresentation does something to suggest that he does not want to rescind the contract, then he is prevented from doing so. Such actions include allowing a period of time to lapse after the contract was made.

A party cannot contract out of his liability for misrepresentation or any appropriate remedy unless it satisfies the test of reasonableness (see 9.8.4).

9.6 DURESS AND UNDUE INFLUENCE

9.6.1 Duress

Contracts may be alleged to have been entered into as a result of duress on the part of one party. The duress must be such that it prevents the person who complains of it from having a free will to enter the contract voluntarily. The effect of duress is to render a contract void (ie unenforceable) or voidable (ie a party complaining of duress has a choice of whether to affirm the contract or avoid it).

Duress is a combination of pressure and the lack of freedom to choose. Pressure is commonplace in commercial transactions and so long as the party being 'pushed' is not forced to enter without freedom of choice, then it is considered perfectly proper and an everyday commercial activity.

Duress may be exerted on a person through threats of violence or actual threat and imprisonment; on goods (ie unlawful detention of a person's goods, or a threat to detain them); or by 'economic duress'.

Duress administered to a person renders the contract void in serious cases and voidable in others. So far as duress to goods is concerned, a person who handed over money as a result of actual or threat of detention of goods can recover that money from the other party.

Economic duress

One party may exert economic pressure on the other which is such that the latter has no realistic choice but to enter the contract on the terms required by the first party. In *North Ocean Shipping v Hyundai Construction* [1979] QB 705, HC who were building a ship threatened, without justification, to terminate the contract unless NOS agreed to increase the price for the work being done. NOS needed the ship urgently and reluctantly agreed. Although they stated that they reserved their rights, at no later stage did they raise any objections. They continued to make stage payments to NC and eventually took delivery of the ship. The court decided that economic duress had been used by HC and therefore NOS would have been entitled to refuse to pay 10% and to enforce the original contract if they so wished. However, under the circumstances they were regarded as affirming the new price terms. They should have raised further objections not only throughout the contract when the stage payments were made but more particularly at the time of expected delivery.

In *Universe Tankships of Monrovia v International Transport Workers' Federation and Laughton (The Universe Sentinel)* [1983] AC 366, UT's ship was 'blacked' by ITWF. In order to secure its release, UT paid a sum of money into ITWF's welfare fund. The House of Lords held the agreement was vitiated by economic duress. Lords Scarman and Diplock concluded that economic duress might arise where there is an intentional submission to the inevitable and that the pressure used to secure such submission was illegitimate in that there was suppression of the will of the victim.

In *Atlas Express v Kafco (Importers and Distributors)* [1989] 1 All ER 641, AE, a firm of road hauliers, contracted with K(ID) to deliver cartons of basketware to Woolworth branches. Prior to entering into the contract, a manager of AE estimated that each load would comprise between 400 and 600 cartons. On this basis he agreed a contract rate of £1.10 per carton. The first load fell well below his estimations, comprising only 200 cartons. The manager then stated they would be unable to transport any more loads unless K(ID) agreed to a minimum price of £440 per load. K(ID), a small concern that was heavily dependent on its contract with Woolworth, was unable to find another carrier willing to transport its goods and so agreed reluctantly to pay the minimum charge. It later refused to pay that charge and, when sued, claimed economic duress as a defence. The court held that where a defendant had no alternative but to accept revised terms that were detrimental to its interests, this amounted to economic duress that vitiated the apparent consent to the renegotiated terms.

CTN Cash and Carry v Gallaher [1994] 4 All ER 714 illustrates the limits of economic duress. CTN bought cigarettes from G under a long-standing contract, with each purchase a separate transaction. G regularly gave credit to CTN. A consignment of cigarettes worth £17,000 due to be delivered was stolen from a warehouse and there was a disagreement about which party bore the risk. It later became clear that the risk was with G, but before this a representative of G made it clear that if CTN did not pay the £17,000, all credit facilities would be withdrawn. CTN decided that paying was the lesser of two evils. They later sought to recover on the grounds that they had only paid as a result of economic duress. The court did not uphold the claim. It was accepted that the threat to remove credit facilities was coercive, but not improper. The defendants were using the threat as a means of getting money they believed was due to them and not as a means of extorting money they knew not to be due.

Where, say, *A* owes *B* money, *A* may offer a lower amount than he actually owes, forcing *B* to accept it where perhaps his financial circumstances are such that he has no choice. Such an agreement cannot be forced upon *B* and he should be entitled to recover the balance he is actually owed (*D and C Builders v Rees* [1966] 2 QB 617; *Ferguson v Davies* (unreported, 21 November 1996)). As mentioned above, not all threats can be considered to be duress as some may be commercially legitimate. There seems to be no doubt that where the threat is one to commit an act that is unlawful, it is considered to be duress. However, a threat by a party to break a contract where it can be shown that that threat did not force the other party to enter into the contract may not be considered to be duress. Furthermore, a threat not to supply goods unless a higher price is paid is not duress if it can be shown that the other party could have bought a plentiful supply of those goods elsewhere. Therefore, where the threat to do something is lawful but is clearly in excess of that which is regarded as commercially acceptable, it is held to be duress. In *Hughes v Peter Cremer* (unreported, 21 October 1988), it was held that the 'minimum basic test of subjective causation in economic duress ought to be a "but for" test. Good or bad faith [is] also relevant, but not decisive'.

A situation could occur where *C* has a right to bring a prosecution lawfully but threatens *D* with a prosecution unless *D* enters a contract or agrees to more certain terms. This may be regarded as being duress, as a threat amounts to excessive pressure which is not acceptable. Furthermore a court will not condone a situation where a party agrees to anything being done on the basis that a prosecution may be stifled.

In a threat to issue civil proceedings (ie where *E* threatens to sue unless *F* agrees to certain clauses), a court will not interfere where *E* is in fact threatening to enforce its legal right.

Where eg *G* can show that *H* entered into a contract irrespective of the duress, a contract will be valid. However, it is the person accused of duress who is responsible for showing that the other would have entered the contract anyway.

What is the effect of duress?

The person who is subjected to the duress can normally choose whether he affirms or avoids the contract. If duress has occurred and he has taken no steps to set aside the contract, he may be held to have affirmed it.

9.6.2 Undue influence

This is an equitable doctrine that arose to deal with the situation where donations and gifts are allegedly made as a result of one party exerting unreasonable pressure on another. The basic principle arose to prevent one person profiting from his own fraud or wrongful act. A presumption of undue influence arises where the transaction is manifestly disadvantageous to the person who has been influenced.

Where a special relationship exists (eg with a parent and child or solicitor and client), undue influence is likely to be presumed. Therefore, where one party is shown to be disadvantaged, the presumption arises. Family arrangements are treated far more leniently than, say, a relationship between solicitor and client. However, where a parent has exercised undue influence over a child, the transaction is likely to be set aside.

To rebut the presumption of undue influence, a party must show that the donor was acting independently of any influence from the donee. Perhaps the best way of showing this is to show that he had received independent advice from a third party. That advice must be such that an honest and competent adviser would give if acting solely in the donor's interests.

A contract made under undue influence is voidable, and not void. The party influenced has the right to decide whether to affirm or avoid the contract. Yet he may lose the right to set aside the contract if he does something to affirm the contract in any way or leaves matters for such a substantial period that he may be deemed to have acquiesced and therefore be bound by the transaction.

In a number of more recent cases, particularly concerning the husband and wife relationship, the wife has been persuaded to enter some surety contract or guarantee with a bank or similar creditor on the basis of undue influence or misrepresentation not by the creditor, but by a third party (ie the husband). In *Barclays Bank v O'Brien* (below), the Court of Appeal created a special class of surety that would apply mainly to wives, but also to other cohabitees.

Whether the bank/creditor is bound by the wrongdoings of the husband (the principal debtor), and thereby unable to enforce security against the wife (the guarantor), depends on whether the bank/creditor had actual or constructive notice of the wife's equitable right to have the surety agreement set aside on the basis of undue influence or misrepresentation. The informality of the dealings between a wife and husband means there is a higher likelihood of the husband misrepresenting the liability of the contract to the wife in order to secure her agreement to the undertaking. Thus where the bank/creditor is aware that the transaction is manifestly disadvantageous to the wife, and there is a substantial risk of the husband using undue influence or misrepresentation, then the bank/creditor is put on notice. In which case, the creditor/bank should explain to the wife privately the implications of the transaction and advise her to take independent advice. If this is not done, and if there was undue influence or misrepresentation, the creditor will be unable to enforce the security free of the wife's interest.

In *National Westminster Bank v Morgan* [1985] 1 All ER 821, Mr and Mrs M jointly owned the family home. Mrs M agreed to sign a remortgage of the house in favour of NWB to prevent the original mortgagee repossessing the house because of mortgage arrears due to Mr M's business problems. The bank manager visited Mr and Mrs M and she made it clear she had little confidence in her husband's business. The manager, in good faith but incorrectly, told her that the mortgage only secured liabilities in respect of the house. In fact, it covered all Mr M's debts to NWB. When the loan was not repaid NWB sought to repossess the home. Mrs M pleaded undue influence. The House of Lords found no undue influence. The relationship between Mrs M and NWB was an ordinary one: no relationship of trust existed and so there was no onus on NWB to advise her to take independent advice. Neither was the transaction manifestly disadvantageous to her: indeed, it helped her to keep her home.

In *Barclays Bank v O'Brien* [1994] 1 AC 180, Mr O'B wanted to increase the overdraft facilities for his business. BB agreed to a loan of £120,000 provided it was secured by his house, which he owned jointly with his wife. He told her that the loan was only £60,000. The bank manager gave instructions that both Mr and Mrs O'B should be advised on the nature of the transaction and to take independent advice. These instructions were not complied with and Mr and Mrs O'B signed the documents without reading them. The business later collapsed and the issue of whether Mrs O'B was bound by the contract arose when BB took proceedings to repossess the house. The Court of Appeal held BB was aware that the parties were husband and wife, and as such were put on notice as to the circumstances in which Mrs O'B would have been asked to sign the surety. BB failed to warn her of the risks she ran in entering into the surety contract or as to her potential liability in respect of Mr O'B's debts. Furthermore, BB had not properly advised her to seek independent advice. On this basis BB was fixed with constructive notice of the misrepresentation made by Mr O'B to induce Mrs O'B into the contract, and therefore she was entitled to have the legal charge set aside.

The principles are not confined to married couples. They extend to cohabitees and any situation where the creditor is aware that the surety places a confidence and trust in the principal debtor. In *Avon Finance v Bridger* [1985] 2 All ER 281, a son persuaded his parents to act as surety for his debts by means of a misrepresentation. It was held that the surety was unenforceable by AF, *inter alia* because AF had knowledge of the trust the parents reposed in their son with regard to their financial dealings.

In *Lloyds Bank v Bundy* [1974] 3 All ER 757, B and his son both used the same bank, LB. The son's business ran into difficulties and B was asked to guarantee his son's overdraft, putting up his farm as security. He did this and when the son could not pay, LB sought to repossess the farm. B claimed the contract should be set aside on the grounds of undue influence. He had banked with that branch for many years and had placed total trust in them, yet LB had not warned him of the possible consequences of the guarantee. The Court of Appeal held that the presumption of undue influence does not usually arise between a bank and its customers, and thus it would usually have to be proved, but the facts in this case did raise the presumption. There was a relationship of trust and LB was unable to rebut the presumption.

See further *CIBC Mortgages v Pitt* [1993] 4 All ER 433, in which the House of Lords made it clear that the directions in *O'Brien* need only be followed if the lender knows that the transaction is manifestly disadvantageous to the wife.

9.7 TERMS OF CONTRACT

Assuming it can be established that a contract has been made, it is important to know what terms of a contract have been agreed upon and are therefore binding on the parties.

Not all contracts are expressed in writing: some may be oral or may have terms that are partly oral or partly in writing. Generally, a party is bound by the terms of an agreement if he has agreed to them being incorporated in writing.

Prior to a contract being agreed, representations may be made by one party to encourage the other to enter into the contract. These representations are not usually considered to be the terms of a contract.

9.7.1 Standard form of contract and incorporation of terms

A party may be keen to show that the agreement terms are those contained in a pre-prepared standard contract form, perhaps in a ticket or enclosed with a letter containing an offer. These standard terms are very often handed to a person at the time a contract is made. The question of whether the terms are then incorporated into the contract is an important one since the standard form frequently tends to impose obligations on the parties and contains clauses that purport to exclude or limit liability in many situations so far as the party who prepared the conditions is concerned.

The conditions must be brought to the notice of the party who receives them either before or at the time the contract is made. If not, they cannot be incorporated into the contract. In *Olley v Marlborough Court* [1949] 1 KB 532, a person who checked into a hotel found that some of his property had been stolen. He sued the hotel, which placed reliance on a notice that disclaimed liability for any lost or stolen article but which was on the back of his bedroom door. On arriving at the hotel when he had signed the hotel register, there had been no mention of any exemption clauses. The court held that the notice was ineffective since it had not been brought to his attention until after the contract had been made.

The conditions must be contained in a document which it would be reasonable for the receiving party to expect to contain conditions. For example, conditions contained on a deckchair hire ticket or a parking ticket issued by an automatic machine from a car park are ineffective for bringing attention to the party receiving it (*Chapleton v Barry UDC* [1940] 1 KB 532; *Thornton v Shoe Lane Parking* [1971] 2 QB 163).

It is common that two parties engaged in trade enter into several contracts with each other. Where it can be shown that the parties intended the conditions that had been used in previous contracts should continue to be used throughout the course of dealing between them, those conditions are likely to be effective in the most recent agreement. See eg *Henry Kendall & Sons v William Lillico & Sons* [1968] 2 All ER 444, concerning verbal contracts followed by 'sold notes' that contained an exclusion clause that the recipient was aware of but had never read. Held, the recipients' readiness to be bound by the printed conditions, despite not having read them, meant they had accepted them. Thus, the general conditions became part of the oral contract. Contrast the findings in *McCutcheon v MacBrayne* [1964] 1 All ER 430, where the plaintiff's agent, who had dealt with the defendants on a number of occasions, sometimes signed a risk note containing the relevant exclusion clauses and sometimes did not. Held, it is the consistency of a course of conduct that gives rise to the implication that in similar circumstances a similar contractual result will follow. When the conduct is not consistent, there is no reason why it should still produce an *invariable contractual result*. See also *Hollier v Rambler Motors* [1972] 2 QB 71; *Knight Machinery (Holdings) v Rennie* [1995] SLT 166; and *Petrotrade v Texaco* (unreported, 21 December 1999).

Similarly, conditions used in a particular trade or business may be incorporated where both parties are in the same trade and are aware that those conditions are used, even when they do not actually refer to them in the contract between themselves (*British Crane Hire v Ipswich Plant Hire* [1975] QB 303).

It is not essential that the party receiving the conditions (*A*) should have read them. In order for the other party (*B*) to rely on them being incorporated, he must be able to show that *A* knew that there was writing or printed matter on the document and that it contained or referred to the conditions on which *B* intends to rely. *B* must take reasonable steps to give notice to *A* of the conditions. If *A* knew that there was writing or printed matter on the document and sufficient steps were taken to give him notice of the conditions, then even if he did not actually know that it contained conditions, he is still likely to be bound by the contract's terms.

The steps to be taken to give reasonable notice of the conditions depends on the facts of each case. It is not always necessary for a set of conditions to be sent to *A*; it may be sufficient that *B* had made specific mention of any pre-contract documents.

If the term on which *B* intends to rely is considered onerous, then he must show that he has taken reasonable steps to bring the effect of that clause to *A*'s attention. What *B* must do depends on the fact of each case, but the court would have to be satisfied that clear steps were taken to draw the effect of that clause to *A*'s attention before it is allowed to be incorporated (*Interfoto Picture Library v Stilleto Visual Programmes* [1988] 1 All ER 348; *AEG (UK) v Logic Resources* (*The Buyer*, December 1995).

An interesting, and unusual, example of both the question of reasonableness notice and the onerous nature of a contract term arose in *O'Brien v MGN* (unreported, 1 August 2001). In outline, the case was about a scratch-card game launched in *The Daily Mirror* dated 29 April, which OB had bought, containing the rules of the game and then later extended to the *Sunday Mirror* and *The People*. There were numerous ways of winning, one of which was to match two figures with the same figure as stated on a premium rate 'phone line. A printing error in the game for the 3 July *Mirror* resulted in 1,772 people (including OB) claiming the £50,000 prize. The rules, which had been published on various dates before (but not on) 3 July in those papers, stated: 'Should more prizes be claimed than are available in any prize category for any reason, a simple draw will take place for the prize'. A statement on the card read 'FULL RULES AND HOW TO CLAIM SEE DAILY MIRROR'. Other statements also referred to 'rules as previously published' and 'Normal Mirror Group rules apply'. OB was entered into the draw and won just £33.97.

The High Court held that there was sufficient indication that the rules applied as they had been set out in the *Mirror* dated 29 April. OB had seen the rules in the 29 April edition, and it was up to him to read them carefully. He must also have seen the words on the scratchcard, and he accepted that he must have seen the references to the rules in the 3 July edition and that there was a need to check them. He did this by buying a back issue. The court held that the contract between MGN and OB had been made on 3 July when OB rang the premium rate number and accepted to participate in that day's offer. OB must also have appreciated that there would be a limit on the number of prizes, and that there would be few in the higher categories. Further, the rules were not unusual or uncommon. The Court of Appeal generally upheld the decision. However, the issue was whether the above rule of the game rules, on which the case turned (similar to the argument in *Interfoto*), was sufficiently onerous or outlandish for something special to have been done before it could be said to have been brought to OB's attention. It was held by the Court of Appeal not to place an extra burden on OB, nor did it absolve MGN from liability for personal injuries caused by negligence. There had been no special action called for by MGN to bring OB's attention to that rule.

If one party intends to rely on printed notices to bring to the other party's attention certain clauses they must be in a clearly visible place and must be brought to the party's attention prior to entering into the contract.

9.7.2 The battle of the forms

A common situation is where *A* sends to *B* an offer, perhaps asking for supply of goods and/or services, and indicates in that letter that he intends to be bound by his own standard terms and conditions, a copy of which will be enclosed with the letter. *B* then replies, indicating that the order is accepted but that he intends to trade on his own terms only. Whose terms are incorporated into the contract? In the example described, neither of the parties' terms are incorporated. *B*'s reply to the order is regarded as a counter offer and not an acceptance.

If after having received *B*'s counter offer, *A* confirms the order, this may be regarded as being his acceptance to *B*'s counter offer and the contract is governed by *B*'s standard terms. The terms must satisfy all the rules relating to incorporation, such as reasonable notice. If these are satisfied, the terms are likely to govern the contract.

There is relatively little case-law on this specific area. What often happens is that each party writes to the other indicating that he intends to contract only on his own standard terms. At some stage a contract is made and the difficulty is determining whose conditions apply. It is often described as the 'battle of the forms'.

The general principle that has arisen is known as the 'last shot' doctrine: in other words, a court looks into the communication between the parties and tries to establish at which point one set of conditions was unconditionally accepted by the other party (*Butler Machine Tool v Ex-Cell-o* [1979] 1 WLR 401). However, subsequent case-law has placed slight variations on the principle, and in *British Steel v Cleveland Bridge & Engineering* [1984] 1 All ER 504 the court found it impossible to identify an offer that had been accepted. Even though the goods had been delivered and 'accepted' by the receiving party, it was clear that party would never have agreed to the seller's standard terms. In that case the court found that no contract was concluded.

See also *Chichester Joinery v John Mowlem* (1987) 42 BLR 100, in which numerous terms and conditions were referred to in correspondence regarding a subcontract, and where it was held, distinguishing *Butler Machine Tool*, under such circumstances that counter offers had been made, and that the subcontractor's counter offer had 'killed' the defendant's previous counter offer.

It is important therefore that any party who intends to contract on his own standard terms should ensure that all correspondence and contractual documents contain a copy of, or reference to, his standard terms.

9.7.3 Conditions and warranties

Once it is established that a certain term has been incorporated into a contract, it is important to know whether that term will be classified as a condition or a warranty. A condition is an essential stipulation of the contract in which one party guarantees to the other that it is true or that certain promises will be fulfilled. Breach of the condition permits the innocent party, if he wishes, to treat himself as being free from any obligation to be bound by the contract and claim damages for any loss he sustains as a result. A warranty is a term of the contract that is not regarded as so essential as a condition. Breach of a warranty does not allow a person to treat the contract as discharged but to claim damages only – even if he has suffered no prejudice by the breach.

Furthermore, certain terms may not be clearly defined as either a condition or a warranty (often referred to as an 'intermediate term'). The consequence of the breach of that term simply depends on the nature of the breach itself. If it is a minor one, it can be remedied by an award of damages. If it is so important or fundamental it affects the whole contract, the contract must be regarded as discharged (*Hong Kong Fir Shipping v Kawasaki Kisen Kaisha* [1962] 2 QB 26). Some terms are categorised automatically as warranties and conditions (see Chapter 10).

9.7.4 Meaning and construction of term

It is important that the terms on which the party intends to rely can be easily understood. Therefore where any technical or unusual words are incorporated into a contract, there should be a clear explanation of their meaning to avoid any ambiguity. If there is ambiguity a court may delete that part of the contract or, if the majority of the contract is not clearly intelligible, all of it.

The court looks at the whole context of an agreement to establish the meaning of any particular term or clause. It is not open to a court to alter the words used or to impose a meaning that it believes the parties ought to have included, unless it is clear that that is actually what the parties had intended. In other words, a court will not rewrite the terms of a contract.

The modern approach to the interpretation of contract terms has been stated as follows in *Investors Compensation Scheme v West Bromwich Building Society; Alford v West Bromwich Building Society* [1998] 1 All ER 98:

(1) Interpretation is the ascertainment of the meaning that the document would convey to a reasonable person having all the background knowledge that would reasonably have been available to the parties in the situation in which they were at the time of the contract.

(2) The background, subject to the requirement that it should have been reasonably available to the parties and to the exception in (3) below, includes absolutely anything that would have affected the way in which the language of the document would have been understood by a reasonable man.

(3) The law excludes from the admissible background the parties' previous negotiations and declarations of subjective intent. They are admissible only in an action for rectification. The law makes this distinction for reasons of practical policy and, in this respect only, legal interpretation differs from the way utterances are interpreted in ordinary life. The boundaries of this exception are in some respects unclear. But this is not the occasion on which to explore them.

(4) The meaning that a document (or any other utterance) would convey to a reasonable man is not the same thing as the meaning of its words. The meaning of words is a matter of dictionaries and grammars; the meaning of the document is what the parties using those words against the relevant background would reasonably have been understood to mean. The background may not merely enable the reasonable man to choose between the possible meanings of ambiguous words but even (as occasionally happens in ordinary life) to conclude that the parties must, for whatever reason, have used the wrong words or syntax.

(5) The 'rule' that words should be given their 'natural and ordinary meaning' reflects the commonsense proposition that we do not easily accept that people have made linguistic mistakes, particularly in formal documents. Yet if one would nevertheless conclude from the background that something must have gone wrong with the language, the law does not require judges to attribute to the parties an intention that they plainly could not have had.

This statement was adopted by Morritt LJ in *WRM Group v Wood* [1998] CLC 189 and approved by Thomas J in *Kumar v AGF Insurance* [1998] 4 All ER 788.

9.7.5 Extrinsic evidence

In an ideal world all the terms that affect a contract would be supported by written evidence in the contract itself.

One party may wish to adduce evidence that is extrinsic to the written contract on the basis that the written terms themselves clearly do not show all the points agreed between the parties. If after hearing the evidence a court determines that terms additional to those contained in the document were agreed upon and were intended by the parties to be incorporated into the contract, that contract will consist partly of the terms of the document and partly those outside it. If, however, the court finds that the document is a complete record of the contract, it will reject the extrinsic evidence produced. This latter situation is known as the 'parol evidence rule'. Therefore, where a document appears to be a complete contract, a party will have great difficulty convincing a court that further terms outside the agreement were intended to be incorporated into the contract.

Where certain contracts must by law be evidenced in writing, then any extrinsic oral evidence is likely to be excluded.

The exceptions to the parol evidence rule are as follows:

(1) Evidence adduced to determine the written agreement's validity or effectiveness.
(2) Evidence used to determine the agreement's true nature.
(3) Evidence to interpret or explain parts of the written agreement.
(4) Evidence of custom or trade usage.

9.7.6 Collateral contracts

In certain circumstances, although the party intended to be bound by all the terms in a written document, there may be a collateral contract of agreement outside the main agreement which gives efficacy to matters on which the main contract may be silent. This collateral agreement may be oral. A court may determine that it does have effect and that it runs alongside the main contract (see *Shanklin Pier v Detel Products* [1951] 2 KB 854).

9.7.7 Implied terms

Although it is always hoped that any terms incorporated into the contract are expressed either in writing or openly agreed between the parties before the contract is made, it is possible that terms are implied into the contract. This is particularly so in certain types of contracts (eg sale of goods, landlord and tenant, and employment).

Terms implied into the contract do not necessarily reflect the party's intention, although this is possible. Certain contracts might be silent about particular aspects of the contract. However the court does not imply a meaning simply because it improves the contract. It must be a necessity.

Certain statutes impose implied terms or a term may be implied from general usage or custom in any particular trade or activity. Similarly, evidence of a previous course of dealing between the parties may give rise to certain terms being implied.

Where there is an express term which clearly contradicts that which might be considered to be customary in the circumstances, the general rule is that the express term will prevail.

9.8 EXEMPTION AND EXCLUSION CLAUSES

It is common for parties to want to exclude or limit their liability in the terms of any contract they enter into. Furthermore, they may want to provide time limits in which the other party can lodge a claim.

Exclusion clauses are generally construed strictly. The court takes into account the circumstances of the case and tries to give effect to what they believe to be the parties' intentions. The words must therefore be clear and unambiguous. Where a clause is ambiguous a court infers whichever meaning favours the party against whom the clause is intended to operate, to the detriment of the party seeking to rely on it. This principle is known as 'contra proferentem'.

Where an exclusion clause is drafted so widely that, if interpreted literally, it defeats the main purpose of the contract, the court attempts to interpret it to reflect the parties' intentions.

9.8.1 Liability for negligence

It is possible to exclude or restrict a party's liability for negligence, but the parties must ensure that the words are clear and it is made certain that they intended to exclude such liability (*Smith v South Wales Switchgear* [1978] 1 WLR 165). It has also been said that it is 'inherently improbable' that a private person would wish to exempt a business with which it was dealing from liability for his own negligence. Any party who wishes to achieve this end 'must do it clearly so that the point is brought to the attention of the other contracting party' (*Casson v Ostley* (unreported, 29 June 2001)).

It is, however, not possible, in most cases, to exclude liability for death or personal injury (see 9.8.4).

9.8.2 Burden of proof

This is placed upon the person who intends to rely on the exemption or exclusion clause. He must show that the clause covers the liability that he intends to restrict or exclude. If he satisfies a court of this, the other party will try to convince the court that the loss or damage that arose emanated from an act or omission that falls outside the scope of the clause.

9.8.3 Exemption clause and a third party

A third party (ie one that is not a party to the contract) cannot at common law rely on an exemption clause contained in the contract; the exemption clause is intended to apply to the relationship *vis-à-vis* the parties to the contract (*Scruttons v Midland Silicones* [1962] AC 446). However, a situation could arise, say, where the duty of care owed by *C* to *D* arises as a result of a contract between *D* and *E*. An exemption clause in the contract between *D* and *E* which purports to exclude or restrict liability may be regarded as applying to any liability attaching to *C*. The condition that must be proven is that it was the intention of all the parties that such a clause should apply to *C*'s liability.

The position described above has been affected considerably by the Contracts (Rights of Third Parties) Act 1999 (see 9.11.1).

9.8.4 Statutory control and exemption clauses

Unfair Contract Terms Act 1977

The Act seeks to control terms contained in the contract (and also non-contractual notices that seek to exclude or restrict liability in tort) where those terms purport to exclude or restrict liability. The Act may make the clause ineffective or may mean that it must satisfy the requirement of reasonableness to be effective.

Dealing as a consumer

The Act draws a distinction between situations where a party deals as a consumer, in which case the three conditions below must be satisfied, and where he does not:

(1) he must not make the contract in the course of the business or hold himself out as doing so;
(2) the other party must make a contract in the course of a business; and
(3) the goods must be of a type ordinarily supplied for private use or consumption.

An illustration to this rule arose in *R & B Customs Brokers v United Dominions Trust* [1988] 1 WLR 321. The court held that a freight forwarding company dealt as a consumer when it entered into an agreement with a finance company to purchase a motor vehicle for a director's personal and business use. The decision was made on the basis that the company had not held itself out as making the contract in the course of a business.

Section 3 of the Act applies to a contract where one of the parties deals as a consumer or on the other party's written standard terms of business. No definition is provided in the Act for the meaning of 'written standard terms', presumably because these can be easily recognised in the instant case. It has been held that a contract can be on written standard terms even if some of those terms have been negotiated individually (*McCrone v Boots Farm Sales* [1981] SLT 103; *The Salvage Association v CAP Financial Services* [1995] FSR 654). The party cannot by reference to any contract term, except in so far as the term satisfies the test of reasonableness, exclude or restrict any liability in respect of his breach of contract, or claim that he is entitled to render a contractual performance that is substantially different from that which is reasonably expected of him, or render no performance at all for all or some of his contractual obligations.

Section 4 states that a person who deals with a consumer cannot by way of any contract term be made to indemnify another person in respect of any liability for negligence or breach of contract, except in so far as the contract term satisfies the test of reasonableness. Indemnities given by people who do not deal as a consumer are not affected by this section.

Liability for negligence

Section 2 prevents a person excluding or restricting his liability (arising from business liability) for death or personal injury resulting from negligence. Any such clause is totally ineffective. Nor can he exclude or restrict his liability for any other loss or damages that arise out of his negligence unless the term satisfies the test of reasonableness.

Consumer guarantees

Section 5 states that any clause that attempts to exclude or restrict business liability for loss or damage resulting from the negligence of the manufacturer or distributor of any goods is ineffective. Here, 'goods' means those ordinarily supplied for private use or consumption. The loss or damage must arise from the goods being defective while in use by a person other than exclusively for business.

'Business liability' is defined by s 1 as applying to liabilities for breach of any obligations arising from something that occurs in the course of a person's business or from the occupation of premises used for business purposes.

Sale, supply and hire purchase

Section 6 prevents the person who sells or lets out his goods under HP agreements from excluding or restricting liability for any of the undertakings as to title implied by the Sale of Goods Act 1979, s 12 or the Supply of Goods (Implied Terms) Act 1973, s 8. Furthermore, s 6 provides that the terms implied by those enactments as to description, quality and fitness for purpose cannot be excluded where the other party deals as a consumer. The use of an exclusion clause seeking to avoid these provisions in a consumer contract is also rendered a criminal offence by the Consumer Transactions (Restrictions on Statements) Order 1977. If that party deals as a business, those provisions can be excluded subject to the reasonableness requirement.

Section 7 applies to other contracts such as those for hire of goods or work and materials.

As against a consumer, liability in respect of description, quality or fitness cannot be excluded. Against a business, such provisions can be excluded subject to the reasonableness requirement. Terms relating to title implied by the Supply of Goods and Services Act 1982 cannot be excluded regardless of whether the other party is a consumer or business. Where a term seeks to exclude terms as to title which are not implied by that Act, it is valid only if reasonable, again regardless of the other contracting party's status.

Reasonableness test

To be effective, many of the clauses governed by the Act must satisfy the test of reasonableness. To satisfy the test, s 11 states that 'the term shall have been a fair and reasonable one to be included having regard to the circumstances which were, or ought reasonably to have been, known to or in the contemplation of the parties when the contract was made'. The reasonableness of the term is determined at the time when the contract was made; therefore any facts not known at that time are likely to be irrelevant in determining whether a clause is reasonable.

Schedule 2 lays down guidelines (which are not exhaustive) to assist in determining whether a clause satisfies the test. The guidelines apply to contracts dealing with the sale of goods and HP, and contracts for the supply of goods, but they are often regarded as being of general use in assisting to determine whether a clause is reasonable (see eg *Flamar Interocean v Denmac* [1990] 1 Lloyd's Rep 434; *St Albans City and District Council v ICL* [1995] FSR 686). The guidelines are as follows:

(a) the strength of the bargaining positions of the parties relative to each other, taking into account . . . alternative means by which the customers' requirements could have been met;

(b) whether the customer received an inducement to agree to the term, or in accepting it had an opportunity of entering into a similar contract with other persons, but without having to accept a similar term;

(c)   whether the customer knew or ought reasonably to have known of the existence and extent of the term (having regard . . . to any custom of the trade
and any previous course of dealing between the parties);

(d)   where the term excludes or restricts any relevant liability if some condition
is not complied with, whether it was reasonable at the time of the contract
to expect that compliance with that condition would be practicable;

(e)   whether the goods were manufactured, processed or adapted to the special
order of the customer.

Limiting liability

Section 11 provides that where a person, by use of a contract term, seeks to
restrict liability to a specified sum and the question arises whether that term
satisfies the test of reasonableness, consideration must be given (without
ignoring the guidelines listed above) to:

(1) the resources he could expect to be available to him to meet the liability if it arises, and

(2) how far it was open to him to cover himself by insurance.

A court must determine whether a clause is reasonable. It cannot rewrite the
term, nor can it delete words to render reasonable what it believes is an
'unreasonable' term.

Exceptions

Certain contracts are not affected by ss 2–4 of the 1977 Act (Sch 1). They
relate to contracts for insurance; creation or transfer of an interest in land,
patents, trademarks and copyright; formation or dissolution of a company or
the rights or obligations of its members; and any contract relating to creation
or transfer of rights in securities. For illustrative cases on the scope of those
exclusions, see *Micklefield v SAC Technology* [1990] 1 WLR 1002 and
Electricity Supply Nominees v IAF Group [1993] 1 WLR 1059.

Schedule 1 qualifies the Act's effect on any contract of marine salvage or
towage, a charterparty, and for the carriage of goods by a ship or hovercraft.
It further qualifies any contract of employment in that any attempt to
exclude liability for negligence will not be effective unless it favours an
employee.

Misrepresentation

Section 8 of the 1977 Act provides that where a term or clause attempts to
exclude or restrict any liability of or any remedy available to a party arising
from a misrepresentation, then that term or clause has no effect in so far as
it satisfies the test of reasonableness in s 11.

Unfair Terms in Consumer Contracts Regulations 1999

These regulations implement EC Directive 93/13/EC, which attempts to
harmonise the laws on safeguarding the consumer with regard to unfair

contract terms. They repealed the 1994 Regulations of the same name and came into force on 1 October 1999.

The Regulations do not affect the provisions of the 1977 Act; nor do they apply to non-consumer contracts. Therefore in some circumstances a party only has the choice of an action under that Act.

The Regulations prohibit the use of unfair terms in consumer contracts, whether oral or written. They apply to any term or contract concluded between a seller or supplier and a consumer where the term has not been individually negotiated (ie where it has been drafted in advance and a consumer has not been able to influence the term's content).

Whereas the Act applies only to specific types of clauses, the Regulations apply to all contract clauses that are not individually negotiated.

Plain intelligible language

Regulation 6 provides that terms must be drafted in plain intelligible language. If there is any doubt about the meaning of a written term, the most favourable interpretation to a consumer prevails. By using plain intelligible language, contract provisions relating to definition of the subject-matter, the price or remuneration are not subject to any test. However, these may be factors that must be taken into account in considering whether another term is fair.

The Regulations require that any term satisfies the test of 'fairness' (unlike the 1977 Act's test of reasonableness). If a term is regarded as unfair then it is not binding on a consumer. However, the Regulations stipulate that although one term may be ineffective, where the balance of the contract can continue without that term, it shall be binding on the parties.

What is unfair?

Under reg 5, 'an unfair term is one which contrary to the requirement of good faith causes a significant imbalance in the parties' rights and obligations under the contract to the detriment of the consumer'. When assessing the unfair nature of a term, the following must be considered (reg 6):

(1) the nature of the goods and services to which the contract applies;
(2) all the circumstances at the time the contract was concluded; and
(3) all other terms of the contract or of another contract on which that contract may be dependent.

Schedule 2 to the Regulations lists 17 terms which it is stated may be unfair. The list, although lengthy, is not exhaustive, and includes:

(1) inappropriately excluding or limiting the consumer's legal rights;
(2) irrevocably binding the consumer to terms with which he had no real opportunity of becoming acquainted before the conclusion of the contract;
(3) obliging the consumer to fulfil his obligations where the seller/supplier does not perform his;

(4) enabling the seller/supplier to alter the contract's terms unilaterally without a valid reason specified in the contract.

In *Director General of Fair Trading v First National Bank* [2002] 1 All ER 97, a credit agreement provided that the lender was entitled, on default of an instalment, to demand payment of the balance and interest outstanding. It further provided that interest on the amount that became payable would be charged at the contract rate until payment, after as well as before judgment, and that such obligation was to be independent of and not to merge with the judgment. In the absence of such a provision, a lender seeking to enforce an agreement in the county court would have been unable to recover post-judgment interest. The House of Lords, reversing the Court of Appeal, held that this term was not unfair. The essential bargain was that the bank would make funds available to the borrower which the latter would repay, with interest, over time. Neither party could suppose that the bank would willingly forgo any part of the principal or interest. If the bank thought that such was the likely outcome, it would not lend. The House of Lords also said that, if there were any room for doubt about the borrower's obligation to repay the principal in full with interest, that obligation was very clearly and unambiguously expressed in the conditions of the contract. See also *Falco Finance v Michael Gough* [1999] CCLR 16

The examples are guidelines only; each term must be assessed on its own merits. It is always possible for a listed term to be fair in the specific circumstances of any one case.

Complaints to qualifying bodies

The reg 11(1) provisions are new to the 1999 Regulations. Where a qualifying body notifies the Director General (DG) in writing that it agrees to consider a complaint that any contract term drawn up for general use is unfair, that body is obliged to consider that complaint. It is then obliged to give reasons for any decision whether to apply for an injunction and, in so deciding, to take account of any undertaking that might be forthcoming.

The relevant qualifying bodies are the Information Commissioner, the DG of Gas and Electricity Management (along with the Northern Ireland counterpart), the DG of Telecommunications, the DG of Water Services, the Rail Regulator, the Financial Services Authority, every weights and measures authority in Great Britain, and the Department of Enterprise, Trade and Investment. There is nothing in the Regulations to restrict these bodies to terms arising in their own field of interest, though this is no doubt how it will operate in practice. While the DG of Fair Trading must be notified by a qualifying body of intended action, the former has no powers to stay any action.

The OFT has signed certain agreements with the Consumers' Association, the Department of Enterprise, Trade and Investment, the Office of Telecommunications and with LACOTS (the Local Authority Co-ordinating Committee on Food and Trading Standards).

Application for an injunction

Regulation 12(1) gives the DG of Fair Trading and any of the above quali-fying bodies, and also the Consumers' Association, the power to apply for an injunction, including an interim injunction, against any person appearing to be using, or recommending, an unfair term drawn up for general use in consumer contracts.

Before a qualifying body applies for an injunction, reg 12(2) requires it to notify the DG in writing at least 14 days before the date on which the application is made, beginning with the date on which such notification is given. The DG can consent to a shorter period of notice.

Regulation 12(3) provides that the court may grant an injunction on such terms as it thinks fit, and reg 12(4) further provides that the injunction may relate not only to the use of a particular contract term drawn up for general use, but to any similar term, or term having like effect, used or recom-mended by any person.

Obtaining documents and information

Regulation 13 gives extensive powers to the DG and the qualifying bodies (but not the Consumers' Association) to obtain documents and informa-tion. Under reg 13(3), such parties have the right to require any person to supply:

(1) a copy of any document which that person has used or recommended at the time when notice is given as a pre-formulated standard consumer contract; and

(2) information about the use or recommendation by that person of that or any other document in dealings with consumers.

These powers are to be exercised by a written notice that may specify the way and the time within which the notice is to be complied with; further, any such notice can be varied or revoked by a subsequent written notice (reg 13(4)). The court, when approached by the party issuing the notice, may make such order as it thinks fit in the event of non-compliance (reg 13(6)). Under reg 13(5), nothing in these provisions can compel any person to supply a document or information that he would be entitled to refuse to produce or give in civil proceedings.

Notification of undertakings and orders

Under reg 14, a qualifying body must notify the DG of any undertakings it has obtained under regs 10 and 11. The qualifying body is also required to give the DG written notice of the outcome of any application made for an injunction, and of the terms of any undertaking given to, or order made, by the court. Such body must also give the DG written notice of the outcome of an application made to enforce any previous court order.

Dissemination of information on the Regulations

The 1999 Regulations require the DG to arrange for the publication, in such form and manner as he considers appropriate, of any:

(1) undertaking or order notified by a qualifying body;
(2) undertaking given as to the continued use of a term which he considers unfair in consumer contracts;
(3) application made by him for an injunction and of the terms of any undertakings given to, or order made by, the court;
(4) application made by him to enforce a previous court order.

Regulation 14(2) obliges the DG to inform any person, on request made in whatever form, whether a particular term covered by the Regulations has been the subject of an undertaking given or notified to him by a qualifying body, or the subject of a court order made on application by or as notified to him by such body. When responding, the DG is to provide the person making the request with details of the undertaking, or a copy of the order, together with a copy of any amendments that the person giving the undertaking has agreed to make to the term in question. It would appear that, only when providing such a copy, this is the only time when the DG's response must be in writing.

Under reg 14(3), the DG may (not must) arrange for the dissemination in such form and manner as he considers appropriate of such information and advice as to the operation of the Regulations as may appear to him expedient to give to the public and to all persons likely to be affected by the Regulations.

The OFT published a regular series of bulletins on its activities under the Regulations.

9.9 BREACH OF CONTRACT

There are many ways in which a contract can come to an end other than by way of the parties discharging their obligations and promises under the contract's terms. Perhaps one of the most important is by breach of contract.

Breach generally gives rise to a cause of action for the person who has been aggrieved. This does not mean that whenever there is a breach, the aggrieved person is entitled to treat himself as discharged from any further obligation to accept the other party's performance of his contractual duty or any attempt to perform them. However, the aggrieved party usually prefers this course of action, although in some situations he may wish to treat the contract as continuing. Furthermore, he may decide to waive his rights to treat the contract as discharged, except for the other party's performance even though it is defective, and instead sue for damages.

9.9.1 Affirming the contract

The aggrieved party may treat the contract as continuing, in which case he is said to have 'affirmed' the contract. Affirmation may be express or implied if, with knowledge of the breach and of his right to choose between the alternatives open to him, he does some unequivocal act that suggests he intends to go on with the contract regardless. Nevertheless, by affirming the contract the aggrieved party does not lose his right to claim damages for any resulting loss by him.

An aggrieved party may lose his right to treat the contract as repudiated if he conducts himself in such a way that the other party believes that he does not intend to exercise his right. The aggrieved party must have shown unequivocal representation in either words or conduct that he does not intend to do so. Furthermore, it must be shown that the aggrieved party knew of the circumstances giving rise to the breach and of his right to treat the contract as repudiated. Another condition that must be satisfied is that the party who claims that the other has waived his right has relied to such an extent on the action which he regards as being the waiver, that it is unjust not to allow the contract to continue. The facts of each case decide whether a court accepts that an aggrieved party waived his right.

9.9.2 Repudiation must be accepted

Where an aggrieved party decides to treat himself as discharged of his obligation under the contract, he must accept repudiation. Otherwise, the contract continues to exist. In other words, he must indicate to the other party that he considers that that party is in breach and that he intends to treat the contract as repudiated. Once acceptance has been communicated, it cannot then be withdrawn. Therefore, if the parties decide to resume the contract's performance, the contract is regarded as renewed, even if the terms are the same.

9.9.3 What if both parties are in breach?

The effect of this depends on the order of the breaches by each party. If *A* admits the breach and *B* follows with an act that is also a breach of contract, then if *B* informs *A* that he intends to treat the contract as repudiated on the basis of *A*'s breach, failure to perform does not give rise to a breach of contract to *A*.

If both parties commit a breach of contract simultaneously, it is suggested that neither party is entitled to treat the contract as repudiated.

9.9.4 Anticipatory breach

If one party indicates to the other that he intends to do or not do something that leads a reasonable person to believe that he does not intend to fulfil his obligations under the contract, this could be regarded as an 'anticipatory breach'. In these circumstances, the 'aggrieved' party may indicate to the other that he 'accepts' the repudiation and sue for damages immediately, or he may wait and see whether the breach does occur and then sue for damages.

9.10 FRUSTRATION

Despite the best intention of both parties to the contract, an event may occur once the contract is entered into which makes it physically or commercially impossible for the contract to be performed. The principles of frustration were illustrated in *Taylor v Caldwell* (1863) 32 LJQB 164, in which the defendants had agreed to allow the plaintiffs to use a music hall for concerts on four specified nights. Before the first night, but after the contract was made, the music hall was completely destroyed by fire. The defendants were sued but the court held that they were not liable in damages to the plaintiffs. It is not necessary that physical destruction of any subject-matter has to take place but merely that an event occurs outside the control of either party and is such that it brings the contract to an immediate end.

A court that is asked to determine whether contracts have been frustrated will try to determine whether the contract's terms are wide enough to enable the contract to continue in the new situation; if it is not, the contract must be regarded as frustrated.

9.10.1 Delay

It is not always easy to determine whether an unexpected delay in the performance of a contractual duty gives rise to the contract being frustrated. To amount to frustration, the delay must be unexpected and abnormal in that its effect or length would not be reasonable for the contracting parties to have contemplated it occurring. Much depends on the length of the delay in relation to the nature of the contract and the effect caused by the delay on the contractual duty. If the delay is held to be within the commercial risks undertaken by the party to the contract, the court will hold that there is no frustration.

9.10.2 Sale of goods

The Sale of Goods Act 1979 makes provision where a certain set of circumstances gives rise to the contract being frustrated. Section 7 provides: 'Where there is an agreement to sell specific goods and subsequently the goods, without any fault on the part of the seller or buyer, perish before the risk passes to the buyer, the agreement is avoided.' Apart from this particular set of circumstances, the normal rule relating to frustration applies where it is claimed an agreement to sell goods has been frustrated.

9.10.3 Consequences of frustration

The common law rules, to deal with the consequences of frustration, can be found in three court rulings: *Chandler v Webster* [1904] 1 KB 493 (room booked to view Coronation procession that did not take place; held, even though the contract had been frustrated, the lessee could not recover the advance payment and remained liable for the balance); *Krell v Henry* [1903] 2 KB 740 (loss to be borne by the debtor if the obligation to pay did not mature until after the discharge of the contract); and *Fibrosa Spolka Akcyjna v Fairbairn Lawson Combe Barbour* [1943] AC 32 (contract frustrated by outbreak of war, where the request for the return of an advance payment was refused because of the considerable amount of work already done; held, the money could be recovered as there had been a total failure of consideration). Note that the ruling in *Fibrosa* applies only in the case of a total failure of consideration. It does not permit the recovery of an advance payment if the consideration has only partly failed (ie if the payer has received even a small benefit for his payment). However, while the payee may be compelled to repay the money on the ground that the payer has received no benefit, he may himself, in partial performance, have incurred expenses for which he has no redress.

While the position was considerably affected by the Law Reform (Frustrated Contracts) Act 1943, the Act does not apply to contracts to which s 7 of the Sale of Goods Act applies (see 9.10.2), nor to any other contract for the sale or the sale and delivery of goods, where the contract is frustrated because the goods have perished. In such cases, the common law rules continue to apply.

Section 1(2) of the Act provides that all sums that have been paid or are payable in pursuance of the contract before the time of the frustration shall, in the case of sums actually paid, be recoverable and, in the case of sums payable, cease to be payable. There is a proviso that where the party to whom the sums were paid or are payable incurred expenses before the time of frustration, in performance of the contract, then a court may allow him to retain or recover a sum up to the level of the expenses incurred.

Benefit acquired under the contract

Section 1(3) states that where a party has, by reason of any performance of another party under the contract's terms, obtained a valuable benefit (other than a payment of money) before the contract is frustrated, then a sum can be recovered from him which should not exceed the value of the benefit and should be such a figure as the court thinks fit, having regard to all the circumstances. The 'benefit' is the product of the services supplied, but it might be the services themselves. It is up to the court to place a value on the benefit received. This is not always easy since a small service may result in something of great value to the receiving party, or a substantial service may produce something of little value.

The court must take into account the amount of any expenses incurred, if any, by the party who benefited, including any sum that he paid to any other party and the effect, in relation to the benefit, of the circumstances giving rise to the frustration. In effect, the court must first identify the 'valuable benefit', then place a value upon it, and finally consider the award of a just sum, which cannot be greater in value than the actual benefit obtained.

Severing part of the contract

Section 2(4) provides that a court can sever any part of a contract that it believes is severable and treat it as if it were a separate contract that had not been frustrated. The rest of the contract is therefore regarded as frustrated. The Act has no effect upon the part of the contract that can be regarded as being completely performed.

Excluding the Act

Under s 2(3), if it is clear that the parties have anticipated that the frustrating event might occur and have provided for what should happen in the event that it did occur, the Act does not apply. But where the circumstances are so unusual and the effect so serious that they fall outside the clauses' intention, the Act may not have been excluded.

Where the parties intend to make provision in the event that the contract is frustrated, they must make it very clear what the alternative consequences of frustration are. Otherwise, it is likely that the common law rule will apply which may be detrimental to eg the paying party.

Exclusions from the Act

Certain types of contract are excluded from the Act; these include charter-parties and contracts for the carriage of goods by sea, for insurance and for the sale of specific perishable goods, whether or not the risk passes to the buyer before the date of perishing.

9.11 PRIVITY OF CONTRACT

The general rule is that only the parties to a contract incur rights and obligations under it, as illustrated by *Dunlop Pneumatic Tyre v Selfridge & Co* [1915] AC 847. The plaintiff supplied tyres to a wholesaler on condition that, if the wholesaler supplied any retailer, the retailer must promise not to sell the tyres to the public below a minimum price. The wholesaler supplied the defendant with tyres on that condition and with an agreement that, should they sell the tyres at a discount, the defendant must pay the plaintiff

£5 per tyre sold at discount. The defendant sold the tyres to the public at a discount and the plaintiff sued to recover £5 per tyre. The House of Lords decided that there was a contract between the plaintiff and the wholesaler and another contract between the wholesaler and the defendant retailer, but none between the plaintiff and defendant. Thus the plaintiff could not recover damages under the agreement between the wholesaler and the defendant because it was not privy to that contract.

This means that no third party can sue or be sued on a contract, even if the contract is made for their benefit. In *Tweddle v Atkinson* (1861) 1 B&S 393, the plaintiff was engaged to be married to the defendant's daughter. His father and prospective father-in-law made a contract that provided that each of them would give a certain sum of money to the plaintiff when the marriage took place. The father-in-law died before making the payment and the plaintiff sued his estate. The court held that even though the contract expressly provided that the plaintiff was to be entitled to enforce it, he could not do so in law.

In *Beswick v Beswick* [1967] 2 All ER 1197, a coal merchant agreed to transfer his business to his nephew on condition that his nephew paid him a pension and, after his death, would pay his widow a weekly annuity. The uncle died and only one payment was made. The widow, as her husband's administratrix, sued for an order of specific performance. She was granted the order, only because of her position as administratrix. If she had sued as an intended beneficiary she would have been unsuccessful because she was not party to the contract. A party to a contract that is for the benefit of a third party can enforce it, but the damages recovered will only be nominal because a plaintiff can only recover damages for losses he has suffered. Remedies other than damages may be available.

If the contract is for the benefit of a third party *and* the contracting party, in certain situations damages may be awarded for their losses (see *Jackson v Horizon Holidays* [1975] 3 All ER 92). In *Woodar Investment Development v Wimpey Construction UK* [1980] 1 All ER 571, however, the House of Lords confirmed that the principle stated by Lord Denning in *Jackson* was not of general application but confined to the special facts in that case.

9.11.1 Contracts (Rights of Third Parties) Act 1999

This Act reforms the common law rule of privity of contract and provides for circumstances in which a third party is to have a right to enforce a contract term effectively where the contracting parties intend this to be so.

9.11.2 Right of third party to enforce

There are effectively two requirements for a third party to have the right to enforce a contract under the Act. These are contained in s 1(1)–(3), as follows:

(1) either:
   (a) where the contract expressly provides that they should have that right, or
   (b) if the contract expressly confers a benefit on them and they are identified expressly (unless it appears on a true construction of the contract that the contracting parties did not intend the third party to have the right of enforcement); and
(2) they must be identified in the contract by name, class or description and do not even have to be in existence at the time the contract is made. This allows those making contracts to confer benefits on eg unborn children, a future spouse or a company that has not yet been incorporated.

The contract can state that the right of enforcement may be limited (ie the contract may provide that a third party can only enforce the contract by way of arbitration, and not litigation). All usual remedies for breach of contract will be available to a third party with the right to enforce (s 1(5)). As well as being able to enforce a term made for their benefit, s 1(6) makes it clear that a third party can take advantage of an exclusion or limitation clause in the contract. Should there be any doubt about whether a contract confers a benefit on a third party, a contractor can, by a term in the contract, expressly exclude a third party from any benefit.

9.11.3 Variation and rescission of contract

Once a third party has a right to enforce a term under the Act, the contracting parties cannot cancel or vary the original contract terms so as to affect that right without the third party's consent (s 2(1)). This is provided where either the:

(1) third party has communicated his assent to the term to the promisor (the party to the contract against whom the term is enforceable by the third party);
(2) promisor is aware that the third party has relied on the term; or
(3) promisor can reasonably be expected to have foreseen that the third party would rely on it and has done so.

The Act restricts this third party right in the following ways:

(a) if the contract states expressly that it can by agreement be rescinded or varied without the third party's consent, then s 2(1) will not apply (s 2(3));
(b) if the contract states expressly that the third party's consent is to be required in circumstances different to those set out in s 2(1), this sub-section will not apply; and
(c) a court or arbitral tribunal may dispense with the need for third party consent if the third party cannot be found to give his consent, if he is mentally incapable of giving it, or if there is no proof that he relied on the term (s 2(4) and (5)).

9.11.4 Defences etc available to promisor

A promisor (the party to the contract against whom the term is enforceable by the third party) has various defences or set-offs available to him if a third party brings a claim against him.

First, he can rely on a defence or set-off that arises out of the contract and is relevant to the term being enforced and would have been available to him had the claim been brought by the promisee (the party by whom the term is enforceable against the promisor) (1999 Act, s 3(2)). The explanatory notes to the Act set out illustrations of how the rule might work in practice:

(1) A third party can no more enforce a void, discharged or unenforceable contract than a promisee could.
(2) P1 (the promisor) and P2 (the promisee) contract that P2 will sell goods to P1, who will pay the contract price to P3 (the third party). In breach of contract, P2 delivers goods that are not of the standard contracted for. In an action for the price by P3 (just as in an action for the price by P2), P1 is entitled to reduce or extinguish the price by reason of the damages for breach of contract.

Secondly, he can rely on a defence or set-off if an express contract term provides for it to be available to him in a claim brought by a third party and if it would have been available to him had the claim been brought by the promisee (who is the party to the contract by whom the term is enforceable against the promisor) (s 3(3)). The explanatory notes to the Act illustrate how the rule might work in practice with one example: P1 and P2 contract that P1 will pay P3 if P2 transfers his car to P1. P2 owes P1 money under a wholly unrelated contract. P1 and P2 agree to an express term in the contract which provides that P1 can raise against a claim by P3 regarding any matter that would have given P1 a defence or set-off to a claim by P2.

Thirdly, he can rely on a defence or set-off, or make any counterclaim not arising from the contract if this would have been possible had the third party been a party to the contract (ie specific to the third party and unavailable to the promisor in an action by the promisee) (s 3(4)). The explanatory notes to the Act set out illustrations of how the rule might work in practice:

(a) P1 contracts with P2 to pay P3 £1,000. P3 already owes P1 £600. P1 has a set-off to P3's claim so that P1 is only bound to pay P3 £400.
(b) P3 induced P1 to enter into the contract with P2 by misrepresentation, but P2 has no actual or constructive notice of that misrepresentation. P1 may have a defence (or a counterclaim for damages) against P3 which would not have been available had the action been brought by P2.

The first and third defences or set-offs above are subject to any express term of the contract that narrows the defences or set-offs, or counterclaims available (s 3(5)).

9.12 DAMAGES

In the event of a breach of contract, damages are assessed according to the rules laid down in *Hadley v Baxendale* (1854) 9 Ex 341. This states that damages are recoverable for all the losses that flow as a natural result of the breach. Further damages are recoverable for losses not so flowing if, given the circumstances prevailing at the time the contract was made, these were contemplated by the contract breaker as a probable result of the breach. In appropriate cases, the innocent party can seek an injunction to prevent the breach, or specific performance to order the contract to be performed. These are discretionary remedies and will generally be granted only where damages are not an adequate remedy. In *Sky Petroleum v VIP Petroleum* [1974] 1 All ER 954, the claimants obtained an interlocutory injunction to restrain the defendants from breaking a contract to supply the claimants with all their petroleum requirements for ten years. The court treated the injunction as in effect a decree of specific performance, saying that the general rule against the grant of such a decree was inapplicable where damages would clearly not be an adequate remedy. In the instant case, there was a real danger that the claimants would be forced out of business if the defendants broke their contract at a time of exceptional disturbance in the oil market.

10

SALE OF GOODS AND CONSUMER PROTECTION

The law of contract for sale of goods was consolidated in the Sale of Goods Act 1979, as amended by the Sale and Supply of Goods Act 1994. Provisions relating to contracts for work and materials exist in the Supply of Goods and Services Act 1982. Agreements of hire purchase, condition of sale and credit sale are governed by the Consumer Credit Act 1974 and the Supply of Goods (Implied Terms) Act 1973.

The law sets out various obligations with which a seller must comply as well as the buyer's corresponding rights. There are more limited obligations imposed on the buyer. There are also provisions affecting the position of a person without title who tries to sell the goods and the rights of the person who takes them.

Statute has also intervened to restrict the validity of exclusion clauses.

This chapter also deals with certain measures of consumer protection, in particularly the statutory controls over the supply of unsafe or dangerous goods. Account is given of the Stop Now regime and of proposed changes in consumer law.

10.1 TERMS IMPLIED INTO A SALE OF GOODS CONTRACT

Section 12 of the 1979 Act states that there is an implied term on the seller's part that he has a right both to sell the goods and, in an agreement to sell, to sell them at a time when the property is to pass. Furthermore, in a contract for sale (other than that in which the seller intends to transfer only such title as he or a third person may have, and which is governed by s 12(3)-(5)) there is an implied term in s 12(2) that:

(a) the goods are free, and will remain free until the time when the property is to pass, from any charge or encumbrance not disclosed or known to the buyer before the contract is made, and

(b) the buyer will enjoy quiet possession of the goods except so far as it may be disturbed by the owner or other person entitled to the benefit of any charge or encumbrance so disclosed or known.

This implied term is regarded as a condition; therefore, if it is breached the buyer can treat the contract as repudiated and claim damages. Alternatively, he may affirm the contract and also claim damages. Under s 12(2), these obligations are warranties and give rise to no more than a claim for damages.

The exclusion of the s 12 provisions is prohibited by s 6 of the Unfair Contract Terms Act 1977.

10.2 DESCRIPTION

Section 13 of the 1979 Act provides that where there is a contract for the sale of goods by description there is an implied term that they will correspond with this description. If the sale is by sample as well as by description, it is not sufficient that the bulk of the goods correspond with the sample if the goods do not also correspond with the description. Care must be taken to ensure the description is as accurate as possible.

In *Arcos v Ronaasen & Son* [1933] AC 470, the contract was for wooden staves which were to be ½″ thick. About 5% of the staves delivered corresponded to this measurement, the remainder being ⁹⁄₁₆″. All the staves were suitable for the buyer's purpose. The House of Lords ruled that there had been a breach of s 13. The court held that when buyers 'descend to minute measurements' ½″ does not mean about ½, though it did add: 'No doubt there may be microscopic deviations which businessmen and therefore the courts will ignore'.

10.3 FITNESS FOR PURPOSE AND QUALITY

10.3.1 Fitness for purpose

Section 14 states that where a buyer expressly or impliedly makes known to

(1) the seller who sold him the goods in the course of business, or
(2) the credit broker who had previously sold the goods to the seller, where the buyer is paying all or part of the purchase price in instalments,

the particular purpose for buying the goods, there is an implied condition that the goods are reasonably suited to that purpose. This applies whether or not the goods are commonly supplied for such purpose, but not if the buyer does not, or it is unreasonable for him to, rely on the seller's or credit broker's skill or judgement. A credit broker is defined by s 61(1) as

> a person who acts in the course of a business of credit brokerage carried on by him, that is a business of effecting introductions of individuals desiring to obtain credit:
> (a) to persons carrying on any business so far as it relates to the provision of credit, or
> (b) to other persons engaged in credit brokerage.

Where the buyer is required to make the purpose of goods known, he is not required to make it known expressly. For example, where an article can only be for one particular purpose, the buyer need not make it clear that he wants the article for that purpose. Where the goods may be used for several purposes, it may be necessary, but not definitely, to indicate the intended purpose.

The seller must prove that the buyer did not rely on his judgement. If the seller informs the buyer that he has no knowledge or expertise of the goods being bought or the buyer has more knowledge of the goods than the seller, the buyer cannot make a successful claim against the seller that the goods were not fit for their purpose.

The duty to provide goods that are reasonably fit for their purpose is strict and a party cannot successfully defend a claim by showing that he took all reasonable care. However, a seller is not liable where the goods are used by the buyer for purposes that are outside the range of those that the seller could reasonably foresee.

Where a buyer purchases goods there is no breach of the implied term where their failure to meet the intended purpose arises from an abnormal feature or idiosyncrasy, not disclosed to the seller, in the buyer or in the circumstances of the goods' use by the buyer, irrespective of whether the buyer was himself aware of the abnormal feature or idiosyncrasy (*Griffiths v Peter Conway* [1939] 1 All ER 685; *Slater v Finning* [1996] 3 All ER 398).

10.3.2 Satisfactory quality

The requirement that the quality of the goods sold should be of 'merchantable' quality as required by s 14 of the 1979 Act was amended by the 1994 Act. Section 14 (as amended) now provides that where a seller sells goods in the course of a business, there is an implied term that the goods supplied are of 'satisfactory' quality.

Goods are of satisfactory quality if they meet the standard that a reasonable person would regard as satisfactory, taking into account any description of the goods, the price (if relevant) and all other relevant circumstances. The 1979 Act states that their quality includes their state and condition, and suggests that some of the things that must be taken into account when considering the quality are:

(a) the fitness for all the purposes for which goods of the kind in question are commonly supplied;
(b) appearance and finish;
(c) being free from minor defects;
(d) safety; and
(e) durability.

This does not apply where their unsatisfactory nature is specifically drawn to the buyer's attention, or where the buyer examines them, but only as regards defects which that examination ought to reveal. This provision applies only if there is an examination: it does not apply if the buyer was offered the chance to examine and rejected it.

10.4 SALE BY SAMPLE

Section 15 of the 1979 Act applies where by purchasing the bulk of the goods the buyer can place his reliance on examination of a sample. It must be clear that the parties intended that the sample, which is exhibited to the buyer at the time of sale, is of the goods that the buyer is purchasing. Section 15 states that the bulk must correspond with the sample in quality and the buyer must have a reasonable opportunity of comparing the bulk with the sample before he is deemed to have accepted the goods.

Further, s 15 (as amended) states that the goods will be free from any defect that might make their quality unsatisfactory, which might not be apparent on reasonable examination of the sample.

10.5 EXCLUSION OF IMPLIED TERMS

Where the buyer is a consumer, as defined in the Unfair Contract Terms Act 1977, the seller cannot exclude or restrict his liability by reference to any contract terms imposed by ss 13–15 of the 1979 Act. It is a criminal offence to employ any such exclusion or restriction in a consumer contract by virtue of the Consumer Transactions (Restrictions on Statements) Order 1976. If the exclusion or restriction clause appears in a contract with a business, the clause will be valid if it can be shown to be reasonable.

The Unfair Terms in Consumer Contracts Regulations 1999 provide that, in consumer contracts, a term is void if, contrary to the requirements of good faith, it causes a significant imbalance in the parties' rights and obligations to the detriment of the consumer. In the present context, the Regulations have no real role to play since the relevant term will be automatically void under the 1977 Act, whether or not it is also unfair under the 1999 Regulations.

10.6 BREACH OF AN IMPLIED TERM

The terms implied by ss 13–15 of the 1979 Act are conditions and as such an aggrieved party is normally entitled to treat the contract as repudiated and reject the goods. However, the 1994 Act made an important amendment for non-consumers: where the breach on the part of the seller is so slight that it is unreasonable for him to reject the goods, 'the breach is not to be treated as a breach of condition but may be treated as a breach of warranty'. The aggrieved party can claim damages only. This provision only applies unless a contrary intention appears, or is to be implied, from the contract.

10.7 STIPULATIONS OF TIME

Section 10 of the 1979 Act provides that unless a contrary intention appears from the contract's terms, stipulation of time of payment is not deemed to be of the essence of a contract of sale. Whether any other stipulation of time is of the essence of the contract depends on the terms of the contract itself. In other words, late payment does not give rise to an action for damages. However, the Act further provides that a court has the power to award interest. Late payment can give a right to interest under the provisions of the Late Payment of Commercial Debts (Interest) Act 1998.

10.8 CONTRACTS SIMILAR TO CONTRACTS OF SALE

The terms as to title, description, fitness for purpose and satisfactory quality implied into contracts for hire purchase, supplying work and materials or for hiring goods, and the provisions as to excluding or restricting these terms, are essentially identical to the terms provided in the Sale of Goods Act (Supply of Goods (Implied Terms) Act 1973; Supply of Goods and Services Act 1982). Under the terms of the latter, those who provide a service must provide it with reasonable care and skill.

10.9 PASSING OF PROPERTY AND RISK

Sections 16–20 of the 1979 Act contain the rules governing the passing of property, in goods sold, from the seller to the buyer. All provisions of ss 16–20 can be varied and in most cases the parties, whether buyer or seller, will want to vary them by way of specific terms in the contract. Section 16 refers to unascertained goods (eg '50 kilograms of flour') and provides that no property in the goods transfers to the buyer unless and until the goods are actually ascertained.

Section 17 provides that for specific or ascertained goods, the property is transferred to the buyer at such time as the parties intend it to be transferred. In other words, consideration must be given to the contract's terms, the parties' conduct and the general circumstances of the case.

Section 18 sets out various rules for ascertaining the parties' intention for the time when the property in the goods is to pass to the buyer, in the absence of any contrary intention by the party. They can therefore be excluded by reference to terms in the contract.

Section 19 states that where there is a contract for sale of specific goods (or where goods are subsequently appropriated to the contract) the seller may reserve the right of the goods' disposal until certain conditions are fulfilled. In those circumstances the property in the goods does not pass to the buyer until these conditions are fulfilled.

10.9.1 'Romalpa' clauses; retention of title

This type of clause puts the seller in a more favourable position than he would normally be if the buyer is unable to pay. Under the 1979 Act the property in specific goods passes to the buyer when the contract is made, irrespective of the time of payment or delivery. Consequently, a seller is advised to include a clause stipulating that he retains property in the goods supplied until he receives payment. The principle arose as a result of *Aluminium Industrie Vaassen v Romalpa Aluminium* [1976] 1 WLR 676. Such a clause is beneficial to the seller if eg the buyer goes into liquidation.

Five broad categories of clause have emerged:

(1) Simple clause: retaining ownership in the goods supplied under the contract until they are paid for.

(2) Current account clause (sometimes called 'all liabilities' or 'all monies'): retaining ownership in the goods until they are paid for, plus all other sums due from the buyer are paid (ie for goods or services supplied under separate contracts). This means that where a supplier makes regular deliveries, the property in goods in earlier deliveries is retained long after they have been paid for, so long as any part of the price on later deliveries is unpaid. The buyer, if continually enjoying credit periods, never gets to own any goods supplied.

(3) Extended clause: claiming ownership against both the buyer and any sub-buyers to whom the goods are sold.

(4) Proceeds clause: retaining ownership in the goods and claiming the proceeds of any resale.

(5) Products clause: retaining ownership in the goods supplied and in any new product into which the goods are incorporated.

Where the buyer is a company, CA 1985, ss 395 and 396 (as amended by CA 1989) arguably apply. These sections provide that certain classes of charge are void against a liquidator or administrator and any creditor of the company unless registered. Where the buyer is an individual or partnership, a trustee in bankruptcy may argue that the clause is in effect a bill of sale which is void unless registered pursuant to the Bills of Sale Act 1878 (see *Re Bond Worth* [1980] Ch 228 and *Stroud Architectural Systems v John Laing Construction* [1994] 2 BCLC 276). Categories of registrable charges for present purposes are floating charges, charges on book debts and charges which, if executed by an individual, would require registration as a bill of sale simple.

10.9.2 Passing of the risk

Section 20 of the 1979 Act states that unless it is otherwise agreed in the contract, the goods remain at the seller's risk until the property in them is transferred to the buyer. Then the goods are at the buyer's risk, whether or not delivery has been made.

10.10 DELIVERY AND ACCEPTANCE

10.10.1 Delivery

Detailed rules for delivery of goods are contained in the 1979 Act. Section 29 deals with the place and time of delivery, goods that may be in possession of a third person and expenses incurred in connection with the delivery. Section 30 sets out what might be regarded as a defective, insufficient or excessive delivery. It has been affected by the Sale and Supply of Goods Act 1994 to the extent that s 30(4) (the buyer's right to reject part of the delivery of goods, some which satisfy the contract description) is repealed. Furthermore, a new provision is inserted for situations in which there is a shortfall or excess in the delivery.

Where there is a shortfall the buyer can either reject the delivery, recover the price paid and sue for any loss suffered, or accept the quantity delivered, paying for this at the contract rate and recovering any additional money paid; he can also claim damages for breach. Where there is an excess, the buyer can either:

(1) reject the whole of the goods delivered; or
(2) select the correct quantity and reject the rest; or
(3) accept the whole delivery and pay for the excess at the contract rate.

A new provision, inserted by the 1994 Act, states that a buyer who does not deal as a consumer is not entitled to reject the goods where there is a shortfall or an excess if it is so slight that it would be unreasonable for him to do so. Whether the shortfall or excess is slight must be proved by the seller.

Section 31 deals with delivery by way of instalment (eg it stipulates when the buyer is not bound to accept delivery by instalments). Section 32 sets out the rules for where delivery is made to a carrier; s 33 makes a buyer take responsibility for the risk of any deterioration in the goods where a seller has agreed to deliver at his own risk to a place other than where they are sold.

All the above rules can be altered by the party by reference to terms of the contract; close consideration should be given to this.

10.10.2 **Acceptance**

Generally, where a buyer accepts the goods, he cannot repudiate the contract at a later stage. Therefore, any rights he may have had with regard to a breach of condition would then have to be treated as a breach of warranty and would entitle him to claim for damages only.

Section 34(2) of the 1979 Act states that when a seller attempts to deliver goods he must allow the buyer, if requested, a reasonable opportunity of examining them to ascertain whether they conform with the contract and, if appropriate, to compare the bulk of the delivery with the sample. Section 35 (as amended) states that the buyer is deemed to have accepted the goods (except as provided below) when:

(1) he intimates to the seller that he has accepted them;
(2) the goods are delivered to him and he does any act which is inconsistent with the seller's ownership; or
(3) after a reasonable period has passed, he retains the goods without intimating to the seller that he has rejected them.

Where goods have been purchased for resale, a reasonable time in which to indicate rejection would usually be the time taken to resell together with a further period for the ultimate buyer to test the particular goods (*Truk (UK) v Tokmakidis* [2000] 2 Comm 594). When considering whether a 'reasonable' time has passed, consideration must be given to whether the buyer has had a reasonable opportunity to examine the goods.

If the buyer has not previously examined the goods, he is not deemed to have accepted them when they are delivered unless he has a reasonable opportunity to examine them as specified in s 34(2). Furthermore, where the buyer deals as a consumer, he cannot lose his right to have a reasonable opportunity of examining the goods. Any attempt by the seller to persuade him to contract out of this right will be ineffective.

A buyer is not deemed to have accepted goods merely because he asks for or agrees to them being repaired or where the goods are delivered to another person under a subsale.

In *AC Daniels & Co v Jungwoo Logic* (unreported, 14 April 2000), the claimant had ordered from the defendant an injection mould for the claimant's plastic medical waste bins. However, the mould had to be returned to the defendant nine times because of faults. The claimant finally rejected the mould and turned to another supplier, and brought an action for repayment of fees and damages for breach of contract against the defendants. Held, the claimant had not accepted the mould and the rejection was effective.

Where the contract relates to the making of one or more commercial units, and a buyer accepts any goods included in a unit, he is deemed to have accepted all the goods comprised in that unit.

A right of 'partial rejection' was introduced by the 1994 Act. Where the buyer has the right to reject goods by virtue of the seller's breach which affects some or all of the goods, but he accepts some of the goods including all those unaffected by the breach, he is not regarded as losing his rights to reject the rest. The rule also applies where the buyer is faced with an instalment of goods rather than the entire delivery. Goods are 'affected by a breach' if, as a result of the breach, they do not conform to the contract. The right to partial rejection can be amended or deleted by agreement in the contract.

Section 36 provides that where goods are delivered to the buyer and he refuses to accept them, having the right to do so, he is not bound to return them to the seller; it is sufficient if he intimates to the seller that he refuses to accept them. He cannot, however, exercise a lien over the goods to obtain repayment from the seller.

Where the buyer refuses to take delivery within a reasonable time from a request by the seller that he should take delivery, s 37 makes him liable to the seller for any loss occasioned by his neglect or refusal to take delivery and also for a reasonable charge for the care and custody of the goods.

10.11 SALES BY A NON-OWNER

The fundamental principle is that no one can transfer a better title to property than he has. So if eg the seller has stolen the goods, obtained them by deception or has them under an HP agreement (whereby ownership remains with the creditor until all instalments have been paid), the true owner should be able to recover those goods. The rule also covers less obvious situations where the seller has a defective title, or where some other person has a limited interest in the goods (eg where the seller has obtained goods subject to a reservation of title clause (see 10.9.1)), where the goods have been used as security for a loan, or some other charge or encumbrance exists to give a third party rights over the goods.

In such situations the seller will be in breach of s 12 of the 1979 Act, the implied condition that the seller has a right to sell and the implied warranty that the buyer will obtain goods free from encumbrances (see 10.1). The buyer will therefore have a claim against the seller for a refund and/or damages. Such a claim may prove fruitless if the seller is a thief who promptly disappears having sold the goods. Unless one of the exceptions to the rule applies, then the true owner can recover the goods. The owner may also have a claim against the seller in the tort of conversion (ie a person without authority dealing with goods intending to assert a right to them inconsistent with his right).

10.11.1 Exceptions to the rule

These exceptions under the 1979 Act give protection to innocent parties who buy in good faith without notice of the lack of title:

(1) The seller may have the owner's authority or consent to sell (eg if acting as an agent (s 21(1)).

(2) Where an agent has the status of a 'factor' or 'mercantile agent', he need not have the owner's authority to sell. A mercantile agent is one whose customary business is to be entrusted with goods in order to sell or otherwise dispose of them. If he has possession of goods (or documents of title) but is instructed not to sell, but nevertheless does so, then he passes on good title (s 21(2)).

(3) The owner may represent by his words or conduct that the seller is the owner or has the authority to sell (ie by giving that impression to the buyer). The owner is then estopped (ie he cannot deny the authority of the seller to sell: s 21(1)).

(4) The seller has a voidable title that the true owner has failed to avoid at the time of sale (eg if the seller paid the owner by a cheque that is dishonoured, and the owner fails to take steps to reclaim the goods before they are resold: s 23).

(5) A person may have sold goods but remain in possession of them. Property (title) has legally passed to the buyer, but nevertheless if the seller then resells to someone else, that second buyer gets good title (s 24).

(6) A buyer may have obtained possession of the goods with the seller's consent, but the property has not passed (as with a reservation of title clause). If he then resells he can pass on a good title to the subsequent buyer (s 25).

A special exception applies to motor vehicles sold when under HP or conditional sale agreements. Generally a person who acquires goods under such agreements cannot pass on title because ownership does not pass until he has paid all the instalments and, for HP, exercised the option to purchase (sometimes requiring an additional payment). The Hire Purchase Act 1964, Pt III, however, makes an exception for a private purchaser of a motor vehicle (as opposed to a trader) who, subject to certain provisos, will obtain a good title.

10.12 REMEDIES OF THE SELLER

An unpaid seller normally sues the buyer for the price of the goods or for damages for non-acceptance of them. Section 39 of the 1979 Act provides that notwithstanding the property in the goods may have passed to the buyer, the unpaid seller of the goods has a lien on the goods or right to withhold the price while he is still in possession of them. Furthermore, where the buyer becomes insolvent, the seller has a right to stop the goods in transit after he has parted possession with them. The Act also gives him a right of resale as defined by s 48. The unpaid seller must be regarded as being in possession of the goods to exercise his right of lien (ie he must retain general control of them).

Section 43 states that the unpaid seller may lose his right of lien or of retention when he delivers the goods to a carrier to transport them to the buyer without reserving the right of the goods' disposal or by his agent lawfully obtaining possession of the goods or by waiving his lien (eg by agreeing to a subsale or when making a new arrangement with the buyer which is inconsistent with his right to a lien). The lien may also be lost if the seller refuses to deliver the goods on some ground other than the buyer's failure to pay. However, an unpaid seller does not waive his lien when he obtains judgment for the price. Only when judgment is satisfied can his lien be defeated.

Where the property and goods do not pass to the buyer, the seller is likely to seek remedy in an action for damages for non-acceptance under s 50, or for consequential losses or expenses under s 54 or 37.

Section 50 states that the measure of damages is 'the estimated loss directly and naturally resulting, in the ordinary course of events, from the buyer's breach'. Where there is an available market for the goods in question, the measure of damages is likely to be the difference between the contract price and the market price at the time, if there is one, when the goods ought to have been accepted.

10.13 REMEDIES OF THE BUYER

10.13.1 Damages for non-delivery

Section 51 states that where the seller wrongfully neglects or refuses to deliver the goods, the buyer may maintain an action for damages. The measure of damages is the estimated loss directly and naturally resulting in the ordinary course of events from the seller's breach. Where there is an available market for the goods, the measure of damage is similar to that contained in s 50 (see 10.12 above).

Where the loss suffered by the buyer does not result directly and naturally in the ordinary course of things from the breach, he can recover for such loss only if the seller, given what he knew or should have known when the contract was made, contemplated such loss as the probable result of the breach (s 55; *Hadley v Baxendale* (1854) 9 Ex 341).

10.13.2 Damages for delay in delivery

Where there is a delay in delivery, the buyer may still accept delivery. If he suffers consequential losses (eg additional expenses or loss of profit), he is entitled to sue the seller for such sum that would put him in the financial position he would have been in had the seller made delivery on the expected day.

10.13.3 Damages for defective quality

The buyer may have an action for damages for breach of warranty under s 53. He may be entitled to claim damages for diminution in the goods' market value, and for the cost of adaptations or of substituted goods.

Where a buyer, despite having received defective goods, can nevertheless sell the goods to a sub-buyer, his damages should not be reduced by taking the subsale into account. He can rely on the normal measure of damages.

Other items of damage a buyer may wish to claim for are loss of profits under a subsale; wasted expenses; possible fines imposed from the buyer because the goods are defective; and any compensation he may have to pay to a third party because of the defect.

This is subject to the proviso that the relevant head of damage was contemplated by the seller as a probable consequence of breach (*Re Hall and Pim's Arbitration* [1928] All ER Rep 763).

10.13.4 Other remedies of the buyer

Rejection of goods

Where the seller breaches a condition of the contract, the buyer may choose to treat it as terminated, reject the goods and sue the seller for damages (see also 10.10.2 (partial rejection)). However, where there is a breach of a condition, and the buyer is not a consumer and normally has the right to reject the goods under ss 13–15 of the 1979 Act, but the breach is so slight that it would be unreasonable for him to reject them, that breach cannot be treated as a breach of condition but may be treated as a breach of warranty. This prevents a non-consumer buyer from objecting to goods in those circumstances. He is entitled to a claim for damages.

The seller must show that the breach is slight. This provision can be deleted or amended by an appropriate clause in the contract.

Recovery of money paid to the seller

Section 54 states that nothing in the Act shall affect the buyer's right to recover money paid, whether or not consideration for the payment of it has failed.

Specific performance

The buyer may wish to insist on the performance being carried out by the seller. Section 52 provides that a court may direct that this should happen. It is always within the court's discretion whether such an order is made. It is not lightly made where the goods are likely to be of an ordinary type and where similar goods could be obtained elsewhere.

Other claims the buyer may wish to make include an application for an injunction, perhaps to prevent the seller from disposing of the goods elsewhere; a declaration from the court of the buyer's position as against his legal rights against the seller; or he may issue proceedings against the seller claiming damages for his wrongful interference with the goods.

10.13.5 The Consumer Guarantees Directive

Considerable changes will be made in the rights and remedies available to consumer buyers when the UK implements the EU Consumer Guarantees Directive 1999/44 (see 10.14.4).

10.14 CONSUMER PROTECTION

10.14.1 Cancellation rights

The Consumer Credit Act 1974 enables a buyer who is a consumer to cancel a contract for sale of goods where that contract is within the definition of a consumer credit or hire agreement within the Act. The agreement itself may be generally defined as a credit agreement where the buyer is not a corporate body and where the credit provided or the rental amount does not exceed £25,000 (other than an exempt agreement), or one financed wholly or partially by a loan under a regulated agreement connected with arrangements made between the lender and seller. The Act stipulates when the right of cancellation arises and how it should be exercised. There is generally a 'cooling off' period that starts when the buyer receives a statutory copy of the credit agreement, so that the consumer is free to decide whether he wishes to enter the contract.

Further provisions exist to protect the consumer from the effects of any contract arising as a result of 'cold calling' (ie where a consumer receives an unexpected visit from the seller and/or his employees). The Consumer Protection (Cancellation of Contracts Concluded Away from Business Premises) Regulations 1987 allow a cooling off period that permits cancellation and the return of any money to the consumer. The Regulations do not apply to contracts for the supply of food, drink and other goods for current consumption, certain contracts concluded on the basis of a trader's catalogue, contracts that do not require the consumer to make total payments exceeding £35, and contracts cancellable by virtue of the 1974 Act.

Rights of cancellation are also provided under the Timeshare Act 1992 and by the Consumer Protection (Distance Selling) Regulations 2000.

10.14.2 Product liability: civil law

The Consumer Protection Act 1987 imposes liability on manufacturers and certain other people for death, personal injury and physical damage to property which arises from defective products. The liability imposed does not depend on proof of negligence and (subject to certain defences) is therefore strict.

The claimant must show that the injury or damage suffered was caused by the product and that the product was defective. Once these conditions are satisfied, the manufacturer or other person is likely to be liable unless he comes within the defences provided for by the Act. The products covered are virtually all goods.

The following people can be held jointly and severally liable:

(1) the manufacturer of the finished product;
(2) the manufacturer of any part of the product which is defective;
(3) any person who permitted his name or logo to be placed on the product and thereby held himself out to be a producer;
(4) the importer of the product into the EU;
(5) the supplier of the product who may be unable to trace the product back to its manufacturer.

Section 4 of the Act sets out six available defences, notwithstanding the strict liability imposed. A person is afforded a defence if he can show that:

(a) the defect is attributable to compliance with any requirement imposed by or under any enactment or with any EU obligation; or
(b) he did not at any time supply the product to another; or
(c) the supply of that product by him was otherwise than in the course of his business and that he is not caught within the definition of identifiable people who should be liable; or
(d) the defect complained of did not exist in the product at the relevant time (ie it arose after the time when he supplied the product); or
(e) the state of the technical and scientific knowledge at the time of the supply was such that he would not be able to discover the defect (sometimes known as the 'state of the art' defence); or
(f) the defect was contained in a product that eventually became comprised in a final product and was fully attributable to the final product's design or due to compliance with the requirements made by the final product's producer.

It is also possible for the person being sued to rely on a claim for contributory negligence on the part of the person complaining of the damage.

Case-law

In *Worsley v Tambrands* (1999) 96(48) LSG 40, W brought an action against T Ltd, a tampon manufacturer, claiming damages for personal injuries suffered as a result of toxic shock syndrome after inserting a regular tampon, a type she had used since age 15. W contended that the warnings on the packet were defective. Held, the box gave unambiguous instructions to read the detailed leaflet inside, and the leaflet was true and accurate. The claim failed.

In *Richardson v LRC Products* (unreported, 2 February 2000), R had given birth to a baby despite using a condom. She brought an action against LRC on the basis that ozone damage to the rubber condom's surface while still in the factory had caused it to split. Held, on consideration of the expert evidence, that method of contraception had never been claimed to be 100% effective, the condoms were manufactured to the required standard, and sufficient warnings had been given of the chance of them splitting. The claim failed.

In *Abouzaid v Mothercare* (unreported, 21 December 2000), A was involved in an accident in 1990: a product called Cosytoes had been purchased from M. It was attached to a child's pushchair by elasticated straps, which were joined by a metal buckle attached to one of the straps. As A attempted to join the straps, the buckle hit him in the eye, causing severe injury. The question arose whether the product was defective within the 1987 Act.

Section 3 requires this to be answered by a consideration of the standard that persons generally are entitled to expect in all the circumstances. Expert evidence was that anyone manufacturing the product today would be producing a defective product unless the potential risk of eye injury was removed by design or the product was accompanied by a suitable warning. This advice was given in 1999, and the Court of Appeal stated that this raised the question whether, if the product would be defective in 1999, it would also have been defective in 1990.

The court concluded that it would have been, since there had been no material changes in public expectations in the meantime. Elasticated products had been in use for many years, and there was no suggestion of any relevant technical advances that might have reasonably affected the expectations of members of the public.

In *A & Others v National Blood Authority & Others* (QBD, 26 March 2001), the claimants had been infected with Hepatitis C in blood given to them in transfusions. They claimed in relation to the period from 1 March 1988 when the Consumer Protection Act came into force. They said the blood was defective within the meaning of the Act and NBA was therefore liable even though the virus had not been identified until May 1988 and a screening test not introduced until 1989.

The court ruled that the fact the blood was infected with the virus, before it was identified, was not generally known to the public which, in consequence, did not accept any risk that it was not 100% clean. The reference in the Act to the safety that persons were entitled to expect related to the safety of the blood and not to whether tests were available or had been carried out. Any other ruling would reintroduce the concept of fault, which the Act was designed to eliminate. It was, furthermore, not necessary for the court to consider whether a reasonable producer could or would have avoided the defect, since avoidability was not a relevant circumstance under the Consumer Protection Act.

In *Bogle v McDonald's Restaurants* [2002] EWHC 49, a group of claimants sued for personal injuries caused by the spillage of hot drinks served by M. In all of the cases, the hot drink had been bought by an adult and, in all but one, it was alleged that the lidded cup with its hot drink had fallen over either on or from a tray or a table, that the lid had come off and that at least part of the contents had spilled over a claimant. The claimants contended that M was liable in negligence under the Occupiers' Liability Act 1957 and/or the Consumer Protection Act 1987.

The High Court dismissed the action. There would be occasions when hot drinks were spilled, even in lidded cups. The risk would not have been avoided or reduced had the drinks been served at a lower temperature, as the claimants contended. It was a part of M's business to sell hot drinks, with the inherent risks that entails. As regards the lidded cups themselves, it was held that M was entitled to assume that consumers would know that the drinks were hot not simply by touching the outside of the cup, which has a high thermal efficiency. Furthermore, they were adequately designed to retain a hot drink if the cup was tipped over. As regards the claimants' argument that M was under a duty to warn, the court held that hot drinks are bought by teenagers and adults who could be expected to know that such drinks were sometimes spilled and were served at temperatures that could cause serious burns. There was no duty on M to warn its customers, even though it had in fact warned its staff about hot drinks and had, since 1995, printed a warning on the cups.

10.14.3 General product safety: the criminal law

Under the 1987 Act and the General Product Safety Regulations 1994, a criminal offence can arise if unsafe goods are placed on the market. In addition, under the 1987 Act, a number of safety regulations have been enacted setting out standards for various goods. Details of the current list of regulations can be obtained from the Department of Trade and Industry, Consumer Safety Unit, Victoria St, London SW1H 0ET.

The 1987 Act also provides for prohibition notices and notices to warn. These are notices issued by the Secretary of State for Trade and Industry which, respectively, serve a notice on a party banning the supply by him of goods considered to be unsafe; and on a party requiring him to give notice that he has supplied goods that are considered unsafe.

10.14.4 The Consumer Guarantees Directive

Although the Directive 1999/44 should have been implemented in the UK by the beginning of 2002, it has not, at the time of writing, been formally adopted. The rights proposed under the Directive are as follows:

(1) Goods must show the quality and performance normal in goods of the same type and which can reasonably be expected, taking account of their nature and the seller/producer's public statements.

(2) Goods must be fit for the purposes for which that type is normally used.

(3) Goods must be fit for any purpose made known to the seller, which he accepts.

(4) Goods must be installed correctly by the seller, or those under his control, if part of the sale contract. Any installation instructions, intended for consumers, must be without shortcomings.

(5) Goods must comply with descriptions given by the seller or possess the qualities shown by a model or sample.

(6) If goods fail these tests, consumers may require repair or replacement unless this is disproportionate, taking into account the value of the goods without a fault, the significance of the fault and the remedy's level of inconvenience to the consumer.

(7) Any lack of conformity that emerges in the first six months after delivery is assumed to have been present at delivery. It is the seller's task to prove to the contrary.

(8) A price reduction or rescission may be required if the seller cannot complete the other remedies in a reasonable time or if they would involve significant inconvenience for the consumer.

(9) The liability for second-hand goods can be reduced to not less than 12 months.

(10) Contracts where consumers commission the goods are included.

(11) Goods do not lack conformity if the consumer was aware, or could not reasonably have been unaware, of the lack of conformity at the time the contract was made, or if the consumer supplied faulty materials for their manufacture.

(12) There is a liability of at least two years, but consumers might have to report faults within two months of detection.

(13) Retailer/manufacturer guarantees are to be available on request and will be legally binding.

Discretionary provisions

The Directive allows member States certain options when implementing the Directive:

(1) They can legislate that consumers must inform sellers of the lack of conformity within two months from the date of detection.

(2) They can, in the case of second-hand goods, permit a shorter liability period than two years, providing it is not less than one year.

(3) They can adopt or maintain more stringent measures offering a higher level of consumer protection.

10.14.5 Stop now orders

On 1 June 2001 new regulations, Stop Now Orders (EG Directive) Regulations 2001, came into effect. They bring into force in the UK Directive 98/127. The Regulations create a new enforcement mechanism under which certain 'qualified entities' (listed in Sch 3 to the Regulations) can seek orders to stop infringements of a wide range of UK consumer protection laws. They also provide certain public bodies in the UK with power to bring action, in the UK on behalf of other member States and in other member States on behalf of UK consumers. A detailed description of this subject is beyond the scope of this book, but the general scope is as follows.

The Regulations address measures, defined as 'Community infringements', that are against the provisions of certain consumer protection directives which harm the collective interests of consumers. The ten directives are listed in Sch 1 to the Regulations. The Regulations also contain a non-exhaustive list of the UK legislation that brought those relevant EU directives into force. Provision is made for dealing with persistent offenders and power is given to the Director General of Fair Trading and any qualified entity to bring proceedings against them. Such power may be used without recourse to court action and without the need for written assurances to be sought from the trader. The intention is for the activity to be stopped without further delay. However, only a court can issue an authorised 'stop now' order.

OFT's co-ordination role

The OFT's role is to ensure action is taken by the most appropriate body. All qualified entities (both UK and EU) must notify the OFT and the business concerned of their intention to take action at least two weeks before bringing proceedings; this gives the OFT an opportunity to stop the infringement without the need for court action. Where more than one UK body applies to take the same action, the OFT can direct which entity may bring proceedings or that only it may do so. If the OFT directs that only it may bring proceedings, it may take into account whether the infringement could be stopped by other existing means.

The OFT will seek to ensure that any action taken by qualified entities or approach by the OFT is necessary and proportionate. Where local action is required to 'prevent what is a local problem', the OFT will expect the relevant local authority to take the action. It would expect other qualified entities to take action only in relation to matters that fall within the normal ambit of their activities. The OFT would expect to act where major consumer detriment or substantial national issues arise, either through the need to clarify the law or where the business activity concerned is nation-wide.

There will be occasions when the same business activity results in infringements of more than one of the provisions under the Regulations. In these situations, where the OFT acts it will ensure that the most appropriate enforcement tool is used and that action is proportionate.

10.14.6 The Enterprise Bill

This is currently going through Parliament. Its main features in the area of consumer protection are as follows.

Stop Now Orders

This regime (see 10.14.5) will be extended to protect consumers from traders who do not meet their legal obligations. The new enforcement regime will apply to infringements of all legislation protecting consumers' economic interests, such as failing to carry out a service (eg building work or home maintenance) to a reasonable standard. This will also ensure that honest traders, especially small businesses, do not face unfair competition from those who engage in unlawful conduct.

OFT approved Codes of Practice

The OFT will be able to give formal approval to codes of practice helping consumers identify businesses they can trust. Businesses involved in the scheme will also gain a marketing advantage.

Super-complaints

Consumer bodies will be able to make 'super-complaints' to the OFT, which will be required to respond within 90 days. The Government believes this will significantly strengthen the voice of consumers on competition matters.

Enforcement of consumer laws

Part 8 of the Bill deals with improving consumer protection. It gives enforcement bodies increased powers and will replace Pt III of the Fair Trading Act 1973 and the Stop Now Orders Regulations (see 10.14.5). Part III of the 1973 Act gives the DG of Fair Trading the right to apply for an order that the trader refrain from continuing a course of conduct that is unlawful and detrimental to consumers (see 10.14.5). This has caused some difficulties, because most infringements are local, but local trading stan-dards officers then have to refer them to the DG in London. In addition, the DG has to try to obtain written assurance first, which wastes time. The Bill will bring Pt III and the Regulations together.

BUSINESS PREMISES

NICHOLAS MARSHALL, MARSHALL HATCHICK SOLICITORS

11.1 INTRODUCTION

Even in these days of virtual reality and e-commerce, most businesses need premises. Leasehold premises provide greater flexibility and less capital commitment and so are more attractive for most businesses than freehold premises. This chapter accordingly also looks at various aspects of lease-hold premises. We assume a direct landlord/tenant relationship. There are further complications involving eg underleases and various parties who may be involved apart from the landlord and the tenant and space does not permit these to be dealt with here. In all cases readers should seek special-ist professional advice.

The statutory framework for business tenancies in England and Wales is contained largely in the Landlord and Tenant Act (LTA) 1954, Pt II of which has remained on the statute book for nearly 50 years, in large part untouched. However, at the time of writing major changes to certain areas of the Act are under consideration by the Government. Following a pro-longed period of consultation of the Office of the Deputy Prime Minister, a draft Order was issued in July 2002 setting out the proposals as then envis-aged. The Order would be issued under the Regulatory Reform Act 2001 as the Regulatory Reform (Business Tenancies) (England and Wales) Order. Note that references in this chapter to the Regulatory Reform Order are to the July 2002 proposal only.

The case-law on business tenancies is significant, largely because of the large sums of money that can be involved, the major impact on a business which can result from problems with its premises, and the contrasting com-mercial pressures of boom and recession.

11.2 WHAT IS A PROTECTED BUSINESS TENANCY?

It is important for a tenant to establish whether a business premises tenancy is 'protected' under LTA 1954. Broadly, if protected, the tenant will be enti-tled to remain in the premises and call for a new lease on expiry. Subject to certain exceptions as set out below, LTA 1954 applies to 'any tenancy where the property comprised in the tenancy is or includes premises which are occupied by the tenant and are so occupied for the purposes of a business carried on by him or for those and other purposes' (s 23(1)).

11.2.1 Tenancy

There must be a 'tenancy'. This is distinct from a 'licence' to occupy land. The leading case is *Street v Mountford* [1985] AC 809, which (although it is a judgment in respect of residential accommodation) sets out the tests that are clearly applicable to commercial premises. This case is regarded as a watershed in the development of the lease/licence distinction. It came at a time when there was an increased tendency (in both residential and commercial premises) for contracts to be entered into purporting to be a 'licence to occupy' rather than a tenancy, and thereby avoiding the statutory protection that would otherwise be available to the tenant.

Street v Mountford established that a tenancy, as opposed to a licence, is created where there is:

- exclusive possession of the premises;
- a fixed or periodic term; and
- the payment of rent and/or a premium.

The principal test for distinguishing between a lease and licence in business tenancies is that of 'exclusive possession', which is a question of fact in each case to be determined on the evidence. Today, in many cases most landlords would regard it as too risky to attempt to grant a licence: the fear is that if challenged the court would look behind the form of the document, or the veneer of its title, and construe the existence of a lease where the landlord had not intended this. Accordingly landlords will use other means to ensure the tenant will not obtain statutory protection, eg by granting a lease for a term not exceeding six months or by contracting outside LTA 1954 (see below).

Care must be taken over the six-month exception: eg if a second term of six months or less is granted which follows on from a previous term and the total of the two exceeds 12 months, the second term will be protected (s 43(3)).

A 'tenancy at will' is excluded from LTA 1954. This can be created expressly or by implication of law. A tenancy at will is a popular method of letting business premises by a landlord for an undefined term. Such tenancy will also often arise when a contracted out tenancy comes to an end and the tenant remains in occupation temporarily.

A tenancy at will is a purely personal relationship that can be determined by either party at any time, although the court would look carefully to discover whether it is a true tenancy at will, or is in fact periodic or for a term certain. If it is correctly drafted the tenant will not have the benefit of statutory protection.

Some tenancies are, by their nature, excluded from LTA 1954, such as an agricultural tenancy, a tenancy created by a mining lease and a service tenancy. Nor does it apply to a tenancy granted for a term certain which cannot exceed six months unless the tenant has been in occupation for a period which, together with any period during which any predecessor in the carrying on of the business carried on by the tenant was in occupation, exceeds 12 months.

11.2.2 Premises

It is for the benefit of both landlord and tenant that the precise extent of the premises comprised in the tenancy is defined clearly. If not, dispute could arise over whether certain parts of the building are within the tenancy, and therefore within the scope of the tenant's liability to repair them. In extreme circumstances, the tenancy can be void for uncertainty and therefore unenforceable.

This is particularly the case where a tenant is taking a suite or floor of offices in a block. Does the tenancy include the kitchen, the toilets or the boiler or are these the landlord's responsibility in terms of cleaning and maintenance? It is insufficient to say merely that the 'interior' of the premises is demised: the fabric of the building from the glass in the windows to the structural beams or girders should be described and allocated clearly to either the landlord or the tenant. A well-drawn plan should also be attached to the lease, but this will often only be to identify the property leased – its precise extent being described in words.

The lease should provide clear details of the tenant's rights or 'easements', eg the right to use the kitchen and toilets not leased to the tenant and to use the common parts of the building or the estate.

11.2.3 Occupied by the tenant

Only an occupying business tenant is protected by LTA 1954. If the business tenant occupies only part of the premises let to him, statutory protection applies to that part only. Usually there are no difficulties in establishing whether a tenant does occupy the premises, but problems can arise (eg where there is seasonal occupation, such as holiday resorts, occupation is normally presumed during the out-of-season months provided it is resumed each season). In *Hancock and Willis v GMS Syndicate* [1982] 265 EG 473, a firm of solicitors acquired additional accommodation and let out the basement and ground floor of their original building under a licence and used the remainder of the building for storing files and for the occasional lunch. The court held that this was insufficient and the 'thread of continuity' had been broken for the purposes of business use. Therefore the tenant lost security under LTA 1954.

The question of occupation by the tenant is also relevant in cases involving termination of leases by the tenant at the end of the term (see below).

This has been an uncertain area of law in recent years, although the situation is now judicially more certain. Great care is needed on this point.

11.2.4 For the purposes of a business

In order to attract the statutory protection, business premises must be occupied 'for the purposes of a business . . . or for those and other purposes' and therefore it is necessary to consider whether what is being carried on at the premises falls within the meaning of a 'business'.

In LTA 1954, s 23(2), 'business' is defined as a trade, profession or employment and also includes any activity carried on by a body of persons whether corporate or incorporate. This wide interpretation was held soon after the Act came into being to cover a tennis club in *Addiscombe Garden Estates v Crabbe* [1958] 1 KB 513, but was held in *Abernethit v AM & J Klieman* [1970] 1 QB 10 not to cover a Sunday school held in a house loft. It will be a question of fact for the court to resolve in each case.

Problems arise with mixed residential/business uses. The tenant must show that the business is a 'significant purpose' of his occupation of the building. It is a question of law whether he occupies the premises for the purposes of a business carried on by him. In *Royal Life Savings Society v Page* [1978] 1 WLR 1329, a doctor who had consulting rooms in Harley Street, but who occasionally saw patients at his rented home with the landlord's consent, was held to be not protected under LTA 1954. This is to be contrasted with *Cheryl Investments v Saldanha* [1978] 1 WLR 1329, where an accountant used his flat for the purposes of a seafood importers without his landlord's knowledge and was held to occupy the premises for the purposes of LTA 1954. The more common situation is a single lease of a shop, with a flat above; this generally falls squarely in the ambit of LTA 1954, even if the area of the flat exceeds that of the shop.

11.2.5 'Contracting out' of LTA 1954

Letting business premises 'outside' of LTA 1954 has become increasingly popular in recent years, and in some sectors it is usual for leases to exclude the security of tenure provisions under ss 24–28 of the Act. There may be various reasons for this, eg the landlord may be unwilling to commit itself long term in times of economic uncertainty, or may wish to be sure of being able to regain possession on expiry of the lease, or may simply wish to retain flexibility.

In order to contract out in this way the lease must contain a simple clause declaring that the relevant LTA 1954 provisions will not apply to the tenancy. However, as the tenant is giving up potentially valuable rights, and his business could be badly affected by being forced to relocate at the end of the term, it was felt at the time that the contracting out provisions were introduced (by the Law of Property (Miscellaneous Provisions) Act 1969, which amended LTA 1954 in this regard) that safeguards must be built in to protect the tenant. Accordingly, the 1969 Act inserted s 38(4) into LTA 1954, which required the parties to obtain a court order before contracting out. Any provision to contract out of a lease which was not authorised by such order in this way is invalid (ie the tenancy will take effect as a protected tenancy). The order will only be granted if the court is satisfied that both parties, in particular the tenant, have either taken appropriate legal advice or understand the nature of the rights they are giving up.

The existing legislation will be significantly changed in this regard by the Regulatory Reform Order. The increasing popularity of contracted out leases has led to the court becoming clogged up with applications for contracting out, and in some areas the whole process has become a bureaucratic rubber stamping exercise. Accordingly, the Order proposes that court orders will no longer be required. Instead, the landlord will have to serve the tenant with a 'health warning' at least 14 days before the parties are committed to a lease. Alternatively, to cater for emergencies, the parties may proceed within that period but as an additional safeguard the tenant must sign a statutory declaration before a solicitor that he has read the health warning and has accepted its consequences. The new procedures would ensure that the tenant becomes aware of the consequences of excluding security of tenure, while removing the need for court approval.

Although losing his rights to security of tenure in this way, there is an advantage for the tenant, in that it will usually be possible to negotiate a more favourable rent than would be the case were the lease to have security. Contracted out leases tend to be for shorter periods than would otherwise be the case and so it may also be that the tenant can negotiate less onerous repairing obligations.

11.3 PRIVITY AND CONTINUING LIABILITY

In contrast to a recessionary background where a tenant is able to demand a short-term lease, in more buoyant economic circumstances it is the landlord who often has the upper hand and bargaining power. The landlord will seek high quality tenants willing and able to take full repairing and insuring (FRI) leases, maybe for a 20-year term. Such tenants are said to be a 'good covenant'.

It is clear that any tenant wishing to take on such a long-term contract needs to consider extremely carefully whether it is willing to take on such a potentially onerous liability. Even if the tenant assigns the lease during the term, that may not be an end of its liabilities. Unless the position has been changed by agreement in the lease (which was none), a tenant under a lease signed before 1 January 1996 would always ultimately be liable to the landlord even after assignment of the lease, if the assignee defaulted.

Example

> In 1967 Mr and Mrs A took a lease on a small industrial unit at a relatively low rent for 21 years. The business prospered and in 1977, after the rent had increased on review comfortably in line with inflation, Mr and Mrs A sold their business, which provided them with sufficient funds to buy a bungalow by the coast and to invest a lump sum in the bank on which to live on. In 1987, after two more rent reviews the company that took over the lease of the premises from Mr and Mrs A went into liquidation owing £50,000 in rent and service charges to the landlord. The landlord exercised its right to pursue Mr and Mrs A as the original tenants for the rent arrears: after all, they had signed a lease for 21 years. The capital that they had saved was insufficient to cover the debt and they were forced to sell the bungalow and take rented accommodation to raise the funds to satisfy the debt. They would still have been liable, as original tenants, no matter how many times the lease had been assigned.

Many (mainly tenants) would say this is iniquitous; others (mainly landlords) would say that when a lease is taken for 21 years it means exactly that and the tenant should not be able to walk away from the contract. After many years of political lobbying by pressure groups on both sides, the law was changed with effect from 1 January 1996. The Landlord and Tenant (Covenants) Act (LT(C)A) 1995 had the effect of abolishing privity of contract (the legal doctrine under which original tenants were liable for the whole term) in the case of new leases. Although an ongoing tenant may be required to guarantee the performance of the party taking over the lease (ie its immediate assignee), the liability cannot extend beyond that second assignment (if both assignments are lawful). Such a guarantee is called an 'authorised guarantee agreement' (AGA) and is likely to apply in the case of most first assignments of business leases. The onus is still on the original tenant to find a good assignee that is likely to fulfil its obligations. The original tenant is concerned to ensure not only that the first assignee's references are sufficiently strong to prevent the landlord from being able to withhold its consent (which will probably be required), but also that he will be able to pay the rent and generally be a good tenant.

In the case of insolvency of the first assignee and eventual disclaimer by its liquidator, the original tenant may be required to take up a new lease on the same terms and for the same duration as the original lease.

There is a provision in LT(C)A 1995 that relates to both new and existing leases. A landlord who wishes to pursue the original tenant or guarantor must serve a default notice under s 17 notifying him of the potential claim for what is called a 'fixed charge' (ie rent, service charge, liquidated damages and interest) within six months of the current tenant's default. Arrears accrued more than six months prior to a default notice will not be recoverable from the original tenant or guarantor.

Once the former tenant or guarantor has received a default notice, he is entitled to take some control over the problem by paying the arrears and other sums demanded in full and calling upon the landlord to grant to him an overriding lease of the premises. This places the former tenant/guarantor in a contractual position between the landlord and the defaulting tenant. The terms of the overriding lease will include all the provisions of the defaulted lease with the exception of any personal covenants given by the defaulter.

Once in possession of the overriding lease, the former tenant/guarantor can then take proceedings against the defaulting tenant to recover the arrears discharged by him under the default notice. If he fails, the former tenant/guarantor will be entitled to recover possession of the premises to enable him to relet or possibly retain for his own use.

LT(C)A 1995 also has the effect of amending LTA 1927, s 19(1) in relation to assignment of commercial leases. Effectively, in exchange for the above changes that improve the tenant's position, landlords have been able to exercise more control over who the lease is assigned to. They can now specify in advance the circumstances in which consent to an assignment can be withheld or any conditions subject to which consent can be granted. If the provision is worded so that there is no subjective element, the landlord is deemed to be acting reasonably if the agreed terms are adhered to. For example, if there is a requirement that any assignee must be able to produce the most recent set of accounts showing net profits before tax of at least three times the passing rent, then this would be acceptable. Alternatively, if the circumstances or conditions are to be determined by an independent third party or by the landlord who is required to act reasonably, this will also be acceptable.

11.4 COVENANT STRENGTH

The strength of the tenant's covenant is all important to the landlord. The businessman offering his company as a tenant, whether on taking a new lease or on taking an assignment of an existing lease, may not provide sufficient comfort for the landlord.

The landlord will be concerned about how the quality of the tenant's covenant is to affect the value of its investment. A tenant company listed on the Stock Exchange is likely to enhance the freehold value.

Where the tenant's covenant is not strong enough (eg a start-up company or an individual of limited means), the landlord would generally require some security to persuade it to accept the prospective tenant.

11.4.1 Personal guarantees

Many commercial leases provide that on assignment the landlord can require two directors of any assignee company to provide personal guarantees. References should be taken up for the directors or any prospective guarantors. A landlord would normally require two guarantors providing joint and several liability, ie each guarantor can be held responsible for the defaulting tenant's total debt if the landlord chooses. In the past, over-confident businessmen have sometimes provided personal guarantees without a second thought, only subsequently to have to pay the price (often of bankruptcy) for their optimism. As in the case of any previous tenants who may still be liable, a landlord will not hesitate to pursue guarantors where there is any chance of recovery of the tenant's indebtedness.

Under LT(C)A 1995, the guarantors under the AGA are released when the guaranteed tenant is released. Guarantees under pre-1996 laws (unless released by the landlord or as stated otherwise in the lease) generally subsisted for as long as the term itself.

11.4.2 Security deposit

The landlord may require a lump sum deposit as security, generally representing three or six months' rent. This sum is placed on bank deposit (with interest normally accruing to the tenant) and a deed drawn up between the landlord and tenant records in what circumstances the landlord is entitled to withdraw funds.

The tenant will be required by the deposit deed to repay any sums withdrawn, but the drawback from the landlord's point of view is that once the fund has been used up and assuming the arrears persist, there is no guarantee that any excess sums will be recovered. At least in these circumstances the landlord will have had time to consider his options and, in the case of an empty building and an insolvent tenant, have an opportunity of seeking a new tenant.

The problem for a tenant, of course, particularly in the case of a new business venture, is the immediate tying-up of capital that provides no benefit to the start-up company except nominal interest. If VAT is payable, or could become payable, on the rent then it is likely the landlord will require a deposit of a sum equivalent to the VAT as well as the rent itself. As this is merely a security deposit and not a VAT payment as such, no VAT invoice can be issued by the landlord, so the tenant will have to find the equivalent VAT amount as well as the rental deposit itself.

The protection of the director of the new company from the risks of providing personal guarantees usually makes it worthwhile. It may be possible for the tenant to negotiate repayment of the fund in certain circumstances (eg after three years of net profits of the tenant company exceeding an agreed multiple of the annual rent). The deed should state that upon expiry or lawful assignment of the lease, the fund will be returned to the tenant.

11.4.3 Bank guarantees

Less common now than previously, bank guarantees are usually an expensive option for a tenant as banks generally now require both deposit of assets to cover the amount of the guarantee and payment of a procuration or arrangement fee.

11.4.4 Break clause

Inclusion of a break clause provision enables the landlord to determine the lease before its expiry, should it wish to be rid of the tenant for any reason. The tenant should obviously beware here as, assuming its rights to renewal of the lease under LTA 1954 are excluded (see below), it will be vulnerable to being evicted or financially exploited by the landlord.

A tenant-only break clause provides the tenant with an opportunity to determine the lease, normally on a fixed date (eg the first or some subsequent rent review date). The tenant has the peace of mind of knowing that if the business does not work out it has an opportunity to terminate the lease on the relevant date. The only items that it has to worry about are to ensure that

(1) sufficient care is taken in serving notice at the right time and on the right person in accordance with the break clause provisions; and

(2) there are no subsisting breaches of covenant at the time of service of such notice and until termination of the lease.

If the landlord is reluctant to accept the tenant's notice, he will take every opportunity to keep the tenant 'on the hook'. He may eg argue that because of a subsisting (albeit minor) breach of covenant, he is not obliged to accept the notice. The tenant should take care to ensure that the rent is paid on the due date and that at the very least the repair covenant has been complied with if it has any intention of exercising the break provision.

It was held in *Trane (UK) v Provident Mutual Life Assurance* (1995) 03 EG that the requirement in a lease that the tenant had to observe the tenant's covenants up to the intended termination date had the effect of being what is called a 'condition precedent'. Accordingly, any subsisting breach, however minor, would prevent the break clause from being exercised.

11.5 RENT REVIEWS

Except in the case of short-term leases of about five years or less, it is likely that there will be provision for the rent to be reviewed from time to time. This ensures the landlord continues to receive a market rent and not simply the historical rent fixed at the beginning of the term. Rent reviews are usually fixed by reference to the open market, but there are other alternatives.

11.5.1 Open market rent review

This amounts to a reappraisal of the rent for the same premises on the assumption that a willing landlord wishes to grant to a willing tenant the premises in good condition for either the original length or the unexpired length of term. The formula for rent reviews differs from one lease to the next and often depends on the landlord's solicitors' drafting preferences. Care must be taken by the tenant's solicitor to ensure the landlord does not have an unfair advantage at the negotiating table on rent review. A large amount of law has evolved, largely as a result of judicial decisions, in this field.

Example – Typical scenario of a rent review

The lease provides for a rent review on 29 September. The landlord is required to serve a notice of intention to review the rent not more than six months and not less than three months before the review date. In his notice the landlord, having taken the advice of his surveyor, suggests an increase to £X to take effect from the rent review date. The tenant acknowledges receipt of the notice but suggests a far smaller rental increase from the current rent of £Y. The lease provides that if one month after service of the notice of intention to review the rent, no rent has been agreed between the landlord and tenant, then either party may refer the matter to either an expert or an arbitrator as stated in the rent review formula. In this case the negotiations between the landlord and tenant are unproductive and their respective surveyors are brought in to endeavour to negotiate an agreement.

A starting point for surveyors is often 'comparables' – ie rents agreed on other comparable properties at around the relevant time. This is easier in a shopping parade or business park than with restaurants or hotels. The parties should give careful consideration to the wording of the rent review clause and in particular the factors or circumstances to be assumed and disregarded. The review procedure and the negotiation of the rent operate as if a notional or hypothetical lease was being granted and there are certain assumptions behind that hypothetical lease. For example, it may be required to assume the premises are 'fit' and 'available for immediate occupation and use' and that improvements carried out at the tenant's expense are disregarded when assessing the rent. On occasions the landlord may agree to a substantial rent-free period at the beginning of the lease in exchange for a higher rental figure, so as to retain/enhance the building's investment value. This practice can have a major impact on rent reviews, as shown by a number of cases to have come before the courts in recent years. The landlord will wish to disregard all such rent-free periods or other inducements at each rent review, in order to perpetuate what might be an artificially high rent. A well-advised tenant will wish to restrict any such disregard to rent-free periods granted to compensate it for fitting out the premises.

Despite efforts by The Law Society and the RICS to introduce model forms of rent review, these are not widely used and therefore it is dangerous to assume that any two different leases have identical rent review clauses.

A cornerstone of the rent review formula has been that reviews are usually 'upwards only'. Accordingly, even in the time of falling rents, if a landlord called for a review the rent would not fall. As in the case of negative equity for homeowners, upwards-only rent reviews have resulted in premises being over rented where there is no possibility that the passing rent can fall to the market rent on review. If the premises are surplus to requirements, an assignment of that lease becomes virtually impossible unless there are substantial inducements such as rent-free periods and reverse premiums. The tenant may also find that any opportunity for underletting at less than the passing rent is prohibited by the lease terms and therefore the landlord can reasonably withhold his consent to any underletting on this basis. Although properly advised, there may be ways around this for a tenant.

11.5.2 Turnover rents

Rents linked to the turnover of the tenant's business are an alternative to market rents. This is now not uncommon, eg in shopping precincts and also hotels and restaurants. In this case the landlord monitors each retailer's turnover and the rent is calculated by reference to that turnover. If the tenant suffers, then so does the landlord, and he may feel it incumbent to see what he can do to help that tenant's trading. For example, a landlord decided to improve a 1960s shopping precinct by providing a covered area for pedestrians at one end where it was previously exposed to the elements. The effect was to secure and in some cases improve the turnover of those shops within the covered area, while those outside of it began to suffer. As a result, the landlord extended the covering to all the shops in the precinct for mutual benefit. Another advantage from the tenant's point of view is the saving on professional fees. It follows that the involvement of the professional adviser is likely to be minimal where negotiation is largely unnecessary.

Note that reference is made to 'turnover', not 'profit'. Turnover may be perceived to increase simply as the rate of VAT goes up, whereas this may not have a similar effect upon profits. In *Tucker v Granada Motorways Services* [1977] 3 All ER 865, the Minister of Transport granted a lease to a tenant of a motorway service area. The tenant paid a fixed rent together with an additional variable rent based on the takings from the petrol station and catering services. The gross takings included the tobacco duty payable on cigarettes, cigars etc. Accordingly, when tobacco duty rose so did the tenant's rent, even though its profit remained the same. Therefore, advice should be taken on the definition of 'turnover'. For the tenant, as far as possible this should be linked to the business's profit, although opportunities for abuse and difficulty in policing may cause landlords to resist this.

11.5.3 Index-linked rents

One advantage of index linking is that both landlord and tenant can monitor the rent relatively easily. As in the case of an open market rent review, it is often the case that the review date is fixed by reference to an anniversary and, if the formula in the lease is correctly worded, the new rent will reflect the rate of inflation rather than property values. Although index linking is cheap to operate for landlord and tenant, it may well not reflect the reality of market conditions. If the tenant is in a depressed area where there is a number of empty units around him, this would work in his favour in an open market rent review, but would have no influence on the RPI. For a unit situated in an affluent and popular area, the converse would be the case. Index linking is not recommended for anything but short- to medium-term leases.

11.5.4 Fixed increases

For shorter leases of anything up to three or five years the parties may agree to fixed increases, perhaps on an annual basis, and so expose each party to a certain degree of risk. As in the case of a homebuyer locking himself into a fixed-rate mortgage, it is likely that one of the two parties may regret such a commitment at some stage in the lease.

11.6 DURING THE LEASE

11.6.1 Implied and express covenants

A lease or tenancy agreement is a contract between landlord and tenant, and various express obligations, mainly of the tenant, but some of the landlord too, are set out in the document. Alongside the express obligations on each party in the lease are various implied obligations, but well-advised parties will prefer to set out matters expressly, rather than rely on the 'grey areas' that implied obligations create.

The bulk of the lease is likely to be made up of the 'tenant's covenants' requiring in particular the rent to be paid on certain days and for the tenant to acknowledge certain obligations and responsibilities. The five most important areas of liability that the tenant will incur are considered below.

11.6.2 Payment of rent

Generally this will be quarterly in advance and most modern leases will specify that the tenant must pay by direct debit/standing order if the landlord requires. Interest will be payable on rent not paid on time. Importantly, particularly in a multi-occupied building with service charges where there is most potential for landlord/tenant dispute, the lease will probably require

419

payment *without deduction or set-off*. Put simply, if eg the tenant has a claim against the landlord for inadequate services that the landlord is required to provide, the tenant may not deduct rent to cover this. The landlord can pursue the tenant, by various means, for payment of the outstanding rent without regard to the tenant's claim in respect of service charge.

11.6.3 Repair

The tenant's repair responsibility generally applies either to the whole building or, where the lease is for part only of a building, merely the interior. As a general rule, the longer the lease, the greater the tenant's repair responsibility. The lease may state that the tenant is required 'to keep the demised premises in good and substantial repair'. The definition of 'demised premises' is important here and will show whether the repair responsibility is full repairing or simply internal. There is also likely to be a requirement on the tenant to decorate the demised premises on fixed dates. The tenant may be in a position to negotiate something less than a full repairing liability if eg the lease is for a short term and is contracted out of LTA 1954. The obligation may eg be to return the premises to the landlord in no worse a state or condition than they are at the beginning of the term, as evidenced by an agreed schedule of condition, preferably with photographs.

If the tenant neglects his duties, the landlord is entitled to seek a remedy against the tenant. Modern leases generally provide him with the power to enter the premises to carry out these works at the tenant's cost. His claim would be for a debt against the tenant. *Jarvis v Harris* (Court of Appeal, 1997) resolved an uncertainty that previously surrounded this important point: it is now clear that if the landlord is prepared to risk incurring the cost of repairing the premises where the tenant is in breach of covenant, that cost will be reasonable as a straightforward debt due from the tenant to the landlord. This assumes the lease contains the appropriate express provisions, as most leases do.

The alternative of suing for damages or for an order requiring the tenant to comply with its covenant is more complex. For example, if the lease was granted for seven years or more (and at the time of service of the landlord's notice of dilapidations or a notice under the Law of Property Act 1925, s 145 there are three or more years of that term unexpired), the tenant is entitled to the protection provided by the Leasehold Property (Repairs) Act 1930. In this case, leave of court is required before the landlord can enforce a right to damages or forfeiture and the onus is on the landlord to establish a ground to secure leave of the court. Such lease can only be granted in certain specified grounds and will generally not be given unless the breach of covenant is very substantial.

11.6.4 Alterations

Usually, a lease provides that no alterations can be carried out to the premises except internal alterations, which require the landlord's consent. In this case there is an 'absolute' covenant against external alterations, building of extensions etc and a 'qualified' covenant against internal alterations. In the case of the absolute prohibition, this does not prevent the tenant from asking the landlord for consent. The landlord can refuse permission and is under no obligation to justify its refusal. Equally, the landlord may agree to the alteration (which would be evidenced by a suitable licence) on the basis of receipt of an appropriate premium.

If the tenant wished eg to erect internal partitioning, the landlord would not be able to withhold his consent unreasonably. This is the case whether or not words such as 'such consent not to be unreasonably withheld' are included, as by virtue of LTA 1927, s 19(2) that qualification is deemed to apply in any event. LTA 1927 provides that not only cannot the landlord unreasonably withhold his consent, but also that the landlord cannot demand a premium for doing so, apart from a reasonable sum 'in respect of any damage to or diminution in the value of the premises' or any legal or other expenses incurred in providing its consent. Again this would be evidenced by a licence to alter. Typically the licence will provide that the tenant must comply with all planning and any other statutory obligations in carrying out the alterations and reserve the right in favour of the landlord to require the tenant to reinstate the premises to their previous condition at the end of the term.

11.6.5 User

User covenants are either expressed positively (eg only 'to use the demised premises as . . .') or negatively ('not to use the demised premises except as . . . and for no other purpose'). The user may express specific terms and refer to the proposed use of that tenant, or express broad terms and eg refer to the most recent Use Classes order. As in the case of alterations there may be an absolute restriction against change of use or a qualified restriction. In this case, there is no statutory implication that consent is not to be unreasonably withheld. However, if the landlord does consent, the conditions he is entitled to impose on the tenant are limited by LTA 1927, s 19(3). Should he decide to withhold consent, there is little more the tenant can do. In the event of breach of this covenant, the landlord can apply to the court for an injunction to stop an unauthorised use where it is clear that damages are not an adequate remedy.

11.6.6 Alienation

The two most important ways in which a tenant can dispose of all or part of its interest under a lease are assignment and subletting.

Assignment

It is possible to assign part only of a lease, but this is unusual, gives rise to various problems, and the lease generally prohibits this.

Assignment of the whole of the premises will generally be permitted, and the terms on which this can happen are likely to depend on whether the lease was completed before or after 1 January 1996 (ie whether LT(C)A 1995 applies). The circumstances in which the tenant can assign, and the conditions of any assignment, are likely to be more stringent in the case of post-1996 leases, namely to compensate the landlord for the fact that the tenant will be released from further liability on the occasion of the second lawful assignment.

Subletting

Creating a sublease leaves the landlord/tenant relationship in place and creates a third interest below that of the tenant, ie the subtenant. The tenant's liability to the landlord is thereby unaffected, but this arrangement provides more flexibility: the tenant can sublet the property for a temporary period with a view to regaining possession at a later date when it is anticipated the business will again require the premises. That in turn raises the question of whether the subtenant will be entitled to LTA 1954 protection, thereby depriving the tenant of the right to resume occupation. The tenant generally will be entitled to resist any application for a new tenancy on the grounds that it needs the premises for its own use, but in this situation it is better to contract the sublease outside the LTA 1954 security of tenure provisions (see 11.2.5); this will avoid the subtenant making any application for a new lease in the first place.

A further aspect of flexibility provided by the subletting route is the facility, subject to the lease terms, to be able to sublet part, if the configuration of the building is such that a part can be sublet conveniently (eg if a tenant takes a lease of two floors of an office building the lease might permit a sublease of part as long as that part comprises the whole of either of the floors). Again, it would be advisable for the sublease to be contracted outside LTA 1954 and it is probable that the landlord will also require this by means of a provision in the lease. The landlord's concern will be to prevent the indefinite fragmentation of occupation that could arise if a subtenant part became entitled to renew the sublease. Arrangements such as this tend to be of relatively short-term duration.

Where a landlord has other premises in the area, he will be concerned to ensure that the rent on any sublease, of whole or part, is at the higher of the market level at the time, or the passing rent payable under the lease. There are two reasons for this. First, any subletting at less than market rent would adversely affect the landlord's position as regards rent reviews or lease renewals in respect of both the premises themselves and other premises owned nearby – the lower rent on the sublease could be quoted as a comparable by other tenants to justify a lower rent. Secondly, in the event of premature termination of the headlease, in certain circumstances the landlord could be left with a subtenancy in place at lower rent.

Accordingly, alienation clauses generally contain detailed and complex provisions to protect the landlord from various adverse consequences that could arise as a result of assignment or subletting, while at the same time giving the tenant the requisite freedom and flexibility it will need if it is to enter into a lease for anything other than a very short term.

11.7 EXPIRY OF THE LEASE

Where the tenant does *not* have security (eg a lease which is excluded from LTA 1954 as referred to in 11.2.5), the tenant is *not* entitled to remain in occupation beyond the expiry of the contractual term. This is not always so under LTA 1954. The assumption is made in this part of the chapter that the tenant wishes to remain in occupation and has security of tenure.

11.7.1 Right to renew

A tenant protected under LTA 1954 has an automatic right to renew his tenancy at the current market rent. As long as the tenancy meets the definition referred to in s 23(1) (see 11.2), the lease continues indefinitely until either landlord or tenant serves statutory notices, assuming the premises continue to be occupied by the tenant for business purposes (see 11.7.6). In this case the tenant is 'holding over', during which time the terms of the expired contractual tenancy continue as before.

If the tenant is no longer in occupation for business purposes, he will have no automatic right to renew the lease.

At a time of falling rents, it may well suit the landlord to 'overlook' serving any notice to determine the lease. If it is likely that on a renewal the market rent will be less than the passing rent under the current lease, there may be no point in him determining the lease. It follows that at a time of rental growth, he may suffer significant losses in rental income if he fails to serve his notice in good time. When the commercial property market is relatively stagnant there is often a stand-off between landlord and tenant: the landlord is not confident that he will be able to negotiate any increase in the rent on renewal and the tenant is equally not inclined to commit itself to a new lease during times of uncertainty. In the meantime, the lease continues on the same terms.

11.7.2 The landlord's notice

Under LTA 1954, s 25(1), 'The landlord may terminate a tenancy . . . by a notice given to the tenant in the prescribed form specifying the date at which the tenancy is to come to an end'. The date specified in the notice must be not less than six months and not more than 12 months from the date the notice is issued.

Example – Landlord's notice

A lease is due to expire on 25 December 2000 and the landlord wishes it to be determined on that date. A notice must be served before 24 June 2000 and after 25 December 1999. If the matter was overlooked, a notice could be served, say, in August 2000, citing the date for determination as 1 March 2001 (ie at least six months ahead). In the meantime the tenant continues paying the rent at the current rate, but the landlord has lost the right to receive a higher rent (assuming a rising market) for the period from December 2000 to March 2001.

The landlord's notice must specify whether he opposes the grant of a new tenancy. If he does wish to oppose, the notice must set out the grounds of such opposition (see 11.7.6).

Under the Regulatory Reform Order as currently proposed, changes with regard to the landlord's termination notice will be made. There will be a new requirement for landlords who are not opposing renewal to set out their proposals for a new tenancy in the termination notice. There is no such requirement under the current legislation and it is hoped that the change will speed up the renewal process. A 'health warning' would explain to the tenant that the proposals are for the purposes of negotiation only and do not bind either party.

11.7.3 Tenant's response to landlord's notice

If the tenant wishes to renew the lease it must serve written counter-notice on the landlord, stating that it is not willing give up possession of the property on the date stated in the landlord's notice. The counter-notice must be given within two months of the date of the landlord's notice; if it is not given, the tenant will lose all rights to renew the lease.

Within four months of (but not earlier than two months after) the date of the landlord's notice, the tenant must commence proceedings in the court for a new tenancy unless a new lease has been granted in the interim. If the tenant fails to do so he will lose all rights under LTA 1954.

However, changes to the above are proposed by the Regulatory Reform Order. Under the current proposals, if and when they come into effect, there will be no requirement for the tenant to serve the counter-notice and, although the deadline of applying to the court no later than four months after the s 25 notice remains, the proposals enable the parties to agree to extend that deadline, so giving them more time to negotiate an agreement without having to go to court. Such agreements would remove the need for tenants to make applications to the court solely to retain their legal rights to renew, thus reducing unnecessary court business and legal costs.

Where the landlord and tenant have taken all the correct steps and proceedings have commenced, the terms of the new lease are a matter for negotiation. Failing agreement, the court will take such decisions as it thinks fit not only on whether a tenancy should be granted but also with regard to the terms of the tenancy and the rent.

At present, the court has power to order the grant of a new lease up to a maximum term of 14 years. Under the proposals in the Regulatory Reform Order, this period will be extended to 15 years, this being more compatible with modern leasing patterns, where leases tend to have five-yearly rent reviews.

11.7.4 Tenant's request for a new tenancy

It is possible for the tenant to take the initiative, which in the days of the rising market was called a 'pre-emptive strike'. If it is certain it wishes to renew (particularly in a situation where the market rent is likely to be less than the passing rent), it has power to terminate the contractual tenancy. A tenant is entitled to serve a notice under LTA 1954, s 26 which, as in the case of s 25, may be served not more than 12 months and not less than six months before the date of termination. It has to propose the terms of the new lease (eg rent, length of term etc), and a s 26 notice cannot be served if the landlord has already served a s 25 notice. Within two months of the date of the tenant's notice, the landlord must give notice to the tenant whether he will oppose an application to the court for the grant of a new tenancy. If he does oppose, the grounds for such a position must be stated. Any ground referred to is significant in that it determines whether any compensation is payable to the tenant (see 11.7.7) and the landlord may not be able subsequently to claim the benefit of other grounds not stated in the original notice.

If the landlord fails to respond to the notice within the two-month period, he cannot prevent the grant of a new lease on the basis of the statutory grounds of opposition.

11.7.5 Application to court for new tenancy

Under LTA 1954, s 24(1):

> the tenant . . . may apply to the court for a new tenancy –
> (a) if the landlord has given notice under [s 25 of this Act] to terminate the tenancy, or
> (b) if the tenant has made a request for a new tenancy in accordance with section 26 of this Act.

The application should be made not less than two months and not more than four months after serving either of the above notices. It is essential that these time periods are adhered to as failure to do so could mean that a tenant will lose the premises it needs for its business.

At present, only the tenant may apply to the court for a new tenancy. The landlord can only prompt proceedings indirectly by serving a notice triggering renewal or termination. Under the proposals in the Regulatory Reform Order, the landlord will be able to apply for either

(a) a renewal, thus being able to counter any tactical delay by the tenant, or
(b) termination without renewal.

If the court agreed that the landlord has grounds to oppose a new tenancy it would refuse to order the grant of a new lease. If, however, the landlord failed to establish grounds for opposition, the court would order the grant of a new tenancy and fix its terms if necessary without the need for any separate application by the tenant.

In the majority of cases the court procedure goes no further than the issue of the application to preserve the tenant's right to a new lease. Often the summons issued by the court provides for a date to be fixed to enable negotiations to continue between the parties. This is assuming the landlord is happy for the renewal to take place. However, he can oppose the application.

11.7.6 Landlord's opposition to renewal

There are seven specified grounds, set out in LTA 1954, s 30(1), under which a landlord can oppose an application to renew.

Disrepair
(LTA 1954, s 30(1)(a))

'The tenant ought not to be granted a new tenancy in view of the state of repair' because of a breach of its obligations under its lease. It was held in *Lyons v Central Commercial Properties London* [1958] 1 WLR 869 that 'the neglect of repair to which the section refers should be substantial'. A court has discretion to consider the seriousness of the breach, the tenant's overall conduct and the reasons for the breach that has arisen.

Rent arrears
(LTA 1954, s 30(1)(b))

'The tenant ought not to be granted a new tenancy in view of his persistent delay in paying rent . . .' Again the court must exercise its discretion in deciding whether this ground has been established. If it feels the landlord should not be required to experience the problems and expense of recovering the rent if the lease were renewed, his application may well be granted.

Breaches of other obligations
(LTA 1954, s 30(1)(c))

'The tenant ought not to be granted a new tenancy in view of other sub-stantial breaches by him of his obligations under the current tenancy, or for any other reason connected with the tenant's use or management of the holding.' This provides a wider ground for the landlord to oppose renewal in that eg it could include breaches of planning regulations. The question that the court asks is whether his interest has been prejudiced by the breach.

Alternative accommodation
(LTA 1954, s 30(1)(d))

'The landlord has offered and is willing to provide or secure the provision of alternative accommodation for the tenant . . .' Such accommodation must be available on terms that are reasonable, having regard to the provisions of the current tenancy and to all other relevant circumstances. This ground is rarely cited and there are few reported cases.

Uneconomic subletting
(LTA 1954, s 30(1)(e))

'Where the current tenancy was created by the sub-letting of part [and] that the aggregate of the rents reasonably obtainable on separate lettings of the holding and the remainder of that property would be substantially less than the rent reasonably obtainable on a letting of that property as a whole.' This is not a common ground and is a purely financial one. It is only open to the 'competent landlord' if he is a superior landlord and is not available to the immediate landlord. The court will agree to this ground if the landlord, by letting the tenanted premises together with the rest of the property in the head lease as a single unit, could expect more rent than by letting the indi-vidual units separately.

Demolition or reconstruction
(LTA 1954, s 30(1)(f))

'The landlord intends to demolish or reconstruct the premises comprised in the holding or a substantial part of those premises or to carry out substantial work of construction on the holding or part thereof and it could not reason-ably do so without obtaining possession of the holding.' This is a common ground for opposition by a landlord. His intention to carry out these works must be genuine and settled, and established by the date of the hearing. Considerable case-law exists for whether the landlord had the necessary intention (eg it is often recommended that a landlord that is also a company passes a formal board resolution referring to the intention to demolish or reconstruct the premises). The landlord also needs to show a legal and financial ability to proceed (ie legal in the sense of planning consent and financial in the sense of either having the finance or being able to raise it). Contractors' tenders should be obtained and made available to the court as further evidence of intention to proceed with the work.

Owner occupation
(LTA 1954, s 30(1)(g))

'On the termination of the current tenancy the landlord intends to occupy the holding for the purposes, or partly for the purposes, of a business to be carried on by him therein or as his residence.' There is 'a five-year rule' to be satisfied, ie that the landlord cannot rely on this ground if his interest was purchased or created within five years ending with the termination of the current tenancy. If he granted the tenancy himself, the five-year rule does not apply. He will have the same problems in establishing 'intention' as under s 30(1)(f) above. His occupation does not have to be immediate upon the termination of the lease, so long as it is within a reasonable time after the end of the term; nor does he have to occupy all of the premises – a substantial part normally will be sufficient. Note that this ground can also be used if he wishes to occupy the premises as his own residence, although there are few if any reported cases on this. The writer had a case where, acting for the tenant in receipt of a notice under this ground, the landlord wished to use the subject premises not 'as his residence' but as part of his residence. Could he rely on the ground? The case was settled before going to court and so the question remained open.

11.7.7 Compensation

Compensation for non-renewal

Where the landlord is successful in denying the tenant a new lease on one of the last three grounds referred to above (ie uneconomic subletting, demolition and reconstruction, or owner occupation), compensation is payable to the tenant.

The amount is based on the rateable value of the holding multiplied by an 'appropriate multiplier' prescribed by the Secretary of State for the Environment by statutory instrument. The rateable value is ascertained at the date of the service of the s 25 or 26 notice so that the multiplier is *one*, except in a case in which the tenant elects to be paid compensation by reference to the rateable value of the holding on 31 March 1990, in which case the multiplier is *eight*. The tenant will make this election if the holding includes a residential element, but cannot do otherwise.

The compensation is doubled if for the 14 years ending with the current tenancy's date of termination all or part of the premises have been occupied for business purposes and on any change of occupier each is a successor to his predecessor's business. Any agreement in the lease to exclude or reduce compensation where the occupation for carrying on the business has lasted for five years prior to the date when a tenant is to quit is void under LTA 1954, s 38(2).

Compensation for improvements

A tenant is rarely entitled to compensation for any improvements he has carried out unless specific provisions have been written into the documentation. There is machinery in LTA 1927 for statutory compensation, but this is impractical, cumbersome and rarely used.

Tenant's notice to determine

Until recently it was thought that a tenant could not walk away from its obligations under a lease simply by giving up possession and surrendering the keys to the landlord at the end of the term. It was thought that it must give three months' notice to the landlord and that the lease would continue if it did not do so. The Court of Appeal decision in *Esselte v Pearl Assurance* [1997] 02 EG 124 has thrown a lifeline to tenants.

If the lease is contracted out of LTA 1954, neither party is required to serve notice and the lease will determine on the contractual expiry date.

In other cases, whether or not a landlord has served a s 25 notice (and provided the tenant has been in occupation under the tenancy for at least one month), the tenant can give not less than three months' notice to end the lease on its contractual expiry date (LTA 1954, s 27). A s 27 notice cannot be served after a tenant's request for a new tenancy has been served on the landlord unless the procedure under the s 26 notice has been followed by formal discontinuance through the court.

If there is less than three months to go before the contractual expiry date, a tenant can still serve notice under s 27(2) by giving not less than three months' notice to expire on a quarter day *after* its contractual expiry date. The notice under s 27(2) may be served before the contractual expiry date (in anticipation of the lease being continued under the Act) or after the contractual expiry date.

Example – Notice to determine less than three months before contractual expiry date

Where the contractual expiry date is 25 December 1998, the tenant can serve a s 27(1) notice to expire on 25 December 1998, on any day up to 24 September 1998. After that day, the earliest date the lease can be determined using s 27(2), is the following quarter day, ie 25 March 1999.

This somewhat unsatisfactory situation will be rationalised by the Regulatory Reform Order if and when this comes into effect. Under the current proposals a tenant wanting to end a tenancy that is continuing under LTA 1954 (ie where the contractual term has expired) will not have to give more than three months' notice. The requirement that such notice expires on a quarter day would be removed.

12

EMPLOYMENT LAW

Over recent years, domestic employment law has undergone a metamorphosis with the result that a considerable body of law now exists governing the relationship between an employer and its workforce. EU legislation and ECJ decisions have had an increasing influence on domestic employment law and this trend is set to continue. Over a similar period, the number of disputes coming before employment tribunals has risen steadily. It is therefore important for employers to be aware of this complex body of law that governs all employment relationship aspects from recruitment to termination (and in some instances beyond). This chapter concentrates on the areas governing the individual employment relationship as they affect the rights and obligations between employer and employee. It does not attempt to deal with collective employment law except where this affects individual employment law in such areas as redundancy and transfer of undertakings.

12.1 THE IMPACT OF EU LAW

EU law has had a profound effect on UK employment law and the rights afforded to individual employees. Much of the law affecting UK employers has been implemented to give effect to EU legislation. Indeed, in certain circumstances, employees may be able to rely directly upon EU law provisions to enforce rights where they would have no claim under UK law. The main sources of EU law are as follows.

12.1.1 Treaty of Rome 1957, as amended

Article 141 of the Treaty provides that men and women should receive equal pay for equal work (see 12.22).

12.1.2 Legislation in the form of directives

Directives take the form of instructions to EU member countries to pass national legislation, by a specified date, to implement each directive's provisions.

Certain EU law provisions have 'direct effect'. This means that individuals can rely directly on these provisions in UK courts. For direct effect to be established, the EU law provision must be unconditional, clear and precise. The most important of these provisions is Art 141 (see above).

In contrast to Art 141, directives do not have general direct effect and therefore cannot generally be relied on by individuals directly in UK courts. However, a directive has direct effect where the individual seeking to rely on its terms is employed by the State, or by a body that is 'an emanation of the State' (ie public sector employees). In contrast, private sector employees cannot rely on a directive's provisions, but they may have a claim against the UK Government for its failure to implement fully the provisions of any directive into national legislation by the specified date (see *Francovich v Italian Republic* [1992] IRLR 84).

Furthermore, it has been held that the national courts must, as far as possible, interpret national law in the light of the wording and purpose of any relevant EU directive (known as 'the purposive approach'). This is the case whether the national law was passed before or after the directive's adoption. This approach should only be adopted where the national legislation can be interpreted consistently with the directive without distorting the meaning of the domestic legislation itself.

Some of the most important provisions in the context of employment law are:

(1) Equal pay: Art 141 and the Equal Pay Directive.
(2) Sex discrimination: Equal Treatment Directive.
(3) Transfer of undertakings: Acquired Rights Directive.
(4) Maternity rights: Pregnant Workers Directive.
(5) Contracts of employment: Proof of Employment Directive.

The importance of EU law in the field of UK employment law cannot be overstated. Throughout this chapter, references are made to relevant EU provisions, where appropriate.

12.2 EMPLOYMENT: THE WORKER'S STATUS

The employer must first consider whether a worker is to be an employee: is he to be employed under a contract of service (ie an employee) or a contract for services (ie an independent contractor)? This important distinction forms the basis of the employment relationship and the parties' rights and obligations arising from it. The vast majority of workers are employees, but in certain circumstances an employer may not feel this is appropriate. Some of the important consequences of the distinction, by which the employer can make a reasoned decision on the employee's status, are listed below.

Employee rights

- Written statement of employment terms and conditions
- Protection against unfair dismissal
- Entitlement to redundancy pay
- Statutory minimum notice entitlement or agreed contractual notice
- Right to statutory sick pay
- Maternity rights, including statutory maternity pay entitlement
- Not to be discriminated against on grounds of sex, race or disability
- Not to be discriminated against on grounds of membership or non-membership of a trade union
- Time off for trade union activities
- Medical suspension payment entitlement
- Guarantee payment entitlement
- Equal pay
- Protection in connection with a transfer of an undertaking
- Right to be consulted on health and safety issues.

Employee obligations

- To work in accordance with the employer's instructions
- To work with due diligence
- To pay income tax through PAYE
- To pay employee NICs.

Self-employed rights

- Entitlement to contractual benefits
- Not to be discriminated against on grounds of sex, race or disability
- Where appropriate, to work within a safe system of work and place.

Self-employed obligations

- To work with due skill and diligence
- To pay own tax under Schedule D
- To pay self-employed NICs.

The obligations and consequently the costs placed upon an employer are far greater in relation to an employee. However, balanced against this is the high level of control that an employer has over an employee.

12.2.1 Distinguishing between contract of service and contract for services

Once the employer reaches a decision on the worker's status, it is important to ensure that the intended status is actually achieved. As can be seen above, a number of factors such as tax and NICs obligations and statutory employment protection flow from the definition of the relationship. The mere description of the relationship by the parties as being one of employer-employee or employer-independent contractor is not decisive. The label put on the relationship is not conclusive and, over the years, the courts have developed a number of tests in an attempt to ascertain the true nature of employment relationships.

Mutuality of obligation

This test was first expounded by the courts in *Nethermere (St Neots) v Gardiner* [1984] IRLR 240, where it was stated that for there to be a contract of service there must be 'an irreducible minimum of obligation on each side'. There must be an obligation on the employer to provide work for the employee and on the employee to perform such work for the employer. Without this element, there could not be a contract of service.

The control test

This was the first test developed by the courts and looked at the level of control exercised by the employer over the worker, not only about the particular work that the worker was required to do, but also whether the employer controlled how and when the work should be done. The greater the control, the more likely the worker is an employee. This test was not sufficient when dealing with more skilled workers (eg brain surgeons), and so the courts developed what is known as the 'integration test'.

The integration test

This test was set out by Denning LJ in *Stevenson, Jordan & Harrison v McDonald and Evans* [1952] 1 TLR 101: it looks at whether the worker is an integral part of the business. The closer the connection between the worker and the business, the more likely the worker is an employee, whereas an independent contractor is more likely to be merely an accessory to the business.

The multiple test

Ready Mixed Concrete (South East) v Minister of Pensions and National Insurance [1968] 2 QB 497 stated that a contract of service exists if:

(1) The worker agrees, in consideration of a wage or other remuneration, to provide his own work and skill in the performance of some service for his master.

(2) He agrees expressly or impliedly that in performance of the service he is sufficiently subject to the control of the other to make him a master.

(3) All the other provisions of the contract are consistent with it being a contract of service.

Note that an obligation to work subject to the other party's control is not the overriding factor, if all the other provisions of the contract are inconsistent with a contract of service. Therefore, it is important to look at the relationship as a whole, and not just at isolated factors.

Subsequently, in *Market Investigations v Minister of Social Security* [1969] 2 QB 173 it was again reiterated that control is not the decisive test and that the most important question to ask is whether 'a person was in business on his own account'.

It was stated in *Hall (Inspector of Taxes) v Lorimar* [1994] 1 All ER 250 that the question of whether a person is in business on his own account, though often helpful in distinguishing between a contract *of* service and a contract *for* services, might be of little assistance in the case of a person carrying on a business or profession. In such cases the traditional distinction between an employee and an independent contractor should be borne in mind, ie the extent to which the individual is dependent or independent of a particular paymaster for the financial exploitation of his talents.

The overview approach

There is 'no single path to a correct decision': As the *Ready Mixed Concrete and Market Investigations* decisions show, although control is still an important factor, each case will turn on its own facts. Factors that are important are:

(1) degree of control;
(2) the chance of profit and the risk of loss;
(3) method and payment of tax;
(4) exclusivity of service;
(5) the parties' intention;
(6) the worker's integration into the business;
(7) the employer's right to suspend and/or dismiss;
(8) whether the worker provides his own equipment; and
(9) whether the worker is free to hire his own helpers.

When deciding to take on a worker as an independent contractor, legal advice should be sought to ensure that the way the relationship is structured is one of employer-independent contractor. Failing to define the relationship correctly can have financial implications. For example, the Inland Revenue has wide ranging powers to recover tax from an employer who has failed to make the appropriate deductions through the PAYE system as he incorrectly thought his worker was an independent contractor and therefore responsible for his own tax and NICs. In doubtful cases, it is always advisable to seek prior clearance from the Revenue as regards the tax treatment.

12.3 THE EMPLOYEE

In many instances, employers may wish to employ employees on a part-time, temporary or seasonal basis. Particular matters should be borne in mind when engaging such employees.

12.3.1 Temporary employees

Temporary employees who obtain the necessary year of continuous employment will attain statutory employment protection rights.

There are essentially two types of temporary employees. First are those commonly known as 'temps', who are employed through an employment agency that charges its client a fee from which it pays the temp directly. The employment agency is treated as the primary employer and the agency's client as a secondary or quasi employer. Any claim for unfair dismissal or a redundancy payment is unlikely in these circumstances to be successful against the secondary employer.

Secondly, there are temporary employees who are employed for a certain fixed period, often to cover staff absence (eg maternity leave). If, at the time of employing a temporary employee, the employer informs him that his employment is temporary and is to be terminated on the first employee resuming work, such termination is likely to be a fair reason for some other substantial reason. A tribunal would then consider if the employer acted reasonably within the Employment Rights Act (ERA) 1996, s 98(4) and (6) (see 12.10).

Under s 106 of that Act, where an employer employs a temporary replacement to cover an employee in the case of pregnancy, childbirth or medical suspension, and if at the time of employing the replacement the employer advises the employee in writing that employment will be terminated when the other employee resumes work, this is deemed to be for some other substantial reason and the tribunal will then assess reasonableness in accordance with s 57(3).

12.3.2 Seasonal employees

These are employees who are taken on for a limited period to cover eg busy periods in the tourism industry for the summer months. Seasonal employees, subject to the necessary qualifying conditions, are entitled to all the normal employment protection rights. Accordingly, their contracts can be terminated only on the employer providing them with the statutory minimum notice requirement (if there is not a longer contractual period).

There is one particular area of concern that employers should bear in mind. If the period between seasons of work is short and a particular worker is habitually re-engaged, continuity of employment may be preserved in accordance with the rules dealing with absence due to temporary cessation of work (see 12.8.2). This is obviously important with a view to the employee gaining statutory employment protection rights, especially the right to claim unfair dismissal and a redundancy payment.

12.3.3 Part-time employees

The Part-time Workers (Prevention of Less Favourable Treatment) Regs 2000 came into force on 1 July 2000. They transpose requirements of the Part-time Work Directive (97/81/EC) into UK law.

12.3.4 Directors

Directors are not automatically employees of a company. However, a director who is paid a salary and devotes his whole time and attention to the business of the company will normally work under an employment contract and be an employee.

The company's board must approve a director's contract. Under CA 1985, s 319, a company is prohibited from entering into a contract with a director which it cannot terminate by notice (or can only terminate in specified circumstances) for a period exceeding five years, unless the term has been approved by a resolution of the company in general meeting. Any term not so approved is void and deemed to be replaced by a term entitling the company to terminate on reasonable notice.

For a fuller discussion of the role of directors, see 18.5.

12.4 THE CONTRACT OF EMPLOYMENT

The contract of employment governs the employer-employee relationship. Although in practice a single document is referred to as 'the contract of employment', in reality it need not be in writing – it can be oral. Indeed, it can, and in most instances does, include terms expressly agreed between the parties, implied terms, terms implied by custom and practice or arrangement and terms incorporated from other documents such as collective agreements (where a collective agreement contains terms appropriate for incorporation into an individual contract).

12.4.1 The terms of the contract

Express terms

These are terms that the parties specifically agree upon between themselves.

Implied terms

Frequently many terms of an employment contract are left unspecified, but nevertheless are implied into it. This occurs where implied terms are necessary to give effect to the contract or if such terms are customary in a particular trade or are a usual arrangement for a particular employer. There are terms that are commonly implied into a contract and affect both the employer and employee. A number of these are listed below.

Employers' duties

To maintain the relationship of mutual trust and confidence

There is a duty on an employer not to destroy the trust and confidence that exists in an employment relationship. Breach of this implied term may entitle the employee to treat himself as having been constructively dismissed (see 12.10.1) and bring a claim for unfair dismissal as a result of a fundamental breach of a term of the contract by the employer.

To safeguard the employee's health and safety

An employer owes a duty to all his employees to safeguard their health and safety. This includes a duty to provide safe equipment and a safe system of work. For a fuller discussion on health and safety and the employer's duties, see Chap 15.

To terminate the contract on reasonable notice

This term is implied where there is no express agreement between the parties. Either party may terminate the contract on reasonable notice; what is deemed 'reasonable' depends on the particular employment circumstances.

To provide work

In general terms, provided the employer fully remunerates his employee, it is not a breach of contract for the employer not to provide work. A term to provide work for an employee is, however, implied where eg the level of remuneration is dependent on the amount of work done or where an employee has particular skills that will deteriorate through lack of use.

Employee duties

Fidelity

An employee is under a duty to act faithfully on behalf of his employer and to act in the interests of his employer's business. For example, the employee must be honest and not steal from his employer. It is also a breach of the implied duty of fidelity for an employee to compete with his employer's business while still employed. Where, however, an employee merely takes steps in his own time to compete at the end of the employment relationship, there would not be a breach of the implied contractual duty of fidelity (*Ixora Trading v Jones* [1990] FSR 251).

Obedience

It is an implied term of the contract that an employee obeys his employer's *lawful* orders; not to do so is a breach of the contract. It is not a breach to disobey an unlawful order.

To work with due diligence and care

An employee is under a duty to take reasonable care when performing tasks for his employer. Where he fails to take such reasonable care, the employer may be vicariously liable (see Chap 15).

Not to use or disclose trade secrets or confidential information

Another breach of the implied duty of fidelity is for an employee to use or disclose to third parties confidential information of his employer during employment. In the absence of an express term in the contract, on termination of employment the implied duty is not as extensive as during employment and only extends to information that is not merely confidential but can be described as a trade secret. The circumstances of each case have to be assessed in deciding whether any information amounts to a trade secret, but in *Faccenda Chicken v Fowler* [1986] ICR 297 a number of factors were stressed to be important in deciding whether the implied duty of fidelity applied to confidential information after the termination of employment, as follows:

(1) Nature of the employment – did the employee work in a business (or part of a business) where he regularly handled sensitive information?
(2) Nature of the information – was the information such as to be so highly confidential as to amount to a trade secret?
(3) Did the employer impress upon the employee the confidential nature of the information? What was the employer's attitude?
(4) Could the particular information be isolated easily from other information that the employee was free to use or disclose?

While the employment relationship subsists, the implied duties on employees are wide ranging. On termination of employment, however, apart from the implied duty not to disclose trade secrets, an employee is free to set up a competing business and in theory to solicit customers and employees of his former employer. In many cases, therefore, employers will wish to incorporate into employment contracts express covenants restricting an employee's activities on termination.

12.5 THE DOCTRINE OF RESTRAINT OF TRADE

Express covenants in an employment contract restricting an employee's activities after termination of employment are governed by the doctrine of restraint of trade. Such covenants are prima facie void on public policy grounds.

To be valid, this type of covenant must be reasonable in the interests of both the parties and the public (*Nordenfelt v Maxim Nordenfelt* [1894] AC 535). A covenant will be upheld only to the extent that it is reasonably required for the protection of the employer's legitimate interests. A protectable interest must first be established, and then the clause must be limited to what is reasonably necessary to protect that interest. Restraint of trade covenants fall into two main categories.

12.5.1 Non-competition covenants

Although a blanket non-competition covenant after termination will not be upheld by the courts, an employer is free to seek to uphold a covenant restricting an employee from working for a trade rival. Such a covenant is likely to be upheld provided it is limited to a reasonable period (*Littlewoods Organisation v Harris* [1977] 1 WLR 1472). A 'reasonable period' is likely in most circumstances to be one not exceeding one year after termination.

Employers can also seek to prohibit a former employee from working in the same business as that for which he worked for his former employer within a specific geographical area and for a specific period. Such clauses are extremely restrictive and are only upheld by the courts where the employer can show he has a large concentration of customers within a particular area that it is necessary for him to protect. If the employer can show this, the covenant is still only reasonable to the extent that the area it seeks to cover is limited and that the covenant runs only for a certain length of time. It is important to remember that a valid covenant covering a particular radius in one part of the country may not be valid covering the same radius in another area. Contrast a highly populated urban area with a rural area with a low population level (*Scorer v Seymour-Johns* [1966] 3 All ER 347, CA).

12.5.2 Non-solicitation covenants

Such a covenant will seek to restrict the former employee from soliciting his former employer's customers or clients. Again, such covenants must be reasonable in relation to the time that they run and should be limited to those customers with which the former employee dealt with. Furthermore, it was standard practice for employers to include a covenant in contracts prohibiting the poaching of fellow employees. Following the Court of Appeal decision in *Hanover Insurance Brokers v Schapiro* [1994] IRLR 82, however, such covenants are generally unenforceable. In order to try and enforce such a covenant, it should be limited to very senior employees or those employees who have a particular expertise that it is necessary for the employer to protect and should only cover individuals who were employees at the same time as the departing employee. In addition, covenants frequently were specified to apply however the contract was terminated. Again, this has been held to be too wide and covenants are only enforceable if a contract is terminated lawfully (*Living Design (Home Improvements) v Davidson* [1994] IRLR 69).

The drafting of restrictive covenants is extremely tricky and legal advice should be sought on every occasion. The above is only a brief summary of the relevant law; failure to carefully consider with appropriate advice when drafting covenants may result in them being unenforceable because they are too wide in nature.

In certain circumstances the courts are willing to sever an unenforceable covenant or part of a covenant providing that what remains makes sense without the need for modifying the wording and that the sense of the contract itself is not altered. However, it is far preferable to insert into a contract a correctly drafted limited covenant that is likely to be upheld by the courts than to seek reliance on a widely drafted covenant that will fail and cannot be altered at a later stage.

If an employer, after termination of an employee's contract, wishes to rely on any express covenants contained within that contract, there are two remedies available:

(1) *An injunction.* This is the usual and most effective remedy by an employer seeking to enforce a term. Application for an injunction can be made once evidence of any breach has come to light. A successful application will result in the employee being restrained from breaching any of the terms of the covenant.
(2) *Damages.* An employer can also bring a claim against his employee for damages for breach of contract or breach of confidence. In such cases the employer, in order to recover damages, has to show that he has incurred a loss. There is also a potential claim against the employee's new employer for inducing the breach of contract, if the new employer was aware of the employee's breach.

12.5.3 Intellectual property rights

A complex body of law exists to deal with intellectual property rights that arise during the course of the employment relationship. This legislation governs copyright, patent and design rights.

Copyright is governed by the Copyright, Designs and Patents Act 1988. Section 11(2) of the Act states that, subject to contrary agreement, the first owner of any copyright in a work made by an employee during the course of his employment is his employer.

The Patents Act 1977 governs the protection of an original invention capable of industrial application by means of a patent. Section 39 of that Act states that an invention made by an employee belongs to his employer if:

(1) it was made in the course of the employee's normal duties; or

(2) it arises out of duties specifically assigned to him, in circumstances where an invention might reasonably be expected to result from the performance of those duties; or

(3) it was made in the course of the employee's duties and at that time the employee had, because of the nature of his duties and the particular responsibilities arising from them, a special obligation to further the interest of his employer's undertaking.

Further, s 40 of the 1977 Act states that in certain circumstances, where a patent is granted in relation to an invention made by an employee, but which belongs to an employer, and the patent is of outstanding benefit to the employer, compensation may be payable to the employee. The object of the compensation is to award the employee with a fair share of the benefit that the employer has derived or can be reasonably expected to derive from the patent.

Finally, s 42 of the 1977 Act states that any attempt by an employer to diminish the employee's rights in relation to inventions is unenforceable.

The 1988 Act introduced for the first time a design right. Section 215(3) of the Act states that where a design is created by an employee in the course of his employment, the employer is the first owner of the design right.

12.6 WRITTEN PARTICULARS OF EMPLOYMENT

A contract of employment contains both express and implied terms and need not be set out in writing (see 12.4).

Under ERA, s 1, however, an employer is now under a duty to provide each employee (whose employment is to continue for more than one month) with a written statement of certain terms and conditions of his contract of employment within two months of the commencement of employment. The following exceptions apply:

(1) Where the employment contract is for one month or less.

(2) Crown servants where issues of national security may be involved.

(3) Seamen in a ship registered in the UK under a crew agreement the provisions and form of which are of a kind approved by the Secretary of State.

(4) Employment during any period when the employee is engaged in work wholly or mainly outside Great Britain unless the employee ordinarily works in Great Britain and the work outside Great Britain is for the same employer, or the law which governs their contract of employment is the law of England, Wales or Scotland. Note that the right to receive

a written statement of the terms and conditions of employment has been extended to employees who work wholly or mainly outside Great Britain, if that employment began on or after 25 October 1999.

Contents of the written statement

The written statement must contain the following specific information:

(1) The names of both the employer and the employee.
(2) The date employment began.
(3) The date continuous employment began (if applicable).
(4) The employee's job title or a brief description of the job.
(5) The place or places of work.
(6) The scale or rate of remuneration together with payment intervals and the method of calculating remuneration.
(7) The hours of work.
(8) Holiday entitlement (including public holidays) and holiday pay containing sufficient information to enable an employee to calculate entitlement to accrued holiday pay on termination of employment.

With regard to (6) above, in *Lange v Georg Schunemann* [2001] IRLR 244 the ECJ confirmed that the written statement of terms and conditions of employment should (if applicable) state that an employee is obliged to work overtime whenever requested to do so by his employer, even though there was no reference relating to overtime in 91/533/EEC, Art 2(2).

The details listed in (1)-(8) above must be provided in a single document, known as the 'principal statement'. Further additional information that must be provided must include:

(1) Terms and conditions for sickness, injury and sick pay.
(2) Pensions.
(3) Length of notice required from both employer and employee to terminate the contract.
(4) Where the employment is not intended to be permanent, the period for which it is expected to continue, or if for a fixed term the date when that term will end.
(5) Details of any collective agreements that directly affect the terms and conditions of the employment.
(6) Disciplinary rules and procedures, together with details of a person to whom an employee can appeal against any disciplinary decision.
(7) Details of a person whom an employee can approach seeking redress of any grievance relating to his employment.

These further provisions may be contained in other documentation which either the employee has reasonable opportunity of reading in the course of his employment or which are made reasonably accessible to him in some other way.

Where there are no provisions relating to any of the matters listed above, this fact must be stated in the written statement.

Small employers' exemption

Small employers (ie those with fewer than 20 employees) must provide written statements of terms and conditions but are not required to have a disciplinary or grievance procedure. They are, however, expected to observe the recommendations of the ACAS Code of Practice if a disciplinary or a grievance situation arises. The Government is proposing to remove the small employer's exception.

12.6.1 Changes to statement of terms and conditions of employment

Where there is a change to any of the terms contained in the written statement, the employer is under an obligation at the earliest opportunity, and in any event not later than one month after the change, to provide the employee with a written statement containing particulars of the change. It is important for the employer when altering an employee's contractual terms to remember that as a general rule this should only be done with the employee's consent. A unilateral variation by the employer will constitute a breach of contract and may give rise to a claim for unfair dismissal. (See 12.10 and in particular 12.10.10.)

It was held in *Cantor Fitzgerald International v Callaghan* [1999] 2 All ER 411 that where an employer unilaterally reduced his employee's pay or diminished the value of his salary package, the entire foundation of the contract of employment was undermined; thus, an emphatic denial by the employer of his obligation to pay the agreed salary or wage, or a determined resolution not to comply with his contractual obligations in relation to pay and remuneration, would normally be regarded as repudiatory. Similarly, where an employer imposed an apparently slight change on a reluctant employee by economic pressure, the employer would be entitled to treat the employment contract as discharged by the employer's breach.

The House of Lords held in *Carmichael v National Power* [1999] 4 All ER 897 that, unless it appeared from the terms of documents, or from what was done or said at the time or subsequently, that the parties intended those documents to form an exclusive memorial of their relationship, it was not appropriate to determine the nature of that relationship solely by reference to the documents. Moreover, the question whether the parties intended a document or documents to be the exclusive record of the terms of their agreement was a question of fact.

12.6.2 Unlawful terms

A contract must not contain any term that is unlawful or contrary to public policy, eg contracts entered into knowingly with a view to defrauding the Revenue or contracts for an immoral purpose.

12.6.3 Remedies for failure to provide written particulars

If an employee has not been provided with a written statement under the ERA, or if the written statement provided raises a query as to certain terms or conditions that should have been included or referred to in it, the employee can make a complaint to an employment tribunal. Where there is no express or implied agreement concerning a particular term, a tribunal, if it considers the complaint well founded, will state the particulars that should have been given and the employer is then deemed to have provided a statement containing such particulars. Thereafter, if the employer has been in breach of any of those terms, the employee can bring an appropriate action against the employer. There is no right to claim compensation for failure on the part of an employer to provide a written statement.

A claim before the tribunal can be brought by any employee who has more than 13 weeks' continuous employment at any time during employment or, where employment has ended, before the end of three months beginning with the date when employment ceased.

Although the written minimum statement is relied on in many cases, there is benefit to be obtained by the employer in providing a more detailed contract of employment. The employer can make provision for such matters as restraint of trade clauses (the importance of which is noted at 12.5) and any other special rules which that particular type of business may require.

Furthermore, under ERA, s 13, it is unlawful for an employer to make deductions from an employee's wages unless such deduction is required or permitted by a statutory or contractual provision, or the worker has given his prior written consent to the deduction. In consequence, incorporation into the contract of a term entitling the employer to make deductions from an employee's wages in certain circumstances ensures that the employer does not breach the Wages Act provisions (see 12.18).

Finally, as a matter of good practice, an employer should ensure his employees sign a copy of their employment contract to prove receipt.

12.7 WORK PERMITS AND IMMIGRATION MATTERS

12.7.1 Introduction

Decisions on immigration are referred to the Home Office, but the position concerning work permits vests with the Department for Education and Employment (DfEE). If the DfEE refuses to grant the permit, there is no

445

formal appeal against this decision (other than possibly requiring a judicial review of such decision where appropriate).

Under the Asylum and Immigration Act 1996, employers who employ a person who does not have the right to work in the UK commit a criminal act and may be subject to a fine of £5,000 per offence. The employer's defence is that he asked for documentary proof of the right to work in the UK during the selection process.

Documents that are acceptable are set out in the Immigration (Restrictions on Employment) Order 1996 and are:

(1) A document issued by a previous employer, the Inland Revenue, the Benefits Agency, the National Insurance Contributions Office (NICO) or the Employment Service, which contains the person's NI number.
(2) A passport describing the individual as a British citizen or as having the right of abode in or re-admission to the UK.
(3) A passport containing a certificate of entitlement to right of abode.
(4) A certificate of registration or naturalisation as a British citizen.
(5) A birth certificate issued in the UK or in the Republic of Ireland.
(6) A passport or national identity card issued by a member state of the European Economic Area (EEA) which describes the person as a national of that state. EEA countries as at June 2002 are Austria, Germany, Liechtenstein, Spain, Belgium, Greece, Luxembourg, Sweden, Denmark, Iceland, The Netherlands, the UK, Finland, Ireland, Norway, France, Italy and Portugal.
(7) A passport or other travel document endorsed to show that the person is exempt from immigration control, or has indefinite leave to enter or remain in the UK, or has no time limit on his stay; or a Home Office letter confirming this.
(8) A passport or other travel document endorsed to show that the person has current leave to enter or remain in the UK and is not precluded from taking the employment in question; or a Home Office letter confirming this.
(9) A UK residence permit issued to a national of an EEA member state.
(10) A passport or other travel document endorsed to show that the person has a right of residence in the UK as a family member of a named person who is a national of an EEA member state and resident in the UK.
(11) A letter issued by the Home Office indicating that the person has permission to take employment.
(12) A letter issued by the Home Office confirming that the person is a British citizen or has permission to take employment.
(13) A work permit or other approval to take employment issued by Work Permits UK (part of the Home Office).
(14) A passport which describes the holder as a British Dependent Territories' citizen and which indicates that that status derives from a connection with Gibraltar.

12.7.2 Work permits

The work permit arrangements, operated by the Immigration and Nationality Directorate of the Home Office, allow employers based in England, Scotland and Wales to employ people who are not nationals of an EEA country and are not entitled to work in this country.

There are three main categories under which work permit applications may be made: business and commercial; sportspeople and entertainers; and training and work experience.

The Directorate can also give permission for multinational employers to provide internship placements to overseas students who are studying at an institution outside the UK. Students studying at a UK institute who want to do casual work in their spare time or vacation or a work placement that is part of their course do not need permission, but should be aware of restrictions on the type of work they may do.

There is also a special concessionary arrangement within the normal work permit rules enabling people whose employer does not have a commercial presence in the EU to work in this country on a service contract awarded to their employer by a British-based organisation. This is known as the General Agreement on Trade in Services (GATS).

12.7.3 How to apply for a business and commercial work permit

Eligibility to apply for a work permit

A work permit application can be made by an employer based in this country, needing to employ a person to work in England, Scotland or Wales. The employer should make a work permit application for a named person to do a specific job for the employer, normally on a full-time basis. The person cannot transfer a work permit to a different job or to work for a different employer.

While in this country, the relevant worker is expected to be the applicant's employee. If the employer temporarily transfers the worker from an overseas branch or subsidiary (intra-company transfers) or if the person is seconded to work for the employer from an overseas employer, it may be appropriate for the overseas contract of employment to continue. For work permit purposes, the applicant will be treated as the employer. If an individual wishes to employ someone, he will need to do so on a Class 1 NICs basis.

The employment contract should already exist and not have been created for the purpose of making a work permit application. It will not normally apply to workers employed by their own overseas service companies, or engaged through other third parties (including overseas companies) whose main involvement with the worker is to hire his services to others.

An application for a work permit where the applicant provides services to clients under a contract may mean the person needs to work at the client's premises. This does not apply if the service is to supply staff only.

Work permits are not issued to recruitment agencies, employment agencies and other similar businesses, as the UK does not approve this type of employment. This also applies where the employment is supplementary to the job for which a work permit has been issued. Agencies may be used to help recruit staff, but the employer must apply for a work permit that must be in respect of a specific job within a company.

If an applicant has not applied for a work permit in the past five years, it should send documents that show it is a British-based company. The Directorate requires:

(a) A copy of the British company's latest audited accounts with the accountant's name clearly shown, or a copy of the latest annual report.

(b) If neither of these is available, any other relevant documents that clearly show the company is a British-based employer, eg a certificate of incorporation, a lease, invoices, utility bills, VAT returns and accounts submitted to the Inland Revenue. (This is not an exhaustive list and the Directorate may need to ask for further information.) In the case of hotel and catering establishments, the Directorate also requires menus, wine lists and hierarchy charts.

(c) For professional partnerships such as solicitors and veterinary surgeons, the Directorate will accept a copy of one of the partner's registration with an appropriate organisation (eg The Law Society, The Royal College of Veterinary Surgeons).

A person who has held a Training and Work Experience Scheme (TWES) permit will not normally be eligible for another work permit until he has completed a period of time outside the UK. If he was on a TWES permit for up to 12 months, he will not normally be eligible to return for a further work permit until he has spent 12 months outside the UK. If he was on a TWES permit for over 12 months, he will not normally be eligible to return for a further work permit until he has spent 24 months outside the UK.

12.8 CONTINUITY OF EMPLOYMENT

A number of statutory employment protection rights are dependent on the employee having worked continuously under a contract of employment for a minimum period. The main statutory employment rights that are subject to a qualifying period of continuous employment are as follows:

Right	Qualifying period
Redundancy payment	Two years
Unfair dismissal	One year

The right to up to 29 weeks' maternity leave	One year. There is no length of service requirement for the basic 18 weeks' maternity leave)
Statutory maternity pay	26 weeks before the beginning of the 14th week before the expected week of confinement
Written particulars of employment	Two months
Minimum notice period	One month (for one week's notice)
Guarantee payment	One month ending with the day before the workless day or more than three months if engaged on a fixed term or specific task contract for three months or less
Medical suspension payment	One month ending on the day before suspension begins or more than three months if engaged on a fixed term or specific task contract for three months or less

An employee's period of continuous employment is determined on a week-by-week basis, although it is the total number of calendar months or years of employment attained that is important for qualifying periods or statutory rights. The period begins with the day on which the employee actually commences work and ends on the day that is to be ascertained in accordance with the appropriate rules. In most cases this will be the last day the employee works. Once an employee has commenced work there is, subject to contrary evidence, a presumption that employment is continuous. It is, therefore, important to look at the rules for calculating what weeks count towards a period of continuous employment and under what circumstances continuity will be broken.

12.8.1 Weeks that count

ERA sets out detailed rules regarding what weeks counted in calculating an employee's period of continuous employment. Continuous employment is calculated in the same way for part-time and full-time employees, irrespective of hours worked.

Any week during which an employee's relations with his employer are governed by a contract of employment count in calculating continuity.

12.8.2 Periods where no contract of employment exists

Periods in which there is no contract of employment may nevertheless count as periods of employment for continuous employment purposes. The situations in which continuity of employment are preserved are set out below. If in any week the employee is for the whole or the part of that week:

(1) incapable of work in consequence of illness or injury, a period of not more than 26 weeks under this provision counts in preserved continuity;

(2) absent from work on account of a temporary cessation of work, this covers the situation where an employee is habitually re-engaged by an employer and the periods of no employment in between are relatively short;

(3) absent from work in circumstances such that, by arrangement or custom, he is regarded as continuing in the employment of his employer for all or any purpose, this would cover such instances as where an employee is absent on unpaid leave;

(4) absent from work wholly or partly because of pregnancy or childbirth, and furthermore in relation to the right to return to work after absence for pregnancy or childbirth, if an employee exercises her right to return in accordance with s 71 of the Act (see 12.13.5), all weeks during that period of absence count in calculating continuity.

Further instances in which continuity is preserved are as follows:

(1) Under ERA, ss 94 (unfair dismissal) and 193 (redundancy payment), when employment is terminated in a situation where notice should have been given, but was not, and as a result the employee did not attain the qualifying condition of one or two years' service, respectively, for claims for unfair dismissal or a redundancy payment, the employee's employment is treated as continuing until the expiry of the statutory minimum notice period that that employee would have been entitled to.

(2) ERA, s 210(5) applies to preserve continuity of employment where an employee's contract of employment is renewed or he is re-engaged under a new contract of employment in pursuance of an offer made by his employer before the ending of his employment under a previous contract or within four weeks thereafter.

(3) An employee who is dismissed and then reinstated or re-engaged pursuant to an industrial tribunal award or by a settlement through ACAS has continuity preserved, notwithstanding the period between dismissal and reinstatement.

(4) On the transfer of a trade or business from one person to another, the period of employment of an employee with the transferor company counts as a period of employment with the transferee company and consequently continuity of employment is preserved (see 12.24).

(6) If an employee's employment is transferred to another employer who at the time the employee enters his employment is an 'associated' employer of the former employer, again that employee's continuity of employment is preserved. Employers are treated as associated if one is a company of which the other (directly or indirectly) has control, or if both are companies of which a third person (directly or indirectly) has control.

12.8.3 **Weeks that do not count, but do not break continuity**

Certain weeks do not count in the calculation of continuous employment, but do not operate so as to break continuity. Where an employee's period of employment includes intervals which do not count in calculating continuity, but which do not break it, the commencement of the employee's continuous employment is treated as having been postponed by the number of days which do not count. Circumstances where these rules apply are any week during which an employee:

(1) takes part in a strike or is absent from work because of a lock-out;
(2) is employed overseas.

This applies only in calculating the qualifying period and amount for redundancy payment purposes.

12.8.4 **Statutory maternity pay (SMP)**

For the purposes of calculating entitlement to SMP, continuous employment is defined in Statutory Maternity Pay (General) Regs 1986. The definition is, however, much the same as discussed above.

12.9 WORKING TIME

The Working Time Regs 1998, as amended by the Working Time Regs 1999, provide as follows.

12.9.1 **Weekly limits**

Workers have the right not to work more than an average of 48 hours in any seven-day period. The average is calculated, normally, using a 17-week period of assessment, but this can be extended to 26 weeks if the workers are covered by derogations of up to 12 months by a collective and/or workforce agreement between employer and works. 'Working time' means the time when a worker is working and at his employer's disposal and carrying out his activities or duties.

12.9.2 **Night work**

Night workers have the right not to be required to work more than an average of eight hours in any 24-hour period. The standard averaging period is again 17 weeks, but can be extended by the derogations or by an agreement between employer and workers. If the work involves special hazards or heavy physical or mental strain, the eight-hour limit is absolute.

Adult night workers have the right to a free health assessment (and a young worker to a health and capacities assessment) before being required to perform night work, and periodically thereafter. All night workers are entitled to be transferred to day work if a registered medical practitioner has advised that the worker is suffering health problems associated with night work and if there is suitable day work available.

12.9.3 Daily rest periods

Adult workers are entitled to 11 hours of consecutive rest in each 24-hour period. Young workers are entitled to 12 hours of consecutive rest in each 24-hour period unless periods of work are split up over the day or are of short duration.

12.9.4 Weekly rest periods

Adult workers are entitled to an uninterrupted rest period of not less than 24 hours in each seven-day period. This may be averaged over a two-week period. Young workers are entitled to two days of rest in each week. This cannot be averaged over a two-week period, but can be reduced to 36 hours where justified by 'technical or organisation reasons'.

12.9.5 Rest breaks

Adult workers who work more than six hours in any day are entitled to a rest break. The length of the rest break may be determined by a collective or workforce agreement. If, however, there is no agreement, the worker's break must be at least 20 minutes long. Young workers are entitled to a minimum 30-minute rest break if they work for longer than 4 hours.

12.9.6 Paid annual leave

Subject to the exclusion identified below, workers have the right to four weeks' annual leave. The annual leave cannot be paid in lieu except in the event of termination.

12.9.7 Qualifications

The Regulations apply to workers over the minimum school-leaving age. The definition of 'worker' covers those with a contract of employment plus a wider group who undertake work under other forms of contract (eg agency and temporary workers, freelancers, etc). To qualify for the rights relating to night work, the worker's daily working time must include at least three hours of night time (generally 11 pm to 6 am).

To qualify for the right to paid annual leave, the worker must have continuous employment of not less than 13 weeks.

To qualify as a 'young worker' for the purposes of the Regulations, the worker must be over the minimum school-leaving age but under 18.

12.9.8 General exclusions

The Working Time Regs do not cover workers employed in, or engaged in, the following sectors of activity:

(1) Air, rail, road, sea, inland waterway and lake waterway transport (see Transport Workers)
(2) Sea fishing
(3) Other work at sea
(4) The activities of doctors in training
(6) Where characteristics peculiar to certain specific services – such as the armed forces, or the police, or to certain specific activities in the civil protection services – inevitably conflict with the provisions of the Regulations, eg undercover police work (civil protection services includes the police, fire brigades and ambulance services, the security and intelligence services, customs and immigration officers, the prison service, the coastguard, and lifeboat crew and other voluntary rescue services.

Note that:

(a) The Working Time Directive has been amended to cover transport workers, and these amendments are expected to be in force in the UK by 1 August 2003. These changes, however, will not cover 'mobile workers', that is to say a member of flying or travelling personnel employed by an undertaking which operates transport services for passengers or goods by road, air or inland waterway. Rail or sea transport workers are outside the definition.
(b) The Directive has also been amended to cover doctors in training. From 1 August 2002. There will then be a five-year transitional period, with an optional further three years. Under the amendment, the average working time week for the first three years of the transitional period will be 58 hours, 56 hours for the following two years, and 52 hours for any remaining transitional period.

12.9.9 Specific exclusions

In specified circumstances workers will not have the rights they would otherwise have in respect of rest breaks, daily rest, weekly rest and night work. The specified circumstances include workers engaged in security and surveillance activities, activities involving the need for continuity of service of production (such as dock work, hospital services, the provision of utilities, civil protection services, agriculture) and where there is a foreseeable surge of activity such as in tourism. Workers will, however, be entitled to compensatory rest of an equivalent period or where this is not possible appropriate protection.

Workers whose working time is not measured or pre-determined, or who can themselves determine the duration of their working time, are excepted from provisions of the Regulations relating to weekly working time, night work, rest periods and breaks. Where a worker's working time is partly measured, predetermined or determined by the worker and partly not, the provisions relating to weekly working time and to that part of the night work will only apply in relation to that part of the worker's work which is measured, predetermined or cannot be determined by the worker himself.

Shift workers are excluded from taking their entitlements to daily or weekly rest where this is impossible. There is a similar exception for those engaged in activities involving periods of work split up over the day. In both cases, the workers will be entitled to compensatory rest.

The maximum weekly working time limit and the entitlements in respect of night work will not apply to domestic servants employed in a private household.

Workers' entitlements under the provisions in relation to night work, rest breaks, daily rest and/or weekly rest may be modified or excluded by a collective agreement and/or a workforce agreement. A workforce agreement is one reached between the employer and workers the terms and conditions of which are not determined by reference to a collective agreement or their representatives. Compensatory rest must be given if there is any such modification/exclusion.

The maximum weekly working hours limit will not apply in respect of workers who enter into an individual voluntary arrangement with their employer that the limit will not apply. Any such agreement must be terminable upon notice (maximum of three months, but in default of express provision, seven days).

12.9.9 Remedies

Complaint may be made to an employment tribunal where there has been a failure to provide paid annual leave, rest breaks, daily rest or weekly rest. The complaint must be brought within three months of the act or omission complained of unless the tribunal considers it was not reasonably practicable to do so. The tribunal may make a declaration that the complaint is well founded and award compensation.

Note also that there are additional restrictions on the working time of children (essentially 12- to 18-year-olds) which are contained in the Children and Young Persons Act 1993, as amended by s 2 of the Children (Protection) at Work Regs 1998.

12.10 UNFAIR DISMISSAL

Sections 94–110 of the 1996 concern the right of an employee, subject to certain qualifying conditions, not to be unfairly dismissed by his employer.

An affected employee may bring a claim of unfair dismissal before an industrial tribunal. If the claim is successful, the tribunal may order the employer to reinstate or re-engage the employee and/or to pay compensation.

The interpretation of the law of unfair dismissal has resulted in substantial case law, but many decisions can only be explained on their own specific facts. However, the decisions do give guidance and reference has been made to leading cases in particular areas of unfair dismissal law.

12.10.1 The basis of a claim

Preconditions

In order for the employee to be able to bring a claim for unfair dismissal before a tribunal he must first show that he was employed by the employer under a contract of employment; that he was dismissed by the employer; and that he has attained the necessary one-year period of continuous employment. No minimum period is required where an employee is dismissed for reasons which are automatically unfair (see 12.10.5).

Certain employees are excluded from bringing a claim, eg when the employee is over the normal retirement age in the particular employment in question; or he is working abroad; or he has been dismissed in connection with a lock-out or strike. The burden of proof rests with the employee to show that he satisfies the necessary qualifying conditions.

Dismissal by the employer

ERA, ss 95 and 136 state that an employee is to be treated as having been dismissed if and only if:

(1) the contract under which he is employed by the employer is terminated by the employer with or without notice; or
(2) where under that contract he is employed for a fixed term and that term expires without being renewed under the same contract; or
(3) the employee terminates that contract with or without notice, in circumstances in which he is entitled to terminate the contract without notice by reason of the employer's conduct (what is known as 'constructive dismissal').

Termination by the employer

It is important to note that once an employer gives notice of dismissal to an employee, as a general rule this cannot be withdrawn without the employee's consent. Likewise, the same principle applies to notice of resignation given by the employee.

Expiry of a fixed term contract

The expiry of a fixed term contract which is not renewed by the employer is a dismissal for unfair dismissal purposes. However, under s 197 of the Act an employer and employee can agree in writing to exclude the employee's right to claim unfair dismissal arising out of the non-renewal of the contract where the employee is employed under a fixed term of one year or more. If it is intended to exclude such rights, provision should be made in the contract of employment itself.

It was held in *BBC v Kelly-Phillips* [1998] 2 All ER 845 that the reference to a contract for a fixed term included a contract which had been varied by an extension of the term under the same contract.

In *Puncher v Bishop Grossteste College* (EAT, 6 November 2001), the applicant was engaged by way of a series of fixed term contracts beginning in September and ending July the following year. The contract of employment contained a waiver clause whereby he waived the right to claim unfair dismissal and statutory redundancy payments on termination of the fixed term contract without renewal. Section 108 of the Act provides that the right not to be unfairly dismissed did not apply if the period of employment was less than one year. In July 1999, the applicant's employment was ended when the respondents opted not to renew his contract. It was held that the waiver term applied only if it could be shown that the applicant's contract was for a fixed term of one year or more. None of the contracts signed by the applicant was for such a term, each being for less. The contract could not be added up for the purposes of a claim for unfair dismissal, to obtain an employment period of more than 12 months. The waiver clause was therefore invalid as none of the contracts was for a fixed period of more than one year.

Constructive dismissal

Constructive dismissal occurs where an employer has committed a repudiatory breach of the employee's contract of employment, which entitles the employee to resign. The leading case in this area is the Court of Appeal decision in *Western Excavating (ECC) v Sharp* [1978] IRLR 27. There must be an intention by the employer to break one or more of the essential terms of the employee's employment. It is not sufficient that the employer has merely acted unreasonably.

The repudiatory breach by the employer need not be of an express term of the contract, but could be a breach of an implied term such as that of mutual trust and confidence (see 12.4.1). Examples of actions by an employer which may justify an employee claiming constructive dismissal are a unilateral reduction in an employee's pay or a substantial change in the nature of the employee's job.

It is important that an employee must not affirm the breach of contract by his employer by delaying his resignation for a substantial period of time or by doing some other act which is inconsistent with his acceptance of the breach.

12.10.2 Qualifying period

An employee must have been continuously employed for a period of at least one year at the effective date of termination to be able to bring a claim for unfair dismissal. The period of continuous employment is calculated from the date of commencement to the effective date of termination. There is, though, no qualifying period where the dismissal is automatically unfair (see 12.10.5). The effective date of termination is defined in s 97(1) of the Act as:

(1) where an employee's employment is terminated by notice, either by the employer or the employee himself, the date on which that notice expires;

(2) where an employee's employment is terminated without notice, the date on which that termination takes effect;

(3) where an employee is employed under a fixed term contract which expires without the term being renewed, the date on which that term expires.

In most instances the effective date of termination is the date on which the employee finishes work. Where, however, an employee is dismissed without notice or with notice that is less than the statutory minimum, the effective date is the date on which the minimum statutory notice would have expired if it had been given (see 12.8.2). Accordingly, an employee who is dismissed without notice one week short of attaining one year's continuous employment is nevertheless, under the operation of this rule, deemed as having one year's continuous employment and therefore is entitled to bring a claim for unfair dismissal.

12.10.3 The reasons for dismissal

Once the employee has established that he has been dismissed and that he satisfies the other qualifying conditions, the burden of proof switches to the employer to show:

(1) the reason or the principal reason for the dismissal; and
(2) that reason was one of the prima facie fair reasons set out in ERA, s 98.

Section 98 sets out the following prima facie fair reasons for dismissal:

(1) a reason related to the capability or qualifications of the employee to carry out the particular job which he was employed to do;

(2) a reason relating to the employee's conduct;

(3) the employee's redundancy;

(4) that the employee could not continue in his position without contravening a duty or restriction imposed by or under an enactment;

(5) some other substantial reason of a kind such as to justify the dismissal of an employee holding the position which that employee held.

12.10.4 Fairness: has the employer acted reasonably?

If the employer has established one of the prima facie fair reasons set out in s 98 of the Act, the tribunal will then go on to consider the question of whether the dismissal was fair or unfair in all the circumstances of the particular case (having regard to equity and the substantial merits of the case). The question is whether the employer acted reasonably in treating the reason for dismissal as a sufficient reason for dismissing the employee.

The burden of proof does not rest on either party, but it is for the tribunal to be satisfied that the employer acted reasonably when dismissing the employee. A leading case on this point is *Iceland Frozen Foods v Jones* (1982) IRLR 439, in which the EAT stated that it was the function of an employment tribunal to determine whether in the particular circumstances of each case the decision by the employer to dismiss the employee fell within the band of reasonable responses which a reasonable employer might have adopted. If the dismissal falls within the band, then it is fair; if it does not, then it is unfair. It is not for the tribunal, in judging whether the employer acted reasonably, to substitute for the employer's decision what they believe the right course of action should have been. In many instances one employer might have dismissed whereas another might have taken some other form of disciplinary action, but either decision could fall within the band of reasonable responses.

It is also for an employer, to show that he has acted reasonably, to have adopted fair procedures when taking a decision to dismiss an employee. Until the House of Lords' decision in *Polkey v AE Dayton Services* [1988] ICR 142, it was believed that if the employer had adopted an unfair procedure in dismissing an employee, but established that if he adopted a fair procedure, the employee would still have been dismissed, then that dismissal could still be fair. In *Polkey,* however, the House of Lords held that this was the wrong approach and that fair procedures must be followed regardless of whether or not a failure to do so would in fact not affect the ultimate outcome.

In *Foley v The Post Office* and *HSBC Bank v Madden* (2000] IRLR 827, the Court of Appeal held that the test tribunals should apply in assessing unfair dismissal cases was whether the employer's decision fell within the 'band of reasonable responses' (as set out in the case of *Iceland Frozen Foods v Jones* [1983] ICR 17; [1982] IRLR 439), unless the law was changed by Parliament or interpreted by the House of Lords in a different way. Tribunals could not substitute their own views for the employer's.

12.10.5 Automatically unfair dismissals

Certain dismissals are deemed to be automatically unfair and are not subject to the reasonableness tests set out in the Act. In addition, in certain cases, an employee may be able to bring a complaint despite the fact that he does not satisfy the necessary qualifying condition regarding continuous employment.

Trade union related dismissals

It is automatically unfair for an employer to dismiss an employee for either:

(1) being or proposing to become a member of an independent trade union; or
(2) refusing to join or remain a member of a trade union; or
(3) taking part or proposing to take part in union related activities at an appropriate time, ie outside working hours or within working hours if agreed with the employer.

An employee can bring a claim under this heading irrespective of the fact that he may not have two years' continuous service or that he may be over age 65 or the normal retiring age in his employment. In such a case, the burden of proof rests upon the employee to show that the reason for the dismissal was union related. However, if he does satisfy the necessary qualifying conditions, it is for the employer to prove the reason for dismissal in the usual way.

Maternity related dismissals

Under ERA, s 99(1), it is automatically unfair for an employer to dismiss any woman irrespective of her hours of work or length of service if the sole or principal reason for her dismissal is that she was pregnant or was for any other maternity related reason. For further discussion, see 12.13.7.

Health and safety related dismissals

Section 100 of the Act makes it automatically unfair for an employer to dismiss an employee for certain health and safety reasons. Again, no qualifying period of employment is required.

Assertion of statutory rights

Under s 104 of the Act, it is automatically unfair to dismiss an employee if the reason or principal reason for the dismissal was the allegation by an employee that his employer had infringed a statutory right or that the employee had brought proceedings to enforce a particular right. The relevant statutory rights include eg claims made under s 13 of the Act (protection of wages) and claims to a written statement of terms under s 1. Again, no qualifying period of employment is required.

Spent convictions

Where under the Rehabilitation of Offenders Act 1974 a conviction has been spent, it is automatically unfair for an employer to dismiss an employee for failure to disclose such a spent conviction.

Transfer of undertaking related dismissals

It is automatically unfair to dismiss an employee where that dismissal is for a reason connected with the transfer of an undertaking unless such dismissal can be justified as being for an 'ETO' reason entailing changes in the workforce (see 12.24.4 and 12.24.5).

Redundancy – unfair reasons for selection

It is automatically unfair for an employee to be selected for redundancy because he is a trade union member or has refused to become one, or an employee is selected for redundancy because she is pregnant; or where the employee is selected for redundancy in breach of an agreed practice or customary arrangement.

Sunday working

The Sunday Trading Act 1994 provides that if a protected shop worker is dismissed or selected for redundancy, and the reason or principal reason was a refusal to work on a Sunday, or the worker opted out of such work, the dismissal will be unfair. No service qualification is required for an unfair dismissal claim to be brought in such a case.

Whistleblowing

Under the ERA, as amended by the Public Interest (Disclosure) Act 1998, the dismissal of an employee because, or principally because, he made a protected disclosure is automatically unfair. There is no qualifying period nor upper age limit.

12.10.6 Grounds for dismissal

Capability

Capability is defined as being assessed by reference to skill, aptitude, health or any other physical or mental quality. Capability falls into two classes:

(1) the inability of an employee to carry out his particular job to the required standard (ie incompetence), and

(2) ill health.

Incompetence

In competency cases it is important for the employer to show:

(a) what was required of the employee;

(b) that the employee was aware of what was required; and

(c) that he fell short of the required standard.

Complaints about an employee's incompetence must relate to 'work of the kind which he was employed by the employer to do'. Therefore, in certain circumstances a single act of incompetence or negligence may be sufficient to justify dismissal in some cases. For example, in *Alidair v Taylor* [1978] ICR 445 an airline pilot who landed his aircraft negligently so as to put the lives of his passengers at risk was fairly dismissed by his employer in view of his gross incompetence and the potentially calamitous consequences that his actions could have had.

However, most incompetency cases involve a number of relatively minor incidents, which taken in isolation are relatively unimportant but which accumulated over a sufficient period of time may constitute a reason for dismissal. In cases of this kind, it is important for an employer to adopt a fair procedure in dealing with the employee and such procedure should include the following steps:

(1) Where an employee falls short of the required standards, the employer should arrange a meeting with him (and his representative) at which he should be informed of the areas in which he is falling short of those standards and the time period during which his performance must improve. The employee should also be told that if the required improvement does not occur, he will receive a formal written warning and that if after that time further improvement is not seen, the ultimate sanction of dismissal may be considered.

(2) If no improvement is apparent, the employee should be called to a second meeting, together with his representative, at which he should be warned of the areas in which he has failed to improve and he should be given the opportunity to explain why there has been no improvement. The employee should be given a formal written warning. At the conclusion of that meeting he should be informed that he will be given a further period in which to improve, but that if there is no substantial improvement within that time then such failure will result in his dismissal.

(3) When no further improvement occurs, a third meeting should be called at which the employer should be given the opportunity to state his case and notice of dismissal will be given. The employee should then be given the opportunity to appeal against the decision to dismiss him.

In certain circumstances, the employer should consider further training for the employee. If the employee can show that the reason for his incompetence is that the employer failed to provide adequate training or adequate tools to perform the task satisfactorily, then a dismissal may well be unfair. The provision of further training and supervision is particularly important where an employee has been recently promoted. Furthermore, an employer should consider whether he has other work available to which the employee would be better suited.

Whether an employer follows all the procedural steps outlined above depends upon the circumstances of each particular case. In the case of a senior employee, he should reasonably be expected to be aware of the standards that are required of him and therefore several warnings may not be appropriate. However, it is advisable that, except in cases of clear gross incompetence, warnings should always be provided.

Illness

Frustration   Where ill health may make future performance of the employment contract impossible, the contract may be frustrated and there will be no dismissal of the employee. Frustration of a contract is, however, rare in these circumstances. For a discussion of the law relating to frustration of contracts, see 12.12.1.

Long-term sickness   As it is not normally difficult to show that the reason for dismissal was ill health, attention is generally focused on whether the employer acted reasonably in treating ill health absenteeism as sufficient grounds for dismissal. The adoption, therefore, by the employer of a fair procedure is of primary importance.

Before dismissing an employee for ill health the employer should be aware of the current medical position. With the employee's consent, he should obtain a report from the employee's doctor and in many circumstances also have the employee examined, with his consent, by the employer's own doctor.

In *Spencer v Paragon Wallpapers* [1976] IRLR 373 and *East Lindsey District Council v Daubney* [1977] ICR 566 various principles were set out which would indicate a fair procedure had been adopted in relation to the dismissal of an employee on ill health grounds. The employer having informed himself of the employee's medical condition should consider the following factors:

(1) The nature of the illness.
(2) The likelihood of the illness recurring.
(3) The requirements of his business and the need for the job to be done. Is it essential, because of the nature of the job, that the position needs to be filled quickly, or can the remaining employees cover the work for a period of time?
(4) The employee's past sickness record.

(5) Whether there is an alternative position within the company which would be more suitable to the employee.

In addition, throughout the period of illness the employer should consult with the employee on a regular basis. Failure to consult with the employee will in most cases render a dismissal unfair.

Persistent short-term absenteeism In cases where there is persistent short-term absenteeism due to unrelated illnesses, a medical examination may not be appropriate. In such circumstances the employee should be told what level of attendance he is expected to attain and be warned that if there is no improvement within a set period, this may result in his dismissal. The situation should then be monitored for a period of time (*International Sports v Thompson* [1980] IRLR 340).

Misconduct

Cases of misconduct fall into two categories: first, single acts of misconduct not sufficient by themselves to justify dismissal, and secondly, gross misconduct which may entitle an employer to dismiss an employee summarily (without notice). Examples of categories of gross misconduct would include theft, fraud, deliberate falsification of records, fighting, serious incapability through alcohol, being under the influence of illegal drugs, serious negligence which causes loss, damage or injury and serious acts of insubordination. Whereas any of the above examples may justify summary dismissal, in contrast a one-off incident of bad timekeeping would not.

It was stated in *British Home Stores v Burchell* [1980] ICR 303 that where an employer dismisses an employee for misconduct, the employer must establish that he had a belief that the employee was guilty of misconduct. Furthermore, the employer must have had reasonable grounds for that belief, and that in forming that reasonable belief he had carried out a reasonable investigation into all the circumstances of the matter.

Accordingly, it can be seen that the burden of proof in such cases is not as high as the burden of proof of reasonable doubt in a criminal court. Therefore, if an employer has a reasonable belief that one of a number of employees is guilty of dishonesty and following a full and proper investigation into the matter it cannot identify the particular employee responsible, it may be reasonable for the employer to dismiss all those who could have been responsible (*Frames Snooker Centre v Boyce* [1992] IRLR 472).

Furthermore, in cases where an employee is arrested by the police and criminal charges are pending, an employer does not have to wait for the outcome of the criminal case before deciding what action to take. If the employer carries out his own investigation and as a result dismisses the employee for dishonesty, such dismissal may be held to be reasonable, even if the employee is subsequently acquitted at trial.

The conduct for which an employee is dismissed usually relates to his behaviour during his employment. In certain instances, however, behaviour outside of employment may affect his continued employment. For example, a teacher who has a conviction for indecent assault on a child, even though such conviction was for an offence outside his normal working hours, may be unsuitable to continue on his employment.

12.10.7 Dismissal procedures

Even in cases of serious misconduct, it is important that employers follow a fair procedure when dealing with cases of misconduct by employees. Failure to follow a fair procedure is likely to result in the dismissal being unfair. It is therefore important for all employers to have properly set out disciplinary procedures.

The essential features of a fair disciplinary procedure, as outlined in the Advisory, Conciliation and Arbitration Service (ACAS) Code of Practice, are that it should:

- Be in writing.
- Specify to whom it applies.
- Provide for matters to be dealt with quickly.
- Indicate the disciplinary actions which may be taken.
- Specify the levels of management which have the authority to take the various forms of disciplinary action, ensuring that immediate superiors do not normally have the power to dismiss without reference to senior management.
- Provide for individuals to be informed of the complaints against them and to be given an opportunity to state their case before decisions are reached.
- Give individuals the right to be accompanied by a trade union representative or a fellow employee of their choice.
- Ensure that, except that for gross misconduct, no employees are dismissed for a first breach of discipline.
- Ensure that disciplinary action is not taken until the case has been carefully investigated.
- Ensure that individuals are given an explanation for any penalty imposed.
- Provide a right of appeal and specify the procedure to be followed.
- Specify that in cases of appeal against immediate dismissal the employee is dismissed with the possibility of reinstatement on appeal not suspended pending appeal.

When a matter of misconduct arises, the incident should be fully investigated immediately and witness statements taken if appropriate. Where witness statements are taken and these are the main evidence which are relied upon in taking disciplinary action against an employee it is appropriate for copies of the statements to be provided to the employee in question.

In cases of suspected serious misconduct, an employer should consider a brief period of suspension with pay. It is, however, important to note that unless there is express provision in an employer's disciplinary procedures which are incorporated into a contract of employment, the employer does not have the right to suspend an employee. In the absence of this being an express term of the contract, any suspension is a fundamental breach of the contract of employment by the employer which entitles the employee to resign and claim constructive dismissal.

Before a disciplinary decision is taken, a hearing should be held at which the employee is given an opportunity to state his case. He should be given the opportunity of having a fellow employee or trade union representative present at the meeting.

An employer, before deciding on the appropriate penalty, must take account of the employee's record and any other relevant factors. It is good practice for an employer to adjourn the hearing to consider a case before giving his decision. Once a decision has been made, this should be notified to the employee in writing and the employee should be informed of his right of appeal. The letter should state how the appeal should be made and to whom. Any appeal should be conducted by a member of senior management who has not been involved in the previous decision or investigation. It is essential that records are kept of all disciplinary proceedings and copies of letters are retained on an employee's personnel file as this will be important evidence should an unfair dismissal claim be made to an industrial tribunal.

12.10.8 Redundancy

Where the reason or the principal reason for an employee's dismissal is redundancy it may be unfair in two circumstances.

First, a dismissal is automatically unfair if the circumstances constituting the redundancy applied equally to one or more employees in the same undertaking who held positions similar to that held by the dismissed employee and who have not been dismissed by the employer, and the reason for the selection for dismissal was either

(i)   trade union related,
(ii) health and safety related,
(iii) related to an assertion by him of his statutory rights,
(iv) maternity related, or
(v)   he was selected in contravention of a customary arrangement or agreed redundancy procedure and there were no special reasons justifying a departure from that arrangement or procedure.

Secondly, where the dismissal is not automatically unfair under the above principle, it may be still be unfair in that it does not fulfil the reasonableness tests contained in ERA, s 98(4). For example, the failure to consult may render a dismissal unfair (see 12.11.3).

In *Williams v Compair Maxam* [1982] ICR 156 the EAT sought to lay down certain principles on which a fair selection procedure for redundancy should be based. These principles were laid down in a case where there was a recognised trade union, but are generally accepted as good practice (although failure to follow all the steps would not necessarily render a dismissal unfair). The employer should:

(1) give as much warning as possible of impending redundancies to enable the employees concerned or the recognised trade union (if appropriate) to take early steps to inform themselves of the relevant facts, consider possible alternative solutions and, if necessary, find alternative employment;

(2) consult the recognised trade union (if appropriate) of the best means by which the desired result can be achieved fairly and with as little hardship to the employees as possible;

(3) seek to establish criteria for selection which so far as possible do not depend solely upon the opinion of the person making the selection, but can be objectively checked against such matters as attendance record, efficiency at the job, experience or length of service;

(4) ensure that the selection is made fairly in accordance with those criteria;

(5) see whether instead of dismissing an employee he can offer him alternative employment.

These principles have to be considered in the light of the Collective Redundancies and Transfer of Undertakings (Protection of Employment) (Amendment) Regs 1995 and the Collective Redundancies and Transfer of Undertakings (Protection of Employment) (Amendment) Regs 1999. These apply only when 20 or more employees are to be made redundant.

12.10.9 Contravention of any enactment: illegality

If an employee is dismissed by his employer because the employee could not continue to work in the position he held without breaking the law, such dismissal will be for a prima facie fair reason. This must be a matter of fact; it is not enough that the employer genuinely believes that he would be breaking the law by continuing to employ the employee.

The employer must still act reasonably in all the circumstances, having regard to the size and administrative resources of his organisation. An employer should arrange a meeting at which the employee should be informed of the situation and invited to express his views. In appropriate cases an employer should consider whether it or an associated company has a suitable vacancy which the employee can be offered instead.

A common example of a fair dismissal under this head would be where it is an integral part of an employee's job to drive a motor vehicle and he has been disqualified from holding a valid licence.

12.10.10 Some other substantial reason

ERA, s 98 provides a 'catch all' potentially fair reason for dismissal which is for 'some other substantial reason of a kind such as to justify the dismissal of an employee holding the position which that employee held'. The employer is required to show only that the other substantial reason for dismissal was a potentially fair one. Once the reason has been established, the industrial tribunal must then decide whether the employer acted reasonably under s 98(4) in dismissing for that reason.

The most common example of a prima facie fair dismissal falling within this category is where an employer has had to undergo a necessary reorganisation of his business. This may apply in cases eg where as a result of the reorganisation he has had to alter his employees' terms and conditions of employment. Usually such alteration would be a fundamental breach of the contract of employment entitling the employee to resign and claim constructive dismissal. However, if the employer can show that it was prima facie fair because of the necessity of the business reorganisation, then the tribunal will go on to consider whether the employer had acted reasonably in accordance with all the circumstances under s 98(4) of the Act.

12.10.11 Remedies

Procedure

Where an employee considers that he has been unfairly dismissed, providing that he satisfies the necessary qualifying conditions, he should present a claim for unfair dismissal to an employment tribunal within three months of the effective date of termination. The tribunal has a discretion to allow a complaint outside the three-month time limit if it considers that it was not reasonably practicable for the employee to bring the claim within the appropriate time limit.

Tribunal awards

If a tribunal considers that an employee has been unfairly dismissed, it must then decide which remedy is appropriate. There are three basic remedies available, as follows:

Reinstatement

This is an order that the employer should treat the employee in all respects as if he had not been dismissed. If the tribunal makes a reinstatement order the employee is entitled not only to be restored to his previous position with the company, but also to an amount equal to the salary he would have received had he continued to be employed, together with any benefits he would have been entitled to (eg Christmas bonus, wage increase). The tribunal in making such an order must spell out the relevant terms and conditions which apply to the employee and the date by which reinstatement is to take effect.

Re-engagement

This is an order that the employee be re-engaged by the employer (or the employer's successor or an associated employer) in employment that is comparable to that from which he was dismissed or in other suitable employment. If the tribunal makes such an order it must state the employer's identity, the nature of the employment, the rate of pay, the amount of arrears of pay which the employee is entitled to and other benefits and privileges which must be restored to the employee, and the date on which the re-engagement order is to take effect.

Reinstatement and re-engagement

In considering whether to make both orders, the tribunal must consider a number of factors including whether the employee wishes to be reinstated and whether it is practicable for an employer to comply with an order for reinstatement or re-engagement. In most instances such orders are not appropriate because the working relationship has broken down so completely that it is not practicable to expect the employer and the employee to work together again.

Compensation

Compensation consists of:

Basic award

This is a sum of up to £7,500, determined by reference to age, length of service and a week's pay (as for redundancy payments), a week's pay being up to a maximum of £250. Under the Employment Relations Act 1999, s 34, the limit on a week's pay is index-linked to the retail prices index for September each year, and shall, depending on whether the RPI is higher or lower, be increased or decreased by a percentage equivalent to the rise or reduction in the index. The resulting figure will then be rounded up to the nearest £10. Under certain limited circumstances there is a statutory minimum on the level of the basic award, the current minimum level being £3,400.

Compensatory award

This is a sum of up to £52,600 to take account of loss of earnings and other benefits. Under the Employment Relations Act 1999, s 34, the limit on the compensatory award is index-linked to the retail prices index for September each year, and shall, depending on whether the RPI is higher or lower, be increased or reduced by a percentage equivalent to the rise or reduction in the index. The resulting figure will then be rounded up to the nearest £100. the compensatory award for unfair dismissal is unlimited if the employee is dismissed for a health and safety reason listed in ERA, s 100.

Additional awards are between 26 and 52 weeks' pay, with a maximum of £13,000. In assessing the compensatory award the main heads of compensation (see *Norton Tool Co v Tewson* [1972] ICR 501) are:

(1) Loss of earnings from the date of dismissal to the date of the tribunal hearing. This figure is calculated net of tax and NICs, and any payment in lieu of notice that the employee received is taken into account. Furthermore, if an employee has found a new job, his earnings in that new employment are also taken into account.

(2) Future loss of earnings. If an employee is still unemployed at the date of the hearing, or is earning less than he previously earned, the tribunal will award a sum for future loss of earnings for such period as it considers reasonable.

(3) Loss of benefits in kind. These would include such things as loss of company car, medical insurance and free or subsidised accommodation. In calculating the loss suffered by an employee as a result of losing such benefits, the correct approach in calculating the loss is the cost to the employee in replacing the lost benefits. In calculating the loss of benefit of using a company car, reference can be made to AA guidelines. See *Shore v Downs Surgical plc* [1984] ICR 532.

(4) Loss of pension rights.

(5) Loss of statutory rights. The tribunal awards a nominal figure for loss of the protection from unfair dismissal or the right to a redundancy payment for the first one or two years of any new employment.

(6) Expenses reasonably incurred as a result of the dismissal. In *Leech v Berger Jonsen and Nicholson* [1972] IRLR 58, expenses incurred in looking for new employment were a recoverable loss.

A tribunal may also award compensation for loss of the accrued right to the statutory minimum period of notice.

Reduction of the compensatory award

A tribunal may reduce the level of any compensatory award for the following reasons:

(1) *Contributory fault* Where a tribunal finds that an employee has to any extent caused or contributed to his own dismissal by his actions it reduces the amount of the compensatory award by such proportion as it considers just and equitable (see *W Devis & Sons v Atkins* [1977] ICR 662). In rare cases the reduction may be as much as 100%.

(2) *Where the employee has failed to take reasonable steps to mitigate his loss* The employee is under a duty to mitigate his loss. He should

therefore take all reasonable steps to find alternative employment. If he does not do so, this may be taken into account in reducing the compensatory award. It is important to note that an employee is not obliged to accept the first job offered irrespective of pay and conditions.

(3) *Where the tribunal considers a reduction just and equitable*   The tribunal has the power to reduce the compensatory award to reflect general considerations of fairness. The cases where tribunals may decide that it is just and equitable to reduce compensation under this head can be divided roughly into two groups:

(a) where, by the time of the hearing, the employer can show that the employee is guilty of misconduct which would have merited dismissal, even if the employer did not know about that misconduct at the time of the dismissal; and

(b) where the employee could have been fairly dismissed at a later date or if the employer had followed a fair procedure. See *Chaplin v HJ Rawlinson* [1991] ICR 553.

Additional award

If a tribunal makes an award for reinstatement or re-engagement but the employee is not reinstated or re-engaged, in breach of the order, the tribunal will make a basic and a compensatory award. In these circumstances, the normal maximum of £50,000 may be exceeded, if necessary, to ensure that the award fully reflects the terms of the original order relating to loss of pay and benefits with which the employer failed to comply. Unless the employer can show that it was not practicable to comply with the order, or except in the case of dismissal relating to Sunday trading or for trade union activities, it will also make an additional award of an amount not less than 26 and not more than 52 weeks' pay. The current maximum weekly pay is £250. Under the Employment Relations Act 1999, s 34, the limit on a week's pay is index-linked to the retail prices index for September each year, and shall, depending on whether the RPI is higher or lower, be increased or decreased by a percentage equivalent to the rise or reduction in the index. The resulting figure will then be rounded up to the nearest £10. Where an employee is unfairly dismissed because that employee made a protected disclosure, the compensatory award for unfair dismissal is unlimited (ERA, s 124(1A), as amended by the Public Interest Disclosure (Compensation) Regs 1999).

Trade union and, health and safety dismissals

Where dismissal is to be regarded as automatically unfair when it relates to trade union and health and safety related matters, and the employee is not reinstated or re-engaged, the award will consist of a basic award (calculated as above), a compensatory award (unlimited in relation to dismissal related to health and safety reasons) and an additional award (see above).

The recoupment provisions

If an employee who has brought a claim for unfair dismissal has received unemployment benefit, job seekers allowance or income support between the date of his dismissal and the employment tribunal hearing, the employer may be ordered by the Department of Employment, in a recoupment notice, to pay part of the compensation awarded not to the employee but to the Department of Employment or DSS so that the benefit money can be recovered.

Interest on tribunal awards

Employment tribunal compensation awards now carry interest which starts to run 42 days after the tribunal's written decision is sent to the parties.

12.10.12 Settlement

An employer may wish to settle a claim for unfair dismissal rather than proceed to a hearing. In order for any agreement that is reached with the employer to be binding it must be in one of the following forms:

(1) An agreement reached through the auspices of an ACAS conciliation officer. Once a complaint of unfair dismissal has been presented, an ACAS conciliation officer is appointed to the case to conciliate between the employer and the employee (or their representatives) to establish whether a settlement is possible. Any agreement to settle should be recorded in writing and on a form designed for the purpose (form COT3). Once the COT3 has been signed by both parties and the settlement sum paid, an employee is then precluded from bringing any further claims to an industrial tribunal.

(2) Under ERA, s 203, an unfair dismissal claim may be settled if the conditions governing a statutory compromise agreement are fulfilled. The most important of these conditions are that the agreement must be in writing and the employee must have received independent legal advice from a qualified lawyer as to the terms and effects of the proposed agreement and, in particular, its effect on the employee's ability to pursue his rights before an industrial tribunal. If the conditions are not fully satisfied, the employee will not be precluded from bringing further claims. The following claims can also be settled by means of a compromise agreement:

- itemised pay statements
- guarantee payments
- medical suspension pay
- time off for public duties
- time off for training while under redundancy notice
- time off for ante-natal care
- written reasons for dismissal
- unlawful deduction from pay under the ERA

- sex discrimination
- race discrimination
- equal pay
- rights not to suffer a detriment in health and safety cases
- rights to alternative work and pay in maternity suspension cases.

12.11 REDUNDANCY

An employee who is dismissed by his employer in certain circumstances is entitled to a redundancy payment as set out in ERA, s 139(1). To qualify for a redundancy payment an employee must satisfy certain qualifying conditions. The Part-time Workers (Prevention of Less Favourable Treatment) Regs 2000 implement the Part-time Work Directive (97/81/EC) into UK law and require part-time workers to be treated no less favourably than their full-time equivalents in the event of redundancy.

12.11.1 Qualifying conditions

To be entitled to a redundancy payment, a person must be:

(a) *An employee* Only employees are entitled to redundancy payments. The burden is upon the person applying for the payment to show that he is an employee. He must have been continuously employed for a period of two years ending with the relevant date. The relevant date is defined in the same way as the effective date of termination for unfair dismissal purposes. For redundancy purposes, however, an employee is not entitled to count any period of employment before his 18th birthday in calculating his period of continuous employment.

In addition, as for unfair dismissal purposes, where an employee has been dismissed with no notice or less than the statutory minimum period of notice, the relevant date for the purpose of calculating continuous employment is extended to the date upon which the statutory minimum notice would have expired had it been given (see 12.8.2).

(b) *Dismissed* The employee must have been dismissed. The statutory definition of dismissal for redundancy payment purposes is the same as that for unfair dismissal (see 12.10.1). The employee must have been dismissed by reason of redundancy. ERA, s 139(1) contains the definition of redundancy and provides that an employee who is dismissed shall be taken to have been dismissed by reason of redundancy if the dismissal is attributable wholly or mainly to:

'(a) the fact that his employer has ceased, or intends to cease, to carry on the business for the purposes of which the employee was employed by him or has ceased or intends to cease to carry on that business in the place where the employee was so employed; or

(b) the fact that the requirements of that business for employees to carry out work of a particular kind in the place where he was so employed have ceased or diminished or are expected to cease or diminish.'

Sub-paragraph (a) covers the situation in which the place of business where the employee could be required to work under his contract is shut. Where, therefore, the contract contained a mobility clause entitling the employer to transfer an employee, it was thought that the employer could invoke the mobility clause to transfer the employee from the workplace which had closed down to one where there was work. If the employee refused, he could then be dismissed for misconduct and a redundancy payment avoided.

Following the EAT decision in decision in *Bass Leisure v Thomas* [1994] IRLR 104, however, this approach has been doubted. It was held that an employee's place of work is not wherever an employer can require him to work under his contract. A factual enquiry should be undertaken to ascertain where the employee's true place of work is and if work has ceased there, and the employee is dismissed, he is redundant and can claim a redundancy payment. The exception would be when the new location represents suitable alternative employment which the employee unreasonably refuses (see (g) below).

Sub-paragraph (b) refers to circumstances of a reduction in the business requirements for employees to carry out work of a particular kind, (ie the employer has a surplus of labour). It is important to note that there is no requirement for the work to reduce, but only a requirement that the number of employees carrying out that particular work can be reduced. This would be the case where an employer ascertains that there is over-manning.

(c) *Below retirement age*   To claim a redundancy payment the employee must be below age 65 or the normal retiring age in the business in which he is employed. For employees over age 64 the amount of any redundancy payment payable is reduced by $\frac{1}{12}$ for each month by which his age exceeds 64.

(d) *Not ordinarily working outside Great Britain.*

(e) *Must not have contracted out of his rights to claim a redundancy payment*   Where an employee is employed under a fixed term contract for a minimum of two years and he has agreed in writing to contract out of his right to a redundancy payment, then he is dismissed on the expiry of that fixed term without it being renewed, and he is not entitled to a redundancy payment. See the discussion of the *Bishop Grossteste College* case at 12.10.1.

(f) *Eligible*   Certain employees such as civil servants and other public employees are specifically excluded from the right to a redundancy payment.

(g) *Redundant without an offer of suitable alternative employment*   An employee who has been offered employment either on the same terms and conditions as he previously enjoyed or has been offered suitable alternative employment and he has in either case unreasonably refused the new offer of employment, loses his right to a redundancy payment. The offer of alternative employment must be made by his original employer or an associated employer before his previous employment comes to an end and must start immediately upon the ending of his previous employment or within four weeks thereof.

Where the terms and conditions of the new contract differ wholly or partly from those which the employee previously enjoyed, then he is entitled to a statutory trial period of four weeks, which can be extended by mutual agreement, in which to decide whether the alternative employment is suitable.

Where the employee accepts the offer of alternative employment there is no redundancy situation. However, fie may reject the new offer of employment if it is not suitable and, provided the rejection is reasonable, he is entitled to a redundancy payment.

12.11.2 The redundancy selection process

Once an employer has decided that a redundancy does exist he must then implement that redundancy. It is important that when implementing a redundancy an employer adopts a fair procedure. Failure to do so can result in an employee who satisfies the necessary qualifying conditions bringing a claim for unfair dismissal.

An unfair dismissal may result where an employer has selected an employee or employees for redundancy in contravention of a customary arrangement or agreed selection procedure. Where such an arrangement or procedure exists the employer must adhere to it. Furthermore, an employer must not select an employee for redundancy for an inadmissible reason such as his membership of or participation in the affairs of a trade union. In these circumstances a selection for redundancy is automatically unfair.

Where there is no customary arrangement or agreed procedure, the employer is free to use his own selection criteria, which must be reasonable and properly applied. One of the standard criteria for selection is that known as 'last in, first out', but other factors which may also be considered are the type of skills of an employee for which there is a continuing employment need and the suitability of individual employees to perform those tasks; the employee's competence, and his past conduct.

12.11.3 Consultation and notification requirements

The Collective Redundancies and Transfer of Undertakings (Protection of Employment) (Amendment) Regs 1995 require an employer proposing to make 20 or more employees redundant to consult recognised trade unions, or any appropriate representatives elected by the employees, about ways of avoiding the dismissals, reducing the numbers to be dismissed and mitigating the consequences of the dismissals.

Failure to consult could lead to a claim for compensation known as a 'protective award', where the affected employees are compensated by ordering the employer to make payments for the protected period, or any portion of it for which they have not been paid. The amount of award is what the employment tribunal considers reasonable taking into account the seriousness of the breach and will be up to:

(1) 90 days where 90 days' minimum notice should have been given;
(2) 30 days where 30 days' minimum notice should have been given;
(3) 28 days in any other case.

The period of the award begins on the date on which the first dismissals take place or the date of the award, whichever is the earlier. This is known as the 'protected period'. Consultation must be undertaken 'with a view to reaching agreement'.

Notification should be delivered in writing to each of the appropriate representatives or, in the case of trade union representatives, by post to the union's head office. The appropriate representatives must be given access to the employees being made redundant and be provided with appropriate accommodation and other facilities.

The definition of 'redundancy', for the purposes of trade union consultation and Department of Trade and Industry notification only, is a 'dismissal for a reason not related to the individual concerned or for a number of reasons all of which are not so related'.

12.11.4 Redundancy checklist

The following is a checklist that an employer should consider before implementing any redundancies:

(1) Once the decision to make redundancies has been made the employer should first consult with any recognised trade union representatives, bearing in mind the appropriate time limits, and should provide them with all the appropriate information. Where there is no recognised trade union, the employer should consult with the individual employees.
(2) He should notify the Department of Employment where appropriate, again bearing in mind the appropriate time limit.
(3) Having decided on the numbers to be made redundant he should invite volunteers for redundancy.
(4) He should then establish the selection criteria with the agreement (if possible) of the recognised union. He should consider whether the numbers of employees to be made redundant can be reduced and should also consider whether there is any suitable alternative employment within the company or associated company for the affected employees.
(5) He should consult with the individual affected employees.

(6) He should then send out the notices of dismissal informing the employees of their impending redundancies. He should allow the affected employees time off to look for other employment.

12.11.5 Claim for a redundancy payment

The claim for a redundancy payment must be made within six months of the relevant date by either submitting a claim in writing to the employer claiming a redundancy payment, or by bringing a claim for a redundancy payment to the employment tribunal, or by submitting an unfair dismissal complaint. If a claim is not brought within six months the tribunal has a limited discretion to allow a claim to be brought within a further six months.

12.11.6 Calculation of the redundancy payment

The redundancy payment is calculated along similar lines to that of the basic award for unfair dismissal purposes. It is therefore calculated by multiplying one week's gross pay (subject to the statutory maximum of £250) by a factor depending upon the employee's age and the number of completed years of service (subject to the statutory maximum of 20 years). Therefore, for every year during the whole of which the employee is aged:

(1) 41 or over – a multiplier of one and a half;
(2) between 22 and 40 – a multiplier of one;
(3) between 18 and 21 – a multiplier of one half.

The employer should give the employee a statement showing how the redundancy payment has been calculated.

Finally, it should be remembered that in addition to any statutory redundancy payment, an employee may be entitled to a contractual redundancy payment under his contract of employment and will also be entitled to work out his notice period or be paid in lieu of notice.

12.11.7 Rights on insolvency of an employer

The insolvency provisions of the ERA apply when a company has become legally insolvent. This can mean liquidation, receivership, an administration order or voluntary arrangement approved by the court or bankruptcy. If the company merely ceases trading, these provisions may not apply.

When an employer becomes insolvent, the following payments owed to his employees will be regarded as preferential debts:

- Arrears of wages or salary
- Guarantee payments
- Remuneration for suspension on medical grounds

- Time-off payments
- Remuneration under a protective award.

Employees can apply to the Redundancy Payments Office of the Department of Trade and Industry covering the employer's area. If satisfied that the employer is insolvent and the employees are entitled to the payments, the Department will make the following payments, for a period of up to eight weeks, out of the National Insurance Fund. Note that there is a statutory limit on the amount for anyone week of £250.

(1) Any arrears of pay up to eight weeks (includes guarantee payments, remuneration for suspension on medical grounds, time-off payments, remuneration under a protective award): up to £1,920.
(2) Any money due to employees who have received notice (maximum 12 weeks' statutory notice after 12 years' service): £2,880 maximum.
(3) Holiday pay up to six weeks: £1,440 maximum.
(4) Basic compensation for unfair dismissal: £7200 maximum (calculated in the same way as a redundancy payment: see above).
(5) Reimbursement of fees, etc paid by apprentices.

Provision is also made for the payment of unpaid contributions to occupational pension schemes out of the National Insurance Fund, and for liability to statutory maternity pay and statutory sick pay to be met by the President of the Board of Trade.

12.12 TERMINATION OF EMPLOYMENT

There are three kinds of claim potentially available to an employee on termination of his contract of employment:

(1) unfair dismissal;
(2) a redundancy payment; and
(3) a claim for damages for wrongful dismissal derived from the common law relating to contract.

12.12.1 Lawful methods of termination

A claim for wrongful dismissal arises where an employer has terminated an employee's employment in breach of the employee's contract. A claim for wrongful dismissal, however, does not arise where the contract is terminated in accordance with one of five common law methods:

By agreement

An employer and employee may agree to terminate the contract of employment and thereby release each other from their obligations. Any agreement is, however, void if it purports to exclude the rights conferred on all employees by employment protection legislation (eg unfair dismissal/redundancy).

By effluxion of time

A fixed term contract or a contract to perform a specified task automatically terminates at the end of the term or when the task is completed.

By notice

A contract of employment usually contains an express term setting out the notice period. Where, however, the contract fails to specify a notice period then the contract is deemed to be terminable by either party giving reasonable notice. What amounts to reasonable notice depends on the particular circumstances of the employment concerned. Such factors which are taken into account in deciding what is a reasonable notice period are: the type of job; the employee's status; the period by which the employee's pay is calculated; and any custom or practice which is established in the industry or profession.

Whatever period of notice is specified it must not be less than the statutory minimum period of notice laid down by ERA, s 86. This states that where an employee is continuously employed for at least one month but less than two years he is entitled to one week's notice. Thereafter he is entitled to one week's notice for each complete year of employment up to a maximum of 12 weeks' notice, after 12 years' employment.

Following repudiatory breach

Following a repudiatory breach of the employment contract, an employee can be dismissed immediately without notice. This is known as summary dismissal. Typical examples of conduct which may entitle an employer to dismiss summarily include theft by an employee of his employer's property and gross insubordination.

Frustration

A contract is frustrated where its performance becomes impossible or substantially different from that which the parties envisaged at the time of entering into the agreement by reason of an unforeseen event which has occurred and which is not the fault of either party. Where the contract is held to be frustrated, there is no dismissal and therefore there can be no claim for wrongful dismissal, unfair dismissal or a redundancy payment. The question of whether a contract has been frustrated most frequently occurs in the cases of illness and imprisonment, although it must be said that the doctrine of frustration is not frequently applied in illness cases.

12.12.2 Written reasons for dismissal

Under ERA, s 92, an employee is entitled to be provided by his employer, within 14 days of his request, with written reasons for his dismissal. The statement giving the written reasons is admissible in evidence at any proceedings and it is therefore important that the statement is consistent with the employer's case before an employment tribunal.

An employee must have one years' continuous employment to be entitled to written reasons for dismissal: The Unfair Dismissal and Statement of Reasons for Dismissal (Variation of Qualifying Period) Order 1999.

An employee dismissed at any time while pregnant or after childbirth during maternity leave is entitled to a written statement without having to request it.

Where a request for written reasons for dismissal has been made by an employee and the employer has failed to comply, an employee can bring a claim to a tribunal on the grounds that his employer has unreasonably failed to provide written reasons for his dismissal or that the reasons given are inadequate or untrue. The claim must be brought within three months from the effective date of termination of the employment. This period can be extended if the tribunal is satisfied that it was not reasonably practicable to bring the claim within that period.

If the tribunal finds the claim well founded it may make a declaration as to what it believes the employer's reasons were for dismissing the employee, and will award a sum equal to the amount of two weeks' pay (not subject to the statutory maximum of £250 pw).

12.12.3 Wrongful dismissal

Where an employer dismisses an employee in breach of his contractual or statutory obligations to give that employee notice or any other contractual obligation, it may become liable to pay the employee damages for breach of contract. Examples of actions by an employer which can lead to a claim for damages for wrongful dismissal are as follows:

(1) Where an employer terminates an employee's contract without proper notice, either contractual or statutory.
(2) Where an employer terminates a fixed term contract before the expiry of the term. It is, however, usual to make provision in a fixed term contract for earlier termination by including a provision that the contract may be terminated by either side giving a specified period of notice.
(3) A claim for wrongful dismissal can arise when an employer is found to have repudiated the contract in breach of one of the fundamental contractual obligations. Repudiation occurs where an employer, by his conduct, displays an intention not to be bound by the contract. For example, where an employer insists on imposing new terms and conditions on an employee without that employee's consent, this can

amount to a breach of a fundamental term of the contract entitling the employee to treat the contract as discharged and then sue his employer for wrongful dismissal for breach of contract.

(4) Disciplinary procedures may form part of a contract of employment. If an employer dismisses an employee without following contractual disciplinary procedures this may amount to a serious breach of contract (*Boyo v Lambeth LBC* [1994] ICR 727, CA).

12.12.4 Damages for wrongful dismissal

Once an employee has established that he has been dismissed in breach of contract or without being given the proper statutory minimum period of notice, he must then show that he has suffered loss as a result of the breach by the employer.

The employee's remedy for his employer's breach of contract is damages, the aim of which is to place the employee in the same situation he would have been in if the contract had been properly performed. The amount of damages that an employee receives is based upon the amount of pay and other fringe benefits (such as company car, pension and medical insurance) that he would have been entitled to had the employer complied with his contractual and statutory obligations. Therefore, the courts cannot award compensation beyond the time when the contract could have been brought to an end by the employer in accordance with its terms. For example, in the case of a fixed term contract where the fixed term is for a period of five years and the contract is brought to an end after three years, the employee is entitled to compensation for pay and fringe benefits for the unexpired two-year term.

As stated, an award of damages is based upon contractual entitlements. This means that benefits that are merely discretionary should be excluded from a damages calculation (*Lavarack v Woods of Colchester* [1967] 1 QB 278).

Where an employer has dismissed an employee in breach of the disciplinary procedures laid down in the contract of employment, the level of damages are based on the length of time it would have taken for the employment to be terminated lawfully by the employer if he had followed the correct disciplinary procedures.

12.12.5 Mitigation

An employee must take all reasonable steps to mitigate his loss by seeking other employment. If he fails to take such steps his level of damages may be reduced accordingly. If the employee finds alternative employment then such payments that he receives are taken into account in reducing the level of any compensation that he may be entitled to. Furthermore, statutory benefits received are taken into account in assessing damages.

12.12.6 Accelerated receipt

A further deduction in the level of compensation may be made under this heading. This is particularly relevant where an employee on a long fixed term contract is wrongfully dismissed after the contract has run only a short period of time. For example, where an employee is employed under a five-year fixed term contract and is dismissed after only one year then he is entitled to receive his pay for the further four remaining years. By awarding such a large lump sum which could be invested to produce an income, however, the employee is actually better off than he would have been if the contract had been properly performed. As a result, as the courts do not allow an employee to make a profit, a deduction is made to account for the employee receiving the money in advance, and having the opportunity to benefit by investment.

12.12.7 Interest

Interest may be awarded on the damages from the date when the cause of action arose to the date of judgment, or in the case of payment made before that date, the date of payment.

12.12.8 Payment in lieu of notice

An employer who intends to dismiss an employee may in certain circumstances consider it desirable that the employee should not work out his notice period. The employer pays that employee in lieu of notice instead.

There has been considerable case law over recent years concerning whether a payment in lieu of notice is taxable. The following is a summary of the position.

Payments in lieu of notice will normally be taxable if:

(1) the contract provides for its payment;
(2) there is some prior arrangement for the payment in lieu;
(3) there is a general expectation based upon custom and practice that such payments will be made;
(4) the employer makes it known in advance that a payment in lieu will be available; and
(5) the employee remains employed for the notice period even without working.

Payments in lieu will be taxable under TA 1988, s 148 and eligible for the £30,000 threshold under TA 1988, s 188 if:

(1) the contract does not provide for the payment;
(2) there is no clear prior arrangement for the payment in lieu;
(3) there is no general expectation that such payments will be made;
(4) the employer does not make the availability of such a payment known in advance; and

(5) the employee does not remain employed for the contractual notice period.

In *Thorn EMI Electronics v Coldicott (Inspector of Taxes)* [1996] STC (SCD) 455, the issue was whether payments in lieu to senior managers could be considered emoluments within TA 1988, s 19.

The company made staff redundant and made payments to them equivalent to the salary that would have been payable over the notice period. For senior management the right had been set down contractually to make such payments, for junior staff, it was agreed with the inspector that the payments were compensation for breach of contract under TA 1988, s 148. For senior managers, the Inland Revenue regarded the payments as being emoluments 'from' their employment within TA 1988, s 19 so that the company should have deducted income tax at source.

The payments to the senior managers were emoluments from their employments. These moneys were paid on the occasion of redundancy, but not for redundancy. The managers were contractually entitled to the payment. The employee had provided itself with two methods of lawfully terminating the contracts, and determining what was to be paid in each case.

It was held in *Abrahams v Performing Right Society* (1995) The Independent, 25 May that the employee is not under a duty to mitigate his loss in relation to periods of notice (see 12.12.5). The employee is therefore entitled to be paid for the whole of his notice period. This is because a payment in lieu is not treated as a claim for damages (as the employer has the express right to lawfully terminate by making a payment in lieu), but is rather a debt due under the contract. Where, therefore, the employee is under a long notice period or on a fixed term contract where there is a lengthy period of the contract still unexpired, the amount due may be substantial, where there is no duty on the employee to mitigate.

An express payment in lieu clause is, however, extremely important where an employee is subject to restrictive covenants. Where an employer dismisses an employee by making a payment in lieu, he is in breach of contract unless the contract expressly allows termination with a payment in lieu. If not, the breach by the employer prohibits him from enforcing clauses in the contract intended to survive termination, such as restrictive covenants (see *General Billposting Co v Atkinson* [1909] AC 118).

12.12.9 Wrongful dismissal claims – procedure

Actions for wrongful dismissal have to be brought in the county court or High Court or employment tribunals. The tribunals have a limited jurisdiction to hear breach of contract claims, but the maximum that a tribunal can award in respect anyone claim or any number of claims relating to the same contract is £25,000.

Where an employee would have met the necessary service qualification to claim unfair dismissal, but for the fact that his employment was terminated prematurely by the employer's failure to follow a contractual disciplinary procedure, the EAT has held that damages awarded for wrongful dismissal can include a sum to compensate the employee for the loss of the right to complain of unfair dismissal (*Raspin v United News Shops* [1999] IRLR 9).

A breach of contract claim is brought by presenting an Originating Application to an employment tribunal within three months of the effective date of termination of the contract.

There is therefore now a dual procedure available to employees in bringing breach of contract claims. It may be that employees will still bring breach of contract claims in the county court as they will be entitled to their costs from the employer should they be successful, whereas they will not if the claim is in an employment tribunal.

12.13 MATERNITY RIGHTS

This is an extremely complex area of the law and it is possible to give here only an outline of the rights protecting pregnant employees. Not only is the law relating to statutory maternity leave and maternity pay relevant, but also the law relating to sex discrimination and equal pay. Furthermore, individual employees' own terms and conditions of employment may be more favourable than the statutory minimum protection.

12.13.1 Time off for ante-natal care

An employee who is pregnant and who, on the advice of a registered medical practitioner, registered midwife or registered health visitor, has made an appointment to attend at any place for the purpose of receiving antenatal care, has the right not to be unreasonably refused time off during her working hours to enable her to keep the appointment. The employee also has the right to be paid for that period of absence at the appropriate hourly rate. There is no minimum qualifying period for employees to attain this right.

An example where an employer can reasonably refuse to allow an employee time off to attend an ante-natal class could be in respect of a part-time employee who could be expected to attend when not at work. Where an employer has unreasonably refused an employee time off for ante-natal care or where he has failed to pay the employee the amount due to her while attending the ante-natal appointment, the employee may present a complaint to an industrial tribunal. If the complaint is well founded the tribunal will make a declaration to that effect and can order the employer to pay to the employee the amount of money which would have been due under the statutory provisions.

12.13.2 Maternity leave

All women expecting a baby have the right to 18 weeks' statutory maternity leave. This right applies to all women irrespective of their length of service or the number of hours they work each week. Furthermore, employees who have more than one year's continuous employment can delay their return to work for up to 29 weeks after the beginning of the week in which their baby was born.

During the 18-week maternity leave period all employment rights other than 'remuneration' must be preserved. There is no statutory definition of remuneration and its scope is uncertain, but it is obvious that it covers the normal wage, commission and bonus payments, if these are contractual.

To identify the maternity leave period the employer must have regard to two sets of rules governing both its start date and when it ends. The commencement of the maternity leave period is usually within the particular woman's control as it is the date on which she notifies her employer as the date she wishes her maternity leave to begin. This date must not be before the 11th week before the expected week of childbirth (EWC). A woman is not, however, free to choose the start date of her maternity leave where she is absent from work wholly or partly because of pregnancy or childbirth after the beginning of the sixth week before the EWC. In this instance the maternity leave period is triggered on the first day of absence.

Additional maternity leave

The rules as to extended or additional maternity leave are governed by the Maternity and Parental Leave etc Regs 1999 and the ERA, as amended by the Employment Relations Act 1999. Women who have at least one years' continuous service at the beginning of the 11th week before the EWC are entitled to take additional maternity leave. This gives them the right to return to work up to 29 weeks after the baby is born.

12.13.3 Notice requirements

To qualify for the basic maternity leave period of 18 weeks, the employee must:

(1) as required by the employer, produce a doctor's or midwife's certificate stating the expected week of confinement;

(2) notify the employer at least 21 days before her absence begins, or as soon as is reasonably practicable, that she is pregnant, and of her expected week of childbirth (or if it has occurred, the date when it occurred); and

(3) notify the employer of the date when she intends the maternity leave to begin or, where maternity leave has been triggered automatically, details of the event which caused it to begin (this information is to be given only if the employer requests).

In the case of additional maternity leave, the employee must:

(a) have continuous employment for at least one year immediately before the beginning of the 11th week before the expected week of the confinement, unless dismissed because of pregnancy before that time where, but for the dismissal, she would have been so employed;

(b) produce, if requested by the employer, a doctor's or midwife's certificate giving the expected week of confinement; and

(c) at least 21 days before the employee wishes to start her leave, notify the employer of her pregnancy; the expected week of confinement; and when she wishes to start her leave. There is no requirement for her to state that she wishes to take additional maternity leave, the presumption being that she will unless she notifies her intention to return early.

Where the employee has not been in touch to notify the date of birth, the employer may write to her not earlier than 21 days before the end of the ordinary maternity leave seeking confirmation of the date of birth and of her intention to return. The employee must respond within 21 days of receiving the request. The employer must then confirm the last possible date by which she must return. Where the employee fails to respond to the employer's request for confirmation within the time limit, the employer can take appropriate disciplinary action.

12.13.4 Compulsory maternity leave

An employee must not work during the period of 2 weeks beginning with the date on which the baby was born; nor must the employee permit her to work.

12.13.5 The right to return to work

An employee has the right:

(1) to return to work with her former employee at any time before the end of the period of 29 weeks beginning with the week in which the date of confinement falls; and

(2) on her return, to be employed on terms and conditions not less favourable than those which would have been applicable if she had not been absent; or

(3) if she is not able to return to work by reason of redundancy, to be offered alternative employment (where there is a suitable vacancy) under a new contract, involving suitable work on not substantially less favourable conditions.

12.13.6 Statutory maternity pay

Most women are entitled to statutory maternity pay during their maternity leave. This benefit is administered and paid directly to eligible employees by their employers.

Eligibility

To be eligible for statutory maternity pay an employee must:

(1) be pregnant and have reached, or have been confined before reaching, the commencement of the 11th week before the expected week of confinement.

(2) have 26 weeks' continuous service at the start of the qualifying week, ie the 15th week before the expected week of childbirth;

(3) have normal weekly earnings of at not less than the current lower earnings limit on which Class 1 NICs is payable. The current limit is £72 pw in the eight weeks preceding the 14th week before the expected week of confinement.

Period and rate of payment

SMP is payable for 26 weeks. The maternity pay period starts no earlier than 11 weeks before the expected week of confinement, or if a woman works beyond this then the week following the week in which she stops work. Where, however, a woman is absent from work wholly or partly because of pregnancy or confinement in the six weeks before her expected week of confinement, then the maternity pay period commences in the week on which that day falls.

For the first six weeks of the maternity pay period, statutory maternity pay is payable at 90% of the employee's normal weekly earnings. Thereafter, it is payable at the rate of £75.00 (£100 from April 2003).

Recovery of statutory maternity pay by the employer

An employer can recover up to 92% of the statutory maternity pay paid by making appropriate equivalent deductions from its NICs. A 'small employer', defined as one whose total NICs for the qualifying tax year do not exceed £40,000, may recover the full amount of statutory maternity pay and an additional sum equal to 4.5% of the statutory maternity pay paid for the tax year 2002–03. All forms of compensation are paid by making deductions from Class 1 NICs.

12.13.7 Maternity allowance

Maternity allowance is a state benefit payable to a pregnant woman who does not satisfy the eligibility criteria for statutory maternity pay. In order to qualify the pregnant woman must satisfy the following conditions:

- She must be pregnant at the start of the 11th week before the expected week of confinement or have given birth prior to that date.
- She must have been employed or self-employed for at least 26 out of the 66 weeks immediately before the expected week of confinement.

• She must have paid Class 1 or 2 NICs for at least 26 weeks of the 66 weeks immediately before the expected week of confinement.

Rate of allowance

For women with an expected week of confinement on or after 20 August 2000, maternity allowance was extended so that a woman with average earnings of £30 pw in any 13 weeks in the 66 weeks before the expected week of childbirth now qualifies. Earnings with more than one employment can be aggregated together for this purpose. From April 2002 onwards those earning at least £75 pw are entitled to the standard rate of maternity allowance, £75.00 pw. Those with average earnings between £30 and the lower earnings limit (£75 pw) receive maternity allowance at 90% of their average earnings (Welfare Reform and Pensions Act 1999, s 53).

Maternity allowance is not taxable and not treated as earnings for NICs purposes. A woman is entitled to a national insurance credit for each week that the allowance is payable.

12.13.8 Protection from dismissal

Under ERA, s 99, it is automatically unfair for an employer to dismiss any woman, irrespective of her hours of work or length of service, if the sole or principal reason for her dismissal is one of the following:

(1) That she is pregnant or is dismissed for any other reason connected with her pregnancy.

(2) She is dismissed at any time during her 14-week maternity leave period and the sole or principal reason for that dismissal is that she has given birth or is for any other reason connected with her having given birth.

(3) She is dismissed at the end of her maternity leave period and the sole or principal reason for her dismissal is that she was away from work during her maternity leave period, or that she had the benefit of her usual terms and conditions (excluding remuneration) during her maternity leave period.

(4) She is dismissed because she has given birth or for any other reason connected with her having given birth within four weeks of the end of her maternity leave period. The woman must submit a medical certificate during her maternity leave period which states that she will be incapable of work at the end of her maternity leave period by reason of ill health. Also at the date of the dismissal the incapability must continue and the certificate must remain current.

(5) The sole or principal reason for her dismissal is a requirement or recommendation to suspend her on health and safety grounds.

(6) She is made redundant during her maternity leave period and is not offered a suitable alternative available vacancy.

The new s 60 gives women greatly increased rights to protection from dismissal on the grounds of pregnancy or for a reason related to pregnancy. A claim under s 60 must be brought within three months of the dismissal or such other period as the tribunal considers reasonable if it was not reasonably practicable to bring the claim within three months.

12.13.9 The right to return to work

If at the end of a woman's extended maternity leave (ie up to 29 weeks after the week of the birth) an employer refuses to allow the woman to return to work there will be a deemed dismissal under ERA, s 96 on the date that she had notified her employer that she wished to return to work. The employer then has to establish that the reason why the woman was not permitted to return fell within one of the prima facie fair reasons for dismissal contained in s 98 of the Act. If the tribunal considers that the dismissal was for one of the maternity related reasons set out in the Act the dismissal is automatically unfair.

There are two situations in which a woman will in any event lose her right to return to work after extended maternity absence. These are:

(1) If her employer can show that it has fewer than six employees and it was not reasonably practicable for it to allow the woman back or to offer her suitable and appropriate alternative work.
(2) If the employer can show that it was not reasonably practicable for a reason other than redundancy to give her back her old job, and he offered her suitable and appropriate alternative work which she has either accepted or unreasonably refused.

It should be noted that the onus lies on the employer to show that there was no suitable and appropriate alternative work.

Where a woman is dismissed while pregnant, or where dismissal ends her maternity leave period, she is automatically entitled to receive written reasons for her dismissal, regardless of her hours of work or length of service (ERA, s 92(4)). No continuous employment is required in relation to this right.

12.13.10 Maternity protection and health and safety

Employers are under a general duty to take reasonable care for the health and safety of their employees. These duties are laid down both in common law and in statute; for a fuller discussion on an employer's health and safety obligations in general see Chapter 15. Employers should also make reference to guidelines issued by the HSE.

Under ERA, s 99, it is automatically unfair for an employee to be dismissed if the reason for doing so was a requirement or recommendation to suspend that employee on health and safety grounds, irrespective of the employee's hours or length of service. As a result of the implementation of the Pregnant Workers Directive by the Management of Health & Safety at Work (Amendment) Regs 1994, further stringent obligations are laid upon employers in relation to the health and safety of new or expectant mothers in their employment.

Under these amended regulations an employer, whose workforce includes women of child-bearing age, is under an obligation to carry out risk assessments in relation to that risk group. Where any risks are identified, an employer must take preventative or protective measures to avoid those risks. If these measures will not be effective in avoiding such risks, then the employer must alter the woman's working conditions or hours of work. Furthermore, if this alteration is not reasonable or still does not avoid the risks, then the employer must offer the woman any suitable alternative work which is available. If no alternative work is available, the woman must be suspended from work on full pay.

Where there is suitable alternative work available, and the employer fails to offer it to the affected employee, she has the right to bring a complaint to an employment tribunal. Such a claim must be brought within three months beginning with the first day of the suspension or if this was not reasonably practicable within such time as the tribunal considers reasonably practicable. Where the complaint is upheld the tribunal can award such compensation as it considers just and equitable. Where a woman is suspended on the grounds that there is no suitable alternative work and the employer fails to pay her her full remuneration during the suspension period, again she can bring a complaint to an industrial tribunal within three months, or such further period as the tribunal considers is reasonably practicable.

If a pregnant woman works nights and it is necessary for her to be moved off night work for health and safety reasons, the employer must ensure that this is done.

There are further specific regulations which place obligations upon employers in relation to pregnant workers. Employers are advised to contact their local Health & Safety Office for advice if they have any queries as to their obligations in this respect.

In *Day v T Pickles Farms* [1999] IRLR 217, the EAT confirmed that the duty to carry out a risk assessment under reg 13A arises as soon as a female of childbearing age enters the workforce, not just when an existing employee becomes pregnant or is breast-feeding. If this is not done at the start of employment, an employee may, depending on the facts of the case, be able to argue that she has been subjected to a detriment by the employer's failure in this respect. If an employee suffers such detriment, this could amount to unlawful direct discrimination under the SDA.

The EAT also held that the requirement to notify the employer in writing of the fact of pregnancy under the Management of Health and Safety at Work Regs could potentially be fulfilled by the employee providing the employer with a series of doctor's sick notes indicating the fact that she was pregnant. The employer would then have to prove that the doctor's certificates did not amount to written notification of pregnancy.

12.13.11 Interrelationship with sex discrimination law

Although the dismissal of a woman for pregnancy or for a pregnancy related reason is automatically unfair under ERA, s 99, a woman may also be able to obtain a remedy under the Sex Discrimination Act (SDA) where she is either refused employment or treated unfavourably as a result of her pregnancy.

As there is no statutory cap on the amount of compensation for sex discrimination, it may well be desirable to bring a claim under the SDA rather than under s 99 where the statutory limit on unfair dismissal compensation applies. *In Webb v EMO Air Cargo (No 2)* [1995] 4 All ER 577, the House of Lords held that the terms of the test of unlawful discrimination set out in the SDA were to be construed in accordance with the ruling of the ECJ on the Equal Treatment Directive as meaning that, in a case where a woman was engaged for an indefinite period, the fact that the reason why she should be temporarily unavailable for work at a time when, to her knowledge, her services would be particularly required, pregnancy was a circumstance relevant to her case, being a circumstance which could not be present in the case of the hypothetical man. It did not, however, follow that pregnancy would be a relevant circumstance in the situation where the woman was denied employment for a fixed period in the future during the whole of which her pregnancy would make her unavailable for work, nor in a situation where after engagement for such a period the discovery of her pregnancy led to the cancellation of the engagement.

12.14 PARENTAL LEAVE

The UK has adopted the Parental Leave Directive (96/34/EC) through the Employment Relations Act 1999 and the Maternity and Parental Leave Regs 1999. The Regulations add to the existing rights for natural mothers and give rights for the first time to fathers and adoptive parents. An employee must have been continuously employed for a period of not less than one year.

The parental rights are only in relation to unpaid leave. If an employee is entitled to paternity or parental leave under their terms and conditions of employment then the employee can choose the more generous option, but the statutory entitlement will be reduced pro rata. If, therefore, a company paternity scheme allows one week's paid leave to fathers then an employee can take that week as paid leave but will only be entitled to 12 weeks' parental leave under the Regulations.

12.14.1 Amount of leave

The basic entitlement is to 13 weeks' unpaid leave per child (therefore 26 weeks for twins). This increases to 18 weeks unpaid leave for a disabled child. The leave can be taken any time before the 5th birthday or the 5th anniversary of the placement of the child for adoption with the employee, with three exceptions:

(1) In the case of an adopted child, if the child's 18th birthday falls before the 5th anniversary of the placement then entitlement to parental leave ends on the 18th birthday.
(2) If the child (natural or adopted) is entitled to a disability living allowance then parental leave can be taken anytime up to the child's 18th birthday.
(3) If any leave requested by an employee is postponed by the employer in accordance with the Regulations to a date after entitlement would otherwise have expired, then that leave may still be taken.

Protection of employees on parental leave

An employee on parental leave is protected from suffering any detriment through the action or deliberate inaction of the employer (ERA, s 47C).

An employee can also claim automatic unfair dismissal if the reason for dismissal was connected with the employee taking parental leave.

An employee taking parental leave of less than four weeks is entitled to return to the same job. An employee taking parental leave of more than four weeks (in a single continuous period) is entitled to return to the same job or a similar job if it is not reasonably practicable to return to the original job. The alternative similar job must be suitable and appropriate to the employee's circumstances and on terms not less favourable than the original job.

Parental leave is included for the purposes of calculating continuous employment

12.14.2 Workforce agreements and default provisions

The specific provisions governing the parental leave scheme for a particular organisation can be contained in a workforce agreement or collective agreement. The requirements for the creation of a workforce agreement are set out in Sch 1 to the 1999 Regs. The agreement should cover:

- Conditions relating to providing evidence of entitlement
- Notice to be given by the employee
- Postponement of leave requested by an employee
- Minimum periods of leave
- Maximum annual leave.

Where there is no agreement in force, the default provisions contained in Sch 2 to the Regulations will apply.

12.14.3 Right to time off to deal with family emergencies

The Parental Leave Directive also included rights for employees to unpaid leave to deal with emergencies involving dependants. The ERA has been amended by the insertion of a new s 57A to give this right in the UK. An employee is entitled to take a reasonable amount of time off during working hours in order to take action necessary:

(1) to provide assistance on an occasion when a dependant falls ill, gives birth, or is injured or assaulted;
(2) to make arrangements for the provision of care for a dependant who is ill or injured;
(3) in consequence of the death of a dependant;
(4) because of the unexpected disruption or termination of arrangements for the care of a dependant;
(5) to deal with an incident which involves a child of the employee and which occurs unexpectedly in a period during which an educational establishment, which the child attends, is responsible for him.

There is no statutory right to payment for the time off and any payment is to be determined by the contract of employment.

12.14.4 Review of maternity and parental rights

The Government has undertaken a review of maternity and parental rights including publishing a green paper under the title Work and Parents: Competitiveness and Choice. The consultation period on the paper ended in March 2001 and in May 2001 the DTI issued three framework documents. These are:

(1) The simplified framework of maternity pay and leave.
(2) The framework for adoption leave.
(3) The framework for paternity leave.

The main points of the frameworks are as follows.

Simplified framework of maternity pay and leave

Under the framework to be effective from April 2003:

(1) All women will be entitled to 26 weeks ordinary maternity leave.
(2) Women who have been employed for 26 weeks at the notification week (which is 15 weeks before the expected week of childbirth) will be entitled to 26 weeks ordinary maternity leave with statutory maternity pay plus another 26 weeks unpaid additional maternity leave.

(3) Additional maternity leave starts immediately ordinary maternity leave ends, so there is no overlap (under the current system ordinary leave runs from when the employee stops work but additional leave runs from the date of birth so there is an apparent overlap).

(4) The qualification period date for maternity pay and additional maternity leave will be harmonised as the 15th week before the expected week of childbirth to be known as the notification week.

(5) Average earnings for the purposes of calculating maternity pay will be the average of the 26 weeks before the notification week.

(6) The notice an employee must give of the date for starting maternity leave will increase from three to four weeks.

(7) An employee will be assumed to be taking her full entitlement to leave unless and until she gives four weeks notice of her intention to return earlier. The employer will not be required to write to the employee asking for her expected date of return to work.

(8) The automatic triggering of the start of maternity through a maternity related illness will be restricted to four weeks before the expected week of childbirth (currently six weeks).

(9) Adoptive parents will be able to benefit from the same entitlements so that one parent (it can be either parent not necessarily the mother) can take leave and statutory pay on the same terms as a woman on maternity leave. The other parent will be entitled to pay and leave equivalent to the paternity entitlement to be introduced in April 2003.

Framework for adoptive leave

Under the framework to be effective from April 2003:

(1) One adopting parent in a couple will be entitled to leave equivalent to maternity leave with the same entitlements to pay and additional leave subject to the same qualifications.

(2) The other adopting parent will be entitled to leave equivalent to paternity leave with the same right to pay subject to the same qualifications.

(3) The adopting couple can choose which parent takes which type of leave.

(4) The adopting parents must give notice to their employers as soon as they have been approved for adoption with an indication of when the adoption will take place. This will have the effect of the notification week for maternity in calculating entitlement to pay.

(5) The letter from the adoption agency takes the place of the MAT B form.

(6) The leave element equivalent to maternity leave must start on the day the child is placed with the parents and the paternity element within two months of that date.

(7) The right applies to any child adopted under age 18 but if two or more siblings are adopted at the same time (whether twins or not) only one period of each type of leave is available.

(8) Step-family adoptions and adoptions by persons already acting as foster carers to the child are not covered by the right.

Framework for paternity leave

Under the framework to be effective from April 2003:

(1) The father of a newborn baby will be entitled to two weeks paid leave.
(2) The leave must be taken as a single block within two months after the date of birth.
(3) To qualify the employee must have been continuously employed by the employer for 26 weeks prior to the notification week and earning more than the lower NICs limit.
(4) Notice of the intention to take paternity leave must be given during the same notification week as for maternity leave (ie 15 weeks before the expected week of childbirth).
(5) If the notice states that the employee wishes to start the leave on the day of the birth then he may do so even if the birth is earlier or later than the expected date. If a specific date is given then this can only be changed by four weeks notice.

In each case any contractual entitlement which is more beneficial than the statutory requirement is deducted from the statutory requirement. For example if an employee is entitled to one week paternity leave on full pay under his contract of employment then the statutory requirement is reduced to one further week at the statutory rate of pay.

An employer is therefore free to give enhanced entitlements under the contract of employment over and above the statutory minimums and to place restrictions and qualifications on these enhancements. An example might be giving maternity pay at full pay (rather than 90% of pay) during part of the maternity leave period for women employed for over five years

12.15 STATUTORY SICK PAY (SSP)

Where an employee is absent from work due to sickness he may be entitled to:

(1) contractual sick pay as set out in his written statement of terms and conditions of employment;
(2) SSP.

There are numerous regulations governing this complex area, but the main provisions are contained in the Social Security Contributions and Benefits Act 1992 and the Statutory Sick Pay Act 1994.

12.15.1 Qualifications for statutory sick pay

The main requirements for an employee to be entitled to statutory sick pay are that he must:

(1) have four or more consecutive qualifying days of sickness;
(2) notify his absence to his employer;
(3) supply evidence of his incapacity for work. This is usually agreed between the employer and employee and normally involves a self-certification by the employee for periods of absence of four to seven days and thereafter a doctor's certificate.

The following groups are specifically excluded:

(1) Pensioners.
(2) Employees on short-term contracts of three months or less. (Employers should note, however, that a series of short-term contracts would be likely to create an entitlement.)
(3) Employees whose average earnings are lower than the point at which NICs become payable, ie the lower earnings level (£75 pw for 2002–03).
(4) Those receiving a sickness or invalidity benefit or maternity allowance in the 57 days preceding the first day of sickness.
(5) Employees who have not yet started work.
(6) Any employee affected by a trade dispute at his workplace, unless the employee was:
    (a) sick before the dispute began, or
    (b) able to prove that he was not participating in, or directly interested in the dispute.
(7) An employee who had already received 28 weeks of statutory sick pay and had stopped getting the sick pay less than eight weeks before.
(8) An employee who becomes sick while entitled to maternity allowance or statutory maternity pay, or falls sick with a pregnancy-related illness on or after the start of the sixth week before the week in which the baby is due.
(9) An employee who is in legal custody.

12.15.2 The period of payment

As mentioned above an employee is only entitled to statutory sick pay once he has been absent for four or more qualifying days. This period is known as a period of incapacity for work. Statutory sick pay is therefore payable on the fourth qualifying day and thereafter until either the employee has reached his full entitlement of 28 weeks' statutory sick pay or returns to work. An employer's liability to pay statutory sick pay ends once the employee has received 28 weeks' statutory sick pay during a three-year period.

Once the employee's entitlement to SSP has terminated, if the employee is still sick, he will then be entitled to incapacity benefit.

12.15.3 The amount payable

Employees who earn less than the lower weekly earnings limit for NI liability (£75 for 2002–03) are not entitled to statutory sick pay. There is one rate of SSP (£63.25 for 2002–03) payable to all qualifying employees.

An employer is entitled to recover any amount by which the payments of statutory sick pay made by him in any month exceed 13% of the amount of the employer's liabilities for NICs payments in respect of that month.

Where an employee also has a contractual right to sick pay, an employer is well advised to include within an employee's written statement of terms and conditions that he is only entitled to contractual sick pay as is appropriate to top up wages to the normal level of remuneration after payment of statutory sick pay or any sickness benefit received afterwards.

An employer is obliged to keep minimum information on record for statutory sick pay purposes for at least three years. Furthermore, when an employee leaves in certain circumstances an employer is under a duty to issue the employee with a 'leaver's statement'.

12.16 FURTHER STATUTORY PAYMENTS TO EMPLOYEES

12.17.1 Medical suspension payment

Where an employee is suspended from work on medical grounds in compliance with any law or regulation concerning workers' health and safety, that employee may be entitled to be paid by his employer during each week of the period of suspension for a maximum of 26 weeks (ERA, ss 64–70). To claim such a payment the employee must have been continuously employed for a period of one month ending with the day before that on which the suspension begins. It should be noted that an employee who is employed under a contract either:

(1) for a fixed term of three months or less, or
(2) made in contemplation of the performance of a specific task which is not expected to last for more than three months

is not entitled to a medical suspension payment unless he has been continuously employed for a period of more than three months ending with the day before the day on which the suspension begins. An employee is not entitled to such a payment where either he is absent from work because of illness during the period where such a payment would be due or is offered suitable alternative work which he unreasonably refused to perform.

If an employer fails to pay a medical suspension payment where due, an employee can bring a claim to an employment tribunal within three months of the date on which the claim for a payment was made, or within such further reasonable period, if the tribunal considers it not reasonably practicable to bring the claim within the three-month time limit. If the complaint is well founded, the tribunal will make an order for the employer to pay the employee the amount considered to be due.

12.16.2 Guarantee payments

Where an employee, on any day which in accordance with his contract of employment he is normally required to work, is not provided with work by his employer by reason of either:

(1) a diminution in the requirements of the employer's business for work of the kind which the employee is employed to do, or

(2) any other occurrence affecting the normal working of the employer's business in relation to work of the kind which the employee is employed to do,

that employee may, subject to certain exceptions, be entitled to a guarantee payment. The qualifying conditions are the same as those for a medical suspension payment (see 12.8). An employee is not entitled to a guarantee payment where the employer's failure to provide work is as a result of a strike, lock-out or other industrial action, not necessarily involving the employee concerned.

An employee is not entitled to a guarantee payment for a workless day if his employer has offered to provide alternative work for that day which is suitable in all the circumstances and the employee has unreasonably refused the offer or he does not comply with reasonable requirements imposed by his employer with a view to ensuring that his services are available.

Amount of payment

There are detailed rules governing the calculation of guarantee payments. At the present time, the maximum amount of any guarantee payment is £17.00 per day at the time of writing and such payment cannot exceed five days in any period of three months. This is periodically adjusted to reflect the movement in the retail price index.

Where an employer fails to make payment to an employee, that employee may present a claim to an employment tribunal. The time limit for presenting the claim is the same as for a medical suspension payment. If the tribunal finds the complaint well founded, it will order the employer to pay the amount of the guarantee payment to the employee that is found to be due.

12.17 ITEMISED PAY STATEMENTS

An employee is, subject to certain statutory exceptions, entitled to a written pay statement from his employer detailing:

(1) the gross amount of salary;
(2) the amount of any variable or fixed deductions from that amount and the reasons for which they are made; this can however be done under a separate statement of fixed deductions;
(3) the net amount of wages;
(4) where parts of the net amount are paid in different ways, the amount and method of each part payment.

If an employer does not provide an employee with a pay statement, the employee can apply to an employment tribunal and the tribunal can make a declaration concerning the particulars to be included in any statement. Furthermore, where the tribunal finds that any unnotified deductions have been made from the employee's pay, during the period of 13 weeks immediately preceding the date of the application made by the employee, the tribunal may award a sum not exceeding the amount of the unnotified deductions during that period.

An application can be brought at any time while employment continues or within three months after the termination of employment. The tribunal does not have the power to extend the time limit in any circumstances.

12.18 WAGES: PAYMENT AND DEDUCTIONS

The payment of wages is governed by an individual's contract of employment. If there is no express term governing how wages are to be paid, then payment is determined by an implied term and such implied term is likely to be that which is customary for the payment of wages in a particular industry.

12.18.1 Deduction from wages

Under ERA, s 13, an employer is not entitled to deduct sums from an employee's wages unless either:

(1) such deduction is required or permitted by a statutory or contractual provision; or
(2) the worker has given his prior written consent to the deduction.

Therefore, if in certain circumstances an employer wishes to make deductions from an employee's wages, the right for him to do so should, for the sake of clarity, be in writing and contained within the contract, a copy of which should be given to the employee.

It is important to note that the provisions of the Act apply not only to employees, but also to persons working under a contract for services. The following deductions are excluded from the operation of the provisions:

(1) deductions made to reimburse an employer for any overpayment of wages or expenses;
(2) deductions made pursuant to any statutory disciplinary proceedings;
(3) statutory payments due to a public authority;
(4) sums payable to third parties, made either pursuant to a contractual term to which the worker has agreed in writing or to which he has otherwise given his previous written agreement or consent (the most common example of this would be trade union dues);
(5) deductions made as a result of participation in a strike or other industrial action;
(6) deductions made for the purpose of satisfying a court or tribunal order for the payment of an amount by a worker to his employer; this requires the worker's prior written agreement or consent.

The definition of wages for ERA purposes includes all sums payable to a worker in connection with his employment including any fees, bonuses, commission and holiday pay or other emoluments referable to his employment.

There are however a number of payments that are specifically excluded from the definition of wages and these include advances under loan agreements or by way of an advance of wages; payments for expenses incurred in carrying out employment; payments by way of pension, allowance or gratuity in connection with the worker's retirement or as compensation for loss of office; any payment in relation to the worker's redundancy; or any payment otherwise than in the worker's capacity as a worker.

12.18.2 Retail workers

Special rules regarding wage deductions apply to retail workers. The employer of such a worker cannot deduct wages for cash shortages or stock deficiencies that amount to more than one-tenth of the worker's gross wages payable on a particular pay day. An employer must make any deduction below that limit not more than 12 months after the date on which he discovered the shortage or deficiency or ought reasonably to have discovered it.

The employer of a retail worker cannot receive any payment from the worker on account of a cash shortage or stock deficiency unless he has:

(1) notified the worker in writing of his total liability in respect of that shortage or deficiency, and
(2) made a demand for payment which is both in writing and on a pay day.

The demand must be made not earlier than the first pay day after the date of the written notification and not later than 12 months after the date when the employer discovered the shortage or deficiency or ought reasonably to have done so. As stated above, the amount demanded must not exceed one-tenth of the worker's gross wages payable on the particular pay day.

The restriction of deductions to one-tenth of gross wages does not apply to deductions from a final wages payment.

12.18.3 Worker's remedy for unlawful deduction

The worker's remedy is by way of complaint to an employment tribunal. The complaint must be brought within three months of the date of the deduction, or within such further period if it was not reasonably practicable for the complaint to be brought within the time limit. If the tribunal finds that the complaint is well founded, a declaration is made to that effect and the employer is ordered to repay to the worker the amount of the deduction. It is important for employers to note that where sums have been wrongfully deducted and they have been ordered by a tribunal to repay such sums to an employee, the employer cannot at a later stage seek to recover those same sums by lawful means, even if the sums were properly owing to the employer. It is therefore important for employers to ensure that they deduct money correctly on the first occasion to ensure that any sums owing to them will be recovered.

12.19 THE MINIMUM WAGE

The provisions as to the minimum wage are governed by the National Minimum Wage Act 1998 and the National Minimum Wage Regs 1999. A person qualifies for the national minimum wage if they are an individual who:

(1) is a worker;
(2) is working or ordinarily works in the UK under their contract subject to condition (3) below being satisfied, such a worker will be entitled to the NMW when temporarily working outside the UK; and
(3) has attained age 18.

The coverage of the 1998 Act extends beyond an employee and also covers a worker who has entered into, works or has worked under a contract, whether express or implied, whereby the worker undertakes to do or perform personally any work or services for another party to the contract whose status is not by virtue of the contract that of a client or customer of any profession or business undertaking carried on by the worker. The 1998 Act may cover agency workers, homeworkers, teleworkers, and casual and temporary workers, but will not cover self-employed persons.

A worker's length of employment or the country in which his employer is based does not affect his entitlement to the national minimum wage.

A worker who has not yet reached age 18 does not qualify for the national minimum wage. For workers over 18, there are at the time of writing three different rates of the national minimum wage: £4.20; or £3.60 for workers aged 18–21 and for accredited trainees.

An employer must keep records that show that a worker is paid at least the national minimum wage. These records must be included in one document and may be computerised.

12.20 SEX AND RACE DISCRIMINATION

Discrimination on the grounds of sex or marital status is made unlawful by the Sex Discrimination Acts 1975 and 1986; discrimination on racial grounds is unlawful under the Race Relations Act (RRA) 1976. These Acts make discrimination unlawful in every stage of employment, from recruitment to dismissal. Furthermore, the Acts apply to self-employed workers as well as employees. (Disability discrimination is dealt with at 12.21.)

The scope of the 1975 Act has been extended by the Sex Discrimination (Gender Reassignment) Regs 1999. By virtue of these Regulations, s 2A of the 1975 Act makes it unlawful to discriminate against a person and treat him or her less favourably than others on the grounds that he or she intends to undergo, is undergoing or has undergone gender reassignment (ie sex change). A 'genuine occupational qualification' defence applies specifically to such cases. In *Smith v Gardner Merchant* [1998] 3 All ER 852, CA, it was held that, for the purposes of the 1975 Act, there was a difference between discrimination on the ground of sex and discrimination on the ground of sexual orientation, and a person's orientation was not an aspect of his or her sex. It was still possible, however, for discrimination based on a man's homosexuality to be discrimination against him as a man if the same would not have been directed against a homosexual woman. The EAT, however, declined to follow this ruling in *MacDonald v Ministry of Defence* [2001] 1 All ER 620.

M, an officer in the Royal Air Force, was required to resign after declaring his homosexuality to an officer conducting a vetting interview. Those declarations led to his compulsory resignation. He subsequently brought proceedings under the SDA 1975 for unlawful discrimination on grounds of sex in respect of his dismissal (the termination claim) and intrusive questioning by the vetting officer (the sexual harassment claim). The employment tribunal dismissed those proceedings, holding, on the basis of decisions by the English courts, that the word 'sex' in the 1975 Act was concerned with gender rather than sexual orientation, that accordingly the reason for the termination of M's employment fell outside the discrimination envisaged by the 1975 Act, that a female homosexual was the correct comparator in a claim for sexual harassment brought by a male homosexual and that the vetting officer would have treated a female homosexual no differently than M. On his appeal to the EAT (which was heard before the implementation of the Human Rights Act 1998), M relied on Art 14a of the European Convention for the Protection of Human Rights and Fundamental Freedoms 1950 which protected the enjoyment of convention rights and freedoms from discrimination on various grounds including 'sex'. The European Court of Human Rights had construed that word as applying, in Art 14, to sexual orientation as well as gender (for Art 14, see below).

It was held that, for the purposes of the 1975 Act, the word 'sex' included sexual orientation, and accordingly discrimination on the grounds of such orientation fell within the scope of the Act. The word 'sex' could mean 'gender' or could refer to homosexuality in both men and women. There was therefore an ambiguity on the face of the record, and that ambiguity would be resolved, on established common law principles, by construing the 1975 Act in conformity with the wider definition given to the word 'sex' under art 14 of the convention. The EAT went on to say that, if comparators were relevant in respect of the termination claim, the issue was not as between a male and female, but rather the true comparator was between a male or female homosexual and a female or male heterosexual in order to determine not whether one homosexual was being treated less favourably than another, but whether homosexuals of either gender were being treated, in the context, less favourably than heterosexuals of the opposite gender. Similarly, in a sexual harassment claim, comparisons with other homosexuals were irrelevant.

The distinction was between how the employer treated a homosexual, whether male or female, on the one hand, and a heterosexual, whether female or male, on the other. Accordingly, in the case of a male, it was necessary to look for a female heterosexual comparator. The lower court had misdirected itself and the appeal was allowed.

Article 14 of the Convention provides:

> 'The enjoyment of the rights and freedoms set forth in this Convention shall be secured without discrimination on any ground such as sex . . . or other status.'

12.20.1 Recruitment

Discrimination can occur in recruitment in a number of ways – either in the arrangements that an employer makes for determining who should be offered employment (ie job specifications), or in the terms on which an employer offers employment, or by the employer directly refusing or omitting to offer employment. For example, a question at interview to a female employee as to whether she has any plans to start a family could amount to sex discrimination.

It is important for employers to ensure that any of their staff who are involved in conducting job interviews should be aware of the potential pitfalls. The Equal Opportunities Commission has issued a Code of Practice for the elimination of discrimination on the grounds of sex and marriage through the promotion of equality of opportunity in employment. In recruitment situations, it suggests that the following considerations should be borne in mind:

(1) Applications from both men and women should be processed in the same way.
(2) There should not be separate lists of male and female applicants, or those that are married and those that are single.
(3) Any questions asked at interview should relate to the requirements of the job.
(4) Questions about plans for marriage or family intentions are liable to be interpreted as discriminatory.
(5) There should be proper training of staff involved in conducting interviews so that potential discriminatory questions can be avoided.
(6) Records should be kept showing the reasons why particular applicants were or were not appointed. Such records could prove to be important evidence if queries ever arose.

Once employment has commenced, discrimination can occur in a number of ways, either in the terms of the employment afforded to an employee or the denial or limited provision afforded to an employee regarding access to promotional opportunities, training facilities or any other benefits or by subjecting a person to any detriment, or by dismissing them.

12.20.2 Types of discrimination

Discrimination can occur in three ways: directly, indirectly, or by victimisation. In ascertaining whether there has been discrimination, the position of the person alleging discrimination is compared with someone of similar ability and qualifications in a similar situation. In all circumstances 'like will be compared with like'.

Direct discrimination

Direct discrimination occurs where a person is treated less favourably than another on the grounds of sex, marital status or racial grounds. It is important to note that the employer's intentions are irrelevant. Even if, therefore, the employer feels that he is acting in the best interests of the person concerned, if that person is treated less favourably by the employer, then there is direct discrimination. The test is simply one of whether the treatment was less favourable. In *R v Birmingham City Council, ex p EOC* [1989] IRLR 173, it was held that denying girls the same number of places in selective secondary education as boys amounted to direct discrimination. It was not necessary to show that selective education was more desirable than non-selective education.

In *Anyanwu v South Bank Student* Union [2001] 2 All ER 353, the complainants, who were of black African origin, were students at, and members of, the respondent university. They were engaged to serve as full-time salaried officers of the university's student union for a one-year term beginning on 1 August 1995. In that capacity, they were trustees of the funds of the student union. The university raised questions about their conduct as trustees, and instituted disciplinary proceedings. After initially suspending them, the university expelled the complainants by letters dated 29 March 1996. By those letters, the complainants were forbidden from entering any university building, including the student union. That prohibition made it impossible for the complainants to perform their duties as employees of the union, and by letters of 2 April 1996 the union treated their employment contracts as at an end. The complainants sought to challenge their suspension and expulsion in judicial review proceedings, but were refused permission to apply. They also brought complaints of unlawful racial discrimination against the student union and the university, relying on their suspension, subsequent expulsion and the termination of their employment. At a preliminary industrial tribunal hearing, during which the complainants clarified their case, the university, relying on the earlier judicial review proceedings, applied for the proceedings against it to be struck out on the ground of res judicata. The tribunal granted that application, but the EAT reversed that decision. On the university's appeal, the Court of Appeal raised the issue whether the allegations against the university could, in any event, fall within RRA, s 33(i), which provided that a person who knowingly 'aids' another person to do an act made unlawful by the 1976 Act was to be treated for the purposes of that Act as himself doing an unlawful act of the like description. By a majority, the court held that the word 'aids' in s 33(1) contemplated a 'primary actor', who was a 'free agent' in the matter, setting out to do an act or achieve a result, and a secondary party helping him to do it. The court further concluded that the university was the 'prime mover', and that accordingly it had not aided the student union to dismiss the complainants, even though it might well be said that it had brought about the dismissals. Accordingly, the university's appeal was allowed, and the complainants appealed to the House of Lords.

It was held that the word 'aids' in s 33(1) was a familiar word in everyday use and bore no technical or special meaning in the context of that provision. A person aided another if he helped or assisted him. He did so whether his help was substantial and productive or whether it was not, provided the help was not so insignificant as to be negligible. While any gloss on the clear statutory language was better avoided, the subsection pointed towards a relationship of co-operation or collaboration; it did not matter who instigated or initiated the relationship. It was plain that, depending on the facts, a party who aided another to do an unlawful act might also procure or induce that other to do it. The expressions 'procure' and 'induce', however, were found in other sections of the 1976 Act, not in s 33, and were differently enforced; they meant something different from 'aids' and there was no warrant for interpreting 'aids' as comprising those other expressions. It was not helpful to introduce the concepts of 'free agents' and 'prime movers', which could only distract from the essentially simple test under s 33(1). Accordingly, the Court of Appeal had erred in its construction of that provision, but it was still necessary to consider whether the claims against the university could fall within s 33(1) as correctly construed.

The House of Lords also said that it was important not to strike out discrimination claims as an abuse of process except in the most obvious cases. Such cases were generally fact-sensitive, and their proper determination was always vital in the UK's pluralistic society. In the field of discrimination, perhaps more than any other, the bias in favour of a claim being examined on the merits or demerits of its particular facts was a matter of high public interest. In the instant case, the Court of Appeal, perhaps because of its concentration on the 'prime mover' and 'free agent' issues, had not considered the complainants' case as amplified and clarified at the preliminary hearing in the industrial tribunal. Fairly considered, the complainants' allegations raised an arguable case under s 33(1) against the university, and it would be wrong to strike it out. Accordingly, the appeal would be allowed and the matter remitted to an employment tribunal.

Indirect discrimination

Indirect discrimination occurs where an employer applies a requirement or condition which applies equally to all persons, but:

(1) the proportion of women, married persons or persons of a particular race who can comply with that condition is considerably smaller than the proportion of men, unmarried persons or persons not within that race; and

(2) the employer cannot show that condition to be justifiable irrespective of the sex, marital status or race of the person to whom it is applied; and

(3) the requirement is to that person's detriment because he or she cannot comply with it.

In considering whether an employer has indirectly discriminated against an employee, it is necessary to consider carefully the different concepts involved in the above definition of indirect discrimination.

First, a requirement or condition imposed by the employer must operate as a bar preventing the employee concerned from obtaining what is sought. For example, in *Home Office v Holmes* [1984] IRLR 299 an obligation on an employee to work full time was held to be a requirement for the purposes of the definition of indirect discrimination.

Secondly, when deciding whether the requirement or condition has had a disproportionate impact on one particular sex or racial group, it is necessary to define the appropriate pool for comparing members of one sex or racial group with members of the other sex or another racial group. The choice of the appropriate pool for comparison is a question of fact for an employment tribunal and will turn on the particular circumstances of each case.

In *Jones v University of Manchester* [1993] IRLR 218, however, the Court of Appeal indicated that any pool for comparison should be defined broadly, so as to cover all men and women to whom the employer applied or would apply the requirement.

In deciding whether a particular employee 'can comply' with a requirement or condition, the question is not whether the employee is physically able to comply but whether he can in practice comply, having regard to custom and usual behaviour. For example, in *Mandla v Lee* [1983] IRLR 209 the House of Lords rejected an argument that Sikh employees could comply with a prohibition on wearing turbans, as in accordance with custom and cultural conditions they could not comply, although theoretically they could have done.

Thirdly, the requirement or condition must be shown to operate to the particular employee's detriment because he cannot comply with it. This is an objective test and it would be sufficient for the employee concerned to show that he could not comply with the requirement or condition at the time when his claim arises.

Even when the above requirements are satisfied, an employer may still avoid liability for indirect discrimination if it can show that the requirement or condition was justifiable irrespective of sex or race.

Justifiability

The question of whether a particular discriminatory condition is justifiable depends upon an objective test. The correct approach was stated by the ECJ in *Bilka-Kaujhaus GmbH v Weber van Hartz* [1987] ICR 110. The employer in order to justify a discriminatory practice must put forward objective economic grounds relating to the management of the business.

The practice must also be necessary and in proportion to the objectives pursued by the employer. It is a matter for determination by an employment tribunal on the facts of each case when striking a balance between the requirement's discriminatory effect and what are the employer's reasonable needs. For example, in *Singh v Rowntree Mackintosh* [1979] ICR 554, the employer imposed the rule that none of his employees could have beards. This condition effectively excluded Sikhs from employment at the company and Mr Singh complained of indirect discrimination. The tribunal held that indeed the condition was discriminatory, but that it was justifiable on the grounds of hygiene.

Two examples where an employer has been held to indirectly discriminate against an employee are as follows:

(1) A refusal by an employer to allow a request from an employee returning from maternity leave to work on a part-time basis after the birth of

her baby amounted to indirect sex discrimination, even though the employee had worked on a full-time basis prior to maternity leave. The employer could not justify the requirement of full-time work as it needed only to have made a relatively minor adjustment within the organisation of its department to accommodate the employee's request for part-time work (*Guthrie v Royal Bank of Scotland* (Case No 31796/86), 10 March 1987).

(2) A blanket mobility clause imposed on all staff may amount to indirect sex discrimination as it is likely to have a disproportionate adverse effect on women. This is because women tend to earn less than their husbands and a higher proportion of women than men would find it impossible to relocate as their husbands, the main breadwinners, could not realistically give up their jobs (*Meade-Hill & The National Union of Civil and Public Servants v The British Council* (1995) *The Times*, 7 April).

Victimisation

It is also unlawful for an employer to treat any person less favourably than another due to the fact that that person brings proceedings, gives evidence or information or takes or threatens to take any action, or makes any allegation concerning his employer with reference to either the SDA, the Disability Discrimination Act (see 12.21), the RRA or the Equal Pay Act 1970.

In *Khan v Chief Constable of West Yorkshire Police* [2002] 4 All ER 834, the facts were as follows. K, a detective sergeant of Indian origin, was a long-serving member of the West Yorkshire police force. Over the years, he made a number of unsuccessful applications for promotion to the rank of inspector. Following the last such rebuff, K brought industrial tribunal proceedings for racial discrimination against the appellant chief constable, alleging that he had been treated less favourably, on grounds of race, than other applicants contrary to the RRA 1976.

While the proceedings were pending, K applied to another police force for an inspector's post. That force asked the West Yorkshire police for a reference.

Such a reference would normally have been given, but the force's solicitor advised the chief constable that it would be inappropriate to provide a reference for K because the pending litigation raised issues that would be relevant to the reference. Acting on that advice, the West Yorkshire police informed the other force that the chief constable was unable to comment on K's application for fear of prejudicing his position in the discrimination proceedings. K subsequently amended his claim to add a claim under s 2(1)(a) of the 1976 Act for discrimination by way of victimisation, based on the refusal to provide a reference. Under s 2(1)(a), a person (the discriminator) discriminated against another person (the person victimised) in any circumstances relevant for the purposes of any provision of the Act if he treated the person victimised less favourably than in those circumstances he treated or would have treated other persons, and did so 'by reason that' the person victimised had brought proceedings against the discriminator under the Act. K's claim for direct discrimination failed, but his claim for victimisation succeeded. The chief constable's appeal was dismissed by the EAT. That decision was in turn affirmed by the Court of Appeal which held that K had been treated less favourably than other employees for whom a reference had been sought, and that the less favourable treatment had been by reason of his having performed an act protected by s 2(1) of the 1976 Act, namely the bringing of discrimination proceedings. The chief constable appealed to the House of Lords.

Upholding the appeal, the House of Lords said that where an employer, acting honestly and reasonably, took steps to preserve his position in pending proceedings for racial discrimination, those steps would not have been taken 'by reason that' the proceedings had been commenced, and accordingly they would not constitute discrimination by way of victimisation within the meaning of s 2(1)(a) of the 1976 Act. Such a conclusion accorded with the spirit and purpose of the Act. Moreover, the statute accommodated that approach without any straining of language. An employer who conducted himself in that way was not doing so because of the fact that the complainant had brought discrimination proceedings. He was doing so because, currently and temporarily, he needed to take steps to preserve his position in the outstanding proceedings, ie the reason for the employer's action was the existence of the proceedings, not their commencement. The act protected by s 2(1)(a) could not have been intended to prejudice an employer's proper conduct of his defence, so long as he acted honestly and reasonably. Acting within that limit, he could not be regarded as discriminating by way of victimisation against the employee who brought the proceedings. In the instant case, K had been treated less favourably than other employees since the West Yorkshire police ordinarily provided references for members of the force who were seeking new employment. It was, however, necessary to look further than that. The industrial tribunal had failed to do so, and had therefore fallen into error.

12.20.3 Genuine occupational qualification

An employer also has a defence to an allegation of sex or race discrimination where he can show that the discrimination is as a result of a genuine occupational qualification. If, therefore, the defence can be established, an employer can discriminate in relation to advertisements, interviewing procedures and in job offers. Once the employment relationship has been established, again if the defence is available, an employer can refuse individual opportunities for promotion, training or transfer. In the context of sex discrimination, a genuine occupational qualification can be established where eg the essential nature of the job calls for a man for reasons of physiology. This does not relate to physical strength or stamina but would eg apply in the case of an employer seeking male models or in the case of theatrical performances, for reasons of authenticity, male actors. It can also be a genuine occupational qualification where the need for the job to be held by a man is important in order to preserve decency or privacy. In *Etam v Rowan* [1989] IRLR 150, where a man applied for a shop assistant's job in a ladies fashion shop, the EAT decided that it was not appropriate to apply the decency/privacy general occupational qualification because an adequate number of female employees was already employed to deal with female customers in the changing rooms. The Tribunal judged that the male applicant could have carried out the bulk of the job, whilst attending to customers in the changing rooms could be done without any difficulty by one of the female assistants

In the context of race discrimination, an example of a genuine occupational qualification would be where for reasons of authenticity an employer may require members of only one race (eg Indian waiters in an Indian restaurant).

12.20.4 Liability for discriminatory acts

Both the individual concerned and his employer are liable for discriminatory acts carried out by an employee during the course of his employment, whether or not those acts are done with the employer's knowledge or approval. An employer does, however, have a defence to vicarious liability where he can show that he has taken such steps as were reasonably practicable to prevent an employee from doing such acts during the course of his employment. It is therefore important for an employer to be seen to be proactive in this field. If allegations of discriminatory acts are brought to his attention he should deal with these immediately.

12.20.5 Remedies

An individual who is alleging sex or race discrimination can bring a complaint to an employment tribunal. Such complaint must be brought within three months of the discriminatory act. A tribunal can, however, consider an application out of time if it considers that it is just and equitable to do so.

If the complaint is well founded, the tribunal can make a declaration declaring the complainant's and the employer's rights in relation to the act of discrimination which has been complained about. For example, the declaration can state that certain training facilities should be made available to an employee. Furthermore, an award of compensation can be made. The amount of compensation awarded may include a sum for injury to feelings which results from the employee's knowledge that it was a discriminatory act which brought about the employer's action.

By virtue of the Industrial Tribunals (Interest on Awards in Discrimination Cases) Regs 1996, there is no limit on the award that can be made in discrimination cases, and a tribunal power also has the power to award interest on compensation. Interest is awarded from the date of discrimination.

Finally, a tribunal can make a recommendation that the employer within a specified period of time takes such action as appears to be practicable for the purpose of obviating or reducing the adverse effect on the complainant of any act of discrimination to which the complaint relates.

12.20.6 Roles of the EOC and CRE

The Equal Opportunities Commission and the Commission for Racial Equality are both extremely active in the fields of sex and race discrimination. They have the power to carry out formal investigations and as a result of those investigations serve non-discrimination orders on employers. Such an order is made if a Commission is satisfied that an employer has committed or is committing a discriminatory act or maintaining a discriminatory practice. The terms of the non-discrimination notice require the employer to cease committing such acts and institute any necessary changes in any of its practices to avoid any discriminatory effects. If this order is not complied with, it can be enforced in a county court. The Commissions also adopt a proactive role in advising individuals about their rights in relation to discriminatory matters. Where appropriate, they can support individuals in claims against an employer.

Where a person has brought a claim for discrimination to an employment tribunal, they can serve on the employer concerned a questionnaire that has been compiled by the Commissions. If then an employer does not answer the questions on the questionnaire or provides inadequate answers, its replies can be taken into account in the tribunal proceedings and a tribunal has the discretion to draw adverse inferences from them.

The field of potential discriminatory acts is very wide and extends from recruitment right through training, promotion, transfer, redundancy selection procedures through to dismissal. In all cases an employer should consider carefully whether action that it proposes to take could have a potential discriminatory effect. Legal advice is important in this area and should certainly be sought, for instance before the placing of job advertisements in local or national newspapers.

12.21 DISCRIMINATION ON GROUNDS OF DISABILITY

The Disability Discrimination Act 1995 (DDA) made it unlawful for employers (with certain exceptions (see 12.21.5)) to discriminate against those with disabilities. The key elements of the Act that are relevant to employers are that:

(a) it is now unlawful to discriminate against current or prospective employees with disabilities because of a reason relating to that disability; and

(b) the Act obliges employers to make reasonable adjustments if their employment arrangements or premises place the disabled employee or disabled applicant at a substantial disadvantage.

As with the SDA and RRA, there is no qualifying period of employment before a claim may be presented and that the tribunals are able to award unlimited compensation for discrimination.

12.21.1 Definition of 'disability'

The definition of 'disability' is particularly wide and goes beyond those who are registered as disabled to include all persons who have a 'physical or mental impairment which has a substantial and long-term adverse effect on [that person's] ability to carry out normal day-to-day activities'. The meaning of 'mental' or 'physical' impairment is intentionally not specifically defined so that the Act is able to potentially cover all physical and mental impairments. Certain conditions are, however, excluded from the Act by virtue of reg 4 of the Disability Discrimination (Meaning of Disability) Regs 1996. Excluded conditions include kleptomania, pyromania, a tendency to physical or sexual abuse of other persons, exhibitionism, voyeurism, hay fever and addiction to alcohol, nicotine or other drugs.

To be a 'substantial and long-term condition', it must either:

(a) have lasted at least 12 months;
(b) be likely to last at least 12 months; or
(c) be likely to last for the rest of the lifetime of that person.

To affect normal day-to-day activities the condition must affect at least one of the following activities:

- Mobility
- Manual dexterity
- Physical co-ordination
- Continence
- Ability to lift, carry or otherwise move everyday objects.
- Speech, hearing and sight.
- Memory or ability to concentrate, learn or understand perception of the risk of physical danger.
- Severe disfigurement is also treated as having a substantial and long-term adverse effect on the person's ability to carry out normal day-to-day activities.

12.21.2 Types of discrimination

Unlike the Sex Discrimination and Race Relations Acts, which cover three types of discrimination (direct, indirect and victimisation) the DDA only defines discrimination as (1) direct discrimination (s 5) and (2) victimisation (s 55).

It was held in *Clark v TDG* [1999] 2 All ER 977 that, having regard to the provisions of the Act, a disabled person was treated less favourably than others if the reason for the treatment did not or would not apply to others. Since that test was not based on the fact of disability, a tribunal was not required to compare the treatment of the disabled person and others in similar circumstances, but had simply to identify others to whom the reason for the treatment did not or would not apply.

Direct discrimination is defined in a similar way to that of the other Acts, as is victimisation (see 12.20.2). The 1995 Act, however, has also introduced a new obligation on an employer that is specific to disability discrimination. This is the employer's duty to make reasonable adjustments in order to accommodate the disabled person (s 6).

12.21.3 Employer's duty to make reasonable adjustments

Under DDA, s 6(1) the employer is required to take such steps as are reasonable in all the circumstances to prevent the disabled person from being placed at a substantial disadvantage compared to others. Examples of steps that an employer would be expected to take are eg altering premises (such as providing ramps and widening doorways for wheelchair access), altering working hours or allocating certain duties to another person. The list of steps that an employer may be expected to take is not exhaustive but an employer is only expected to make such adjustments that are reasonable in the circumstances.

In determining whether an action is reasonable in the circumstances, s 6(4) provides that an employer should consider:

A. The extent to which taking the step would prevent the effect in question;

B. The extent to which it is practicable for the employer to take the step;

C. The financial and other costs which would be incurred by the employer in taking the step and the extent to which taking it would disrupt any of its activities;

D. The extent of the employer's financial or other resources;

E. The availability to the employer of financial or other assistance with respect to taking the step.

The duty to make reasonable adjustments does not mean an employer has to act in anticipation of employing persons with disabilities. The employer only has to make the adjustments if he employs or is considering employing a disabled person.

12.21.4 Remedies

The remedies under the 1995 are similar to those available for sex and race discrimination claims (see 12.20.5).

12.21.5 Exemptions

Certain employers are exempt from the requirements of the Act. The main exemption is for employers who employ less than 15 people. Section 68(1) of the DDA, however, does classify apprentices and self-employed workers as employees.

Partners are also outside the Act. Although employees of a partnership that has more than 15 employees will be protected by the Act, the partners themselves are not given such protection. Other exemptions include police officers, persons working in the armed forces, fire-fighters and prison officers.

12.21.6 The Disability Code

The Disability Code explains in more detail the operation of the Act, gives practical examples of the circumstances which employers may find themselves in, and the actions they must take in order to avoid liability under the Act. Section 51 provides that the Code does not impose specific legal duties, but it is admissible as evidence in any proceedings under the Act, and the tribunal or court must take it into account where it is relevant in deciding a question arising in proceedings.

12.21.7 The Disability Commission

The Disability Rights Commission Act 1999 establishes a Disability Rights Commission. Its functions are broadly comparable to those of the Equal Opportunities Commission and the Commission for Racial Equality. Its general functions are to:

- work towards the equalisation of opportunities for disabled persons;
- take such steps as it considers appropriate with a view to encouraging good practice in the treatment of disabled persons; and
- keep under review the working of the 1995 Act.

In addition to its general functions, the Commission has a number of specific functions. These include undertaking formal investigations; issuing non-discrimination notices; entering into agreements in lieu of enforcement action; providing assistance in relation to proceedings under the Act; facilitating conciliation in relation to disputes under the Act; and the preparation and issue of codes of practice.

12.21.8 **Remedies**

A complaint may be made to an Employment Tribunal. It must be brought before the end of three months beginning with the act complained of, though the Tribunal can extend the time limit if it considers it just and equitable. The Tribunal may make such of the following orders as it considers just and equitable:

(a) a declaration of the complainant's rights;
(b) ordering the respondent to pay compensation;
(c) recommending that the respondent take such actions as the Tribunal thinks are reasonable for the purposes of obviating or reducing the adverse effect on the complainant in relation to any matter to which the complaint relates.

Compensation may be awarded, including compensation for injured feelings. There is no limit on the compensation.

12.22 **EQUAL PAY**

The Equal Pay Act 1970, as amended, sets out the domestic provisions underpinning a woman's right to equal pay to that of a man (or vice versa) for like work or work rated as equivalent or work of equal value. EU law is also very important in this area, especially art 141 of the EC Treaty which sets out the principle that men and women are entitled to equal pay for equal work. Article 141 can be enforced directly by individuals in the UK courts.

There is also the Equal Pay Directive 1975 (75/117/EEC) which can be used as an aid in construing domestic law, where this falls short of EC law requirements. The Directive prohibits discrimination between men and women when it comes to levels of pay for the same work or work of equal value.

It is important to note that, in line with the Sex Discrimination and Race Relation Acts, the Equal Pay Act 1970 applies to the self-employed as well as employees.

All complaints regarding discrimination in contractual pay or benefits should be brought under the Equal Pay Act and not the SDA.

The Equal Pay Act deems an equality clause to be included in a woman's contract, where it is not incorporated expressly. Such a clause operates so that if a term in a woman's contract is less favourable to her than a similar term in a man's contract, then the appropriate term in the woman's contract is modified so as to make it as favourable as the term in the man's contract. Again, if a woman's contract does not include a beneficial term which is within a man's contract, then again the woman's contract is modified to include that term. The equality clause applies not only to pay but to all terms and conditions of employment. It applies equally to men.

The EOC has issued a Code of Practice on Equal Pay.

The Act has been extended to workers posted to Great Britain by an undertaking established in an EU member state under certain circumstances to perform at least part of their work in Great Britain, even if their work is performed mainly outside Great Britain.

12.22.1 Like work

A woman is treated as employed on like work to that of a man if her work is the same or of a broadly similar nature to that of a man's, and any differences in the work are not of practical importance in relation to the performance of her contract. As to what amounts to a difference of practical importance, this depends upon the facts of each particular case, but regard will be had to the nature, extent and the frequency with which such differences occur in practice. If the difference is, however, merely incidental to the main employment, such difference is not of practical importance.

12.22.2 Work rated as equivalent

A woman can claim equal pay even if not employed on like work if, after a job evaluation study has been carried out, the woman's job has been rated as equivalent to a man's in terms of the demand made on the worker. There are various headings for evaluation within such a scheme such as effort, skill and decision. All job evaluation schemes must be carried out on an objective basis and if as a result of the scheme the woman's work has been rated as equivalent, the woman is entitled to equal pay. If, however, the work has not been rated as equivalent, her case for equal pay may fail. A woman may, however, challenge a job evaluation scheme if it is discriminatory in itself.

12.22.3 Work of equal value

Even if a woman is not employed on like work or work that has been rated as equivalent under a job evaluation scheme, she may now claim equal pay if her work is of equal value to that of a man's. Equal value is assessed in relation to the demands placed upon a worker under headings such as effort, skill and responsibility. It is important to note that a claim can still be brought under this heading even if a man is paid the same as a woman for doing like work, but there is another man doing a different job who is paid more but the work is deemed to be of equal value.

12.22.4 The comparator

The basis of any claim for equal pay is that of a comparison between a man and a woman (or vice versa). The comparator must be a person of the opposite sex employed in the same employment (or in the employment of an associated employer) at the same place of work, or at another place if there are common terms and conditions of employment observed at the different places of work. Again, under Art 141 of the EC Treaty a comparison can be made with a previous employee who has subsequently left the employment.

In *Preston v Wolverhampton Healthcare NHS Trust* [2001] 3 All ER 947. a question arose in relation to the operation of the Equal Pay Act. Section 2(4) required proceedings to be brought within a period of six months following the cessation of the employment. The claimants said that such provisions were incompatible with EU law because they made it excessively difficult to exercise the rights conferred by Art 141 and because they were more restrictive than other UK provisions relating to discrimination. The ECJ held that the procedural rule in s 2(4) was not contrary to EU law so long as the limitation period was not less favourable for actions based on EU law than for those based on domestic law. The principle of equivalence required a comparison not between an action under Art 141 and one under the 1970 Act, but an objective consideration of the purpose and essential characteristics of allegedly similar domestic actions in the field of employment law.

12.22.5 The material factor defence

Even if a woman has succeeded in showing that she is entitled to equal pay as she is performing either like work, work rated as equivalent or work of equal value, it is possible for an employer to justify the difference between the man's and the woman's contract by showing that the variation is genuinely due to a material factor which is not the difference in sex. In *Rainey v Greater Glasgow Health Board* [1987] ICR 129 it was held that in establishing the material factor defence, the material difference need not be restricted to the personal qualities of the employee and the relevant comparator, but can extend to other factors such as market forces.

In *Barry v Midland Bank* [1998] 1 All ER 805, the Court of Appeal, in a ruling upheld by the House of Lords, ruled that the defence had been made out when the amount paid out under a voluntary redundancy scheme depended on the number of completed years' service, and on the employee's pay at the date of termination of the employment. The main objective of the scheme was to cushion employees against unemployment and job loss, and to compensate them for loss of job and loyalty to the bank.

The Court of Appeal held such an objective was legitimate and non-discriminatory and did not fail to take into' account to a significant effect the full service of an employee or to meet its objectives. Furthermore, the form of the scheme was both appropriate and reasonably necessary, since basing the award on the pay at termination of the employment was not a mere matter of convenience but was designed to promote the scheme's primary objective. It followed that any discrimination was because of a genuine material factor other than the difference of sex.

In *Glasgow City Council v Marshall* [2000] 1 All ER 641, the claimants, seven women and one man, worked as instructors at special schools. They were paid less than teachers at these schools. They brought an action under the 1970 Act, contending that they did like work to that done by teachers of the opposite sex in the same schools and that, accordingly, they were entitled to the same pay as their respective male and female comparators. The defendants explained that the pay disparity was because, for historical reasons, teachers and instructors were paid according to two different nationally agreed pay scales. The House of Lords ruled that the defendants had identified the factor which had caused the pay disparity, and no one questioned the genuineness of that explanation or suggested that the pay disparity was tainted with sex discrimination. The employers had therefore made out the material factor defence.

12.22.6 Remedies

Any claim under the Equal Pay Act 1970 must be brought before an employment tribunal. If the claim is successful, the woman is entitled to the insertion of an equality clause into her contract of employment which then entitles her to be paid at the same rate as that of her male comparator. The woman is also entitled to recover arrears of wages for up to two years before the commencement of proceedings. Employment tribunals also have a discretion to award interest on the amount of any award of compensation; this to be calculated with effect from the date of the discriminatory act. Even if equality has been achieved at the time of the application, arrears of pay may be awarded for any inequality that existed during the preceding two years.

12.22.7 Pension schemes

Pension schemes now come within the definition of pay for the purposes of legislation relating to equal pay for men and women. This was confirmed in the ECJ in the ruling relating to *Bilka-Kaujhaus v Karin Weber von Hartz* [1986] 5 ECR 1607. The employer must, therefore, not discriminate on grounds of sex, in any aspect of the scheme, including the conditions for joining the scheme, the level and type of benefits available and their timing. This applies to all benefits in respect of periods of employment from 17 May 1990, which was the date of the ruling in the ECJ on the *Barber v Guardian Royal Exchange Assurance Group* [1990] IRLR 240. This ruling states that sex discrimination in occupational scheme benefits is unlawful.

The equality requirements that are now largely incorporated in the Pensions Act 1995. Section 62 specifies that the equal treatment rule applies both to the terms on which employees join the scheme, and how they are treated once they have joined. This requirement is broad, and outlaws both direct and indirect discrimination. Thus, although it remains possible for the employer to determine the categories of employees eligible to join the scheme, and to provide different benefits for different categories, this must not be on a basis which unfairly differentiates between the sexes. For example, it is not permitted to discriminate on the basis of the number of hours worked, if to do so would result in one sex being disproportionately favoured in comparison with the other. This would be regarded as indirect discrimination.

Where equalisation of benefits has not been fully applied under a scheme from that date, levelling up applies, ie the benefits for the disadvantaged sex must be increased to the level available to the advantaged sex.

In *Preston v Wolverhampton Healthcare NHS Trust* (see 12.22.4), it was held that EU law precluded a national rule of procedure which had the effect of requiring a claim for membership of an occupational pension scheme to be brought within six months of the end of each contract of employment to which the claim related where there had been a stable employment relationship resulting from a succession of short-term contracts concluded at regular intervals in respect of the same employment to which the same pension scheme applied.

The tribunal may make an award equal to the difference in pay between that of the claimant and the equal or equivalent employee for a period of up to two years before the date of the complaint to it.

12.23 INSOLVENCY OF EMPLOYER

On an employer becoming insolvent, it is likely that a number, if not all, of the employees will have outstanding claims. Under the Insolvency Act 1986 certain claims by employees are treated as preferential debts. In many cases, though, there will be insufficient funds to meet even those preferential debts and consequently an employee may be left in an unsatisfactory position. Employees do, however, now have the right to make an application to the Secretary of State for Employment for payments from the National Insurance Fund under the ERA.

The insolvency provisions of the ERA apply when a company has become legally insolvent. This can mean liquidation, receivership, an administration order or voluntary arrangement approved by the court or bankruptcy. If the company merely ceases trading, these provisions may not apply. When an employer becomes insolvent, the following payments owed to his employees will be regarded as preferential debts:

- Arrears of wages or salary
- Guarantee payments
- Remuneration for suspension on medical grounds
- Time-off payments
- Remuneration under a protective award.

Employees can apply to the Redundancy Payments Office of the Department of Trade and Industry covering the employer's area. If satisfied that the employer is insolvent and the employees are entitled to the payments, the Department will make the following payments, for a period of up to eight weeks out of the National Insurance Fund. Note that there is currently a statutory limit on the amount for any one week of £250.

(1) Any arrears of pay up to eight weeks (includes guarantee payments, remuneration for suspension on medical grounds, time-off payments, remuneration under a protective award) (£2,000 maximum).

(2) Any money due to employees who have received notice (maximum 12 weeks' statutory notice after 12 years' service (£3,000 maximum)).

(3) Holiday pay up to six weeks (£1,500 maximum).

(4) Basic compensation for unfair dismissal (£7,500 maximum)

(5) Reimbursement of fees etc paid by apprentices.

Provision is also made for the payment of unpaid contributions to occupational pension schemes out of the National Insurance Fund, and for liability to statutory maternity pay and statutory sick pay to be met by the President of the Board of Trade.

This does not apply to:

- Non-employees
- Employees who ordinarily work outside the European Union
- Merchant seamen
- Certain share fisherman

An employee who feels that he has been refused a payment to which he is entitled can complain to an employment tribunal.

12.23.1 Redundancy payments

An employee can also make a claim under the ERA against the National Insurance Fund where he claims that his employer is liable to pay him a redundancy payment and that his employer is insolvent and that the whole or part of his redundancy payment remains unpaid.

12.23.2 Remedy

Where an employee has applied for payment from the National Insurance Fund and his application has been refused, he may present a complaint under the ERA to an employment tribunal to the effect either that the Secretary of State has failed to make any payment or that the amount of any payment made is less than the amount that should have been paid. The complaint should be brought within three months of the date on which the Secretary of State's decision is given to the employee, or if the tribunal considers that it was not reasonably practicable to bring a complaint within that time, within such further period as is considered reasonable.

If the complaint is well founded, a declaration is made to that effect and the amount that is due from the Fund is stated.

12.24 TRANSFER OF UNDERTAKINGS (PROTECTION OF EMPLOYMENT) REGS 1981 (TUPE)

The TUPE Regs, which implement the Acquired Rights Directive (EEC) 77/187, are designed to protect the rights of employees on a change of employer, whether such change results from a takeover or merger or from contracting out.

12.24.1 Application

The Regulations apply whenever there is a transfer from one person to another of an undertaking or part of an undertaking which is situated in the UK immediately before the transfer. For there to be a relevant transfer there must be a transfer of an undertaking or part of an undertaking as a 'going concern'.

It was originally thought, therefore, that, the TUPE Regs only applied to undertakings which were commercial ventures. Following the case of *Dr Sophie Redmond Stichting v Bartol* [1992] IRLR 366, however, the exclusion of undertakings that were not in the nature of a commercial venture from the operation of the TUPE Regs was seen as contrary to the Acquired Rights Directive. Accordingly, the Regulations were amended by the Trade Union Reform and Employment Rights Act 1993 so that this inconsistency with the Directive was removed.

In deciding whether there has been a transfer to which the Regulations will apply, the ECJ in *Spijkers v Gebroeders Benedik Abbatoir CV* [1986] 2 CMLR 296 stated that the important question was whether there was a separate identifiable economic entity which was transferred and which continued after the transfer by the new employer in substantially the same manner.

In answering this question, the circumstances of each particular case should be examined, including:

(a) the type of undertaking in question;
(b) whether tangible assets, such as buildings and stock, are transferred;
(c) whether goodwill is transferred;
(d) whether customers are transferred;
(e) whether there is an intention to transfer employees;
(f) whether there is any suspension in the carrying on of the activities, and if so for what period of time;
(g) the degree of similarity of the activities carried on before and after the transfer.

There has been considerable litigation as to whether there is a transfer of an undertaking to which the Regulations apply when a service which has previously been carried on 'in house' is 'outsourced' to an external contractor or when a new contractor takes over the provision of those services from the previous contractor. Case law indicates that such circumstances can amount to a transfer falling within the ambit of the Regulations (see *Rask v ISS Kantineservice* [1993] IRLR 133 (the contracting-out of an in-house catering service to a private contractor); *Kenny v South Manchester College* [1993] IRLR 265 (contracting-out of the provision of prison education services); and *Dines v Initial Health Care Services* [1994] IRLR 336 (change of contractor for the provision of hospital cleaning services after competitive tendering).

There can be a transfer to which the Regulations apply even where there is no transfer of assets or customers. For example in *Kenny v South Manchester College* [1993] IRLR 265, on the College successfully tendering to provide prison education services, there was a relevant transfer for the purposes of the Regulations, despite the fact that the premises, books and other items required to provide the education services would remain the property of the Home Office or the local education authority. Nevertheless, the Regulations applied as the education department in the prison was a clearly identifiable entity and would continue after the transfer in substantially the same manner as it did beforehand. Furthermore, in *Schmidt v Spar Und Leuhkasse: Der Fruheren* [1994] IRLR 303, it was confirmed that the Acquired Rights Directive, and as a consequence TUPE, can apply to a business or operation carried on by just one person.

The test laid down in *Spijkers*, however, (of whether there is a separate economic entity which is in existence after the transfer, carrying on the same economic or similar activity as it carried on prior to the transfer) will be the decisive criterion in deciding whether there has been a transfer to which TUPE applies. In *Isles of Scilly Council v Brintel Helicopters* [1995] IRLR 6, it was stated that the question of retention of identity could be supplemented by enquiring whether the job previously done by the employee was still in existence after the transfer. In this context, it is important to note that TUPE only applies to a transfer from one legal person to another. As a result, the Regulations will not apply where there is merely a change in ownership by way of share transfer.

There have also been a number of developments that affect the application of TUPE. For example, *Suzen* [1997] IRLR 255 has transformed the general approach to transfers. This case involved the transfer of a school cleaning contract from one contractor to another. The employer who won the contract dismissed its employees and the question arose whether the transfer of the cleaning activity to a new contractor equated to the transfer of an undertaking.

The case was referred to the ECJ which held that a transfer of activities does not, in itself, constitute a transfer of undertaking.

This ruling has since been accepted by the Court of Appeal in *Betts v Brintel Helicopters* [1997] IRLR 361, in which the court drew a distinction between labour intensive activities and other types of activities. The court suggested that with labour intensive activities, if the activity continued with 'substantially the same staff after the alleged transfer the court may well conclude that the undertaking was transferred . . .'. This effectively takes the ruling in *Suzen* one step further, as where an undertaking is transferred with 'substantially the same staff' as before the transfer then there may very well have been a transfer regulated by TUPE. circumstances of the transfer should be considered before concluding that a transfer is not regulated by TUPE.

These matters were considered afresh by the Court of Appeal in *ECM (Vehicle Delivery Service) v Cox* [1999] 4 All ER 669. It was held that, to determine whether an undertaking had continued and retained its identity in different hands, a tribunal has to consider all the facts characterising the transaction in question. In carrying out that exercise, the tribunal had to take account of the similarity of the pre- and post-transfer activities, the type of undertaking concerned and whether the majority of employees had been taken over by the new employer to enable it to carry on the activities of the undertaking on a regular basis. A transferee's failure to appoint any former employees of the transferor, however, did not point conclusively against a transfer, and a tribunal was entitled to take into account the reason for that failure. The Court of Appeal upheld the decision, distinguishing *Suzen* in that the present case was not one of the loss of a contract with one customer being said to amount to a transfer; and distinguishing *Bett* as being of the loss of a contract for one location being said to be a transfer of an undertaking.

12.24.2 Transfer of employment

The most important consequence of a transfer to which the Regulations apply is contained in reg 5 which provides that those employees employed in the undertaking immediately before it is transferred are transferred to the new employer (the transferee) on the same terms and conditions of employment that they enjoyed with their previous employer (the transferor). Subject to certain limited exceptions, all the transferor's rights, powers, duties and liabilities under or in connection with the contract of any transferring employee are transferred to the transferee. Furthermore, anything done by the transferor in respect of a transferring employee is deemed to have been done by the transferee. Accordingly, the transferee inherits:

(1) all existing contractual terms, both express and implied;
(2) liabilities for past breaches of contract;
(3) statutory liabilities such as unfair dismissal compensation, redundancy payments and claims for compensation under discrimination legislation;
(4) continuous employment with the transferor;
(5) tortious liability, such as liability for personal injuries.

The transferee does not, however, inherit criminal liability and liabilities relating to the provisions of occupational pension schemes which relate to old age, invalidity or survivor's benefits. In *Walden Engineering v Warrener* [1993] IRLR 420, an argument that transferring employees should be entitled to equivalent pension benefits after the transfer was specifically rejected.

In *British Fuels v Baxendale* [1998] 4 All ER 609, the question arose whether dismissals of employees prior to the transfer of an undertaking, including a trade or business, were nullities so that, on the transfer, the employees were entitled to retain the benefit of the terms and conditions of their previous employment despite their dismissal by their old employer and re-engagement by the new employer on different terms. The House of Lords ruled that the dismissals were not nullities, nor was there an automatic obligation on the transferee's part to continue to employ the employees who had been dismissed. The court also held that, although on a transfer the employee's rights against the previous employer are enforceable against the transferee, and cannot be amended by the transfer itself, there can be a variation of the terms of the contract for reasons which are not due to the transfer either on or after the transfer of the undertaking.

In *The Chancellor, Master and Scholars of the University of Oxford v Humphreys* [2000] 1 All ER 996, the House of Lords held that the Regulations did not extinguish the right of action of an employee who had objected to a transfer of his employment contract on the grounds of a detrimental change in working conditions. It was rather the case that, in such circumstances, the Regulations preserved an employee's common law rights to sue for dismissal in accordance with the provisions of the Acquired Rights Directive. The House also held that the right to terminate and sue for constructive dismissal preserved by the Regulations had to be asserted against the transferor, and not against the transferee. The remedy against the transferor was not transferred. In *Martin v Lancashire County Council* [2000] 3 All ER 544, the Court of Appeal held that when an undertaking was transferred under TUPE, a transferor's liability in tort to an employee in respect of a personal injury which had accrued before the transfer would be transferred to the transferee. Where the transferor had effected an employer's liability policy, the transferor's right of indemnity under that policy would also be transferred to the transferee by virtue of the Regulations.

12.24.3 'Immediately before the transfer'

An employee only transfers to the transferee company if he is employed by the transferor 'immediately before the transfer'. Until the House of Lords' decision in *Lister v Forth Dry Dock and Engineering (in Receivership)* [1989] IRLR 161, there had been considerable case law regarding the meaning of the phrase 'immediately before'. If a transferor were to dismiss certain employees eg three hours before a transfer would this avoid the application of the Regulations?

The House of Lords, in *Lister*, adopted a purposive approach in construing reg 5 of the TUPE Regs and stated that it referred not only to a person employed immediately before the transfer, but also to an individual 'who would have been so employed if he had not been unfairly dismissed for a reason that was connected with the transfer which was not an economic, technical or organisational reason entailing changes in the workforce' (see 12.24.4). If, therefore, the transferor dismisses employees prior to a transfer, but for reasons connected with it, the TUPE Regs will apply. Where, however, an employee is dismissed before, on or after the effective transfer of a business, he does not have a right to demand that the transferee continues to employ them or find them work. This was decided by the House of Lords in *Wilson v St Helens BC* [1998] 4 All ER 609; [1998] IRLR 706 and *Meade v British Fuels* [1996] IRLR 541.

12.24.4 Unfair dismissals and business transfers

Regulation 8 provides that a dismissal, the reason or principal reason for which is the transfer or a reason connected with it, is automatically unfair whether the dismissal occurs before or after the transfer. Reg 8(2), however, provides a defence for an employer where the dismissal is because of an 'economic, technical or organisational reason entailing changes in the workforce of either the transferor or the transferee before or after the transfer'. Where the dismissal can be shown to be for such an 'ETO reason' this does not make the dismissal automatically fair, but the tribunal will go on to consider whether the dismissal was fair and reasonable in all the circumstances in accordance with the reasonableness tests under Employment Protection (Consolidation) Act, 1978, s 57(3).

Under the Regulations an employee must bring a claim for unfair dismissal within three months of the date he was dismissed.

A dismissed employee may also have claims for a redundancy payment or wrongful dismissal.

12.24.5 What amounts to an ETO reason?

An employer can establish a defence to a transfer related dismissal if it can show that it was for an ETO reason entailing changes in the workforce. In *Wheeler v Patel* [1987] ICR 631, it was stated that an economic reason must relate to the conduct of the business itself. It follows that a dismissal which is made to facilitate a transfer or which is made at the request of the transferee does not amount to a relevant economic reason.

The ETO reason must also entail 'a change in the workforce'. In *Berriman v Delabok Slate* [1985] ICR 546, this phrase was held to mean a change in the number of employees or a change in the functions that the employees are required to perform. It does not cover the situation where an employer merely dismisses those employees who do not agree to changes in their terms and conditions of employment. Accordingly, where an employer seeks to harmonise the terms and conditions of the transferring workforce with those of its present employees, any such attempt at harmonisation is connected with the transfer and does not amount to an ETO defence. However, where a number of employees are not required by the transferee, and in a non-transfer situation would be deemed to be redundant, then the ETO defence should apply.

12.24.6 Redundancy payments

Where an employee is automatically transferred to the transferee in accordance with the Regulations, he is not dismissed by the transferor and therefore is not entitled to a redundancy payment. Where, however, an employee is either dismissed by the transferor before the transfer for a genuine redundancy reason or where following the transfer, the transferee dismisses the employee for a genuine redundancy reason, the employee is still entitled to a redundancy payment, even though the dismissal is for an ETO reason connected with the transfer.

12.24.7 Avoiding the Regulations

Regulation 12 provides that any agreement that attempts to exclude or limit the operation of the Regulations is invalid. In transfer documentation, however, it is usual for the transferor and the transferee to agree certain warranties and indemnities that provide who is liable for payment of any sums deemed to be payable as a consequence of any transfer related dismissal, or any liability that may transfer as a result of the operation of the Regulations.

From an employee's point of view, following *Katsikas v Konstantinidis* [1993] IRLR 179, an employee cannot be forced to transfer to a new employer against his will. Accordingly, reg 5 now provides that an employee's contract is not transferred if the employee informs either the transferor or the transferee that he objects to becoming employed by the transferee. It is, however, unlikely that an employee would exercise this right to object as the Regulations further provide that if an employee exercises his right to object, then his contract of employment is automatically terminated and he is not treated as having been dismissed by the transferor and therefore is not be entitled to any compensation.

12.24.8 Collective agreements and trade union recognition

Regulation 6 provides that any collective agreement which has been made between a transferor and a trade union which is recognised by the transferor, and which applies to transferring employees, continues to have effect after the transfer as if made by the transferee with the relevant trade union. The effect of this regulation is, however, minimal as collective agreements are unenforceable unless the contrary is stated in the agreement itself.

Furthermore, reg 9 provides that where, after a transfer, the undertaking transferred retains an identity distinct from the remainder of the transferee's undertaking, any trade union which the transferor recognised with regard to the transferring employees is deemed to be recognised also by the transferee.

12.24.9 Provision of information and consultation with trade unions

The 1981 Regs, as amended by the Collective Redundancies and Transfer of Undertakings (Protection of Employment) (Amendment) Regs 1999, apply to business transfers completed for redundancies on or after 1 November 1999. An employer must inform the appropriate representatives of any employees who may be affected by the transfer or any measures taken in connection with it of:

(1) the fact that the transfer is to take place, approximately when it will occur and the reasons for it;
(2) the legal, economic and social implications of the transfer for the affected employee;
(3) whether he expects to 'take measures' in relation to those employees in connection with the transfer, and if so what measures; and
(4) if the employer is the transferor, whether or not the transferee expects to 'take measures' in relation to any employees it is taking over and, if so, what measures.

Such information must be given to the representatives long enough before the transfer to enable consultations to take place.

The 'appropriate representative', where a union has been recognised, is a union representative. Where no union is recognised, elected representatives are to be consulted. If affected employees fail to elect representatives within a reasonable time of being asked to do so, the employer must give the employees the required information individually. Requirements are laid down for the election process, such as ballots being in secret and principles of fairness being observed.

If there are special circumstances which render it not reasonably practicable for the employer to comply with the above duties, he must take all such steps as are reasonable in the circumstances. In the event of a breach of these duties, a tribunal may make a declaration to that effect and award compensation of up to 13 weeks' pay for each affected employee mentioned in the award.

12.24.10 References

An employer is under no legal duty to provide a reference for an employee (*Gallear v J F Watson & Son* [1979] IRLR 306). Where, however, an employer agrees to provide a reference, it should exercise great care when compiling that reference. In *Spring v Guardian Assurance* [1994] IRLR 460, the House of Lords held that employers owe a duty of care to employees in respect of the preparation of a reference. Although, when providing a reference to a prospective employer, the former employer does so for the benefit of that person, it also does so to assist the employee who has to rely on his former employer to, exercise due skill and care. The implication of this decision is that it is now far easier for employees to challenge references given by a former employer if they can show that the employer has not taken all reasonable care in compiling a reference.

An employee may also have actions in defamation or malicious falsehood where his previous employer provides an inaccurate reference. However, these claims are far more difficult to prove and are not very common.

Furthermore, when an employer supplies a reference to a prospective employer, he will owe that employer a duty to exercise a reasonable degree of care and skill to ensure that the reference is accurate and not misleading (see *Hedley Byrne and Co v Heller and Partners* [1963] AC 465). Consequently, if the prospective employer suffers loss as a result of its reliance on an inaccurate reference, the old employer may be held liable to pay damages on account of its negligence, if the mistake was due to carelessness.

An employer, when providing a reference, may therefore include a disclaimer of any liability arising out of a result of a potential new employer relying on the reference. Any such disclaimer, however, is subject to the provisions of the Unfair Contract Terms Act 1977 and of the Unfair Terms in Consumer Contracts Regs 1999, and will only be enforceable if the disclaimer is reasonable or, respectively, fair.

12.25 DATA SUBJECTS' RIGHTS

Employees (as data subjects) are given rights by the Data Protection Act 1998. The rights of the data subject enable them to:

(1) submit a subject access request to:
    (a) determine whether a data controller is processing personal data held on them;
    (b) be given a description of the personal data, the purpose(s) for which they are being processed and who will receive the data
    (c) have the information constituting the personal data sent to them;
    (d) be informed of the logic behind any automated decision-taking that has been or could be the sole basis for any decision significantly affecting him, unless it is a trade secret;

(2) serve a written notice on a data controller requiring them within a reasonable time to cease, or not to begin, processing of their data that may cause damage or distress;

(3) serve a written notice on a data controller requiring them within a reasonable time to cease, or not to begin, processing of their data 'for the purposes of direct marketing';

(4) serve a written notice on a data controller requiring them to ensure that no decision is taken that would significantly affect them (which would be based solely on the processing by automatic means of personal data about them) for the purpose of evaluating matters relating to them. This might cover matters such as their performance at work;

(5) the right to apply to court to have data corrected or erased if inaccurate;

(6) obtain court orders to force a data controller to comply with the Act; or

(7) submit a complaint to the Data Protection Commissioner and claim compensation through court action.

12.26 ACCESS TO MEDICAL REPORTS

The Access to Medical Reports Act 1988 gives employees (and the self-employed) considerable rights as regards access to medical reports prepared for employment purposes.

The Act gives individuals rights in relation to 'any medical report relating to the individual which is to be, or has been, supplied by a medical practitioner for employment purposes'. However, the Act further states that it applies to medical reports that are 'prepared by a medical practitioner who is or has been responsible for the clinical care of the individual'. The Act therefore limits employees' rights of access to medical reports prepared by their own doctor or specialist consultant. The definition within the Act clearly excludes reports prepared by company-nominated doctors unless the doctor has been responsible for the clinical care of the individual concerned.

Rights of employees under the Access to Medical Reports Act 1988 – employees have the following rights conferred on them by the Access to Medical Reports Act 1988:

(1) To refuse to allow the employer to apply to their GP for a medical report.

(2) To gain access to the report. (A doctor does not have to disclose the contents of the report if they consider it would be likely to cause serious harm to the physical or mental health of the individual.)

(3) To ask their doctor to amend the report, if it is inaccurate or misleading.

(4) To refuse to allow the report to be passed to the employer.

Since the Access to Medical Reports Act 1988 does not normally apply to medical reports prepared by independent company doctors, employers do not require the employee's permission to gain access to a medical report prepared by a company-appointed doctor.

Employers may require employees to consent to undergo medical examinations by a company doctor at their request where there is a clause in their contracts of employment to that effect. Whilst this does not enable employers to force employees to undergo a medical examination, it may provide them with a fair reason for dismissing the employee who refuses. If no such written clause exists in the contract, the employer would have no authority to require employees to be examined by a company doctor, and no grounds for disciplining or dismissing employees who refuse to consent.

Employers wishing to seek a medical report from an employee's or job applicant's GP must seek the individual's written consent before making such an application. This request must be made to the employee in writing and must also inform the individual of their rights under the Act.

Employers should also note that any contractual term obliging an individual to provide a GP's report will be void, because such a term would contradict the freedom given to individuals under statute.

The Access to Medical Records Act 1990 took the issue of access to medical records one stage further. This Act enables individuals to make a written request for access to any health record from the holder of that record. Thus, while the Access to Medical Reports Act 1988 normally applies only to medical reports held by the person's GP, the Access to Health Records Act covers records held by a range of health professionals, including:

- Any registered medical practitioner
- A registered dentist
- A registered optician
- A registered nurse, midwife or health visitor
- A registered pharmacist
- A registered chiropodist, dietician, occupational therapist, speech therapist, orthoptist or physiotherapist
- A clinical psychologist or psychotherapist
- An art or music therapist employed by a health service body.

To qualify under the Act, a health record must consist of information 'relating to the physical or mental health of an individual'. The only other stipulation is that the health record must have been made in connection with the care of the individual. On analysis of these stipulations, it is evident that where a company-nominated doctor examines an employee for the sole purpose of providing information to the employer, the record produced would probably be excluded from the Act because it has been made for a purpose that is not connected with the care of the individual.

Employers may request an employee's consent to obtain a copy of their health record from any relevant health professional in two ways:

(1) By asking the employee to obtain the record and pass it on to the employer.

(2) By gaining the employee's written consent for the employer to make direct application for access to the health record.

The employee has the right of refusal under the Act, and employers cannot force employees or job applicants to agree to provide such information, or to consent to the employer making a direct application for information.

Specialist records may prove to be more useful to an employer than a GP's report in assessing an employee's fitness for employment in a specific job, and employers may wish to use this route as a means of obtaining relevant information in the event of an employee who is suffering (or has suffered) from long-term ill-health.

13

TAX AND EMPLOYEE COMPENSATION

This chapter deals with an employer's obligations to operate PAYE and national insurance contributions (NICs), and also covers the tax treatment of benefits-in-kind and other forms of employee compensation. Legislative references are to TA 1988 unless stated otherwise.

13.1 SCHEDULE E

13.1.1 Scope of Schedule E
(TA 1988, ss 19 and 192)

The basic rule of Schedule E is that income tax is charged on the emoluments of an office or employment that fall under one or more than one of the following Cases:

Case I: Any emoluments for any tax year in which the person holding the office or employment is UK-resident and ordinarily resident (excepting the emoluments of a non-UK domiciled person from an office or employment under any person, resident outside, and not resident in, the UK).

Case II: Any emoluments for duties performed in the UK, for any tax year in which the person holding the office or employment is not resident (or, if resident, not ordinarily resident) in the UK (excepting the emoluments of a non-UK domiciled person from an office or employment under any person, resident outside, and not resident in, the UK).

Case III: Any emoluments for any tax year in which the person holding the office or employment is UK-resident (whether or not ordinarily resident there) so far as the emoluments are received in the UK.

There are rules to identify the tax year to which to relate emoluments received before an employment starts, or after employment has ceased.

Schedule E is also chargeable directly by other provisions of TA 1988 (eg gains from share options (s 135)). Such charges are outside the three Cases.

13.1.2 Assessment of employee earnings
(TA 1988, ss 202A and 202B)

Income tax is charged under Schedule E Cases I and II on the full amount of the emoluments (wherever received) from the employment in a tax year from the office or employment concerned (s 202A(1)). Under Case III, income tax is charged on the full amount of the emoluments received in the UK in a tax year from the office or employment concerned. This applies whether the emoluments are for that year or for some other year of assessment, and whether or not that office or employment is held at the time the emoluments are received or (as the case may be) received in the UK (s 202A(2)).

There are rules to be followed to ascertain when emoluments are treated as received (taking the earlier or earliest time in a case where more than one rule applies):

(1) the time when payment is made of or on account of the emoluments;
(2) the time when a person becomes entitled to payment of or on account of the emoluments;
(3) where the emoluments are from an office or employment with a company, the holder of the office or employment is a director of the company and sums on account of the emoluments are credited in the company's accounts or records, the time when sums on account of the emoluments are so credited; any fetter on the right to draw the sums is disregarded;
(4) where the emoluments are from an office or employment with a company, the holder of the office or employment is a director of the company and the amount of the emoluments for a period is determined before the period ends, the time when the period ends;
(5) where the emoluments are from an office or employment with a company, the holder of the office or employment is a director of the company and the amount of the emoluments for a period is not known until the amount is determined after the period has ended, the time when the amount is determined.

Rules (3)-(5) above apply to all of a director's emoluments whether or not the office or employment is that of director. They also apply if the holder of the office or employment is a director of the company at any time in the tax year of assessment in which the time there mentioned falls.

A 'director' is, in relation to a company whose affairs are managed by:

(1) a board of directors, a member of that board,
(2) a single director, that director, and
(3) the members themselves, a member of the company.

'Director' in relation to a company also includes any person in accordance with whose directions or instructions the company's directors are accustomed to act. However, this does not apply where the company's directors only act on advice given by him in a professional capacity.

There are special rules dealing with the time of receipt for vouchers, living accommodation, expenses and benefits-in-kind (in particular cars made available for private use, car fuel provided, beneficial loan arrangements, employee shareholdings and director's tax paid by the employer). For non-cash vouchers, credit tokens and cash vouchers taxable under PAYE, see 13.2.9. Living accommodation provided for the employee (s 145(1)) is treated as received for the period for which it is provided.

In all of the following cases, the benefits concerned (for employees earning more than £8,500 and directors) are treated under TA 1988 as received in the tax year concerned at the amount of their cash equivalent for that year:

- General charging provision (s 154(1))
- Cars available for private use (s 157(1))
- Car fuel (s 158(1))
- Beneficial loan arrangements (s 160(1))
- Loans written off (s 160(2))
- Disposal of employee shares in excess of market value (s 162(6))
- Directors' tax paid by employer (s 164).

If emoluments take the form of a benefit not consisting of money, and the special rules set out above do not apply, the emoluments are treated as received at the time when the benefit is provided.

Amounts deducted in arriving at pay
(TA 1988, s 202)

Contributions made by an employee to an approved retirement benefit scheme and contributions of unlimited amount to a payroll giving scheme ('give as you earn') are deducted from an individual's salary in arriving at taxable pay for the purposes of both PAYE and Schedule E. A 10% supplement is added by the Government on donations made between 6 April 2000 and 5 April 2003.

Note that NICs are based on pay *before* such amounts are deducted (see 13.17 below).

The point in time at which PAYE should be applied can, in certain circumstances, be earlier than the date of actual payment.

13.2 PAYE

13.2.1 Introduction
(TA 1988, s 203)

When an employer makes a payment of any income assessable under Schedule E, PAYE is deducted or repaid by the person making the payment.

There are detailed regulations dealing with the assessment, charge, collection and recovery of income tax deducted, under PAYE, from income assessable under Schedule E (see Income Tax (Employments) Regulations 1993). The deductions of income tax made under these Regulations are at the basic or other rate(s) in such cases or classes of cases as are provided for by the Regulations.

Tax tables are used to calculate the required PAYE deductions. These are constructed with a view to securing so far as possible that the total income tax payable on any income assessable under Schedule E for any tax year is deducted from such income paid during that year. The tables are cumulative so that the income tax deductible or repayable on any payment is such that the total net income tax deducted since the beginning of the tax year is in proportion with that part of the tax year which ends with the date of the payment. This is achieved by a provisional deduction for allowances and reliefs, and subject also, if necessary, to an adjustment for tax overpaid or remaining unpaid on account of income tax under Schedule E for any previous tax year. In estimating the total income tax payable, it is assumed the income paid in the part of the tax year which ends with the making of the payment is pro rata for that part of the tax year.

Interest required to be paid on unpaid tax is paid without any deduction of income tax and is not taken into account in computing any income, profits or losses for any tax purposes.

13.2.2 Meaning of payment for PAYE
(TA 1988, s 203A)

There are rules to be followed in ascertaining when emoluments are treated as paid under the PAYE rules. These are broadly similar to those applying to ascertain the time of receipt of income (s 202B).

13.2.3 Payment by intermediary
(TA 1988, s 203B)

Where any payment of assessable income of an employee is made by an intermediary of the employer, the employer is treated as the payee under the PAYE rules. This treatment is not required if the intermediary deducts income tax from the payment he makes and accounts for it under the PAYE regulations. This procedure is intended to stop the deferment of tax by making payments through an offshore entity.

13.2.4 Employee of non-UK employer
(TA 1988, s 203C)

This applies where:

(1) an employee works for a person in the UK who is not his employer;

(2) any payment of assessable income to the employee for work done in that period is made by a person who is the employer, or an intermediary (s 203B(4)) of the employer, but who is resident overseas;

(3) the PAYE regulations do not otherwise apply to the person making the payment; and

(4) income tax is not deducted or accounted for by the person making the payment.

The person in the UK for whom the employee works is treated, under the PAYE rules, as making, if the recipient is entitled to a net payment after deduction of any income tax, the gross amount of that payment and the amount of any income tax due; and in any other case, the payment actually made is taken.

13.2.5 Employee non-resident, etc
(TA 1988, s 203D)

A special rule deals with the case where, in a tax year, an employee is not resident or, if resident, not ordinarily resident in the UK; and he works in *and* outside the UK. Here, some of the employee's income is assessable under Schedule E Case II, but an unknown proportion of the income may prove not to be assessable. On an application, the Revenue gives a direction as to the proportion of any payment made which is to be treated, under the PAYE rules, as a payment of the employee's assessable income. If no such direction is made, the entire payment is treated as assessable income and PAYE is operated accordingly.

13.2.6 Mobile UK workforce
(TA 1988, s 203E)

This applies where:

(1) a person has entered into an agreement that employees of a contractor will, in any period, work for, but not as employees of, that person;

(2) payments of the employees' assessable income for work done in that period are likely to be made by or on behalf of the contractor; and

(3) PAYE regulations would apply on the making of such payments but the Revenue considers that it is likely that income tax will not be deducted or accounted for by the contractor in accordance with the regulations.

In such a case, the Revenue may direct that, if:

(1) any employees of the contractor work in any period for, but not as employees of, the person concerned, and

(2) any payment is made by that person for work done by the employees in that period,

income tax must deducted by that person on making that payment.

13.2.7 **Tradable assets**
(TA 1988, ss 203F, 203FA and 203FB)

Where any assessable income of an employee is provided in the form of a 'readily convertible asset', the employer is treated, for the purposes of the PAYE regulations, as making a payment of that income of an amount equal to that which, on the basis of the best estimate that can reasonably be made, is the amount of income likely to be chargeable to tax under Schedule E in respect of the provision of the asset. 'Readily convertible assets' are assets:

(1) which are capable of being sold or otherwise realised on a recognised investment exchange or on the London Bullion Market;
(2) which are capable of being sold or otherwise realised on a market specified in the PAYE regulations;
(3) which are rights which can be passed by assignment, or any other rights, in relation to a money debt that is or may become due to the employer or any other person;
(4) which consist in, or in any right in relation to, any property that is subject to a fiscal warehousing regime (VATA 1994, ss 18–18F);
(5) which are likely (without anything being done by the employee) to give rise to, or to become, a right enabling a person to obtain an amount or total amount of money (other than sterling or euro) which is likely to be similar to the expense incurred in the provision of the asset (eg a reversionary interest in a trust);
(6) for which trading arrangements exist; or
(7) for which trading arrangements are likely to come into existence in accordance with any arrangements of another description existing when the asset is provided or with any understanding existing at that time.

'Trading arrangements' also exist if there are arrangements that enable a person, or a member of his family or household (s 168(4)), to obtain an amount of money that is similar to the expense incurred in the provision of that asset. 'Asset' does not include:

(1) any payment actually made of, or on account of, assessable income;
(2) any non-cash voucher, credit token or cash voucher (see 13.2.9); or
(3) any description of property for the time being excluded from the scope of this rule by PAYE regulations.

There are useful articles in *Tax Bulletins*, February 1997, p 385 (updated article addressing some of the practical considerations of operating PAYE on payments in the form of tradable assets), and August 1998, p 563 (applying PAYE to remuneration in the form of readily convertible assets).

Enhancing an asset's value
(TA 1988, s 203FA)

It may be that an employee's assessable income includes something which enhances the value of an asset in which the employee or a member of his family or household already has an interest. It may further occur that the asset, with its value enhanced, would be treated as a readily convertible asset (s 203F) if assessable income were provided to the employee in the form of that asset at the time of the enhancement. In such event, the above rule is applied as if the employee had been provided, at that time, with assessable income in the form of the asset (with its value enhanced), instead of with whatever enhanced its value.

Where any assessable income of an employee is provided in the form of a 'readily convertible asset', and its value is enhanced as above, the employer is treated, for the purposes of the PAYE regulations, as making a further payment of that income of an amount equal to that which, on the basis of the best estimate that can reasonably be made, is the amount of income likely to be chargeable to Schedule E tax in respect of that enhancement.

The PAYE regulations may exclude certain matters from the scope of what constitutes enhancing the value of an asset for these purposes.

13.2.8 PAYE: gains from share options
(TA 1988, 203FB(1))

These rules are further modified whereby an amount is assessable as a result of an event giving rise to the realisation of a gain from share options etc (s 135, 140A(4) or 140D). Such amount is that which, on the basis of the best estimate that can reasonably be made, is income likely to be chargeable to tax under Schedule E as a result of the event, reduced by the amount of any relief likely to be available under s 187A (relief for NICs in respect of share option gains).

13.2.9 PAYE: non-cash vouchers, credit tokens and cash vouchers

Non-cash vouchers
(TA 1988, s 203G)

Where a non-cash voucher (as described below) is received by an employee, the employer is treated, under the PAYE regulations, as making a payment of assessable income of the employee of an amount equal to the expense incurred by the person at whose cost the voucher and the goods, etc for which it can be exchanged are provided (s 141(1)(a)). This applies if either of the two conditions set out below is fulfilled with respect to the voucher;

and the voucher is not of a description for the time being excluded from the scope of this treatment by PAYE regulations:

(1) The first condition is fulfilled if a non-cash voucher is capable of being exchanged for anything which, if provided to the employee at the time when the voucher is received, would be regarded as a readily convertible asset (s 203F).

(2) The second condition is fulfilled with respect to a non-cash voucher if (but for it being excluded by s 203F(4)(b) because it falls within the definition in s 141(1)) it would itself fall to be regarded as a readily convertible asset under s 203F.

On each occasion on which an employee uses a non-cash voucher to obtain money, or anything which, if provided to him at the time when the non-cash voucher is used, would be regarded as a readily convertible asset under s 203F, the employer is treated, under the PAYE regulations, as making a payment of assessable income of the employee of an amount equal to the expense incurred by the person at whose cost the goods, etc are provided (s 142(1)(a)).

Credit tokens
(TA 1988, s 203H)

On each occasion on which an employee uses a credit token (s 142(4)) provided to him by reason of his employment to obtain money, or anything which, if provided to the employee at the time when the credit token is used, would be regarded as a readily convertible asset under s 203F, the employer is treated, under the PAYE regulations, as making a payment of assessable income of the employee of an amount equal to the expense incurred by the person at whose cost the money, goods or services are provided (s 142(1)(a)). This applies where the credit token is not of a description for the time being excluded from the scope of this treatment by PAYE regulations.

Cash vouchers
(TA 1988, s 203I)

Where a cash voucher is received by an employee, the employer is treated, under the PAYE regulations, as making a payment of assessable income of the employee of an amount equal to the sum of money for which the voucher is capable of being exchanged (see s 143(1) and (3)).

13.2.10 Accounting for tax
(TA 1988, s 203J)

Where an employer makes a notional payment of assessable income of an employee, the obligation to deduct income tax requires him to so deduct it from any payment he actually makes to that employee.

13.2.11 Agency workers

Where the remuneration receivable by an individual under any contract is treated by s 134 (agency workers) as the emoluments of an office or employment, the rules described in ss 203B–203K (except s 203E (PAYE: mobile workforce)) apply as if that person held that office or employment under or with the agency.

13.2.12 PAYE repayments
(TA 1988, s 204)

Regulations provide that no repayment of income tax is made to any person if at any time he:

(a) has claimed unemployment benefit for a period including that time; or
(b) has claimed a jobseeker's allowance for a period including that time; or
(c) has claimed a payment of income support under the Social Security Act 1986 or the Social Security (Northern Ireland) Order 1986 for a period including that time and his right to that income support is subject to the condition of availability for employment; or
(d) is disqualified at the time from receiving unemployment benefit because of loss of employment owing to stoppage of work or would be so disqualified if he otherwise satisfied the conditions for entitlement; or
(e) is prevented at the time from being entitled to a jobseeker's allowance because of a trade dispute or would be so prevented if he otherwise satisfied the conditions for entitlement.

13.2.13 Returns of expenses and benefits
(Income Tax (Employments) Regulations 1993)

By 6 July following the end of each tax year, the employer must provide the Revenue with details on form P11D for employees earning £8,500 or more and directors, and on form P9D (for other employees) showing for each employee:

(1) emoluments received other than in money;
(2) payments made on behalf of the employee and not repaid;
(3) emoluments in the form of non-cash vouchers;
(4) emoluments in the form of credit tokens;
(5) the amount of any tax on a notional payment which is treated as an employee's income because the employer is unable to deduct it from an actual payment;
(6) living accommodation provided for the employee or for members of his family or household;
(7) qualifying removal expenses and benefits to a relocated employee to the extent that they exceed the qualifying limit; and

(8) emoluments relating to business entertainment (s 577(5)) disallowed in computing the employer's taxable business profits.

For employees earning £8,500 or more and directors (s 167), the return must also show particulars of

(9) payments made by the employer to the employee by reason of his employment for expenses (except for qualifying removal expenses as in (7) above);
(10) any sums put at the employee's disposal by the employer by reason of his employment and paid away by him; and
(11) any benefits provided by the employer for the employee (or for any other person) by reason of his employment such as give rise to any charge to tax under special circumstances (see below).

If, or to the extent that, the payments referred to in (1) and (10) above are for qualifying travel expenses, or for amounts expended 'wholly, exclusively and necessarily' in the performance of his duties, the employee may claim relief under s 198. Claims of expenses and benefits for which the inspector has issued a dispensation (s 166(1)) need not be included in the return.

The amount to be entered by an employer on returns of expenses payments on forms P9D and P11D, or by an employee when claiming a deduction for expenses, should include any amount paid by way of VAT, which is reimbursed, whether or not the employer may subsequently recover all or part of that VAT by repayment or set-off (SP A6, A7).

A return P46(Car) is required at the end of any quarter in which a car is first made available or replaced, if a second car is provided, if the employee begins to earn £8,500+ pa or becomes a director, or if a car is withdrawn without replacement.

When a company grants to a director or employee an option to acquire shares or allots or transfers shares under such a right which might give rise to liability under s 135, it must make a return of particulars of such transactions to the Revenue (s 136(6)).

13.2.14 Accounting to the Revenue for PAYE

Regulations impose an obligation on the employer to pay tax deducted under PAYE to the Collector of Taxes or Accounts office within 14 days of the end of the tax month in which the deduction was required. Employers with a monthly liability below £1,500 may choose to account for such deductions on a quarterly basis instead.

The Collector is provided with powers to recover such amounts of PAYE and NICs which are overdue. Further provisions enable such sums to be recovered from the employee rather than employer in certain circumstances.

It is also worth remembering that where an employer has not paid over the PAYE tax to the Collector of Taxes within 14 days of the end of the year of assessment (ie by 19 April), that unpaid tax or NICs automatically carries interest from 19 April until the date of payment.

13.2.15 End of year returns

In addition to paying over the tax and NICs, the employer is required to submit certain documents to the Inspector of Taxes providing details of the employees, their emoluments and tax and NICs due. Individuals' end of year summaries (form P14) and the employer's end of year return or annual return (form P35) are required to be submitted by 19 May following the end of the year to which they relate. Penalties may be charged for late submission. Additional documents may be required where, for example, payments are made to casuals or where students have been employed.

13.3 BENEFITS IN KIND

13.3.1 General rules

The legislation distinguishes between 'P11D employees' (ie directors and employees earning £8,500 or more pa) and other employees. An employer is required to submit form P11D in respect of each P11D employee who may then be assessed on the cost to the employer of benefits-in-kind received by them. Other employees are normally taxed on benefits only if they are convertible into cash.

Directors are normally within the P11D regime, regardless of whether their remuneration reaches or exceeds the £8,500 limit. An employee falls within the P11D category where remuneration, *together with benefits and reimbursed expenses*, is £8,500 pa or more. Such employees were formerly called 'higher paid' employees. The threshold of £8,500 was set in 1979 and, in accordance with the Government's intentions that all employees should pay income tax on the whole of their earnings, whether received in cash or in kind, this limit has not been increased. By 1989 the term 'higher paid' had become inappropriate and consequently, while there was no change made in the level of the threshold, references to higher paid employees were deleted from the legislation.

Employees are treated as earning £8,500 or more if they are remunerated *at the rate of* £8,500 pa or more. For example, a person whose employment began on 1 January 2000 and who had received a salary of £2,000 and reimbursed expenses of £200 by 6 April 2000 would be within the P11D category as the total amount of £2,200 would give an annual rate greater than £8,500.

Unless a dispensation applies, all reimbursed expenses and other benefits have to be reported on form P11D and count towards the £8,500 limit, even though they may be justified as being for business purposes and no taxable benefit-in-kind ultimately arises.

Dispensations
(TA 1988, s 166)

The Revenue may grant a dispensation so that certain reimbursed expenses need not be reported on form P11D. This is clearly useful in reducing administration and accounting work and, wherever possible, employers should apply for a dispensation. The expenses covered by it will be set out by the Revenue and any expenses not covered must still be reported. Any changes in the method of reimbursing expenses or scales of allowances must be notified to the Revenue.

13.3.2 Benefits that may result in a tax charge for non-P11D employees

The general rule is that employees who are not within the P11D category are assessable only on benefits capable of being converted into cash or on any benefits provided through an employer meeting an employee's own personal liability. This principle has been modified to some extent so that, for instance, credit vouchers are an assessable benefit even if the employee is not within the P11D category. However, the principle continues to hold good with regard to benefits such as the provision of a company car, free use of assets, beneficial loans etc. Table 13.1 below sets out the position.

Table 13.1 Treatment of benefits received by non-P11D employees

	Taxable	Non-taxable
Benefits capable of being turned to pecuniary account ie convertible to cash	✔	
Luncheon vouchers in excess of 15p per working day		
Credit tokens and vouchers	✔	
Transport vouchers (ie any ticket, pass or other document or token intended to enable a person to obtain passenger transport services)	✔	
Living accommodation	✔	
Payment of employees' personal liabilities	✔	
Relocation expenses (over £8,000)	✔	
Round sum allowances	✔	
Company cars		✔
Free use of assets		✔
Beneficial loans		✔
Medical insurance		✔

13.3.3 Tax treatment of specific benefits received by non-P11D employee

Benefits capable of being converted into cash

Where the benefit is convertible into cash, the measure of assessable benefit is the amount of cash which could be realised, not the cost to the employer. For example, an employee provided with a new suit by the employer would be taxable only on its second-hand value.

Payment of employee's personal liabilities

A liability arises where the employer pays a personal liability of the employee. This includes such items as home heating and lighting bills and water rates, but special rules apply where the employee is in representative accommodation (see 13.3.4).

Credit tokens and vouchers
(TA 1988, s 142)

The taxable amount on credit tokens and vouchers is the cost to the employer of providing them. Vouchers other than cheque vouchers are deemed to be taxable emoluments as and when they are *allocated* to a particular employee, not when they are *used* by that employee.

Transport vouchers
(TA 1988, s 141)

There is specific legislation to ensure that season tickets provided by employers are taxable. Once again, the measure of the assessable benefit is the cost to the employer of providing the voucher.

Living accommodation
(TA 1988, s 145)

The assessable amount is the greater of the gross rateable value of the property or the rent payable by the employer, less any amount made good by the employee. Following the abolition of domestic rates, estimated values are used for new or substantially altered properties. No assessable benefit arises where the employee occupies representative accommodation (see 13.3.4).

Relocation expenses
(TA 1988, s 191A and Sch 11A)

See 13.3.4 below.

13.3.4 Benefits not taxable for any category of employees

There are certain benefits that are not usually taxable even when the employee is within the P11D category. The most common items are described below.

Retirement benefits

Payments by an employer to an *approved* occupational pension scheme to secure retirement benefits for an employee do not give rise to an income tax liability for that employee. Payments into a non-approved scheme are taxable as additional remuneration for the year that the employer makes the relevant contribution. To secure approval, a pension scheme must be established for the sole purpose of providing 'relevant benefits' (ie pensions, death-in-service payments, and widows' and dependants' pensions). In addition, an employee's contributions must not exceed 15% of his remuneration. The pension benefits payable by an approved scheme must not exceed certain limits. Pension schemes are covered in more detail in Chap 14.

Luncheon vouchers

Non-transferable luncheon vouchers (ie vouchers which are not capable of being exchanged for cash) are exempt from income tax up to a limit of 15p per working day. Vouchers for larger amounts are partly exempt, with the excess over 15p being taxable in full, whether or not the employee is within the P11D category.

Staff canteen and dining facilities

No taxable benefit-in-kind arises where the canteen etc is used by all staff. Furthermore, the use of a separate room by directors and more senior staff does not prejudice this exemption, unless the meals provided are superior. The Revenue may also accept, in certain cases, that facilities provided by the employer for staff to use a local restaurant may come within the definition of a 'canteen', provided that *all* staff are eligible to use these facilities on the same terms.

There are requirements which need to be strictly observed. For example, there must be no voucher or form of identification which employees need to produce on entering the restaurant. Furthermore, the Revenue may try to withhold exemption from directors and employees earning £8,500 or more who use such a restaurant facility.

Sports facilities
(TA 1988, s 197G)

No taxable benefit arises on the use or availability of sports facilities owned by the employer. Similarly, no taxable benefit generally arises where an employer takes out corporate membership of an outside sports club so that *all* the employees are able to use the club's facilities. An assessment will, however, be made if the employer takes out a subscription for a particular director or employee earning £8,500 or more, or if the subscription covers a small group of such employees and directors.

Works buses and public transport
(TA 1988, ss 197AA and 197AB, respectively)

There is no charge for the use of a works bus (more than 17 seats) provided for journeys between home and work or between workplaces. A similar relief is given for support for public transport bus services for such journeys.

For 2002–03 and later years, this exemption is modified so that where employees benefit from their employer's subsidy of a bus service by receiving free or reduced price travel there is no tax charge on this benefit. This extension only applies to journeys on local stopping services. It means the tax treatment of employee travel on subsidised local bus services is the same of that for travel on employer-provided works buses.

Cycles and cycle safety equipment
(TA 1988, s 197AC)

The provision of a cycle and safety equipment is not chargeable if use thereof is restricted to journeys between home and work and between places of work.

Workplace nurseries and crèches
(TA 1988, s 155A)

Employees are exempt from income tax on the benefit derived from the use of a workplace nursery provided by the employer. The exemption applies only to nurseries run by employers alone or jointly with other employers or bodies, either at the workplace or elsewhere. The provision by an employer of cash allowances to employees for childcare, or the direct meeting of an employee's childcare bills by an employer, are taxable benefits.

Relocation expenses
(TA 1988, s 191A & Sch 11A)

Section 191A and Sch 11A provide for a ceiling of £8,000 for the amount which may be paid tax free for any one move. It is not necessary for the individual to dispose of his former residence in order to qualify for the exemption. Payments made to compensate employees for losses on the sale of their old houses are now regarded as taxable. Many practitioners still regard this as debatable and base their arguments on a decision by the House of Lords, *Hochstrasser v Mayes* [1960] AC 376.

Since 5 April 1998, relocation expenses exceeding £8,000 are subject to NICs.

Long service awards
(ESC A22)

Awards to directors and employees to mark long service are exempt provided the period of service is at least 20 years and no similar award has been given to the employee within the previous ten years. The gift must not consist of cash and the cost should not exceed £20 per year of service. An Inland Revenue concession has extended the exemption to gifts of shares in the company which employs the individual or in another group company.

Awards under suggestion schemes
(ESC A57)

Provided the employee is not engaged in research work, he may receive a tax-free payment under a firm's suggestion scheme. Making suggestions should not, however, be regarded as part of the employee's job. The size of the award should be within certain limits (ie £25 or less where the suggestion, although not implemented, has intrinsic value). Where the suggestion *is* implemented, the amount should be related to the expected net financial benefit (ENFB) to the employer. The current limits are:

(1) 50% of the ENFB during the first year of implementation, or
(2) 10% of the ENFB over a period of up to five years.

The overriding maximum is £5,000; any excess of £5,000 is taxable.

Pool cars
(TA 1988, s 159)

No tax charge arises by reason of the use of a pooled car. A car qualifies as a pooled car only if *all* the following conditions are satisfied:

(1) It is available for, and used by, more than one employee and is not ordinarily used by any one of them to the exclusion of the others.
(2) Any private use of the car by an employee is merely incidental to its business use.
(3) It is not normally kept overnight at or near the residence of any of the employees unless it is kept on premises occupied by the employer.

These requirements are strictly interpreted. Note that a car only qualifies as a pooled car *for a tax year*. There is a danger therefore in a car being taken out of pooled use and allotted to a specific employee towards the end of a tax year. As the car now no longer qualifies as a pooled car, any employee who has had the car available for private use during the same tax year may be assessed. Therefore, if the car is ordinarily parked overnight near the home of one of the users, it will not qualify as a pooled car and will create tax problems for any other employees who use it.

Representative accommodation
(TA 1988, s 145(4))

Living accommodation qualifies as representative accommodation if *any one* of the following conditions is satisfied:

(1) It is necessary for the performance of the employee's duties that he should reside in the accommodation.
(2) The accommodation is provided for the better performance of the employee's duties and it is customary to provide accommodation for such employees.
(3) The employee has to live in the accommodation because of a special threat to his security.

The exemption under the first two conditions is usually only available to directors who (together with their associates) hold 5% or less of the company's ordinary share capital and are full-time working directors. Where the employer pays for heating, lighting, repairs, maintenance etc, the representative occupiers cannot be assessed in respect of such benefits on more than 10% of their emoluments of the employment.

Re-training
(TA 1988, ss 588–589)

Where an employer pays the cost of a course undertaken by an employee (or former employee) to provide him with skills for future employment elsewhere (or self-employment), the cost of the course can be a deductible expense of the employer, and may not be a taxable benefit of the employee. Furthermore, ss 200B–200J provide restricted relief to training related to the current employment.

Counselling
(TA 1988, ss 589A and 589B)

Relief in similar form to that available for re-training costs is available for qualifying counselling services for outplacement, coming to terms with redundancy, etc.

Sandwich courses
(SP4/86, re-issued November 1992)

Where an employee is released by his employer to take a full-time educational course at a university, technical college or similar educational institution which is open to the public at large, payments for periods of attendance may be treated as exempt from income tax. There are various conditions that attach to this exemption, ie:

(1) The course must last for at least one academic year with an average of at least 20 weeks of full-time attendance.
(2) The rate of payment must not exceed the greater of £7,000 and the rate of payment that an individual would have received had he been granted a public grant.

Where the rate of payment exceeds the above limits, the full amount is taxable but where the amount of payment is increased during a course, only subsequent payments are taxable.

Computer equipment
(TA 1988, s 156A)

There is a limited exemption for computer equipment and peripheral devices. Relief is limited to the first £500 of the cash equivalent of such equipment made available to an employee.

13.3.5 Free use of assets
(TA 1988, s 156)

A taxable benefit arises where an asset is made available by an employer for use by a director or P11D employee. The annual benefit is 20% of the asset's market value when it was *first* made available for use by the employee. Assets that may be involved include yachts, furniture, television sets, stereo equipment, company vans etc, ie virtually any asset apart from living accommodation and company cars. If the employer rents or hires the asset for a sum in excess of 20% of its original market value, the higher rental charge is substituted as the assessable benefit. A deduction is allowed for any contribution or rental payable by the employee.

A further charge may arise if the ownership of assets is eventually transferred to the employee. The amount may be determined either by the market value of the asset at the time of transfer of ownership, or, where a higher figure results, by the original cost of the asset at the time it was first made available as a benefit for *any* person, less any amounts already charged as benefits in connection with the availability of the asset.

The second alternative does not apply to cars.

Example – Transfer of assets

XYZ Ltd provides *A* with the use of a yacht which costs £40,000 with *A* paying a rental of £2,000 pa. After two years the yacht is sold to *A* for its second-hand market value of £20,000. The assessable benefit would be:

	Benefit £
Year 1	
£40,000 × 20%	8,000
Less rental paid	2,000
	6,000
Year 2	
40,000 × 20%	8,000
Less rental paid	2,000
	6,000
Year 3	
Cost of yacht	40,000
Less benefits assessed in years one and two	(12,000)
Amounts paid by employee	(24,000)
	4,000

Where an asset, previously made available to an individual, is transferred at no cost to him (or to another employee), at a time when its market value is still high, it is possible that the overall effect is that the total cost of the benefit for tax purposes exceeds the original cost. In other cases, the rules may operate to impose a high benefit charge upon the transfer of an asset despite the value of the asset having rapidly depreciated during the period of use.

Such rules must therefore be considered carefully when planning the provision of an asset for use by or arranging for its transfer to an employee. It may be that transfer of ownership should be avoided where assets have a relatively short useful life if a tax-efficient remuneration package is desired.

Example – Ownership of assets

A company provides employees with the use of suits which remain the property of the company. The suits cost £200 and have a useful life of two years, after which they are scrapped.

An employee could therefore have an effective benefit of £200 but would be charged tax on only £40 for each of the two tax years.

13.4 TRAVELLING, SUBSISTENCE AND ENTERTAINING

13.4.1 General rules

Travel between home and the ordinary place of work does not rank as business travel. Where an individual is 'on call' and assumes the responsibilities of the employment upon leaving home, it may be possible to argue that home to work travel is business and not private travel, but this usually applies only in exceptional cases.

In order to secure tax relief on reimbursed travelling expenses, the employee must keep adequate records so as to distinguish business from non-business travel. Ideally, expenses claims to the employer should show the actual cost of such travel and, if the employer is to obtain a dispensation, the Revenue needs to be satisfied that such internal controls exist.

Mileage allowances should not be so large as to create a 'profit' element which would of course be taxable. The Revenue has introduced a Fixed Profit Car Scheme setting maximum rates of reimbursement which can be treated as tax free. These are *reduced* when the business mileage exceeds 10,000 miles pa. The rates for 2002–03 are:

Amount per mile

Up to 10,000 miles	*Over 10,000 miles*
40p	25p

Provided these rates are not exceeded and mileage is for business purposes, no benefit-in-kind will arise. Interest paid on a loan taken out for the purchase of a car used for business purposes may qualify for tax relief. Relief for such interest is not included in Fixed Profit Car Scheme rates and needs to be claimed separately.

13.4.2 Subsistence

The Revenue view is that it is strictly only the extra costs of living away from home which are allowable. If there are continuing financial commitments at home, the whole cost of living away from home is normally allowed. This concession is not available if the employee has no permanent residence, for example an unmarried person who normally lives in a hotel or club and who gives up that accommodation when away on a business trip. There is a specific exemption where an employee performs his duties wholly overseas and needs board and lodging abroad in order to do so.

There is, however, a statutory *de minimis* exclusion for incidental overnight expenses, where an individual is away from home on a 'qualifying absence' and the expenses, which would not otherwise be deductible, do not exceed a £5 nightly maximum for absences elsewhere in the UK and £10 if the absence is abroad (s 200A).

13.4.3 Overseas travelling expenses
(TA 1988, ss 192–193)

Where some or all of the duties of an employment are performed abroad, the expenses of travelling to and from the UK to carry out these duties are specifically regarded as having been necessarily incurred in the performance of the overseas employment. It follows, therefore, that if those expenses are reimbursed by the employer, no benefit-in-kind arises. Recent legislative changes have relaxed the rules further, so that, while the employee is serving abroad, the employer may pay for an unlimited number of journeys made by the employee to and from the UK without any tax charge arising. However, these journeys must be made wholly and exclusively for the purpose of performing the duties of the employment.

Moreover, where an employee travels between places where different jobs are performed, and one or more of these jobs is performed wholly or partly overseas, the expenses incurred in travelling overseas are also deemed to be necessarily incurred in performing the duties carried out overseas, so that once again no benefit-in-kind arises. In many cases, there is dual purpose in travelling and a taxable benefit-in-kind arises on the private element. Consequently, where travel expenses relate partly to a foreign holiday taken at the end of the business trip, there would be a taxable benefit-in-kind.

Similarly, a benefit-in-kind may be assessed on some or all of the expense where a spouse accompanies a director or employee and where this is not necessary for business purposes.

Maintenance of records

A director or employee who travels overseas should be able to substantiate a claim that expenses were necessarily incurred for business purposes by producing details of the expenses and the time spent away from home. A brief itinerary should be available where travel is undertaken within the overseas country or countries. The Revenue normally expects that an employer will properly control expenditure but in certain cases it may wish to see receipted bills or other vouchers.

13.4.4 Spouse's travelling and subsistence expenses

Where a spouse or other family member accompanies the director or employee abroad on a business trip, it is helpful in satisfying the Revenue that no benefit-in-kind arises if the board of directors minute their decision that he should be so accompanied. However, this is not generally sufficient in itself and it must be shown that the spouse or relative was able to perform certain tasks that could not be performed by the director.

It may be possible to show this if the spouse has some practical qualification, for example an ability to speak the foreign language concerned. A relative's expenses might also be allowable where the director or employee is in poor health and to travel alone would be impracticable or unreasonable. Where the individual's presence is for the purpose of accompanying his or her spouse at business entertainment functions, the expenses of the trip may be disallowed in calculating the employer's tax liability under the entertainment legislation, even though the expenses may be allowable in determining the employee's tax liability.

13.4.5 Employees working overseas: family visits
(TA 1988, s 194)

Where an employee is abroad for a continuous period of 60 days or more, there is an exemption for amounts borne by the employer for travelling expenses for visits by the employee's spouse and minor children. The exemption is only available for two journeys by the same person in each direction in a tax year. There is no relief if the employee ultimately bears the expense personally.

13.4.6 Entertaining expenses and round-sum allowances

It is not uncommon for directors or employees to have a round-sum allowance to cover such things as travelling, subsistence and entertaining. In the case of travelling and subsistence, the allowance counts as the taxable income of the director or employee, but a tax deduction may be claimed for any part of the allowance which can be shown to have been spent for business purposes. It is very important to have a record-keeping system which enables such claims to be substantiated. It may be better for the employer to dispense with round-sum allowances and reimburse the director or employee for properly substantiated expenditure. In this way, no benefit-in-kind should arise.

In the case of entertaining expenditure, the situation is rather more complex. If an employer reimburses a director's or employee's entertaining expenditure or pays a round-sum allowance which is specifically intended for entertaining, the expense to the employer is disallowed for tax purposes. The reimbursement or allowance is entered on the director's or employee's P11D but a deduction may be claimed for all the expenditure which is for genuine business purposes. If, on the other hand, the director or employee is given a round-sum allowance not specifically designated as being for entertaining, there is no question of the allowance being disallowed in the employer's tax computation. However, the director or employee would only escape liability on any part of the allowance which could be shown to have been used for business expenditure *other than* entertainment.

13.4.7 Private use of company vans
(TA 1988, ss 159AA–159AC and Sch 6A)

An employee may be assessed on a standard amount of £500 per year for private use of a company van. The amount is reduced to £350 for vans which are four or more years old at the end of the tax year. Any vehicles in excess of 3.5 tons are exempt from tax altogether (unless the vehicle is used wholly or mainly for the employee's private purposes). Where an employee has two or more vans made available for private use at the same time, tax is charged on the scale figure for each van. The standard amount will be reduced *pro rata* where the van is only available part of the year. A reduction is made for any contributions made by the employee towards the private use. Where a van is shared amongst several employees, the standard amount is apportioned among the employees.

13.5 COMPANY CARS

13.5.1 Car benefits
(TA 1988, ss 157, 168A–168G and Sch 6)

Prior to 6 April 2002, the taxable benefit was based on the list price of the car at the time that it was first registered, and not on the cost of the car. The taxable benefit was 35% of the list price which includes delivery charges, standard accessories and optional accessories fitted when the car was first made available to the employee. A separate addition to the list price is also made where accessories are fitted after the car has been made available, but accessories with a list price of less than £100 and accessories installed before 1 August 1993 are left out of account. Where the car is at least four years old at the end of the tax year the benefit is reduced by one-third.

Where the list price of a vehicle exceeds £80,000, the excess is not taken into account.

Where a car is more than 15 years old at the end of the tax year, the car has a market value of at least £15,000 and the market value exceeds the list price, the benefit-in-kind is calculated by reference to the market value rather than original list price.

The assessable benefit is reduced by one-third where there is at least 2,500 business miles pa. There is a reduction of a further one-third where the business mileage is at least 18,000 miles pa.

Prima facie, if an employee is offered a car in return for a reduction in salary, he may well be taxable under Schedule E on the amount of remuneration foregone (*Heaton v Bell* (1969) 46 TC 211, HL). However this charge is specifically prevented by s 157A.

A new system for evaluating the taxable benefit, based on CO_2 emissions, applies for 2002–03 and subsequent years.

Cash equivalent

The cash equivalent of the benefit is the appropriate percentage for the year of the price of the car as regards the year. However, this is subject to reductions for periods when the car is unavailable and payments for use of the car. The appropriate percentage for the year is determined as follows.

Car with CO_2 emissions figure

This rule applies where the car is first registered:

(1) after 31 December 1997 but before 1 October 1999, and when so registered conformed to a vehicle type with an EC type-approval certificate, or had a UK approval certificate, that specifies a CO_2 emissions figure in terms of grams per kilometre (g/km) driven, or

(2) after 30 September 1999, and is so registered on the basis of an EC certificate of conformity or UK approval certificate that specifies a CO_2 emissions figure in terms of g/km driven.

Hear, 'the applicable CO_2 emissions figure' means if the car:

(a) is within (1) above, to the specified CO_2 emissions figure mentioned there, and

(b) is within (2) above, to the specified CO_2 emissions figure mentioned there:

    (i) where the EC certificate of conformity or UK approval certificate specifies only one CO_2 emissions figure, that figure, and

    (ii) where it specifies more than one, the figure specified as the CO_2 emissions (combined) figure.

This is subject to modifications for bi-fuel cars and cars for disabled drivers.

Where the applicable CO_2 emissions figure does not exceed the lower threshold for the year, the appropriate percentage for the year is the basic percentage of 15%.

Where the applicable CO_2 emissions figure exceeds the lower threshold for the year, the appropriate percentage for the year is whichever is the smaller of:

(1) the basic percentage increased by 1% for each 5 g/km by which the applicable CO_2 emissions figure exceeds the lower threshold for the year, and

(2) 35%.

This is subject to a diesel car supplement and any regulations to provide for discounts.

The lower threshold

The lower threshold is ascertained from Table 13.2.

Table 13.2

Year of assessment	Lower threshold (in g/km)
2002–03	165
2003–04	155
2004–05 and subsequent years of assessment	145

The applicable CO_2 emissions figure (if it is not a multiple of five) is rounded down to the nearest multiple of five.

Bi-fuel cars

Where the car:

(1) is first registered after 31 December 2000, and
(2) is so registered on the basis of an EC certificate of conformity, or UK approval certificate, that specifies separate CO_2 emissions figures in terms of grams per kilometre driven for different fuels,

then 'the applicable CO_2 emissions figure' is the lowest figure specified or, if there is more than one figure specified in relation to each fuel, the lowest CO_2 emissions (combined) figure specified.

Automatic cars made available to disabled drivers

The following rule applies where:

(1) the car has a CO_2 emissions figure, and is appropriately certified and registered;
(2) the car has automatic transmission;
(3) at any time in the year when the car is available to the employee, he holds a disabled person's badge (see s 168AA(3)); and
(4) by reason of his disability he must, if he wants to drive a car, drive one that has automatic transmission.

For this purpose the car is not at any time available to the employee by reason only of its being made available to a member of his family or household.

If the applicable CO_2 figure for the car is more than it would have been had the car been an equivalent manual car, the above applies as if the applicable CO_2 emissions figure in relation to the relevant car were the same as that in relation to an equivalent manual car.

An 'equivalent manual car' means one that:

(a) is first registered at or about the same time as the relevant car, and
(b) does not have automatic transmission, but otherwise is the closest variant available of the make and model of the relevant car.

For the purposes of this paragraph a car has automatic transmission if:

(1) the driver is not provided with any means whereby he may vary the gear ratio between the engine and the road wheels independently of the accelerator and the brakes, or

(2) he is provided with such means, but they do not include a clutch pedal or lever that he may operate manually.

EC certificate of conformity, EC type-approval certificate and UK approval certificate

Here:

(1) 'EC certificate of conformity' means a certificate of conformity issued by a manufacturer under any provision of the law of a member state implementing Art 6 of Council Directive 70/156/EEC, as amended;

(2) 'EC type-approval certificate' means a type-approval certificate issued under any provision of the law of a member state implementing Council Directive 70/156/EEC, as amended; and

(3) 'UK approval certificate' means a certificate issued under the Road Traffic Act 1988, s 58(1) or (4), or the Road Traffic (Northern Ireland) Order 1981, art 31A(4) or (5).

Car with no CO_2 emissions figure

The rules set out below apply where the car is first registered after 31 December 1997.

If the car has an internal combustion engine with one or more reciprocating pistons, the appropriate percentage for the year is ascertained from Table 13.3.

Table 13.3

Cylinder capacity of car in cubic centimetres	Appropriate percentage
1,400 or less	15%
More than 1,400 but not more than 2,000	25%
More than 2,000	35%

A car's cylinder capacity is the capacity of its engine calculated as for the purposes of the Vehicle Excise and Registration Act 1994.

Where this does not apply the appropriate percentage for the year is:

(a) 15% if the car is an electrically propelled vehicle, and

(b) 35% in any other case.

This is subject to diesel car supplements and any power to provide for discounts.

Diesel car supplement

Where the car is propelled solely by diesel, and is first registered after 31 December 1997, the appropriate percentage for the year is whichever is the smaller of:

(1) the percentage which is 3% greater than the appropriate percentage for the year, and
(2) 35%.

This is subject to any power to provide for discount.

Discounts

The Treasury may by regulations provide for the value of the appropriate percentage as determined above to be reduced by such amount as may be prescribed in the regulations, in such circumstances and subject to such conditions as may be so prescribed.

Car registered before 1 January 1998

Where the car was first registered before 1 January 1998, and has an internal combustion engine with one or more reciprocating pistons, the appropriate percentage for the year is ascertained from Table 13.4.

Table 13.4

Cylinder capacity of car in cubic centimetres	Appropriate percentage
1,400 or less	15%
More than 1,400 but not more than 2,000	22%
More than 2,000	32%

For this purpose a car's cylinder capacity is that of its engine calculated as for the purposes of the Vehicle Excise and Registration Act 1994.

Where the above does not apply, the appropriate percentage for the year is:

(1) 15% if the car is an electrically propelled vehicle, and
(2) 32% in any other case.

Electrically propelled vehicle

A vehicle is not an electrically propelled vehicle unless:

(1) it is propelled solely by electrical power, and
(2) that power is derived from:
  (a) a source external to the vehicle, or
  (b) an electrical storage battery which is not connected to any source of power when the vehicle is in motion.

Reduction for periods when car unavailable

Where for any part of the year concerned the car is unavailable, the cash equivalent of the benefit is the amount ascertained as above multiplied by the fraction:

$$\frac{A}{B}$$

where: A = the number of days in the year on which the car is available; and
B = the number of days in the year.

13.5.2 Tax treatment of employee contributions

Contributions made by an employee towards the cost of the car can be deducted from the list price, subject to a maximum deduction of £5,000.

Example – Employee contributions to company cars

Two employees are entitled to company cars. One contributed £4,000 towards a car with a list price of £18,000 while the other contributed £11,000 towards a car with a list price of £25,000. Their assessable benefits-in-kind for 2002–03 are:

	A £	B £
List price	18,000	25,000
Less capital contribution income of:		
(A) amount contributed	(4,000)	
(B) deduction for capital contribution limited to		(5,000)
	14,000	20,000
35% thereof	4,900	7,000
Assessable benefits	4,900	7,000

Annual payments made by employees for private use of a car may still reduce the assessable benefit on a £1 for £1 basis. In the above example, *B* would have been better off if he had reduced his initial capital contribution and made annual payments in return for being allowed to use the vehicle for private purposes.

13.5.3 Returns

So as to enable coding notices to be amended to reflect changes in an employee's car benefit, employers have to submit returns for directors or employees who either:

(1) have a car provided for the first time;
(2) change vehicles;
(3) have the use of an additional car;
(4) have the use of a car withdrawn;
(5) qualify to be assessed on an existing car either by being appointed a director, or by coming within the 'higher paid' employee category.

Returns, using Inland Revenue form P46 (car), should be returned on a quarterly basis covering the following periods:

Period of return	Latest date for submission
6 April to 5 July	2 August
6 July to 5 October	2 November
6 October to 5 January	2 February
6 January to 5 April	3 May

The return provides details as to the make of car, engine size, list price, accessories, capital contributions and anticipated annual business mileage.

The maximum penalty for failing to submit a return by the due date is £300 plus £60 per day until the return is submitted.

The maximum penalty for submitting an incorrect return, either fraudulently or negligently, is £3,000.

13.5.4 Private petrol
(TA 1988, s 158)

An additional scale benefit applies where an employer provides private petrol for use in a car to which a scale benefit charge arises. The scale charge depends entirely on engine size. The scale for 2002–03 is as follows:

Engine size (cc)	Petrol £	Engine size (cc)	Diesel £
Up to 1400	1,930	Up to 2000	2,460
1401 to 2000	2,460	2000+	3,620
2000+	3,620		

The scale figures apply regardless of the amount of private fuel provided. If *any* is provided, the fuel scale charge always applies unless the employee reimburses his employer for the full cost. In some cases it may be cost effective for an employee to do this and the position should therefore be reviewed before the start of each new tax year.

13.5.5 Other related costs

The scale benefit does not cover the salary of a chauffeur. If a director is allocated a chauffeur, the full cost to the employer of providing the chauffeur should be included on the director's form P11D and will therefore be potentially assessable as a benefit-in-kind (subject to a claim for business mileage).

13.5.6 Car parking spaces
(TA 1988, s 197A)

The provision of a car parking space at or near the employee's place of work is not a taxable benefit. Where, however, an employee pays for car parking himself, he cannot claim a deduction for those charges.

13.5.7 Cash alternative
(TA 1988, s 157A)

Where a car is made available to an employee, the mere fact that he is offered a cash alternative to the benefit of the car does not make the benefit chargeable.

13.6 BENEFICIAL LOANS
(TA 1988, s 160)

13.6.1 Type of loans which are caught

A charge generally arises for directors and P11D employees on the annual value of beneficial loan arrangements. The annual value of a loan is taken as interest at the 'official rate' less the amount of interest (if any) paid by the employee. The official rate is revised regularly to keep pace with movements in interest rates generally. An additional taxable benefit arises if the loan is subsequently written off or forgiven.

The beneficial loan provisions can also apply if a loan is made to a member of an employee's family.

Moreover, the Revenue is able to assess benefits even though there may be no formal loan, where credit has been involved. In particular, a director who overdraws his current account with the company is regarded as having obtained a loan and is subject to an assessment.

Almost all loans by employers (and persons connected with them) are caught as the legislation deems such loans to have been given by reason of the employment. Until 6 April 1994, there was only a single exception in that this rule did not apply where the employee was related to the employer and it could be shown that the loan was given for family reasons. There were no other exceptions and there have been cases where bank employees etc have paid a normal commercial rate of interest on money lent to them, but have been assessed on a benefit because the interest they have paid has been less than the official rate.

For 1994–95 and subsequent years, loans made by an employer whose business includes lending money to the general public do not give rise to a charge on the employees provided the loans are made on similar terms to the public.

13.6.2 Beneficial loans used for a qualifying purpose

No charge arises on a cheap loan where the money borrowed has been applied for a qualifying purpose, eg to purchase shares in a close company in which the individual has a material interest or where he is employed full time in the conduct and management of the company's business.

13.6.3 *De minimis* exemption

There is an exemption for all cheap or interest-free loans not exceeding £5,000 made to an individual employee. This figure excludes loans that qualify for tax relief, eg loans of up to £30,000 for house purchase.

13.6.4 Employee loans written off

If the loan is written off, the amount forgiven is treated as assessable income for that year even if the person is no longer employed by that company. The only exception here is if the loan is forgiven on the employee's death.

Some care needs to be taken if it is decided to clear a loan by making an *ex gratia* or compensation payment to an employee upon the termination of the employment. An income tax liability arises if the loan is formally written off. On the other hand, no liability normally arises if the employee receives a cheque as an *ex gratia* or compensation payment and uses that sum to clear his outstanding loan. It is recommended that professional advice be taken in such circumstances.

13.7 LIVING ACCOMMODATION
(TA 1988, ss 145–146)

13.7.1 Introduction

The income tax charge which generally applies where an employee is provided with accommodation (unless it is representative accommodation – see 13.3.4) depends on whether the property is owned or rented by the employer. In the past, where the employer owned the property, the assessable amount was usually the gross annual value for rating purposes. Despite the abolition of domestic rates, this treatment continues to apply for properties on existing rating lists. For new properties, and those where there have been major improvements, the Revenue makes an estimate of what the gross annual value would have been had rates continued.

Where the property is rented by the employer, the assessable amount is the greater of the rent paid and the annual value as above. In addition a charge may arise on the annual value of any furniture and fixtures, and on any occupier's expenses borne by the company such as water rates, decorations, gardener's wages etc.

An additional charge may arise where the employer paid more than £75,000 to acquire the property. The amount assessable is a percentage of the excess of the cost of the property over £75,000. The percentage to be applied is the official rate of interest used for beneficial loans (see 13.6) as at the *beginning* of the tax year.

Example – Charge on living accommodation in excess of £75,000

A company director occupies a property owned by the company which has a gross annual value of £2,000. The cost of the property was £100,000.
  The director is assessed on the following amount for 2002–03:

	£
Gross annual value	2,000
£25,000 × (say) 8% =	2,000
	4,000

13.7.2 Properties owned for more than six years

Where the property is made available to an employee and has been owned by the company for at least six years, the figure taken into account in computing the additional charge is the market value at the time it was made available rather than the cost. The actual cost (including improvements) to the employer is still used to determine whether the provisions will apply. Consequently, properties whose actual cost (including any improvements) was less than £75,000 are not within the scope of this additional charge even if their market value exceeds £75,000. Where the actual cost exceeded £75,000, the additional charge is based on the market value.

Example – Charge on living accommodation purchased over six years ago

In the example in 13.7.1, assume that the company has owned the property for more than six years and that in May 1997, when the director first occupies it, the market value is £200,000. As the original cost of the property exceeded £75,000, the director is assessed on the following amount for 2002–03:

	£
Gross annual value	2,000
£125,000 × (say) 8% =	10,000
	12,000

13.7.3 Possible reduction in assessable amount

It may be possible to reduce the assessable amount where the employee is required to occupy a property which is larger than would normally be needed for his or her own purposes. In *Westcott v Bryan* (1969) 45 TC 476 a director was required to live in a large house so that he could entertain customers. He was allowed a reduction in the assessable amount to cover the relevant proportion of the annual value and the running expenses.

Some care is needed if it is intended to claim relief in this way. This claim succeeded because the house was larger than needed for the director and his family. It would not have succeeded had the property merely been more expensive than he would have chosen. It was also helpful that the directors of the company had approved board minutes setting out their requirement and the business reason for it.

13.7.4 Holiday accommodation and foreign properties

Some employers buy holiday flats or cottages etc for use by staff. In practice, the Revenue generally apportions the assessable amount for the year amongst those employees who have occupied the property. The assessment can be reduced by letting the accommodation to third parties when it is not required by directors and employees. A practical problem arises with regard to overseas properties. Because there is no rateable value, the benefit is the annual rent which the property would normally command on the open market.

13.8 MISCELLANEOUS BENEFITS

13.8.1 Council tax

Where an employer pays the council tax on behalf of an employee, this is normally chargeable as part of the employee's remuneration package, resulting in a charge to both income tax and NICs. The one exception to this is where the employee is a representative occupier (see 13.3.4).

13.8.2 Medical insurance
(TA 1988, s 155(6))

The cost of medical insurance is normally assessable on P11D employees. Where the employer has a group scheme, a proportion of the total premiums is related to individual employees. There is an exception in that the premiums are exempt to the extent that they provide cover for an employee working outside the UK.

13.8.3 Telephone rental

The Revenue treats the full amount of the rental paid by the employer as a taxable benefit-in-kind even though the telephone may be partly (or mainly) used for business calls. The decision in *Lucas v Cattell* (1972) 48 TC 353 was that the expenditure on rental had a dual purpose (ie that a telephone is intended to be used for both business and personal use) and therefore no part of it was allowable.

13.8.4 Club subscriptions

A benefit-in-kind is deemed to arise where an employer pays or reimburses an employee's subscription to a club, even though the employee may only belong to the club in order to entertain the employer's customers.

13.8.5 In-house tax and financial advice

This is a type of expenditure which the Revenue has ignored in the past, but is now treated as a benefit-in-kind where the cost can clearly be allocated to particular employees. Similarly the Revenue will seek to assess directors on a benefit-in-kind where work on their personal taxation affairs has been carried out by the company's auditors, the cost being recovered in whole or in part from the company.

13.8.6 Christmas parties and other annual functions
(Extra-Statutory Concession A70)

The Revenue has said that it will not assess a benefit in respect of 'modest' expenditure on a Christmas party for staff, provided the party is open to all staff. The limit for expenditure to be regarded as modest in this context is currently £75 per head. Although this rule is generally attributed to Christmas parties, it may apply to a function at another time of year.

Where there is more than one annual function and their total costs per head exceed £75, the functions that total £75 or less are not taxed. All other functions are taxed in full.

13.8.7 Legal fees

There may be expenditure which is incurred for the benefit of the company's business but nevertheless is deemed to give rise to a benefit-in-kind. A leading case in this connection concerned a director of a company who was accused of dangerous driving. It was necessary for the company's business that he should not be imprisoned and the company paid his legal expenses. Although the lawyers engaged by the company were more expensive than the director would have used himself, the expenditure by the company was treated as a benefit-in-kind.

13.8.8 Outplacement counselling
(TA 1988, s 589B)

The value of outplacement services provided to employees made redundant is exempt from income tax. Such services may include assistance with CVs, job searches, office equipment provisions and advice on interview skills. These costs are not treated as part of a termination payment (see 13.19).

13.8.9 Goods and services provided at a discount to the normal price ('in-house benefits')

Where employees are allowed to purchase goods or services from their employer, no tax charge arises provided they pay an amount equal to the employer's cost. The House of Lords has decided that 'cost' meant marginal cost, not average cost (*Pepper v Hart* [1992] STC 898). This normally produces a significantly lower benefit.

Following this, the Revenue published a statement in January 1993 setting out its practice for the future with regard to teachers, employees within the transport industry and other employees who receive goods or services from their employer. The relevant press release stated that Treasury Ministers had the matter under review but, in the event, the decision has not been disturbed.

The Revenue has stated that the decision in *Pepper v Hart* means that:

(1) rail or bus travel by employees on terms which do not displace fare-paying passengers involves no or negligible additional costs;

(2) goods sold at a discount which leave employees paying at least the wholesale price involve no or negligible net benefit;

(3) where teachers pay 15% or more of a school's normal fees, there is no net benefit;

(4) professional services which do not require additional employees or partners (eg legal and financial services) have no or negligible cost to the employer (provided the employee meets the cost of any disbursements).

13.8.10 Director's tax paid by employer
(TA 1988, s 164)

Any tax (as NICs) paid by an employer on behalf of a director must be included as part of his emoluments.

13.8.11 Scholarships
(TA 1988, s 165)

Although scholarships are not taxable upon the recipient (s 331), they are taxed as benefits if he is a member of an employee's family. This does not apply if no more than 25%, in value, of the scholarship is granted to such persons, and it is not awarded because of the employment.

13.9 END OF YEAR RETURNS

Form P11D can be obtained from the local Revenue office. The form needs to be submitted by 6 June following the end of the tax year. If the forms are submitted late there can be a penalty of up to £300 for each late return, and a continuing daily penalty of up to £60 may be imposed under similar procedures as for forms P35/P14. Penalties up to £3,000 may be charged for each incorrectly completed return.

13.10 PERSONAL SERVICE COMPANIES
(FA 1988, s 60; FA 2000, Sch 12)

13.10.1 Application of the rules
(FA 2000, Sch 12, paras 1–6)

Engagements to which the rules apply

The special rules apply where:

(1) an individual 'worker' personally performs (whether or not by obligation) services for the purposes of a business carried on by the 'client';
(2) the services are provided not under a contract directly between the client and the worker but under arrangements involving a third party (the 'intermediary'); and
(3) the circumstances are such that, if the services were provided under a contract directly between the client and worker, the worker would be regarded for income tax purposes as the client's employee.

Here, 'business' includes any activity carried on by a government or public body or a local authority (in the UK or elsewhere), or a body corporate, unincorporated body or partnership. A third party includes a partnership or unincorporated body of which the worker is a member.

The circumstances referred to in (3) above include the terms on which the services are provided, having regard to the terms of contract forming part of the arrangements under which they are so provided. The fact that the worker holds an office with the client does not affect the application of these rules.

Worker treated as receiving Schedule E income

If, in the case of an engagement within these rules, in any tax year

(1) the conditions specified below are met in relation to the intermediary, and
(2) the worker, or an associate of his:
    (a) receives directly or indirectly from the intermediary a payment or benefit not chargeable to Schedule E tax, or
    (b) has rights entitling him to receive such a payment or benefit from the intermediary,

the intermediary is treated as making a 'deemed Schedule E payment' to the worker in that tax year. The deemed payment is treated as made at the end of the tax year unless an earlier date of deemed payment applied in certain cases (Sch 12, para 12; see 13.10.3). A single payment is treated as made in respect of all relevant engagements in relation to which the intermediary is treated as making such payment in the tax year.

Conditions of liability where intermediary is a company

Where the intermediary is a company, the conditions are that the intermediary is not an associated company of the client and either the worker has a material interest in the intermediary, or the payment or benefit not chargeable under Schedule E:

(1) is received by the worker directly from the intermediary, and
(2) can reasonably be taken to represent remuneration for services provided by the worker to the client.

An associated company is one where the client and the intermediary are both under the worker's (whether alone or with associates) control. A material interest means:

(a) beneficial ownership of, or the ability to control, more than 5% of the company's ordinary share capital;
(b) possession of or entitlement to acquire rights entitling the holder to receive more than 5% of any distributions that may be made by the company; or
(c) in the case of a close company, possession of or entitlement to acquire rights that, should the company be wound up or under any other

circumstance, entitle the holder to receive more than 5% of the assets that would then be available for distribution among the participators (s 417(1)).

Conditions of liability where intermediary is a partnership

In relation to payments or benefits received by a worker as a member of the partnership, the conditions are that:

(1) the worker (alone or with relatives) is entitled to 60% or more of the partnership profits; or
(2) most of the profits derive from services provided under engagements that apply to a single client (whether alone or with associates); or
(3) under the profit-sharing arrangements the income of any partner is based on the amount of income generated by him in providing services to the partnership.

'Relative' means husband or wife, parent of remoter forebear, child or remoter issue, or brother or sister.

With regard to a worker who is not a member of the partnership, the conditions are that the payment or benefit:

(1) is received by the worker directly from the intermediary, and
(2) can reasonably be taken to represent remuneration for services provided by the worker to the client.

Conditions of liability where intermediary is an individual

The conditions under these circumstances are that the payment or benefit:

(1) is received by the worker directly from the intermediary, and
(2) can reasonably be taken to represent remuneration for services provided by the worker to the client.

Exception of certain payments subject to deduction of tax

These rules do not apply to payments subject to deduction of tax under s 555 (payments to non-resident entertainers and sportsmen).

13.10.2 Deemed Schedule E payment
(FA 2000, Sch 12, paras 7–11)

Calculation of deemed payment

There are nine steps to be taken in calculating the deemed Schedule E payment for a tax year.

Step 1   Find the total amount of all payments and other benefits received by the intermediary in that year in respect of the relevant engagements, and reduce it by 5%.

Step 2   Add the amount of any payments and other benefits received by the worker in that year in respect of the relevant engagements, other than from the intermediary, that are not chargeable to Schedule E income tax, and would not be so chargeable if the worker were employed by the client.

Step 3   Deduct the amount of any expenses met in that year by the intermediary that would have been deductible from the emoluments of the employment if the worker had been employed by the client and the expenses had been met by the worker out of those emoluments.

Step 4   Deduct the amount of any capital allowances in respect of expenditure incurred by the intermediary that could have been claimed by the worker under CAA 1990, s 27 (plant and machinery: extension of allowances to employments etc) if the worker had been employed by the client and had incurred the expenditure.

Step 5   Deduct any contributions made in that year by the intermediary for the worker's benefit to a retirement benefits scheme approved under ss 590–612, or to a personal pension scheme approved under ss 630–655, that if made by an employer for an employee's benefit would not be chargeable to income tax as employee's income. This does not apply to excess contributions made and later repaid.

Step 6   Deduct the amount of any employer's NICs paid by the intermediary for that year in respect of the worker.

Step 7   Deduct the amount of any payments or other benefits received in that year by the worker from the intermediary:

(1) in respect of which the worker is chargeable to Schedule E income tax, and
(2) which do not represent items in respect of which a deduction was made under Step 3.

If the result at this point is nil or a negative amount, there is no deemed Schedule E payment.

Step 8   Find the amount that together with the employer's NICs on it is equal to the amount resulting from Step 7.

Step 9   The result is the amount of the deemed Schedule E payment.

Treatment of payments made under construction industry scheme

Where s 559 applies (construction industry subcontractors: payments to be made under deduction), the intermediary is treated for the purposes of

Step 1 above as receiving the amount that would have been received had no deduction been made under that section.

Apportionments

In calculating the deemed Schedule E payment, any necessary apportionments are made on a just and reasonable basis of amounts received by the intermediary that are referable to the services of more than one worker, or partly to the services of the worker and partly to other matters.

Application of Schedule E rules

The following provisions apply to calculating the deemed Schedule E payment.

A 'payment or other benefit' includes anything that, if received by an employee for performing his duties of employment within Schedule E, would be an emolument of the employment, or chargeable to tax as such an emolument. The amount of a payment or other benefit is taken to be the amount of payment or cash benefit received, or the cash equivalent of a non-cash benefit. In the case of the latter, the cash equivalent is taken to be the greater of:

(1) the amount that would be chargeable to tax under s 19(1) if the benefit were an emolument chargeable to tax under Schedule E Case I, and

(2) the cash equivalent determined under the rules in s 596B (benefits under non-approved retirement benefit schemes).

A payment or benefit is treated as received when, for a payment or cash benefit, payment is made of or on account of the payment or benefit, or for a non-cash benefit, to be used or enjoyed.

Application of income tax acts: deemed Schedule E payment

The income tax acts (in particular the PAYE provisions) apply in relation to the deemed Schedule E payment as if the worker were employed by the intermediary, and the relevant engagements were undertaken by the worker in the course of performing his duties in that employment. The worker is not chargeable to tax in respect of the deemed payment if or to the extent that any combination of the following factors apply:

(1) the worker is resident, ordinarily resident or domiciled outside the UK,

(2) the client is resident or ordinarily resident outside the UK, or

(3) the services are provided outside the UK.

A deemed Schedule E payment is treated as an emolument of an employment for the purpose of:

(a) determining whether it is employment to which ss 153–168G apply (benefits-in-kind: provisions applicable to higher paid employment), and

(b) s 198 (deductions for necessary expenses defrayed out of emoluments).

Where the intermediary is a partnership or unincorporated association, the deemed payment is treated as received by the worker in his personal capacity and not as income of the partnership or association.

Where the worker is UK resident, the services are provided in the UK and the client or employer carries on business in the UK, the intermediary is treated as having a place of business in the UK, whether or not it in fact does so.

The deemed payment is treated as the worker's relevant earnings for the purposes of s 644 (relevant earnings for purposes of permissible personal pension contributions).

13.10.3 Supplementary provisions
(FA 2000, Sch 12, paras 12–24)

Earlier date of deemed Schedule E payment in certain cases

If in any tax year:

(1) a deemed Schedule E payment is treated as made, and
(2) before the date on which payment would be treated as made any relevant event occurs in relation to the intermediary,

the deemed payment for that year is treated as having been made immediately before that event or, if there is more than one, immediately before the first of them.

Where the intermediary is a company, the 'relevant events' are where the worker:

(a) is a member of the company, ceases to be a member;
(b) holds an office with the company, ceases to hold such office; or
(c) is employed by the company, ceases to be so employed.

Where the intermediary is a partnership, the relevant events are:

(i) the dissolution of the partnership or its ceasing to trade or a partner ceasing to act as such; or
(ii) where the worker is employed by the partnership, his ceasing to be so employed.

Where the intermediary is an individual and the worker is employed by him, it is a relevant event if the worker ceases to be so employed.

The fact that the deemed payment is treated as made before the end of the tax year does not affect what receipts and other matters are taken into account in calculating its amount.

Relief in cases of distributions by intermediary

A claim for relief may be made where the intermediary:

(1) is a company;
(2) is treated as making a deemed Schedule E payment in any tax year; and
(3) either in that tax year (whether before or after that payment is treated as made), or in a subsequent tax year, makes a distribution.

A claim for relief must be made by the intermediary by notice in writing given to the Revenue.

If on a claim being made the Revenue is satisfied that relief should be given so as to avoid a double charge to tax, relief is given by way of amending any assessment, by discharge or repayment of tax, or otherwise, as appears to it appropriate. Relief is given by treating the amount of the distribution as reduced, not the amount of the deemed Schedule E payment.

The Revenue is to exercise this power so as to secure that so far as practicable relief is given by setting the amount of a deemed Schedule E payment against relevant distributions:

(a) of the same tax year before those of other tax years;
(b) received by the worker before those received by another person; and
(c) of earlier years before those of later years.

Where the amount of a distribution is reduced, the amount of any associated tax credit is reduced accordingly.

Provisions applicable to multiple intermediaries

Avoidance of double counting

Where a payment or other benefit has been made or provided, directly or indirectly, from one relevant intermediary to another in respect of the engagement, the amount taken into account in relation to Step 1 or 2 of the calculation in 13.10.2 is reduced to such extent as is necessary to avoid double counting.

Joint and several liability for PAYE deductions

All relevant intermediaries in relation to an engagement are jointly and severally liable to account for any amount required under the PAYE provisions to be deducted from a deemed Schedule E payment treated as made by any of them. An intermediary is not so liable if it has not received any payment or benefit in respect of any engagement.

Calculation of intermediary's profits

In calculating for tax purposes the profits of a business carried on by an intermediary that is treated as making in connection with that business a deemed Schedule E payment, a deduction is allowed for the amount of the payment and of any employer's NICs paid by the intermediary in respect of it. No deduction in respect of these matters may be made except in accordance with this rule. This deduction must be taken into account for the period of account in which the deemed payment is treated as made.

There are special rules for partnerships. Here, the amount of the deduction allowed is limited to the amount that reduces the partnership's profits for the tax year to nil. To the extent that in any tax year the expenses in connection with the relevant engagements exceed the sum of:

(1) the amounts that would be deductible for Schedule E purposes if the worker had been employed by the client and the expenses had been incurred by the worker, and

(2) 5% of the amount taken into account in Step 1 of the calculation as the intermediary's receipts in respect of the relevant engagements,

they shall be left out of account in calculating the partnership's profits.

Meaning of 'associate'

An associate in relation to:

(1) an individual has the meaning given by s 417(3) and (4), subject to the provisions detailed below;

(2) a company means a person connected with the company within the meaning of s 839; and

(3) a partnership means any associate of a partnership member.

Where an individual has an interest in shares or obligations of a company as a beneficiary of an employee benefit trust, the trustees are not regarded as associates of his by reason only of that interest. However, there is an exception where the individual (either alone or with any associate) or any associate of his (with or without any other associate) has at any time on or after 14 March 1989 been the beneficial owner of, or able (directly or through other companies or by other indirect means) to control more than 5% of the company's ordinary share capital. Here 'associate' does not include the trustees of an employee benefit trust by reason only that the individual has an interest in shares or obligations of the trust.

References in these rules to payments or benefits received or receivable for a partnership or unincorporated association include payments or benefits to which a person is or may be entitled in his capacity as a member of the partnership or association.

In these rules, anything done by or in relation to an associate of an intermediary is treated as done by or in relation to the intermediary. Furthermore, a payment or other benefit provided to a member of an individual's family or household is treated as provided to the individual. 'Family or household' refers to an individual's spouse, his sons and daughters and their spouses, his parents, his servants, his dependants and his guests (s 168(4)). A man and a woman living together as husband and wife are treated here as if they were so married.

Transitional provisions

These rules apply for the tax year 2000–01 and subsequent years and apply in relation to services performed, or to be performed, on or after 6 April 2000. Payments or other benefits in respect of such services received before that date are treated as if received in 2000–01.

Deemed discontinuance of business

This applies where an individual or partnership is:

(1) carrying on a business at the beginning of the tax year 2000–01, and
(2) treated as making one or more deemed Schedule E payments for that year in connection with that business.

Where this rule applies, the individual or partnership may elect that:

(a) the business be deemed to have been permanently discontinued at the end of the year 1999–2000, and
(b) a new business is deemed to have been set up and commenced on 6 April 2000.

Notwithstanding the deemed discontinuance, the old business and the new business are treated as the same for the purposes of s 385 (carry-forward of losses against subsequent profits). Any such election must be made by being used in a return made and delivered on or before the due date (TMA 1970, ss 8, 8(1A), and 12AA(2) and (3)).

Agency workers

These rules do not affect the operation of s 134 (workers supplied by agencies).

13.11 GIFTS OF SHARES

A gift of shares to an employee is normally a taxable benefit, the tax charge being based on the shares' market value. If the shares are given to the employee by a shareholder, he is normally treated as if he had made a disposal of the shares at their market value, and he may therefore be liable for CGT.

The tax position where an employee is allowed to subscribe for new shares at an undervalue is broadly the same.

The employee is taxed on the difference between the amount he pays to subscribe for the shares and their market value. Dealing with matters in this way usually avoids any CGT problems for the shareholders (since there is no disposal by the existing shareholders or the company, merely an issue of new shares).

A company normally needs to report the acquisition of shares by an employee within 30 days of the end of the tax year.

13.12 NON-APPROVED SHARE OPTIONS

13.12.1 Introduction

A Schedule E income tax charge may arise on the exercise of a share option or on the growth in value of shares which have been acquired by reason of the individual's office or employment (and, in particular, shares in dependent subsidiaries). The legislation was introduced on a piecemeal basis and it is often difficult to discern any clear or logical structure or principles that underlie the legislation.

13.12.2 Non-approved share options
(TA 1988, s 135)

A tax charge may arise on either the grant or the exercise of the option.

Grant of the option

A charge may arise only if the option has a potential life of more than seven years. Even if the option is capable of being exercised more than seven years later, the Revenue is unlikely to assess a value greater than the difference between the value of the shares at the time the option is granted and the aggregate of the amount (if any) paid for the grant of option and the amount payable under the option.

Exercise of the option

A person who is subject to tax under Schedule E Case I may be subject to an income tax charge when he exercises a non-approved share option which has been granted to him by reason of his office or employment. The charge is not dependent upon his selling the shares but arises on any profit or gain that he is deemed to have made by exercising the option. Normally the profit is simply the difference between the market value of the shares at the time that he exercises his option and the price payable under the option.

Example – Exercise of share options

A was granted an option to acquire 1,000 shares in XYZ Ltd at a price of £2 per share. After five years have elapsed, he exercises the option and pays £2,000 to acquire the 1,000 shares. By this time the shares have grown in value to £5 per share.

A will be assessed for the year in which he exercises the option. His profit will be assessed as £3,000, ie:

	£
Market value of 1,000 shares	5,000
Less amount paid	2,000
	3,000

13.12.3 Residence status of the employee

No charge arises under these provisions if the employee was not resident and ordinarily resident in the UK at the date that the option was granted. This is because the individual has to be UK-resident and ordinarily resident if he is to be chargeable to tax under Schedule E Case I.

The charge, however, still arises where an individual who was resident and ordinarily resident when the option was *granted* ceases to be UK-resident before the option is *exercised*.

13.12.4 Other employee share options
(TA 1988, s 162)

Where an individual exercises an option which was granted to him as an employee, but at a time when he was not chargeable to tax under Schedule E Case I, and he retains the shares, an income tax charge may arise on the eventual disposal of the shares. The legislation on beneficial loans contains deeming provisions which treat the difference between the shares' market value at the time that the option is exercised and the amount payable to exercise the option as if it were a loan. On a subsequent sale or disposal of the shares the loan is deemed to be written off and a Schedule E charge arises if the individual is resident in the UK at that time.

13.12.5 Returns by employer

A company which grants an option to an employee must make a return within 30 days of the end of the tax year.

13.13 PROFIT-SHARING SCHEMES
(TA 1988, ss 186–187)

These operate by means of a trust, with the trustees receiving payments from the company's profits to enable them to buy shares on the employees' behalf. In computing its profits, the company should get a deduction for the sums paid so long as the trustees apply the money in accordance with the approved scheme rules. The amount that may be appropriated to an employee under the scheme cannot exceed £3,000 or, if greater, 10% of his remuneration for PAYE purposes, with an overall limit of £8,000.

The employee is entitled to dividends paid on the shares during the period of retention by the trustees. The trustees *must* retain the shares for a period of two years; if the shares are then retained by the trustees for a further three years, there is no income tax charge on the employee. If they are sold by the employee within three years of appropriation, an income tax charge arises based on the percentage of the 'locked-in value' ie the lower of the market value of the shares when they were appropriated by the trust fund or the sale proceeds. The percentages are as follows:

Date of disposal	Appropriate %
Before release date	100
After cessation of employment due to injury, disability or redundancy	50
After relevant age*	50
Excess or unauthorised shares	50

*ie the applicable pensionable age

Provided the shares are held in trust for three years, normally the only liability arising to the employee is to CGT when he disposes of the shares appropriated to him. The capital gains liability arises on the difference between the disposal proceeds of these shares less their open market value on the day they were appropriated to him. The growth in value from the date of acquisition by the trust to the date of appropriation is tax free.

Examples – Disposals of shares in a profit sharing scheme

(1) In March 1996, the trustees of an approved scheme appropriated 500 £1 shares to an employee at a time when the market value was £1.25 each. The locked-in value is therefore 500 at £1.25 = £625.

In June 1998 the shares are sold for £2.35 each. The sale was made between years four and five and consequently an income tax liability arises based on 50% of the locked-in value, ie £312.50.

(2) The facts are as in example (1) but the sale is delayed until June 1999. The sale is after the end of year five; therefore there is no Schedule E liability. A CGT charge could arise on a disposal of the shares. The gain is the difference between £2.35 per share and £1.25 as adjusted for indexation.

Such schemes are being phased out and replaced with a new approved profit-sharing scheme by FA 2000, Sch 8.

13.14 SHARE OPTION SCHEMES

13.14.1 Introduction

There are two main types of approved share option schemes for employees: save as you earn (SAYE) linked share option schemes and executive share option schemes.

Approved SAYE linked share option schemes were introduced in 1980. The main features of these schemes are that there is a limit on the value of the shares which may be allocated to an employee and that participation in the scheme must be open to all full-time employees who have completed five years' service.

In 1984 the Government introduced a further category of approved share options intended to cover special arrangements for senior executives. The maximum amounts involved are much more generous and there is no requirement that the option be granted to all employees.

It is possible for an employer to establish both types of scheme and, indeed, to grant non-approved share options as well.

13.14.2 SAYE option schemes

These schemes entail the grant of an option for employees to purchase company shares at a price which must not be 'manifestly less' than 80% of their market value at the time that the options are granted. The employee is required to take out an SAYE linked savings scheme (maximum £250 per month) and may use the proceeds to exercise the share option either five or seven years later, depending on the rules of the particular scheme. No income tax liability arises on the grant of the options or upon their exercise. CGT is charged on an eventual disposal of the shares.

13.15 EXECUTIVE SHARE OPTION SCHEMES

The general principle is that an income tax charge may arise on the exercise of a share option, but certain approved share option schemes may be established which avoid such an income tax liability. CGT may still apply but only on a subsequent disposal of the shares concerned. However, following the Greenbury report, the tax benefits only apply to a restricted extent for options granted after 17 July 1995.

13.15.1 **Conditions for approval**

The following conditions must be satisfied to receive Revenue approval:

(1) Participation in the scheme must be open only to full-time directors or employees or to part-time employees working at least 20 hours a week. Part-time directors may not participate in this scheme. The Revenue has indicated that it regards a director who works 25 hours per week as full time. The employer may choose which of the employees are to be permitted to participate in the scheme.

(2) Where the employer is a close company, no participant must own (or be entitled to acquire as a result of the grant of the option) more than 10% of the company's shares. Furthermore no individual who has owned more than 10% of the company's shares within the previous 12 months is able to participate.

(3) The price at which the option is to be exercised must not be 'manifestly less' than the value of the shares at the time that the option is granted. With effect from 1 January 1992, it became possible for options to be granted at a discount of up to 15% of the market value of shares at the time of granting where the company also operates an approved profit-sharing scheme or savings-related share option scheme.

For options granted from 29 April 1996, the discount feature is no longer available, and it is only necessary to compare the aggregate consideration and the market value.

(4) There is a limit on the number of shares over which a particular employee may be granted options. The scheme must limit his options to shares with a market value at the time the options are granted which does not exceed £30,000. Remuneration for PAYE purposes excludes benefits-in-kind and reimbursed expenses and is after deducting contributions to an approved pensions scheme.

(5) The shares issued under the scheme must be fully paid ordinary shares of the company or its parent company. They must either be shares quoted on a recognised stock exchange or shares in a non-close company which is controlled by a quoted company or shares in a company not under the control of another company.

(6) Options must not be transferable and must be exercisable only between three and ten years after they are granted. There is an income tax charge on individuals who exercise options under the scheme more than once every three years. This three-year time limit is waived if a director or employee dies, in which case the option must be exercised by the personal representatives within one year of death.

13.16 SPECIAL EMPLOYEE SHARES

There are circumstances where a tax charge may arise on the disposal of shares, or on their being made more valuable by the removal of restrictions. The relevant legislation particularly needs to be borne in mind where the director or employee has acquired shares in a company which is a subsidiary of another company.

Liability to income tax under Schedule E may arise:

(1) when any restrictions affecting the employee's shares are removed; or
(2) when the shareholder receives any special benefit by virtue of owner-ship; or
(3) where the shares are in a 'dependent subsidiary'.

13.16.1 Shares in a dependent subsidiary

A company which is a subsidiary is deemed to be a dependent subsidiary unless the directors certify each year that it is not a dependent subsidiary and the auditors confirm their agreement to this. A company is regarded as a dependent subsidiary if there is any significant amount of trading with the parent company or another member of the group.

Where an employee holds shares in a dependent subsidiary, a tax charge may arise on the growth in the value which takes place at the earliest of the following times:

(1) the time when he actually disposes of the shares;
(2) the date that the company ceases to be a dependent subsidiary;
(3) the expiry of seven years from the date of acquisition.

A charge may arise even though the company was not a dependent sub-sidiary when the person acquired his shares if it subsequently becomes a dependent subsidiary.

13.17 NATIONAL INSURANCE CONTRIBUTIONS (NICs)

13.17.1 Introduction

Outline of contributory system
(Social Security Contributions and Benefits Act (SSCBA) 1992, s 1)

NICs are levied under various classes. Employers are concerned with those relating to 'employed earners' (see below):

Class 1:   Earnings-related (SSCBA 1992, s 6), being:
             (i)   primary Class 1 contributions from employed earners; and
             (ii) secondary Class 1 contributions from employers and other persons paying earnings.

Class 1A: Cars (s 10), payable by persons liable to pay secondary Class 1 contributions and certain other persons.

Class 1B: PAYE settlement agreements (s 10A), payable by persons who are accountable to the Revenue for income tax on emoluments under a PAYE settlement agreement.

The amounts and rates of contributions and the other figures which affect the liability of contributors are subject to alteration from year to year. Modified rules apply in the following special cases under SSCBA 1992:

- Women married or widowed before 6 April 1997 (s 19(4))
- Crown employees (s 115)
- HM Forces (s 116)
- Mariners, airmen etc (s 117)
- Married women and widows (s 118)
- Persons outside Great Britain (s 119)
- Employment at sea (continental shelf operations) (s 120).

There are also reductions in state scheme contributions and benefits for members of certified schemes under the Pension Schemes Act 1993.

The rules for computation, collection and recovery of contributions of Classes 1, 1A and 1B otherwise with respect to contributions of those classes are set out in SSCBA 1992, Sch 1.

A person is only liable to pay Class 1, 1A or 1B NICs if he fulfils prescribed conditions as to residence or presence in Great Britain.

Categories of earners
(SSCBA 1992, s 2)

An 'employed earner' is a person gainfully employed in Great Britain either under a contract of service or in an office with emoluments chargeable to Schedule E income tax. By contrast, a 'self-employed earner' is a person gainfully employed in Great Britain otherwise than in employed earner's employment (whether or not he is also employed in such employment).

The Social Security (Categorisation of Earners) Regulations 1978 provide for certain prescribed descriptions of employment to be categorised as being an 'employed earner' or 'self-employed earner' notwithstanding that such employment would not otherwise fall within that category. The occupations concerned are teachers, lecturers and tutors; office cleaners; ministers of religion; and people employed by their spouses in connection with their spouses' employment.

'Earnings' and 'earner'
(SSCBA 1992, ss 3 and 4)

'Earnings' include any remuneration or profit derived from an employment; 'earner' is construed accordingly (s 3(1)). Regulations set out how the amount of a person's earnings are calculated or estimated.

The regulations make special provision for directors and senior employees for certain categories of income that are not earnings for NICs purposes:

(1) rent paid to a director or an employee who owns the premises and leases them to the company;
(2) payment of a dividend, but the rules for intermediaries may apply;
(3) payment of interest on a current account balance.

The following are treated as remuneration derived from an employed earner's employment:

(1) any sum as:
    (i) statutory sick pay; or
    (ii) statutory maternity pay; and
(2) any sickness payment made:
    (i) to the employed earner; and
    (ii) under arrangements by which the secondary contributor makes payments towards the provision of that sickness payment (where the funds for making sickness payments under such arrangements are attributable in part to contributions made by the employed earner, a prescribed part thereof is disregarded).

Additionally, the regulations treat as remuneration derived from an employed earner's employment any payment made by a body corporate to or for the benefit of any of its directors where that payment would, when made, not otherwise be earnings under SSCBA 1992, and also treat any amount on which an employed earner is chargeable to Schedule E income tax as remuneration derived from the earner's employment.

13.17.2 Personal service companies etc
(SSCBA 1992, s 4A)

The rules by which NICs are applied where a worker performs services for a client through an intermediary in circumstances, whereby if the intermediary were ignored the worker would be classified as an employed earner of the client, are set out in the Social Security Contributions (Intermediaries) Regulations 2000. The Regulations are virtually identical to the provisions set out in FA 2000, Sch 12 whereby such earnings are chargeable for Schedule E income tax (see 13.10).

13.17.3 Class 1 Contributions

Earnings limits and thresholds
(SSCBA 1992, s 5)

For each tax year, the limits and thresholds set out below are specified for that year by regulations:

(1) for primary Class 1 NICs:
    (a) a lower earnings limit,
    (b) an upper earnings limit, and
    (c) a primary threshold; and
(2) a secondary threshold for secondary Class 1 NICs.

The amounts for 2002–03 are:

	Weekly (£)	Monthly (£)	Annual (£)
Lower earnings limit	75	325	3,900
Upper earnings limit	585	2,535	30,420
Primary threshold	89	385	4,615
Secondary threshold	89	385	4,615

The amount specified as the lower earnings limit for any tax year is an amount equal to or not more than £0.99 less than the weekly rate of the basic pension in a Category A retirement pension; or that sum as increased by any Act or order passed or made before the beginning of that tax year and taking effect before 6 May in that tax year.

The amount specified as the upper earnings limit for any tax year is an amount which either:

(a) is equal to seven times the sum which is the primary threshold for that year; or

(b) exceeds or falls short of seven times that sum by an amount not exceeding half that sum.

There are equivalent limits or thresholds for earners paid other than weekly.

Primary contributors
(SSCBA 1992, s 6)

Where earnings are paid to or for the benefit of an earner over age 16 for any one employment of his which is employed earner's employment:

(a) a primary (earner's) Class 1 contribution is payable if the earnings exceed the current primary threshold; and

(b) a secondary (employer's) Class 1 contribution is payable if the earnings exceed the current secondary threshold.

No primary or secondary Class 1 NICs are payable on earnings covered by a PAYE Settlement Agreement (PSA).

No primary (earner's) Class 1 NICs are payable on earnings paid to or for the benefit of an employed earner above pensionable age. However, secondary Class 1 NICs are still payable.

There are special rules whereby reduced primary or secondary Class 1 NICs are payable for persons to whom the Employment Rights Act 1996, Pt XI (redundancy payments) does not apply.

Notional payment of primary Class 1 contribution where earnings not less than lower earnings limit
(SSCBA 1992, s 6A)

Where employees are paid an amount which is not less than the current lower earnings limit, but does not exceed the current primary threshold:

(a) the earner is treated as having actually paid a primary Class 1 contribution for that period, and

(b) the earnings are treated as earnings upon which such a contribution has been paid.

This protects the employee's entitlement to benefits.

Secondary contributors
(SSCBA 1992, s 7).

The 'secondary contributor' in relation to any payment of earnings to or for the benefit of an employed earner is, under s 7(1), in the case of an earner employed:

(1) under a contract of service, his employer;

(2) in an office with emoluments, either:
   (a) such person as may be prescribed in relation to that office; or
   (b) if no person is prescribed, the government department, public authority or body of persons responsible for paying the emoluments of the office.

For employed earners who:

(a) are paid earnings in a tax week by more than one person for different employments; or

(b) work under the general control or management of a person other than their immediate employer,

regulations provide who is to be treated as the secondary contributor for any particular employment.

Calculation of primary Class 1 NICs
(SSCBA 1992, s 8)

Where for earnings from employed earner's employment a primary Class 1 contribution exceeds the current primary threshold, but does not exceed the current upper earnings limit, the amount of that contribution for 2002–03 is 10%. The amounts and rates for 2002–03 are:

	Weekly earnings (£)	Rate of primary contributions
Up to primary threshold	0.00–89.00	No contribution
Between primary threshold and upper earnings limit	89.01–585.00	10%
Above upper earnings limit	Over 585.00	No further contribution

Alternative rules apply for contracted-out employees (Pensions Act 1993, ss 41 and 42A), airmen, continental shelf workers, mariners, members of HM Forces, married women and widows who have elected for reduced rates, persons resident abroad, and volunteer development workers (Social Security (Contributions) Regulations 1979, regs 81–123F).

Calculation of secondary Class 1 NICs
(SSCBA 1992, s 9)

Where earnings from employed earner's employment exceed the current secondary threshold, the amount of the secondary Class 1 contribution for 2002–03 is 12.2%. The amounts and rates for 2002–03 are:

	Weekly earnings (£)	Rate of primary contributions
Up to secondary earnings threshold	0.00–89.00	No contribution
Above secondary earnings threshold	89.00 and over	11.8%

Alternative rules apply for contracted-out employees under Pensions Act 1993, ss 41 and 42A and the 1979 Regulations, regs 81–123F (see above).

Calculation of earnings
(1979 Regulations, regs 2–22)

The rules for calculating the amount of Class 1 NICs are set out in detail. Particular attention is drawn to regs 18 (calculation of earnings), 19 (payments to be disregarded) and 19A (certain payments by trustees to be disregarded).

13.17.4 Class 1A NICs

Benefits-in-kind etc
(SSCBA 1992, ss 10–10ZB)

Class 1A liability is imposed on benefits-in-kind received by an employed earner employee and who is employed as a director or has annual emoluments, including benefits, of more than £8,500. Such benefits-in-kind are now subject to Class 1A NICs; prior to 2000–01, the Class 1A liability arose only on the provision of cars and fuel. A deduction is available for business expenses which are allowable for income tax under Schedule E (TA 1988, s 198). Personal expenses paid for an employee by an employer continue, as before, to be included as emoluments subject to Class 1 NICs.

Benefits provided by third parties (including non-cash vouchers) are also subject to Class 1A NICs.

Class 1A NICs are payable at the rate applicable to secondary Class 1 contributors (generally employers) (ie 11.8%).

No Class 1A NICs are payable for any tax year on so much of any emoluments that are taken into account in a PSA (see 13.17.4).

Calculation of earnings
(1979 Regulations, regs 22A–22H)

The rules for calculating the amount of Class 1A NICs with reference to cars are set out in detail in these sections.

13.17.5 Class 1B NICs
(SSCBA 1992, s 10A)

A person who is accountable to the Revenue for income tax on emoluments of his employees under a PSA is also liable to make Class 1B NICs for that tax year. Class 1B NICs are payable on:

(1) the amount of any of the emoluments included in the PSA which are chargeable emoluments; and
(2) the total amount of income tax for which he is accountable for the tax year in question under the PSA.

Class 1B NICs are payable at the rate applicable to secondary Class 1 contributors (generally employers) (ie 11.8%).

Regulations may provide for persons to be excepted in prescribed circumstances from liability to pay Class 1B NICs.

Exception for employees subject to social security system of foreign states
(1979 Regulations, regs 22A–22H)

Certain employees who are subject to the social security system states within the European Economic Area, and under reciprocal agreement arrangements, are not liable to Class 1A NICs.

13.18 ENTERPRISE MANAGEMENT INCENTIVES

13.18.1 Introduction
(FA 2000, Sch 14, paras 1–7)

From 28 July 2000, enterprise management incentives (EMIs) that take the form of non-taxable share options can be granted over shares to key employees of qualifying trading companies. The qualifying rules are similar to those for enterprise investment relief, venture capital trusts and corporate venturing. The option must meet a number of general requirements (set out in Sch 14, paras 8–11), the company must be a qualifying company (paras 12–26), the individual must be an eligible employee (paras 27–36) and the option must comply with certain terms (paras 37–41).

13.18.2 General requirements
(FA 2000, Sch 14, paras 8–11)

An option does not qualify unless it meets the following requirements:

(1) It must be granted for commercial reasons to recruit or retain a key employee in the company and not as part of an arrangement to avoid tax.
(2) The upper limit on options that can be held by an employee in a company or group is £100,000 worth (by market value) of unexercised options. Once that limit is reached, no further qualifying options can be granted for three years. Account must be taken of options under a non-savings related company share option plan (TA 1988, Sch 9). These are treated as unexercised qualifying options against the £100,000 limit.
(3) The number of employees who can hold EMI options in a relevant company at the same time is limited to 15.

13.18.3 Qualifying companies
(FA 2000, Sch 14, paras 12–26)

The company must be 'independent', and must not be a 51% subsidiary of another company nor under the control (s 840) of another company. Any subsidiaries must be at least 75% owned and must be qualifying subsidiaries. The company or group gross assets must not exceed £15,000,000.

Throughout the qualification period, the company or the group must exist wholly for the purpose of carrying on one or more qualifying trades, or be preparing to do so. In applying this test, there may be disregarded any incidental purposes such as the holding or managing of property used for its qualifying trades. A company intending to carry on a qualifying trade must commence its trade within two years of the share issue.

The company's or group's trade must be carried on wholly or mainly in the UK on a commercial basis with a view to profits. It must not consist substantially of excluded activities. Research and development carried out for a qualifying trade are not excluded. The following activities are excluded:

- Dealing in land, commodities or futures or in shares, securities or other financial instruments
- Dealing in goods other than in the ordinary course of a wholesale or retail trade
- Banking, insurance, money lending and other financial activities
- Leasing or receiving royalties or licence fees
- Providing legal or accountancy services
- Property development
- Farming or market gardening
- Holding, managing or occupying woodlands, any other forestry activities or timber production
- Operating or managing hotels or comparable establishments or managing property used as a hotel or comparable establishment
- Operating or managing nursing homes or residential care homes or managing property used as a nursing home or residential care home.

13.18.4 Eligible employees
(FA 2000, Sch 14, paras 27–36)

To be an 'eligible employee', an employee must work for the company or for one of its qualifying subsidiaries.

The employee must be committed to work at least 25 hours a week for the company or for one of its qualifying subsidiaries, or, if less, 75% of his working time for the company. However, this does not include non-working by reason of injury, ill health, disability, pregnancy etc.

The employee personally, or together with his associates, must not have a material interest (more than 30%) in the company or its parent or other group company. Options and other rights to acquire shares are included in determining a right to control. However, shares held under approved profit-sharing schemes (TA 1988, Sch 9) or all employee share ownership plans (FA 2000, Sch 8) are disregarded.

13.18.5 Requirements as to terms of option etc
(FA 2000, Sch 14, paras 37–41)

The shares to which the options apply must form part of the ordinary share capital of the company, be fully paid up and not redeemable. The option must be capable of being exercised within ten years from the date of grant and must be non-transferable other than to personal representatives within one year of death.

13.18.6 Income tax treatment
(FA 2000, Sch 14, paras 42–55)

There is no income tax charge on the grant or exercise of the option, provided that the option is exercised within ten years after its grant. However, there is an income tax charge if the shares are acquired at a discount on market value. The charge arises on an amount equal to the lower of the discount, or the excess of the value on exercise over the acquisition cost. If the option is to acquire shares at a nil cost, the charge arises on the lower of the market value at the time of grant or the time of exercise.

An income tax charge also arises if a disqualifying event occurs, eg:

(1) a relevant company coming under the control of another company;
(2) a relevant company ceasing to meet the trading activities requirement;
(3) the employee ceasing to meet the employment or working time requirements;
(4) variations in the terms of the option whereby there is an increase in the shares' market value subject to the option or the requirements of Sch 14, paras 37–41 ceasing to apply;
(5) an alteration to the company's share capital;
(6) a conversion of shares not complying with Sch 14, para 50;
(7) the grant of an option under TA 1988, Sch 9 (Sch 14, para 10);
(8) the company ceasing to prepare to carry on a trade; or
(9) the employee ceasing to work for the requisite period.

13.18.7 Capital gains tax treatment
(FA 2000, Sch 14, paras 56–58)

Qualifying shares also include replacement shares treated as original shares under TCGA 1992, s 127. However, the normal rights issue provisions (TCGA 1992, ss 127–130), which treat the acquisition date of such shares as being the date of purchase of the original shares, do not apply.

The base date for taper relief is the date of the original grant of the original option, not the date of exercise.

13.18.8 Company reorganisations
(FA 2000, Sch 14, paras 59–63)

There are special rules dealing with company reorganisations, takeovers etc.

13.19 TERMINATION PAYMENTS

13.19.1 Redundancy payments
(TA 1988, s 579)

A statutory redundancy payment made under the Employment Rights Act 1996 (ERA) is exempt from tax although it may need to be taken into account in computing the tax payable on a termination payment (see 13.19.3).

Payment to an employee under a non-statutory redundancy scheme is generally treated by the Revenue as exempt under SP1/81 where the following conditions are satisfied:

(1) Payments are made only on account of redundancy as defined in ERA 1996, s 166.
(2) The individual has at least two years' continuous service.
(3) Payments are made to all relevant employees and not merely to a selected group of employees.
(4) The payments are not excessively large in relation to earnings and length of service.

In *Mairs v Haughey* [1993] STC 569, the Revenue sought to tax a payment made to an employee for giving up contingent redundancy rights. The Revenue argued that the payment constituted an emolument of the employment, but it was held that a redundancy payment is not an emolument and a lump sum paid in lieu of a right to receive such a redundancy payment is equally not an emolument.

This case has also cast doubt on the view generally held within the Revenue that a termination payment is always taxable where the employee is contractually entitled to it. SP1/94 was issued after *Mairs v Haughey*.

13.19.2 *Ex gratia* payments

There has been concern that *ex gratia* payments may be subject to tax under Schedule E as unapproved retirement benefits taxable under s 596A. If this charge arises, the amount received is taxed in full under Schedule E. The Revenue issued SP13/91 in October 1991 and has subsequently clarified the position. An *ex gratia* payment is normally regarded as a retirement benefit taxable under s 596A only where it is paid in connection with an individual's retirement. The Revenue has also given the following guidelines on hypothetical situations:

(1) A person who has worked for a company for 20 years leaves at age 54 to take a senior executive position in another company: 'golden handshake'.
(2) A long-service employee leaves to take a senior executive position in another company at the age of 60: borderline, probably retirement.
(3) A division of a company is sold and the 55-year-old manager responsible for running it leaves to take a job with the purchaser: 'golden handshake'.
(4) A person in his 50s has a heart attack and is advised by his doctor to leave and seek a less stressful position: 'golden handshake'.
(5) An employee aged 35 is involved in an accident and suffers disabilities that make him unable to continue with his job: 'golden handshake'.

(6) An employee aged 50 leaves to take a job nearer home to be able to nurse her aged parents: borderline, 'golden handshake'. If the employee did not take a new job, or was nearer normal retirement age, this situation would be treated as retirement.

Ex gratia payments not caught under s 596A are normally treated in the same way as compensation for loss of office (see below).

13.19.3 Compensation for loss of office

Golden handshakes and other termination payments
(TA 1988, s 148)

Where a director's or employee's contract of service is terminated, it may be possible for a compensation payment to be made which is either wholly or partly tax free *provided* the employee is not entitled to the compensation under a contract of service. Where the individual receives compensation, under a term of his contract of employment, the Revenue's view is that it is taxable under Schedule E in the usual way. A payment made to a director as compensation for accepting a reduced salary or any other variation of his service contract is not regarded as a termination payment, and the amount received is normally taxable in full.

13.19.4 Payments for restrictive covenants

A payment made to an employee in return for his giving a restrictive covenant is chargeable to tax under Schedule E (s 313). The employer should operate PAYE.

13.20 HOW THE INLAND REVENUE ENSURES COMPLIANCE

13.20.1 The Collector's audit division

The division exists to monitor the operation of tax deduction and payment under the PAYE and construction industry subcontractors schemes and to monitor NIC compliance.

Method of operation

The Collector of Taxes has a statutory right to inspect documents and records relating to tax deductions. This does not mean Collectors have an automatic right of entry to business or other premises but given their power to inspect documents such a right of entry must to a certain extent follow on. The PAYE Regulations give the Collector the power to specify that the documents should be made available for inspection at a reasonable time at:

- A place agreed by the employer and Collector.

- In default of such agreement, the place in the UK where the documents are normally kept.
- In default of such a normal place, the employer's principal place of business in the UK.

There is no statutory limit to the number of years for which the Collector may ask for documents or records, but the employer is only obliged to keep records for three years after the end of the year to which they relate. It could therefore be said that it is safe for the employer to destroy records after that period has elapsed. The argument against this is that if the Collector finds irregularities in the records for the three most recent years it would be extremely difficult for the employer to refute the suggestions that similar irregularities took place in earlier years. It is therefore advisable that records should be kept for a minimum of six years.

The Revenue booklet IR71 entitled 'PAYE Inspections' provides brief information on the way such inspections are undertaken, while IR109 explains how settlements are negotiated at the end of an inspection.

Problem areas

From his previous experience of investigations, and knowledge of the type of business the records of which are being examined, the Collector can identify, in advance, those areas which are likely to be a fruitful source of additional liability. The areas most commonly investigated are:

(1) casuals;
(2) part-timers;
(3) bonuses (eg at Christmas);
(4) round-sum expense allowances including entertaining;
(5) directors emoluments of all types;
(6) payments out of petty cash;
(7) termination payments;
(8) self-employed consultants, out-workers etc.

The Collector will check for failure, or under-deduction, of tax either deliberately or through ignorance, as well as being concerned (and this applies particularly to directors) with the timing of deductions. His responsibility extends to Class 1 and 1A NICs as well as to income tax.

Where employers engage subcontractors in the construction industry the inspection also covers the operation of the Construction Industry Tax Deduction Scheme.

Settlement

Provided the employer agrees with the Collector's conclusions, the unpaid tax and NICs are quantified and the employer is asked to make an offer in settlement of that tax, interest, and possibly penalties.

13.20.2 Role of Schedule E compliance units

While the monitoring of compliance with PAYE and NIC regulations is officially the responsibility of the Collector's PAYE audit teams, visits are increasingly made to employers by Schedule E compliance units.

The units specialise in reviewing the provision of expenses and benefits to directors, and employees earning £8,500+ pa. Reviews of P11Ds therefore form a large part of their work. Officers also examine employees' own tax returns however, and focus on aspects of the employer's records which indicate or suggest the provision of benefits that have not been declared.

Compliance visits

During the visit, the employer is asked about the possible provision of benefits by third parties to employees or payment of salaries direct to third parties. Questions may also be asked about the provision of inducement and termination payments. The status of individuals treated as casual employees and as self-employed may also be explored.

The principal inquiries however focus upon an examination of the provision of expenses and benefits to directors or employees and members of their family or household with a view to identifying benefits previously undeclared or undervalued.

PAYE Settlement Agreements
(TA 1988, s 206A)

As with PAYE audit inspections, minor errors may result in settlements confined to that year. In other cases settlements, to include in some cases penalties and interest, may cover the previous six years, with earlier years' adjustments estimated on the basis of the errors discovered for the one year reviewed.

The tax liabilities exposed are normally employee liabilities. In the majority of cases both the Revenue and employer are keen to settle matters in such a way that the employer meets the additional liability.

Care should be taken in such cases to ensure employees' tax rates are taken into account in computing the tax due, although use of a composite rate may sometimes be administratively beneficial and prove acceptable to the Revenue.

While in strictness the liabilities should be grossed up to take into account the additional benefit of the employer meeting the employee's tax liability, the Revenue may be persuaded to forego this for the sake of a quick settlement with the employer as opposed to raising separate Schedule E assessments on all employees involved.

At the close of their inquiries steps are taken to ensure the employer's procedures are now acceptable, and employers should take the opportunity to review existing dispensations, or apply for new dispensations.

14

LIFE ASSURANCE, PENSIONS AND PERMANENT HEALTH INSURANCE

VINCE JERRARD, ZURICH FINANCIAL SERVICES

14.1 INTRODUCTION

Although the fine print can appear daunting, life assurance, pension and permanent health insurance policies are really just evidence of a contract between the policyholder and the company issuing the policy. In exchange for payment of a contribution or premium, the company promises to make one or more specified payments in certain defined circumstances.

Depending on the type of contract entered into, the payment from the company may be, for example, a lump sum on the death of an individual, an income in retirement for a pensioner, or a replacement income for a person prevented from earning by reason of sickness or disability. Despite the technical appearance of many of these policies (often due to complex tax rules offering relief on payment of premiums or benefits), it is useful to bear in mind the essential simplicity of the idea: payment of premiums (usually regular payments) to the company in exchange for the guarantee or expectation of payments back on the happening of some future event.

With life assurance contracts, there must be an 'insurable interest' before a policy can be effected. Broadly, before a person can effect a life policy he must be able to demonstrate that the death of the person whose life is being insured will cause him financial loss. In addition the amount of the assurance must not exceed the amount of that loss.

Individuals have an automatic and unlimited insurable interest in their own life and the life of their spouse. In other cases an insurable interest must be demonstrated before a person can effect a policy on someone else's life (a 'life of another' policy).

This chapter, in Part I, looks at the contracts themselves and gives an outline of the rules which apply to them. Part II then goes on to consider some basic uses of the contracts with reference to sole traders, partners and small companies.

PART I – THE BASICS

14.2 LIFE ASSURANCE

14.2.1 Types of policy

There are three basic types of life assurance policy.

Whole of life policies are protection-orientated policies which pay the guaranteed sum assured on the death of the life assured, whenever death occurs. As such, they are most appropriate where long-term protection is needed, for example to meet the inheritance tax liability on an individual's death or to protect the family from the consequences of the 'breadwinner's' death. Whole of life policies may, over the years, also acquire cash values, although they are not primarily investment vehicles.

Endowment policies pay a guaranteed sum on the death of the life assured during the policy term, or on survival to the end of the term. Such policies provide a valuable mixture of protection and investment and have often been used in conjunction with a mortgage to provide for a lump sum which will pay off the loan at the end of the mortgage term, or on the borrower's prior death. The economic climate in recent years has raised significant issues around the ability of endowments to meet intended maturity values, and new business levels of endowments are low,

Term assurance policies pay a guaranteed sum assured only if death occurs before the end of the term. They are for protection purposes only and usually provide no return to the policyholder if the life assured survives the policy term. Term assurance policies are usually the cheapest form of life assurance protection. The cover provided by them can be widened by use of renewal or conversion options. A renewal option allows the policyholder to renew the policy at the end of the original term, without further evidence of health being required. A conversion option allows a policyholder to turn his policy into a whole of life assurance or an endowment policy, free of underwriting, should his needs change. A convertible term assurance is particularly useful if the need is for life assurance protection for the whole of the individual's life but it is not possible to afford a whole of life policy at the time. Term assurance policies can also be effected under some pensions legislation (see 14.3.6). These policies have the advantage of tax relief on the premiums paid.

A more recent development in the UK has been what is commonly called 'critical illness' protection. This cover may be written as an additional benefit to a whole life, endowment or term policy, or on a stand alone basis, and provides for payment of the sum assured on the life assured suffering one of the several specified diseases or events. Typical dread diseases and events are heart attack, stroke, cancer, major organ transplant, certain types of heart surgery and total permanent disability.

14.2.2 Traditional and unit-linked policies

There are two bases on which policies are offered.

Traditional policy

Under a traditional policy the life assurance company estimates future mortality experience, investment return and company expenses. Using these factors the actuary determines the premium rate for a given sum assured, both of which are then guaranteed by the company. As the assumptions made by the company are, of necessity, conservative, the premiums may often be higher than necessary. To counter this, traditional companies developed 'with profits' policies so that those contracts could share in the extra profits being made by the life company.

Extra profits are allocated to the policy by means of bonuses, either during the policy's term (reversionary bonuses) or on the policy's maturity (terminal bonuses). Once a bonus has been allocated it cannot be taken away, although the level of future bonuses is not guaranteed.

With profits policies offer the prospect of a smoothed investment return with part of the fund performance in good years being retained to bolster bonus declarations in poorer years. However, such policies have attracted criticism recently, partly because of their opacity, and quite radical changes in with profits business might be anticipated.

In 1999 the Government introduced the Individual Savings Account (ISA), an investment vehicle to stimulate savings, particularly among the lower paid and those who do not currently have any significant savings. Life assurance is included as an asset capable of being held in an ISA but only to the extent of £1,000 contribution pa (against an annual contribution of up to £7,000 until April 2006).

Unit-linked policies

These are a more recent innovation introduced to the UK in the 1960s. They offer fewer guarantees to the policyholder. Premiums are invested in pooled investment funds maintained by the life company and the policy's performance is linked directly to the fund's actual performance. Freed from having to set up the policy with long-term investment guarantees, the company can adopt an investment policy which is not unduly conservative and so may be able to provide a more realistic level of cover from the outset. The direct linking of the policy and the investment performance of the underlying fund also mean that the policyholder is not subject to the company's discretion in deciding the level of bonuses it should declare.

As unit-linked policies do not usually carry the same investment guarantees as traditional contracts, they usually incorporate the system of reviews by which the company can ensure that the policy stays 'on track'. A review compares the original assumptions about mortality, expenses and investment return with the actual performance achieved. Unfavourable performance usually leads to an increase in premium and favourable performance to an increase in benefits.

14.2.3 Qualifying and non-qualifying policies

The other main method of categorising life assurance contracts is according to whether they are 'qualifying' or 'non-qualifying'. This categorisation arises solely for the purpose of the taxation of the policy proceeds.

The qualifying rules are detailed and complex but, very broadly speaking, a qualifying policy is a regular premium policy with a minimum duration of ten years. The premiums remain fairly level and the sum assured satisfies certain minimum requirements to ensure that it provides a realistic level of life cover protection.

The 1994 Budget announced impending changes to the life policy tax regime, with an implementation date of May 1996. After a postponement of the implementation schedule, consultation on the Revenue proposals closed in April 1997. The stated intention was to remove pre-certification and to simplify and modernise the current regime, but the proposals set out in the Consultation Document attracted widespread concern among many in the industry for their complexity, the likely high cost of implementation and their failure adequately to protect the legitimate expectations of existing policyholders, particularly in the areas of part surrenders (see 14.2.5) and the taxation of trust-held policies. At the end of 1997 the Revenue confirmed that the proposed radical changes to the policy tax regime would not be implemented. Instead, legislation was introduced in FA 1998 to address the specific issues of the taxation of trusts (specifically, so called 'dead settlor trusts'), personalised portfolio bonds and the fiscal representation in the UK of offshore insurance companies; all areas where the Revenue believed legislation was deficient and abuse could exist.

More recently, a number of these issues have re-emerged as a result of the Sandler Review of the industry, conducted for the Treasury. Sandler recommendations included the removal of the qualifying policy regime and the part surrender rules (see 14.2.5).

Certain proposals in the corporation tax area have also led to a questioning of the tax structure for the whole industry in the future and quite radical changes could take place over the next few years.

One constant aim for the industry in these possible changes will be the maintenance of all benefits enjoyed by existing policyholders.

14.2.4 The advantages of qualifying policies

Premiums paid under qualifying policies issued before 14 March 1984 attracted Life Assurance Premium Relief (LAPR). Qualifying policies issued before that date continue to benefit from LAPR provided that neither the benefits secured are increased nor the term extended after that date.

Subject to meeting the conditions for LAPR, relief was given at approximately half of the basic rate of income tax in force at the time, on up to the greater of ⅙th of the policyholder's income or £1,500 pa. Where LAPR is still available, currently it applies at the rate of 12½%.

The other key advantage of qualifying policies concerns the taxation of policy proceeds. In general, the proceeds from a qualifying policy are entirely free of tax, provided premiums are kept up for at least 10 years (or three-quarters of the term of an endowment policy, if less).

14.2.5 Tax treatment of policies

While a policy is in force all the tax on income and gains attributable to the policy is the responsibility of the life company which pays tax on them according to its own corporate taxation position.

The life company

Life companies are generally taxed on the excess of the investment income and realised capital gains over the management expenses (the 'I-E' basis). For proprietary companies there is a formula to determine the proportion of income and gains to be allocated to policyholders and shareholders, the former's share being taxed at 22% (20% for income from directly held equities) and the latter's share at 30%.

The individual policyholder

The taxation of the individual in connection with income tax and life assurance policies revolves around the concept of the 'chargeable event'. For non-qualifying policies the five chargeable events are:

(1) death of the life assured;
(2) the maturity of the policy;
(3) the total surrender of the policy;
(4) the assignment of the policy for money or money's worth (eg the sale of the policy);
(5) excesses (the system of 'excesses' allows partial surrenders each year of up to 5% of the premiums paid, on a cumulative basis, up to a total of 100% of the premiums paid; only if the cumulative 5% 'allowances' are exceeded does a chargeable event occur).

Chargeable events in the case of qualifying policies are the same as those listed above but with the following amendments:

(a) death or maturity is a chargeable event only if the policy has previously been paid-up within the first 10 years (or three-quarters of the term of an endowment policy, if less);

(b) a surrender or an assignment for money or money's worth or an excess is a chargeable event only if it occurs before the expiry of 10 years (or three-quarters of the term of an endowment policy, if less) or if the policy was made paid-up within that period.

Assignments between spouses or as security for debts are not chargeable events and nor are payments of critical illness claims.

Part assignments for no consideration are also not chargeable events (but note that such assignments taking place on divorce are, in the Revenue's opinion, almost invariably for consideration).

As far as the policyholder is concerned, in most cases life assurance policies (qualifying or not) are free of any personal liability to CGT. Only if the policy is in the hands of someone other than the original owner who gave consideration for it (ie who bought it or gave something of value for it) are proceeds liable to CGT.

Note the comments in 14.2.3 concerning discussions taking place over the future of the qualifying rules and the rules on taxation of policy part surrenders.

Company-owned policies

Special rules apply to post-13 March 1989 policies owned by companies, those assigned to secure a debt owed by a company and those held on trusts created by a company. Broadly speaking, such policies are treated as non-qualifying policies and so may give rise to a tax charge on death, maturity, surrender, part withdrawal or assignment for money or money's worth.

However, policies which would otherwise be qualifying endowments receive more favourable treatment in respect of calculation of the chargeable gain, in certain circumstances where the policy has, throughout its term, been issued to secure a loan to the company which was used to purchase land (or construct, extend or improve buildings) used for the purposes of the company's trade.

14.2.6 Gain on the happening of a chargeable event

Where a chargeable event occurs the gain arising on the event must be computed. The calculation depends on the event's nature but, broadly speaking, it is the investment profit made under the policy, taking into account previous capital benefits enjoyed and the total premiums paid. Any extra amount received by way of death benefit is mortality profit and is not included in the gain for tax purposes.

The rules for calculating the gain as a result of an excess following a withdrawal or partial surrender are somewhat different and take into account the 5% allowable withdrawals. The more favourable treatment for company-owned policies referred to in the previous section is that the amount of the loan (or the lowest amount of the loan during the policy term) is used in place of the sum of total premiums paid when calculating the chargeable gain. Thus, if the loan has remained constant during the policy term and the policy proceeds do not exceed the loan, there is no chargeable gain.

14.2.7 Taxing gains on chargeable events

In outline, tax is payable on a chargeable gain as follows:

(1) Gains made on life policies do not give rise to a tax liability at the basic rate of income tax. Accordingly if the taxpayer's income, including the gain, does not fall into the higher rate tax band there is no income tax charge on the gain.

(2) If the policyholder's income (including any chargeable gain) is taxable at the higher rate, the gain made on the life policy is liable to tax at 18% (the higher rate of 40%, less the basic rate of 22%).

(3) As the gain has accrued over the life of the policy, it would be rather harsh to treat the total gain as the taxpayer's income in the year of receipt. This could push him into the higher rate tax band in that year despite a relatively low income level. Therefore, a measure of relief is afforded by a process known as 'top-slicing'. This involves calculating the rate of tax appropriate to a part of the total gain (a 'slice') and then applying that rate of tax to the whole of the gain.

(4) The taxpayer is usually the policyholder. Exceptions to this are that if the policy is held on trust the charge falls upon the settlor (ie the person who established the trust) if the settlor is alive, otherwise it will fall on the trustees or, if they are not UK-resident, the beneficiaries; if the policy is owned by or held on trusts created, or held as security for a debt owed, by a company, the amount of the gain is treated as part of the company's Schedule D Case VI income (and top-slicing relief does not apply).

Further details of the qualifying rules and taxation of life policies can be found in the *Zurich Tax Handbook.*

14.3 PENSIONS

14.3.1 Introduction

Pensions are usually regarded as one of the most attractive investments available. Within limits, contributions are deductible up to the highest rate of tax paid by the contributor; the underlying pension funds grow, in the main, free of UK taxes on income and gains; and in most cases the pension plan can provide a tax-free cash lump sum to the planholder together with a retirement income in 'old age'.

Over the years UK pensions legislation has undergone substantial reform and development. The Social Security Act 1986 created the framework for 'Personal Pensions' and 'Free-Standing Additional Voluntary Contribution

Schemes'; reduced the benefits provided by the State Earnings Related Pensions Scheme (SERPS); increased the scope for individuals to contract out of SERPS; and removed the ability of Occupational Pension Schemes to require compulsory membership for employees.

The legislation also allowed, for the first time, banks, building societies and unit trust groups to offer pension plans.

Further changes took place in 1997, this time by virtue of tax changes to the treatment of pension funds. It is now no longer possible for such funds to reclaim the Advance Corporation Tax (ACT) paid by a company when it pays a dividend. This has reduced the overall return from an average pension fund and has had real consequences for pensions funding by companies and individuals.

From April 2001, a new form of pension became available. Stakeholder pensions are available for many individuals as an alternative to personal pensions and, in some cases, in addition to occupational pension schemes. For the first time, children and adults without earnings have been able to contribute to personal pensions and stakeholder pensions.

From April 2002, SERPS was replaced by the State Second Pension (S2P). Although existing SERPS entitlements remain unaffected, future benefits will accrue under S2P, which is designed to offer greater benefits to those on below average earnings.

14.3.2 The state pension scheme

The benefit the state provides to those in retirement falls into two main parts: the basic retirement pension and an earnings related additional state pension.

Everyone is entitled to the basic retirement pension, subject to payment of the necessary NICs. Currently, for a married man with earnings at the national average level, the aim is to provide a basic pension of approximately 20% of his final earnings level. The basic state pension is increased in line with price inflation each year.

Between April 1978 and April 2002, SERPS provided an additional state pension which was based on earnings (within certain limits) rather than the flat benefit provided by the retirement pension. SERPS also provided a widow's benefit if a husband died after retirement and also, in certain circumstances, if he died before retirement. SERPS was funded by the higher rate NICs payable by both employers and employees. The self-employed did not contribute towards, or benefit from, SERPS.

In recent years the state pension scheme has come under pressure from increases in life expectancy and large numbers of retired people in the population. These concerns led the Government to reduce the benefits originally provided under SERPS. Those reaching state retirement age in or after the year 2010 will receive a pension of only 20% of their relevant earnings, instead of the 25% originally intended, and the relevant earnings to be taken into account will be the average of lifetime earnings and not the best 20 years of earnings, as was the original rule for SERPS.

A sliding scale operates for those retiring between the years 2000 and 2010.

SERPS was replaced by S2P from April 2002. S2P is targeted primarily at low and moderate earners (ie those earning less than £10,800 pa (at the time of writing)). Those earning less than that will receive at least double the amount that SERPS paid to a person on the same earnings.

S2P also provides benefits for those who are unable to work through long-term disability or illness and for some carers.

14.3.3 Contracting-in and contracting-out

Since SERPS was introduced it has been possible to opt out of the scheme (referred to as 'contracting-out') in which case NICs are reduced for both the employer and employee but with the loss of SERPS benefits. It is also possible to contract out of S2P.

Contracting-out is possible through an occupational scheme providing a level of benefits at least broadly equivalent to the SERPS benefits being up or through a contracted-out money purchase occupational scheme (COMPS), or an appropriate personal pension (APP) or stakeholder pension plan used by an employee not in an occupational scheme or a member of a contracted-in occupational scheme.

With APP and stakeholder pension schemes, the individual and the employer continue to make full NICs and the DSS make payments which are age related direct to the relevant pension plan. Contracting-out through an occupational scheme means lower NICs for employer and employee but the employer is required to make payment of the NICs reduction to the occupational scheme with further age related payments made by the DSS.

If the individual is contracting-out on a money-purchase basis these NICs reductions are known as 'protected rights contributions' and the fund built up from them must be used to purchase protected rights benefits. It is these benefits which, in effect, replace the SERPS or S2P being lost through contracting-out and they are treated more restrictively than benefits built up through the employer's or employee's additional contributions. For example, a protected rights pension cannot commence before state retirement age and cannot be commuted for cash.

Whether contracting-out of SERPS or S2P is advisable is a decision to be taken by each employee according to his or her personal circumstances. The key factors to be taken into account are the individual's age, sex, earnings and attitude to risk. The decision has to be reviewed each year before the end of the tax year.

14.3.4 Occupational pension schemes

These are schemes sponsored by an employer and to which the employer must make a contribution. Schemes are established on one of two bases: either money-purchase (defined contribution) or final salary (defined benefit schemes).

With defined benefit schemes the employee is guaranteed a level of pension benefit based on a fraction (typically $\frac{1}{60}$ or $\frac{1}{80}$) of his final salary, multiplied by the number of years' pensionable service. A money-purchase scheme does not carry a guarantee of a specific level of pension but invests the contributions and uses the accumulated fund to provide whatever pension can be purchased with the fund at retirement.

To be tax efficient an occupational pension scheme should be approved by the Pension Schemes Office (PSO) which is a branch of the Inland Revenue. 'Approval' prevents contributions paid by the employer being taxed in the employee's hands but the preferable status of 'exempt approval' offers significant further benefits. An exempt approved scheme is able to invest in a fund free of all UK income and capital taxes (although the fund can no longer reclaim ACT paid on company dividends); the employee can claim tax relief on contributions he makes to the scheme; and employers' contributions are deductible business expenses.

Contributions

In general, there are no specific limits on the amount of contributions which can be paid into an occupational scheme but monitoring is necessary to ensure that the scheme does not become 'over-funded'. In other words, contributions may have to be limited if projected funds in the scheme are likely to exceed the amount necessary to meet its obligations. (See below under 'Benefits' for details of the remuneration cap introduced in 1989 for some scheme members.)

Employees may make personal contributions (of up to 15% of 'eligible' remuneration) to the scheme. This may be done on a voluntary basis (by way of additional voluntary contributions to the scheme or by the employee effecting his own Free Standing AVC plan) but the scheme may require some personal contribution from the employee as a condition of membership.

Benefits

To be exempt approved, the scheme must be set up under irrevocable trust for the sole purpose of providing 'relevant benefits'. These are benefits such as an income in retirement, the option to commute part of that income for a lump sum, an income for the employee's widow etc. As a result of the generous tax benefits available to such schemes, there are strict limits on the benefits which may be provided. For example, the maximum pension which can be provided to the scheme member is usually two-thirds of final remuneration and the minimum period of service required to achieve this level of benefits is now 20 years.

A pension for a spouse or dependant can also be provided of up to two-thirds of the deceased member's maximum pension at normal retirement date. A similar pension can be provided on death after retirement.

An employee's pension can be commuted for a lump sum, also based on final salary and years of service. The maximum lump sum is ³⁄₈₀ of final salary for each year of service up to 40 years' service or 2.25 times the pension available before commutation, if greater.

FA 1989 introduced new rules for members of schemes established on or after 14 March 1989 and members joining older schemes after 31 May 1989. For such members no benefits can be provided for any remuneration in excess of a specific amount (increased in line with the RPI) which is £97,200 for 2002–03. This remuneration 'cap' restricts funding of such schemes (by the employer and by the employees' personal contributions) as well as payment of the various benefits the scheme can provide.

Schemes may also provide a lump sum of up to four times final remuneration (capped where necessary) on the death, in service, of the employee. This can be paid together with a refund of any personal contributions paid by the employee. It is usually possible to pay the death benefits free of inheritance tax.

The eligibility, contribution and benefit rules changed more than once in the late 1980s and some members of existing schemes will have had their positions protected from some of the subsequent changes. Further details can be found in the *Zurich Pensions Handbook*.

Top-up occupational schemes

FA 1989 also introduced the concept of unapproved top-up occupational pension schemes. These schemes, for example, allow employers to provide highly paid employees with pension benefits in respect of salary which exceeds the earnings cap, and to provide more than the usual maximum pension benefits.

14.3.5 Personal pensions and stakeholder pensions

Prior to October 1987 the main personal plan was the retirement annuity contract (also called s 226 plans). In October 1987 FSAVC schemes were introduced, enabling an occupational scheme member to effect his own top-up pension as an alternative to making personal voluntary contributions to the employer's scheme. In July 1988 the s 226 plans were replaced by the new personal pension plans. From April 2001, a new type of pension, the stakeholder pension, became available. At the same time, significant changes were made to the eligibility and contribution rules for personal pensions.

Retirement annuity contracts

Although it has not been possible to effect a retirement annuity contract since 30 June 1988, plans in force by that date are allowed to continue.

An individual was eligible for one of these plans if he had relevant earnings. These are earnings which do not carry pension rights, eg the earnings of sole traders, the self-employed, partners and employees in non-pensionable employment. Controlling directors of investment companies are excluded from eligibility.

Unlike occupational schemes, these 's 226' contracts are not controlled by reference to the maximum benefits which can be provided; rather, restrictions are applied to the amount of contributions which can be made. The contribution limit is 17.5% of net relevant earnings, with larger percentages applicable for those over 50 (up to a maximum of 27.5% for those aged over 60). Net relevant earnings (NRE) are, broadly speaking, an individual's earnings after deduction of any business expenses. The earnings cap applicable to other schemes does not apply. Contributions made to these plans up to the limits are fully tax-deductible and the funds in which the plans invest are free of all UK income and capital taxes. Employers are not able to pay contributions to employees' s 226 contracts and they cannot be used to contract out of SERPS or S2P.

The plans are issued on a money-purchase basis, the fund accumulated at retirement being used to provide a lifetime annuity for the planholder. The planholder need not actually retire to take the benefits from these plans but the benefits must be paid between the ages of 60 and 75 (earlier for some specified occupations).

The annuity paid can be in various different forms, guaranteed or not, flat rate or increasing etc. If the planholder dies before taking his annuity a lump sum can be paid, not exceeding the contributions made to the plan plus a reasonable amount of interest or bonuses. Alternatively, an annuity can be paid to the individual's widow or dependants. Annuities can also be effected on a 'joint life basis' for the planholder and spouse, so that the annuity payments continue until the surviving spouse's death. The annuity is treated as earned income when it is paid, and the planholder can elect to commute part of his annuity at retirement. This commutation permits a maximum lump sum of three times the remaining annual annuity, but limited to a £150,000 lump sum per contract for contracts entered into on or after 17 March 1987.

In addition to pension benefits, such plans can provide life assurance protection. The maximum contribution which can be used to provide life cover is 5% of NRE (any such contribution is taken into account in determining the overall contribution limit applicable to the individual).

Death benefits payable under such plans can be assigned or put in trust so that payments of benefits on death can be arranged in a way effective for inheritance tax planning.

If, in any year, an individual pays less in contributions to a plan than would be permitted, it is possible to carry forward the shortfall in contributions for up to six years. It is also possible to 'carry back' a contribution to the previous tax year (and sometimes the year before that). Carry-forward ceased from the beginning of the tax year 2001–02.

Personal pension plans and stakeholder pensions

Personal pension plans (PPPs) were introduced on 1 July 1988. In many ways they are more flexible than the s 226 contracts which they replaced. For example, employers may make contributions to an employee's PPP; an 'appropriate' PPP can be used by employees to contract out of SERPS; and benefits can be taken between the ages of 50 and 75 (earlier for some specified occupations). Employees' contributions to PPPs are payable net of basic rate income tax under the pension relief at source (PRAS) rules.

PPPs are, like s 226 contracts, money-purchase arrangements with controls on the maximum contributions which can be made. Where an employer contributes to an employee's PPP, the employer's contributions must be taken into account in determining the employee's maximum permissible contributions.

With effect from 1989/90 the maximum contributions allowed (as a percentage of net relevant earnings) are:

Age at beginning of year of assessment	%
below 36	17½
36–45	20
46–50	25
51–55	30
56–60	35
61+	40

However, PPPs are also, with effect from 1989–90, subject to a similar income cap to that referred to in relation to occupational pension schemes (see 14.3.5) and earnings over the appropriate limit must be ignored in calculating entitlement to pay contributions. The benefits provided by a PPP are, again, very similar to those available under a s 226 plan, although the tax-free cash that can be taken is a maximum of 25% of the fund. Prior to April 2001, it was also possible to use up to 5% of net relevant earnings to provide life assurance protection.

Unlike s 226 contracts, it is possible to defer taking an annuity but still receive income withdrawals from the fund.

From April 2001, a new tax regime was introduced for stakeholder pensions. The new tax regime also applies to other types of 'defined contribution' (or money purchase) pension plans, including personal pensions and some occupational pensions.

Contribution limits and benefits are similar to those for personal pensions. However, for those who contribute less than £3,600 pa there will be no link with earnings for the first time ever. In addition, it is possible to have a stakeholder pension, or a personal pension, alongside an occupational pension scheme if you are not a 'controlling director' and earnings are less than £30,000 pa. This is known as 'concurrency'. Contributions to provide life assurance benefits are now restricted to 10% of the total pension contributions.

Broadly speaking, all employers with more than four employees who do not offer an occupational scheme need to provide access to a stakeholder pension scheme. There are, however, exemptions available where the employer contributes more than 3% of its employees' earnings into a suitable personal pension scheme. Employers are not obliged to make contributions to their designated stakeholder scheme, but they must make available the facility to collect contributions by deductions from their employee's salaries.

14.3.6 Moving between different types of pension arrangement

If a self-employed individual effects a PPP or stakeholder pension but then moves into employment, for example a sole trader incorporating his business, he can continue with his PPP or stakeholder pension. The same is true with an employee who has a PPP or stakeholder pension and moves into self-employment. In some cases, however, it is not possible to continue with the same pension plan; for example an employee who is a member of an occupational scheme cannot remain in that scheme if he becomes self-employed. Similarly, if a person with a PPP or stakeholder pension joins an employer's occupational scheme he cannot continue to pay contributions into the PPP unless his earnings are less than £30,000 pa and he is not a controlling director (in which case, it is possible to contribute to both schemes on a concurrent basis).

In those cases where a change of status affects pension planning it is usually possible for a transfer payment to be made from one scheme to another.

Further details of pension plans and planning can be found in the *Zurich Pensions Handbook.*

14.4 PERMANENT HEALTH INSURANCE

Typically, permanent health insurance (PHI) policies are a means of providing a replacement income if an individual is unable to work through illness or disability. Policies are usually available to those aged between 16 and 60 and cover usually ends no later than the normal retirement date for the individual's occupation.

In the event of sickness or disability the policy usually provides for a deferment period and payment of benefits only commences at the end of this period. Deferment periods may be between one month and one year (usually selected by the policyholder at the outset) and are valuable to the company offering the policy because they reduce the number of short-term claims they have to meet. The longer the deferment period, the cheaper the policy. In some cases, especially those occupations where short-term illnesses affect earnings almost immediately (eg professional sportsmen), the company may decline to offer policies with very short deferred periods.

The benefits payable under the policy are usually limited to approximately 75% of the individual's pre-claim earnings, often taking into account any benefits received from the State and any other policy during the period of claim. Limiting the maximum benefit in this way provides the incentive to the individual to return to work as soon as possible.

Benefits paid by such policies are tax free where the policies are owned by individuals. Where PHI policies are effected by companies to cover their employees, the income is taxable in the employee's hands in the same way as salary would have been.

One of the most important things about PHI policies is the definition of 'disability' which is used in the policy. Under some policies a person is not treated as being disabled if he can do any part of his former job. Others may not treat a person as disabled if he is capable of doing some other job for which he is reasonably suited, even if he is completely unable to do his previous job.

The most flexible PHI policies allow the level of benefit to be increased as salary increases and also give the policyholder the option of paying a higher contribution in exchange for disability income which increases to offer protection against inflation during the period of disability.

PART II – THE USES

14.5 INTRODUCTION

In this second part of the chapter the uses of life assurance, pensions and permanent health insurance are considered with particular emphasis on the business needs of sole traders, partners and small companies. The chapter does not consider more personal uses of life assurance but it is most important that they are not overlooked.

Life assurance is a unique product in the paying of a lump sum on an individual's death at some unknown time in the future. As such it plays a vital role in protection of the family on the breadwinner's death and loss of the family's income. The inclusion of 'critical illness' benefits can also be extremely beneficial as a breadwinner's serious illness can have just as severe an impact as his or her death.

Although most people can see the need for life assurance on the family breadwinner's life, it should not be forgotten that many people are only able to go out and earn an income because their partners are devoting themselves to looking after children and the family home. The non-earning partner's death or serious illness can also cause major financial difficulties such as the need for boarding school fees, a cleaner, a nanny – perhaps even the need for the surviving partner to give up work to look after the family.

Life assurance is also important in inheritance tax planning, being able to provide a fund from which the liability may be met, thus preserving the deceased's estate intact.

Life assurance may be used as a means of investment, even though qualifying endowment policies and single premium savings bonds may have advantages for the individual investor and, in some cases, corporate investment.

14.6 SOLE TRADERS

14.6.1 Life assurance

Keyman assurance – loss of profits

Although the sole trader himself usually is the driving force behind the business's profitability, there may be cases in which an employee is also essential to the undertaking's well-being. Where the death or disability of such a key person would weaken the business's profitability or reduce its capital value as a going concern, the business's owner should consider effecting a life policy (with dread disease benefit) on the keyman's life. The individual's status usually satisfies the requirement for an insurable interest, providing this sum assured is reasonable in view of the keyman's value to the business.

Receipt of the policy proceeds on the life assured's death or disability does not normally constitute a chargeable event, and so does not trigger a tax charge on the policy, if the policy is a qualifying policy. However, it is important to consider whether the policy is an asset owned by the sole trader personally or is a business asset. This determines the ultimate tax treatment of both the premiums paid and the sums received.

If the policy is a business asset contributions paid to it, in general, are tax-deductible provided:

(a) the policy is a short-term assurance; and
(b) the insurance is intended to meet the loss of profit resulting from the employee's death; and
(c) the sole relationship between the policyholder and the life assured is that of employer and employee.

These principles were laid down in a statement in 1944 by the then Chancellor of the Exchequer, Sir John Anderson. In general, the first requirement is an indication that premiums paid on a policy with a term of more than five years will not be tax-deductible.

609

If premiums are tax-deductible, this usually means that the policy proceeds are, in turn, taxable as a trading receipt of the business. If the premiums do not attract tax relief, usually the proceeds are received as a capital sum, taxable (through Revenue practice) only under the policy tax regime as discussed in 14.2.5. In cases of doubt it may be wise to contact the local tax inspector.

Security for loans

If a sole trader has to borrow money for business purposes, the lender may often require assignment of a life policy on the sole trader as security. The policy should ensure that such loans are repaid on the sole trader's death. Premiums are unlikely to be tax-deductible as a business expense because the plan's purpose is to satisfy a capital liability so that the premiums are not an income expense at all.

Insurance for redundancy payments

If a sole trader's business ceases on his death, his personal representatives are liable for making redundancy payments to eligible employees (see 12.10.8). The amount of any payment depends on various factors, such as salary level and length of service, but for a sole trader employing several staff, such payments could be a significant burden on his estate.

14.6.2 Pensions

For the sole trader

Pension provision for a sole trader can be through a PPP or stakeholder pension (unless a s 226 contract had been effected prior to July 1988). As a sole trader is not an employee, occupational pension schemes are not available and the question of contracting-out of SERPS or S2P does not arise.

Establishing a self-invested personal pension (SIPP) may allow the sole trader a wider range of investment choices, including the option to invest in commercial properties for rental.

For his employees

For a sole trader's employees the choice is wider. As an alternative, the employer could establish an occupational scheme for his staff. If the employer has more than four employees, he may be obliged to designate a stakeholder pension plan and make available the facility to collect employee contributions from salary. Most sole traders, however, do not want to assume the responsibility of establishing and running an occupational pension scheme but may well be able to make contributions to their employees'

PPPs. As long as the employer's contributions to the employees' PPPs exceed 3% of earnings, there is no requirement to designate a stakeholder pension.

Some pension providers offer a group PPP arrangement which is particularly suitable in these circumstances. Members of staff still own individual plans but some aspects of the administration are centralised. If the employer does decide to set up an occupational scheme for his employees, a money-purchase arrangement is likely to be preferable because of the absence of long-term guarantees which have to be met by the employer.

Employees should consider whether contracting-out of S2P will be beneficial to them. This can be effected in a variety of ways: the employer may offer contracting-out under the main occupational scheme; those in a contracted-in occupational scheme and those not in the occupational scheme can use a PPP or stakeholder pension to contract out on an individual basis.

If the sole trader's spouse is employed in the business, he or she is like any other employee as far as pension planning opportunities are concerned, but may be treated more favourably by the employer.

For the sole trader's spouse and children

From April 2001, even if the spouse has no earnings, it is possible to contribute up to £3,600 pa into a PPP or stakeholder pension. It is also possible to make a similar level of contributions to a PPP or stakeholder pension for the sole trader's children.

Prior to April 2001, if the spouse did not have any earnings that could be pensioned, consideration needed to be given to whether the spouse could be paid a salary for work done in the business.

The salary paid by the sole trader could be deductible up to the top rate of tax and, if it was less than the spouse's personal allowance and the lower rate for NICs, no income tax or NICs had to be made by either the sole trader or the spouse in respect of that salary. Of course, it had to be possible to justify the employment and the salary being paid by reference to the duties undertaken by the spouse.

Once the spouse was employed in this way, s/he could contribute to a PPP, or an occupational scheme could be set up for him/her by the sole trader. Although the occupational scheme might have been a little more expensive to run and, if it was an insurance company scheme, might have had higher minimum contribution levels, it usually offered the chance to provide higher pension benefits for the spouse than would a PPP, where the contribution was limited to a percentage of a salary.

To obtain the benefit of tax relief through PPP contributions, the spouse needed to earn more than his/her tax allowances, but this could lead to payment of NICs. In such cases, it might have been better for the sole trader, as employer, to have made the PPP contributions for him/her.

Although, in theory, it is still possible for the spouse to be employed in this way, the ability to contribute up to £3,000 pa to a PPP or stakeholder plan is a much simpler means of providing pension benefits.

14.6.3 Permanent health insurance

For the sole trader

It is often the case that if the sole trader is not able to work, the business soon becomes unprofitable. Although state benefits do exist (the sickness and incapacity benefits) they are designed more to avoid poverty than to maintain an individual's standard of living. Accordingly, a PHI policy is one of the first things which the sole trader should consider.

For his employees

A sole trader's employees are will usually be entitled to the same state benefits (with the addition of statutory sick pay) but may be treated more favourably under the terms of their contract of employment.

If the employer has undertaken to maintain the full, or a proportion of, salary during periods of sickness, he should consider effecting a PHI policy on the employee's life, so as to 're-insure' the liability for continuing salary. Benefit received from the policy by the employer is taxable as a trading receipt but normally deductible as a trading expense when paid to the employee.

Even if the employer has not agreed to maintain salary payments beyond that required by statute, he may still consider effecting a PHI policy on key employees to maintain the profitability of the business during their absence from work.

14.7 PARTNERS

14.7.1 Life assurance

The majority of the uses of life assurance applicable to sole traders also apply to partners. Perhaps the main difference with partnerships is that they are more likely to involve key people and that consideration should be given to the partnership's future on the death of one of the partners.

Quite apart from loss of a deceased partner's earning potential, the surviving partners may, subject to the provisions of the Partnership Deed, be faced with having to pay the beneficiaries the value of the deceased's partnership share. For partners who have made no provision, this burden can be acute and might necessitate expensive borrowing or even the sale of vital partnership assets.

Life assurance can help in these circumstances. The partners can set up an arrangement so that each of them has life cover which is paid to the survivors on his death. The survivors then have the funds to pay the deceased partner's share to his heirs, without affecting other aspects of the business's viability.

This partnership assurance arrangement may be achieved by each partner owning a life assurance policy on the life of every other partner, but this can be unwieldy and expensive where there are more than three or four partners. An alternative is for each partner to effect a policy on his own life and write it in trust for the benefit of the other partners.

Both sorts of arrangement should be accompanied by a cross-option agreement by which the surviving partners can compel the deceased's personal representatives to sell the deceased's partnership share to them and vice versa. The cross-option agreement can also contain further provisions to deal with the valuation of the partnership share, time for payment, the destination of surplus policy proceeds and payment of additional capital, should the policy proceeds be insufficient.

A policy incorporating critical illness benefits can also be particularly useful in partnership arrangements where a partner's serious illness can have effects equally severe as his or her death.

14.7.2 Pensions

For the partners

The pension planning routes available to partners are the same as those available to the sole trader, ie a PPP (or through a s 226 contract if one had been effected before 1 July 1988). Again, an SIPP can offer the ability to invest in a wider range of investments.

For their employees

For partnership employees the position is the same as for employees of a sole trader (see 14.6.2); see also that paragraph for the comments made on spouses and children.

14.7.3 Permanent health insurance

Partners are in much the same position as sole traders when considering PHI policies (see 14.6.3). A partnership may be better placed to absorb the loss of profits resulting from a partner's long-term absence through injury or illness but a PHI policy can secure the position still further. A policy can be taken out by each partner for his own benefit with the Partnership Deed providing for a corresponding reduction in that partner's share of profits for the period of absence. Alternatively, policies can be owned by all the partners as partnership assets to replace the income at the partnership level. The former method has the advantage of the availability of a tax holiday and of putting this provision into the hands of each individual.

14.8 COMPANIES

14.8.1 Life assurance

Keyman assurance

Keyman assurance is particularly important for small companies where, for example, the managing director, sales director etc may be fundamental to the business's profitability and continuance.

Frequently, small companies effecting keyman policies are not able to obtain tax relief on the premiums but are not taxed on the proceeds other than through the life policy taxation regime (see 14.2.5). Often this is because the keyman being insured has a material interest in the company so that the relationship between the life assured and the policyholder is not only that of employee and employer.

In the absence of such an interest in the company on the keyman's part, deductibility of premiums might be achieved if the policy is a short-term assurance. A policy of this nature might be appropriate in the early days of the company's existence (eg where it is expected that the company will grow sufficiently over the next five years so as to absorb the loss of the keyman after that time). Although keyman policies are caught by the rules described in 14.2.5, the high level of life cover being provided usually means that any investment profit under the policy will be small, so that any tax charge on a chargeable event will not cause undue difficulties.

Loan protection and repayment

A form of keyman assurance might also be appropriate where the company is obtaining a loan and the lender requires a life policy on a key executive by way of additional security. Even where the lender has not required a life policy as security for a loan, life assurance has a key role to play in company borrowings. Although the company is usually the borrower, it is common for lenders to require a personal guarantee from one or more directors to ensure repayment of any loan.

By having to give a personal guarantee the director is losing one of the main benefits of trading through a company – that of limited personal liability. Bearing in mind that a key person's death in the company organisation may well precipitate profitability difficulties and so make a calling in of the loan more likely, this is another good reason to effect life assurance on the lives of key individuals. Receipt of the policy proceeds will enable the company to repay its borrowings and so free the guarantor's personal estate from the potential liability.

Repayment of loans should also be considered for any company overdraft which could be called in on a key person's death and in relation to directors' loan accounts where the director's estate may require repayment on the director's death.

Note that the rules described in 14.2.5 mean that policies effected after 13 March 1989 (or older policies which are varied after that date to increase their benefits or extend their term) are treated as if they were non-qualifying and may give rise to a chargeable gain unless they are qualifying endowments and have been used to secure specific types of borrowing.

Key shareholder assurance

Another aspect of small companies which needs to be considered is that of transfer of shares on the death of one of the shareholders. In many cases small companies do not declare dividends on the shares, but those involved in the running of the company draw benefits by way of salary and directors' fees. On a director's death, those inheriting the deceased's shares may find that they have a minority shareholding in the company. The shares may be producing no dividends and may be insufficient to enable the new shareholder to become a director. In such a case the shares may be virtually unsaleable except to the other shareholders who may be able to use their position to depress the value of the shares.

Although in exceptional cases minority shareholders may have some rights against an oppressive majority under company law, the problem can be tackled by life assurance arrangements in at least two specific ways.

The company could effect life policies on the individual shareholders so that, on a shareholder's death, it receives a capital sum to buy the shares from the deceased's heirs. It has been possible for companies to buy their own shares since 1982. An agreement can be entered into between the shareholders and the company itself in which various matters can be addressed; for example, options can be given to both sides to require a sale or purchase of the shares and to determine the method of calculating a fair price for them. The existence of such options usually creates the necessary insurable interest to sustain the life assurance. However, the deceased's personal representatives may have difficulty in enforcing their option to require the company to buy the deceased's shares in some circumstances, eg where the purchase price is to come out of the company's capital. In addition, there are various legal procedures to be gone through before an agreement to buy a company's own shares can be set up and further clearances from the Revenue need to be obtained when the purchase is made to ensure there are no adverse tax consequences.

An alternative and relatively simple method of arranging a share purchase scheme is to establish an arrangement similar to that used for partnership assurance (see 14.7.1). In this way each shareholder effects a policy on the life of each of the others, or each effects a policy on his own life and puts it in trust for the benefit of the other shareholders. The life policies are accompanied by a cross-option agreement which enables both the deceased's personal representatives and the surviving shareholders to enforce the sale and purchase of the deceased's shares and tackles such questions as valuation of the shares etc.

14.8.2 Pensions

For directors and other top executives

The company's directors may plan for their own pension benefits through an occupational scheme, a PPP or stakeholder pension. In most cases the directors and key executives join a company occupational scheme to enable them to maximise their pension benefits in a tax-efficient way. PPPs and stakeholder pensions with direct contributions from the company are also efficient for the purposes of income tax and NICs, but the limit on the PPP and stakeholder pension contributions which can be made can tip the balance in favour of an occupational scheme.

Directors and executives looking for the ability to invest in a wider range of assets may choose whether a small self-administered scheme (SSAS) or an SIPP (see 14.6.2). An SSAS is a type of occupational scheme; an SIPP, as its name implies, is a personal pension. Both plans can offer a wide range of investments, including the flexibility of investments in commercial property.

For other employees

The choices are very much the same as for the employees of sole traders and partners. If the company has more than four employees, it may be obliged to designate a stakeholder pension for them. If the company does not want to make pension provision for its staff through an occupational scheme, it will need to at least make contributions to its employees' PPPs of 3% of earnings if it is to be exempted from the designation requirement. A group PPP arrangement 'sponsored' by the company in this way indicates a greater commitment to the provision of pensions for its employees, as well as securing exemption from the stakeholder designation rules.

For spouses and children of the directors

The comments made in 14.6.2 apply equally to pensions for spouses and children of directors and top executives of small companies.

14.8.3 Permanent health insurance

As with sole traders and partnerships, the smaller the company the more vulnerable it is to the long-term absence of a key individual. The company may effect PHI policies on its directors and top executives either to enable the company to maintain payment of salary or to cushion the company itself from the possible loss of income due to the key person's absence. The question of whether premiums paid on such a policy are tax deductible for the company is not entirely clear.

Despite the policy's long-term nature it seems likely that premiums paid by a company on a PHI policy on an employee, to enable the company to maintain payment of salary to the employee during a period of disability, should be tax-deductible. Certainly it appears that the receipt of payment by the company from the policy would be taxable in the company's hands (although matched by tax relief on the payment of the salary) even though the payment would be made gross by the life company. In cases of doubt, companies should consult their local tax inspector.

15

HEALTH AND SAFETY

JEREMY STRANKS, SAFETY & HYGIENE CONSULTANTS

15.1 INTRODUCTION

Increasingly, health and safety at work is being seen as an important part of business life. It is a multidisciplinary subject that has both direct and indirect influences on many of the issues dealt with in this book – contract law, sale of articles and substances, safety of premises that are workplaces, employment law and insurance.

In particular, in the last decade there has been a greater emphasis by the enforcement authorities on the role and function of directors and senior managers in terms of their responsibilities for health and safety, the need to promote the right safety culture, the level of commitment shown and the potential for the individual prosecution of directors and other members of the body corporate within the concept of corporate liability. Moreover, society has become more litigious, especially in the case of death, injury and ill-health arising from work, and damages awarded in civil claims for negligence are increasing constantly.

Clearly there is an intention on the part of Government and the HSC to reduce accidents and ill-health arising from work. In *Revitalising Health and Safety*, the Government and HSC have set targets for improving health and safety performance over the next ten years. These targets are to:

(a) reduce by 30% the number of working days lost per 100,000 workers from work-related injury and ill-health by 2010;
(b) reduce by 20% the incidence rate of cases of work-related ill-health by 2010;
(c) reduce by 10% the incidence rate of fatalities and major injuries by 2010; and
(d) achieve half the improvement under each target by 2004.

This chapter covers the following issues, all of which are relevant to directors, company secretaries and senior managers:

(1) The Health and Safety at Work Act 1974.
(2) Enforcement procedures.

(3) Management of Health and Safety at Work Regs 1999.
(4) Civil and criminal liability under health and safety law.
(5) Negligence and breach of statutory duty.
(6) The main areas of the criminal law in relation to
    (a) workplaces;
    (b) work equipment;
    (c) personal protective equipment;
    (d) fire precautions;
    (e) lifting operations;
    (f) substances hazardous to health;
    (g) reporting of injuries, diseases and dangerous occurrences; and
    (h) consultation with employees.

15.2 HEALTH AND SAFETY AT WORK ETC ACT 1974 (HSWA)

Under the HSWA, employers, employees, occupiers of premises and people who manufacture and design articles and substances for use at work have both general and particular duties.

15.2.1 General duties of employers to their employees
(HSWA, s 2)

It is every employer's duty, so far as reasonably practicable, to ensure the health, safety and welfare at work of all his employees. More particularly, this includes:

(1) providing and maintaining plant and systems of work that are, so far as is reasonably practicable, safe and without risks to health;
(2) arrangements for ensuring, so far as is reasonably practicable, safety and absence of risks to health in connection with using, handling, storing and transporting articles and substances;
(3) providing such information, instruction training and supervision as is necessary to ensure, so far as is reasonably practicable, the health and safety at work of employees;
(4) so far as is reasonably practicable as regards any place of work under the employer's control, maintaining it in a condition that is safe and without risks to health, and providing and maintaining means of access to and egress from it that are safe and without such risks;
(5) providing and maintaining a working environment for his employees that is, so far as is reasonably practicable, safe, without risks to health, and adequate as regards facilities and arrangements for their welfare at work.

Every employer must prepare and, as often as is necessary, revise a written Statement of Health and Safety Policy, and bring the Statement and any revision of it to the notice of all his employees.

Every employer must consult appointed safety representatives with a view to making and maintaining arrangements which will enable him and his employees to co-operate effectively in promoting and developing health and safety at work measures and in checking their effectiveness.

15.2.2 General duties other than to employees
(HSWA, ss 3 and 4)

Every employer must conduct his undertaking in such a way as to ensure, so far as is reasonably practicable, that persons not in his employment are not exposed to risks to their health or safety. Similar duties are imposed on self-employed persons. The employer must give such persons information about aspects of his undertaking which might affect their health and safety.

Further, a person who controls premises must ensure, so far as is reasonably practicable, that the premises, access to and egress from them and all plant and substances on them are safe and without risk to non-employees.

15.2.3 Articles and substances for use at work
(HSWA, s 6)

Any person who designs, manufactures, imports or supplies any article for use at work must:

(1) ensure, so far as is reasonably practicable, that the article is designed and constructed to be safe and without risks when properly used;
(2) carry out or arrange to carry out such testing and examination as may be necessary to comply with (1) above; and
(3) provide adequate information about the use for which it is designed and test it to ensure that, when put to that use, it will be safe and without risks to health.

In undertaking the design or manufacture of such article, research must be carried out to discover and, so far as is reasonably practicable, eliminate or minimise any risks to health or safety which may arise. An article must be erected or installed to ensure it is safe and risk-free.

Similar provisions as to proper use, testing and the provision of adequate information apply to substances.

15.2.4 General duties of employees at work
(HSWA, s 7)

It is the duty of every employee while at work:

(1) to take reasonable care for the health and safety of himself and of other persons who may be affected by his acts or omissions at work; and

(2) as regards any duty or requirement imposed on his employer, to co-operate with him so far as is necessary to enable that duty or requirement to be performed or complied with.

15.2.5 Duty not to interfere or misuse
(HSWA, s 8)

No person shall intentionally or recklessly interfere with or misuse anything provided in the interests of health, safety or welfare in pursuance of any of the relevant statutory provisions.

15.2.6 Duty not to charge employees

No employer shall levy or permit to be levied on any employee of his any charge in respect of anything done or provided in pursuance of any specific requirement of the relevant statutory provisions.

15.2.7 Enforcement procedures
(HSWA, ss 20 and 21)

The enforcing authorities for the HSWA and other health and safety legislation are:

(1) the Health and Safety Executive (HSE), which is split into a number of specific inspectorates (eg Nuclear Installations, Agricultural, etc) and national industrial groups (NIGs);
(2) local authorities, principally through their environmental health departments; and
(3) fire authorities, for certain fire-related legislation.

Actual enforcement is undertaken by inspectors appointed under the Act and authorised by written warrant from the enforcing authority.

Under HSWA, s 20 an inspector has the power to enter premises at any reasonable time and, where obstruction is anticipated, to enlist the support of a police officer. On entering a premises, he may take with him any person duly authorised by his enforcing authority, and any necessary equipment or materials. He may make such examination and investigation as may be necessary.

The inspector may direct that premises, or any part of them or anything in them, must remain undisturbed while the examination or investigation takes place. He may take any measurements and photographs and make any recordings he considers necessary, and take samples of any articles or substances found in any premises and of the atmosphere in them or in their vicinity.

Where it appears to him that an article or substance has caused or is likely to cause danger to health or safety, he may have it dismantled or subjected to any process or test. He may also take possession of it and detain it for so long as is necessary to examine it, to ensure it is not tampered with before his examination is completed and to ensure it is available for use as evidence in any proceedings for an offence under the relevant statutory provisions.

The inspector may require any person whom he has reasonable cause to believe to be able to give any information relevant to any examination or investigation to answer such questions as he thinks fit and to sign a declaration of truth. He may require the production of, inspect and take copies of any entry in any books or documents which by virtue of the relevant statutory provisions must be kept, and any other books or documents which it is necessary for him to see for the purposes of any examination or investigation. He may require any person to afford him such facilities and assistance with respect to any matter or things within that person's control or in relation to which that person has responsibilities as are necessary to enable the inspector to exercise any of the powers conferred on him.

After an inspector has completed an investigation or examination, he has a duty to inform safety representatives of the actual matters he has found (s 28(8)) and must give the employer similar information.

Improvement notices

If an inspector is of the opinion that a breach of the relevant statutory provisions has or is likely to occur, he may serve an improvement notice on the employer, occupier or employee. The notice must state which statutory provision he believes has been contravened and the reason for this belief. It should also state a time limit within which the contravention should be remedied.

Prohibition notices

Where an inspector is of the opinion that a work activity involves or will involve a serious risk of personal injury, he may serve a prohibition notice on the owner and/or occupier of the premises or the person having control of that activity. The notice will direct that the specified activities in it shall not be carried on by or under the control of the person on whom the notice is served unless certain specified remedial measures have been complied with. Note that it is not necessary for an inspector to believe that a legal provision is being or has been contravened. A prohibition notice is served where there is an immediate threat to life and in anticipation of danger.

Such notice may have immediate effect after its service. Alternatively, it may be deferred, thereby allowing the person time to remedy the situation, undertake works, etc. The duration of a deferred prohibition notice is stated on the notice.

Prosecution and penalties

Prosecution is frequently the outcome of a failure to comply with an improvement or prohibition notice. Conversely, an inspector may simply institute legal proceedings without service of a notice. Cases are normally heard in a magistrates' court, but there is also provision in the HSWA for hearing on indictment (in the Crown Court). Much depends on the gravity of the offence.

Magistrates may impose fines of up to £20,000 for a breach of ss 2–6 of the Act, and for breach of an improvement or prohibition notice. The maximum fine for other offences is £5,000. Fines in a Crown Court are unlimited.

15.2.8 Hierarchy of duties under health and safety law

Under health and safety law there are three distinct levels of statutory duty.

'Absolute' requirements

Where risk of injury or disease is inevitable if safety requirements are not followed, a statutory duty may well be strict or absolute. An example of an absolute duty is in the Provision and Use of Work Equipment Regs 1998, reg 5(1), which states:

> 'Every employer shall ensure that work equipment is so constructed or adapted as to be suitable for the purpose for which it is to be used or provided.'

Absolute duties are qualified by the terms 'shall' or 'must' and there is little or no defence available when charged with such an offence. Most of the duties under recent legislation, such as the Management of Health and Safety at Work Regs 1999, are of an absolute or strict nature.

'Practicable' requirements

A statutory requirement qualified by the term 'so far as is practicable' implies that, if in the light of current knowledge and invention it is feasible to comply with this requirement, then, irrespective of the cost or sacrifice involved, such a requirement must be complied with (*Schwalb v Fass H & Son* (1946) 175 LT 345).

'Reasonably practicable' requirements

A duty qualified by the term 'so far as is reasonably practicable' implies a lower or lesser level of duty than one which is qualified by 'so far as is practicable'. 'Reasonably practicable' is a narrower term than 'physically possible' (ie 'practicable'), and implies that a computation must be made in which the quantum of risk is placed in one scale and the sacrifice involved in the measures necessary for averting that risk is placed in the other. If it can be shown that there is a gross disproportion between these two factors (ie the risk being insignificant in relation to the sacrifice), a defendant discharges the onus upon himself (*Edwards v National Coal Board* [1949] 1 All ER 743).

The mythical reasonable man

A further level of duty is qualified by the term 'reasonable'. For instance, under HSWA, s 7, every employee has a duty while at work to take 'reasonable care' for the safety of himself and other persons who may be affected by his acts or omissions at work. But what is a reasonable person? What is considered 'reasonable' in terms of behaviour changes with time according to society and the norms prevalent at the time.

15.3 CURRENT TRENDS IN HEALTH AND SAFETY LEGISLATION

All modern health and safety legislation is driven by European Directives. For instance, in the UK:

(1) the Directive on the health and safety of workers at work was implemented as the Management of Health and Safety at Work Regs 1992; and

(2) the Directive on temporary and mobile construction sites was implemented as the Construction (Design and Management) Regs 1994.

Regulations produced since 1992 do not, in most cases, stand on their own. They must be read in conjunction with the general duties imposed on employers under the Management of Health and Safety at Work Regs 1999, in particular the duties relating to:

• Risk assessment
• The operation and maintenance of safety management systems
• The appointment of competent persons
• Establishment and implementation of emergency procedures
• Provision of information to employees which is comprehensible and relevant
• Co-operation, communication and co-ordination between employers in shared workplaces (eg construction sites, office blocks)
• Provision of comprehensible health and safety information to employees from an outside undertaking
• Assessment of human capability prior to allocating tasks
• Provision of health and safety information, training and instruction.

Duties imposed on employers tend largely to be of an absolute nature, as opposed to qualified duties, such as 'so far as is reasonably practicable', as with the HSWA. Risk assessment, taking into account the 'requirements and prohibitions imposed on an employer by or under the relevant statutory provisions', is the starting point of all health and safety management systems. Most modern health and safety legislation requires some form of documentation, such as risk assessments and planned preventive maintenance systems, and the maintenance of records.

15.4 MANAGEMENT OF HEALTH AND SAFETY AT WORK REGS 1999

The 1999 Regs, which are accompanied by an HSC Approved Code of Practice, require a management-orientated approach to compliance with health and safety legislation generally. Moreover, duties under other regulations must be read in conjunction with the general duties under the 1999 Regs. Duties on employers are of an absolute or strict nature.

15.4.1 Risk assessment
(1999 Regs, reg 3)

Every employer shall make a suitable and sufficient assessment of the risks to the health and safety of:

(1) his employees to which they are exposed while at work; and
(2) persons not in his employment arising out of or in connection with the conduct by him of his undertaking,

for the purpose of identifying the measures he needs to take to comply with the requirements and prohibitions imposed upon him by or under the relevant statutory provisions and by Part II of the Fire Precautions (Workplace) Regs 1997.

Relevant statutory provisions

These are the statutory provisions (ie the HSWA) and those of any regulations made under the statute (eg Noise at Work Regs 1989).

Principles of prevention to be applied
(1999 Regs, reg 4)

Where an employer implements preventive and protective measures he shall do so on the basis of the principles specified in Sch 1 to the Regulations.

625

Health and safety arrangements
(1999 Regs, reg 5)

This is the 'management' aspect of the Regulations. Having undertaken risk assessments, employers need to install effective systems for managing health and safety at work. The key elements of effective health and safety management systems can be found in *Successful health and safety management* (HSE Guidance Note HS(G)65) and *Guide to Occupational Health and Safety Management Systems* (British Standard publication BS8800). These key elements of such a system are shown in Fig. 15.1.

Figure 15.1: Key elements of successful health and safety management

Health surveillance
(1999 Regs, reg 6)

Every employer shall ensure that his employees are provided with such health surveillance as is appropriate having regard to the risks to their health and safety which are identified by the assessment.

Health and safety assistance
(1999 Regs, reg 7)

An employer must appoint one or more competent persons to assist him in undertaking the measures he needs to take to comply with the requirements and prohibitions imposed upon him by or under the relevant statutory provisions and by Part II of the 1997 Fire Precautions Regs. This regulation does not apply to self-employed persons and those carrying on a business in partnership where that person or a partner has sufficient training, experience or knowledge as to be considered competent.

Recent legislation has attached particular significance to the duty on employers to appoint competent person for a range of tasks. But what is a 'competent person'?

Case-law broadly defines a competent person as someone appointed by an employer with the appropriate level of skill, knowledge and experience directed to ensuring the safety of others. They must be appointed to advise the employer on aspects of compliance with the relevant statutory provisions and to oversee emergency procedures. The level of competence must be related to the significance of the risks and the number of employees exposed to risk. A competent person may be appointed from within an organization or be an external consultant.

Increasingly, enforcement officers are looking for evidence of the competence of health and safety practitioners based on the possession of recognized qualifications in health and safety, such as those administered by the National Examination Board in Occupational Safety and Health (NEBOSH), universities and other institutions.

Procedures for serious and imminent danger and for danger areas
(1999 Regs, reg 8)

Employers must:

(1) establish and where necessary give effect to appropriate procedures to be followed in the event of serious or imminent danger to persons at work;
(2) nominate a sufficient number of competent persons to implement these procedures; and
(3) prevent any employee being given access to a danger area unless he has received adequate health and safety instruction.

Contacts with external services
(1999 Regs, reg 9)

Every employer shall ensure that any necessary contacts with external services are arranged, particularly as regards first aid, emergency medical care and rescue work.

Information for employees
(1999 Regs, reg 10)

Every employer shall provide his employees with comprehensible and relevant information on:

(1) the risks to their health and safety identified by the assessment;
(2) the preventive and protective measures;
(3) the procedures referred to in reg 8(1)(a) and the measures referred to in reg 4(2)(a) of the 1997 Fire Prevention Regs;
(4) the identity of the competent persons nominated in accordance with reg 8(1)(b) and the measures referred to in reg 4(2)(b) of the 1997 Regs; and
(5) the risks notified to him in accordance with reg 11(1)(c) (shared workplaces).

Every employer shall, before employing a child, provide a parent of the child with comprehensible and relevant information on:

(a) the risks to his health and safety identified by the assessment;
(b) the preventive and protective measures; and
(c) the risks notified in accordance with reg 11(1)(c).

Co-operation and co-ordination
(1999 Regs, reg 11)

Where two or more employers share a workplace (whether on a temporary or permanent basis), each must:

(1) co-operate with other employers to enable them to comply with legal requirements;
(2) take all reasonable steps to co-ordinate the measures he is taking with other employers in order to comply with legal requirements; and
(3) take all reasonable steps to inform other employers of risks to their employees' health and safety arising from his activities.

Persons working in host employers or self-employed persons' undertakings
(1999 Regs, reg 12)

Every employer and self-employed person shall ensure that the employer of any employees from an outside undertaking who are working in his undertaking is provided with comprehensible information on:

(1) the risks arising in the undertaking; and
(2) the measures taken by the first-mentioned employer to comply with legal requirements and to protect those employees.

These measures include details of emergency and evacuation procedures and the competent persons nominated to implement such procedures.

Capabilities and training
(1999 Regs, reg 13)

Every employer shall, in entrusting tasks to his employees, take into account their capabilities as regards health and safety. He shall ensure that his employees are provided with adequate health and safety training on their being:

(1) recruited into the employer's undertaking; and
(2) exposed to new or increased risks within the employer's undertaking because of:
    (a) their being transferred or given a change of responsibilities;
    (b) the introduction of new work equipment to or a change of work equipment already in use;
    (c) the introduction of new technology; or
    (d) the introduction of a new system of work or a change of a system of work already in use.

Training shall be repeated periodically where appropriate, be adapted to take account of new or changed risks and take place during working hours.

Employees' duties
(1999 Regs, reg 14)

Every employee shall use any machinery, equipment, dangerous substance, transport equipment, means of production or safety device provided to him by his employer in accordance both with any training in the use of equipment and the instructions respecting that use provided by the employer in compliance with the requirements and prohibitions imposed upon that employer by or under the relevant statutory provisions. Every employee shall inform his employer or any other employee with specific responsibility for the health and safety of his fellow employees (eg competent person, trade union safety representative) of any:

(1) work situation which he reasonably considers represents a serious and immediate danger to health and safety; and
(2) matter which he reasonably considers represents a shortcoming in the employer's protection arrangements for health and safety.

Temporary workers
(1999 Regs, reg 15)

This regulation places an absolute duty on employers to provide any person working under a fixed-term contract or employed in an employment business with comprehensible information:

(a) on any special occupational qualifications or skills required to be held by that employee if he is to carry out his work safely; and

(b) of any health surveillance required,

before the employee commences his duties. Further provisions apply in the case of persons carrying an employment business being required to pass on information to employees before working in another employer's undertaking.

Risk assessment in respect of new or expectant mothers
(1999 Regs, reg 16)

A 'new or expectant mother' means an employee who is pregnant, has given birth within the previous six months, or is breastfeeding.

Where employees include women of child-bearing age and the work could involve risk to the health and safety of a new or expectant mother, or to that of her baby, from any processes or working conditions, or physical, biological or chemical agents, the assessment required by reg 3(1) shall also include an assessment of such risk. If in taking other action required by the legislation such an employee would remain at risk, the employer must alter her working conditions or hours of work.

If it is not reasonable to alter working conditions or hours of work, or if it would not avoid such risk, the employer shall, subject to the Employment Rights Act (ERA) 1996, s 67, suspend the employee from work so long as is necessary to avoid such risk.

In relation to risk from any infectious or contagious disease, references to a level of risk is in addition to the level to which a new or expectant mother may be expected to be exposed outside the workplace.

Certificate in respect of new or expectant mothers
(1999 Regs, reg 17)

Where:

(1) a new or expectant mother works at night, and

(2) a certificate from a registered medical practitioner or a registered midwife shows that it is necessary for her health or safety that she should not be at work for any period identified in the certificate,

the employer shall, subject to ERA 1996, s 67 suspend her from work so long as is necessary for her health or safety.

Notification by new or expectant mothers
(1999 Regs, reg 18)

Nothing shall require the employer to take any action in relation to an employee until she has notified him in writing that she is pregnant, has given birth within the previous six months, or is breastfeeding.

Protection of young persons
(1999 Regs, reg 19)

A 'young person' means any person who has not attained age 18. Every employer shall ensure that young persons employed by him are protected at work from any risks to their health or safety which are a consequence of their lack of experience, or absence of awareness of existing or potential risks or the fact they have not yet fully matured. Subject to reg 19(3), no employer shall employ a young person for work:

(1) which is beyond his physical or psychological capacity;
(2) involving harmful exposure to agents which are toxic or carcinogenic, cause heritable genetic damage or harm to the unborn child or which in any other way chronically affect human health;
(3) involving harmful exposure to radiation;
(4) involving the risk of accidents which it may reasonably be assumed cannot be recognised or avoided by young persons owing to their insufficient attention to safety or lack of experience or training; or
(5) in which there is a risk to health from:
  - extreme cold or heat;
  - noise; or
  - vibration.

In determining whether work will involve harm or risks, regard shall be had to the results of the assessment.

Nothing in reg 19(2) shall prevent the employment of a young person who is no longer a child for work where:

(a) it is necessary for his training;
(b) the young person will be supervised by a competent person; and
(c) any risk will be reduced to the lowest, reasonably practicable level.

Provisions as to liability
(1999 Regs, reg 21)

Nothing in the relevant statutory provisions shall operate so as to afford an employer a defence in criminal proceedings for a contravention of those provisions by reason of any act or default of an employee of his, or a person appointed by him under reg 7 (competent person).

Exclusion of civil liability
(1999 Regs, reg 22)

Breach of a duty imposed by the 1999 Regs shall not confer a right of action in any civil proceedings.

General principles of prevention
(1999 Regs, Sch 1)

Schedule 1 specifies the general principles of prevention set out in Council Directive 89/391/EEC, Art 6(2), ie:

(1) avoiding risks;
(2) evaluating the risks which cannot be avoided;
(3) combating the risks at source;
(4) adapting the work to the individual, especially as regards the design of workplaces and the choice of work equipment and of working and production methods, with a view, in particular, to alleviating monotonous work and work at a predetermined work rate and reducing their effect on health;
(5) adapting to technical progress;
(6) replacing the dangerous by the non-dangerous or the less dangerous;
(7) developing a coherent overall prevention policy which covers technology, organisation of work, working conditions, social relationships and the influence of factors relating to the working environment;
(8) giving collective protective measures priority over individual protective measures; and
(9) giving appropriate instructions to employees.

15.5 CRIMINAL AND CIVIL LIABILITY

15.5.1 Criminal liability

A crime is an offence against the state. Criminal liability refers to the duties and responsibilities under statute, principally the HSWA and regulations, and the penalties that can be imposed by the criminal courts (ie fines, imprisonment and remedial orders). There are two categories of conviction:

(1) *Summary conviction*: for offences regarded as less serious which, in practice, applies to most health and safety offences, and where the case is brought before a magistrates' court (without a jury). The maximum penalty for certain health and safety-related offences is £20,000 and/or six months' imprisonment, and for other health and safety related-offences £5,000.
(2) *Conviction on indictment*: where the case is tried before a judge and jury in the Crown Court. This form of trial is reserved for the more serious offences and offenders can be sentenced to up to two years' imprisonment with unlimited fines.

Thus the criminal courts in question are the magistrates' courts, which handle the bulk of health and safety offences, and the Crown Courts, which deal with the more serious offences. Appeals can be made to the High

Court and beyond, to the Court of Appeal and, assuming leave is given, to the House of Lords. Subject to certain criteria, a case may pass to the European Court of Justice.

Criminal law is based on a system of enforcement. Its statutory provisions are enforced by the state's enforcement agencies, such as the police, the HSE, local authorities and fire authorities.

In contrast to civil liability in tort, criminal liability cannot be insured against by employers, directors or employees. However, it is lawful to insure against court costs and the legal expenses of counsel in connection with a prosecution for health and safety offences.

15.5.2 Civil liability

Most civil claims are based on negligence or breach of statutory duty. A civil action generally involves negligence and/or breach of a statutory duty. In such actions, a claimant sues a defendant for a remedy (or remedies) that is beneficial to the claimant. In most cases, this takes the form of damages, a form of financial compensation. In a substantial number of cases, the claimant will agree to settle out of court.

Civil liability, therefore, refers to the 'penalty' that can be imposed by a civil court (eg the County Court, High Court, Court of Appeal (Civil Division) or House of Lords), and consists of awards of damages for injury, disease and/or death at work.

15.5.3 Negligence

'Negligence' is defined as 'careless conduct injuring another'. It has been defined at common law as:

(1) the existence of a duty of care owed by a defendant to a claimant;
(2) breach of that duty; and
(3) injury, damage or loss resulting from or caused by that breach.

All the above circumstances must be established by an injured person before a civil claim for damages may be brought.

15.5.4 Breach of statutory duty

In certain cases, a breach of a criminal duty imposed by statute or regulations may give rise to civil liability and a claim for damages. In many cases, a statute or regulations will state that such breach shall not give rise to civil liability (eg the 1999 Regs). However, where such a statement of exclusion is not made, civil liability is implied.

The standard test adopted by the courts has been to ask the question: Was the duty imposed specifically for the protection of a particular class of people, or was it intended to benefit the public at large? If the answer to the first part of the question is 'Yes', a civil claim may be allowed.

On this basis, the courts have always viewed legislation, such as the safety provisions of the Factories Act 1961, as being directed towards protecting a particular class and have allowed civil claims for damages by persons belonging to these protected classes, namely employees.

15.5.5 Vicarious liability

Vicarious liability is based on the fact that if an employee, while acting in the course of his employment, negligently injures another employee or the employee of another employer, his employer, rather than the negligent employee, will be liable for that injury. Vicarious liability rests on the employer simply as a result of the fact that he is the employer and is deemed to have ultimate control over his employees (ie the master and servant relationship).

This liability must be insured against under the Employers' Liability (Compulsory Insurance) Act 1969. Employers cannot contract out of this liability as this is prohibited by the Law Reform (Personal Injuries) Act 1948 and the Unfair Contract Terms Act 1977.

See generally Fig 15.2 for an illustration of the criminal and civil action procedures.

Figure 15.2: Legal routes following an accident at work

15.6 WORKPLACE (HEALTH, SAFETY AND WELFARE) REGS 1992

15.6.1 Introduction

'Workplace' is defined broadly as meaning any premises or part of premises which are not domestic premises and made available to any person as a place of work, and including:

(1) any place within the premises to which such person has access while at work; and

(2) any room, lobby, corridor, staircase, road or other place used as a means of access to or egress from the workplace or where facilities are provided for use in connection with the workplace other than a public road.

15.6.2 Duty to maintain the workplace

Under reg 5 of the 1992 Regs, there is an absolute duty on employers to maintain the workplace, equipment, devices and systems (including cleaning as appropriate) in an efficient state, in efficient working order and in good repair.

15.6.3 The working environment

Specific provisions apply with regard to environmental factors:

(1) ventilation must be effective and suitable to maintain comfortable conditions;

(2) the temperature must be reasonable during working hours;

(3) lighting must be suitable in terms of the type of lighting and sufficient with regard to the amount of light provided; emergency lighting must be provided where failure of lighting may create danger;

(4) there is a general duty to keep the workplace clean and surfaces (floors, walls, etc) must be cleanable; there must be adequate control over refuse;

(5) sufficient floor area and space must be provided for employees; and

(6) both indoor and outdoor workstations must be suitable for the work carried out; seats provided must be suitable for the person and for the work undertaken.

15.6.4 Structural safety

Specific provisions applying to structural safety include:

(1) floors and traffic routes must be suitable for the purpose, in good repair and free from obstructions;

(2) measures to prevent risks arising from falls and falling objects must be taken, including marking risk areas and covering pits, tanks, etc;

(3) windows and transparent or translucent doors, gates and walls must be of safety material or protected in certain cases, and be suitably marked;

(4) the design of windows, skylights and ventilators must be such that there is no risk when opening, closing or adjusting, and be suitably positioned;

(5) windows etc must be capable of being cleaned safely, including the fitting of suitable devices to buildings;

(6) traffic routes must be organised in such a way as to ensure safe circulation by pedestrians and vehicles;

(7) doors and gates must be suitably designed and constructed, and fitted with certain safety devices; and

(8) escalators and moving walkways must function safely and safety devices and emergency stop controls must be fitted.

15.6.5 Welfare amenity provisions

The provision and maintenance of suitable and sufficient welfare amenities is an important feature of the Regulations. Sanitary conveniences must be suitable and sufficient, adequately ventilated and lit, and kept in a clean and orderly condition with separation of the sexes. Washing facilities must be suitable and sufficient, located in the vicinity of sanitary conveniences (and changing rooms if required), with hot and cold water, and cleaning and drying facilities. They also must be ventilated and well lit, and kept in a clean and orderly condition with separation of the sexes.

Drinking water supply must be wholesome, readily accessible and conspicuously marked, with cups or drinking vessels provided unless from a jet supply.

Accommodation for clothing must be suitable and sufficient, with security for clothing not worn and separate accommodation in some cases. Facilities for drying must be provided which are suitably located. Facilities for changing clothing must be suitable and sufficient, and ensure privacy with separation of the sexes.

Facilities for rest and to eat meals must be suitable and sufficient, including the provision of rest rooms or areas. There must be separation of smokers and non-smokers, and facilities provided for pregnant women and nursing mothers. Facilities must also be provided for taking meals.

15.7 PROVISION AND USE OF WORK EQUIPMENT REGS 1998

15.7.1 Introduction

'Work equipment' means any machinery, appliance, apparatus or tool or any assembly of components which, in order to achieve a common end, are arranged and controlled so that they function as a whole. 'Use' in relation to work equipment means any activity involving work equipment and includes starting, stopping, programming, setting, transporting, repairing, modifying, maintaining, servicing and cleaning.

15.7.2 Employers' duties

Work equipment must be constructed or adapted to be suitable for the purpose for which it is to be used or provided. It must be maintained in an efficient state, in efficient working order and in good repair. Any maintenance log for machinery must be kept up to date.

Where work equipment incorporates specific risks, its use must be restricted to those persons given the task of using it, and repairs, modifications, maintenance and servicing must be restricted to designated persons. All persons using work equipment must receive appropriate information, instruction and training.

Items of work equipment must conform with any enactment which implements in Great Britain any of the relevant EU Directives applicable to that item of equipment listed in Sch 1 to the 1998 Regs. Effective measures must be taken to ensure the safety of dangerous parts of machinery, and to provide protection against specified hazards and high or very low temperature.

15.7.3 Specific duties of employers

More specific duties cover:

- Controls and control systems relating to machinery
- Isolation from sources of energy
- Stabilising work equipment
- Lighting where work equipment is used
- Safety of maintenance operations
- Marking work equipment
- The provision of warnings and warning devices.

15.7.4 Mobile work equipment

'Mobile work equipment' is defined as any work equipment which carries out work while it is travelling or which travels between different locations where it is used to carry out work. It may be self-propelled, towed or remote controlled and may incorporate attachments. Employers must ensure that no employee is carried by mobile work equipment unless:

(1) it is suitable for carrying persons; and
(2) it incorporates features for reducing to as low as is reasonably practicable risks to their safety, including wheels or tracks.

Employers must:

(a) minimise the risk of rolling over of mobile work equipment;
(b) fit roll-over protective structures where necessary;
(c) adapt or equip forklift trucks to reduce the risk of overturning;
(d) take specific measures in respect of self-propelled and remote-controlled self-propelled work equipment; and
(e) either prevent the seizure of drive shafts or, where seizure cannot be avoided, take every possible measure to avoid an adverse effect on the safety of an employee.

15.8 PERSONAL PROTECTIVE EQUIPMENT AT WORK REGS 1992

15.8.1 Introduction

These Regulations establish the principles for selecting, providing, maintaining and using personal protective equipment (PPE). They do not replace recently introduced law dealing with PPE, such as the Control of Substances Hazardous to Health (COSHH) Regs 1999 and the Noise at Work Regs 1989. Employers need consider only one set of regulations for all their PPE requirements covering a particular risk.

'Personal protective equipment' is defined as all equipment (including clothing affording protection against the weather) which is intended to be worn or held by a person at work and which protects him against one or more risks to his health or safety, and any addition or accessory designed to meet that objective.

15.8.2 Employers' duties

There are a number of general duties on employers, namely:

(1) to ensure the provision of suitable PPE to employees, where risks cannot be controlled by other means;
(2) where more than one item of PPE is worn or used by an employee, to ensure compatibility of those items and that they give effective protection against risks;
(3) a duty to assess the PPE's suitability in protecting against risks;
(4) to ensure any PPE is maintained (including replaced or cleaned as appropriate) in an efficient state, in efficient working order and in good repair;
(5) to provide accommodation for PPE not in use;
(6) to provide information, instruction and training for employees to enable each employer to know the risks, correct use of the PPE and actions to ensure it remains in an efficient state, efficient working order and good repair; and
(7) to enforce the use of PPE by employees.

15.8.3 Employees' duties

Employees must:

(1) use PPE in accordance with any training received by them and the instructions respecting that use; and
(2) report any loss or defect.

15.9 MANUAL HANDLING OPERATIONS REGULATIONS 1992

These Regulations apply to all manual handling operations which may cause injury at work. 'Manual handling operations' means any transporting or supporting of a load (including lifting, putting down, pushing, pulling, carrying or moving) by hand or by bodily force.

15.9.1 Employers' duties

Employers have a general duty to avoid, so far as is reasonably practicable, manual handling operations which involve a risk of injury to employees. Where avoidance is not reasonably practicable, the employer must make a suitable and sufficient assessment of all such manual handling operations, having regard to the factors specified in the Schedule (see 15.9.3).

15.9.2 Employees' duty

Employees must make full and proper use of any system of work provided by the employer arising from the assessment.

15.9.3 The assessment

In accordance with the Schedule, this must take into account:

- the task
- the load
- the working environment, and
- individual capability.

15.10 HEALTH AND SAFETY (DISPLAY SCREEN EQUIPMENT) REGS 1992

The Regulations apply to all identified 'users' and 'operators' of display screen equipment. The following definitions are significant in the interpretation of the Regulations.

'Display screen equipment' means any alphanumeric or graphic display screen regardless of the display process involved. 'User' means an employee who habitually uses display screen equipment as a significant part of his normal work. 'Operator' means a self-employed person who habitually uses display screen equipment as a significant part of his normal work. 'Workstation' means an assembly comprising:

(1) display screen equipment (including software, a keyboard or any other input device);
(2) any optional accessories to the display screen equipment;
(3) any disk drive, telephone, modem, printer, document holder, work chair, work desk, work surface or other item peripheral to the display screen equipment; and
(4) the immediate work environment around the display screen equipment.

The Regulations do not apply to:

(a) drivers' cabs or control cabs for vehicles or machinery;
(b) display screen equipment on board a means of transport;
(c) display screen equipment mainly intended for public operation;
(d) portable systems not in prolonged use;
(e) calculators, cash registers or any equipment having a small data measurement display required for direct use of the equipment; or
(f) window typewriters.

15.10.1 Employers' duties

There are a number of general duties on an employer to:

(1) perform a suitable and sufficient risk analysis of workstations used by users and operators for the purposes of his undertaking;
(2) plan users' activities to ensure regular screen breaks or changes of activity to reduce their workload at that equipment;
(3) provide eye and eyesight tests for existing new users, at regular intervals after the initial tests, and when a user experiences visual difficulties;
(4) provide users with special corrective appliances where normal corrective appliances cannot be used and the eye and eyesight test indicates such need; and
(5) provide information and training in the use of the workstation to users.

15.10.2 Risk analysis

The Schedule covers the requirements to be considered in a workstation risk analysis, namely:

(a) the equipment (display screen, keyboard, work desk or work surface and work chair);
(b) the environment (space requirements, lighting, and reflection and glare, noise, heat, radiation and humidity control); and
(c) the interface between the computer and the operator/user.

15.11 FIRE PRECAUTIONS (WORKPLACE) REGS 1997

These Regulations came into operation on 1 December 1997, bringing the UK into line with the fire safety aspects of the Framework and Workplace Directives. The Regulations place primary responsibility for workplace fire safety on employers and those in control of workplaces, who must assess and provide the measures needed to prevent or control the risks from fire. The necessary and appropriate measures must be determined by the specific circumstances of individual workplaces.

These Regulations incorporate a new approach to the enforcement of fire safety requirements, allowing most significant breaches of the Regulations to be dealt with by civil sanctions, with the burden of proof on the fire authority sooner than an employer. They amend certain regulations, including the Management of Health and Safety at Work Regs 1992 and the Safety Representatives and Safety Committees Regs 1977.

15.11.1 Principal requirements

Every employer and any other person who has control of a workplace, and any person who has an obligation relating to maintenance, repair or safety there, must comply with the Regulations (although see 15.11.5 (excepted workplaces)). In particular, they must:

(1) ensure the workplace is equipped with appropriate firefighting equipment, fire detectors and alarms, and that any non-automatic firefighting equipment is easily accessible, simple to use and indicated by signs;
(2) take measures for firefighting, nominate and train employees to implement those measures, and arrange contacts with external emergency services;
(3) keep emergency routes clear, and comply with specific criteria relating to routes, doors and signs; and
(4) have a suitable system of maintenance for fire precautions in relation to the workplace, equipment and devices, and ensure these are working and in good repair.

15.11.2 Amendment to the Management of Health and Safety at Work Regs 1992

These Regulations are amended to incorporate the provisions of the 1997 Regs on:

- Risk assessment
- Health and safety assistance
- Information for employees
- Co-operation and co-ordination
- Persons working in host employers' undertakings.

15.11.3 Enforcement

The Regulations are enforced by the local fire authority, either through fire brigade officers or through appointed inspectors. Criminal breaches of the Regulations are liable on conviction in a magistrates' court or Crown Court to a fine, imprisonment or both. Anyone who fails, intentionally or recklessly, to comply with the Regulations and puts employees at serious risk in case of fire (ie death or serious injury) commits a criminal offence.

In situations where non-compliance puts employees at serious risk, the authority can serve an enforcement notice requiring work to be undertaken within a specified period. The recipient has 21 days in which to appeal. Except in situations where the risk is so serious that the service of an enforcement notice cannot be delayed, the authority must give written notice of its intention to serve. Failure to comply with an enforcement notice is a criminal offence.

Where there is a breach of Regulations, whether serious or not, a county court may, on receipt of an application from a fire authority, issue an enforcement order requiring compliance. Before making application for an order, the fire authority must give written notice to the alleged offender of its intention to seek an order, and consider any representations made as a result.

15.11.4 Fire Precautions Act 1971

The scope of this Act, which enables a fire authority to serve a prohibition notice to immediately prohibit the use of premises, including an unsafe workplace in a building, is extended to workplaces in movable structures and in the open air. The Act is not amended and duties under it must be read in conjunction with the Regulations.

15.11.5 Excepted workplaces

The following workplaces are excepted from the requirements of these Regulations:

(1) those having a current fire certificate, or for which an application is pending, under the Fire Precautions Act 1971;

(2) those having a current fire certificate under the Safety of Sports Grounds Act 1975 or the Fire Safety (Safety of Places of Sport) Act 1989;

(3) workplaces covered by the Fire Precautions (Sub-surface Railway Stations) Regs 1989;

(4) construction sites within the meaning of reg 2(1) of the Construction (Health, Safety and Welfare) Regs 1996;

(5) ships within the meaning of reg 2(1) of the Docks Regs 1988;

(6) premises covered by the Fire Certificates (Special Premises) Regs 1976;

(7) premises covered by the Mines and Quarries Act 1954;

(8) offshore installations within the meaning of reg 3 of the Offshore Installations and Pipelines Works (Management and Administration) Regs 1995;

(9) aircraft, locomotives and rolling stock, or trailers used as a means of transport, or vehicles having a licence under the Vehicle Excise and Registration Act or which are exempted from duty under this Act;

(10) workplaces which are in fields, woods or other land forming part of an agricultural or forestry undertaking, but which are not inside a building and are situated away from the undertaking's main building.

15.12 LIFTING OPERATIONS AND LIFTING EQUIPMENT REGS 1998

Under these Regulations, lifting equipment provided for use at work should be:

- Strong and safe enough for its use
- Marked with its safe working load
- Installed and positioned to minimise risks
- Used safely
- Thoroughly examined and, where appropriate, inspected by a competent person on an ongoing basis.

All equipment used at work for lifting and lowering loads, including attachments and accessories, but with the exception of escalators, is covered by the Regulations.

The Regulations apply to all employers or self-employed persons who provide lifting equipment for use at work, as well as those who have control over its use. An ongoing requirement of the legislation is that:

(1) lifting operations must be planned, supervised and carried out in a safe manner by a competent person;

(2) equipment used for lifting people must be marked accordingly, and should be safe for such a purpose;

(3) before being used for the first time the equipment should, where appropriate, be thoroughly examined;

(4) it may also need to be thoroughly examined in use at set intervals (eg six months for accessories and equipment used for lifting people);

(5) all examinations must be carried out by a competent person; and

(6) a report must be submitted by the competent person to the employer following a thorough examination or inspection.

15.13 CONTROL OF SUBSTANCES HAZARDOUS TO HEALTH (COSHH) REGS 1999

The COSSH Regs apply to every form of workplace and every type of work activity involving the use of substances which may be hazardous to health to people at work. The Regulations are supported by a number of HSC Approved Codes of Practice, including:

- Control of substances hazardous to health
- Control of carcinogenic substances
- Control of biological agents.

15.13.1 Definitions

'Biological agent' means any micro-organism, cell, culture or human endoparasite, including any which have been genetically modified, which may cause any infection, allergy, toxicity or otherwise create a hazard to human health. 'Substance' means any natural or artificial substance, whether in solid, liquid, gas or vapour form (including any micro-organism). 'Substance hazardous to health' means any substance (including any preparation) which is:

(1) a substance which is listed for supply in Part 1 of the Approved Supply List as dangerous for supply within the meaning of the Chemicals (Hazard Information and Packaging for Supply) Regs 1994 and for which an indication of danger specified for the substance in Part V of that list is very toxic, toxic, harmful, corrosive or irritant;
(2) a substance for which the HSC has approved a maximum exposure limit or an occupational exposure standard;
(3) a biological agent;
(4) dust of any kind when present at a substantial concentration in air; and
(5) a substance, not being one mentioned in (1)–(4) above, which creates a hazard to any person's health which is comparable with the hazards created by substances mentioned in (1)–(4).

15.13.2 Assessment of health risks
(Reg 6)

This regulation places a duty on employers, where employees may be exposed to substances hazardous to health, to make a suitable and sufficient assessment of the risks (a health risk assessment) created by that work to employees and the steps that need to be taken. The assessment must be reviewed if it is no longer valid or there has been a significant change in the work to which the assessment relates, and any changes, as a result of the review, must be made.

15.13.3 Prevention or control of exposure
(Reg 7)

Exposure to substances hazardous to health must be either prevented or, where this is not reasonably practicable, controlled. Except in the case of a carcinogen or biological agent, prevention or adequate control shall be by means other than the provision of personal protective equipment (PPE).

15.13.4 Use of control measures, etc
(Reg 8)

Every employer shall take all reasonable steps to ensure that any control measure is properly used or applied. Every employee shall make full and proper use of any control measures, return PPE to any accommodation provided, and report defects in control measures to his employer.

15.13.5 Maintenance, examination and test of control measures, etc
(Reg 9)

The employer must ensure that any control measure is maintained in an efficient state, in efficient working order and in good repair and, in the case of PPE, in a clean condition.

15.13.6 Monitoring exposure at the workplace
(Reg 10)

Where appropriate, the employer shall ensure that there is a suitable procedure for monitoring the exposure of employees, including keeping records of such monitoring procedures.

15.13.7 Health surveillance
(Reg 11)

Where appropriate, the employer shall ensure that employees who are liable to be exposed are under suitable health surveillance.

15.13.8 Information, instruction and training etc
(Reg 12)

Where employees are exposed to the risk of exposure, they must be provided with such suitable and sufficient information, instruction and training for them to know those risks and the precautions which should be taken.

15.13.9 Defence in proceedings for contravention of Regulations
(Reg 16)

In any proceedings for an offence consisting of a contravention of these Regulations, it is a defence for any person to prove that he took *all* reasonable precautions and exercised *all* due diligence to avoid the commission of that offence.

15.14 HEALTH AND SAFETY (INFORMATION FOR EMPLOYEES) REGS 1999

15.14.1 Posters and leaflets

These Regulations require information relating to health, safety and welfare to be furnished to employees by means of posters or leaflets approved and published by the Health and Safety Executive. Copies of posters and leaflets may be obtained from the HSE and HMSO. The Regulations also require the enforcing authority's name and address and the Employment Medical Advisory Service's address to be written in the appropriate space on the poster. Where the leaflet is given to employees, the same information should be specified in a written notice accompanying it.

15.14.2 Certificates of exemption

The Regulations provide for the issue of Certificates of Exemption by the HSE, provide for a defence for a contravention of the Regulations, and repeal, revoke and modify various enactments relating to the provision of information to employees. The Regulations do not apply to the master and crew of a seagoing ship.

15.14.3 Modification to the Regulations

The Health and Safety Information for Employees (Modifications and Repeals) Regs 1995 amended the 1989 Regs, allowing the HSE to approve, as an alternative to the basic Health and Safety Law poster, a particular form of poster or leaflet for use in relation to a particular employment or class of employment. When applying for approval to display an alternative poster, applicants must demonstrate:

(1) a clearly defined industry or group of employers;
(2) a clear demand for the alternative poster; and
(3) that the poster would meet the same purposes as the basic poster and that the benefit justifies the development costs.

15.14.4 Abolition of statutory requirements

These Regulations also abolish 53 statutory requirements to display health and safety information, notably the Factories Act 1961, s 139 and a series of regulations made under that Act covering specific industries.

15.15 REPORTING INJURIES, DISEASES AND DANGEROUS OCCURRENCES

The Reporting of Injuries, Diseases and Dangerous Occurrences Regs 1995 (RIDDOR) cover the requirement to notify and *report* certain categories of injury and disease sustained by people at work, together with specified dangerous occurrences and gas incidents to the relevant enforcing authority (ie the HSE or local authority). The majority of duties on 'responsible persons' (as defined) are of an absolute nature.

15.15.1 Principal requirements of RIDDOR

The responsible person (eg employer) must notify the relevant enforcing authority by the quickest practicable means and subsequently make a report within ten days on the approved form in respect of death, any defined major injury and dangerous occurrence arising out of or in connection with work (reg 3). It is the employer's duty to report the death of an employee where, as a result of an accident at work, the injured employee dies within one year of the accident (reg 4). The employer must also report cases of disease to employees listed in the Schedule (reg 5).

There are duties on certain persons to report gas incidents (reg 6).

A responsible person must keep records of reportable injuries, diseases and dangerous occurrences (reg 7).

15.15.2 Notifiable and reportable major injuries

These are listed in Sch 1 to RIDDOR, as follows:

(1) any fracture, other than to the fingers, thumbs or toes;
(2) any amputation;
(3) dislocation of the shoulder, hip or knee;
(4) loss of sight (whether temporary or permanent);
(5) a chemical or hot metal burn to the eye or any penetrating injury to the eye;
(6) any injury resulting from electric shock or electrical burn (including such burn caused by arcing or arcing products) leading to unconsciousness or requiring resuscitation or admittance to hospital for more than 24 hours;

(7) any other injury:
    (a) leading to hypothermia, heat induced illness or unconsciousness;
    (b) requiring resuscitation; or
    (c) requiring admittance to hospital for more than 24 hours;
(8) loss of consciousness caused by asphyxia or by exposure to a harmful substance or biological agent;
(9) either of the following conditions which result from absorbing any substance by inhalation, ingestion or through the skin:
    (a) acute illness requiring medical treatment; or
    (b) loss of consciousness; and
(10) acute illness which requires medical treatment where there is reason to believe that it resulted from exposure to a biological agent or its toxins or infected material.

15.15.3 Scheduled dangerous occurrences

A dangerous occurrence is a major incident as a rule which has the potential for significant damage and potential loss of life and which is listed in Sch 2 to RIDDOR. Dangerous occurrences are classified under five headings:

(1) General (eg incidents involving lifting machinery, pressure systems, overhead electric lines).
(2) Dangerous occurrences which are reportable in mines (eg fire or ignition of gas, escape of gas, insecure tip).
(3) Dangerous occurrences which are reportable in respect of quarries (eg misfires, movement of slopes or faces).
(4) Dangerous occurrences which are reportable in respect of relevant transport systems (eg accidents involving any kind of train, incidents at level crossings).
(5) Dangerous occurrences which are reportable in respect of an offshore workplace (eg releases of petroleum hydrocarbon, fire or explosion).

15.15.4 Reportable diseases

These are diseases listed in Sch 3 to RIDDOR under three classifications:

(1) conditions due to physical agents and the physical demands of work (eg malignant diseases of bones due to ionising radiation, decompression illness);
(2) infections due to biological agents (eg anthrax, brucellosis, leptospirosis); and
(3) conditions due to substances (eg poisoning by carbon disulphide, ethylene oxide and methyl bromide).

15.16 COMPULSORY INSURANCE

The Employers' Liability (Compulsory Insurance) Act 1969 deals with employers' duties in terms of insuring themselves against claims which may be made by employees.

15.16.1 Employers' duties

Section 1 of the Act requires that every employer carrying on business in Great Britain shall insure and maintain insurance against liability for bodily injury or disease sustained by his employees, and arising out of and in the course of their employment in Great Britain in that business. This insurance must be provided under one or more 'approved policies'. An approved policy is a policy of insurance not subject to any conditions or exceptions prohibited by regulations.

15.16.2 Cover

Cover is required in respect of liability to employees who either:

(1) are ordinarily resident in Great Britain; or
(2) though not ordinarily resident in Great Britain, are present in Great Britain in the course of employment for a continuous period of not less than 14 days.

The amount for which an employer is required to insure and maintain insurance is £2m in respect of claims relating to one or more of his employees, arising out of any one occurrence.

15.16.3 Issue and display of certificate of insurance

The insurer must issue the employer with a certificate of insurance, which has to be issued not later than 30 days after the date on which insurance was commenced or renewed. The certificate must be displayed prominently.

15.16.4 Penalties under the Act

For failure to insure or maintain insurance, the maximum penalty on conviction is a £1,000 fine. For failure to display a certificate of insurance, the maximum penalty on conviction is a £500 fine.

15.17 CONSULTATION WITH EMPLOYEES

Joint consultation between employers and employees is an important feature of the safety management process and may take place specifically with trade union-appointed safety representatives and/or through the operation of a health and safety committee, or as part of a normal employer/employee consultative process.

15.17.1 Safety Representatives and Safety Committees Regs 1977

The main objective of these Regulations is to provide a basic framework within which each undertaking can develop effective working relationships. These relationships must cover a wide range of work situations (ie different types of workplace and work activity).

Appointment of safety representatives

A recognised trade union may appoint safety representatives from among the employees in all cases where one or more employees are employed by an employer by whom it is recognised. The employer must be notified by the trade union of the names of the safety representatives. Each safety representative has certain prescribed functions, as indicated below.

Functions of safety representatives

Safety representatives have the following functions:

(1) to represent employees in consultation with employers;
(2) to co-operate effectively in promoting and developing health and safety measures;
(3) to make representations to the employer on any general or specific matter affecting the health and safety of
    (a) their members; and/or
    (b) other persons employed at the workplace;
(4) to carry out certain inspections;
(5) to represent members in consultations with the HSE;
(6) to receive information from inspectors; and
(7) to attend meetings of the safety committee if appropriate.

None of these functions, however, imposes a legal duty on safety representatives.

Time off with pay

Employers must give safety representatives time off with pay for performing their functions and for any reasonable training they undergo.

Inspections of the workplace

Safety representatives are entitled to carry out workplace inspections, and employers must give reasonable assistance. Notice to inspect must be given in writing, with a standard inspection every three months. Safety representatives may also inspect the scene of a reportable accident or dangerous occurrence.

Inspection of documents

Safety representatives can inspect any document which the employer has to maintain, other than documents relating to the health records of identifiable individuals.

Approved code of practice

Qualifications and functions of safety representatives

So far as is reasonably practicable, representatives must have two years' experience with the employer or in similar employment. They must keep themselves informed of legal requirements and encourage co-operation between employer and employee. They are entitled to carry out workplace health and safety inspections and must inform the employer of the outcome of these inspections.

Employers' obligations

Employers must provide information to safety representatives on:

- Plans and performance of the undertaking
- Hazards and precautions
- Occurrence of accidents, dangerous occurrences and occupational disease
- Any other information, including the results of any measurements taken (eg from air monitoring).

Safety committees

Basic objectives and functions

The basic objective is to promote co-operation and act as a focus for employee participation. Safety Committees' functions are to consider:

(1) circumstances of individual accidents and cases of reportable diseases; and
(2) accident statistics and trends.

The committee might also:

(a) examine safety audit reports;
(b) consider reports and information from the HSE;
(c) assist in the development of safety rules and systems;
(d) conduct periodic inspections;
(e) monitor the effectiveness of health and safety training, communications and publicity; and
(f) provide a link with the Inspectorate.

Membership

Safety committees should be reasonably compact but allowing for representation of management and all employees. It must be appreciated that safety representatives are not appointed by the safety committee and vice versa. Neither is responsible to or for the other.

Conduct

Meetings should be held as often as necessary; agendas and minutes must be provided.

Arrangements at individual workplaces

Local arrangements should include:

(1) division of conduct of activities;
(2) a clear definition of the committee's objectives, terms of reference, membership and structure; and
(3) publication of matters notified by safety representatives.

15.17.2 Health and Safety (Consultation with Employees) Regs 1996

These Regulations brought in changes to the law with regard to the health and safety consultation process between employers and employees, largely because many employees are not members of a recognised trade union. Under the Safety Representatives and Safety Committees Regs 1997, employers must consult safety representatives appointed by any trade unions they recognise.

Under the 1996 Regs employers must consult any employees who are not covered by the 1997 Regs. This may be by direct consultation with employees or through representatives elected by the employees they are to represent.

HSE guidance

HSE guidance accompanying the Regulations details:

- which employees must be involved;
- the information they must be provided with;
- procedures for the election of representatives of employee safety;
- the training, time off and facilities they must be provided with; and
- their functions in office.

15.18 CONCLUSION

Most employers are good at assessing the cost of measures to ensure the appropriate levels of protection of employees at work. What they are not good at is assessing the extensive costs arising from death, major injuries and ill-health connected with work activities. Such costs can represent a significant loss as a result of, for instance, fines and damages imposed by the courts, together with increased employers' liability insurance premiums. These are only the direct costs, however. The indirect costs, such as poor levels of morale following a fatal accident, damage to plant and equipment and lost time arising from an accident, are frequently not taken into account.

Indeed, no employer can afford to disregard the current legal requirements for the development and implementation of management systems directed at the prevention of these losses. It should be recognised that loyal, well-trained and safety-conscious employees are the organisation's most valuable asset. Without these people, many employers would not be in business.

16

PARTNERSHIP LAW

KEITH HATCHICK, MARSHALL HATCHICK SOLICITORS

Despite the fact that the principal legislation in this area of law dates back to the Partnership Act (PA) 1890, this form of business relationship continues to be the most important after that of the plc. It is particularly popular for professional services like solicitors, surveyors, architects and accountants and smaller concerns where the rigours of maintaining a company and complying with the legislation are inappropriate.

16.1 WHAT IS A PARTNERSHIP?

PA 1890, s 1(1) defines 'partnership' as being the relationship that subsists between persons carrying on a business in common with a view to profit. All forms of company are expressly excluded under s 1(2).

Note that partnership is a *relationship* and does not have a separate legal status (unlike a company). It is the partners themselves who are and remain responsible for the partnership's activities and it is they personally who will if the circumstances require sue or be sued. In other words, whereas a limited company provides the shareholders with limited liability (up to the amount unpaid on their share capital), a partnership gives no such protection to a third party.

This distinction can sometimes be over-emphasised since frequently directors/shareholders of small companies need give personal guarantees before banks will contemplate offering such companies loans etc. Giving such guarantees in effect counteracts the very point of limited liability since if a company fails it may have the same effect as if the partnership failed.

There are at least three different kinds of partnership envisaged by PA 1890 under s 32, ie one formed for:

(1) a fixed term which when completed results in its dissolution;
(2) a particular or defined purpose or undertaking, eg a particular sales promotion: as and when completed the partnership is dissolved;
(3) an indefinite period, eg most forms of professional partnership give each partner an ability to terminate on giving the others a period of notice (see 16.9).

16.2 LIMITED PARTNERSHIP

This vehicle has become increasingly important in the context of offshore planning arrangements. The attractions are various and include the following:

(1) limited liability to certain of the partners;
(2) it is a registered entity that obtains a Certificate of Registration and a registration number from the Registrar of Companies;
(3) in the UK it is not automatically subject to UK tax (unlike a UK company): if the management and control is situated overseas, the partnership is deemed to be non-UK resident for tax purposes;
(4) there are fewer compliance and disclosure requirements than for a company if one of the general partners is an individual.

A limited partnership must have at least one 'general partner' who remains liable for all the partnership's debts and obligations. This partner may be a company. The remaining partners can be limited partners who are liable to contribute a fixed sum of capital to the partnership and their liability is limited to this extent. There is no statutory minimum capital contribution.

The partnership agreement must be signed by all (general and limited) partners and notification must be given to the Registrar of Companies (it is not thought necessary for the agreement to be filed).

The Limited Partnership Act 1907 is the principal governing legislation. This requires notification on Form LP5 to Companies House of its existence; failure to notify converts the limited partnership into a normal partnership in which all partners are completely liable for partnership debts. Changes must be notified on Form LP6.

A limited partnership must be formed with a view to making a profit; simply holding investments is not in itself sufficient.

16.3 LIMITED LIABILITY PARTNERSHIP ACT 2000

The Limited Liability Partnerships Act (LLPA) 2000 received royal assent on 20 July 2000 and came into force by SI on 6 April 2001 together with the Limited Liability Partnership Regs (LLP Regs) 2001.

A limited liability partnership (LLP) is, like its company cousin, a creation of statute. It is different from a company or partnership but shares similarities with both. Once incorporated, the LLP has a different legal status from its shareholders and officers. An LLP's capacity is unlimited, eg it can hold property in its own name, bring actions, be a shareholder, employ staff and retain independent contractors and agents, and borrow and create fixed and floating charges.

An LLP comes into force only when a certificate of registration has been issued. It does not need to promulgate a memorandum or articles of association. It is the LLPA 2000 and LLP Regs that govern its existence. Like directors of a company, members of an LLP can bind it with a third party, but members are not directors and therefore the following examples are not relevant restrictions:

- loans to members
- substantial property transaction rules
- duty to regard employee interest
- upper age limit for members.

Accounts on an annual basis do need to be filed with the Registrar of Companies and then are available to public inspection, but there is no share capital.

An LLP is not a partnership and there are no limits on the trade or business it may do. While members are not automatically employees, though this can be accommodated, although they cannot (unless other factors exist) be judged to be self-employed for tax purposes. Like a partnership, many LLPs will want an LLP agreement to bind the members and the LLP. This is a private document and does not need to be registered. So far as professional firms are concerned, the most important aspect is that individual members will not be liable for the negligence of other members and on a winding-up there is a limit on liability where liabilities exceed assets.

Members can be another LLP or company or individuals; there must be a minimum of two members. Where numbers fall below the minimum, the continuing member becomes personally liable after six months' moratorium and the LLP must be wound up. There must be two designated members, who have largely an administrative role, where their participation is needed. The LLPA 2000 provides that where there are no designated members appointed or where there is only one, each member of the LLP should be considered to be a designated member.

There is no required criterion for membership, but where a person has been disqualified under the Company Directors Disqualification Act 1986 this will also prevent such member from continuing or being a member of an LLP. Similarly, a bankrupt cannot be a member of an LLP or be involved in its formation.

The formation of an LLP is through the filing of forms with the Registrar of Companies. Details of the name (which cannot be the same as another on the Register, and similar rules as for companies exist concerning use of particular words etc), the registered office, the names and addresses of members and details of designated members (at least two – see above) needs to be notified. The application must be signed by at least two members. Accompanying this document must be a compliance document made by a solicitor or other person involved in formation confirming the proper procedures and requirements have been followed, along with a statutory fee of £95.

Any changes to membership need to be notified to the Registrar and consent to membership and acceptance of designated status must be accepted expressly; such acceptance needs to be filed on the relevant form with the Registrar within 14 days. Where the compliance requirements are not complied with, the LLP itself and designated members are potentially liable to prosecution. There is a potential defence for the designated member where under LLPA 2000, s 9(5) if such designated member took all reasonable steps to ensure requirements were complied with.

16.4 IS THERE AN AGREEMENT?

In almost all partnerships there needs to be a partnership deed, ie a contract between the partners setting out the contractual relationship between them. In the past there have been instances where the courts have taken the view that a contract exists even if there is no formal documentation – so long as it can be shown there was a contractual intention and some form of relationship based upon that intention.

For the purposes of this chapter it is assumed the partners wish to enter into a written agreement setting out their relationship. Partners are free to agree upon restrictions between themselves, but this cannot affect the rights of a third party unless they have been made a party to the agreement (under the well-defined contractual rules relating to privity of contract).

The partnership deed is a private document between the partners and does not need to appear on a public register (unlike memorandum and articles of association for a private company, which must be registered at Companies House – there is no such public body to which partnerships need report). A further advantage is that financial information relating to the partnership (eg accounts, partners' drawings and general emoluments etc) remain private and not subject to public inspection. A partner is not an employee since partnership being a relationship between partners, no partner is capable of employing himself. A partnership very commonly employs other people and all the partners have authority to make contracts in the course of a partnership business (eg employing people).

16.5 THE SALARIED PARTNER

The salaried partner is an employee of the partnership who is held out to the outside world as being a partner. He is normally entitled to a fixed remuneration that is not dependent on profits. A common example is within professional firms where having served apprenticeship it is felt by the equity partners to be appropriate to give an individual the status and prestige of being a partner without the need to consider capital contributions etc. His name appears on the notepaper with the other partners and he is able to bind the firm in the same way as any other partner.

It is a question sometimes of great importance whether a person is a partner. The courts have interpreted each case on its own particular circumstances. Irrespective of whether a person is a salaried partner, he is being held out as a partner and as such both he and his fellow partners are jointly and severally liable for his or their actions.

A salaried partner (as a result of his less senior status) is frequently given in the partnership agreement (and if not so given such a partner should insist upon) an indemnity from his fellow partners to compensate him in the event that he suffers liability in his capacity as a partner.

16.6 PARTNERSHIP AND THIRD PARTIES

Since a partnership does not have any separate status under English law, it is important to consider in what circumstances a partner is capable of binding his fellow partners and the relationship generally with outsiders.

The basic rule is that a partner is both a principal and an agent for his fellow partners, eg he can bind his fellow partners to any contract he signs if acting within his authority. In this way he is binding himself since he is a partner and a principal to that contract, and he is also binding his fellow partners since they are bound under the laws of agency by that contract.

PA 1890, s 5 states that each partner acts as an agent for the firm. Where a partner does any act in the usual course of business of the kind carried on by the firm, he binds the firm and his partners unless he has no authority to act for the firm in a particular matter *and the person with whom he is dealing either knows he has no authority or does not know or believe him to be a partner.*

It is a question of construction and circumstance whether a partnership may be bound under the agency rules. Three factors should be considered:

Nature of the business

An example would be that it is unlikely a firm of architects could advise on financial investments, whereas a banking partnership may so do. The Court of Appeal considered this question in *United Bank of Kuwait v Hammond* [1983] 3 All ER 418. A solicitor gave false undertakings to the bank concerning money held by the firm on behalf of a client. On the strength of this undertaking the bank advanced money to that client. The court took the view that the solicitor had acted within his ostensible authority in making the allegation since in normal circumstances it would be quite reasonable to expect such funds would fall within the firm's client account as part of normal day-to-day business. The bank was not required to check further since it was reasonable for the partner to be held out by a firm as having such authority.

Carrying on business in the normal way

In *Higgins v Beauchamp* [1914] 3 KB 1192, it was felt that carrying on a cinema business was not in effect a trading business (ie one for purchasing and selling of goods) and therefore a partner could not bind his fellow partner to a debt incurred by him. Carrying on business in a particular trade or profession can and does over a period of time change and in determining decisions of this nature courts have been flexible.

Knowledge and belief

If a partner has no authority to bind the firm and an outsider dealing with him realises it, the partnership cannot be bound by that partner's acts. If a third party does not have knowledge of the partner's lack of authority he can normally rely on the partner's position as a partner in binding his firm. However, this would not be the case if the outsider did not know or believe that the person he was dealing with was a partner.

16.7 LIABILITY OF PARTNERS

16.7.1 To third parties

Each partner is and remains jointly and severally liable to outsiders for any act or omission committed by any of the partners or their employees in carrying on business. This means an outsider has a choice of suing all or any of the partners for the full amount of such loss in accordance with normal principles of law. This is irrespective that a person so sued may be a salaried, or indeed a sleeping, partner.

16.7.2 *Inter se*

Under PA 1890, s 9, each partner is liable jointly with other partners for debts and obligations of the firm incurred while he is a partner.

Under s 17, a person who becomes a partner does not become liable to creditors of the firm for anything done before he became a partner. Likewise a retiring partner remains liable for debts and obligations incurred before retirement. This rule can be varied if a person either allows himself to be represented as being a partner or represents himself as being one (s 14).

Partnership liability was discussed at length in *Hurst v Bryck* [2000] 2 All ER 193. A solicitor argued that he did not need to contribute to the funds required by his fellow partners since they had repudiated the partnership by entering into a separate agreement without his agreement. Lord Millett accepted the argument that there had been a repudiation, but not that the solicitor was discharged, stating that the rights and obligations as at that date did remain. Being a contractual matter it was important to apply the rules of equity which would not accept a discharge of such liability. The court emphasised the need for proper and detailed accounts and a fair accounting procedure.

16.8 PARTNERSHIP AGREEMENT

The relationship between partners in a firm is normally set out in writing in a partnership deed. PA 1890 also contains a number of implied terms. A partnership agreement typically includes details of the following matters.

16.8.1 Good faith

Like company directors, it is clear that partners owe a fiduciary duty to each other. PA 1890 sets out three such duties in ss 28–30.

Honesty and full disclosure

Partners are bound to 'render true accounts and full information of all things affecting the partnership to any partner or his personal representative'. In *Law v Law* [1905] 1 Ch 140, a sleeping partner's share was bought for a gross undervalue since only certain assets had been disclosed. It was held that the other partner had been in breach of his fiduciary duty and should be entitled to a proper value. In another case involving property development, unbeknown to one of the partners an offer of purchase was turned down by the other. Eventually the property was sold at a lower value. The court took the view that although the partner conducting the sale had used good faith in rejecting the first offer he should have discussed the matter with the other partner and sought additional advice before rejecting it.

No unauthorised personal profit

A partner shall not make a private gain, even if innocent, and should account to his other partners for any profit made. Section 29 states that 'every partner must account to the firm for the benefit derived by him without the consent of the other partners from any transaction concerning the partnership or from any use by him of a partnership property, name or business connection'. This definition is very wide and has been broadly applied by the courts. In one case, a discount was offered to a partner which would not have been obtainable by the partnership as a whole. Since the partner made a private profit he should have disclosed this profit and have accounted for it to the practice.

No conflict of duty and interest

Section 30 states that 'if a partner, without the consent of the other partners, carries on any business of the same nature as and competing with that of the firm, he must account for and pay over to the firm all profits made by him in that business'.

16.8.2 Management and control

Under PA 1890, s 24(5), each partner may take part in the management of the partnership business. This is a corollary of partners having unlimited liability. Note that the limited partner loses his rights to limited liability if he interferes in the business of a partnership. This question of management is also enshrined in s 24(6), which sets out the basic tenet that partners are self-managers in that 'no partner shall be entitled to remuneration for acting in the partnership business'. In larger partnerships it is normal to find at least one partner spending a substantial amount of time in administration and other non-profit making work and the partnership agreement frequently includes special provisions for such a partner to ensure that his drawings and participation in any profit are not thereby affected. Section 24(6) does not prevent a partnership from making its own arrangements in this respect.

16.8.3 Meetings, reaching decisions etc

There is no rule on how decisions should be reached. There may be a voting system whereby certain partners qualify for a greater number of votes than others. More usually each partner is given one vote with basic decisions being decided upon by simple majority, but with complicated or controversial matters requiring specified majorities (eg 75% or in the case of taking in/expelling a partner, 100% of the votes (other than the partner being so expelled)). PA 1890 does not codify this (but see 16.8.6 *re* s 24(7)) and it is left to each partnership to agree this as a matter of contractual negotiation. If a partner feels he is being unfairly treated by the remaining partners, he has very limited remedies. If there has been a breach of contract he may be able to sue. It may also be that he can apply for a receiver to be appointed or possibly for a dissolution on just and equitable grounds. There is, however, no specific statutory protection. It is for this reason that partnership agreements often contain a settlement of disputes mechanism.

16.8.4 Settlement of disputes

It is common for partnership agreements to require disputes to be referred to arbitration. A popular alternative is for the agreement to contain provision for the appointment of an independent third party to act as an expert whose decision shall be binding on all parties (if the parties cannot agree on the appointment of such independent expert, he would normally be appointed by a third party, eg President for the time being of The Law Society of England and Wales).

16.8.5 Financial provisions

These are probably the most important details from a day-to-day practical view. PA 1890, s 24(1) states that unless there is contrary agreement, all partners are entitled to share equally in the capital and profits of a business and should contribute equally toward the losses (of capital or otherwise) sustained by the firm. Frequently the partnership agreement contains contrary provisions to this to take account of differing roles and participation from each partner. In considering the finances of a partnership it is important to understand the distinction between:

(1) the partnership capital; and
(2) undrawn profits.

Partnership capital means fixed capital typically invested in the partnership on its founding or upon new partners being appointed. Upon dissolution or a retirement, this is often returned to the partners or the relevant retiring partner with or without payment of interest. If a partnership is dissolved, the amount of surplus over and above the capital is normally deemed to be profit and as such is distributed to the partners in accordance with the profit-sharing rules. In many cases the relevant proportions for a refund of capital are different to those for the division of profits. Each partnership agreement needs to be drawn carefully to ensure the distinction is clearly provided for. (PA 1890, s 24 states other provisions that are frequently incorporated into the partnership agreement, eg under subs (4) a partner is only entitled to interest on capital when profits have been ascertained. In subs (3), anything paid over and above capital requirements is entitled to interest of 5% pa.)

Of greater importance is the requirement that if one partner is sued for a partnership debt under s 24(2), he is entitled to an indemnity from his fellow partners.

16.8.6 Change of partners

This normally occurs through death, retirement, expulsion or appointment of a new partner. Under s 24(8), unless stated to the contrary (in the partnership agreement), decisions should be taken by majority vote, but where it is proposed to introduce a new partner, s 24(7) requires the consent of all existing partners. Courts have in the past been called upon to interpret a number of provisions regarding nomination and partnership appointments that do not fall within this ambit. The circumstances of each particular case have been considered and the court's ruling has been based on its merits. In one case where a partner had left his partnership to his widow, it was deemed this constituted an assignment of a partner's share and did not entitle the widow to be a partner. Where a partner was entitled to introduce a qualified person as a new partner, subject to the other partners' consent not to be unreasonably withheld, the court ruled that since consent had not been forthcoming the qualified person did not have the right to become a partner (*Re Franklin and Swathling Arbitration* [1929] 1 Ch 238).

In the context of expulsion s 25 states that 'no majority of partners can expel any partner unless a power to do so has been conferred by express agreement between the partners'. In *Walters v Bingham* [1988] 1 FTLR 260, the court was called upon to consider a dissolution provision in the partnership agreement and ruled that three questions should be considered:

(1) Was the expulsion within the ambit of a dissolution provision?
(2) Had the partners exercising the right of expulsion done so in good faith in accordance with the normal partnership duties?
(3) Had the rules of natural justice been complied with, ie had the partner concerned been given details of the precise cause of complaint against him and been given every opportunity to defend himself?

The implication to be drawn is that if all three conditions have been satisfied, a court would uphold any such expulsion. Other cases of expulsion that have come before the courts include *Blisset v Daniel* (1853) 10 Hare 493 (refusal to uphold expulsion clause where the majority were seeking to obtain the partnership share at a discount); *Barnes v Youngs* [1898] 1 Ch 414 (unlawful expulsion of partner in circumstances where no details of the particular act complained of were given); and *Carmichael v Evans* [1904] 1 Ch 486 (expulsion held lawful where partner convicted of travelling on a train without a fare and thereby defrauding the railway company and bringing the partnership into disrepute, being a breach of his duties as a partner).

The partnership agreement in many instances includes provisions requiring retirement once a partner reaches a specified age or when certain other conditions occur (eg he becomes bankrupt or subject to the Mental Health Acts).

It is common in a partnership agreement for there to be provisions setting out what is required for the introduction of a new partner (PA 1890, as mentioned above, requires the consent of all partners and this applies if the partnership agreement does not make another provision). An assignment of partnership does not create a new partner; it merely assigns an existing partner's rights to partnership assets and/or profits to a third party. It may take the form of eg a mortgage or an arrangement made upon the divorce of one partner in favour of his former spouse.

In the case of a voluntary assignment, the assignee (the person in whom the assignment is in favour) has no right to interfere in the management or administration of the partnership or the assets or acquire the delivery or inspection of any accounts or books. The only interest an assignee would have relates to a share of profits for which the assigning partner may otherwise have been entitled if there had been no assignment. If, however, the partnership goes into dissolution, the assignee has the right to receive both his share and the accounting details verifying the amount of that share from the date of dissolution.

16.9 DISSOLUTION AND WINDING-UP

This can occur in two circumstances, ie where:

(1) a partnership splits up: in this case a winding-up of the business would be required;
(2) surviving or continuing partners take over the whole firm: here a valuation is needed of the former partner's share of the business.

Dissolution may or may not arise from insolvency.

Frequently, partnership agreements spell out the procedure for dissolution. There are at least three common situations that are usually provided for:

(1) Ability to expel a partner: a number of circumstances are expressly included which enable the partners to expel one of their colleagues from the partnership in certain specified situations, eg if he is grossly negligent, brings the practice into disrepute or, in a professional practice, becomes barred from continuing to practice in that position. If a partner is charged with an indictable offence, this also enables the others to expel him.
(2) A partner wishes to retire: the agreement usually incorporates a mechanism whereby he can hand in his notice. The notice period is often at least six months or a year and expires on a specified date.
(3) Upon death: since the partner's involvement automatically ceases a procedure is usually inserted for winding up his previous involvement.

Even if nothing is specified in the agreement, a partner can apply to court for dissolution under PA 1890, s 35. This gives the court discretion to dissolve a partnership for the following reasons:

(1) Insanity (ie a partner becomes a patient under the Mental Health Act 1983).
(2) Permanent incapacity.
(3) Prejudicial conduct: this requires proof with regard to the nature of the business that a partner has conducted himself in a manner 'calculated to prejudicially affect the carrying on of the business'.
(4) Where there have been continual breaches of the agreement: s 35 refers to 'wilfully or persistently committing a breach . . . or otherwise so conducts himself in matters relating to partnership business that it is not practicable for the other partners to carry on the business in partnership with him'.
(5) Business being carried on at a loss: there must be some proof that making a profit is not possible.

(6) If just and equitable: this depends on the particular circumstances presented to court, eg refusal to hold partner meetings, unresolvable dispute (ie where trust and mutual confidence have broken down irretrievably).

16.9.1 Appointment of receiver

In a dissolution it is possible for a receiver to be appointed at the court's discretion. Unlike company law, the receiver appointed is responsible for acting in the best interests of all the partners. Courts do not usually authorise the appointment of a receiver where there is only a partial dissolution. (There would therefore need to be a winding-up of the complete partnership as opposed to the buying out of the retiring partner.)

The partnership agreement usually specifies what should occur on dissolution. There is likely to be a valuation of each partner's share (where there is a winding-up) or the respective outgoing partners' shares (where there is a partial dissolution). The valuation needs to take into account such sums as may be owing to creditors etc. It also needs to apply a method for the valuation of goodwill (see 16.9.3).

PA 1890 contains a number of basic provisions for dealing with dissolution.

Section 39

All debts and liabilities of the firm must be paid before the distribution of any surplus (after deducting anything due by the partners to the firm) and gives the right of any partner to apply to court to wind up the business and affairs of the firm.

Section 37

On a dissolution or partial dissolution of a partnership, any partner may make a public notice of the dissolution and has a right to require other partners to concur with this action. (It is important to remember that a retiring/former partner is liable for debts incurred after departure unless he complies with a notice provision under s 36 and avoids being represented as a partner (s 14) (see 16.7.2)). Normally it is prudent for such a partner to inform the firm's existing clients of his departure and put a notice to that effect in the *London* or *Edinburgh Gazette*. A further prudent precaution would be for him to ensure all headed notepaper has been properly altered and any stocks of old paper destroyed.

16.9.2 Assets valuation on dissolution

It is usual for the partnership agreement to contain criteria for the valuation of business assets of the partnership on dissolution, requiring the use of the firm's accountant (or an independent one).

16.9.3 Goodwill

This has been defined as being the difference between the value of a business as a going concern and the value of its assets. Like any other business, a partnership over time attracts goodwill that can and often does form part of its assets. In certain isolated cases it is illegal to sell goodwill, eg s 54 of the National Health Service Act 1977 forbids the sale of an NHS practice's goodwill. The sale of goodwill is important in assessing how much a new partner may need to pay on joining a partnership and how much the continuing partners may need to pay on the retirement of a partner. The valuation of goodwill is normally conducted by a firm of accountants and the procedure and criteria to be adopted are time consuming and complicated. It is for this reason that professional partnerships are often disposed to value goodwill at nil. This not only prevents argument as to the valuation, but also reduces the amount of time spent in settling outstanding affairs.

16.9.4 Sharing profits after dissolution

PA 1890, s 42(1) states that on partial dissolution the surviving/continuing partners should in the absence of any agreement to the contrary share profits made since dissolution which are attributable to the partners' share of partnership assets. Alternatively, such partner or his estate has a right to interest of 5% pa on the amount of his share of partnership assets. A partnership agreement may give continuing partners the right to buy out the former partners in accordance with laid down procedures and valuation provisions, but this would need to be expressly incorporated into the provisions of the agreement.

16.9.5 Insolvency

Assuming the partners are personally solvent, PA 1890, s 44 sets out the order of priority for repayment of partnership debts and requires the partners if necessary to contribute in the same proportions that they are entitled to share profits. The order in which funds should be applied is:

(1) payment of debts and liabilities of the firm to persons, not partners;
(2) payment of each partner rateably of sums due to him from the firm for drawings (not capital);
(3) payment of each partner rateably of amounts due in repayment of capital; and
(4) division of any residue among the partners in the proportion in which the profits are divisible.

It is more complicated where one or more of the partners are insolvent. It is outside the scope of this chapter to consider this matter in any detail, but there are a number of options open to creditors, eg wind up the partnership, wind up the partnership and bring petitions against insolvent partners (and ultimately bankruptcy), bring an action against the individual partners without winding up the firm or bring proceedings against one or more partners without involving others or the firm itself.

16.10 EEIGS

In order to harmonise the laws of EU member States and each UK Companies Act, the UK has acceded to the EU in seeking to achieve this aim by incorporating various EEC directives into UK legislation. Some areas, however, have been otherwise treated. For example in 1985, EC Council Regulation 2137/85 was promulgated providing for the European economic interest grouping (more commonly referred to as EEIGs). This was loosely modelled on a French example. Its aim is to enable existing businesses in different member States to form an autonomous body for the provision of common services ancillary to the main activities of its members. All profits made belong to the members of EEIG and they are all jointly and severally liable for any liability.

EEIGs are formed by a written contract between the members. This needs to be registered in the member State in which the official address is situated.

The UK has added to the Regulation in the form of the European Economic Interest Grouping Regs 1989 under which Companies House is responsible as the registering body. There is provision set out in the Companies Act 1985 and the Insolvency Act 1986, which are applicable.

There are not many examples of EEIGs, but in England there have been a number of firms of solicitors who have used them as a means of association with lawyers elsewhere in the community.

17

HOW AN UNINCORPORATED BUSINESS IS TAXED ON ITS PROFITS

This chapter discusses the tax treatment of a 'sole trader' (ie an individual carrying on business on his own account) and partnerships. These are 'unincorporated' businesses, as opposed to companies that are 'incorporated' businesses. The proprietors of unincorporated businesses are self-employed and taxed under Schedule D.

The chapter also covers some wider issues for proprietors of unincorporated businesses such as sole traders and partners. We address issues such as bringing in a partner or merging with another firm. We also describe some of the advantages (and disadvantages) that might apply if an unincorporated business were transferred to a company. Assuming an unincorporated business has grown to the point where it should be incorporated, we set out some of the tax aspects concerning the best way this should be achieved. Finally, we look at some tax considerations to be borne in mind where the proprietors of an unincorporated business sell out or cease trading.

SELF-EMPLOYED INDIVIDUALS

17.1 CURRENT YEAR BASIS

In broad terms, the 'current year' (CY) basis of assessment normally means that a trader is assessed on the profits for his accounts year which ends in the tax year concerned (there are special rules for the opening years). Thus, if an individual makes up accounts to 31 August, the CY basis of assessment normally means that his tax liability for 2002–03 will be determined by his profits for the year ended 31 August 2002.

17.1.1 Opening years

The CY basis has special rules to cope with a business during the first two tax years since there may not be an accounting year that ends in either of those tax years, or the accounting period that ends in the second tax year may be shorter or longer than 12 months. In broad terms, assessments are generally determined as follows:

- First tax year – 'actual' or 'fiscal year' basis
- Second tax year – profits of the first 12 months
- Third tax year – CY basis.

Example of opening years rules

A starts in business on 6 October 1999. His accounts for the year to 5 October 2000 show profits of £48,000. Profits for the year ending 5 October 2001 are £72,000. A will be assessed as follows:

		£
1998–99	'actual' basis ($\frac{6}{12} \times £48,000$)	24,000
1999–00	First 12 months profits	48,000
2000–01	CY basis	72,000

17.1.2 No accounts for first 12 months

The way in which the opening years rules work is more complicated where the trader does not prepare accounts for a 12-month period ending in the second tax year. It might be that he starts business on 1 March 2000 and makes up his first accounts for a 16-month period ending on 30 June 2001. The assessments in such a case will be:

2000–01 $\frac{4}{16}$ ×   profits for period
2001–02 $\frac{12}{16}$ ×   profits for period
2002–03 $\frac{12}{16}$ ×   profits for period

Similarly, if X makes up her first accounts for a six-month period ending on 30 April 2002 and then has accounts for the year to 30 April 2003, the assessments will be:

2001–02 $\frac{5}{6}$ ×   profits for six months ended on 30 April 2002
2002–03 $\frac{1}{6}$ ×   profits for six months ended on 30 April 2003, *plus*
           $\frac{11}{12}$ ×   profits for year ended 30 April 2003
2003–04   profits of year ended 30 April 2003.

17.1.3 Overlap relief

Because of the way a new business is assessed during the first two tax years, some profits may be taxed more than once. In the last example, $\frac{11}{12}$ of the profits for the year ended 30 April 2002 are assessed twice, once in arriving at assessable profits for 2001–02, and again in arriving at the assessment for 2002–03. To compensate for this, and to ensure that over the life of the business tax is paid only on the actual amount of profits, overlap relief is given when the business is discontinued or, for partners, when they leave the firm. In some circumstances, the relief may also be available if the firm's accounting date is changed (see 17.1.4).

Basis of assessment under opening years rules

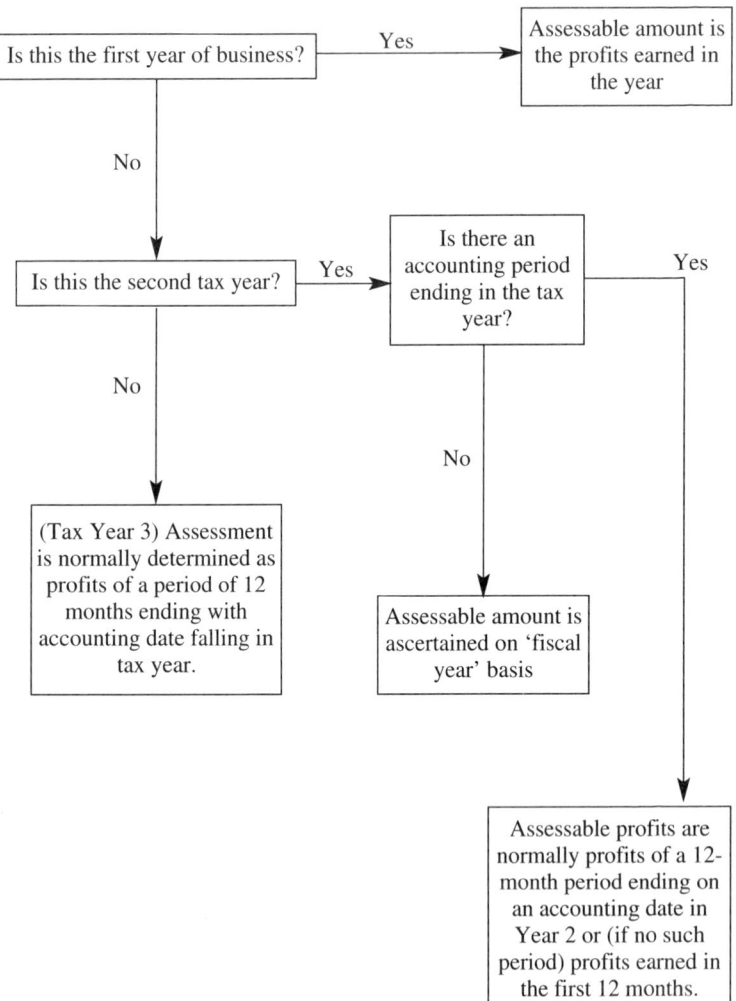

Example of overlap relief

If the profits for the year ended 30 April 2002 were £36,000, $^{11}/_{12}$ would be £33,000. This amount is carried forward and deducted from A's profits for the final year of trading. Thus, if A retires on 5 October 2004, and his final year's profits are £60,000, the assessment for 2004–05 will be:

	£
Current year basis	60,000
Less overlap relief	33,000
Taxable profits	27,000

If the overlap relief exceeds the taxable profits for the final year, the balance may be treated as an allowable loss and either set against the individual's other income for that year or the preceding year, or carried back against Schedule D Case I profits of the last three years (see 17.6.7).

17.1.4 Effect of a change in accounting date

Where a firm changes its accounting date to one that falls earlier in the tax year, an adjustment is required to ensure that 12 months' profits are taxed as income of the year in which the change takes place.

Example of how a change is dealt with

B draws up accounts to 30 June until 2002, when she changes to a 30 April accounting date. This means her accounts which fall in 2002–03 are for a period of only 10 months.

The CY basis requires profits to be ascertained for a 12-month period that ends with the new accounting date. Suppose that the relevant figures were:

Year ended 30 June 2001	profits of £120,000
Period of 10 months ended 30 April 2002	profits of £140,000

B would be assessed for 2002–03 on £160,000 ie $^2/_{12}$ × profits for the year ended 30 June 2001 + profits for the 10 months ended 30 April 2002. Once again, some profits will be taxed more than once (the period of two months ending on 30 June 2001) and therefore B would be entitled to increased overlap relief in due course on $^2/_{12}$ of the profits for the year ended 30 June 2001. The benefit of the overlap relief is enjoyed as and when the firm's accounting date is changed to a date that falls later in the tax year or B ceases business.

17.1.5 Moving accounting date to later in tax year

A different approach is required where a firm extends its accounts to a date that falls later in the tax year. Normally, the assessable profits are those for the entire period that ends in the tax year.

Example of tax treatment of such a charge

C makes up accounts to 31 December. In 2002, he extends his accounting period by three months so that the firm has a 15-month accounting period from 1 January 2001 to 31 March 2002. The whole of the profits for this period is assessed for 2001–02, but *C* can use some or all of his overlap relief. If *C* has a potential entitlement to four months' overlap relief of £20,000, and the profits for the 15 months ended 31 March 2002 are £150,000, *C* would have Schedule D Case I income for 2001–02 of:

	£
Profits for period ended 31 March 2002	150,000
Less $\dfrac{3 \text{ months}}{4 \text{ months}} \times$ overlap relief brought forward	15,000
	135,000

17.1.6 Retirement

Where an individual retires and ceases to carry on a business, he is taxed under the CY basis on his profits for a notional period that starts immediately after the basis period for the previous tax year and ends on the date that he ceases.

Example of how taxable income is ascertained for final year of assessment

D makes up accounts to 30 April. Her profits for the year ended 30 April 2002 are £80,000. She ceases business on 30 November 2002 and her profits for the final six months amount to £50,000. Her assessable income for 2002–03 is her share of profits for the period 1 May 2001 to 30 November 2002, ie £80,000 + £50,000.

17.1.7 Accounting periods must not exceed 18 months

There is a maximum length of 18 months to an accounting period. Accounts covering a longer period are rejected as unacceptable for tax purposes under the CY basis.

17.2 CAPITAL ALLOWANCE BASIS PERIODS

17.2.1 Business on CY basis

Capital allowances are computed on exactly the same basis as profits. Normally this means allowances are computed for the accounts year that ends in the tax year. However, there are special rules that apply for overlapping accounts.

Where there is a gap between accounting periods, the additions and disposals during the intervening period are added to the accounting period that ended before the gap.

Example – Overlapping periods

If a new business is commenced on 1 January 2001 and accounts are drawn up to 31 December 2001, there is an overlap of the period 1 January to 5 April 2001, as this will form part of the profits assessed for 2000–01 and 2001–02 (see 17.1.1).

If the trader spends £10,000 on plant and machinery during the first three-month period, and £40,000 during the period 6 April to 31 December 2001, capital allowances are given as follows:

		£
2000–02	$\frac{3}{12} \times 25\% \times £10,000$	625
2001–02	Pool brought forward	9,375
	Additions	40,000
		49,375
	Allowances ($\frac{9}{12} \times 25\%$)	9,258

PARTNERSHIPS

17.3 ASSESSMENT OF FIRM'S PROFITS: SPECIAL RULES

17.3.1 Assessment under CY basis

Where the CY basis of assessment applies, the Revenue issues separate assessments on each of the individual partners. This is the full extent of their liability; they are not jointly liable for tax payable by their partners (except, possibly, where the partner is not UK-resident).

Because partners are assessed separately under the CY basis, the continuation election cannot apply. Each partner is dealt with as a 'separate taxable unit' and the opening and closing years rules apply separately to him.

Example – CY opening year rules for new partners

A and B have been in partnership since 1 October 2000. They share profits equally and their profits for the first two years are as follows:

			£
Year ended 30 September 2001			90,000
Year ended 30 September 2002			120,000

C joins the firm on 1 October 2002 and thereafter each partner receives one third of the firm's profits, which for the year ended 30 September 2001 amount to £150,000. *B* retires on 5 April 2003 and *A* takes over his share of profits. The three partners are assessed as follows:

			£
2000–01	*A*	5/12 × 50% of £90,000	22,500
	B	5/12 × 50% of £90,000	22,500
2001–02	*A*	First 12 months' profits	45,000
	B	First 12 months' profits	45,000
2002–03	*A*	CY basis	60,000
	B	Final year (profits for period 1 October 2001 to 5 April 2003) 85,000	
		Less: overlap relief (22,500)	62,500
	C	5/12 × 1/3 of £150,000	25,000
2003–04	*A*	CY basis	75,000
	C	First 12 months' profits	50,000

17.4 TREATMENT OF OTHER INCOME

Where a partnership receives investment income (eg untaxed interest, miscellaneous income taxed under Schedule D Case VI or dividends), the normal tax treatment was that the income should be assessed on the individual partners. The principle that partners are jointly and severally liable for tax has never applied to investment income received by the firm.

Under the new CY basis, the way the income assessable on the partners is arrived at has changed. Instead of the income being ascertained by reference to the fiscal year, it is assessable on the CY basis. Thus, if a firm makes up accounts to 30 April, the partners are assessed for 2002–03 on their share of partnership investment income received during the firm's year ended 30 April 2002. This rule applies even where the income actually arose prior to 5 April 2002.

17.5 QUALIFYING LOANS

Tax relief may be obtained on loan interest where the money is to provide capital into a partnership. Relief is available where the loan is applied in:

(1) purchasing a share in a partnership; or
(2) contributing capital or advancing money to a partnership where the

money advanced is used wholly for its trade, profession or vocation purposes; or

(3) paying off another loan the interest on which would have been eligible for tax relief.

In addition, the borrower must be a member of the partnership throughout the period (and not just as a limited partner). He must not have recovered any capital from the partnership since raising the qualifying loan.

17.5.1 Recovery of capital
(TA 1988, s 363)

If, at any time after the application of the loan's proceeds, the partner recovers any amount of capital from the partnership, he is deemed to have used the withdrawal to repay the qualifying loan on which he is claiming interest relief. This is so whether or not he actually uses the proceeds in this manner. It is therefore advisable to segregate the partners' capital and current accounts in the partnership's books so that any withdrawal can be identified clearly.

17.5.2 Replacement capital

Where a partner has a surplus balance on either his current or capital account with a partnership and he does not already have a qualifying loan, he may withdraw the balance due to him (with his partners' consent), use the money to pay off non-qualifying borrowings and then borrow further funds to introduce capital into the partnership with tax relief.

Example – Replacement capital

> B is a partner in the XYZ partnership. He has a credit balance of £100,000 in his capital account. Outside the partnership, he has bought a yacht for his private use with the help of a £40,000 loan from his bank.
>
> B would withdraw £40,000 from his capital account in the partnership and use the money to repay the yacht bank loan. B would borrow £40,000 as a loan (not overdraft) and use the funds to reintroduce capital into the partnership with full tax relief on the interest payable.
>
> Professional advice should be sought in advance on such transactions.

17.5.3 Other partnership loans

Another situation where it may be appropriate to restructure existing borrowings is where there is a partnership loan outstanding in the business's books. The loan might typically have been used to purchase goodwill or the property from which the practice/business is carried on. In this situation, each partner is required to borrow privately his share of the partnership loan and introduce the moneys raised into the partnership. The partner can then claim tax relief on the interest paid personally as a charge on his income on an actual basis.

The partnership collects the moneys raised by each partner's loan and uses the funds to redeem the partnership loan. As a result, each partner's share of profits becomes correspondingly higher because no interest is now payable by the partnership. However, overall, the situation is the same because the higher profits must be used to finance the private borrowing.

This kind of rearrangement needs considerable attention to detail and timing to be successful and tax effective, and professional advice should always be sought. This is particularly necessary during the transition to the CY basis as there is anti-avoidance legislation to be considered.

17.5.4 Purchase of plant or machinery
(TA 1988, s 359)

Where a partner incurs capital expenditure in the purchase of plant or machinery used for the partnership's business purposes, and which is eligible for capital allowances, he can claim tax relief on interest paid if the plant etc is financed by a loan. The relief is only available in the tax year in which the loan is taken out and the following three tax years. Similar relief is also available for employees who are required to purchase plant etc for use in carrying out their duties.

17.5.5 Property occupied rent free by partnership

Where a partner takes out a loan to purchase property occupied by the partnership for business purposes and the interest is paid by the partnership, technically no deduction is due to the partnership as the interest is not its liability but the partner's. However, SP4/85, issued in February 1985, regards the interest paid as rent so that it becomes allowable as a deduction. In the partner's hands, the rent is taxable but the interest paid is normally allowed as a deduction in arriving at his Schedule A income.

MISCELLANEOUS

17.6 RELIEF FOR TRADING LOSSES

Relief may be available for a loss incurred by an individual in a trade or profession. The provisions that govern this relief are complex and there are several ways in which losses may be utilised.

17.6.1 Carry forward relief against subsequent assessments
(TA 1988, s 385)

A loss incurred by a sole trader or a partner's share of his firm's trading loss may be carried forward and deducted in assessments for later years for the same trade or profession. Where losses are carried forward in this way, they must be used against the assessable profits for the first subsequent year in which profits arise. The loss carried forward in this way may also be relieved against certain income connected with the trade even though it is assessed under a different schedule (eg interest earned on temporary investment of trade receipts and dividends from trade investments). There is no limit on the number of years for which a loss may be carried forward provided the same trade is carried on.

17.6.2 Relief against general income
(TA 1988, s 380)

Where a sole trader or partner incurs a loss and the trade was carried on with a view to profit, the loss may be relieved against his general income for the tax year in which it was incurred (ie his total income for the year). Losses are set against an individual's general income for the preceding year.

17.6.3 Relief by aggregation

Where the profits of different accounting periods are time apportioned (eg on commencement of a business), a loss may be relieved by aggregation with a profit. This situation could arise if a first period of trading is less than 12 months.

Example – Loss relief by aggregation

A started business on 1 January 2001. He made a loss of £9,000 for the period ended 30 September 2001 and a profit of £24,000 for the year ended 30 September 2002. Relief by aggregation would produce the following result:

Profits assessable 2000–01	NIL
Profits assessable 2001–02	NIL
Profits assessable 2002–03	NIL

The reason for this is that the first 12 months' trading is deemed to produce a net loss computed as follows:

	£
Loss for period 1 Jan to 30 Sept 2001	(9,000)
$\frac{3}{12}$ of profit for year ended 30 Sept 2001	6,000
	(3,000)

Relief for the same loss may be obtained more than once when the loss is used by aggregation. This can produce effective relief that exceeds the loss actually incurred.

If a loss is set against other income, it cannot also be relieved by aggregation. Thus, if A had claimed relief for the loss that he had incurred in 2000–01, only that part of the loss for the period ended 30 September 2001 which relates to the period 6 April to 30 September 2001 could be taken into account in arriving at the profits of the first 12 months' trading.

Example – Loss set against other income

B commenced trading on 1 August 2000. He has a loss during the nine months ended 30 April 2001 of £36,000. He has profits for the year ended 30 April 2002 of £60,000. If the 2000–01 loss is used by its being set against B's other income, the position is as follows:

2000–01		NIL
2001–02	Profits of first 12 months:	
	nine months ended 30 April 2001	NIL
	$\frac{3}{12} \times$ profits for year ended 30 April 2002	15,000
		15,000
2002–03	Profits of first 12 months	15,000

Contrast this with the situation where relief for the loss is obtained by aggregation.

2000–01		NIL
2001–02	Profits of first 12 months	NIL
2002–03	Profits of first 12 months	NIL

17.6.4 Capital allowances and loss claims
(TA 1988, s 383)

The general principle is that where capital allowances cannot be given because there are insufficient profits, the allowances must be carried forward and given in subsequent years. However, it is possible for an individual to claim for capital allowances to be treated as a deduction in arriving at the loss for the year of assessment. Capital allowances claimed in this way may either increase a loss or convert a profit into a loss.

The capital allowances to be taken into account are those of the normal basis period which relates to the tax year. This still applies even though the loss itself may be arrived at on the strict basis by apportioning the results of the accounting periods which overlap the relevant tax year.

Example – Capital allowances and loss claims

A commences trading on 6 October. His results are as follows:

	£
Year ended 5 October 2001 – profit	4,000
Year ended 5 October 2002 – profit	12,000
Year ended 5 October 2003 – profit	50,000

Assume that capital allowances are as follows:

2000–01	30,000
2001–02	38,000

If *A* claims that his capital allowances for 1998–99 should be deducted and the resultant loss relieved under s 380, the position is as follows:

		£
2000–01	⁵⁄₁₂ × profits for year ended 5 October 2001	2,000
	Capital allowances for 2000–01	(30,000)
	Loss after deducting capital allowances	(28,000)
2001–02	⁵⁄₁₂ × profits for year ended 5 October 2001	2,000
	⁵⁄₁₂ × profits for year ended 5 October 2002	6,000
		8,000
	Capital allowances for 2001–02	(38,000)
	Loss after deducting capital allowances	(30,000)

The £28,000 loss for 2000–01 may be set against *A*'s other income for 2000–01 or 2001–02. The £30,000 loss for 2001–02 is available to be set against *A*'s other income for 2001–02 or 2002–03.

17.6.5 Losses in early years of a trade
(TA 1988, s 381)

In certain circumstances, relief may be claimed against an individual's general income for the three years of assessment preceding the year in which the loss is incurred. Relief is given against income for the earliest year first. The loss may be computed in the normal way, or it may be augmented by capital allowances as described in 17.6.4. There are certain preconditions for a loss to be claimed:

(1) The loss must arise during the first four tax years in which the business is carried on.
(2) Where a trade is acquired from a spouse, the four years run from the date the spouse first commenced trading (unless the trade is taken over on the spouse's death).

(3) The trade must be carried on on a commercial basis *and with a reasonable expectation of profits.*

A claim for a loss to be relieved in this way must be made within two years of the end of the tax year in which it was incurred. Where a loss is carried back in this way, any repayment normally produces an entitlement to repayment supplement.

17.6.6 Relief for trading losses against capital gains
(FA 1991, s 72)

An individual who has incurred a trading loss may have it set against any capital gains that arise in the same year, provided he makes a claim within two years. He cannot claim relief for trading losses in this way without first having made a claim for relief under TA 1988, s 380 for the loss to be set against his general income for the year.

It is also possible for a trading loss to be set against his capital gains for the following year provided a claim is first made under s 380(2) for the trading loss to be set against his general income for that year. A precondition for a loss to be relieved in this way is that he has carried on the relevant trade at some time during the following tax year.

Taper relief, introduced in FA 1998, progressively reduces the amount of a gain that is liable to CGT on the disposal of an asset the longer that asset is held. Allowable losses are set against gains before the application of taper relief. Where the amount of allowable capital losses equals or exceeds the amount of chargeable gains before taper relief, the gains are extinguished by the losses.

However, the maximum amount of trading losses that may be set against gains is equal to the chargeable gain after the application of taper relief. So, where taper relief is applied to a gain, the trading losses do not extinguish it, even if the amount of the losses equals or exceeds the amount of the untapered gains.

Now, under FA 2002, s 47, the maximum amount of trading losses will be worked out before taper relief is applied. So if the trading losses equal or exceed the gains, the gains will be extinguished by the losses.

Table 17.1 shows the calculation under the 'old' provisions and with the change to be made by the 'new' provisions.

Table 17.1

	'Old' provisions	*'New' provisions*
Gain on disposal of an asset	£100,000	£100,000
Trading loss available to be set against gains	£80,000	£80,000

Table 17.1 *Cont.*

	'Old' provisions	*'New' provisions*
Calculate maximum amount of losses that may be deducted from gains	£60,000 (£100,000 × 60%) Restrict maximum deduction of losses to the gain if taper relief was applied (in this example taper relief means 60% of the gain is chargeable to tax)	£80,000 Do not use taper relief calculation to restrict losses.
Gain after deduction of available trading losses up to maximum amount	£40,000 (£100,000 – £60,000)	£20,000 (£100,000 – £80,000)
Gain after taper relief applied	£24,000 (£40,000 × 60%)	£12,000 (£20,000 × 60%)
Chargeable gain after AEA at £7,700 (2002–03 figure used for illustration)	£16,300 (£24,000 – £7,700)	£4,300 (£12,000 – £7,700)
'Unused' trading loss	£20,000 (£80,000 – £60,000)	Nil

FA 2002, s 47 increases the amount of trading losses that may be set against chargeable gains. Under the clause, the maximum amount will be equal to the quantum of gains before taper relief, rather than after taper relief as now. The change will normally reduce CGT liabilities. This change applies for trading losses sustained in 2004–05 and later tax years. Anyone who sustains trading losses in 2002–03 or in 2003–04 may elect for the new treatment to apply.

17.6.7 Terminal loss relief
(TA 1988, s 388)

Where a trade, profession or vocation is permanently discontinued, a loss incurred during the last 12 months can be deducted from the profits charged to tax in the three tax years before the final year. The relief can include a claim for the loss arising in the tax year in which the cessation takes place, and a proportion of the loss for the previous tax year.

Capital allowances for the final tax year may also be claimed, as can an appropriate proportion of the preceding year's capital allowances, representing the allowances due for the period beginning 12 months prior to the cessation.

The terminal loss may be carried back against profits from the same trade for the three tax years preceding the year of cessation. The relief is given against the latest year's profits first. If interest and dividends would have been included as trading profits (except that they were subject to deduction of tax at source), the terminal loss may be set against such income.

17.6.8 Computation of loss under CY basis

The rules for computing losses under the CY basis are much simplified. They preserve most of the principles explained 17.6.1–17.6.7. The exceptions are as follows:

(1) Losses may only be relieved once. The new rules do not allow duplication of loss claims by aggregation, as was possible under the preceding year (PY) basis.
(2) Relief for losses can be claimed against other income of the year of loss and the preceding year. (Under the PY regime, this was the following year.) Thus a trader who makes a loss in the accounting year to 31 December 2002 will be able to claim relief against other income in 2002–03 and/or 2001–02.
(3) It is not necessary to have separate claims for surplus capital allowances to be converted into losses; under the CY rules, capital allowances are allowed as a deduction just like any other allowable business expense.
(4) The rules for claiming loss relief against future profits from the same trade are slightly modified under the CY basis so that it is not now necessary to make a claim each year when the relief is to be given. All that is required is a claim to establish the amount of the loss. Thereafter the loss is carried forward and offset every year until fully utilised, without the need for any claim.

17.6.9 Anti-avoidance provisions

Farming losses
(TA 1988, s 397)

Restrictions may apply to losses suffered by farmers. The legislation may prevent a farming loss being set against the individual's other income where he has suffered losses for each of the preceding five tax years. The only way of avoiding this restriction is for him to show that no reasonably competent farmer would have expected to have made a profit during the period in question.

Losses from limited partnerships
(TA 1988, s 117)

Limited partnerships were widely used in tax avoidance arrangements. The House of Lords decided in *Reed v Young* [1986] STC 285 that a limited partner could be entitled to loss relief for an amount that exceeded his actual liability under the Limited Partnership Act 1907. This led to specific legislation to limit the amount of loss relief to the capital 'at risk'. Any losses incurred beyond this amount have to be carried forward to be set against any future share of profits received by the limited partner from the firm.

The provisions of LPA 1907, s 117 apply to individuals who are limited partners or members of a joint venture arrangement under which their liability is limited to a contract, agreement, guarantee etc.

17.6.10 Schedule D Case V losses
(TA 1988, s 391)

Profits from a trade managed or controlled abroad are taxed under Case V. Loss relief is calculated in the same way as for a loss incurred in a trade, profession or vocation taxed under Schedule D Case I or Case II.

Relief for such losses is given in the same way as for UK trading losses, except that where a loss is to be set against other income, a Case V loss can be deducted only from:

(a) profits from other foreign trades assessable under Case V;
(b) foreign pensions and annuities where a 10% deduction is available (see *Zurich Tax Handbook 2002–03*, para 8.8);
(c) foreign emoluments assessable under Schedule E (see *Zurich Tax Handbook 2002–03*, paras 4.1.1 and 24.2).

17.7 POST-CESSATION RECEIPTS AND EXPENSES
(TA 1988, ss 103–104)

17.7.1 Post-cessation receipts

Where a person has been assessed on the cash basis special rules apply if the trade or profession is discontinued. Subsequent receipts are normally taxed under Schedule D Case VI as income for the year in which they come in, although an election may be made for the post-cessation receipts to be treated as arising in the year of discontinuance.

Expenses may be deducted in so far as they were incurred wholly and exclusively for business and are not otherwise allowable. For example, a solicitor who had post-cessation receipts would be able to deduct premiums paid on a professional indemnity policy where the cover related to the period after he had ceased to carry on his profession.

A similar charge may arise where a change occurs in the treatment of a trader's profits so that the cash basis ceases to apply and his profits are assessed on the earnings basis. Amounts received from customers after the change which relate to invoices issued when the business was dealt with on the cash basis are treated as post-cessation receipts.

17.7.2 Post-cessation expenses
(TA 1988, s 109A)

Relief can be due for expenses incurred by a person after he has ceased carrying on a trade or profession. This relief can be due on any such expenditure incurred within seven years of the date of cessation. The following types of expenditure may qualify for relief:

(a) the costs of remedying defective work done, goods supplied, or services rendered while the trade or profession was continuing and damages paid by the taxpayer in respect of such defective work, goods or services whether awarded by a court or agreed during negotiations on a claim;
(b) insurance premiums paid to insure against the above costs;
(c) legal and other professional expenses incurred in connection with the above costs;
(d) debts owed to the business which have been taken into account in computing the profits or gains of the trade or profession before discontinuance but which have subsequently become bad;
(e) the costs of collecting debts that have been taken into account in computing the trade's profits before discontinuance.

The amount of this relief is reduced by any expense allowed as a deduction in the final accounting period which remains unpaid at the end of the year of assessment in which the relief is given. Expenditure that qualifies for the relief is set against income and capital gains of the year of assessment in which the expense is paid. Where there is insufficient income or capital gains to cover the expenditure, the unrelieved expenditure of that year cannot be carried forward under the new relief arrangements against future income or capital gains. However, the unrelieved expenditure is still available to be carried forward under the existing rules and set against subsequent post-cessation receipts from the trade or profession.

PRACTICAL ASPECTS AND INTRODUCTION OF SELF-ASSESSMENT AND HOW IT AFFECTS SELF-EMPLOYED INDIVIDUALS

17.8 OUTLINE OF NEW REGIME

17.8.1 Background

The 1997 changes amount to a fundamental change to the tax system. The Revenue no longer needs to initiate proceedings by issuing an assessment; liability for tax arises automatically.

Under the new regime, taxpayers are required to submit tax returns that incorporate a calculation of the tax to be paid (or in some cases, to be repaid) and payment of the amount due. In effect, instead of being required to deliver a return, the legislation requires taxpayers to make a self-assessment. This replaces the former system where a taxpayer was sent several different assessments on different sources of income and capital gains.

Because of this, and because the Revenue no longer has to issue estimated assessments and amended assessments, there should be a significant reduction in paperwork.

The self-assessment form is capable of being processed by computerised scanning equipment, which further reduces the clerical work required at the Revenue's offices.

17.8.2 Liability to make self-assessments

Any person served with a notice by an Officer of the Board of Inland Revenue must file a return. Normally, the filing date is 31 January following the end of the tax year. However, if the officer is late in serving notice on an individual for him to make a self-assessment, the filing date may be extended. Basically, the officer must give him at least three months to make the self-assessment. Thus, if the notice requiring the delivery of a self-assessment is served after 31 October, it does not need to be delivered to the Revenue until three months later.

17.8.3 Alternative to self-assessment

Provided a return of income and chargeable gains is delivered to the Revenue not later than 30 September following the end of the tax year, the Revenue calculates the amount of tax payable and issues an assessment.

If the officer is late in issuing the notice to make a self-assessment, the 30 September deadline may be extended.

The taxpayer is given at least two months in which to complete and deliver the return and so if the officer serves the notice after 31 July the deadline for filing the return is later than the normal 30 September deadline.

The Revenue has confirmed that if it receives a return by 30 September, but does not issue a notice of the tax payable by 31 December, the trigger date for interest and surcharge is 30 days after the issue of the statement of tax payable.

17.8.4 Inclusion of estimates

The Revenue has stated its intention that if a taxpayer includes an estimate in his return, the rest of the return becomes final within the normal timescale provided it is completed to the best of his knowledge and belief. The Revenue stated that the estimate should be corrected as soon as the missing information is reasonably available, in accordance with TMA 1970, s 97.

The need for estimates often arises in relation to CGT (eg valuations at 31 March 1982). It should be borne in mind that a valuation is not treated as an estimate, unless designated as such by the taxpayer. On the other hand, not all valuations are estimates, although they may be subject to dispute. The Revenue has agreed that it will not be able to reopen the position where no enquiry into a valuation is made within 12 months and the valuation falls within the range of bona fide valuations that could arise between valuers who were fully instructed on the facts.

17.8.5 Submission of supporting documents

The notice the officer sends asking for the self-assessment may specify that certain accounts, statements and documents relating to information in the return should be filed at the same time. The Revenue will certainly continue to require business accounts for a sole trader or a partnership. Other documents that may be required include books, contracts, deeds, receipts etc.

The legislation specifies that records must be retained for a minimum period after the submission of the self-assessment, in case they are required by the officer. Personal records must be retained for 12 months after the filing date. Business records must normally be retained for a minimum period of five years after the filing date.

FA 1994 also sets out the business records that should be retained for examination:

(a) records of all amounts received and expended in the course of the trade or profession, and the matters in respect of which the receipts and expenditure took place; and

(b) all supporting documents relating to such items.

This requirement is extremely wide and general in nature. The taxpayer is protected if he has preserved information in such a way that original documents can be reproduced. This means that a microfilming system is as acceptable as the retention of the original documents. Moreover, the Revenue has published guidance notes on what records should be retained. A penalty of up to £3,000 can be imposed for failure to keep records.

17.8.6 Amendments after filing self-assessment

A notice may be given to the Revenue amending the self-assessment. This may be given within 12 months of the filing date (ie 31 January or three months after the officer gives notice asking for the self-assessment, whichever is the later). The Revenue may also amend the self-assessment within nine months of receiving it to correct obvious errors of principle, arithmetical errors and the like (called 'repairing' a self-assessment).

17.8.7 Revenue enquiries and right to audit

The Revenue may start an enquiry into a self-assessment (or, where the taxpayer has filed an amendment, into the amended self-assessment). The officer must give written notice of his intention to make an enquiry. That notice must be served within a strict time limit of:

(a) 12 months after the date the self-assessment was delivered; or

(b) where the self-assessment is delivered after the filing date, the quarter date (for this purpose 31 January, 30 April, 31 July and 31 October) following 12 months after delivery. Thus, if a self-assessment due on 31 January is not in fact delivered until 31 March, the time limit for the Revenue starting an enquiry expires on 30 April of the following year.

Note also that the Revenue is not be allowed to institute more than one enquiry during the time limit. Once a return or an amendment has been subject to enquiry, no further notice may be given.

Where a notice of intention to enquire has been issued, the officer may issue a notice requiring the production of documents that are in the power or possession of the person on whom the notice has been served. These must be documents etc that are reasonably required by the officer to determine to what extent, if at all, the self-assessment or amendment is incorrect. The notice may also require accounts or other particulars that he may reasonably require. It must give a time limit for the production of the documents etc and the taxpayer must be allowed at least 30 days to produce them.

An appeal may be made to the Commissioners against such a notice. They can set the notice aside if they think it is invalid. If they decide it is valid, the documents must be produced within 30 days of their decision. Continued failure to comply may result in a penalty of up to £150 per day.

There is no specified time limit in which the officer must complete an enquiry, but the Government has stated that a code of practice will be issued on the conduct of enquiries. One aspect to be covered in the code will be a general requirement for the Revenue to proceed with reasonable speed once it has launched an enquiry and not to drag the process out unnecessarily. The code of practice will also set other ground rules which will apply to Revenue offices when they conduct an enquiry.

Once the officer conducting the enquiry has completed his investigation, he must say so and state his conclusions as to the correct amount of tax that should be in the self-assessment.

17.8.8 Correction of self-assessments

There are provisions for the self-assessment to be amended by the taxpayer in accordance with the conclusions notified by the officer who has conducted the enquiry. However, if the taxpayer does not correct the self-assessment in accordance with the officer's conclusions, the officer issues a notice of amendment (in effect an assessment) against which an appeal may be made within 30 days. If the dispute cannot be settled by agreement, the Commissioners adjudicate.

17.8.9 Requirement to notify chargeability

An individual who is liable for unpaid tax but who has not been served with a notice requiring him to make a self-assessment must notify the Revenue within six months of the end of the tax year.

17.8.10 Payment of tax

An individual is required to pay two equal amounts on account of income tax on 31 January during the year of assessment and on 31 July following the end of the tax year. The total amount is normally equal to the total income tax assessed for the previous year. However, it is open to a tax-payer (or his advisor) to make a claim before 31 January (ie the normal filing date) for the payments on account to be reduced to 50% of the tax believed to be payable for the year. The Revenue generally requires an explanation for why it is believed the tax payable will be less than that for the previous year.

When the self-assessment is delivered on the following 31 January, any difference between the payments on account already made and the amount shown as payable for the year needs to be settled. At the same time, it is necessary to make a payment equal to the CGT liability for the year concerned.

17.8.11 Amended self-assessments

Tax is payable or repayable on the later of:

(a) 31 January following the end of the tax year; and
(b) 30 days from the date on which the amendment to the self-assessment was given.

In cases where the Revenue discovers that a source of income has not been, or has been inadequately, assessed, the officer normally makes an assessment and the tax is payable 30 days after the assessment has been issued.

17.9 PENALTIES AND INTEREST CHARGES

17.9.1 Surcharges

Where tax is paid more than 28 days after it fell due, the Revenue may levy a 5% surcharge. This 28-day period applies both to the payments required on 31 January and 31 July and also to tax due 30 days after an assessment has been made. If the tax remains unpaid more than six months after the due date, there is a further 5% surcharge.

17.9.2 Appeals against the surcharge

The Revenue may mitigate the whole or part of a surcharge where there is a reasonable excuse for the delay. In cases where there is a dispute with the Revenue over whether there is a reasonable excuse, the Commissioners can be asked to adjudicate. FA 1994 specifically states that inability to pay is not to be regarded as a reasonable excuse.

17.9.3 Interest

Interest is payable for periods up to the date on which payment is made and is in addition to any surcharges levied. Interest does not attract any tax relief.

17.9.4 Penalties

A penalty of £100 is due if the self-assessment is not delivered by the filing date. The Revenue may then appeal to the Commissioners for a continuing penalty of up to £60 per day. The starting date for this continuing penalty is the day on which the Commissioners direct that it should be imposed. It is avoided if the self-assessment is delivered before the Commissioners make their decision. Even if no continuing daily penalty is imposed, there is a further £100 penalty if the self-assessment is delivered more than six months after the filing date.

Where the failure continues beyond 12 months the penalty, in addition to anything mentioned above, is a maximum of the tax due as shown in the return.

Penalty determinations may attract an interest charge, where the penalties are not paid promptly, as the determination is treated as if it were an assessment for the purposes of interest charged on late payment of tax.

17.9.5 Appeals

It is possible to appeal against the determination of a penalty by the inspector. However, the Commissioners may only set aside the £100 fixed penalties if there is a reasonable excuse for the taxpayer not having delivered the return throughout the period it was overdue. Where this condition is not satisfied, the Commissioners are required to confirm the penalties in full.

17.9.6 Partnerships

The basic rules are modified to take account of partnerships.

Partners' obligations to make returns

Individual partners are required to deliver self-assessments. The partnership is also required to make a return (not strictly speaking a self-assessment) if the Revenue serves a notice, which it may serve on any partner (the 'representative partner').

The notice asks for delivery of the return together with accounts and such other statements as the Revenue requires. The representative partner is required to make a return and all items relevant to the agreement of profits assessable under Schedule D Case II must be included in that return. It is not possible for individual partners to claim a deduction for expenses incurred by them unless they are shown in the partnership return. The notice requires such return to include:

(a) the names, addresses and tax references of all persons who have been partners at any time during the period covered by the return; where partners have been in the firm for only part of the year, the precise period must be specified;
(b) full details of each partner's entitlement to profits (and losses) from each source of partnership income;
(c) particulars of the disposals of partnership assets as if the partnership itself (not the individual partners) were liable to tax on any chargeable gains and details of each partner's share of such capital gains;
(d) details of acquisitions of property by the partnership;
(e) the amount of annual charges borne by each partner (eg annuities paid to former partners or their dependants).

It is possible for the partnership to amend its return and for the Revenue to amend it after an enquiry.

Revenue investigations into partnership returns

The Revenue can enquire into partnership returns on the same basis as for individuals (see above). A notice must be issued within 12 months of the filing date or, if the return is delivered after that date, at the quarter date following 12 months after the delivery date.

A notice served on the partnership is deemed to include similar notices issued to the individual partners to the extent that they have actually delivered self-assessments.

Partnership returns

Each partner is liable to a £100 penalty if the return is submitted late. This applies to any person who was a partner at any time during the return period. The continuing daily penalties and the six-month £100 penalty also apply to each partner.

Appeals against penalty notices imposed on partners

Where penalty determinations have been made so as to impose either the £100 penalty or the continuing daily penalty on two or more partners, appeals may be brought only by the representative partner. He then makes a composite appeal. Once again, the £100 penalty must stand unless the Commissioners are satisfied that there was a reasonable excuse that applied throughout the period of default.

17.9.7 Incorrect returns

If an incorrect self-assessment is delivered and it is wrong because of negligent or fraudulent conduct, the maximum penalty remains 100% of the tax understated in the self-assessment.

A partnership return, which includes accounts and statements, and which is incorrect due to negligent or fraudulent conduct, can give rise to a penalty on each partner, with the maximum amount of the penalty being the tax under-assessed on him. It is possible for this penalty to apply even though the individual partner has not completed the partnership return and has not himself been guilty of negligent or fraudulent conduct. Basically, the conduct of the representative partner who made the partnership return is all that matters.

17.10 ACHIEVING FINALITY

It has generally been accepted that any new regime should afford taxpayers the same degree of certainty that liabilities have been finalised as exists at present where an assessment is appealed against and there is a determination under TMA 1970, s 54.

The legislation specifically provides that the Revenue may make assessments to correct a loss of tax that has been discovered. However, the Act makes it plain that this may not be done where there has been an error or mistake in a return as to the basis of computing a liability but the basis adopted accorded with the practice generally applying at the time.

The Act makes it clear that no discovery assessment may be made where all the facts were clearly made known to the Revenue and the matter was concluded without an enquiry, or with the officer being satisfied after carrying out an enquiry. The distinction the Revenue presently draws between points that are fundamental to the determination of the liability does not feature in the legislation for the new regime and, therefore, to that extent a taxpayer may have greater certainty once an enquiry has been concluded or the time limit for the officer to initiate an enquiry has passed.

ANNUAL PAYMENTS, NICs ETC

17.11 MISCELLANEOUS PRACTICAL ASPECTS

17.11.1 Class 4 NICs

A deduction is available for half of the trader's liability for Class 4 NICs in arriving at his income tax liability. Contributions are payable by self-employed individuals according to the level of their profits as determined for income tax purposes. For 2002–03, Class 4 NICs are levied at 7% of Schedule D profits between £4,615 and £30,420.

Where an individual pays interest on a business loan or has suffered trading losses, such amounts may be set against his earnings in assessing liability for Class 4 NICs. This situation applies even where the losses have been relieved for income tax purposes by way of offset against his other income.

17.11.2 Annual payments
(TA 1988, ss 349 and 387)

These include any annuity or other annual payment (other than interest) and any royalty or other sum paid in respect of the use of a patent. These payments are normally made out of profits or gains chargeable to income tax.

Example of treatment of annual payments

In 2002–03, *A* has taxable profits of £20,000. He pays an annuity to a former partner, *B* of £10,000 (gross).

A cannot deduct the annuity, but he can take basic rate relief at source. This means that he pays *B* only £7,800, ie £10,000 less 22% tax. The £2,200 tax withheld comes out of the tax he would have paid in any event on his £20,000 profits. Furthermore, *A* may be able to secure higher rate relief on the £10,000 annuity. If eg his total income were £60,000, his liability for higher rate tax would be computed as follows:

	£
10% and basic rate band	29,900
Gross amount of annuity	10,000
	39,900
Income subject to 40% rate is:	
Taxable income	60,000
Less	(39,900)
	20,100

However, where a person making an annual payment has an insufficient tax liability to cover the tax withheld, he must account for this separately to the Revenue. Thus if *A* had taxable income of only £8,000 (after allowances but before the annuity), his 2002–03 normal tax liability would be:

	£
Tax at 10% on £1,920	152.00
Tax at 22% on £6,080	1,377.60
	1,489.60

Because he has deducted tax from an annuity of £10,000 he will instead be required to pay £2,200 to the Revenue to cover the tax relief taken by him at source.

17.12 LIMITED LIABILITY PARTNERSHIPS (LLPs)

17.12.1 Treatment of LLPs
(TA 1988, s 118ZA)

Generally, an LLP's business activities carried out with a view to a profit are treated as carried on in partnership by its members, and not by the partnership itself. Any property held by it is treated as held by its members in partnership and not by the partnership itself. This treatment continues to apply if the business activities cease temporarily and during the time the LLP is being wound up (so long as such period is not unreasonably prolonged and/or the winding-up is connected to avoiding tax to any extent). Treatment ceases to apply on appointment of a liquidator, a winding-up order made by a court, or equivalent procedures carried out abroad.

17.12.2 Restriction on relief
(TA 1988, s 118ZB)

TA 1988, ss 117 and 118 (which impose limitations on the extent of loss relief for individuals and companies) apply to a member of an LLP as as they do for a limited partner. There are further modifications in ss 118ZC and 118ZD.

17.12.3 Member's contribution to trade
(TA 1988 s 118ZC)

The calculation of an individual member's contribution (see s 117(3)) does not apply to a member of an LLP. However, for the purposes of ss 117 and 118, a member's contribution to a trade at any time is the greater of:

(1) the amount subscribed by him, and
(2) the amount of his liability on a winding up.

The amount subscribed is that which he has contributed to the LLP as capital, less so much of that amount (if any) as he:

(a) has previously, directly or indirectly, drawn out or received back;
(b) so draws out or receives back during the five-year period beginning with the relevant time;
(c) is or may be entitled so to draw out or receive back at any time when he is a member; or
(d) is or may be entitled to require another person to reimburse to him.

The amount of the liability of a member on a winding-up is that which he:

(1) is liable to contribute to the LLP's assets in the event of its being wound up; and
(2) remains liable so to contribute for the period of at least five years beginning with the relevant time (or until it is wound up, if that happens before the end of that period).

17.12.4 Carry forward of unrelieved losses
(TA 1988, s 118ZD)

Where the total unrelieved loss relating to a trade carried on by a member of an LLP is, in any one or more chargeable periods, prevented from being given or allowed by TA 1988, s 117 or 118 as it applies otherwise by this rule as it applies in each subsequent chargeable period in which:

(1) he carries on the trade as a member of the LLP, and
(2) any of his total unrelieved losses remains outstanding,

TA 1988, ss 380, 381, 393A(1) and 403 (and ss 117 and 118 as they apply to those sections) have effect in the subsequent chargeable period as if:

(a) any loss sustained or incurred by the member in the trade in that chargeable period were increased by an amount equal to so much of his total unrelieved loss as remains outstanding in that period, or
(b) (if no loss is so sustained or incurred) a loss of that amount were so sustained or incurred.

To ascertain whether any (and, if so, how much) of a member's total unrelieved loss remains outstanding in the subsequent chargeable period, deduct from the amount of his total unrelieved loss the aggregate of:

(1) any relief given under any provision of the Taxes Acts (otherwise than as above) in respect of his total unrelieved loss in that or any previous chargeable period, and
(2) any amount given or allowed out of his total unrelieved loss as above in any previous chargeable period (or which would have been so given or allowed had a claim been made).

17.12.5 Limited partners

Although these sections deal with restrictions on loss relief for limited partners, the LLP rules refer to them by cross reference. They are included here for your convenience in understanding the LLP rules.

Restriction on relief: individuals
(TA 1988, s 117)

An amount that may be given to an individual under TA 1988, s 353, 380 or 381 in respect of a loss sustained by him in a trade, or of interest paid by him in connection with the carrying on of a trade, in a relevant year of assessment may be given otherwise than against income consisting of profits arising from the trade only to the extent that the amount given or (as the case may be) the aggregate amount does not exceed the relevant sum. Here:

(1) 'limited partner' means:
  (a) a person who is carrying on a trade as a limited partner in a limited partnership registered under the Limited Partnership Act 1907;
  (b) a person who is carrying on a trade as a general partner in a partnership, who is not entitled to take part in the management of the trade and who is entitled to have his liabilities, or his liabilities beyond a certain limit, for debts or obligations incurred for the purposes of the trade discharged or reimbursed by some other person; or
  (c) a person who carries on a trade jointly with others and who, under the law of any territory outside the UK, is not entitled to take part in the management of the trade and is not liable beyond a certain limit for debts or obligations incurred for the purposes of the trade;
(2) 'relevant tax year' means a tax year at any time during which the individual carried on the trade as a limited partner;
(3) 'the aggregate amount' means the aggregate of any amounts given to him at any time under s 353, 380 or 381 for a loss sustained by him in the trade, or of interest paid by him in connection with carrying it on, in a relevant year of assessment;
(4) 'the relevant sum' means the amount of his contribution to the trade as at the appropriate time; and
(5) 'the appropriate time' is the end of the relevant tax year in which the loss is sustained or the interest paid or for which the allowance falls to be made (except that where he ceased to carry on the trade during that tax year it is the time when he so ceased).

A person's contribution to a trade at any time is the aggregate of

(a) the amount which he has contributed to it as capital and has not, directly or indirectly, drawn out or received back (other than anything which he is or may be entitled so to draw out or receive back at any time when he carries on the trade as a limited partner or which he is or may be entitled to require another person to reimburse to him), and

(b) the amount of any profits of the trade to which he is entitled but which he has not received in money or money's worth.

(Note: TA 1988, s 117(3) is disregarded in relation to LLPs by TA 1988, s 118ZC(1).)

To the extent that an allowance is taken into account in computing profits or losses in the year of the loss by TA 1988, s 383(1), it is treated as falling to be made in the year of the loss (and not the tax year for which the year of loss is the basis year).

Restriction on relief: companies
(TA 1988, s 118)

An amount which may be given under TA 1988, s 338, 393A(1) or 403 for a loss incurred by a company in a trade, or of charges paid by a company in connection with the carrying on of a trade, in a relevant accounting period may be given to that company otherwise than against profits arising from the trade, or to another company, only to the extent that the amount given or (as the case may be) the aggregate sum does not exceed the relevant sum. Here:

(1) 'relevant accounting period' means an accounting period of the partner company at any time during which it carried on the trade as a limited partner (see s 117(2));

(2) 'the aggregate amount' means the aggregate of any amounts given to the partner company or another company at any time under s 338, 393A(1) or 403 for a loss incurred by the partner company in the trade, or of charges paid by it in connection with carrying it on, in any relevant accounting period;

(3) 'the relevant sum' means the amount of the partner company's contribution (per s 117(3)) to the trade as at the appropriate time; and

(3) 'the appropriate time' is the end of the relevant accounting period in which the loss is incurred or the charges paid or for which the allowance falls to be made (except that where the partner company ceased to carry on the trade during that accounting period it is the time when it so ceased).

OPERATING AS AN UNINCORPORATED BUSINESS

17.13 BRINGING IN A PARTNER (AND BECOMING A PARTNER)

17.13.1 Relief for loans where new partner borrows to finance his capital

Income tax relief is available under TA 1988, s 362 for interest on personal loans taken out by partners in order to contribute partnership capital, or to make a loan to the firm (see 17.5).

17.13.2 Interest on capital

It is generally appropriate for interest to be paid on partners' capital accounts, especially where there is some disparity between the amounts of capital provided by each partner.

'Interest' paid in these circumstances is treated as an allocation of Schedule D Case I profits rather than as interest taxable under Schedule D Case III. This has the effect that the partner's relevant earnings for personal pension purposes (see 14.3.6) are likely to be higher than if the firm borrows from a bank to meet its working capital requirements.

Example – Treatment of partnership interest

A is a sole trader. His profits are running at the rate of £50,000. He brings in a partner and finances the practice by a loan which he raises in his personal capacity. At the end of the year, his position may be:

	£
Interest on capital	12,000
Share of profits	50,000
Interest paid on personal borrowings	(10,000)
	52,000

However, for personal pension purposes (see 14.3.6), his relevant earnings are £62,000 – ie there is no deduction for interest relieved under TA 1988, s 362.

17.13.3 Capital gains tax considerations

There is normally no CGT charge if a sole trader and his new partner each puts in capital on an equal basis – or in proportion to their profit-sharing ratios. However, it is possible that a sole practitioner may require the incoming partner to put in capital to match the value of his interest in the firm. The normal way to account for this is to re-value goodwill, and this could give rise to a capital gain.

Example – Valuation of goodwill

> *A* brings *B* into partnership, sharing profits equally. *B* is required to pay £50,000 capital into the firm, but *A* does not need to pay any money into the firm, and, indeed, is free to withdraw all his undrawn profits. On the other hand, it is agreed that half of the goodwill now belongs to *B*.
>
> A situation like this really amounts to an agreement that *A*'s goodwill is worth £50,000. After admitting *B* as a partner, he is entitled to only half of this, but he is also entitled to half of the £50,000 cash that *B* has put into the firm. So, in effect *A* has received a capital payment for a disposal of half of the goodwill and there may be a CGT charge on this.

17.13.4 Keeping certain property assets outside the firm

A sole trader may wish to retain personal ownership of the office premises etc, rather than share them with the incoming partners. This problem may be more apparent than real since there is no requirement that partners should share capital profits in the same way they share ordinary profits. Nevertheless, many people prefer to keep the premises outside the firm altogether.

In such a situation the former sole trader can rent the premises to the firm, preferably under a formal agreement which gives the firm a tenancy or a licence. He can also charge rent, but if he does so the consequences for CGT retirement relief should be borne in mind (see 6.7–6.8).

It is also possible for the partner to forgo rent, but to receive the benefit of an appropriate adjustment in the partnership accounts, as a prior charge on profits in the same way as interest on capital is charged. If the partnership agreement is drafted correctly, this effectively converts Schedule A rental income for the partner into profits falling under Schedule D Case I. It also avoids any restriction on CGT retirement relief.

17.13.5 Admitting a partner under CY basis rules

Where the firm is already on the CY basis, because either the business was started after 5 April 1994 or a partner retired from the firm after that date and no continuation election was made, matters are much more straightforward.

Basically, the partnership's profits are assessed on the CY basis (bear in mind the opening rules (see 17.1.1)). Each partner is separately responsible for settling his own tax; there is no principle of joint and several liability for the firm's income tax.

Where a firm is assessed on the CY basis, any changes in the partners do not give rise to a cessation as there is an automatic 'continuation' for the ongoing partners. Thus, on a partnership change under the new rules, the tax liabilities of past years are not affected because the change does not trigger a Revenue review of tax assessments for the penultimate and ante-penultimate years.

17.14 BUYING OUT A PARTNER

17.14.1 Change in status to salaried partner

Where circumstances permit, there could be some advantage for the outgoing partner to revert to salaried partner status and be taxed under Schedule E.

There can be other benefits in switching from Schedule D status to Schedule E. The continuing partners could undertake to fund an approved pension scheme (see 14.3.5), which in turn may enable a tax-free lump sum to be provided where the outgoing partner had previously been an employee (or a salaried partner). Benefits under an approved scheme must relate to periods of service as an employee, but there is no statutory requirement that the periods be continuous as opposed to two periods separated by a period as a Schedule D partner.

17.14.2 Consultancy arrangement

It could be that the individual agrees to retire from the firm only if he receives a 'retainer' under which the firm is committed to consult him (and pay him) for a minimum number of days over a specified period. Unless the retainer is substantial, it is unusual for the Revenue to seek to classify an ex-partner consultant as an employee, even though he may not undertake work for many other clients (if any). However, this possibility should be borne in mind and the consultancy agreement carefully drafted to avoid any suggestion of a 'master/servant' relationship (see 12.3). If there is any doubt, the partnership needs to withhold PAYE from the consultancy fees.

While it may suit the individual to be taxed as a consultant under Schedule D Case I, particularly if there are expenses that he can claim against his consultancy income (such as the cost of maintaining an office in his home, payment to a spouse for secretarial services and business use of a car), the firm must protect its position. In particular, where the consultancy fee exceeds the VAT threshold, the firm must obtain a valid VAT invoice.

During the transitional period, it may be better for the continuing partners if the retiring partner is paid an annuity rather than consultancy fees, as this may mean that greater relief is available (see below).

17.14.3 Annuity arrangements

An annuity may effectively be paid out of pre-tax income since the payer is normally entitled to relief at his marginal rate of tax. An annuity of £10,000 is satisfied if the partners pay £7,800 (ie £10,000 less basic rate tax), and

699

they can then claim the full amount as a deduction in arriving at their total income for higher rate tax purposes.

As already mentioned, payment as an annuity may be more tax-efficient than consultancy payments during the transitional basis period. The main drawback with annuity payments is that the continuing partners cannot raise qualifying loans in order to meet these obligations.

So far as the outgoing partner is concerned, a capital sum may be preferable, especially where retirement (see 6.7) or roll-over (see 6.3) relief may be relevant. On the other hand, the annuity should not attract a CGT liability unless it exceeds two-thirds of his average share of profits over a three-year period which falls within the last seven years in which he is a partner.

17.14.4 Payment of a capital sum

A capital sum may be paid direct to an outgoing partner, or an adverse balance on his capital account may be written off –in effect a capital payment by means of a transfer from the continuing partners' capital accounts.

17.14.5 Borrowing by partners to fund the buyout

Where one or more partners raise personal loans to make a capital payment to buy out a colleague, interest normally qualifies for relief under ICTA 1988, s 362. If, exceptionally, the interest on such a loan exceeds the partnership profits, the excess may be carried forward as if it were a Schedule D Case I loss. However, it is important to bear in mind that if the buyout does not take place, and the borrower ceases to be a partner, his loan ceases to qualify for tax purposes. This has been a real problem for the proprietors of firms which have subsequently found themselves in financial difficulties.

17.14.6 Capital gains tax implications

A partner who is being bought out may have a CGT liability unless he can make use of roll-over relief or his gain is covered by retirement relief (see 6.7).

17.14.7 Splitting the practice

In some situations, the outgoing partner effectively takes over one particular office and continues to practice on his own account. This is a 'demerger'; the tax treatment depends on whether continuation elections are made.

17.14.8 Demergers

Where some partners buy out part of a firm's business they are usually treated as starting a new business. The partners who continue in the original firm can avoid a cessation by making a continuation election. Alternatively, it may be possible to satisfy the Revenue that a demerger consists of separating two businesses which were different businesses all along. Thus, if a firm of estate agents consists of five offices in different towns, it could be argued that one particular office was always a distinct business and its separation from the rest of the partnership does not amount to commencing a new business. This enables both the continuing partners in the main firm, and the partner(s) who have taken on the office which has demerged, to make continuation elections. Indeed it also allows the partners in the original firm to have a cessation, even though the partners who have demerged chose to make a continuation election.

Capital gains tax

The partners who have demerged will normally have disposed of their interests in the assets of the main firm and acquired enlarged interests in the assets of the demerged firm. Depending on the relative values, any capital gains may well be covered by roll-over relief (see 6.3).

VAT

As partners are jointly and severally liable for VAT, it is important to notify Customs of the departure of partners immediately the demerger takes effect. Joint and several liability continues up to the date the change is notified.

OPERATING AS A LIMITED COMPANY

17.15 GENERAL TAX CONSIDERATIONS

There is no simple answer to the question 'is it better to operate via a company?' There can be both advantages and disadvantages in carrying on business through a limited company rather than as an unincorporated business, and it is generally appropriate to take professional advice. There are commercial considerations as well as tax aspects, eg limited liability may be an important consideration, either for the current proprietors of the business or to attract finance from an outside investor. However, the apparent protection given by limited liability is often illusory, since banks or other lending institutions normally require personal guarantees from directors for any loans made to the company.

17.15.1 Lower rate of tax on profits

Having a company often means that a lower rate of tax applies to retained profits, ie profits which are not taken out as remuneration or dividends.

The nil rate band (see 19.2.4) applies to profits up to £10,000, with marginal relief of up to £50,000 so long as there are no associated companies.

The small companies rate of 19% (see 19.2.5) applies to profits up to £300,000 provided there are no associated companies. If there are associated companies, the threshold at which profits attract tax at either the full 30%, or the marginal small companies rate, is reduced. If there are no associated companies, the small companies rate can produce a substantial saving.

17.15.2 Possible ways of deferring tax

There is a useful timing difference where a business is carried on through a company in that remuneration can be deducted from the profits of the company even though it is not paid (and is not taxable income of the individuals until it is paid). Provided that the remuneration is actually paid within nine months of the company's year end, the company is normally entitled to a deduction in arriving at its profits.

Example – Timing of tax payments

If a company draws up accounts to 31 March 2002, it may secure a deduction for directors' remuneration of £150,000 even though the remuneration is not paid until 31 December 2002, in which case PAYE tax does not have to be paid over until 14 January 2003 in accordance with the timetable for self-assessment payments.

17.15.3 Other tax considerations

Pension contributions

Another aspect which favours having a company is that it is possible for a company to fund pensions for directors more generously than is permitted for personal pensions. For example, if an individual is aged 44, the maximum personal pension contribution the individual may make for the year is 20% of relevant earnings up to the amount of the earnings cap (currently £97,200 for 2002–03) (see 14.3.5). In contrast, a company would normally be permitted by the Pension Schemes Office to fund a pension scheme for the benefit of the individual at the rate of 100% of remuneration up to the amount of the earnings cap.

Payment of remuneration may prevent personal allowances going to waste

Where an unincorporated business operates at a loss, and the individuals have no other income, the benefit of their personal allowances is lost forever. By trading through a company, it is possible to vote remuneration equal to the individuals' personal allowances, and the remuneration voted in this way increases the amount of the company's loss which can be carried forward and set against subsequent profits.

Greater scope for raising new finance

An outside investor normally prefers to be a shareholder rather than a partner. While he could in theory limit his exposure by being a limited partner, this is not familiar territory. Furthermore, a limited partner loses the protection of limited liability under the Limited Partnership Act 1907 if he takes part in the management of the firm's business. Most outside investors are therefore prepared to invest only if they can acquire shares and act as directors of a company.

Having a company also opens the way to attracting outside investment under the Enterprise Investment Scheme (see 21.10.1) or from investors who wish to secure CGT reinvestment relief (see 6.4).

17.16 POSSIBLE DISADVANTAGES

There are a number of possible disadvantages of operating through a company.

17.16.1 Extra administration

Companies are subject to more statutory requirements concerning the keeping of books, filing of annual accounts, disclosure etc than unincorporated businesses. An unincorporated business does not normally need to file annual accounts at all, whereas a company needs to file accounts with Companies House, and to make an annual return.

17.16.2 Loss of privacy

A limited company must file its accounts annually, and they are available for public inspection. In contrast, an unincorporated business's accounts are a private document which need not be made available to anyone other than the proprietors and the Revenue (and, possibly, the business's bankers).

17.16.3 Relief for losses

A proprietor of an unincorporated business may secure tax relief for any losses by setting them against other income. Losses suffered during the first four tax years in which a business is carried on may be carried back and set against income of the previous three years.

In contrast, losses made by a company can only be set against the company's other profits for the year (or the previous year). Any unrelieved losses may then be carried forward and can be off-set against future trading profits only.

17.16.4 Admitting future partners

If profits are retained, this may make it increasingly difficult for individuals who come up through the business to become shareholder directors. For example, if a company has 100 £1 shares in issue, and retains profits after tax of £15,000 pa for ten years, each share is worth £1,500 more at the end of the ten years than at the start of the period. An individual seeking to acquire a 10% shareholding would normally have to raise sufficient finance to pay for the shares at this increased value. The problem does not, though, arise in the case of a partnership, since the normal procedure is to allocate past profits to partners' capital accounts and then admit a new partner on the basis that he shares in future profits at a specified percentage. Having said this, the disadvantage in having a company can be over-stated. For example, if the shareholders so wished, they could arrange for the company to make a bonus issue of preference shares before allowing an incoming director to subscribe for ordinary shares. This is not always appropriate, but where it can be done, the shareholder/directors are not disadvantaged through having a company rather than a partnership and the new shareholder/ director need not put in very large amounts of new share capital.

17.16.5 Tax savings may only be a deferment

The traditional analysis has been that tax generally becomes payable by shareholders on their share of retained profits, either when the shareholders sell their shares and realise a capital gain, or as and when they extract retained profits by taking a dividend. On this analysis, the saving of tax on retained profits is often little more than a deferment of tax. The validity of this view has been brought into question by the substantial increases in CGT retirement relief during recent years (see 6.7). The fact that gains may be exempt up to £100,000 (for 2002–03) if a husband and wife both qualify for the maximum retirement relief means that the traditional analysis is often no longer valid since shareholder/directors are generally able to enjoy the full value of their shares on a sale or liquidation of the company.

17.16.6 Increased liability for NICs

A company is required to pay Class 1 NICs on all amounts paid as remuneration. There is no ceiling akin to that which applies to employees' own contributions. This can give rise to a substantially increased burden for a company as compared with an unincorporated business. Comparing an unincorporated business owned by four equal partners with a company which has four 25% shareholders (and it is assumed that in both cases the individuals will have income of £75,000 each), the national insurance bill for 2002–03 is as follows:

	Partnership £		*Company* £
Class 2	104.00	Employees' Class 1	2,580.50
Class 4	1,806.35	Employer's Class 1	8,305.43
	1,910.35		10,885.93
× 4 =	7,641.40	× 4 =	43,543.72

While the benefits payable to employees are better than those received by the self-employed the higher NIC costs can be a very expensive way of financing such benefits.

17.17 OTHER TAX ASPECTS

17.17.1 Work in progress

In principle, a professional firm should not include partner time in arriving at the cost of work in progress. This means that the figure brought into account should be lower because of this. However, if a business is carried on by a company, time put in by a director should be included when valuing work in progress.

17.17.2 Potential double charge for capital gains

Where a valuable asset is held within a company, a tax liability may arise at two stages before the shareholders can enjoy the sale proceeds. For example, if a company acquires a property at a cost of £150,000, and five years later it is worth £550,000, there might be a gain for the company (after indexation) of £400,000. The company then pays tax on this capital gain either at the marginal small companies rate or at 30%. If a tax charge at 30% is assumed, the company has net funds available after paying tax of £318,000, ie:

	£	
Profit for accounting purposes	450,000	
Less: tax on gain	120,000	(£400,000 at 30%)
	330,000	

If the company is then wound up, and the cash distributed to the shareholders, they are likely to have a personal CGT liability on the £330,000. If retirement relief is not available, the CGT payable by them could be £132,000 (ie £330,000 at 40%). This figure assumes that other assets and retained profits within the company are such that there would have been capital gains for the shareholders in any event, even if the company had not held the property concerned.

However, once again, the traditional analysis is open to question. If the company had paid a dividend in order to transmit the £330,000 cash to shareholders, their personal liability could not exceed £82,250. Consequently, while it is not generally good policy to have appreciating assets within a company, the extent of the extra tax payable is not as great as it was in the past. Furthermore, while some additional tax is likely to be payable if an appreciating asset is held within a company, this is not in itself an argument against a business operating through a company but rather an argument in favour of shareholder/directors holding such assets in their personal capacities outside the company. It should be borne in mind here that retirement relief is available to a full-time working director who disposes of a property which is used by his family company provided that a disposal is associated with a disposal of shares in the company.

17.18 TRANSFERRING A BUSINESS TO A COMPANY

Where a person transfers a business to a company (ie he 'incorporates the business'), there is a disposal of the assets which are transferred to the company. Not all the assets are necessarily chargeable assets for CGT purposes, but a gain may arise on the transfer of assets such as land, buildings and goodwill to the company. Fortunately, there is a relief which may cover such situations (TCGA 1992, s 162).

17.18.1 Nature of relief

The main relief applies only where a business is transferred to a company in return for an issue of shares to the former proprietors of the business. Where the necessary conditions are satisfied so that s 162 relief is available, the gains which would otherwise arise on the transfer of chargeable assets are 'rolled-over' into the cost of the shares issued.

Example – Transfer of a business to a company

A transfers a business to X Ltd in return for shares which are worth £75,000. There are capital gains of £48,000 on the assets transferred to the company. If TCGA 1992, s 162 relief applies, *A* will not have any assessable capital gain, but *A*'s shares in X Ltd will be deemed to have an acquisition cost of £27,000 computed as follows:

	£
Market value	75,000
Less: rolled-over gain	(48,000)
	27,000

17.18.2 Conditions which must be satisfied

For s 162 relief to be available, *all* the assets of the business other than cash must be transferred to the company. It is not acceptable to the Revenue for certain assets of the unincorporated business, such as trade debts, to be excluded, even though this might otherwise be desirable to save stamp duty.

Relief is available only in so far as the company issues shares rather than other consideration such as loan stock. However, some relief is still available if the business is transferred to the company in return for a mixture of shares and loan stock, or shares and cash. The formula to be used is:

$$\text{Chargeable gain} \times \frac{\text{value of shares received}}{\text{value of whole consideration received}}$$

Thus if *B* transfers a business to Y Ltd and receives shares worth £10,000 and loan stock worth £200,000, only one-third of any capital gains arising on the transfer of the business assets can be rolled-over under TCGA 1992, s 162.

17.18.3 Limitations of s 162 relief

The market value of the shares issued in return for the transfer of the business must be at least equal to the capital gains arising on the transfer of assets, or there will still be a CGT charge on the transfer of the business to the company. Thus if *C* transfers a business with a net value of £400,000 to Y Ltd, a new company specially formed for the purpose, the shares in Z Ltd will have a value of £400,000. However, it may be that closer examination reveals that the business's value is depressed by heavy bank borrowings. If so, it may be that capital gains totalling (say) £490,000 arise on the chargeable assets transferred as part of the business. TCGA 1992 s 162 relief is then limited to £400,000. The balance of £90,000 is taxable in the normal way.

17.18.4 Conditions that do not apply

(1) Relief is not confined to a transfer of a business to a company by a sole trader; the same relief is available where a partnership transfers its business to a company.

(2) The shares which are issued need not be ordinary shares.

(3) Relief is not confined to a business which is classified as a trade which falls under Schedule D Case I or II. It is arguable that the relevant business might, for example, consist of letting a group of properties.

(4) There is no requirement that the company should be incorporated or resident in the UK. It can be both of these, but relief is not prejudiced just because a foreign company is involved.

17.18.5 Election to forego roll-over relief on transfer of business
(TCGA 1992 s 162A)

This provides for individuals and trustees to elect for TCGA 1992, s 162 roll-over relief not to apply on the transfer of an unincorporated business to a company. This applies to transfers of business after 5 April 2002. The right to 'elect out' of receiving incorporation relief, which was previously mandatory where certain conditions were met, could benefit individuals and trustees who incorporate a business that they have previously carried on and dispose of the shares in the new company soon afterwards, before the maximum benefit of business asset taper relief can be realised. This may happen eg where there is an unexpected offer to buy the business soon after incorporation.

This flexibility to opt out of the relief also helps in cases where an individual has incorporated his business as part of the sale of the business and the sale falls through. Under the previous rules he might have structured the sale so as to fall outside incorporation relief so as to maximise taper relief entitlement, and then be faced with an immediate tax charge. One of the effects of the new measure is that such transactions can be structured so that they obtain incorporation relief, but opt out of the relief if the sale goes ahead as planned.

17.18.6 Alternative way of incorporating a business

It may sometimes be possible to transfer a business to a company and avoid any CGT liability by relying on the hold-over provisions for gifts (see 6.4). Thus if A establishes a new company, X Ltd, and he owns all the shares, he could give his business to X Ltd and 'hold over' any capital gain. If A's acquisition cost was £15,000 and indexation relief (see 5.5.5) amounts to £7,000, he is deemed to transfer the business assets for £22,000 and the company takes over the assets for a notional acquisition value of £22,000. This could be a suitable way of transferring a business to a company where the proprietors do not wish to transfer all the assets to the company, as required by TCGA 1992, s 162 (eg where the proprietors wish to retain properties used in the business).

Professional advice is essential to such arrangements. Problems are particularly likely to arise if there is some consideration involved, even if it does not correspond to the business's market value at the time of transfer.

17.18.7 Income tax consequences

Although there are specific CGT reliefs, there are no similar provisions for income tax purposes. Where individuals transfer a business to a company, they cease to carry on the business and the Schedule D closing year rules may apply.

Furthermore, the transfer of stock to the company may give rise to a taxable profit. Normally, stock is deemed to be transferred at market value in these circumstances. However, it is possible for the proprietors of the unincorporated business and the company to jointly elect for the stock to be transferred at the lower of its cost or carrying value in the unincorporated business's accounts.

The transfer of plant and machinery, and other assets that qualify for capital allowances, might give rise to a balancing charge. However, it is possible for the proprietors and the company to make a joint election so that the plant etc are deemed to be transferred at their tax written-down value.

17.18.8 **VAT consequences of the transfer**

The VAT legislation provides that a transfer of a business is not a taxable supply if the following conditions are satisfied:

(1) the assets transferred are to be used by the transferee to carry on the same kind of business as that carried on by the transferor; and
(2) where the transferor is a taxable person the transferee is already, or as a result of the transfer becomes, a taxable person;
(3) where part of a business is transferred, that part is capable of separate operation, ie it must have the substance of a business activity.

The above conditions are normally satisfied where a business is transferred to a limited company as a going concern. Where this happens, it is possible for the unincorporated business's VAT registration number to be taken over by the company if the following conditions are satisfied:

(1) an application on form VAT 68 must be made both by the individuals previously in business and the company; and
(2) the unincorporated business's registration must be cancelled from the date of the transfer; and
(3) the company must not already be registered, although it will of course be liable to be registered as a result of the transfer of the business to it.

The effect of such an application is that the company stands in the shoes of the proprietors of the unincorporated business and takes over all the rights and obligations of those proprietors. Thus, the company becomes liable to furnish any outstanding returns and to pay any VAT due to Customs and Excise at the date of the transfer. This includes any undetected errors in VAT returns which emerge at any subsequent VAT control visit.

17.18.9 **Stamp duty on the transfer**

The general principles of stamp duty in relation to the transfer of a business to a company are set out at 8.3.7. It is appropriate to go into a little more detail here, and in particular to look at possible ways of avoiding stamp duty on the transfer of land and buildings.

Land and buildings can be transferred for a consideration below market value, eg an issue of preference shares. Where this happens, stamp duty is payable only on the actual consideration which passes.

It is also possible that ad valorem duty could be deferred or even avoided if the proprietors of the unincorporated business contract to sell the land and buildings to the company but do not complete that contract.

An agreement for the sale of an interest in land is specifically excluded from the charge to stamp duty under Stamp Act 1891, s 59 and therefore there is no stamp duty on the contract. Beneficial ownership of the property passes to the company as soon as the contract is executed and the company issues its shares as consideration. If the contract were ever completed, stamp duty is then payable. However, it may well be that the directors of the company would be safe to rely on the existence of the contract and allow the legal estate to remain in the names of the proprietors of the unincorporated business. As and when the company wishes to sell the property to a third party, the legal estate can be transferred directly from the former proprietors with only one charge to stamp duty arising, this being the duty payable by the new owner on his purchase consideration. It is essential that professional advice be taken on this.

For instruments executed after 22 April 2002, no stamp duty is chargeable on the sale, transfer or other disposition of goodwill (see FA 2002, s 114).

17.18.10 Carry forward of past trading losses
(TA 1988, s 386)

Where a business has been carried on by an individual (either as a sole trader or in partnership) and the business is transferred to a company, it is possible for any unused trading losses to be relieved against the individual's income from the company in subsequent years. This relief is available only if the business is transferred to a company in return for an issue of shares and the individual has retained ownership of those shares throughout the tax year concerned. In practice, the Revenue does not withhold relief provided the individual has retained at least 80% of the shares.

17.18.11 Other tax aspects

Where CGT incorporation relief is sought under TCGA 1992, s 162 (see 17.18.1 above) it is important to bear in mind that if the limited company takes over the liability of the incorporated business to pay the partners the balance on their current accounts, this counts as a form of consideration and CGT may be payable. It is generally thought advisable for the partners to withdraw the balances on their current accounts shortly before the business is transferred to the limited company. If necessary, short-term bank borrowings may be taken on to bridge the situation, with the individuals then lending money to the company after it has acquired the business. This is clearly another aspect on which professional advice should be taken.

Partners in a firm should plan ahead. Retirement relief is an important consideration (until the end of 2002–03 when it is withdrawn) and there can be some pitfalls. For example, an individual who personally owned an asset used by the partnership can qualify for retirement relief on an associated disposal of the property (see 6.7.2). Directors who personally own an asset used by their personal trading company (see 6.8.1) can also claim relief on an associated disposal, but only if they work full-time for the company.

Inheritance tax should be borne in mind as well. While they were partners, the individuals would have been entitled to 100% business property relief. As shareholders in a company which has taken over their business, the relief is limited to 50% unless the individual concerned has more than 25% of the voting shares. Thus, if five individuals who share profits equally transfer their business to a company, each of them has only a 20% shareholding, and his or her entitlement to business property relief is only 50%.

SALE OF THE BUSINESS AND CESSATION

17.19 SALE

17.19.1 Apportionment of sale consideration

When the proprietors of an unincorporated business dispose of it, they actually make separate disposals of different assets. The contract under which the business is sold normally allocates a specific part of the consideration to each separate asset, eg stock, plant and machinery, land and buildings and goodwill. The Inland Revenue may challenge the way in which the sale consideration is apportioned if it seems unrealistic and, if no apportionment is contained in the contract, a just and reasonable apportionment may be made. This may have income tax implications as well as CGT consequences.

Example – Apportionment

A sole trader, A, sells his business for £180,000. It is decided that this sum breaks down into the following components:

	£
Stock	40,000
Plant and machinery	35,000
Leasehold property	25,000
Goodwill	80,000
	180,000

The £40,000 for stock is brought into account as a trading receipt. The £35,000 for plant and machinery needs to be set against the 'pool' balance (see 4.7) and there may be a balancing charge if it exceeds the pool figure. The £25,000 for the sale of the leasehold property and the goodwill may produce capital gains.

The Revenue usually accepts a given apportionment unless it is blatantly unreasonable.

17.19.2 Transfer of business to company immediately before sale

Where a business is to be sold and the gain is likely to exceed any amount covered by retirement relief, there can be some advantage in first transferring the business to a limited company under TCGA 1992, s 162 (see 17.18), the company later selling on the business.

Example – Transfer to a company

Using the figures in the example in 17.19.1, let us suppose that a disposal of the goodwill for £80,000 would produce a capital gain of £70,000. If A had no entitlement to retirement relief, tax of up to £28,000 might be payable.

However, if A transferred the entire business to A Ltd in return for an issue of shares, A Ltd's acquisition value of the business is its market value at the time of the transfer (ie £180,000). The company would have a capital gain on a sale of the goodwill etc only if the assets appreciated after being transferred to A Ltd.

A would have a capital gain if he disposed of his shares in A Ltd, but in practice he may not need to do so and could use the company for some other purpose (eg as an investment company).

17.20 CESSATION

The proprietors of an unincorporated business may not be able to sell it to anyone else and may simply have to terminate the business themselves. A number of tax points arise in this connection.

17.20.1 VAT

Where assets such as stock or plant and machinery are still held by the business at the date that it ceases to make taxable supplies, there is a deemed supply and the assets are treated as if they have been sold. VAT is then due to Customs based on the open market value (except in the situation where the value is less than £250).

There are minor exceptions to this rule, ie there is no deemed supply where the goods retained by the proprietors are motor cars or goods obtained under a second-hand scheme.

17.20.2 Redundancy costs

Payments made to former employees on the cessation of a business do not qualify for relief under TA 1988, s 74 as the payments are not made for the benefit of the trade but are expenditure incurred in bringing that trade to an end. However, TA 1988, s 90 allows a deduction for payments of up to three times the statutory redundancy payments which are due.

17.20.3 Post-cessation expenses
(TA 1988, s 109A)

Relief is available for expenses incurred by a person after ceasing to carry on a trade or profession provided it is incurred within seven years of the cessation date. The following types of expenditure may qualify for relief:

- the costs of remedying defective work done, goods supplied, or services rendered while the trade or profession was continuing, and damages paid by the taxpayer in respect of such defective work etc, whether awarded by a court or agreed during negotiations on a claim;
- insurance premiums paid to insure against the above costs;
- legal and other professional expenses incurred in connection with the above costs;
- debts owed to the business which have been taken into account in computing the profits or gains of the trade or profession before discontinuance but which have subsequently become bad;
- the costs of collecting debts which have been taken into account in computing the profits of the trade before discontinuance.

The relief is reduced by any expense allowed as a deduction in the final accounting period which remains unpaid at the end of the year of assessment in which the new relief is given.

Expenditure which qualifies for this relief is set against income and capital gains of the year of assessment in which the expense is paid. Where there is insufficient income or capital gains to cover the expenditure, the unrelieved expenditure of that year is not eligible to be carried forward under the new relief arrangements against future income or capital gains. Any unrelieved expenditure is then available to be carried forward under the existing rules and set against subsequent post-cessation receipts from the trade or profession.

18

COMPANY LAW

KEITH HATCHICK, MARSHALL HATCHICK SOLICITORS

This chapter gives an overview of a vast body of corporate law that affects business life.

18.1 WHAT IS A COMPANY?

The fundamental principle of a company is that it is a separate legal entity distinct from its members. Two important points should be noted:

(1) Property belongs to a company and not its members. Directors and shareholders can be prosecuted for theft in appropriate circumstances.
(2) A company's debts and liabilities in themselves cannot in general be enforced against that company's members.

18.1.1 Limited liability

Most companies are formed with limited liability. This means shareholders are only obliged to pay the company such amounts that remain unpaid on any shares they hold. In the case of companies limited by guarantee (ie without a share capital – see 18.1.2) shareholders are only obliged to contribute the amount they have guaranteed to contribute to the company should it be wound up. Other typical characteristics of a company are:

(a) it can be sued in its own name;
(b) a death or change in membership does not affect its continued existence; it continues indefinitely until wound up or dissolved;
(c) members hold shares that constitute property and can be transferred to others without affecting the company's existence;
(d) it has power to give security for its borrowing through the creation of a floating charge over all or any part of its assets.

18.1.2 Types of company

The Companies Act (CA) 1985 provides for three types of company:

(i)   companies limited by guarantee;

(ii)   unlimited companies; and

(iii) companies (either private or public) limited by shares.

Companies limited by guarantee

These are generally formed for non-trading purposes (eg charities, clubs, trade associations). Prior to CA 1980 they could be formed with a share capital. This option was rarely used since it exposed members to liability with respect both to their guarantee in a winding-up and anything unpaid on their shares. Since CA 1980, it has not been possible to form a company limited by guarantee with a share capital.

The memorandum of association must contain a provision stating that each member undertakes to contribute to the company's assets if it should be wound up either while he is a member or within one year thereafter. The liability is limited to a specified maximum (usually £1).

Companies limited by guarantee frequently dispense with the requirement that they should use the word 'limited' in their name. To obtain such an exemption, permission must be sought from the Registrar of Companies. This is usually provided so long as

(a) the company's objects are for the promotion of commerce, art, science, education, religion and charity or any profession, and

(b) the articles or memorandum of association prohibit the payment of dividends to members, and

(c) profits, if any, are applied in promoting its objects, and

(d) on a winding-up any assets must be transferred to another similar body (ie not to its members).

Unlimited companies

These are not widely used since members, as the name implies, have no limitation on potential liability in the event that the company is wound up with debts that it is unable to pay. While the company is a going concern members can only be called upon to pay any sums that remain unpaid on their shares. Creditors of the company can, if debts owed to them remain unpaid, obtain a petition for winding up the company, but they cannot sue the members directly.

Private limited companies

CA 1985 contains an unhelpful definition of a private company being 'one which is not a public company'. Effectively this means that a private company is one that is not allowed to offer shares to the public, eg by seeking admission on The Stock Exchange or by issuing an advertisement offering security to be issued by it. A private company is the most popular form for profit-making business entities.

Public companies

CA 1985 contains a technical definition of a public company. The real differences between a public and a private company are:

(1) Its name must finish with the words 'public limited company' or 'plc' (for a Welsh company 'cwmni cyfyngedig cyhoeddus' or 'ccc'). A memorandum of association also needs to highlight the fact that it is a public company.
(2) There must be an authorised share capital of not less than £50,000 (this figure can be varied by the Secretary of State by statutory instrument) of which at least one quarter and the whole of any premium has been paid up.

The advantage of a public company over a private one is that, subject to certain exceptions, a public company is entitled to issue advertisements offering securities to be issued to members of the public. The disadvantages are that public companies are subject to far more stringent controls than private ones. Public companies do not need to be and frequently are not listed on The Stock Exchange.

Public Companies listed on The Stock Exchange need to comply with the rules of this market, which are largely set out by the Financial Services Authority (FSA). The FSA was created by the Financial Services and Markets Act (FSMA) 2000, which updated and extended legislation that had initially been created by the Financial Services Act 1986. The FSA took over the regulating and enforcement obligations of such companies from The Stock Exchange and now polices such them under the Listing Rules. Companies listed on AIM also need to comply with FSMA 2000, but the day-to-day regulations of this market are still controlled by The Stock Exchange.

18.2 MEMORANDUM OF ASSOCIATION

Every company needs a memorandum of association; it acts as a company's charter and regulates the company's external affairs. Its purpose is to enable persons who invest in or deal with it to establish such facts as:

(a) its name;
(b) whether it is a private or public company;
(c) what its objects are;
(d) whether liability of its members is limited or unlimited;
(e) the location of its registered office (England, Wales or Scotland);
(f) if there is a share capital, and if so the amount and how it is divided (eg £1,000 divided into 1,000 ordinary shares of £1 each).

For a company limited by guarantee the memorandum must also state the maximum guaranteed liability of such members (see 18.1.2 above).

18.2.1 The name

The name chosen must end with the word Limited (or Ltd) or public limited company (or plc) (unless a dispensation has been granted – see 18.1.2 above) or the Welsh equivalent (see 18.1.2) in the case of Welsh companies. It should not be the same as any other registered company or be offensive or commit a criminal offence. It should not be of a 'sensitive nature'. The Registrar keeps a list of sensitive names and under what circumstances they are granted. For example, use of the words 'Group' or 'Holding' requires the company using the name to have at least two subsidiary companies. Use of words like 'Royal' are also restricted, normally to companies holding a royal charter.

A change of name requires the company to pass a special resolution that must be filed at Companies House, together with a fee of £10.

Passing off

In forming a new company or changing the name of an existing one, attention should always be given to the name chosen since use of a similar name to an existing company may give rise to a passing off action. This is where the use of a name is sufficiently similar to another as it may mislead members of the public. For example, if a company is called 'AG Honey Ltd' and a new company is formed called 'G A Huney Ltd' and both are in the same line of business, it may be that the first company would have an action for passing off due to its loss of goodwill. The normal action brought is one of damages, but more frequently the earlier company seeks to obtain an injunction to stop the newer company from continuing under that name. Guidelines were set down in *Warnink v Townend & Sons* [1979] AC 731. To establish a case there needs to be:

(a) a misrepresentation by a trader in the course of his business to a prospective customer or consumer;
(b) damage to goodwill of the existing business: it is sufficient if such damage is reasonably foreseeable as a consequence of any such misrepresentation;
(c) 'a common field of activity' – in one case a radio broadcaster failed to prevent a cereal producer from using the same name for his product (*McCulloch v May* [1947] 2 All ER 845).

18.2.2 Articles of association

The articles of association regulate a company's internal affairs, dealing with such matters as:

(a) issue and transfer of shares;
(b) alteration of share capital;
(c) holding of meetings and voting rights;

(d) directors' appointments and retirements;

(e) appointment of a secretary;

(f) declaration of dividend;

(g) accounts, auditing etc; and

(h) winding-up etc.

Both the memorandum and articles of association form a contract between the company and each member and between the members.

18.2.3 Formation requirements

The following documents should be sent to Companies House together with the relevant statutory fee (currently £20).

(1) A copy of the memorandum and articles of association. For a private company, if no articles are filed Table A of the Companies (Tables A to F) Regs 1985 automatically applies. For companies limited by guarantee, the forms of memorandum and articles of association set out in Tables C and D of the Regulations must be used. These must be signed by all members and witnessed.

(2) Form G10 – This must be completed by each director and the secretary. It also gives the address of the company's registered office.

(3) Form G12 – This must be completed by the solicitors engaged in the company formation (but can also be signed by a person named or a director or secretary in Form G10). It confirms compliance with the companies legislation.

18.3 RE-REGISTRATION

At some stage during the currency of a company it may wish to convert into a company of a different form. Part II of CA 1985 anticipates that by considering four particular forms:

(a) a private company becoming a plc;

(b) a plc becoming a private company;

(c) a limited company becoming unlimited; and

(d) an unlimited company becoming limited.

18.3.1 Private company to plc

A special (or written) resolution must be passed that the company should be registered. The company must be able to show that it has an authorised share capital of at least £50,000 with not less than 25% paid up. There are various other considerations set out in CA 1985, s 45 which may need to be considered.

A copy of the special or written resolution must be sent to the Registrar within 15 days of the date of the meeting (or in the case of a written resolution the date it was signed by the last member). Form 43(3) should also be completed. This needs to be accompanied by:

(a) a printed copy of the up-to-date articles and memorandum;
(b) a statement signed by auditors that in their opinion the balance sheet shows net assets not less than the aggregate of called up share capital and undistributable reserve;
(c) a copy of the balance sheet with an unqualified auditors report. The report needs to state that if there is a qualification it is not material for purposes of determining whether (at the balance sheet date) the net assets exceeded the aggregate of its called-up share capital and distributable reserves.

Form 53(3) should be completed and sent to the Registrar as outlined above. It contains a statutory declaration confirming that all required procedures have been complied with and the share capital requirements have been satisfied.

18.3.2 A plc to a private company
(CA 1985, ss 53–55)

A company must pass a special resolution changing the name from plc to Ltd and amend all references in the memorandum and articles accordingly.
Form 53 needs to be completed and sent with the special resolution to the Registrar within 15 days. A shareholder is entitled to apply to court for an order of cancellation and the court will either cancel or confirm the resolution. In order for a shareholder to apply to court he or it must either

(a) hold not less than 5% of the issued share capital (of any class of share);
(b) consist of not less than 5% of members of a company; or
(c) consist of not less than 50 members.

Where there is a reduction of the plc's share capital which has the effect of bringing the nominal value of the company's allotted shares below the authorised minimum, the company must cease to be a plc under CA 1985, s 138. A court may further order that a company shall be re-registered as a limited company and in this case it dispenses with the necessity for the company to pass a special resolution so re-registering. If a company cancels shares under s 146 and it results in its share capital being below the authorised minimum, the company is obliged to apply for re-registration as a limited company.

18.3.3 Unlimited companies

Under CA 1985, s 49, if a plc wishes to re-register as an unlimited company all members must approve that re-registration and its memorandum and articles must be altered to comply with the Act. Form 49 must be completed and filed with the Registrar of Companies, attached to which must be a confirmation signed by each member and a statutory declaration by the director confirming that all members have agreed. On receipt of this documentation Companies House issues a revised certificate of incorporation.

If an unlimited company wishes to re-register as a private company it must pass a special resolution and complete Form 51. If a limited company has already registered as an unlimited company it cannot again re-register as a limited company.

There are provisions in the Act enabling an unlimited company to register as a plc (or vice versa). These are very rarely used in practice, but the procedure is set out in ss 48–53.

18.3.4 Stamp duty

Stamp duty and stamp duty reserve tax (SDRT) are covered in detail in Chapter 8. Stamp duty is levied at 0.5% on the transfer of shares, debentures and other security. The minimum payable is £5 (increased from 50p in October 1999), with the total payable rounded up to the nearest £5. No duty is charged on the issue of new shares.

Stamp duty is chargeable to the purchaser of shares. In certain cases there may be exemption (eg transactions involving shares in the same group of companies on a reorganisation), but this area of law is complicated and professional assistance should be sought.

SDRT arises when there is no stampable document used (eg when a block of shares is sold on The Stock Exchange). In this case the amount paid would equal that which would arise from stamp duty.

A number of pronouncements concerning the future of stamp duty have been made. It is likely that duty for these transfers and other non-property documents will be limited, but nothing has yet been settled.

18.4 AFTER INCORPORATION

When the above formalities have been completed and a certificate of incorporation has been received (and also in the case of a public company a certificate confirming that the share capital requirements have been complied with), the company should hold its first board meeting, the normal business of which includes:

(1) adoption of the company seal (an impression is normally made in the margin of the minutes);
(2) appointment of a chairman (if appropriate) and any additional directors and the approval of any service contracts;
(3) appointment of auditors;
(4) stock transfer forms transferring subscriber share to intended members of the company;
(5) completion of the company's bank mandate form setting up banking arrangements;

(6) adoption of an accounting reference date (ARD) to which the company's accounts will be prepared (in the event that the Registrar is not notified of the ARD within six months of the incorporation the statutory ARD will apply as of 31 March).

The following company forms typically need to be filed with the Registrar following the first board meeting (and subsequently when appropriate changes are made):

(a) Form 88(2) (details of shares allotted for cash; if there is a non-cash consideration, Form 88(3) must be completed);
(b) Form 288 (appointment of new director or secretary), signed by each new director and the secretary: resignations should also be recorded on the same form;
(c) Form 224 (notification of accounting reference date chosen by the company).

Any completed stock transfer form also needs to be sent to the Revenue for stamping (at the rate of 50p per £100 or part thereof – see further below)). If there are any declarations of trust regarding the holding of such shares, such a declaration of trust form also needs to be stamped at a fixed rate of £5.

18.4.1 Continuing requirements

In addition to notifying the Registrar about day-to-day changes (eg:

(a) the appointment or resignation of a director or secretary (Form 288);
(b) a change of accounting reference date (Forms G225(1) and (2));
(c) a change of registered office (Form 287);
(d) a change of auditor etc),

the company also has an obligation to prepare accounts. For the first accounting reference date, the accounts must be for a period of more than six months but not more than 18 months beginning with the date of incorporation. There is no minimum duration for subsequent periods but no period may exceed 18 months.

In each financial year the company's directors must lay before the company in general meeting copies of its annual accounts and the directors and auditors report. A copy of this material needs to be delivered to the Registrar within ten months of the end of the appropriate accounting reference period for a private company, or within seven months for a public company. In the case of a first accounting period of a company which is more than 12 months, the period allowed is ten and seven months respectively from the first anniversary of the company's incorporation (or three months from the end of the accounting reference period, whichever last expires). If a company fails to deliver accounts to the Registrar within those periods, civil penalties are charged of up to £5,000 for a public company and up to £1,000 for a private company.

A private company may pass an elective resolution (see 18.6.6) to dispense with laying the accounts or reports before the company in general meeting (see 18.6.1). Any such election does not relieve the company from the obligation to send copies of the accounts to all members and other people entitled to receive them (including the Registrar).

There are special provisions for dormant companies that may, by special resolution, resolve not to appoint auditors. A dormant company for this purpose means one that has not had transactions requiring entries in the company's accounting records since the end of the previous financial year (or the date of incorporation as the case may be).

18.4.2 Annual return

Each company must deliver to the Registrar on Form 363a details made up to a date not later than the anniversary of the company's incorporation for a new company, or the anniversary of the date of the last return for other companies. The return must be delivered to the Registrar within 28 days of the relevant date.

The annual return needs to specify the following:

(1) The relevant date as it is made up.
(2) The registered office address.
(3) Details of the company's main business activities.
(4) Names and addresses of the company secretary and each director of the company. For directors, additional information is required (including nationality, date of birth, business occupation and other directorships).
(5) Where the register of members is kept (if not at the registered office).
(6) The share capital of the company and its members.

18.4.3 Borrowing

Trading and commercial companies have employed powers to borrow money for all purposes of its business and this power is invariably enshrined in a company's memorandum of association. A borrowing or loan is an agreement under which one party advances or otherwise makes available to another a sum of money in consideration of a promise, whether expressed or implied, to repay the amount advanced, whether or not at a premium and whether or not with interest. An agreement relating to borrowing must be validly entered into by the company and borrowing must not be unlawful or for some unlawful pursuit.

Borrowing takes two forms:

(a) secured debt (borrowings secured subject to a charge that has been granted on some or all of the company's property); and
(b) unsecured debt, eg bills of exchange, promissory notes and bonds etc issued by the company.

Restrictions on borrowing

Frequently articles of association limit the amount of debt in the form of borrowings that can be outstanding at any time without the shareholders' prior consent. In the case of a listed company, The Stock Exchange no longer requires the articles to restrict borrowings and it is left to the company and its advisors to determine limitations; obviously they need to take a view to ensure marketability of its securities. Listed companies are now subject to Chapter 11 of the Listing Rules (which contains the rules governing fully listed companies). Approval must be obtained from the company's shareholders for any transaction entered into by the company and related parties. In this context, 'related party' means a substantial shareholder (someone who controls 10% of the vote of the company) or a director/shadow director. This is read both currently and during the previous 12-month period. It also applies where 'associates' of such related parties are involved.

Agreements usually require the company to undertake to keep its borrowings and those of any subsidiary within a specified limit. In the event that the company fails to comply with this provision, a lender would have remedies against the company for breach of contract and may also seek to bring an injunction. It may be possible that those who authorised the offending loan may be personally liable.

Privity rules under the law of contract would prevent an interested party from bringing an action unless that party had also entered into an agreement with the relevant party acknowledging its rights. This has been revised in the Contracts (Rights of Third Parties) Act 1999. This allows a third party to sue where it is expressly provided that such party may enforce its rights, and a benefit has been conferred on that party. The Act became law on 11 November 1999, but only applies to agreements made after 11 May 2000; it has no retrospective effect.

18.4.4 Debentures

There is no precise meaning of 'debenture'. The broad legal meaning is that it is a document that either creates or acknowledges indebtedness. For these purposes, debenture is used in its banking context, ie a document signed by the company covenanting to repay all monies that may be due to the lender and creating a fixed charge over the company premises etc and a floating charge over the concern's business and undertaking.

If there is a default in the repayment of an unsecured debenture, the main remedy is for the holder to sue for the debts if it remains unpaid. He needs to obtain a judgment and seek distress against the company's property and possibly present a petition for the company's winding-up. In the case of a secured debenture the holder is in a far stronger position since in addition to the powers already referred to he can also appoint a receiver or administrative receiver.

18.4.5 Mezzanine finance

This is a type of debt that has in recent years become quite popular with highly geared companies. It is a form of subordinated debt that ranks behind all or certain other specified debts of the company. Such debt may be secured by charges, but these invariably rank behind other creditors. The principal advantage to the creditor in offering this form of finance is that since the risk is high, so is the interest chargeable.

18.4.6 Charges and secured debentures

There is a temptation to use the words 'charge' and 'mortgage' interchangeably. There is an important difference between them since a mortgage arises when a property is transferred subject to a right of redemption. Conversely a charge does not transfer or convey anything but just gives the person holding the charge (the chargee) certain defined rights over the property as security or a loan.

A fixed or specific charge is one linked to either existing or future property and which attaches to that property. (For future property it attaches when that property has been ascertained.) When a fixed charge has been given relating to specific property, the owner or company giving the charge is prohibited from dealing with the property without the consent of the company or individual to whom the charge was given.

A floating charge, as its name implies, floats over the relevant property until a specified event happens which would then cause it to fasten on to the subject-matter of the charge. Until this occurs the company can carry on its day-to-day activities and sell or deal with its assets without first requiring the holder's consent. If an event occurs which causes the charge to 'crystallise' (fasten), the chargee becomes entitled to a specific or fixed charge over the property and any further dealing by the company of that property requires his consent. A floating charge crystallises in circumstances including:

(a) upon the winding-up of the company;
(b) if an administrative receiver is appointed;
(c) if a company has sold substantially all its property and assets so that it can no longer carry on business;
(d) if possession of any assets is taken by the holder of a charge; and
(e) any other floating charge that may have been granted crystallises or if the company granting the floating charge failed to repay money on demand.

18.4.7 Registration of charges

CA 1985, s 395(1) requires that if any security of a company's property or undertaking has been granted, such security shall cease to prevail unless details of the charge together with a document creating the charge has been delivered to the Registrar within 21 days. Section 396(1) lists nine types of charges to which the obligation of registration applies. The categories listed are broad, but exclude such items as fixed charges over shares that the relevant company may hold in another company and interest under insurance policies.

To register a charge, Form 395 must be completed as accurately as possible. To ensure the charge is valid, full details of its nature should be set out in the form. A mistake or omission in the completion of the form can prejudice the effectiveness of that security against competing claims in the event of a winding-up. It is most important that professional assistance is sought in the drafting and registration of charges to avoid potential pitfalls. Information that must be inserted on Form 395 includes:

(1) Company name and number.
(2) Date of creation of charge.
(3) Description of the instrument.
(4) Names and addresses of persons entitled to charge.
(5) Particulars of property charged.

18.4.8 Failure to register a charge

If a charge is not registered within the required 21-day period:

(a) it becomes void as against the liquidator and administrator, any creditor of the company and any person who has acquired proprietary rights to an interest in assets that are subject to a charge;
(b) the money that it secures becomes immediately repayable when the time for registration expires;
(c) the company and every officer in default becomes liable to a fine under CA 1985, s 399(3).

If registration is late it is normal to execute a fresh charge etc and duly register that within 21 days (but this may be subject to any others that may have been created in any intervening period). This second charge might also be subject to being set aside by a liquidator or administrative receiver as being a preference or possibly a transaction at an undervalue (see Insolvency Act (IA) 1986, ss 244 *et seq*).

18.4.9 Foreign companies

If a company incorporated outside Great Britain has an established place of business in England and Wales, it is required to submit particulars of any charge on property in England and Wales. Charges etc created prior to an establishment of a place of business remain valid even if the charge subsequently establishes the place of business.

Where a lender takes a charge from a foreign company relating to present or future property in England and Wales he should submit particulars of the charge and relevant documentary evidence to the Registrar. Even if the particulars are subsequently returned to the sender, Companies House now maintains an alphabetical index of the names of overseas companies for which charges for registration have been delivered (known as the 'Slavenburg Index' after an important case involving this foreign bank).

18.5 DIRECTORS

Regulation 70 of Table A of the Companies (Tables A to F) Regs 1985 states the general precept of company law, ie 'subject to provisions of the [companies legislation] and the articles and to any directions given by special resolution, the business of the company shall be managed by the directors who may exercise all the powers of the company'. There is broad statutory definition of 'director' since CA 1985, s 741(1) refers only to a person occupying the position of a director by whatever name called. Directors are those people who have agreed to become directors, eg by completing a company Form 288, but may also include individuals who take that role upon themselves (eg a major shareholder in a small company who meddles in day-to-day business). It could also be deemed to include a senior manager of a larger company who makes significant decisions regarding its day-to-day business. It is clear that just because a person is not called a director may be of little importance in establishing what is the position *de facto*. Such quasi directors are normally referred to as 'shadow directors'. In *Re Tasbian (No 3)* [1992] BCC 358, the Court of Appeal supported the claim that in the circumstances presented to the court the company doctor, who had been required to assist in a corporate recovery case, could have been treated as a director or a shadow director in the context under the Company Directors Disqualification Act 1986.

There is no maximum number of directors that can be appointed to a company and a private company may have one director. A public company must have at least two directors. If a private company has only one director there must be at least two people involved in the running of the company since CA 1985, s 283(2) requires that a sole director cannot also be a secretary. There is nothing to stop a director – and indeed a secretary – being another company, but this should not lead to circumvention in the requirement that there are only two individuals involved.

18.5.1 Appointment of directors

Founding directors complete company Form G10, which must be presented to Companies House before a certificate of incorporation is granted (see 18.2.3). Appointment of subsequent directors is determined in accordance with the company's articles. A typical such provision appears in reg 79 of Table A of the 1985 Regs, which states that the existing directors may appoint such person who is willing to act to be a director; this could either be to fill a vacancy or due to a requirement to have additional directors. Occasionally the articles will provide special provisions relating to a director appointment and it is not unusual for the articles to require a rotating system (ie a proportion of all the main members retire and offer themselves for reselection at each AGM). Sometimes the articles also require a director to hold a number of shares in the company. Such shares are frequently held on the basis that on resignation they are resold to the company's other members.

Neither the managing director (MD) nor the chairman has specific powers accorded to him by law, but reg 84 of Table A does allow the appointment of an MD. Each meeting requires a chairman to preside. Normally one of the directors takes this role, but larger companies appoint a specific person to fill this slot. Table A requires that the chairman be a board member. The position of chairman is a difficult one for he is in charge of the meeting and needs to check it is properly conducted. Table A, reg 50 gives the chairman a casting vote at meetings in addition to any other vote he may have (whether on a show of hands or a poll).

18.5.2 Non-executive directors

This has been a characteristic of larger companies for many years. It refers to a director who is not employed by a company under a service contract. Frequently he is seen as being a useful nexus between the board and the shareholders' interests and is able to offer an independent stand that may not otherwise be available at board level. Company law does not recognise any division between a director and a director's responsibilities and duties. In recent years the importance of non-executives has been underlined by various guidelines on corporate governance, such as the Cadbury, Greenbury and Hampel Reports. These codes have recently been republished as a combined Code on Corporate Governance.

An executive director should have a service contract with the company. Table A, reg 82 provides that the director should be entitled to such remuneration as the company may by ordinary resolution determine. For a director who works without having a service contract there is a presumption that he should be paid for the work done for the company on a merit basis (*Craven-Ellis v Cannons* [1936] 2 KB 403).

18.5.3 Director meetings

A company's day-to-day management is centred around the decisions of the Board of Directors. Directors, unless otherwise required by the articles (or a shareholders' agreement etc), meet at such times and intervals as they feel fit. Frequently meetings, if permitted by the company's articles, are held with little formality. Notice is similarly dealt with on an informal basis, but must be given to each director. Article 88 provides that no notice need be given to a director who is absent from the UK. Table A also permits a director to appoint an alternate to represent him.

The articles will specify what constitutes a quorum. A sole director who can only act in limited circumstances without a meeting will usually need acts by written resolution to be effective. Each director will have a vote and in addition Table A gives the chairman a second or casting vote if votes are equal. There is little law to determine how such a casting vote should be exercised but it is recognised that it should not be exercised arbitarily or capriciously (it does not though need to be exercised in the same way as the chairman's first vote).

Meetings are increasingly held by 'phone: this is tolerated by law, but is not preferable to an actual meeting. The validity of such a meeting depends on ensuring the normal procedures are adopted. Due to the normal requirements of meetings, it is unlikely that they can effectively be held by e-mail.

18.5.4 Resignation or retirement

A director can at any time resign his directorship, but if in so doing he has breached a contract of service this could result in liability for damages. In the case of public companies and private companies that are subsidiaries of private companies, CA 1985, s 293 states that a director must retire from office at the AGM following his 70th birthday. This does not apply if a director's appointment has been approved by a resolution of the general meeting at which special notice giving details of the director's age has been circulated to members (at least 28 days prior to the meeting). If such notice is not practical it can take the form of a newspaper advertisement or any other method allowed by the articles, but this needs to be done at least 21 days before the meeting.

18.5.5 Disqualification

This can take two forms:

(1) The articles normally set out regulations under which a director is required to vacate office in certain circumstances (eg ceasing to hold qualifying shares (if required), becoming of unsound mind, bankruptcy etc).
(2) The Company Directors Disqualification Act 1986 sets out three circumstances:
   (a) misconduct in relation to the company (eg conviction of an indictable offence in connection with the company);
   (b) unfitness (eg persistent breaches of company's legislation, like failing to deliver documents or returns to Companies House on a regular basis); and
   (c) in other cases, eg if a director has participated in fraud or a breach of duty or has participated in fraudulent trading that comes to light during a winding-up.

An application may be sought for disqualification by the Secretary of State, the official receiver or the liquidator, past or present members of a company, or a creditor of a relevant company. It is within the court's discretion whether to make an order. For cases of fraud and misconduct such disqualification can be up to a maximum of 15 years, in other circumstances up to five years. Under s 6 of the 1986 Act, a court must disqualify a director for not less than two years and not more than 15 years in the case where a company becomes insolvent (whether while he was a director or subsequently) and his conduct was such as to make him unfit or to be concerned in the management of the company. Under s 8, the Secretary of State can apply to court for a disqualification order for up to 15 years.

See *Re Sevenoaks Stationers (Retail)* [1991] Ch 164 in which the Court of Appeal set out guidelines on how the Act should be interpreted.

18.5.6 Removal of director

CA 1985, s 3 allows a director to be removed by ordinary resolution of the company so long as at least 28 days' special notice, served on the company, has been given. The director has the right to receive a copy of the notice and be heard at the meeting whether or not he is a company member. He can, if he requires, oblige the company to circulate written representation to the members before the meeting (although there is a right to apply to the court to have this curtailed).

The removal of the person as a director does not deprive him from obtaining compensation damages with respect to determination of his appointment. It may also be open to him to petition for the company's winding-up under IA 1986, s 122(1)(g) on the 'just and equitable' ground. In one case the petition was held to be successful since the director had such a substantial stake in a small family company that it was felt to be based upon a personal relationship involving mutual confidence (this area of law was carefully considered by the House of Lords in *Ebrahimi v Westbourne Galleries* [1973] AC 360).

18.5.7 Directors' duties

The duties can be summarised under two heads: the duty of good faith and loyalty (more usually referred to as fiduciary duties), and the requirement to use skill and care in carrying out their duties.

Fiduciary duties

This is an individual duty imposed upon each director of a company and it is owed to the company. From this fundamental principle certain strands have developed:

(1) In exercising good faith, directors must act in what they believe to be the company's best interests.

(2) They should not prejudice their ability to make decisions or restrict how they should act.

(3) They should not place themselves in the position where their personal interests or relationships to other persons may conflict with their duties to the company.

(4) They should not use the powers placed upon them for different purposes from those with which they were conferred.

The following are illustrations of the case-law in this area.

(a) *Re W & M Roith* [1967] 1 WLR 432 (provision made by controlling shareholder/director for pension to be paid for life of surviving widow on his demise; held, agreement not binding as the provision was not for the company's benefit but solely for the widow)

(b) *Re Kuwait Bank v National Nominees* [1991] AC 187 (the bank, a 40% shareholder in a company, appointed two employees as directors to the company, but continued to pay them for time spent in carrying out their duties; held their primary duty as directors was to the company and the bank's interests and wishes in relation to it should have been ignored)

(c) *Re Aberdeen Railway v Blaikie Bros* (1854) 1 Macq 461 (contract revoked between company and partnership because one of the directors was a partner; held, a director cannot enter into engagements that create a conflict of interest, hence revoking the contract was fair)

(d) *Hely-Hutchinson v Brayhead* [1968] 1 QB 549 and *Guinness v Saunders* [1988] 1 WLR 863 (director failed to declare interest in a contract or a proposed contract as required under CA 1985, s 317)

(e) *Guinness v Saunders*, above (misappropriated funds returned to company; in this case, Mr Ward thought he was entitled to £5.2m from the company – he was not, and was required to return it)

(f) *Re Regal (Hastings) v Gulliver* [1942] 1 All ER 378 (directors' know-how applied to competing venture set up by them while still directors in the original company that had fallen into different hands; held, the directors were liable to account profits to the original company)

(g) *Industrial Development Consultants v Cooley* [1972] 1 WLR 443 and *Canadian Aero Service v O'Malley* [1971] 23 DLR (3d) 632 (director retired to obtain remunerative work that their original companies had been denied; held, he was liable to account his profits to the original company).

CA 1985, s 309 requires directors of a company to have regard in the performance of their functions to the interests of the company's employees in general in addition to those of its members. Section 310 states that 'any provision whether contained in the Company's articles or in any contract with the Company or otherwise which attempts to exonerate an officer (or auditor of the company) from, or indemnify them against liability for negligence, default, breach of contract, breach of trust which he may be guilty in relation to the company is unenforceable'. There is a difficulty reconciling this statutory provision with the wording in Table A, regs 85 and 86.

18.5.8 Directors' remuneration

CA 1985, s 318 obliges a company to keep copies of a service agreement for each director of the company or its subsidiaries. These should be kept at the registered office or its principal place of business and must be open for inspection by any member of the company without charge.

Section 319 makes it unlawful for any provision in a director's contract which may make it last for more than five years without being terminated (ie other than through causing a breach of contract) unless the relevant term is first approved by the company in general meeting. There are special provisions relating to inspection being available without charge to members for a period prior to the meeting and at the meeting itself.

18.5.9 Substantial property transactions

CA 1985, s 322 requires that the company approve in advance any arrangement under which a director or person connected with him will acquire from the company or the company will acquire from him non-cash items of requisite value (ie £100,000 or 10% of the company's net assets if more than £2,000). The need for approval does not apply to intergroup transfers when the property is to be acquired by a holding company from one of its wholly owned subsidiaries or vice versa or from one wholly owned subsidiary to another of that same holding company. If a director authorises an arrangement or transaction in violation he is liable to account to the company for any gain he makes.

18.5.10 Loans to directors

CA 1985, s 330(2) and (3) prevents the company making a loan to a director of it or its holding company or from entering into any guarantee or providing security in connection with a loan made by any person to such director. This also covers a prohibition on 'quasi-loans' (ie when a director makes some financial benefit as a result of the company being party to a transaction), eg a gift of a holiday or some other benefit-in-kind. The grant of credit is also prohibited and the assignment of any rights, obligations and liability could also fall within this scope (s 330(4) and (6)).

There are certain exceptions to these rules and these should be carefully considered prior to any such potential 'loan'.

18.5.11 Directors' duties of care

Re City Equitable Fire Insurance [1925] Ch 407 laid down the standard of care required under three heads:

(1) In the performance of his duties a director does not need to show any greater skill than would reasonably be expected from a person of his knowledge and experience.

(2) His duties are of an intermittent nature and should be formed at periodic board meetings or any committee of that board on which he serves. He is not required to give continuous attention to the company's affairs.

(3) He may rely on agents or employees of the company not being directors to carry on its day-to-day duties. In particular he can only be liable on the basis of his own personal negligence.

There are two important statutory provisions that should be noted which affect the director's duty of care:

(a) IA 1986, s 214; this provision can potentially make a director personally liable if there is 'wrongful trading' (see further 18.5.13)

(b) Company Directors Disqualification Act 1986 (see 18.5.5).

18.5.12 Personal liability of directors

There are a number of circumstances referred to above and also with respect to the insolvency legislation in which directors can potentially be personally liable. The articles cannot relieve directors from their duty to act bona fide in the interests of a company nor can a company resolution in general meeting make good default, but the courts have indicated a transaction may sometimes be validated (and the directors thereby excused from liability) if:

(a) all relevant facts are disclosed in a notice convening a general meeting or in a circular accompanying that notice; and

(b) it can be shown that the resolution was 'bona fide in the interests of the company'.

In *Williams v Natural Law* (1996), inaccurate financial projections were provided to an applicant to a franchise which persuaded him to enter into a franchise. The result was a substantial loss of money. The plaintiff had no difficulty in showing there was gross negligence (there was clearly a duty of care to ensure projections were correct and reasonably and properly prepared). It was held that in the particular circumstances of the case the director had, since the plans were presented relying on the director's personal expertise and experience, effectively assumed a personal duty to the plaintiff (and was therefore personally liable). The court did, however, emphasise that a director who merely had control or ownership of the company in itself was not sufficient to create such a liability.

It is clear that English courts have been extending liability for directors and that a more objective test (common in Australian case-law) is beginning to be recognised (ie directors are expected to use skill and diligence and not just be enthusiastic amateurs).

18.5.13 Insurance

It has been customary for the personal liability of directors and other officers to be covered by insurance. Before CA 1989 it was unclear whether under CA 1985, s 310 such insurance was enforceable. A new provision was inserted by s 137 of the 1989 Act under which a new subs 310(3) was incorporated into CA 1985. This makes it clear that a company can purchase and maintain insurance for its officers if its memorandum and articles of association so allow. The normal form of cover protects past, present and future officers of a specific company (including shadow directors), but does not protect outsiders (eg an auditor or liquidator).

Indemnity insurance normally takes two forms:

(i)   protecting officers of a company where an indemnity from the company is not available, and

(ii) where the company reimburses its officers for liability it would in turn make this good to the company.

It is normal for a company to protect against:

(a) paying damages and costs of any action for a 'wrongful act' (broadly defined and includes actions for wrongful trading under IA 1986, s 214);

(b) legal expense incurred (except the exclusions from policy are normally limited to public policy items such as dishonesty, fraud, malicious conduct, indemnity for fines and penalties);

(c) specific risks that should be insured elsewhere (eg negligence or a breach of professional duty by an auditor or solicitor).

18.6 MEETINGS

18.6.1 General meetings

There are two types:

(a) annual general meetings (AGMs), and
(b) extraordinary general meetings (EGMs).

Every company must hold an AGM each calendar year with not more than 15 months between one AGM and the next. A newly formed company need not hold its first AGM for up to 18 months from the date of incorporation (see generally CA 1985, s 366).

An EGM is any general meeting that is held other than an AGM, and is usually convened by the company's directors when they so require. Under s 368, the directors are bound to convene an EGM if the holder of not less than one tenth of the company's voting shares (or for companies without a share capital, of voting rights) so requires. The people calling the meeting must give written notice setting out the meeting's objects and sign that notice. If the directors are requested to hold an EGM by the shareholders or those with voting rights, they must fix the actual date within 28 days (ie allowing a maximum of 49 days before a meeting is actually held).

The directors of a plc are required to convene an EGM under CA 1985, s 142 if there is a serious loss of capital (where the net assets are half or less of its called-up share capital); the meeting must be convened in 28 days for a date not later than 20 days after such notice.

Before the company can hold an AGM or EGM, written notice must be given to the members:

(a) for an AGM, at least 21 days' notice;
(b) for an EGM, not less than 14 days unless a special resolution is proposed, in which case it must be 21 days. In sending out the notice a company should carefully ensure that extra days are given since frequently the article requires 'clear' days' notice (eg Table A, reg 38).

Shorter notice can be given if agreed by all members entitled to attend an AGM, or by those holding not less than 95% of the voting shares (or having such voting rights) for an EGM.

Notice must be sent to every member of a company, but frequently the articles state that accidental omission to give such notice (or non-receipt of such notice) does not invalidate proceedings of a meeting (eg Table A, reg 39). Table A, reg 38 also requires that the notice should state the:

(a) time and place of the meeting;
(b) general business to be transacted (eg retirement, re-election of directors); and
(c) appointment of auditors.

Where a special resolution is to be proposed, the notice must set this down.

For a company with share capital, the notice must also contain the statement in reasonable prominence that a member is entitled to attend and vote and may appoint a proxy; this proxy need not be a member of the company (s 372). If a company's members wish to include a resolution at an AGM and such member or members hold not less than ¹⁄₂₀th of the voting rights (or 100 members entitled to vote with an average paid-up share capital of not less than £100 per member), the company must circulate:

(a) notice thereof to each member of the company that a resolution will be proposed at the AGM; and
(b) a statement of not more than 1,000 words relating to the proposed resolution (s 376). The company and 'any aggrieved person' have the right to petition the court to prevent any such statement being circulated.

The court has power to call a meeting (s 371). This power is normally used if no quorum can be achieved (eg a shareholder argument) or a meeting may end in violence. An example of such use was a meeting held by the British

Union for the Abolition of Vivisection: the court held that only the executive committee should meet, with all other members having a postal vote.

18.6.2 Special notice

This is required for the:

(a) appointment of a director who has attained age 70;
(b) removal of directors;
(c) appointment and removal of auditors.

Notice must be given to the company not less than 28 days before the meeting and the company must give notice to each of the members when it circulates a notice for the meeting (or if this is not practical through newspaper advertisement or any other form allowed by the articles not being less than 21 days before the meeting).

18.6.3 Quorum

The articles of association normally provide that a specified number of people must be present before a meeting can be held. Under CA 1985, s 370, unless the articles state otherwise, two members must be present in person for a meeting to be held. Table A, reg 41 states that where a meeting cannot be held it should be adjourned to the same day in the following week at the same time and place (or such time and place as the directors may determine) and if after half an hour at that adjourned meeting there is no quorum the members present shall form that quorum (even if it is a single person).

A meeting can be held in more than one room at the same time provided there are audiovisual links (*Byng v London Life Association* [1990] Ch 170).

18.6.4 Voting

This is normally done by show of hand with each person present having one vote, unless a poll is demanded in which case a member has a vote for each share he holds. CA 1985, s 372 gives the right of voting by proxy (ie appointing another person to attend and vote in his place). There are two forms of proxy:

(1) a general proxy appointing a person to vote as he thinks fit having regard to what is said at the meeting; and
(2) a special proxy where a person is required to vote for or against a particular resolution (frequently called 'a two-way proxy').

18.6.5 Minutes

Minutes should be taken of proceedings of general meetings. These are signed by the chairman of that meeting either at the end of the meeting or at the next meeting. Frequently articles state that when signed they are con-clusive evidence of what took place at the meeting, but if the articles do not so provide it does not form conclusive evidence. Members are entitled to inspect the minute book at the registered office without charge; if this is refused or not made available the court can compel inspection.

18.6.6 Resolutions

Ordinary resolution

Unless the company's articles or memorandum state otherwise a motion can be passed by ordinary resolution – by simple majority of votes of members entitled to vote and voting in person.

Extraordinary and special resolutions

These must be passed by at least a three-quarter majority of the voting members entitled to vote in person at a general meeting.

Elective resolution

This was introduced by CA 1989 for use in a private company. It can be used to:

(a) allot shares with respect to authority of directors;
(b) dispense with the laying of accounts and reports for a general meeting;
(c) dispense with the appointment of auditors;
(d) reduce a percentage required before sanctioning short notices of meet-ings or special resolution; and
(e) dispense with holding an AGM.

To pass an elective resolution needs at least 21 days' notice in writing. The notice needs to set out the terms of the resolution that needs to have unani-mous consent of those entitled to attend and vote at the meeting (ie one shareholder can veto it). Any election can be revoked by ordinary resolution and is automatically revoked if eg the company becomes a plc. An elective resolution, or one revoking an elective resolution, must be registered at Companies House in the same manner as a special resolution.

18.6.7 Filing of resolution

Companies House must be sent copies of the following:

(a) special resolutions;
(b) extraordinary resolutions;
(c) elective resolutions;
(d) written resolutions;

(e) other resolutions agreed by all members (which would otherwise not be effective unless passed as a special or extraordinary resolution);
(f) a resolution passed by all members of a class of shareholders;
(g) an ordinary resolution increasing share capital.

Copies of all such resolutions must be sent to the Registrar within 15 days after they are passed or made.

The following are examples of ordinary resolutions:

(a) removal of a director (CA 1985, s 303);
(b) appointment or removal of an auditor (ss 384 and 386);
(c) increase in share capital.

Extraordinary resolution examples are few but do occur in insolvency:

(a) in sanctioning the exercise of certain powers of liquidation and a member's voluntary winding-up under IA 1986, s 165;
(b) for the initiation of a creditor's voluntary winding-up when the company is insolvent under IA 1986, s 84.

A special resolution is required for more important situations:

(a) alterations of the objects clause in the memorandum of association (CA 1985, s 4);
(b) alterations of articles (s 9);
(c) reduction of capital (s 135).

18.6.8 Written resolutions

For some years the courts have accepted it is not necessary that the company should always hold a meeting, and that all shareholders having a right to attend and vote at general meetings and give notice in written form constitute a binding resolution on the company. CA 1989 now formally allows private companies to pass resolutions without holding any meeting provided all those who could have attended and voted sign such a resolution. This can only take effect when the last relevant member signs. A written resolution cannot be used to dismiss a director under CA 1985, s 303 or an auditor under s 391. CA 1985 requires that the written resolution should be sent to the auditor who can, within seven days, notify the company that it should be considered by a formal meeting. In this case a meeting needs to be held to consider the resolution. If the written resolution in effect transacted business that would otherwise be done by special, extraordinary or elective resolutions, it must be sent to the Registrar for filing.

18.6.9 The shareholder

There is no clear definition of what a share is in law, but it is clearly recognised as being an item of property that can be bought, sold, mortgaged and approved. Normally a shareholder's rights consist of three items:

(a) dividends;
(b) in the event of a winding-up, a return of capital (also in the event of an authorised reduction of capital); and
(c) voting and attendance at a meeting.

Unless the articles state to the contrary, all shares confer rights with respect to each of these characteristics.

Either a general meeting resolution or, alternatively, the company's articles must empower the directors to allot shares in the company (right to subscribe, convert etc: CA 1985, s 80). Such authority also needs to state the maximum number of shares etc that can be issued under that power and the power can only be that for up to five years. Thereafter further authorisation must be given by the general meeting.

CA 1985, ss 89–96 grant pre-emptive rights to the existing shareholders, ie giving them the ability to protect the proportion of total equity they may hold at any one stage (the provisions require that the company should not allot shares to any person unless it is first offered, on the same or more favourable terms, to each person who holds relevant shares a proportion of shares which as nearly as practicable equals his existing proportion in nominal value of his aggregate holdings of relevant shares). The difficulty with these pre-emption provisions is that they can be modified or extinguished, since under CA 1985, s 31 the need to offer pre-emptive rights can be excluded in the memorandum and articles of a private company (in each case or in respect of a particular allotment).

With reference to public companies, CA 1985, s 95 empowers directors who have general authority by the articles or through a resolution at general meeting to allot shares as if the pre-emption provisions do not apply.

18.6.10 Types of shares

In a company with more than one type ('class') of share there must be equal treatment for all holders of those shares. Frequently a company has more than one class of share with different rights with respect to

(a) dividends,
(b) return of capital,
(c) voting rights, and
(d) nominal values.

Each class of share has its own rights, referred to more generally at 18.6.14.

Preference shares

These, as the name implies, have a preferential right in comparison with ordinary shares. The preference is normally dividend or return of capital. The rights of the holder of such shares are normally set out in the articles of association. Where this share has priority with respect to dividend it normally takes two forms, either cumulative or non-cumulative. The former safeguards the shareholder in the event that a dividend is not declared since in effect it is added to the next time a dividend is paid. In the latter case, if a dividend is not paid the right is lost forever.

Ordinary shares

If there are special rights given to another class of share (eg preference shares), until these preferential rights have been satisfied claims by the ordinary shareholder are delayed. It is for this reason that ordinary shares are sometimes referred to as 'risk capital'. Sometimes such shares are themselves divided into different classes.

Employee shares

These are normally allotted to full-time employees under an established scheme (frequently taking advantage of tax benefits under approved option schemes). This may include present and past employees within the group and spouses etc. Sometimes a special class of share is created to cater for the rights of these holders, but more usually they form part of an established class with special rules regarding allotment, finance and repurchase. There is often also a trust document setting out various rights.

18.6.11 Debenture holder

This has sometimes been classified as a type of share, but does not really conform to the characteristics of shares discussed above. The relationship is really one of debtor/creditor (frequently coupled with some form of security against some or all of the company's assets). The distinction sometimes becomes blurred, eg where a debenture holder may be able to appoint a director, obtain a share of profit (this may be irrespective of whether a dividend is declared), to attend and vote at meetings and sometimes to have the right to convert his debentures into equity shares.

18.6.12 Bonus issue

This is frequently called a 'capitalisation' issue and sometimes a 'scrip' issue. If a cash rich company wants to increase the network of its share capital to its shareholders it may issue them with bonus shares. It is a method of capitalising reserves by issuing new-paid-up shares to its existing shareholders (eg if a company's book value was, say, £10m and the company had an issued share capital of 5m shares of £1 each the shares are effectively worth £2). If a company then decides to make a one-for-one paid-up bonus issue (which is paid out of the share premium account or any free reserves) the shareholder effectively receives for each of his shares (worth £2) two £1 shares each worth £1. The sole effect is that the company can reduce the amount held in its share premium account and replace it with issued shares. Sometimes a listed company achieves the same effect by allowing shareholders to exercise an option and take shares in place of dividends.

18.6.13 CREST

After nearly ten years of work, settlement of dealing in shares can now be dealt with on a computerised basis, rather than a lengthy paper system. The CREST system was inaugurated on 15 July 1996; it is run by CRESTCo, owned by 69 institutions from various parts of the securities industry.

The computer system in its simplest form works from a computer that receives instructions for the transfer of shares and acts upon those instructions. Companies and shareholders are therefore disassociates and communicate only by electronic media through the centralised computer. Companies will continue to keep registers of members and dividends and voting remains unchanged.

CREST is a voluntary system and an issuer can choose whether to use it – even when a security is dealt with by CREST a shareholder can choose whether to hold it in a certificated or uncertificated format.

18.6.14 Class rights

Three particular types of rights are identified:

(1) Those rights that clearly attach to a class of share (eg dividend and rights to participate in surplus assets on a winding-up).
(2) Where the articles purport to confer rights on individuals not as shareholders (eg a solicitor who becomes a member of a company cannot enforce a provision that he should be the company's solicitor). Rights of this sort are clearly not a class right since it could not be said to attach to a class of share.
(3) Rights that although not attached to any particular share are nonetheless conferred upon the beneficiary in the capacity of member or shareholder of the company (eg the right of the holder of 10% of the issued shares to nominate a director (*Cumbria Newspapers Group v Cumberland & Westmorland Herald Newspaper & Printing Co* [1987] Ch 1); it was felt that this constituted class rights).

Where class rights exist they can only be varied if:

(a) the holders of three quarters of the nominal value of the issued share of that particular class consent in writing; or
(b) a separate general meeting of holders of that class is held and an extraordinary resolution passed; or
(c) in either instance all relevant provision of a memorandum and articles of association or any agreement binding upon the shareholder is satisfied.

If variation provisions of class rights are incorporated in the memorandum and articles of association it is sufficient that variations are carried out in compliance with such provisions. If there is no such variation provision included and the rights are set out in the memorandum, it can only be varied if all members of a company agree to it (CA 1985, s 125(5)).

Strict compliance is necessary to the length of notice to be given for any such class meeting (s 369), for the holding of that meeting and voting (s 370) and the circulation of resolutions (ss 376 and 377).

Under s 127, a dissenting minority of not less than 15% of the issued shares of a class whose rights have been varied in the manner permitted may apply to the court to have any variation cancelled. Such application needs to be made within 21 days after consent was given or the resolution passed. When such an application has been made, the variation has no effect until it is confirmed by the court. If the court is satisfied the variation would unfairly prejudice the shareholder of the class represented by the applicant, it will cancel the variation, but if it does not disallow the variation the court must confirm it.

18.6.15 Members' rights and duties

The company in general meeting has the power to act in place of a board if for any reason the board cannot function. For example, if no quorum can be obtained for a meeting of directors or there is deadlock on the board it is well established that the company in general meeting may act instead. Similarly, if the directors are in breach of duty in some circumstances this can be authorised or ratified by the company in general meeting.

There is an obligation on directors in carrying out their duties to act for the benefit of a company as a whole, but if they are members themselves can they vote in support of their own personal interests? This has led the courts to develop the concept of 'fraud on the minority'. Fraud in this context does not mean deceit, but refers to an abuse of power; the victim of such an abuse does not need to be a 'minority of members' – it is enough if the injured party is a company. There is a large body of cases giving examples of circumstances that have amounted to 'fraud on the minority'. In practice it is likely that a new statutory provision incorporated in CA 1985, s 459 can now be used more frequently (see 18.6.16).

Fraud has taken three particular forms, as follows.

Resolution permitting expropriation of property belonging to company

In *Cook v Deeks* [1916] 1 AC 554, directors diverted to themselves contracts that should have been taken up by the company and passed a resolution ratifying and approving this. The court held that the directors should hold the benefit of such contracts on trust for the company and could not be permitted to make a present of it to themselves. In *Menier v*

Hooper's Telegraph Works (1874) 9 Ch App 350, those holding a controlling interest in a company compromised a pending action to their advantage (in a rival concern), which had the effect of gaining the company's assets to the exclusion of a minority. Again the court supported the minority's case.

Resolutions that relieve directors of liability

It is likely that if a director makes a full and frank disclosure to the company's members and the resolution can be shown to be bona fide in the company's interests, it is unlikely that a minority is now able successfully to bring an action for fraud. Further, under CA 1985, s 35, if directors have failed to observe limitations on their power in the memorandum of association they can now be released from any liability by a special resolution.

Resolution that expropriates members' shares

In *Brown v British Abrasive Wheel Co* [1919] 1 Ch 290, a public company was unable to buy out a 2% minority, so it proposed by special resolution to acquire the shares. Here it was felt that the resolution could not be said to benefit the company as a whole, only the majority. An injunction was granted.

Other similar cases, though, have not followed this particular case and it is clear the courts will look carefully at the circumstances of each particular action. Further discussion on this general principle is outside the scope of this book, but a full discussion of the principles involved is discussed at length by the Court of Appeal in the influential case of *Greenhalgh v Arderne Cinemas* [1946] 1 All ER 512 (especially the judgment of Evershed MR).

18.6.16 Other remedies available to shareholders

CA 1948, s 10 gave protection to minorities where there had been conduct of an 'oppressive nature'. The remedy granted in the circumstances was to petition for a winding-up order on the grounds that such a remedy was just and equitable. The new law is incorporated in CA 1985, s 459, which allows a member of a company to petition a court on the ground that the affairs are being carried out or conducted in a manner that is 'unfairly prejudicial to the interests of its members generally or some part of the members (including at least himself) or that any actual or proposed act or omission of the company (including any act or omission on its behalf) is or would be so prejudicial'.

Once the court is satisfied the petition is well founded, it makes 'such order as it thinks fit for giving relief in respect of the matter complained of'. The section goes on to give some examples:

(a) give instructions regulating the conduct of a company's affairs in future;

(b) give instructions prohibiting the company from doing an act complained of or requiring it to make an omission;

(c) authorise a company to bring in its name civil proceedings;

(d) require the purchase of shares of any member of a company either by the company itself or other members (if the company was to purchase its own shares under this head it would not need to comply with the special requirements for purchase of company's own shares: see 18.7.5).

Recent cases concerned with ascertaining whether there was unfairly prejudicial conduct have indicated there is no need to show either bad faith or a conscious intent to be unfair. It was also not essential to show a reduction in share value, although that could be helpful.

In *Re Noble* [1983] BCLC 273, the judge felt that the shareholder had contributed to his own exclusion from the company's management by showing no interest in its affairs. In *McGuinness v Bremmer* [1988] BCLC 673, it was held that a delay in holding a meeting was unfairly prejudicial even though it was within the terms of CA 1985.

Where a letter from the directors had deprived shareholders the chance of selling shares to the highest bidder or had reduced their chance of doing so this would also justify an action under s 459 (*Re a Company (No 008699 of 1985)* [1986] PCC 296).

Where a member had risked his capital in a small limited company, it was justifiable that he would expect to be retained as a director. When he was dismissed it was held to be an unfairly prejudicial treatment of his interests as a member (*Re a Company (No 00477 of 1986)* [1986] PCC 372), but where a director was causing friction and difficulties his dismissal was not deemed to be unfairly prejudicial (*Re a Company (No 002470 of 1988), ex p Nicholas* [1991] BCLC 480).

In addition to a remedy from the court there remains a broad power of the DTI to investigate where there is some cause of disquiet. This has led to a significant increase in publicity and the number of legal actions that have followed.

18.7 SHARE CAPITAL

The memorandum of association for a company with a share capital must declare the amount of share capital it proposes to be registered and the division of that share capital into shares of fixed amounts. For example, this provision in the memorandum may state that a company's share capital shall be £1,000 divided into 1,000 ordinary shares of £1 each. The level of authorised share capital tends to be a formality and its purpose really is to prescribe the maximum number of shares a company is able to issue without first increasing its authorised share capital. It also indicates the nominal value that it has chosen to place on shares into which the share capital is divided. To increase authorised share capital, the company merely has to pass an ordinary resolution in general meeting. This, together with Form 123, is filed with the Registrar within 15 days of the passing of the resolution.

18.7.1 Issued share capital

The general rule is that shares must not be issued at a discount of a nominal par value (eg £1 shares must be issued at not less than £1). Payment does not necessarily need to be in cash; it can be made in kind and the party's valuation of non-cash consideration is usually accepted as conclusive unless the inadequacy appears on the face of a transaction or there is bad faith. Private companies are, however, required under CA 1985, s 88 to complete a return of allotment form (Form 88) reporting upon how many shares are issued and for what consideration.

There are stricter rules regarding non-cash consideration for public companies. A plc may not accept an undertaking by a person that he will work or perform services for a company in payment for shares; there are other similar rules set out in CA 1985, s 99. Further, under s 103, a plc may not allot shares as fully or partly paid up unless certain circumstances exist:

(a) the consideration needs to be valued;

(b) a report needs to be prepared for the company during the six months preceding such allotment; and

(c) a copy should be sent of this report to the proposed 'purchaser'.

18.7.2 Reductions of capital

The general rule is that a company's capital cannot be reduced without a court order being sought. Under CA 1985, s 135, a company may, if authorised by its articles, reduce its share capital so long as it has obtained court confirmation under ss 136–138. The procedure is as follows:

(1) It must pass a special resolution to reduce its share capital either by reducing or extinguishing an amount of uncalled liability on shares or cancelling any paid-up share capital that it 'lost or unrepresented by available assets', or by paying off any paid-up share capital that is in excess of the company's wants. It needs to alter reference in its memorandum of association to its share capital etc.

(2) After passing such resolution the company needs to apply to court to confirm the resolution. The court will be concerned to ensure that all creditors have been notified and given an opportunity to object. Once it is satisfied that every existing creditor has consented or that his debt or claim has been discharged or secured, it will then make an order confirming the reduction on such terms as it sees fit.

(3) If any creditor has been overlooked or is ignorant of a reduction proceeding and the company goes into insolvent liquidation, the court on the application of that creditor may order members whose uncalled

liability has been reduced to contribute as if it had not been to the extent necessary to pay off the creditor.

In practice this procedure is rarely used since most companies use Companies Act procedures for the purchase of its own shares.

Just because the net asset may fall below a company's capital it does not necessarily indicate that it must cease trading. The usual effect is that the company is not able to pay dividends. In the case of a plc, CA 1985, s 142 states that if net assets become half or less of its called-up share capital it must within 28 days of such becoming known to a director convene an EGM for not later than 56 days thereafter (of it becoming known) to consider what steps should be taken to deal with this problem.

18.7.3 Acquisition of own shares

Traditionally even if there was an express provision in the memorandum it has been held that a company cannot purchase its own shares since this results in a reduction of share capital. This general rule has been eroded by practical necessity over a number of years and in CAs 1980 and 1981 it was formally codified. This is now incorporated in CA 1985, ss 143–181.

The general rule states that a company 'shall not acquire its own shares whether by purchase, subscription or otherwise'. Violation of it renders every officer and company liable to a fine and any purchase carried out is void. There are five exceptions:

(a) where fully paid shares are acquired otherwise than for valuable consideration, eg where the shares were given to the company and held by a nominee for it (see *Re Castiglione's Will Trusts, Hunter v MacKenzie* [1958] Ch 549);
(b) the redemption or purchase of shares in accordance with CA 1985, ss 159–181 (see below);
(c) the acquisition of shares on a formal reduction of capital that has been confirmed by the court (see 18.7.2);
(d) the purchase of shares as a result of an order of court;
(e) where shares have been forfeited due to non-payment.

18.7.4 Redeemable shares

Companies have been allowed to issue redeemable shares since CA 1929. Prior to CA 1981 only preference shares could be issued as redeemable, but under CA 1985, s 159 a company (if authorised by its articles) can issue shares of any class which can be redeemable or liable to be redeemed whether at the option of the company or of the shareholders. A company cannot just issue redeemable shares, but must also issue shares that are not redeemable. It also may not redeem shares until they have been fully paid by the holders of the redeemable shares.

Normally, redeemable shares can only be redeemed out of distributable profits or out of the proceeds of a fresh issue of shares made for that particular purpose. If any premium is payable this should also be made out of distributable profits.

Where shares are redeemed out of profits the amount by which the issued share capital is diminished should be transferred to a reserve called the 'capital redemption reserve' (or the proportion if partly paid out of proceeds).

18.7.5 Purchase of own shares

Up to CA 1981, a company had to issue preference shares to enable it to purchase its own shares (or required a court order).

A listed company cannot make a purchase of its own shares unless under CA 1985, s 166 it has first been authorised by the passing of an ordinary resolution. The resolution when passed needs to be filed at Companies House within 15 days. The authorisation may be a general one or limited to a class of shares and may be conditional if the company so wishes. It must, however, state the maximum number of shares to be acquired and the maximum and minimum prices and give a date on which it expires (not later than 18 months after passing the resolution). There are various other safeguards set out in ss 164–169.

The situation with private companies is more straightforward and is now contained in CA 1985, ss 171–177. If the company is authorised by articles it can make a payment for the redemption or purchase of shares otherwise than out of distributable profits or the proceeds of a fresh issue of shares. It must not though exceed 'the permissible capital payment' – the amount by which available profits exceed the proceeds of any fresh issue made for the purposes of redemption. If the principal capital payment is less than the nominal value of shares redeemed or purchased, the amount of the difference must be transferred to a capital redemption reserve; if it is more, the amount of issued share capital and undistributable reserves can be reduced by a sum not exceeding the extent of such excess.

'Available profits' is defined in CA 1985 as being those available for distribution under the dividend rules (see 18.8) and must be calculated in accordance with the usual accounting procedures used by the company's auditors. The following steps must be carried out:

(1) The directors need to make a statutory declaration in Company Form 173. This needs to contain the following information:
    (a) amount of permissible capital payment;
    (b) confirmation that the directors have enquired into the company's affairs and prospects;
    (c) it is their opinion that 'immediately following payment there will be no grounds on which the company could be found unable to pay its debt and . . . for the year following the company will be able to

continue to carry on business as a going concern and to pay its debts as they fall due throughout that year'.

(2) The declaration needs to have attached to it a report by the company's auditors confirming they have enquired into the company's business and the amount stated as permissible capital payment has been properly ascertained and they are not aware of anything in the directors' statement which is 'unreasonable'.

(3) The capital payment needs to be authorised by special resolution (or one in writing) and should be passed on all within the week immediately following the making of a statutory declaration; the payment of capital must be made no earlier than five nor more than seven weeks after the date of such resolution.

There are also similar statutory protections required for public companies, eg:

(a) a member of the company whose shares are to be redeemed or bought cannot vote (if he does the resolution will be ineffective if it would not have passed without his vote);

(b) the statutory declaration and auditor's report must be available for inspection by members at the meeting;

(c) within a week of a resolution a notice must be published in the *Gazette* and also an 'appropriate national newspaper' (unless it has notified all creditors in writing); the notice must give full details of a resolution and state the creditors may within five weeks of the resolution apply to court under CA 1985, s 176 for an order prohibiting payment;

(d) on or prior to the notice's publication, the company needs to send to the Registrar the completed Form 173 and also the auditor's report (copies must also be available at the company's registered office for inspection by any member or creditor).

A member (who has not consented or voted for the resolution) and creditor may not later than five weeks after the passing of the resolution apply under s 176 to the court for cancellation. The court has wide powers under s 177 to cancel, confirm or make such an order as it thinks fit for the purchase of dissenting members' shares.

18.7.6 Financial assistance by company to purchase own shares

CA 1948, s 54 became notoriously difficult to operate and the 1981 Act sought to clarify the position. The new provisions are found in CA 1985, ss 151–158. Generally, where a person is acquiring or proposing to acquire shares in a company it is unlawful for a company or any of its subsidiaries to give 'financial assistance directly or indirectly for the purpose of that acquisition before or at the same time as the acquisition takes place'. Financial assistance can also take the form of acquiring a liability that directly or indirectly gives financial assistance (eg gifts, loans, guarantees, waivers, indemnities etc). The definition of 'financial assistance' is very broadly worded and even if a form of financial assistance does not expressly fall within the provision it may nevertheless be unlawful if a company has no net assets or the consequence of assistance is to reduce its net assets. This section gives a particularly wide definition to the word 'liability' and seems to suggest that before a company can give any financial assistance to any person (whether or not a potential 'purchaser') it must assess his overall financial position before and after the acquisition and if afterwards it has deteriorated the company must refrain from any form of financial assistance which is not covered by one of the exceptions.

18.7.7 Exceptions

Section 153 sets out a number of exceptions and these include:

(a) bonus shares;
(b) lending money in the ordinary course of business;
(c) contributions to employee share schemes (public companies have an additional net asset test in this case); and
(d) lawful declaration of a dividend.

A complication exists under s 153 since it does not prohibit a company from giving financial assistance if:

(a) the company's principal purpose in giving that assistance is not for the purpose of acquisition of shares of a company or its holding company but is an incidental part of some larger purpose of a company; and
(b) the assistance is given in good faith in the company's interests.

The House of Lords considered this wording in *Brady v Brady* [1989] AC 755, which has narrowly interpreted this wording. Advice should always be sought if seeking to fall within this exception.

Special relaxation provisions apply to private companies under ss 155–158. The underlying principle is that financial assistance can only be given if a company has net assets that are not thereby reduced or to the extent they are reduced assistance is provided out of distributable profits (s 155). The relaxation can only be used by genuine independent private companies (ie those not members of a group where there is a plc). The procedure is as follows.

The relevant company giving financial assistance needs to make a statutory declaration similar in terms to the one referred to at 18.7.5 above for the purchase of shares. This declaration must identify to whom the assistance is to be given and must confirm in their opinion that immediately following such assistance there are no grounds on which a company can be found unable to pay its debt and that this will apply during the preceding 12-month period or if wound up in this period it could pay its debts in full.

The declaration must have attached to it an auditors' report stating in effect that they are not aware of anything unreasonable in the circumstances in the directors' opinion.

A special (or written) resolution needs to be passed by the company giving assistance (and in the case of a subsidiary giving financial assistance to a holding company the holding company also needs to pass a special resolution). The special resolutions must be passed on or within a week of the day on which the directors make the statutory declarations and are not effective unless the declaration and auditors' reports are available for inspection by the members at the meeting.

A copy of a statutory declaration (on Company Form G155(6)(a)) and the auditors' report needs to be delivered to the Registrar within 15 days of the declaration and must be accompanied by copies of a special resolution.

Financial assistance must not be given before the expiration of four weeks beginning the date upon which the resolution was passed (or if more than one on the date of the last such resolution). This enables any member not consenting or voting in favour of the resolution to apply to court to cancel the resolution under s 157. If an application is made, financial assistance must not be given until the court has given a ruling.

The financial assistance provided for must be given not later than eight weeks from the date of statutory declaration. If all members voted in favour of the resolution the assistance may be given immediately after the delivery to the Registrar of the statutory declaration and report, but must not be given after eight weeks from that date.

Application to court under s 157 needs to be made by holders of not less than 10% of the company's issued share capital or if a company has no share capital by 10% of the members. The court has similar rights as set out above in connection with purchase of such shares for determining the position.

18.8 DIVIDENDS

An underlying principle of company law is that the company subscribed money capital (ie issued share capital plus share premium) must be maintained. Dividends should not be paid out except from accumulated realised profits. CA 1985, ss 263–281 set out the position. A distribution covers any payment of the company's assets to members which is not a bonus share, a redemption or purchase of the company's own shares, an authorised reduction of share capital, or a distribution and winding-up. Distributions can only be made out of profits made available for that purpose.

The company's profits available for distribution can be summarised as being the accumulated realised profits (not already distributed or capitalised) less its accumulated realised losses not written off under the capital reduction provisions. This realised profits test applies to all companies. In addition, a plc is subject to a net assets test. Thus even if it has realised profit it can only make a distribution if its net assets are less than the aggregate of its called-up share capital and its undistributable reserves and also the proposed distribution will not reduce the amount of the assets to less than that aggregate.

'Net assets' for this purpose is defined as being the aggregate of its assets less the aggregate of its liabilities (uncalled share capital cannot be used as an asset for determination). Special rules regarding distribution apply to companies in various particular industries (eg investment and insurance companies).

A shareholder who receives a distribution he knows or has reasonable grounds to believe was paid in breach of the rules must repay any amount received by the company in addition to any other liability he may have. Further, a director who is knowingly a party to such payments is jointly and severally liable to the company to replace the amounts of dividends so paid with interest (ratification to bind the company is not possible). The director would, however, be entitled to be indemnified by each shareholder who received dividends knowing they have been paid out of capital to the extent such dividends have been received.

The procedure for declaring dividends is relatively straightforward. The articles normally provide for it. Table A, reg 102 states that a company is made by ordinary resolution to declare dividends, but no dividends should exceed the amount recommended by directors. It is at the AGM that a final dividend is normally declared, but an interim dividend can be paid at any date between AGMs. Table A, art 103 states that directors may pay interim dividends if it appears to them to be justified by the company profits available for distribution, but must act in good faith and not incur any liability to the holders of shares conferring preferred rights etc.

A company director needs to consider carefully a company's assets before recommending a dividend. A declaration of dividend creates a contract to pay a debt that would have become statute barred after six years from the date of declaration. Whether a company is able to forfeit the amount held after this period depends on its articles; eg Table A, reg 108 states that it must be unclaimed for 12 years before a dividend can be forfeited.

The articles usually also provide that dividends payable in cash can be sent by cheque through the post to a shareholder's registered address (or such other address as the shareholder may notify the company).

18.9 *ULTRA VIRES*

This used to be an area of some complication, but since CA 1989 was passed the position has been simplified. '*Ultra vires*' in relation to company law is used largely to explain a situation that arises when a company's officers or employees act beyond their legal power. There are two principal elements of this rule:

(a) where directors, officers or employees act outside their power, eg purport to bind the company when they have no authority to do so; and
(b) when the company acts beyond its objects, ie does an act to which the objects clause of its memorandum of association does not extend.

The effect of the provisions in CA 1985, ss 35A and 35B (as inserted by CA 1989, s 108(1)) is that an innocent third party is entitled to rely on the board of directors or a person authorised by the board and that the transaction agreed and enforceable in the normal way binds the company.

The difficulty that remains is that where eg a company is very small or a transaction is large, a third party may have no dealings with the board and may instead be dealing with an executive of the company or a junior employee. In these circumstances the third party is unlikely to know whether the transaction has actually been authorised by the board, so it would be necessary to look at the laws of agency as interpreted by *Royal British Bank v Turquand* (1856) 6 E&B 327. This case enunciated the rule that when a person conducts a company's affairs, in a manner that seems perfectly normal, the third parties dealing with them are not to be affected by any irregularities that may take place in the internal management of the company.

CA 1985, s 285 states that the acts of a director or manager are valid irrespective of any defect that may be discovered afterwards in that director or manager's appointment or qualification.

It is unlikely that a person dealing with a company is deemed to have notice of who the true directors are, but if that third party is actually aware of the potential *ultra vires* problem he would no longer be said to be acting in good faith and therefore probably not be able to rely on either s 35A or 35B or the common law position. The new legislation does not though protect a third party dealing with the company through an unauthorised officer. In this circumstance the company is only bound if an unauthorised officer acts within his actual or apparent authority or the company ratifies what he has done.

Case-law has recognised that where managerial powers have been delegated by the board to other officers, their acts can be regarded as binding the company.

18.10 AUDITORS

Every company other than a dormant one needs to appoint an auditor. The appointment is done at each general meeting at which the accounts and reports are laid and the appointment must be from the conclusion of that meeting until conclusion of the next such meeting (this would not be the case where a private company has elected to dispense with the laying of accounts). It is to the members of the company that the auditors' report is addressed. Normally an auditor continues to be reappointed until he wishes to retire or the directors wish to appoint someone different.

For private companies that have elected to dispense with the laying of accounts, the appointment of auditors needs to be dealt with within 28 days after the date copies of the accounts are sent to members. If a private company has, by elective resolution, dispensed with the obligation to appoint auditors annually, the auditors are deemed to have been appointed for each succeeding financial year until a resolution is passed ending this appointment. Many small companies are exempted from the requirement for an audit report, although does not affect the statutory requirements to prepare file accounts.

A company is totally exempt from the need to have an audit if it is a small company with a turnover of £350,000 or less (£90,000 or less if it is a charity) and its balance sheet total is not more than £1.4m. Exemptions to audit are *not* available to public companies, banks or insurance companies or those that constitute authorised pension funds under the Financial Services Act 1986 (to be replaced from a date to be announced by FMSA 2000). Companies also qualify as an exception from audit.

An auditor has a statutory right of access at all times to the company's books, accounts and vouchers and can require from the company's officers such explanation as he thinks necessary for the performance of his duties as auditor. In addition he is entitled to receive all notices and other communications concerning general meetings and to be heard with respect to business that concerns him.

A company can by ordinary resolution remove an auditor from office irrespective of any agreement it may have with him, but such a resolution requires special notice to be given to the company of a resolution and copies have to be given to the auditor and to the person to be appointed in his place. The auditor is also entitled to make written representation and may have rights to compensation.

Under CA 1985, s 392 an auditor may resign at any stage by depositing a notice in writing to that effect at the company's registered office. This must be accompanied by a statement providing the reasons why he wishes to resign and should contain any details he feels should be brought before the members or creditors. The company must then within 14 days send copies of it to any person entitled to be sent copies of the accounts. The company has the right if it wishes to apply to court, but must in these circumstances notify the auditor. Where no court application is made the auditor must send a copy of the statement to the Registrar within 21 days.

18.10.1 Auditor's negligence

Primarily, the directors are responsible for the published accounts, but an auditor can be shown to be negligent in certifying the accuracy. Auditors must display care and skill expected from such professionals and this has led to numerous well publicised cases. The House of Lords in *Caparo Industries v Dickman* [1990] 2 AC 605 established:

(a) the general responsibility for preparation of accounts, which should give a true and fair view of the company's position, rests on the directors' shoulders;

(b) the auditors provide independent reports to members on the proper preparation of the balance sheet and profit and loss account and whether these documents give a true and fair view (ie their role is investigative rather than creative);

(c) auditors have a duty to obtain information from directors and officers and failure to do so could amount to negligence.

This chapter largely concerns private companies, but a large number of provisions apply to public companies. In the case of a public company listed on The London Stock Exchange (whether fully listed or admitted to the AIM), such companies need to comply with the rule books and codes of the relevant market and the guidelines produced by recommendations made by the Cadbury, Greenbury and Hampel reports. Plcs are also expected to respect guidelines produced from time to time by the Association of British Insurers (ABI) and the National Association of Pension Funds (NAPF).

The rules produced by The Stock Exchange or under the auspices of one of the regulating authorities have quasi statutory force by the largest private companies and most plcs, since they are seen as being recommendations of good husbandry and reassure investors, shareholders and creditors. The various bodies concerned can provide full details of their recommendations, consideration of which it is outside the scope of this book. For a more detailed commentary see K Hatchick, *Alternative Investment Market Handbook* (2nd edn, 2000, Jordans).

18.11 SELECTION OF ADMINISTRATIVE DOCUMENTS TO BE FILED AT COMPANIES HOUSE

18.11.1 Formation

(1) Copy of memorandum and articles of association

(2) Form 10: Statement of first directors and secretary and intended situation of registered office

(3) Form 12: Statutory declaration of compliance with requirements on application for registration of a company (to be completed by the solicitors engaged in the company formation).

18.11.2 Capital

(1) Form 88(2): Return of allotment of shares for cash (to be filed within one month of making the allotment)

(2) Form 88(3): Return of allotment of shares for non-cash consideration (to be filed within one month of making the allotment)

(3) Form G122: notice of consolidation, division, subdivision, redemption, etc of share capital

(4) Form 123: Increase of share capital (filed within 15 days after passing resolution; resolution should also be filed)

(5) Reduction of share capital forms:
  (a) Form 155(6)A and B: Declaration in cases of financial assistance
  (b) Form 157: Application to court for cancellation
  (c) Form 169: Return to be made by a company purchasing its own shares.

18.11.3 Directors or secretary

(1) Form 288: Change of directors or secretary (notification to be given within 14 days; notification of interests and changes of interest in shares or debentures is to be made by the director to the company within five working days of the event)

(2) Form 288a: Appointment of a director or secretary

(3) Form 288b: Resignation of a director or secretary

(4) Form 288c: Change in particulars of a director or secretary.

18.11.4 Notice of accounting reference date

(1) Form G224: Names an accounting reference date to which statutory accounts are to be prepared. A company has nine months from the date of incorporation to file such a form

(2) Form G225(2): New account reference date given after the end of an accounting reference period by a parent or subsidiary undertaking or by a company subject to an administration order.

18.11.5 Annual return

Every company is required to deliver to the Registrar of Companies successive annual returns, each of which is made up to a date that is not later than the company's 'return date', ie:

(a) the anniversary of the company's incorporation; *or*

(b) if the last return lodged by the company was made up to a different date, the anniversary of that date.

The return must be lodged within 28 days after the date to which it is made up.

18.11.6 Registered office

Form 287: a company can change its registered office by filing this form.

18.11.7 Charges, mortgages and debentures

(1) Form 395: notification of particulars or charges created by a company (filed within 21 days after the date of their creation and the relative instrument creating the charge must also be produced)

(2) Form 397: particulars for the registration of a charge to secure a series of debentures

(3) Form 400: particulars of a mortgage or charge subject to which property has been acquired

(4) Form 403a: declaration of satisfaction when a charge has been wholly or partially redeemed

(5) Form 403b: declaration of satisfaction where the declaration relates to release of part of property or undertaking from the charge; or where the part of the property or undertaking charged no longer forms part of the company's property or undertaking.

18.11.8 Resolutions

Copies of the following types of resolution must be filed within 15 days of their being passed:

(1) Special/extraordinary
(2) Elective
(3) Ordinary:
    (a) authorising increase of capital
    (b) giving, varying, revoking or renewing an authority to allot
    (c) shares under s 80
    (d) revoking an elective resolution
(4) Resolution for winding up voluntarily under IA 1986, s 84(3).

19

HOW COMPANIES ARE TAXED

19.1 LIABILITY FOR CORPORATION TAX AND HOW 'PROFITS' ARE DEFINED

19.1.1 Liability for corporation tax
(TA 1988, ss 11 and 12; FA 1988, s 66)

Corporation tax is levied on the chargeable profits (see 19.1.2) of companies resident in the UK for tax purposes. A company is generally defined as any body corporate or unincorporated association, but does not include a partnership, a local authority or a local authority association.

Corporation tax also extends to non-resident companies carrying on a trade in the UK through a branch or agency. Such companies are chargeable to tax on any income attributable to the branch or agency and on any capital gains arising on the disposal of assets used in the UK for the purposes of the branch or agency.

A company incorporated in the UK is regarded as resident there regardless of where the directors exercise their management and control. However, some of the double taxation conventions negotiated with other countries override this in practice and treat a dual resident company as if it were not resident in the UK. A company incorporated overseas may still be regarded as UK-resident on the basis that its central management and control is exercised in this country. Questions relating to the residence status of a foreign incorporated company are usually determined by reference to the guidelines set out in SP1/90.

19.1.2 Computation of profits
(TA 1988, s 6)

A company's profits are made up of its income and chargeable gains. The computation of chargeable profits can be a very complex process because of the lengthy and detailed tax legislation and the extensive case-law. There are also a multitude of Revenue statements of practice, press releases and extra-statutory concessions which may need to be borne in mind when calculating profits upon which corporation tax is payable.

The general principles for computing taxable profits closely follow the rules for income tax and each different type of income is charged under the relevant schedule.

19.1.3 Capital allowances

Although depreciation is not regarded as an allowable expense for tax purposes, tax relief is given for expenditure on qualifying capital assets by means of capital allowances. Capital allowances in respect of a trade carried on by a company are regarded as trading expenses for the accounting period in which they arise. They are therefore taken into account in arriving at the chargeable profits or allowable loss for the accounting period.

Capital allowances on certain leasing activities are primarily deductible from the income arising from that source.

19.1.4 Interest and other annual payments
(TA 1988, s 338)

A company is liable to account to the Revenue for income tax on certain annual payments it makes. These payments (termed 'charges on income') are deductible from a company's profits in arriving at the amount assessable to corporation tax. The basic principle is that these charges on income are offset against the payer's total profits, not merely against a particular source of income with which the payment is connected. A payment counts as a charge on income only if the following conditions are met:

(1) It has been made out of the company's profits brought into charge to corporation tax.
(2) It is made under a liability incurred for a 'valuable and sufficient consideration' (or the payment is a covenanted donation to charity).
(3) The payment must not be one charged to capital or one not ultimately borne by the company.
(4) It must not be in the nature of a dividend or distribution made by the company.

Payments of interest are not treated as charges on income, but are dealt with under the FA 1996 loan relationship regime. Payment must actually be made in the accounting period for it to count as a charge for that period. Where there is a requirement to deduct and account for income tax on the payment, no deduction is allowed until this requirement is satisfied.

Where the total profits for an accounting period are insufficient to absorb charges on income, excess charges in respect of payments made wholly and exclusively for the purposes of the company's trade may be carried forward and utilised against the company's future trading income. Non-trade charges may not be carried forward in this manner and no further relief is available.

19.2 ACCOUNTING PERIODS, RATES AND PAYMENT OF TAX

19.2.1 Accounting periods for tax purposes
(TA 1988, s 12)

Companies pay corporation tax by reference to their accounting periods and the income included is assessed on an actual or accruals basis. Accounting periods may straddle two financial years (which for corporation tax purposes run from 1 April to 31 March). If this is the case, the chargeable profits are apportioned on a time basis for the purposes of determining the rate of tax to apply to the overall profit. An accounting period begins for corporation tax purposes when:

(1) the company comes within the charge to corporation tax either by becoming resident in the UK or acquiring its first source of income; or
(2) the company's previous accounting period ends without the company ceasing to be within the charge to corporation tax.

An accounting period normally runs for a maximum of 12 months from its commencement. In some instances, the accounts year end may vary slightly for commercial reasons (eg where accounts are made up to the last Friday of a specified month). Provided the variation is not more than four days from the 'mean' date it is normally acceptable to treat each period of account as if it were a 12-month accounting period ending on the mean date.

An accounting period runs for a period of less than 12 months if the company's own accounting date falls within the 12 months; it also ends if the company

(a) ceases to trade;
(b) begins or ceases to be resident in the UK; or
(c) ceases to be within the charge to corporation tax altogether.

Example of how accounting period is ascertained

A Ltd is formed on 1 January 2002. It remains completely dormant until 1 February 2002 when it starts to trade. The first set of accounts are made up for a period of 15 months ending on 31 March 2003.

In strictness, there is a first accounting period of one month from 1 January to 31 January 2002. There is then a 12-month accounting period for the year ending on 31 January 2003. There is then a two-month period from 1 February to 31 March 2003 when the company makes up its accounts.

19.2.2 How profits are apportioned

Where accounts are made up for a period of more than 12 months, the income is usually apportioned on a time basis to the relevant accounting period. Thus, in the above example, if A Ltd had profits of £140,000 in its accounts for the 15 months ending on 31 March 2003, these would normally be apportioned as follows:

Accounting period ended 31 January 2002	Nil
12 months ended 31 January 2003	£120,000
Period 1 February–31 March 2003	£20,000

However, where a more appropriate basis of apportionment is available, the inspector may apply that basis instead (*Marshall Hus & Partners v Bolton* [1981] STC 18).

19.2.3 **The corporation tax rates**
(TA 1988, s 6)

The rate of corporation tax is fixed for each financial year which, for these purposes, starts on 1 April. The rate of tax for the financial year 2002 (ie, 1 April 2002 to 31 March 2003) is 30% and the following table shows the full corporation tax rate applicable for previous financial years.

Financial year	Rate (%)	Financial year	Rate (%)
1997	31	2000	30
1998	31	2001	30
1999	30	2002	30

19.2.4 **Starting rate**

From April 2000, a new starting rate of corporation tax of 10% applies for profits of up to £10,000. From April 2002, the starting rate is reduced to nil. There is marginal rate relief at $^{19}\!/_{40}$ for profits from £10,001 to £50,000, giving an effective marginal rate of 22.5%.

19.2.5 **Small companies rates and associated companies**
(TA 1988, s 13)

A reduced rate of corporation tax (the 'small companies rate') applies to a company's profits where those profits do not exceed a maximum level. The rate of tax from April 2002 is 19% and the current profit level below which the small companies rate applies is £300,000. The following table shows the small companies rate and maximum profit level for earlier financial years:

Financial year	Rate (%)	Max profit level (£)
1997	21	300,000
1998	21	300,000
1999	20	300,000
2000	20	300,000
2001	20	300,000
2002	19	300,000

Where profits exceed the maximum profit limit for small companies rate purposes, an element of marginal relief is given for profits between £300,000 and £1,500,000. This relief operates on a tapered basis at $\frac{1}{40}$ by charging the profits to the full corporation tax rate but gives an element of credit for the reduced corporation tax rate which would have been applicable to the initial tranche of profit.

19.2.6 Restriction where there is associated company

The profit limits applicable to small companies relief are restricted, based upon the existence of any 'associated' companies which the company has during the accounting period concerned. A company is an associated company of another if they are under common control or one has control of the other. 'Control' for this purpose is defined as the ability to exercise direct or indirect control over the company's affairs and in particular:

(a) the possession or entitlement to acquire more than 50% of the share capital or voting rights in the company;
(b) entitlement to receive the greater part of income distributed among the shareholders;
(c) entitlement to receive the greater part of the company's assets in the event of a winding-up.

For example, if a company has one associated company, the small companies profit limits are divided by two, ie one plus the number of associated companies. However, an associated company which has not carried on any trade or business at any time during the accounting period concerned is disregarded. Where a company's accounting period straddles more than one financial year and the marginal relief limits for each financial year differ, the 12-month period is treated as separate accounting periods for the purpose of calculating marginal relief.

19.2.7 Payment of tax
(TA 1988, s 10)

The basic rule is that corporation tax is automatically due and payable nine months and one day after the end of an accounting period. However, 'large companies' must pay the tax by instalments. A large company is one the taxable profits of which are in excess of £1.5m pa, divided by one plus the number of active associated companies (if any) that it has. A company that would otherwise be classified (by reference to taxable profits) as a large company is not so treated if its tax liability for the accounting period concerned does not exceed £10,000 (or £5,000 for accounting periods ending prior to 1 July 2000). Furthermore, it is not classified as a large company if it was not a large company in the 12 months preceding the accounting period in question, and its profits for that accounting period do not exceed

£10m, divided by one plus the number of active associated companies (if any) that it had at the end of the preceding accounting period. These limits are reduced pro rata for accounting periods of less than 12 months.

Payment is required in four quarterly instalments. The first must be made 14 days after the first six months of the accounting period in question. Quarterly instalments for a company with an accounting period ended on 31 March 2003 would fall due on 14 October 2001, 14 January 2002, 14 April 2002 and 14 July 2002.

There are transitional rules whereby a company pays 60% of its liability due by instalments in year one, with the balance due nine months after the end of the accounting period. This increases to 72% in year two, 88% in year three and 100% in year four. Interest is charged on any unpaid tax and is an allowable deduction. Interest is paid to the company on overpayments. This interest is taxable.

19.3 COMPANIES' CAPITAL GAINS

19.3.1 Computation of gains

Capital gains made by companies are included in their chargeable profits and are subject to corporation tax. CGT therefore does not apply to companies, although chargeable gains and losses are computed in accordance with the detailed provisions of CGT (see Chap 5). The main differences between CGT and corporation tax on chargeable gains for companies are, first, that provisions which clearly apply only to individuals (eg annual exemption) have no application as far as companies are concerned, and secondly, that computations of chargeable gains are prepared on an accounting period basis rather than by income tax years of assessment. The total chargeable gains for an accounting period less a deduction for allowable losses are brought into charge to corporation tax in the same way as income.

Capital losses can only be offset against chargeable gains; they cannot be offset against trading or other income.

19.3.2 Roll-over relief
(TCGA 1992, ss 152–158 and 175)

Roll-over relief is available where the proceeds on disposal of a qualifying asset used in the company's trade are reinvested in further qualifying assets (see 6.3). It provides a deferral of the corporation tax that would otherwise be payable on the chargeable gain. Relief is normally dependent on the proceeds being fully reinvested in qualifying assets within a period of 12 months before and three years after the date of disposal.

Where the proceeds are only partly reinvested, a proportion of the gain is deferred or 'rolled over' and the balance (equivalent to the amount of proceeds not reinvested) is left in charge. The part of the gain that is deferred or rolled over is deducted from the new asset's base cost for capital gains purposes. This operates to increase the potential gain on the eventual sale of the new asset acquired, hence the term 'roll-over relief'.

Qualifying assets for this purpose are freehold and leasehold land and buildings, goodwill, ships, aircraft and hovercraft, fixed plant and machinery, satellite space stations and spacecraft, and certain agricultural quotas. Expenditure on an asset acquired from a group company (see 19.7) does not rank as qualifying expenditure for roll-over relief.

19.4 INTEREST AND OTHER CHARGES

19.4.1 Loan relationships
(FA 1996, ss 80–84)

The 'loan relationships' regime covers all loans made to a company (eg bank overdrafts, long-term finance etc) and all loans made by a company (eg holdings of gilt-edged securities and corporate bonds). Thus all interest paid or received by a company is brought into account on an accruals basis (so that account is taken of amounts paid in arrears and in advance – this is the normal basis of accounting for these items). Any profits or losses made on loan relationships are treated as income or expenditure on an accruals basis. Certain companies who deal in gilt-edged securities and bonds prepare their accounts on a 'mark to market' basis, and their profit or loss takes account of the market value of securities and bonds held at the beginning and at the end of the accounting period.

Profits or gains made by a company from loan relationships are taxable as trading income, to the extent that the company is a party to the loan relationships in the course of activities which are an integral part of its trade. Losses or deficits are treated as allowable deductions in arriving at the overall profit or loss of the trade.

In other cases where the loan relationship is for non-trade purposes a surplus is brought into tax under Schedule D Case III. If a deficit is suffered on loan relationships, loss relief can be claimed by:

(1) set-off against profits of the same period;
(2) group relief;
(3) carry-back against loan relationship profits of the preceding accounting period;
(4) carry-forward against all profits, other than trading profits of the next period;
(5) carry-forward against future profits from non-trading relationships.

19.4.2 Annual charges
(TA 1988, ss 338–339)

A company may make annual payments in respect of annuities, royalties, covenanted payments etc, which are available for offset as charges on income against the company's chargeable profits on a paid basis.

19.4.3 Income tax deduction at source

Companies must deduct and account to the Revenue for income tax on payments of charges on income. A return Form CT61 is required to be submitted on a quarterly basis detailing payments made and computing the income tax payable to the Revenue. In arriving at the income tax liability due, any income tax suffered on income received under deduction of tax may be offset. Where the income tax suffered on income received exceeds the income tax payable on annual charges, the surplus may be carried forward to the next quarterly return. If at the end of the accounting period it has not proved possible to obtain credit against income tax payable, credit may be obtained against the corporation tax liability for the accounting period (and if there is no or insufficient corporation tax liability to offset any income tax credit, a repayment may be obtained from the Revenue).

19.4.4 Connected parties
(FA 1996, s 87)

Special rules apply where the other party to a loan relationship is a connected company. For this purpose, companies are connected if they are under the same control, or one controls the other, either in the accounting period concerned or in the two preceding years. A person controls a company by owning the greater part of the shares, voting rights or other capital giving entitlement to more than one-half of the assets in a winding-up.

These rules also apply if the other party, or its 'associate', is or was at any time in the two preceding years a 'participator' in the accounting period. In general, participators are shareholders, and associates are relatives, partners or trustees of settlements where the relative or participator is or was the settlor.

If two parties are connected, then interest is only allowable on an accruals basis when paid to a connected party where the recipient is liable to UK corporation tax on the full amount of interest received, or the interest is paid within 12 months after the end of the accounting period concerned. Therefore, if the recipient is an individual, trustee, non-resident company or exempt body such as a charity, the interest must be paid by the anniversary of the accounting period if a deduction is to be obtained.

No tax relief is available for any bad debts on connected party loan relationships, and conversely no liability to tax arises when a debt is waived.

19.5 TAXATION OF COMPANY DISTRIBUTIONS
(TA 1988, ss 238–241)

Company distributions are defined as any dividends, and any other distribution out of the company's assets, paid by a company in respect of shares in the company. The main exception to this is that any repayment of share capital is not normally regarded as a distribution of assets.

The amount of the tax credit accompanying any dividend or other distribution from a UK company made after 5 April 1999 is 10% of the aggregate of the distribution and the tax credit.

For tax years 1999–2000 onwards there is no further tax to pay for shareholders liable at the lower or basic rate, and no increase in charge for individuals liable at the higher rate. The overall effect of this is that the double taxation effect, by charging corporation tax, as well as income tax, is mitigated to the same extent as it was prior to 6 April 1999.

The system prior to 6 April 1999 went further than simply mitigating any double charge to tax. If a person was exempt from tax, or if the tax credits exceeded their tax liability, the tax credit was paid over to them. The payment of tax credits to certain shareholders meant that profits paid out by a company could actually face a substantially lower effective tax charge than profits which were retained by the company and reinvested.

The first stage in the correction of this distortion removed the entitlement to payment for pension providers and other UK companies with effect from 2 July 1997. The second stage of the change extended the restrictions on payment and set-off of tax credits to nearly all shareholders with effect from 6 April 1999.

There is one class of shareholders who still obtain payment of tax credits. Under the terms of some of the UK's double taxation agreements with other countries, specific provision is made, within the agreements, that tax credits can be paid to shareholders resident in that other country. These agreements have effect as long as there is any tax credit made available to UK-resident shareholders, whether that credit is payable or not. The double taxation agreements normally only pay a proportion of the tax credit, so that the effect of the reduction of the rate of tax credit is that the amount of tax credit paid will be very small.

The rates of income tax charged on dividends and similar income are, from 1999–2000, 10%, while the rate charged on those who are liable at the higher rate is 32.5%.

'Schedule F ordinary rate' applies to certain income of dividends and other distributions of UK companies, and equivalent foreign income. Hitherto savings income has been the top slice of income for the purposes of computing the charge to tax. Under the new rules Schedule F and equivalent foreign income is treated as the top slice above other savings income. There is also a 'Schedule F upper rate' that would otherwise be chargeable at the income tax higher rate. The Schedule F upper rate is set at 32.5%.

Under the new rules, in 1999–2000 on a dividend of £80 there is a tax credit of £8.89. Taxpayers who are not liable at the higher rate are charged to tax at the new rate of 10%. So the tax due is £8.89 (ie the total of the dividend and associated tax credit of £88.89 at 10%). The liability is matched exactly by the tax credit, leaving no tax to pay. For a higher rate taxpayer receiving a dividend of £80 in 1999–2000 the tax due is £28.89 (ie the total of the dividend and tax credit of £88.89 at the new upper rate of 32.5%). The tax credit of £8.89 can be set against the tax liability, leaving the higher rate taxpayer with £20 to pay.

Prior to 6 April 1999, UK recipients of distributions were entitled to a tax credit. This aggregate amount was described as a 'franked payment' and, as far as individuals were concerned, represented the gross equivalent of the dividend received. This amount was taxable income, but the shareholder could set the tax credit against his tax liability on the 'grossed-up' amount.

Dividends received by a company from another UK company were termed 'franked investment income'. This income was regarded as having already borne tax and therefore did not form part of the chargeable profits of a company, and was not taxable.

Until 5 April 1999, there was a liability to account for advance corporation tax (ACT) where a company made a qualifying distribution to the shareholders. The ACT rate of was $^{20}\!/_{80}$ths of the dividend (ie 20% of the 'grossed-up amount). As its name suggests, ACT was treated as an advance payment of corporation tax and relief was obtained by deduction from the mainstream corporation tax liability payable on the profits of the accounting period in which the distribution was made.

The maximum relief against mainstream corporation tax for ACT paid on distributions made in an accounting period was equivalent to the ACT that would have been due on a franked payment equal to the profits chargeable to corporation tax for that accounting period. Where ACT exceeded this maximum amount, relief could be obtained in the following ways:

(1) carry-back to accounting periods beginning in the preceding six years;
(2) carry-forward and treated as ACT payable for the next accounting period, and so on, until utilised;
(3) surrender to a 51% subsidiary resident in the UK, and treated as ACT paid by that subsidiary.

Even after the abolition of ACT on 6 April 1999, surplus ACT remains available for relief. The company must calculate the 'shadow ACT' due on distributions after 6 April 1999.

Shadow ACT is not actually paid to the Revenue, but merely serves as a method to calculate the extent to which surplus ACT can be set against further corporation tax liabilities. The shadow ACT position has to be calculated for each accounting period ending after 5 April 1999 as if ACT were payable on the dividends, and the shadow ACT were then set against mainstream corporation tax as described above.

Shadow ACT is relieved in priority to actual surplus ACT brought forward from before 6 April 1999. If there is spare capacity (ie the 'shadow ACT' is less than the maximum that can be offset against mainstream corporation tax), surplus ACT from prior to 6 April 1999 can be utilised against the available balance of profits. Any unrelieved 'shadow ACT' is carried forward and again must be utilised before any actual unrelieved ACT.

If a company is of the opinion that it will never be able to access actual unrelieved surplus ACT, it need not carry out 'shadow ACT' calculations.

19.6 LOSSES

19.6.1 Losses arising in the accounting period
(TA 1988, s 393)

When a company makes a trading loss for an accounting period, it may claim that the loss arising may be set off against other profits including chargeable gains arising in that accounting period. A tax loss is computed in the same manner as taxable profits, but is restricted to losses arising from trading activities carried out on a commercial basis and with a view to the realisation of profit.

19.6.2 Different ways of claiming relief for losses

There are numerous ways in which a trading loss may be relieved for tax purposes apart from being offset against other profits arising in the accounting period. The loss can be carried forward and offset against trading profits arising in succeeding accounting periods. Losses can be carried forward indefinitely in this manner for as long as the company carries on the trading activity that generated the loss. A loss may also be carried back and offset against total profits for the three-year period that ended immediately before the period in which the losses were incurred (provided the company was carrying on the relevant trade in the earlier periods). Partial relief claims are not allowed, and relief is obtained for later years before earlier years. Relief must be obtained for the loss against other profits of the accounting period before computing the balance of the loss available for carry-back.

F(No2)A 1997, s 39 restricts the period against which a company may claim to carry back trading losses to set against the profits of an earlier period. These rules allow a loss to be carried back only to an accounting period falling wholly or partly within 12 months of the start of the period in which the loss was incurred. For accounting periods ending before 2 July 1997 the carry-back period is three years. Losses made in periods which straddle that date are apportioned, with the new and previous rules being applied appropriately.

However, the 12-month period remains at three years in two circumstances: first, where the trading loss arose in the 12 months immediately before the company ceased to trade (a terminal loss); secondly, where the losses result from the special allowances given for the costs of decommissioning North Sea oil and gas installations.

Example

A Ltd makes a trading loss of £1m in its accounting period ending on 31 August 2000. If A Ltd has other income of £150,000, it can choose between the following:

(1) Carry forward the £1m loss to be set against future profits from the same trade – in this case A Ltd will have taxable profits of £150,000 for 2001.

(2) Set part of the loss against profits of 2000 and carry forward the balance of £850,000 for eventual off-set against future profits from the same trade.

(3) Set off part of the loss against 2000 profits and carry back the £850,000 against profits of the year 1999. Any balance can then be carried forward for off-set against future trading profits.

19.6.3 Capital losses

Capital losses, like capital gains, are computed in accordance with CGT rules, although the net capital gains are subject to corporation tax as part of the overall chargeable profits for the accounting period. Capital losses may be offset against capital gains in computing net chargeable gains, and capital losses which cannot be relieved in this way may be carried forward and offset against gains arising in subsequent accounting periods without limit. The carry forward of capital losses is not dependent upon whether the company continues to carry on its trading activity, and may be offset against gains arising on trade and non-trade assets. There are, however, restrictions on pre-entry losses where a company joins a group of companies.

Certain capital losses realised by an investment company (see 19.8.5) may be set against the company's profits (see 6.2.4 on this).

19.6.4 Surplus charges on income
(TA 1988, s 393(9))

Relief for charges on income is generally given as the last of all reliefs other than group relief (see 19.7). It is given against the total profits of the period in which the charges are paid. If profits are insufficient to absorb the charges, the amount of charges paid wholly and exclusively for the purposes of the company's trading activities may be carried forward to the next accounting period and treated as a trading loss to be offset against future trading income of the company. Non-trade charges on income may not be so carried forward and therefore relief is lost.

19.6.5 Charges paid in company's final accounting period
(TA 1988, s 388)

A trading loss may be carried back and offset against profits of the previous year. A company's charges are normally ignored for this. However, charges paid wholly and exclusively for purposes of the trade are treated as trading expenses in computing a loss for the accounting period in which the company's trade comes to an end, and these can be carried back.

19.6.6 Changes in company ownership
(TA 1988, s 768)

Anti-avoidance provisions ensure that trading losses carried forward can only be utilised against future trading income from the trading activity that generated the losses. Losses may not be carried forward if:

(a) within any period of three years there is a change in the company's ownership preceded or followed by a major change in the nature or conduct of the trade carried on by the company; or

(b) there is a change in the company's ownership at any time after the scale of activities in a trade carried on by the company has become small or negligible, and before any considerable revival in the trade.

A 'change in ownership' means a change in more than 50% of the ownership of the ordinary share capital in the company. A 'major change in the nature or conduct of a trade' includes a major change in the type of property dealt in, or the services or facilities provided in the trade, or in customers, outlets or markets. The Revenue issued SP10/91 on some of the factors that will be relevant in determining whether there has been a major change in the nature or conduct of a trade or business.

19.7 GROUPS OF COMPANIES

19.7.1 Group relationships
(TA 1988, s 402)

There are special rules which apply to groups of UK-resident companies. For corporation tax purposes, a group relationship exists between two companies if one company holds not less than 75% of the ordinary share capital of the other, or if both companies are 75% subsidiaries of a third company. Note that these rules are quite different from those used for VAT and stamp duty purposes (see 7.12.3 and 8.3.8).

19.7.2 Use of losses
(TA 1988, ss 402–413)

Where one company in a group makes a loss for tax purposes, it may 'surrender' that loss as group relief to another member of the group for offset against that company's taxable profits for its 'corresponding accounting period'. For this purpose, losses available for surrender include charges on income to the extent that they exceed profits chargeable to corporation tax. For group relief purposes, the requirement for a 75% shareholding relationship is extended so that the company owning the shares must also be beneficially entitled to 75% or more of the profits available for distribution to equity shareholders, and of assets available for distribution in a winding-up.

Where the accounting periods of the surrendering and claimant companies do not coincide (ie 'correspond'), the amount of loss to be surrendered is restricted on a time basis reflecting the length of the accounting periods common to both companies.

19.7.3 Transfers of assets between group companies
(TCGA 1992, ss 171–174)

Where a trading activity is transferred from one group company to another, relief is available under TA 1988, s 343 to ensure that the company transferring the trade does not suffer balancing charges on assets which have qualified for capital allowances. The successor company takes over the assets at their written-down value for capital allowances purposes relating to those assets. It is also possible to elect under CAA 1990, s 158 that properties may be transferred between group companies at tax written-down value for the purpose of industrial buildings allowances. Where s 343 applies, any unrelieved trading losses pass across to the successor company.

Section 343 can also apply where a trade is transferred to another company which is under common control, even though it is not a member of a group.

19.7.4 Payment and interest
(TA 1988, s 247)

The payment of interest by one company to another normally requires the payer to account for income tax deducted from the interest payment. Where the two companies concerned are members of the same group for tax purposes, relief is available from these procedures by lodging, with the Revenue, an election under TA 1988, s 247. This is effective for as long as both companies remain UK-resident and one company beneficially owns more than 50% of the ordinary share capital of the other.

19.7.5 Capital gains and transfers within a group
(TCGA 1992, s 171)

For capital gains purposes, chargeable assets may be transferred from one group company to another without tax consequences. Such transfers are treated as if made at a 'no gain/no loss' price and the recipient company takes over the capital gains base cost of the asset from the transferor company.

Example of intragroup transfers

> X Ltd has two wholly owned subsidiaries Y Ltd and Z Ltd. X Ltd transfers a property to Y Ltd for its current market value. No chargeable gain arises to X Ltd on this transfer. This is ignored when working out any capital gain or loss when Y Ltd eventually disposes of the property. Y Ltd is treated as if it had acquired the property for *A*'s original cost plus indexation to date.
>
> The same treatment would apply if Y Ltd transferred an asset to Z Ltd, its 'sister company'.

19.7.6 Company leaving a group after an intragroup transfer
(TCGA 1992 ss 179 and 179A)

If a company leaves a group, and it owns an asset transferred to it from another member of the group within the previous six years, a tax charge may arise under TA 1988, s 179 as if the asset had been sold for its market value at the time of the intra-group transfer.

From 1 April 2002, if a company leaves a group all or part of the de-grouping charge can be reallocated to one or more other members of that group.

Example of tax charge on company leaving a group

> If X Ltd had transferred a property in 1997 to Y Ltd which was then worth £10m, and a gain of £2.5m would have arisen to X Ltd were it not for the relief under TCGA 1992, s 171 there would be a notional disposal for Y Ltd if it leaves the X Ltd group in 2002. Basically, Y Ltd would be regarded as having made a chargeable gain of £2.5m at the time that it leaves the group.
>
> Note that the charge is based on the value at the time of the intra-group transfer and the £2.5m gain would still arise even if the property were worth £25m (or £7m) in 2002 when Y Ltd leaves the group.

19.7.7 Roll-over relief and groups of companies

For the purposes of roll-over relief (see 19.3.2), all the trades carried on by group companies are treated as a single trade and therefore it is possible to roll over a gain made on qualifying assets by one member of a group against qualifying expenditure incurred by another within the appropriate timescale. Roll-over relief is generally available only for trading companies within a group although, concessionally, relief is also available for a property holding company where the properties concerned are used for trading purposes by the other members of the group.

From 1 April 2002, TCGA 1992, 179B and Sch 7AB introduce provisions that will enable the degrouping charge (see TCGA 1992, s 179) to be postponed by applying the existing business asset roll-over relief provisions in a modified form.

19.8 CLOSE AND INVESTMENT COMPANIES
(TA 1988, s 13A)

19.8.1 Close companies
(TA 1988, ss 414–415)

Companies which are under the control of five or fewer persons, or under the control of their directors, are known as 'close companies'. There are special provisions which are designed to ensure that such individuals cannot take undue advantage of corporation tax legislation by virtue of their positions of influence over a company's affairs.

A person controls a company if, in fact, he is able to exercise control directly or indirectly over its affairs by owning the greater part of its share capital, voting capital, or other capital giving entitlement to more than half the assets on a winding-up. Shareholders and certain loan creditors in a close company are known as participators. Rights held by certain 'associates' are attributed to participators in order to determine whether they have control.

An associate is defined for these purposes as any relative or partner of the individual concerned, or a trustee of a settlement where the individual (or a relative) was the settlor. A relative is defined as meaning spouse, parent, grandparent, child, grandchild, brother or sister. Where the individual is a beneficiary of a trust, the trustees may also be regarded as his associate.

19.8.2 Loans to participators
(TA 1988, s 419)

Where a close company makes a loan or advances any money to a participator, or to his associate, there is a liability to account for an amount of tax equal to the ACT liability which would arise if the loan or advance were treated as a dividend payment. The tax payable under s 419 is due within 14 days after the end of period for the purposes of interest on overdue tax. The company does not receive any relief even though the tax payable is calculated in the same way as ACT.

If the loan is repaid, the tax is repaid accordingly, but if the loan is wholly or partly written off or released, the borrower is treated as receiving, as part of his total income, an amount equal to the amount so written off, grossed up at the lower rate of income tax. While no basic or lower rate tax liability arises, there may be a further liability to higher rate tax.

19.8.3 Benefits to participators
(TA 1988, s 418)

Where benefits-in-kind are received by a participator (or his associates) in a close company and he is not taxed under Schedule E, the cost to the company of providing the benefit can be treated as a distribution (see 19.5).

19.8.4 Directors' defalcations

Cash diverted by a director and misappropriated by him may have to be written off as irrecoverable. Such losses are not allowable in computing the company's profits for tax purposes.

19.8.5 Investment companies
(TA 1988, ss 75 and 130)

An investment company is any company the business of which consists wholly or mainly of the making of investments and the principal part of its income arises as a result of that activity. The expenses of managing a UK-resident investment company are deductible in computing its total profits for corporation tax purposes. Where management expenses exceed the company's chargeable income and gains for an accounting period, the surplus may be carried forward and treated as management expenses incurred in the next succeeding accounting period, and may continue to be carried forward until relieved. Surplus management expenses may also be surrendered as group relief from one group company to another. Expenses brought forward from previous periods are not available for surrender as group relief. Unrelieved management expenses of an accounting period may also be set off against surplus franked investment income by a claim under TA 1988, s 242(2), for the purposes of claiming repayment of the tax credit attaching to it.

Relief for excess management expenses and charges brought forward is not available where there is a change in the ownership of the investment company and:

(a) after the change there is a significant increase in the amount of the capital of the investment company; or
(b) within the period of six years beginning three years before the change there is a major change in the nature of conduct of the business carried on by the company; or
(c) the change in the ownership occurs at any time after the scale of activities in the business carried on by an investment company has become small or negligible and before any considerable revival of the business.

19.8.6 Close investment-holding companies
(TA 1988, s 13A)

A close investment-holding company means a close company carrying on specific investment-holding activities. For this purpose, investment-holding activities do not include the carrying on of a trade on a commercial basis, property holding, or holding shares in companies carrying on either of these activities.

A close investment-holding company does not qualify for the small companies rate of corporation tax. In addition, the Revenue has power to restrict repayment of tax credit to shareholders receiving dividends from a close investment-holding company where it appears that arrangements have been made in relation to the distribution of profits, the main purpose of which is to enable the individual shareholder to obtain the tax repayment.

19.9 DOUBLE TAXATION RELIEF ON FOREIGN INCOME
(TA 1988, ss 788–806)

19.9.1 The main reliefs

A UK-resident company may claim a credit for foreign tax paid on income or capital gains arising from any overseas source. Credit is available against the corporation tax liability payable on the same income or gains. Relief may be due either under the provisions of a double taxation agreement between the UK and the overseas country concerned, or under the general rules for 'unilateral relief' as provided in TA 1988, s 790. Where credit is due under a double taxation agreement, the relevant agreement takes precedence over UK domestic legislation.

For most types of income and gains, the full amount is brought into charge for the purpose of computing the corporation tax liability on chargeable profits for the accounting period. Any overseas tax suffered is then offset by way of credit against the corporation tax liability. The amount of credit which is available is limited to the corporation tax liability on the source of income or gain which has suffered overseas tax. No relief is due for the excess foreign tax paid.

Where double tax relief would be lost (eg where no corporation tax liability arises for the accounting period), it is possible to obtain relief by treating the foreign tax as an expense in computing profits for the purposes of Schedule D Case I.

19.9.2 Double tax relief on dividends from foreign companies

In addition to relief for withholding or other foreign taxes suffered on payment of the dividend, relief may also be available for the foreign tax suffered on the profits out of which the dividend has been paid. This is known as 'underlying tax', for which relief is given automatically if the UK-recipient company controls, directly or indirectly, 10% or more of the voting share capital in the overseas company paying the dividend. The dividend taxable in the UK is grossed up at the rate of underlying tax applicable to the profits out of which the dividend has been paid. This, together with any withholding and other taxes suffered on payment of the dividend, can then be offset against the corporation tax liability arising on the grossed-up equivalent of the dividend received (subject to the restriction that underlying tax relief cannot exceed the corporation tax liability on the same income).

19.9.3 Unremittable income

Where an overseas source of income is taxable on an arising basis but it is not possible to remit the income due to government policy in the foreign country concerned, it is possible to make a claim to defer the corporation tax liability until such time as sufficient funds can be remitted to the UK to satisfy the liability. A claim under these circumstances may be made to the Revenue at any time within six years of the end of the accounting period in which the income arises.

19.10 CONTROLLED FOREIGN COMPANIES AND ANTI-AVOIDANCE LEGISLATION

19.10.1 Reason for legislation on controlled foreign companies

Legislation was introduced in 1984 with a view to countering the use of tax haven companies. The Government made it clear that the legislation was aimed at the following types of companies:

- 'Money box companies' (ie companies which simply accumulate investment income outside the UK);
- 'Dividend trap companies' (ie companies which are interposed between overseas subsidiaries and a UK parent company and which catch dividends before they reach the UK company and so prevent a UK tax liability);
- Offshore 'captive insurance companies';
- Sales, distribution or services companies which are used to enable profits to be put in a company which is subject to a low tax regime;
- Patent holding companies which enable royalty income to be sheltered from UK tax.

19.10.2 Definition of a CFC

A controlled foreign company (or 'CFC') is a foreign company which is controlled by UK resident persons. Basically, where a UK company has a material interest (ie normally a 10% or greater entitlement to share in the profits of a non-resident company) it may be taxed on a proportion of the overseas company's income. Note that the CFC's income is computed according to normal UK tax principles. It is also worth noting that capital gains realised by such a company are not subject to tax under the CFC legislation (but see 19.10.7).

There are various escape routes which enable a UK company to avoid any tax on its share of a CFC's profits. The escape routes involve the CFC meeting one of the following:

(a) the motive test;
(b) the exempt activity test;
(c) the acceptable distribution test; or
(d) the public quotation test.

19.10.3 Motive test

The legislation provides that no tax charge arises if the Board of Inland Revenue is satisfied that the motive for forming the CFC was not to avoid UK tax. In practice, the Revenue accepts that the test is satisfied if the CFC is resident in certain countries which impose tax at a rate comparable to UK tax. Companies which are resident in the following countries are therefore outside the legislation altogether.

A limited exclusion is available for certain other countries (eg Eire and The Netherlands).

Quite separately from the above, a company is not treated as a CFC if its tax liability in the country in which it is resident amounts to at least 75% of the tax which would be payable if it were a UK-resident company.

19.10.4 Exempt activity test

This test requires that the CFC should have premises in the country in which it is resident and use these premises for carrying on a business. Furthermore, the exempt activity test is satisfied only if it can be shown that the CFC's business is effectively managed in the country in which it is resident and that there are a number of employees based there who are adequate to deal with the volume of the company's business.

This test cannot be satisfied where the CFC's main business consists of any of the following:

(a) the holding of securities, patents or copyrights;
(b) dealing in securities;
(c) leasing;

(d) dealing in goods for delivery to or from the UK;
(e) dealing in goods for delivery to or from a connected or associated person.

19.10.5 Acceptable distribution test

This test applies in the following way. Provided the CFC distributes an acceptable proportion of its profits within 18 months of the end of its accounting period, no tax charge can arise for the UK companies who have a material interest.

Where the CFC is a trading company, the requirement is that the CFC should distribute at least 50% of its profits. Where the CFC is an investment company, the requirement is that it should distribute at least 90% of its income.

19.10.6 Public quotation test

There is also an exemption from the CFC legislation where the subsidiary is quoted on a recognised overseas stock exchange.

19.10.7 CGT legislation on non-resident companies

Shareholders in a non-resident company may be subjected to tax on its capital gains. The legislation is contained in TCGA 1992, s 13 and applies if the company would be a close company (see 19.8) if it were a UK-resident company. Basically, any shareholder who has at least 5% of the shares in the non-resident company may be charged tax as if a proportion of the non-resident company's capital gains belonged to him. The proportion is determined by the shareholder's entitlement in a winding-up.

Capital gains may not be apportioned in this way where any of the following conditions are satisfied:

(1) The non-resident company distributes the capital gain within two years, whether the distribution takes the form of a dividend, capital distribution or a payment by the liquidator etc on the winding-up of the company.
(2) The capital gain arises on the disposal of tangible property which is used (and used only) for the purposes of a trade carried on by the non-resident company wholly outside the UK.
(3) The capital gain accrues on the disposal of foreign currency where that currency represents money in use for the purposes of a trade carried on by the non-resident company wholly outside the UK.
(4) A non-resident company is charged tax on the capital gain because the gain arises on the disposal of an asset used by that non-resident company in connection with a UK branch or agency (see 19.1.1).

19.11 FOREX TRANSACTIONS

19.11.1 Outline of the basic rules

The main rules are set out in the flow-chart overleaf. These rules apply to:

(1) Qualifying assets such as currency, cash or bank accounts, and debts.
(2) Qualifying liabilities, including money debts, and provisions for trading liabilities.
(3) Currency contracts involving simultaneous exchange of two currencies such as currency swaps and forward and future contracts. It includes transactions where settlement is made by a single payment instead of actual exchange of currencies.

Forex gains and losses on the above items are taxed as income on an accruals basis. Generally the accounts figures are recognised for tax purposes so long as accounts are prepared using normal accountancy practice. Transactions entered into for trading purposes are taxed as trading profits or losses under Schedule D Case I. Where this is not the case (eg where the company is an investment company) they are taxed as Schedule D Case VI income. Special rules provide for Forex losses arising under Schedule D Case VI to be relieved first against other Case VI profits and then:

(a) offset against other current period profits;
(b) group relieved;
(c) carried back against other Forex or Financial Instruments (FI) profits of the three preceding years;
(d) carried forward against other Forex or FI profits;

The new rules apply from a company's 'commencement date' ie the first day of its accounting period which starts on or after the 'appointed day' which was 23 March 1995. Thus the commencement date of a company will be 1 January 1996.

There are important reliefs available in respect of the above rules.

19.11.2 Matching

An election is available to match Forex gains and losses on certain borrowings and currency contracts with Forex gains and losses on certain categories of non-qualifying assets such as holdings in shares or convertible securities in non-UK resident companies, and net investments in overseas branches where a local currency election has been made (see below). The election can also be made in respect of ships and aircrafts. The effect of the election is that Forex gains and losses on the matched borrowings or currency contracts are taxed on realisation of the asset as capital gains or losses, or in the case of net investments in overseas branches are left out of account altogether. The election is irrevocable and only applies to assets and

New Forex regime for companies

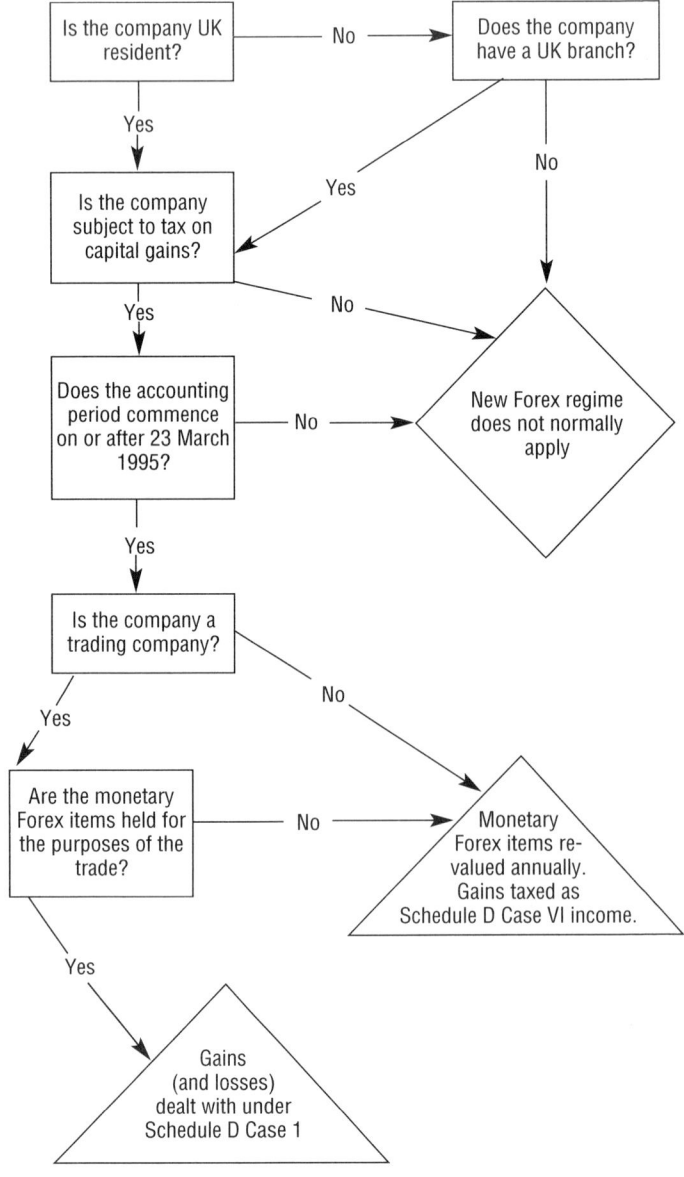

liabilities matched within the same company. This may be of concern to groups of companies where assets and liabilities are not economically matched within the same company.

19.11.3 Local currency election

Generally Forex gains and losses are calculated by reference to sterling but, in certain circumstances an election can be made to calculate *trading* profits by reference to other currencies. For example, a company which carries on an overseas trade may elect to calculate Forex gains and losses by reference to the relevant overseas currency. An overseas company with a UK trade may elect to use its 'home currency'. The effect of the election is that the trading profits or losses, including Forex gains and losses, are first computed in the local currency, then translated to sterling and adjusted for capital allowances.

19.11.4 Deferral relief

Relief is available to enable unrealised Forex gains on long-term capital assets and liabilities to be deferred for tax purposes. The amount available for deferral is the excess of the lower of either the *unrealised* Forex gains (net of losses) or *total* Forex gains (net of losses) in so far as they exceed 10% of taxable profits for the period.

A claim must be made for the relief and the excess is then carried forward and included in taxable profits of the next accounting period (when a further claim may be appropriate). Where the claimant is a member of a UK group, the amount available for deferral is calculated after taking into account gains and losses of other group companies.

19.11.5 Transitional rules

There are detailed rules dealing with the transition to the new regime. These cover the following aspects:

(1) Generally speaking qualifying assets and liabilities and currency contracts in existence at commencement date are revalued as if there had been a disposal at that date.

(2) No adjustment should be required for items previously included in trading profits unless the gains and losses were previously recognised on a realisation rather than an accruals basis.

(3) Pre-commencement gains and losses on qualifying assets previously dealt with under the capital gains regime are carried forward and offset against post commencement gains and losses. Similar rules apply to pre-commencement gains and losses on trading items previously dealt with on a realisation basis.

(4) There are special rules to deal with qualifying assets and liabilities previously outside the scope of tax, such as capital borrowings.

Pre-commencement Forex gains and losses arising on fixed debts are not recognised, but there is a 'kink' test to ensure that the post-commencement gain or loss does not exceed the overall gain or loss over the entire life of the debt. Fluctuating debts are 'grandfathered' for six years with the result that gains and losses are not recognised during that period. If the latter treatment is not favourable a claim can be made to include the fluctuating debts within the new regime.

(5) Currency contracts entered into prior to commencement date are dealt with by a combination of the Forex and the Financial Instrument rules (see 19.11.6). These are intended to ensure that gains and losses are not taxed twice under both the new rules and under pre-commencement capital gains rules.

As might be expected, there are anti avoidance rules which may deny or restrict relief for Forex losses, where the loss is the main benefit expected to accrue from the transaction, or the transactions involved are not on arm's length terms. There are also rules dealing with benefits obtained from changing the company's accounting reference date.

19.11.6 Financial Instruments

The new rules which were included in FA 1994, but came into operation on the same date as the Forex rules, apply to currency contracts (eg swaps), currency options, interest rate contracts and interest rate options. The payments and receipts covered include periodic payments, premiums, fees, costs and payments for variation, termination and compensation.

The overall objective, as with Forex, is to tax the instruments as income, using the accruals or 'market to market' basis. The treatment of trading and non-trading transactions is exactly the same as for Forex transactions and the same rules apply for relief of Schedule D Case VI losses (see above).

Once again there are special transitional rules for contracts in existence at commencement date. The new rules apply to currency contracts but there are provisions to ensure that gains and losses are not taxed twice, under both the new and the old regime. Interest rate contracts and options in existence at commencement date are not dealt with under the new regime until six years after commencement date, unless the company elects to include them within the new rules.

There are anti-avoidance rules which may deny or restrict relief where a transaction is not on arm's length terms or a benefit is given by a transfer of value to an associated person.

19.11.7 Tax planning for Forex and Financial Instrument transactions

It is vital to review the existing position of a company before the commencement date to establish what, if any, measures need to be taken before commencement date and to assess the impact of the new legislation after commencement date. In particular, the following need to be considered:

(1) Whether existing borrowing arrangements need to be restructured to take best advantage of reliefs available and the impact of the transitional rules.
(2) Whether it is beneficial to terminate existing contracts or arrangements before commencement date.
(3) Whether matching relief is beneficial and whether relevant assets and liabilities are located and structured in the best way.
(4) Whether intra-group arrangements are affected by the new rules.
(5) Whether there is potential exposure to anti-avoidance provisions.
(6) The time limits for making the various claims and elections available, which in some cases are within 92 or 183 days of the commencement date.

19.12 CLAIMS AND ELECTIONS

19.12.1 General

Throughout the Taxes Acts, there are various claims for relief from corporation tax which must be lodged with the Revenue and, in practice, are made to the Inspector of Taxes dealing with the company's affairs. Unless otherwise specified by legislation, claims must be made within six years of the end of the accounting period to which they relate. The most common claims and elections are set out below together with the time limit by which the claim or election must be made. The Inspector does not generally have discretion to accept claims made after the time limit has expired for a particular claim unless the legislation (or Revenue practice) allows otherwise.

Relief may be claimed within the normal six-year time limit against any over-assessment to corporation tax due to an error or mistake in, or an omission from, any return or statement. No relief is due where the information was not used to form the basis of an assessment, or where the assessment was made in accordance with practice generally prevailing at the time of issue. An error or mistake claim under TMA 1970, s 33 should be made to the Revenue.

For accounting periods ended after 30 September 1993, group relief and capital allowances claims are no longer made by submitting formal claims to the Inspector. Such claims are made in the pay and file return Form CT200, as are claims for repayment of tax deducted at source.

Table 19.1 – Time limit for claim submission reference

Claim	Period (years)	Legislation	Paragraph reference
Trading losses carried forward	6	TA 1988, s 393	19.6.2
Trading losses offset against other income of accounting period	2	TA 1988, s 393A	19.6.2
Trading losses carried back	2	TA 1988, s 393A	19.6.2
Terminal loss relief	2	TA 1988, s 393A	19.6.2
Disclaimer of capital allowances	2	CAA 1990, s 24	19.1.3
Group relief	2	TA 1988, s 412	19.7
Surrender of ACT	6	TA 1988, s 240	19.5
Carry back of ACT	2	TA 1988, s 239	19.5
Surplus franked investment income	2 (6 for charges on income and management expenses)	TA 1988, s 242	19.5
Roll-over relief	6	TCGA 1992, s 152	6.3 and 19.3.2
CGT rebasing at 31 March 1982	2 after the end of the accounting period in which the first relevant disposal is made after 31 March 1988	TCGA 1992, s 35	5.5 and 19.7.7

20

ENVIRONMENTAL TAXES

This chapter summarises a number of levies, all administered by the Commissioners of Customs & Excise, that can broadly be described as 'environmental taxes'. The following environmental taxes are currently in force:

(1) Landfill tax
(2) Climate change levy
(3) Aggregates levy.

A tax on the use of pesticides was proposed in 1999, but has not yet been enacted.

20.1 LANDFILL TAX (LFT)

20.1.1 Basic provisions

All references below regarding LFT are to FA 1996 unless otherwise stated.

LFT was introduced from 1 October 1996 to encourage businesses to produce less waste and to recycle. LFT is charged on waste disposed by way of landfill (s 40). The liability falls upon the site operator (s 41). In-house sites where waste producers dispose of their own waste are exempted.

LFT applies to both active and inert waste, although insignificant amounts of active waste may be ignored (s 63). Active waste is subject to the standard LFT rate; inert waste is subject to a lower rate. Landfill site operators can claim tax credit for contributions they make to approved environmental bodies (enrolled by Entrust) for spending on projects that benefit the environment.

20.1.2 Disposal of material as waste

LFT applies to all waste (unless it is specifically exempted) 'disposed of' at a landfill site. This means waste materials that are discarded or thrown away (s 64), even if the waste could be used or recycled later. Liability is not avoided if waste material is in fact used later (see *CC&E v Parkwood Landfill* (2001) L00011).

Where before such disposal waste is processed so that its chemical properties are changed (eg composting), the original producer's intention ceases to be relevant. It becomes the intention of the producer of the new material that counts. Crushing, bailing, sorting or screening waste does not change the chemical properties and it remains waste.

Note that soils brought in specifically for site engineering are not treated as waste.

Waste containing both active and inactive materials is taxed on the whole load at the standard rate. However, an incidental amount of active waste in a mainly inactive load is ignored, and the whole is then taxable at the lower rate.

Various activities, such as temporary removal of waste materials to another part of a site pending incineration, recycling or removal for use elsewhere are not treated as taxable disposals (s 62; Landfill Tax Regs (LTR) 1996, regs 38–40).

20.1.3 Landfill sites

Land can only be treated as a landfill site if it is licensed under the Environmental Protection Act 1990 and related or equivalent legislation (s 60) unless the land is exempt under the Waste Management Licensing Regs 1994. The 'operator' of a landfill site is the holder of licence concerned (s 67).

20.1.4 Charge to LFT

LFT is charged by weight (ss 42 and 68 and LTR 1996, regs 41–44). There are two rates.

(1) A lower rate of £2 per tonne on 'qualifying material'. This applies to inactive (or inert) wastes listed in the Landfill Tax (Qualifying Material) Order 1996, including foundry sand (see C&E News Release 48/96).

(2) The standard rate applies to all other taxable waste. This rate is being increased progressively since LFT was introduced, as follows:

	£
From 1 October 1996	7
From 1 April 1999	10
From 1 April 2000	11
From 1 April 2001	12
From 1 April 2002	13
From 1 April 2003	14
From 1 April 2004	15

20.1.5 Exemptions

Certain disposals are exempt from LFT. These are, in brief:

(1) Dredged waste, though not naturally occurring mineral material dredged from the sea for commercial purposes (s 43).
(2) Waste cleared from contaminated land as certified by the C&E Commissioners (s 43B; Landfill Tax (Contaminated Land) Order 1996) and carried out in a qualifying period (s 43A(1)-(3) and (7)).
(3) Disposal of inert waste listed in the Landfill Tax (Qualifying Material) Order 1996 used for required site restoration, other than capping (s 43C; Landfill Tax (Site Restoration and Quarries) Order 1996), as notified to the Commissioners.
(4) Naturally occurring material waste from mining operations (s 44).
(5) Qualifying material disposed of at a 'qualifying landfill site', eg a quarry with planning consent to be refilled (s 44A).
(6) Pet cemeteries licensed as landfill sites (s 45).

The Commissioners have further power to order what is and what is not a taxable disposal. This additional exemption is conferred by issuing a certificate (s 46).

20.1.6 Registration

The requirement to register is set out in s 47, and detailed requirements regarding registration are found in the LTR 1996, regs 4–6.

The registration rules apply to partnerships and unincorporated businesses (FA 1996 s 58(1) and (2); LTR 1996, reg 8). A company which carries on its business through a number of divisions may apply for the separate registration of those divisions (s 58(3)). Each division is given a separate LFT registration number and makes its own tax return, but the company remains legally responsible for the tax.

If a person who is not already registered for LFT acquires an LFT-registered business as a going concern, he must, within 30 days, notify his liability to be registered (using Form LT68). It may be possible to request the transfer of the existing tax registration number. This is not possible if the person selling or transferring the business continues to trade as a VAT- or LFT-registered business, or the acquirer is already registered (s 58(5) and (6); LTR 1996, reg 7).

Companies are eligible to be treated as members of an LFT group if one of them controls each of the others, or an individual, a company or a partnership controls all of them. One of the members of the group must act as the 'representative member', which must have an established place of business in the UK and must complete Forms LT1, LT1A and LT50. Form LT51 must also be completed and signed by all group members. If group treatment applies, any taxable business carried on by a group member is treated as carried on by the representative member. All group members are jointly and severally liable for any LFT due from the representative member. Unlike VAT group treatment, LFT must be accounted for and paid on all taxable disposals made between LFT group members. The detailed rules are set out in s 59.

20.1.7 Accounting for LFT

The accounting and record-keeping requirements for LFT are broadly similar to those for VAT.

A registered person must account for LFT by reference to accounting periods, make returns covering those periods and pay over LFT as and when required by the LTR 1996, regs 11 and 15 (s 49). The Commissioners have powers to raise assessments for unpaid LFT, and overpaid LFT credits (see below). The basic limit for assessment is two years after the end of the accounting period, or later if additional evidence comes to the Commissioners' knowledge. There is an overriding limit of three years after the end of the accounting period (s 50 and Sch 5, paras 11–14 and 33). In raising assessments there is no requirement for the Commissioners to use their best judgement, but they should take into account all relevant factors and use the best evidence available (see *Thomas v CC & E* (2001) L00012, unreported).

Account may be taken against LFT liabilities for various forms of credit (s 51; LTR 1996, regs 17–21). Relief for LFT on bad debts is given by s 52 and LTR 1996, regs 22–29. In addition, there is a scheme whereby credit is given for qualifying contributions made to approved bodies concerned with the environment for spending on an approved object. Up to 90% of qualifying contributions are available for credit, but the maximum claim in a contribution year is 20% of the liability for that year. The rules of the scheme are set out in s 53 and LTR 1996, regs 30–36.

The tax point is the time when the tax becomes due. LFT must be accounted for in the accounting period in which the tax point occurs. Two types of tax point can be used, dependent on the accounting system employed. Different tax points can be used for different customers or types of waste.

The disposal tax point is the date waste is disposed of to landfill. If an LFT invoice is issued within 14 days (longer at Customs' discretion) of the taxable disposal, the date of issue is the tax point unless a notification is made for the date of disposal to be the tax point (s 61; LTR 1996, regs 37).

20.1.8 Appeals

The review and appeals procedure is, broadly, similar to that applying under VAT (ss 54–57).

20.1.9 Information, powers, penalties, secondary liability etc

The various requirements relating to information, powers and penalties are broadly similar to those for VAT, and are set out in FA 1996, Sch 5 as follows:

- Requirements to provide information, keep records and produce and copy of documents (paras 1–3; LTR 1996, regs 12 and 16).

- Commissioners' powers in relation to entry and inspection, entry and search, arrest, access to recorded information, removal of documents and power to take samples (paras 4–10).
- Criminal offences and proceedings and penalties (paras 15–17).
- Civil penalty regime (paras 18–25).
- Interest and penalty interest (paras 26–30).
- Secondary liability on controllers of landfill sites (paras 48 and 49).
- Administrative matters (paras 31–47 and 50–60).

LFT is recoverable as a debt due to the Crown (Sch 5, para 11). The usual order of priority of debts applies in cases of insolvency (para 12).

LFT overpaid can be recovered (paras 14; LTR 1996, regs 13 and 14, with further details set out in regs 14A–14H). The Commissioners can raise assessments where there has been an excessive repayment of LFT. Regard should also be had to the provisions relating to 'unjust enrichment' (FA 1997, Sch 5).

20.2 CLIMATE CHANGE LEVY (CCL)

20.2.1 Basic provisions

The CCL rules by which CCL is charged on 'taxable supplies' are introduced by s 30. Any supply of a 'taxable commodity' is a taxable supply (FA 2000, Sch 6, para 2). The following are taxable commodities for CCL (para 3(1)):

- Electricity
- Natural gas as supplied by a gas utility
- Petroleum and hydrocarbon gas in a liquid state
- Coal and lignite
- Coke, and semi-coke of coal or lignite
- Petroleum coke.

Hydrocarbon oil and road fuel gas are not taxable commodities (Sch 6, para 3(2)). Likewise, waste within the Environmental Protection Act 1990, s 75 or Waste and Contaminated Land (Northern Ireland) Order 1997, art 2(2) is not a taxable commodity (FA 2000, Sch 6, para 3(2)). 'Waste' in this context includes any substance that constitutes a scrap material, or effluent or other unwanted surplus substance arising from any process. It also includes any substance or article that has to be disposed of because it is broken, worn out, contaminated or spoiled in some other way. It does not include substances defined as explosives under the Explosives Act 1875.

20.2.2 Taxable supplies

Under FA 2000, Sch 6, para 4, a supply of a taxable commodity is a taxable supply if CCL is chargeable thereon, ie:

(a) a supply of electricity (para 5);
(b) a supply of gas (para 6); or
(c) any other supply made in the course or furtherance of business, other than electricity, or gas in a gaseous state (para 7).

There is an exclusion for supplies for domestic or charity use (paras 8 and 9) and for supplies made before 1 April 2001 (para 10).

20.2.3 Exempt supplies

A number of categories of supplies are exempt. These are too numerous to list here, but see generally FA 2000, Sch 6, paras 11, 11A and 12–22, the Climate Change Levy (Electricity and Gas) Regs 2001, the Climate Change Levy (Combined Heat and Power Stations) Prescribed Efficiency Percentage Regs 2001, the Climate Change Levy (Use as Fuel) Regs 2001, and the Climate Change Levy (General) Regs (CCL(G)R) 2001.

20.2.4 Deemed supplies

There are also deemed supplies where there is a producer of a taxable commodity other than electricity, or is electricity produced from taxable commodities which does not supply the commodity to another person but consumes or burns it, himself, in the UK (FA 2000, Sch 6, para 23; CCL(G)R 2001, reg 52). Furthermore, there is a deemed supply if, due to a change of circumstances or of intentions, a supply that was not taxable becomes so (para 24).

In the above cases relief from CCL is only given if the consumer provides the supplier with a supplier certificate (CCL(G)R 2001, regs 34–45).

20.2.5 Time of supply

The general rules regarding time of supply and when CCL is charged and accounted for are based on those for VAT. Special rules apply to the supply of gas and electricity because they are 'continuous' supplies, based on the date of issue of a CCL Accounting Document. A detailed discussion of time of supply is beyond the scope of this book, but see generally FA 2000, Sch 6, paras 26–39.

20.2.6 Accounting for CCL

The accounting and record-keeping requirements for CCL are broadly similar to those applying for VAT. Again, a detailed discussion of this subject is beyond the scope of this book, but see FA 2000, Sch 6, paras 40–52 and the various CCL Regs for further information.

The detailed rules for dealing with credits for CCL and repayments are set out in FA 2000, Sch 6, paras 62–76 and CCL(G)R 2001, regs 10–25 and 29–32.

20.2.7 Registration

The requirement to register is set out in FA 2000, Sch 6, para 53. A person is liable to be registered if a taxable supply is made for which he is the person liable to account for CCL charged, and must notify the C&E Commissioners of that fact on Form CCL1. For detailed requirements regarding registration, see Sch 6, paras 54–60 and Climate Change Levy (Registration and Miscellaneous Provisions) Regs (CCL(RMP)R) 2001, regs 2–15.

The registration rules apply to partnerships and unincorporated bodies (FA 2000, Sch 6, para 117; CCL(RMP)R 2001, regs 2, 3, 12 and 13). In addition to Form CCL1, partners must complete Form CCL2.

See also Sch 6, para 118 and CCL(G)R 2001, regs 55 and 57 (person carrying on business of person who has died or become incapacitated); and Sch 6, para 120 and CCL(G)R 2001, regs 56 and 58 (persons who are bankrupt or in administration or liquidation and are represented by the trustee, administrator or liquidator).

Companies eligible to be treated as members of a CCL group are treated in much the same way as for LFT (see 20.1.6); the provisions are detailed in FA 2000, Sch 6, para 116 and CCL(RMP)R 2001, regs 5–10.

If a business is transferred as a going concern then, in certain circumstances it may be possible to transfer the existing registration (and liabilities) to the transferor. The detailed rules are set out in FA 2000, Sch 6, para 119 and CCL(G)R 2001, reg 59.

Non-resident taxpayers must appoint tax representatives to act for them for any purpose of the CCL rules (FA 2000, Sch 6, paras 114 and 115; and CCL(RMP)R 2001, regs 14–18).

20.2.8 Recovery and interest

The recovery and interest requirements for LFT are broadly similar to those applying for VAT.

CCL is recoverable as a debt due to the Crown (FA 2000, Sch 6, para 77). The Commissioners have power to raise assessments where there is default in payment of CCL due (paras 78–80). Such assessments carry ordinary interest for the period of default (paras 81 and 84). Penalty interest, at 10% above the ordinary rate of interest, compounded and with monthly rests (subject to reasonable excuse – para 86), is payable on unpaid CCL where no return is made, on unpaid ordinary interest (para 85). Ordinary and penalty interest are charged for the period of default where CCL is under-declared (para 84). Other provisions relating to assessments to interest are set out in paras 87–89.

There are also provisions relating to walking possession agreements (para .90).

20.2.9 Evasion, misdeclaration and neglect

Criminal offences, proceedings and penalties are dealt with in FA 2000, Sch 6, paras 92–97. Civil penalties in relation to evasion and secondary liability can also fall upon directors, etc for contributory conduct (paras 98 and 99). There are also civil penalties relating to misdeclaration and neglect (para 100) and for incorrect notification (para 101). There are, however, relieving provisions which allow for the correction of errors and, in particular for the correction of aggregate errors of less than £2,000 (CCL(G)R 2001, regs 26 and 29). The civil penalty regime, generally, is found in paras 103–113.

20.2.10 Appeals

The review and appeals procedure is, broadly, similar, to that applying under VAT (FA 2000, Sch 6, paras 121–123).

20.2.11 Information and evidence

The requirements to provide information, keep records and produce and copy documents are set out in FA 2000, Sch 6, paras 124–128. Paras 129–138 set out the Commissioners' powers in relation to entry and inspection, entry and search, arrest, access to recorded information, removal of documents and power to take samples.

20.2.12 Miscellaneous and supplementary matters

A variety of administrative matters are dealt with in FA 2000, Sch 6, paras 139 – 146 and interpretive matters are dealt with in FA 2000, Sch 6, paras 147 – 157.

20.3 AGGREGATES LEVY (AL)

20.3.1 Basic provisions

AL was introduced with effect from 1 April 2002 whenever taxable aggregate is subject to commercial exploitation. It is the person who subjects aggregate to commercial exploitation who is charged with AL. A single flat rate of AL is charged at £1.60 per tonne.

20.3.2 Meaning of aggregates

Generally, 'aggregate' means any rock, gravel or sand, and any substances for the time being incorporated into it or naturally occurring in it. Quantities of aggregate not liable to AL are those:

(a) that are exempt;
(b) previously used for construction purposes (whether before or after 1 April 2002);
(c) that are, or are derived from, any aggregate already subjected to AL;
(d) that on 1 April 2002 are on a site other than their originating site, or a site that must be registered under the name of a person who is the operator, or one of the operators, of that originating site.

20.3.3 Exempt aggregates

A detailed list of exempt aggregates is beyond the scope of this book. The exemptions are listed in FA 2001, ss 17(3)(b)-(f), 17(4) and 18(3).

Aggregate subjected to exploitation in the UK that has already been subjected to AL is exempt under s 17(5) if, and only if:

(a) there has been a previous occasion on which a charge to AL on that aggregate has arisen; and
(b) at least some of the AL previously charged on that aggregate is either AL in respect of which there is or was no entitlement to a tax credit, or AL in respect of which any entitlement to a tax credit is or was an entitlement to a tax credit of an amount less than the amount of AL charged on it.

Any credit the entitlement arising from any of the aggregate being used in a prescribed industrial or agricultural process, or (transitionally) used in Northern Ireland for a prescribed purpose, or is otherwise prescribed, is disregarded (s 17(6)).

Exempt processes of aggregates are listed in s 18.

20.3.4 Other matters regarding aggregates

Again, a detailed discussion of many of the terms used and defined in the commercial exploitation of aggregates is beyond the scope of this book. See further under FA 2001:

(1) Quantity of aggregate subjected to exploitation (s 19(1)).
(2) Sites (s 19(2)), originating sites (s 20(1) and (2)) and s 21).
(3) Definition of 'commercial exploitation' (s 19(3) and (3A)).
(4) Other uses of the site, ie agriculture and forestry (s 19(4)).
(5) Whether quantity of aggregate is 'in the UK' (s 19(5)).
(6) Agreement to supply quantity of aggregate (s 19(6)).s 19(7)).
(7) Responsibility for exploitation of aggregate (s 22(1)-(3)).
(8) Weight of aggregate (s 23).

20.3.5 Accounting for AL

In most cases it is the registered person who must account for AL on returns made for specified accounting periods (FA 2001, s 25). The detailed rules, including those dealing with credits and repayments are set out in FA 2001, ss 25 and 30–32, Sch 8 and Aggregates Levy (General) Regs (AL(G)R) 2002, regs 5–30. Security may be required for the protection of the revenue (s 26).

20.3.6 Registration

Details for registering for AL liability are provided in FA 2001, s 24(2) and Sch 4, para 1(1), (1A) and (1B)). The relevant forms are AL1 (application for registration) and AL1A (site details) (Aggregates Levy (Registration and Miscellaneous Provisions) Regs (AL(RMP)R) 2001, reg 2). Exemptions from registration are detailed in FA 2001, s 24(4) and reg 3 of the Regulations. The Commissioners register a person who is required to be registered for AL with effect from the time when the requirement arose (FA 2001, Sch 4, para 2(1)). Penalties apply where there is failure to comply with the registration and deregistration requirements (paras 1(2)-(4), 3 and 4(1); see also the AL(RMP)R 2001, reg 5).

The registration of persons carrying on a business in partnership, or an unincorporated body, may be in the name of the firm or body concerned; Form AL2 must be signed by all partners. The detailed rules are set out in FA 2001, s 36 and Sch 4, para 2(4) and AL(RMP)R 2001, regs 7–11.

A company that carries on its business through a number of divisions may apply for the separate registration of those divisions (FA 2001, Sch 4, para 2(3)). The company remains legally responsible for AL.

Companies eligible to be treated as members of an AL group are treated in much the same way as for LFT (see 20.1.6). For AL, the provisions are detailed in FA 2001 s 35, Sch 5, para 2(2) and Sch 9; AL(RMP)R 2001, regs 6–13. See also FA 2001, s 37 and AL(G)R 2002, regs 34–36 (persons who are bankrupt or in administration or liquidation represented by a trustee, administrator or liquidator) and FA 2001, s 38 (personal representatives treated as carrying on the deceased's business for a limited time).

If a person who is not already registered for AL acquires an AL-registered business as a going concern, he must within 30 days notify his liability to be registered. It may be possible to request the transfer of the existing tax registration number. This is not possible if the person selling or transferring the business continues to trade as a VAT- or AL-registered business, or the acquirer is already registered. The detailed rules are set out in FA 2001, s 39 and AL(G)R 2002, reg 37.

Non-resident taxpayers must appoint tax representatives to act for them for any purpose of the AL rules (FA 2001, ss 33 and 34; AL(RMP)R 2001, regs 14–18).

20.3.7 Recovery and interest

The recovery and interest requirements for AL are broadly similar to those applying for VAT.

AL is recoverable as a debt due to the Crown (FA 2001, Sch 5, para 1). The Commissioners have power to raise assessments where there is default in payment of AL due (paras 2–4). Such assessments carry ordinary interest and in some cases penalty interest for the period of default (paras 5–13). Penalty interest, at 10% above the ordinary rate of interest, compounded and with monthly rests (subject to reasonable excuse – para 10), is payable on unpaid AL and on unpaid ordinary interest (paras 5–9). There are also provisions relating to walking possession agreements (para 15) and to the extent of priority of AL in cases of insolvency (paras 17 and 18).

20.3.8 Evasion, misdeclaration and neglect

Criminal offences, proceedings and penalties are dealt with in FA 2001, Sch 6, paras 1–6. Civil penalties may arise in relation to evasion and liability can also fall upon directors, etc for contributory conduct (paras 7 and 8). There are also civil penalties relating to misdeclaration and neglect (para 9) and for incorrect notification (paras 9 and 9A). There are, however, relieving provisions that allow for the correction of errors and in particular for the correction of aggregate errors of less than £2,000 (AL(G)R 2002, reg 15). The civil penalty regime, generally, is found in FA 2001, Sch 10.

20.3.9 Appeals

The review and appeals procedure is, broadly, similar to that applying under VAT (FA 2001, ss 40–42).

20.3.10 Information and evidence

The requirements to provide information, keep records and produce and copy documents are set out in FA 2001, s 29 and Sch 7, paras 1–5. Paragraphs 6–13 set out the Commissioners' powers in relation to entry and inspection, entry and search, arrest, access to recorded information, removal of documents and power to take samples.

20.3.11 Miscellaneous and supplementary matters

A variety of administrative matters are dealt with in FA 2000, Sch 6, paras 139–146; interpretive matters are dealt with in paras 147–157.

21

TAX AND THE COMPANY PROPRIETOR

In this chapter, we look more closely at tax planning for proprietors; points to bear in mind when buying a company; the treatment of shareholder directors, and the way in which they are assessed on benefits received by them (and by members of their family); how cash may be extracted from the company in the most tax-efficient manner; and the tax implications of various transactions with the company.

21.1 BUYING A COMPANY

There are several points to bear in mind where an individual or group of individuals are purchasing an existing company.

21.1.1 Relief for financing costs

Where an individual finances such a purchase through a qualifying loan, the interest payable on the loan may qualify for income tax relief under TA 1988, s 360. The conditions that need to be satisfied for a loan to be a qualifying loan are:

(1) The loan must be a formal loan and not merely an overdraft.
(2) The loan must be used to acquire ordinary share capital of a close trading company or ordinary share capital of a company which is the holding company of a trading group or to make a loan to such a company.
(3) The borrower must have a material interest in the close company or be employed full-time by the company at the time the interest is paid.

As can be seen from the above, it is a requirement that the company is a close company and that the individual has a material interest. Close companies are defined at 19.8.1. An individual is regarded as having a material interest if he owns more than 5% of the ordinary share capital of the company. In fact, the 5% test applies to the individual taken together with his associates, so that if an individual held 4% personally and his wife owned 2%, he is deemed to have a material interest.

The requirement that the individual should have a material interest does not apply if he works full time for the company. Working full-time means that the individual works for the greater part of his time in the management of the company, and he must therefore be a director or a person who has a wider management role that affects the company as a whole and not merely a particular department within the company.

21.1.2 Income tax relief for capital losses

As explained at 6.2, a UK-resident individual who has subscribed for ordinary shares in an unquoted company may be able to claim income tax relief for any loss realised on a disposal of those shares. This contrasts with the normal position where capital losses may be set only against an individual's capital gains and not against income.

In practice, where an individual or group of individuals are considering purchasing an existing company, they may be better advised to form a new company, subscribe for shares in that company, and have that company ('Newco') purchase the target company. If Newco has no assets or activities apart from holding shares in the target company, there would be a very close relationship between the value of the shares in Newco and the shares in the target company. If the target company fails, the shares in Newco are likely to become worthless and this produces a capital loss. Because the individuals will have subscribed for shares in Newco, and the other requirements of TA 1988, s 574 are satisfied, it should be possible for them to secure income tax relief (see 6.2).

21.1.3 Checklist of tax points when buying a company

(1) Establish whether the target company has any assets which have been the subject of a roll-over relief claim (see 6.3).
(2) Ensure that none of the company's assets have been transferred to it from another group company within the past six years as this could give rise to a tax charge on the company under TCGA 1992, s 179 (see 19.7.6).
(3) Obtain appropriate indemnities against any tax payable for back years because of failure to make PAYE and NIC deductions, failure to make correct end of year returns, problems in operating the sub-contractors scheme, or interest or penalties payable under the VAT legislation following an investigation.
(4) Take professional advice if the vendors are to receive compensation for loss of office or *ex-gratia* payments, as these payments are not always an allowable deduction for corporation tax purposes.
(5) Take professional advice on possible ways to minimise stamp duty (see 8.3).

21.2 CORPORATION TAX PLANNING

21.2.1 Maximising benefit of small companies rate

There can be a tax penalty where there is more than one associated company (see 19.2.6) and the profits of the two companies are not equally distributed. Even though the combined amount may fall within the limits which would apply for small companies rate if there were only one company, the way in which the rules work can produce a situation where one company's profits suffer tax at the full 30% rate.

Example – Adverse tax position

A Ltd and its wholly owned subsidiary B Ltd may have total profits of £300,000 which would attract corporation tax at only 20% if they arose within A Ltd and A Ltd had no associated companies. If, however, A Ltd has profits of £250,000 and B Ltd has profits of £50,000, the total corporation tax payable is as set out below.

	£
A Ltd	
£250,000 at 30%	75,000
Less: Marginal relief $\frac{1}{40} \times$ (£750,000 – £250,000)	12,500
	62,500
B Ltd	
£50,000 at 20%	10,000
Total corporation tax payable	72,500

The effect in this particular case of having two companies rather than a single company is that the overall rate of tax is increased from 20% to 24.17%.

21.2.2 Commercial considerations

Tax is not, however, the only consideration. There may be good commercial reasons why the directors prefer to keep certain trading operations in a separate company. For example, this may be a way of ensuring that valuable properties within a holding company are not put at risk if those trading operations result in insolvency.

It is sometimes possible to have the small companies rate computed on the basis that a company is left out of account. In particular, if the company is a pure holding company which has no business operations apart from holding shares in one or more subsidiary companies, or holding property used by such subsidiary companies, and the holding company has no profits for corporation tax purposes, it may be left out of account.

21.2.3 Companies controlled by associates

The Revenue also operates a concession where there is no trading interdependence or connection between two companies and they are technically associated companies only because the individuals who control each of the companies are associated with one another (eg an individual controls company A and his brother controls company B). This is an area where professional advice should be taken in the light of the precise wording of ESC C9.

21.2.4 Avoiding disallowable expenditure

If it is decided to have a group of two (or more) companies or associated companies (ie companies which are under common control but are not parent/subsidiary), each company should avoid incurring expenditure which is partly or wholly for the benefit of the other company's trade. Such expenditure is not allowable in computing profits for corporation tax purposes.

21.2.5 Managing a group's tax affairs

It is most important that the necessary elections are in place to enable interest and other annual payments to be paid from one member of a group of companies to another, and for any dividends to be paid within the group, without the company which declares the dividend having to account for ACT. Bear in mind that such elections do not take effect automatically. The proper procedure is to submit the elections to the Inspector of Taxes. They then take effect after three months, or at some earlier date if the Inspector gives notice that he agrees that the elections are valid.

Care is needed if any shares in a subsidiary company are held by outside shareholders. Certain reliefs, and specifically group relief, are dependent on the holding company being entitled to at least 75% of the ordinary share capital of subsidiaries. Other tests also have to be satisfied and group relief might not be available if an outside investor holds preference shares or convertible loan stock, which might mean that less than 75% of the subsidiary's profits, or assets available for distribution on a winding-up, would belong to the holding company (see 19.7.2).

Group relief is available only to cover profits of a corresponding accounting period. It cannot be carried back and set against a subsidiary's profits for an earlier accounting period. There may also be problems where a subsidiary has a different accounting date from that of its parent company.

Some of the above points would be dealt with by the company's tax advisors, but a prudent director will wish to understand the statutory requirements and to ensure that the advisors are on top of the matter. The following checklist may be of assistance in this connection.

21.2.6 Checklist of tax considerations for group of companies

(1) The position should be monitored to identify cases where a subsidiary may have a loss for tax purposes. It may be possible to maximise tax relief if certain action is taken before the end of the accounting period in which the loss will arise. Professional advice is appropriate.

(2) The company's accountant should be consulted before a subsidiary company pays a dividend.

(3) A valid group dividend election should be in place. It is also worth checking with the group's accountant that it will not be more beneficial for the dividend to be paid outside the group election.

(4) Annual charges such as interest should actually be paid by the company's year end as no tax relief is otherwise available.

(5) Advice on the tax implications of any transfers of assets between group companies should be taken. Tax on a gain which is covered by TCGA 1992, s 171 may become payable if a subsidiary leaves the group within six years (see 19.7.6).

(6) The deadlines for submitting formal claims to the Revenue, explained below, should be kept in mind.

21.3 TREATMENT OF REMUNERATION FOR PAYE AND NICs PURPOSES

In essence, shareholder directors are treated in the same way as all other directors and P11D employees (see 13.3.1) in that their remuneration is taxed under Schedule E, and the same rules govern the tax treatment of benefits-in-kind. However, directors who are also significant shareholders in the company are likely to be affected more by certain aspects of the legislation.

21.3.1 How receipts basis applies to shareholder/directors

Where remuneration is deemed to have been received, PAYE must be accounted for and it is assessable as income in the year of receipt.

Special provisions define the date on which an individual is deemed to receive remuneration, as the earlier of:

(1) the date when payment is actually made; and
(2) the time when the employee becomes entitled to payment.

In the case of directors, the date can be earlier than above, in that payment is deemed to take place on the earliest of (1) and (2) and

(3) the date that income is credited to the director in the company's accounts or records; and
(4) the date when the accounts of income for a period is determined.

21.3.2 NIC problem areas

One major problem concerns directors' drawings. The DSS takes the view that where a director arranges for a personal liability to be settled by his company and charged to his drawings account, the payment constitutes earnings for national insurance purposes unless the drawings account is in credit. Thus, payments are treated as earnings for PAYE purposes if:

- payment has actually been made;
- the individual has become entitled to payment;
- the individual is a director;
- the money has been credited to the director's account with the company; and
- the amount of income for a period has been determined.

Example – Directors' drawings

> *A* has a drawings account with his company which is £60 in credit. The company pays a personal bill for *A* of £100 and debits his drawings account with £100, thus turning the credit balance into an overdrawn balance of £40.
>
> The Contributions Agency takes the view that £60 of the payment of the £100 bill is a repayment of a loan and attracts no national insurance liability, but the balance of £40 is a payment of earnings and the grossed up amount is subject to NICs.

21.3.3 Loans by the employer

Curiously, the Contributions Agency takes the view that if an individual arranges for a loan from his employer and the loan is used to settle a personal liability, there is no liability for NICs unless (and until) the loan is written off by the employer.

There is clearly a need for considerable care in dealing with any documentation and structuring the arrangements to minimise liability for NICs on payments of this nature. It should, though, be borne in mind that in general it is unlawful under the Companies Acts for an individual to be given a loan from a company of which he is a director.

21.4 BENEFITS-IN-KIND

21.4.1 Benefits for a director's family
(TA 1988, s 154(1))

A tax liability may arise even though the director or employee has not personally received a benefit-in-kind, as where a benefit is made available to a member of the director's or employee's household by reason of his employment. The Revenue may say that substantial benefits-in-kind enjoyed by a

director's family are provided by reason of that person's employment even though the recipient may also be a company employee. The Revenue is especially likely to argue this where a director's spouse is employed by the company and receives abnormally large benefits-in-kind for employees of that category.

21.4.2 Benefits for 'participators'
(TA 1988, s 418)

The legislation also covers a slightly different situation where shareholders receive benefits because they are shareholders, or associates of shareholders, rather than by reason of their own or anyone else's employment. The legislation applies only to *close* companies (see 19.8) and effectively treats the individual as if he or she had received a dividend equal to the value of the benefits as measured for Schedule E purposes (see 13.1). This is a complex subject on which professional advice should be taken.

21.5 DIVIDENDS

The usual reason why directors take cash from their company in the form of dividends rather than remuneration is because of the national insurance savings. Where the company is subject only to the small companies rate (see 21.2.1) there can be a considerable saving by taking dividends.

21.5.1 Possible drawbacks

There are other aspects to bear in mind, in particular the potential effect on the director's pension entitlement. Where the director is within ten years of normal retirement date, his final remuneration may have to be determined as the average of the three best consecutive years' remuneration. Taking dividends rather than remuneration may have the effect of reducing the individual's potential pension benefits.

21.6 LOANS TO THE COMPANY

21.6.1 Qualifying loans to the company

Where an individual borrows from a bank (other than under an overdraft) and then lends the money on to a company, he is entitled to income tax relief on the interest paid on the borrowings, provided:

- the company concerned is a close company (see 19.8) and the individual is a full-time director or employee involved in the management of the company's business; or

- the company concerned is a close company and the individual has a material interest in it (normally this means having more than 5% of the ordinary share capital); or
- the company is 'employee controlled' and the individual is a full-time employee.

However, the interest ceases to qualify for tax relief to the extent that the individual recovers capital from the company.

Example – Effect on a qualifying loan recovering capital

A has a 'material interest' in a close trading company. He borrows £150,000 from the bank and lends this money to the company for use in its business.

In year one, all the interest that A pays to the bank is an allowable deduction in arriving at taxable income. In year two, A withdraws £70,000 as part repayment of the loan to the company, but uses this for personal expenditure and does not clear his bank borrowings. From this point, only part of the interest payable on the bank loan qualifies for income tax relief.

21.6.2 Consequences if the company fails

Where an individual has raised a qualifying loan, his entitlement to income tax relief ceases when the company ceases to qualify. Thus, if an individual has borrowed £100,000 to finance his investment in a close trading company, and the company is wound up, the individual is not entitled to relief for any interest paid after the company ceased trading. If he is unable to repay the borrowings, he is left with having to pay interest which does not qualify for any tax relief whatsoever.

21.7 LOANS BY THE COMPANY

In the past, many companies operated on the basis that a director drew sums from the company in anticipation of bonuses or other remuneration which would be voted after the end of the company's year, perhaps when draft accounts were available. In many cases, the directors' account was effectively overdrawn at the year-end, and was restored to credit only because of the bonus approved after the year-end at the company's annual general meeting.

The Revenue normally maintains that bonuses should be treated as having been credited to a director only when the accounts were approved at the annual general meeting, and not at the company's year-end. It is generally difficult to resist such an argument since a director normally becomes entitled to a bonus only when the accounts are approved, and credit for such a bonus should not be applied retrospectively.

Where a director's loan account is effectively rewritten and is found to be overdrawn at the year-end, the Revenue is likely to seek to assess a benefit-in-kind as if the director had received a beneficial loan (see 13.6). Furthermore, there may be a liability on the company under the provisions of s 419 (see 19.8.2).

21.8 SALE AND PURCHASE OF ASSETS BY THE COMPANY

Where a director, or some other person connected with the company (eg a shareholder or an associate of a shareholder) purchases an asset from a company, there may be an income tax charge on any benefit enjoyed by the purchaser. Furthermore, the CGT legislation often requires the company's capital gain to be calculated if the company had disposed of the asset for its market value.

The company law aspects also need to be borne in mind. The purchase of an asset by a director normally needs to be disclosed in the company's annual accounts. It may be necessary, or at the very least advisable, for the transaction to be approved by the members of the company in a general meeting.

21.8.1 Purchase of assets by a director

Where a director (or other employee) acquires an asset from the company, the Revenue needs to be satisfied that the price paid is market value. If, in fact, the asset has been purchased at less than market value, the undervalue is treated as a benefit subject to income tax under Schedule E (see 13.1). Thus, if *A* acquires a property from A Ltd for £150,000, but its market value is £250,000, he is charged income tax on a benefit of £100,000. The fact that the buyer has purchased the property at an undervalue needs to be disclosed on form P11D (see 13.3).

In addition to the above, TCGA 1992, s18 means that the company is deemed to have disposed of the property at its market value (ie £250,000). Thus, the company may have a tax charge based on value which it has not in fact received.

In the past, the Revenue made matters worse in such cases by resisting a claim by the company for a tax deduction in arriving at its profits. It is thought that this is not correct, and in the above example A Ltd ought to be entitled to a deduction of £100,000 (ie matching the amount assessed on *A* under Schedule E). However, the position remains uncertain and problems of this type are best avoided if at all possible.

21.8.2 Purchase of assets by associate of a director

Much the same treatment applies if, in the above example, the property had been purchased by *A*'s wife rather than by *A* himself. In general, the Revenue normally argues that a benefit obtained by a close relative or other associate of a director should be treated for tax purposes as if the director had enjoyed the benefit himself.

21.8.3 Capital gains tax treatment of the director

Where a director etc has acquired property from his company, and has been assessed under Schedule E on any undervalue, he should be able to deduct the property's market value at the time of acquisition in arriving at any capital gain when he eventually disposes of the property.

Example – Value of capital gain

> If *B* acquires a property worth £300,000 from his employer but pays only £180,000, he is assessed to income tax under Schedule E on £120,000.
>
> If he later sells the property for £350,000, his capital gain is £50,000 (before indexation), and not £170,000.

21.8.4 Acquisition of property by shareholder

An individual who is a shareholder in a company, but not a director or employee, may likewise purchase an asset at an undervalue. In this situation, the amount of the undervalue is treated as if it were a distribution (ie dividend). The company needs to account for ACT on the amount of the undervalue. Moreover, the company's capital gain is once again calculated as if it had in fact received market value.

Thus, if *B* in the above example had been not a director or employee, but a shareholder, the company may need to account for ACT on £120,000, and *B* would be treated as receiving £150,000 income, less tax at the basic rate.

21.8.5 Sales of assets to the company

Much the same considerations arise where a director or shareholder sells an asset to the company. If the company is deemed to pay too much, the amount of the overvalue is treated as subject to income tax.

21.8.6 Capital gains aspects

Where an individual gives an asset to a company or sells it at an undervalue, he is often treated as if he were making a disposal to a connected person. This is particularly likely where the individual controls the company, or he and his associates, when taken together, have control. In such a case, TCGA 1992, s 18 normally requires the individual's capital gain to be calculated as if he had in fact received market value.

Where the asset concerned is a business asset, however, used either by the individual in a trade carried on by him personally, or by the company in the course of its own trade, it is possible for any gain to be avoided by the two parties making a joint election under TCGA 1992, s 165 (see 6.4 on holdover relief).

Example – Transfer for no consideration

> *C* is the main shareholder in C Ltd. He owns a warehouse used by C Ltd which is currently worth £1m. His original cost was £100,000, the 31 March 1982 value is £300,000, and indexation relief amounts to £200,000. If *C* transferred the warehouse to C Ltd for no consideration, and an election were made under TCGA 1992, s 165, *C* would not have a capital gain and C Ltd would be deemed to acquire the property for £500,000.

21.8.7 Sale at an undervalue

The treatment is slightly different in the case of a sale at an undervalue. The excess of the amount paid to the transferor over the unindexed cost must be deducted in arriving at the amount of the gain which is eligible for hold-over relief. Thus if, in the example above, *C* had sold the warehouse to C Ltd for £700,000, the hold-over relief would be limited to £300,000 and *C* would have a chargeable gain of £200,000.

21.8.8 Interaction with retirement relief

Retirement relief (not available after 2002–03) (see 6.6) is mandatory, ie it does not have to be claimed. Thus, if *C* met all the conditions in relation to the disposal described in the example in 21.8.6, his held-over gain would be reduced by £375,000 retirement relief and this relief is not then available to cover gains on any other disposal.

21.8.9 Company law aspects

The Companies Acts contain many provisions intended to ensure that directors do not obtain personal benefits at the expense of their companies. The main safeguards which apply where a director buys or sells an asset are contained in CA 1985, s 320. This provides that the company may not enter into an arrangement for the purchase/sale of a non-cash asset of the 'requisite value' unless the arrangement is approved in advance by the company's shareholders. The requisite value is 10% of the company's net asset value, subject to a minimum of £1,000 and a maximum of £50,000. The CA 1985 also requires such transactions to be disclosed in the company's accounts.

There are specific rules which preclude a public company from entering into a 'credit transaction' with a director or connected person. A credit transaction is defined as including the sale of an asset on terms such that payment may be deferred. Thus, where a public company sells an asset to a director or connected person, it is normally necessary for full payment to be made at the time the purchase contract is entered into.

21.9 SELF-ADMINISTERED PENSION SCHEMES

In the past, one way in which directors arranged their affairs to best advantage was by having the company form a small self-administered pension scheme, with the trustees making loan-backs to, or other investments in, the company. In effect, a company could secure tax relief while still having the use of the money paid into the pension scheme. There are now, however, special rules which apply to small self-administered schemes (ie schemes which have fewer than 12 members). The Revenue is particularly anxious to monitor such schemes to ensure that they operate as pension schemes and not for the benefit of the directors or as a way of financing the company.

The Revenue requires one of the trustees to be a pensioneer trustee, ie an individual or body widely involved in pension scheme work and having regular dealings with the Pension Schemes Office (PSO). A pensioneer trustee is required to give an undertaking to the PSO not to acquiesce in any arrangements which are considered by the PSO to be inconsistent with a scheme operating as a *bona fide* pension scheme.

21.9.1 Prohibition on loans to members

Loans to scheme members, or anyone connected with a scheme member, are specifically prohibited. Moreover, there are restrictions on the purchase of assets from scheme members.

21.9.2 Loans to the company (and associated companies)

There is a general rule that not more than 25% of the self-administered pension fund's assets may be lent to the company within the first two years. Moreover, the 25% rule applies to the value of the fund contributed by the company (and the members), and does not include any value arising from a transfer to the fund from another approved scheme. After the first two years, the proportion of the fund which may be invested in this way increases to 50%.

Even where a loan is not barred by the above rules, there are other conditions which need to be satisfied. The money must be lent to the company for business purposes and not for a purely speculative purpose such as the purchase of shares or other investments. Any such loan must be for a fixed period and on arm's length terms. The Revenue has indicated that in general such loans must carry a commercial rate of interest, equivalent to clearing bank base rate plus 3%.

21.9.3 Investment in shares in the company

This is another area where the Revenue has tightened the rules. The 50% ceiling referred to in 21.9.2 applies to both loans to the company and investment in its shares. Moreover, there is a separate limit in that a self-administered pension scheme's investment in any unlisted company must not exceed 30% of the shares in that company. Furthermore, where a self-administered scheme purchases shares from a director, it is normally advisable to seek prior clearance, and, indeed, for the directors to seek clearance under TA 1988, s 707 (see 21.14.1). This is very much an area where specialist advice is required.

21.9.4 Investment in property used by the company

The PSO is less difficult where a small self-administered pension scheme acquires a property to be used by the company. The relevant memorandum issued by the PSO states:

> it is not for the Inland Revenue to interfere in the way the trustees invest trust monies, except where tax avoidance is in point, or where the investment appears to be irreconcilable with the *bona fides* of the scheme having regard to its cash needs for purchasing annuities. Investment in land or buildings may be a good long term investment for a scheme where the members are many years from retirement, but even so, questions would need to be asked if the property purchased appeared to be an important part of the employers own commercial premises, and thus potentially difficult to realise.

One particular point is that the PSO does not normally sanction a situation where the trustees take on borrowings which exceed three times their equity in the property.

There is a specific prohibition for residential property. The PSO Memorandum states that investment in residential property is prohibited except where it is for occupation by:

- an unconnected employee as a condition of employment (eg a care-taker), or
- someone unrelated to the members of the scheme (or to a person connected with a scheme member) in connection with his or her occupation of business premises (eg the occupier of a shop with an integral flat above) where the business premises are held by the trustees as a scheme asset.

21.9.5 Overall limit on borrowings by trustees

The Revenue has a well established rule that any borrowings by the trustees should not exceed 45% of the market value of the investments held by the trustees plus three times the ordinary annual contributions payable by the employer.

21.10 RAISING BUSINESS FINANCE

A successful private business often finds itself prevented from fully developing and expanding its business because of lack of finance. There may be a limit on the finance available from a bank in the form of medium-term loans, and in practice many companies survive on overdraft. The proprietors may come to see that they can develop the company to its full potential only if they can attract new equity finance.

There are various commercial aspects to raising new business finance and directors should take professional advice from an accountant and a solicitor who are experienced in venture capital work. From a tax point of view there are three major aspects to bear in mind.

21.10.1 Enterprise Investment Scheme

It may be possible to raise new equity finance from business 'angels' by issuing shares which qualify under the Enterprise Investment Scheme (EIS). An individual who invests at least £500 under the EIS may secure 20% income tax relief, and may also be able to secure CGT deferral relief which may be worth another 40%.

The provisions governing EIS relief which apply to an investor are set out in the *Zurich Tax Handbook 2002–03* at 11.6. From the company's point of view, the following provisions are relevant in determining whether the company can issue shares which qualify under the EIS.

21.10.2 Qualifying companies

A qualifying company is defined as an unquoted company which either:

(1) exists wholly for the purpose of carrying on one or more qualifying trades 'or which so exists apart from purposes capable of having no significant effect (other than in relation to incidental matters) on the extent of the company's activities'; or
(2) has a business which consists wholly of:
   (a) the holding of shares or securities of, or the making of loans to, one or more qualifying subsidiaries of the company; or
   (b) both the holding of such shares or securities, or the making of such loans, and the carrying on of one or more qualifying trades.

There are also certain other conditions which need to be satisfied if it is to be a qualifying company:

(1) The company's share capital must not include any issued shares that are not fully paid up or would not be fully paid up if any undertaking to pay cash to the company at a future date were disregarded.
(2) The company must not control another company apart from a qualifying subsidiary, either on its own or together with a connected person,

and there must not be any arrangements in place under which the issuing company can acquire such control.

(3) The company must not be under the control of another company or under the control of another company and persons connected with it, and once again there must be no arrangements in place whereby such a company may acquire control of the issuing company.

21.10.3 Qualifying trades

There are certain trades which are excluded under TA 1988, s 297, ie the company's business must not consist to any substantial extent of any of the following:

(1) dealing in land, in commodities or futures or in shares, securities or other financial instruments;
(2) dealing in goods otherwise than in the course of any ordinary trade of wholesale or retail distribution;
(3) banking, insurance (but not insurance broking), money-lending, debt-factoring, hire-purchase financing, or other financial activities;
(4) oil extraction activities;
(5) leasing (except for certain short-term charters of ships) or receiving royalties or licence fees;
(6) providing legal or accountancy services;
(7) providing services or facilities for any trade carried on by another person (other than a parent company) which consists to any substantial extent of activities within any of paragraphs (1)-(6) above and in which a controlling interest is held by a person who also has a controlling interest in the trade carried on by the company.

21.10.4 Wholesale and retail distribution trades

Wholesale and retail distribution trades qualify only if they are 'ordinary' trades. Section 297(3) states that a trade does not qualify as an ordinary trade of wholesale or retail distribution if:

(1) it consists to a substantial extent of dealing in goods of a kind which are collected or held as an investment; and
(2) a substantial proportion of those goods are held by the company for a period which is significantly longer than the period for which a vendor would reasonably be expected to hold them while endeavouring to dispose of them at their market value.

The following are taken as indications that a company's trade is a qualifying trade:

(1) The goods are bought by the trader in quantitites larger than those in which he sells them.

(2) The goods are bought and sold by the trader in different markets.

(3) The company incurs expenses in the trade in addition to the costs of the goods, and employs staff who are not connected with it.

The following are 'indications' that the trade is not a qualifying trade:

(1) There are purchases or sales from or to persons who are connected with the trader.

(2) Purchases are matched with forward sales or vice versa.

(3) The goods are held by the trader for longer than is normal for goods of the kind in question.

(4) The trade is carried on otherwise than at a place or places commonly used for the type of trade.

(5) The trader does not take physical possession of the goods.

The above are only indications and are not conclusive that a company's trade is or is not a qualifying trade, but it will be difficult to persuade the Revenue that a trade qualifies if there are a number of indications to the contrary.

21.10.5 Qualifying subsidiaries

A qualifying subsidiary is one in which the issuing company or one of its subsidiaries holds at least 90% of the share capital (TA 1988, s 308(2)). In addition, the company must meet one of the following tests:

- it must be carrying on a qualifying trade; or
- it must exist to hold and manage a property used by the parent company, or by a fellow 90% subsidiary, for the purposes of a qualifying trade; or
- it must be dormant.

21.10.6 Three-year period

EIS relief is withdrawn if a company, having initially satisfied the requirements set out in 21.10.2–21.10.5, ceases to satisfy them within three years.

21.10.7 Individuals excluded from EIS relief

A qualifying investor is defined as an individual who is not 'connected with the company'. This means that he must not own more than 30% of:

- the issued ordinary share capital of the company, or any of its subsidiaries;
- the loan capital and issued share capital of the company or any subsidiary; or
- the voting power in the company or any subsidiary; or
- any loan capital in a subsidiary of the company.

An individual is also connected with the issuing company if he directly or indirectly possesses, or is entitled to acquire such rights as would, in the event of the winding-up of the company (or any of its subsidiaries), mean that he is entitled to receive more than 30% of the assets available for distribution to equity holders of the company.

Rights of 'associates' need to be taken into account. For these purposes, an 'associate' means partner, spouse, parent, grandparent, great grandparent, child, grandchild, great grandchild and certain family trusts.

21.10.8 Individual must not be previously 'connected with the company'

An individual is also deemed to be connected with the company if he is:

- a paid director of the issuing company or any of its subsidiaries;
- an employee of the issuing company or any of its subsidiaries;
- a partner of the issuing company or any subsidiary; or
- an associate of someone who is a director or an employee or a partner of the issuing company, or any of its subsidiaries.

An individual is disqualified if he falls into any of the above categories during the two years prior to the date that the EIS shares are issued. Furthermore, an individual does not qualify for EIS relief if he is connected with the issuing company at the time the shares are issued, unless he is a business angel who qualified for EIS relief on his original investment and is now acquiring additional shares and he is connected only because he is a paid director.

21.10.9 Five-year period

EIS relief is withdrawn if the individual breaches the 30% limit within a period of five years.

21.10.10 Purchase of own shares/redemption of shares

There may be a partial withdrawal of EIS relief if the company (or a subsidiary) purchases its own shares or redeems shares within the five-year period. See further *Zurich Tax Handbook 2002–03* at 11.6.12.

21.10.11 Approved investment funds

As well as seeking investment from business angels and other private individuals, it is possible for a company to issue shares to an approved EIS fund which operates in a similar way to a unit trust. From the point of view of the directors of the company which issues the shares, the same requirements apply as for shares issued to individuals direct.

21.10.12 Venture capital trusts

It may also be possible for an unquoted company to attract new equity finance from a venture capital trust (see *Zurich Tax Handbook 2002–03* at 11.7). The following parameters apply in determining whether a venture capital trust may invest in a company.

(1) The company must exist wholly for the purpose of carrying on wholly or mainly in the UK one or more qualifying trades (defined as for the EIS).

(2) Venture capital trusts may count annual investments of up to £1m in total in any one qualifying unquoted company as a qualifying holding.

(3) The gross asset of the unquoted company must not exceed £10m, immediately prior to the investment by the venture capital trust.

21.10.13 The Alternative Investment Market

The Alternative Investment Market (AIM), provides smaller companies, including companies which have only recently been set up, with a way of raising new equity finance. AIM shares qualify for the following reliefs:

- income tax relief under the EIS;
- CGT reinvestment relief;
- income tax relief for capital losses realised by an individual who sub-scribed for shares in an AIM company;
- CGT hold-over relief for gifts of shares;
- IHT business relief, provided the shares have been held for at least two years.

In addition, the Revenue has announced that venture capital trusts are permitted to invest in AIM securities.

In practice the availability of CGT reinvestment relief and IHT business relief are the most important tax incentives for investors. EIS relief is not available for investment in *all* AIM companies, only those carrying on qualifying trades and having no quoted securities. Thus, shares dealt in on AIM do not qualify for EIS relief if the company has preference shares or loan stock which are quoted on the main market. Where the necessary conditions are satisfied, however, investment in an AIM investment could qualify for 60% tax relief.

21.11 PURCHASE OF OWN SHARES

Since 1980, it has been possible for a company to purchase its own shares. The tax legislation contains specific provisions covering such transactions.

The general rule is that any amount paid by the company in excess of the amounts originally paid for the issue of the shares may be treated as a distribution (TA 1988, s 209). Where certain strict conditions are satisfied, however, it is possible for an unquoted trading company to buy in its own shares without the payment being treated as a distribution.

21.11.1 Conditions for capital treatment to apply

The following conditions need to be satisfied if a purchase by a company of its own shares is not to be treated as giving rise to a distribution:

(1) The company must be an unquoted company.
(2) It must be a trading company or the holding company of a trading group.
(3) The vendor shareholder must be resident and ordinarily resident in the UK.
(4) The vendor must have owned his shares for at least five years.
(5) The vendor's interest in the company must be substantially reduced.
(6) The company must purchase its own shares to benefit its trade.

21.11.2 Definition of unquoted company

For these purposes, a company is regarded as a quoted company if any of its securities are quoted on the Stock Exchange. On the other hand, the fact that shares are dealt in on the USM or the AIM does not make the company a quoted company.

21.11.3 Ownership of shares for five years

The legislation provides that the vendor shareholder must have owned his shares throughout a period of five years ending with the purchase. There are exceptions to cover situations where an individual acquired the shares by a gift from his or her spouse, or inherited them.

Section 220(6) of TA 1988 provides that an individual may count any period of ownership by his spouse towards the five-year period, provided they are not separated or divorced at the time the company purchases its own shares.

Section 220(7) reduces the five-year period to three years in cases where the shareholder inherited his shares. Moreover, it is also possible to include the period during which the shares were owned by the person from whom he inherited them.

21.11.4 Substantial reduction

The legislation states that a shareholder shall be regarded as substantially reducing his interest in the company only if his interest is reduced by at least 25%. Furthermore, in looking at an individual's interest in the company, it is necessary to take account of his interest as a loan creditor (ie someone who has lent money to the company) as well as a shareholder. Although the legislation refers to a minimum reduction of 25%, the Revenue normally expects a much greater reduction.

21.11.5 Benefit to the company's trade

The legislation states that a purchase of own shares by a company is regarded as a distribution unless the purchase is made wholly or mainly for the purpose of benefiting a trade carried on by the company or by any of its 75% subsidiaries. The legislation also requires that the purchase must not be part of a 'scheme or arrangement' the main purpose of which is to enable the individual to avoid tax or to participate in the profits of the company without receiving a dividend.

21.11.6 Advance clearance procedure

It is possible to submit details of the commercial reasons for a proposed purchase of own shares with a view to securing confirmation from the Revenue that the purchase will be treated as a capital transaction and not as a distribution. The basic information required by the Revenue is set out in SP2/82.

21.12 DEMERGERS

It often happens with family companies that different members of the family wish to develop the business in different directions. If the founding generation has passed control to their children, a company may be run by two cousins or more distant relatives who have markedly different ideas and ambitions. There is a way in which the businesses can be separated in a tax-efficient way so that each of the different sides of the family can have a separate company with a distinct business.

Demergers are not confined to family companies and may also be appropriate where individuals who have been business partners wish to go their separate ways.

21.12.1 Form of the demerger

Demergers may take one of three forms, but they all involve the distribution of assets to shareholders out of distributable profits. The three types of transaction are as follows:

- distribution of shares in a subsidiary company to shareholders (ie the holding company declares a dividend);
- transfer of shares in a subsidiary to another company ('Newco') in return for its issuing shares to the shareholders of the holding company;

- transfer of a business to another company (again Newco) in return for that company's issuing shares to the shareholders in the holding company.

Where the Revenue gives approval to a demerger, the value transferred to the shareholders in one of the above three ways is not subject to income tax or CGT.

21.12.2 Conditions which must be satisfied

Demerger relief is available only where the purpose of the demerger is to separate two distinct trading activities. Relief is not intended to be available where the purpose is to separate trades from investments or other assets. It is also necessary to show that the purpose of the demerger is to benefit the trade being demerged. This condition is normally satisfied if it can be shown that the directors have irreconcilable differences as to business policy and the trade of the company to be demerged is being inhibited or held back because of these policy differences.

The demerger reliefs are not available where the demerger forms part of a scheme or arrangement where the main purpose is either:

- the avoidance of tax, or
- the acquisition by any person other than a shareholder of the distributing company of control of that company or any other company involved in the demerger.

21.12.3 Advance clearance

It is possible to secure advance clearance from the Revenue that a proposed demerger qualifies for the tax reliefs. In practice, it is necessary to make out a case to the Revenue that there are good commercial reasons for the demerger and there is no immediate likelihood of one of the demerged companies being sold.

21.12.4 Informal demergers

It may sometimes be possible to achieve a demerger which separates assets from trading activities, but this is not possible under the above rules for statutory demergers.

Informal demergers are a type of reconstruction which relies on SP5/85. Specifically, the transactions involved are normally as follows:

(1) the company's ordinary share capital is re-classified so that A shares carry the right to participate only in the profits of one trade or business and B shares carry similar rights over another business;
(2) the company is put into liquidation;
(3) the liquidator transfers the assets and undertakings which relate to the A shares to a company ('Newco') which issues its share to the A shareholders. The process is repeated in relation to the B shareholders.

In some circumstances it is shares in a subsidiary which are transferred to the new company, which issues shares to the A and B shareholders.

The transfer of the business or undertaking to Newco A and Newco B does not normally give rise to a tax charge for the transferor company because this is specifically covered by TCGA 1992, s 139. Similarly, the issue to the A and B shareholders of shares in Newco A and Newco B does not normally give rise to a CGT charge because of reliefs available under s 136. However, both these sections apply only where the transactions are carried out for *bona fide* commercial reasons and not for the avoidance of tax.

Once again there is a clearance procedure, which clearly should be contemplated only after taking appropriate professional advice.

21.13 LONGER TERM CAPITAL GAINS TAX PLANNING

Inevitably, medium- to long-term CGT planning depends upon a person's particular circumstances, and the following are merely suggestions to be borne in mind.

21.13.1 Should investments be held by trustees?

There is a major distinction between capital gains realised by an individual and gains made by trustees of an interest in possession trust. An individual's capital gains are effectively added to his taxable income and, if the aggregate amount for 2002–03 exceeds £29,900, the gains are subject to 40% tax (see 5.1.4). In contrast, where gains are realised by trustees, the rate of CGT is 34%, regardless of the amount of the gain. It follows that if an individual is a beneficiary of an interest in possession trust, whether this be a trust created by another person's Will, or a settlement created by a relative etc, then it may well be more appropriate from a tax point of view if the trustees, rather than the individual himself, hold shares in a private company.

Example – Shares held by trustees

A has 500 shares in X Ltd. His brother does not have any shares but is the life tenant of a trust created by his father which owns the remaining 500 shares.

If X Ltd is taken over and *A* and the trustees both have a capital gain of £400,000, *A* pays tax of £160,000, but the trustees are liable for CGT of only £100,000.

21.13.2 Special rules where settlor or spouse a beneficiary

The treatment described in 21.13.1 does not apply if the settlor or his spouse can benefit. If so, the trustees' gain is taxed as if the settlor had realised it himself.

21.13.3 Forward planning for retirement relief

Both spouses may qualify for the full measure of retirement relief (see 6.6–6.8) provided they meet the conditions for that relief. In practice, this means that both husband and wife should hold at least 5% of the voting shares for a period of ten years up to the time of a disposal, and they should both be full-time officers or employees of the company.

Example – Maximising retirement relief

A and his wife both work full-time for their private company, X Ltd. A holds 99% of the shares and his wife holds only 1%.

In 2002–03, a capital gain of £1m arises on the sale of the company. A's share is £990,000 and his tax is as follows:

	£
Capital gain	990,000
Less: exemption	(50,000)
	940,000
Less: 50% exemption on £200,000 – £50,000	(75,000)
	865,000

If he has used his annual exemption elsewhere, the tax normally amounts to £346,000.

If A and his wife had each held 50% of the shares, the tax would instead have been calculated as follows:

	£
Capital gain for both husband and wife	500,000
Less: exemption	(100,000)
	400,000
Less: 50% exemption on (£200,000 – £50,000)	(75,000)
	325,000

The maximum tax payable would then be £260,000 (ie £130,000 each).

21.13.4 Assets owned privately but used by personal company

In many situations, the company concerned is not particularly valuable and the proceeds which are likely to arise on a disposal are insufficient to allow retirement relief to be taken up in full. On the other hand, the individual may have charged rent for making a valuable asset (eg a property owned by the director concerned) available to the company for use in its business. A gain on the disposal of the property does not qualify for retirement relief at all if a market rent has been charged (see 6.8.3), so retirement relief may go to waste.

One solution may be for the individual to transfer the property to the company by way of a gift, or a sale at an amount equal to his acquisition value. There should be no problem from the point of view of IHT provided all the shares in the company are held by the individual and spouse. The overall effect is that the individual realises a larger gain on the eventual disposal of his shares and this should qualify for retirement relief in full.

In some situations, it may also be possible for the individual to sell the property to the company for full consideration and to cover any capital gain which arises by using the sale proceeds to subscribe for new shares in the company concerned. Such an investment should qualify for reinvestment relief (see 6.4) and this should mean that no CGT is payable on the disposal of the property. In due course, when the shares and the company are sold, retirement relief should be available to cover any capital gain (subject to the normal limits).

21.14 ANTI-AVOIDANCE LEGISLATION

21.14.1 Transactions in securities

Section 703 of TA 1988 enables the Revenue to treat certain capital sums as if they were income. This section has particular application to a sale of shares in a private company.

For the Revenue to invoke s 703, one of the five prescribed circumstances set out in s 704 must apply. Several of these prescribed circumstances refer to an abnormal dividend and it is therefore particularly dangerous for a person to sell shares as part of a series of transactions under which another person (eg the purchaser) receives an abnormal dividend. However, s 704D can also apply to a series of transactions which does not involve an abnormal dividend but has the effect of extracting cash which could have been distributed as dividend.

There is an exemption for transactions which are carried out for *bona fide* commercial reasons or in the ordinary course of making or managing investments. However, it needs to be shown that none of the transactions was entered into with the main object, or one of the main objects, of obtaining a tax advantage.

Fortunately, s 707 provides an advance clearance procedure whereby a taxpayer may require the Revenue to state whether s 703 would apply to a proposed transaction. The taxpayer must set out all the material facts in his application. If the Revenue is not satisfied that clearance can be granted, or if it requires further information, notice must be given within 30 days. Once the Revenue has given clearance, an assessment cannot be made under s 703 unless it can be shown that the application did not fully and accurately disclose all the proposed transactions.

21.14.2 CGT anti-avoidance provisions

There are two anti-avoidance provisions in respect of CGT, both relating to value shifting.

21.14.3 Controlling shareholders

Section 29 of TCGA 1992 can apply where a controlling shareholder takes actions (or refrains from action) so as to cause value to pass out of his shares and into shares held by some other person with whom he is connected. Section 29 allows the Revenue to treat such a controlling shareholder as if he had disposed of his shares for their value at the time when he exercised his control to shift value into the other shares.

Example – Value shifting

A holds 51% of the ordinary shares in X Ltd and his son holds the remaining 49%. *A* arranges for the company to offer ordinary shareholders the option of converting their shares into preference shares. *A* accepts this offer but his son does not. This means that control of the company shifts from *A* to his son since, after the conversion of ordinary shares into preference shares, all the ordinary shares are held by his son. If the Revenue invokes s 29, it will assess *A* as if he had disposed of his 51% shareholding at its market value before the shares were converted into preference shares.

21.14.4 Section 30 of TCGA 1992

This legislation can apply to a scheme or arrangement under which the value of an asset which has been transferred has been materially reduced and a tax-free benefit has been obtained. Fortunately, there are specific exemptions for the following transactions:

- disposals between husband and wife;
- disposals by personal representatives to legatees;
- disposals within a 75% group of companies.

Nevertheless, this anti-avoidance section is important in connection with any transactions which may affect the balance of control within a family over a private company. Proprietors of companies should therefore take appropriate professional advice.

21.14.5 Share exchanges and take-overs

The exchange of shares or securities in Company A for shares in Company B which is making a take-over bid or acquiring a 25% shareholding in Company A can give rise to a CGT liability for shareholders in Company A unless they had no more than 5% of Company A or advance clearance had been obtained (see 5.4.4). This legislation therefore needs to be borne in mind where shareholders in an unquoted company take shares or loan stock issued by an acquiring company.

21.15 SALE OF THE COMPANY

Once again, the purpose of this section is to outline some of the more common ways in which CGT may be mitigated.

21.15.1 Pre-sale dividends

Vendors of a private company may have a choice. They can sell their shares for a capital sum or they can take a pre-sale dividend and a reduced amount on the sale of their shares. There may be a significant benefit if the shareholders organise a pre-sale dividend.

21.15.2 Using CGT hold-over relief

Where an individual makes a gift of shares in an unquoted trading company, it may be possible to secure hold-over relief. The conditions which must be satisfied are basically that:

- the company is an unquoted company;
- it is a trading company or the holding company of a trading group;
- the recipient of the gift is UK resident;
- the recipient joins in a hold-over election.

A restriction on hold-over relief may apply where the company has chargeable assets which are investment assets. (See 6.4.)

Where hold-over relief is obtained, the person transferring his shares does not normally have a capital gain but the recipient of the gift takes over his acquisition cost for the purposes of CGT.

Where substantial amounts are involved, it may be worthwhile for an individual to use this relief to make gifts to his children, or to a settlement for the benefit of his children.

Example – Hold-over relief

A receives an offer for his shares in X Ltd and stands to realise a capital gain of £2m. If he transfers a quarter of his shares to an interest in possession trust for his children, and makes a hold-over election, the trustees take over his CGT acquisition value. The position on the sale to the third party is that A now realises a gain of £1.5m and the trustees realise a gain of £500,000. Their rate of tax is 25% rather than 40% so A's family saves £75,000 at the Revenue's expense.

21.15.3 Taking loan notes or other paper from the acquirer

Where a public company is acquiring an unquoted company, it may be attractive for the vendors to take loan stock (or other securities) issued by the quoted company. Provided that clearance has been obtained under TCGA 1992, s 138 (see 21.14.5) no capital gain arises to the extent that the vendors take such consideration. They do, however, realise a capital gain as and when they dispose of the loan stock or other securities.

Taking loan stock can be attractive where the vendors anticipate that they may subsequently cease to be resident or where they can cash in the loan stock in stages, so as to realise modest gains in different tax years to take advantage of the CGT annual exemption for those years.

21.15.4 Consideration payable by instalments

One potential problem area is where a person sells shares (or any other asset) with the sale consideration being receivable in instalments. The CGT legislation requires the full amount to be brought into account for the year in which the disposal takes place. In some cases this might cause hardship in that a vendor is assessed for CGT but does not yet have sufficient cash to cover this liability. The legislation caters for this by allowing payment of CGT to be made by instalments over a period of up to seven years. However, this is not automatic and the basis on which payment may be made by instalments needs to be negotiated with the Inspector of Taxes.

Where it subsequently transpires that not all the consideration is actually received, the CGT assessment may be reduced.

21.15.5 Contingent liabilities

If a person sells shares (or any other assets) but is under an obligation to return part of the money in certain circumstances, the legislation requires that his capital gain should be computed without reference to the contingent liability. However, if and when the contingent liability becomes an actual liability, the CGT assessment is then adjusted to reflect this (see 5.5.1).

21.15.6 Earn-outs

It is also possible for a person to sell his shares for an amount in cash, plus a further amount based on the future result of the company's business. The House of Lords decision in *Marren v Ingles* [1980] STC 500 has established that such a vendor must be deemed to have received two types of consideration at the time of his disposal: the cash amount, plus the contingent right to receive further sums in the future. The technical term for the right to receive sums in the future is a *chose in action*. The House of Lords decided that CGT must be charged on the cash received plus the market value of the *chose in action*.

Example – Tax treatment of earn-out transaction

A sells out for £1.5m plus a contingent right to receive up to another £1m if his company achieves profit targets.

The present value of this contingent right or chose in action is £450,000 and so *A* is assessed as if he had received £1.95m. If the full amount of £1m is eventually received, he then has a further gain in the year that this is paid out. His gain in that year is:

	£
Proceeds	1,000,000
Less market value of chose in action when acquired	(450,000)
Capital gain before indexation	550,000

TCGA 1992, s 138A deals with the above problem and states that where the earn-out consideration consists only of shares or other securities to be issued by the acquiring company, those securities may be treated as if they were securities issued by the acquiring company on the take-over.

Example

If the sale contract in the example immediately above provides that *A*'s further £1m consideration must be satisfied by an issue of shares by the acquiring company, he would then be taxed only on the £1.5m cash, and tax would not be payable on the *chose in action* or on the issue of the shares, but only as and when he disposes of those shares.

21.15.7 Qualifying corporate bonds

Some caution is required where a private company is being disposed of and the vendors are offered a share exchange involving the issue of qualifying corporate bonds (QCBs). A QCB is a special type of loan stock (see 5.3.2). It is called a *qualifying* corporate bond because no capital gain may normally arise on its disposal (similarly, no allowable loss normally arises on its disposal).

However, where a company has been taken over, and the acquiring company issues a security which is a QCB, the legislation provides that the vendors' capital gain may be deferred only until such time as the QCB is disposed of.

This can cause real problems if the acquiring company gets into financial difficulty and cannot redeem the QCB. The deferred gain may become chargeable, as a disposal is deemed to take place when the acquiring company is wound up, and there is no relief for the loss due to the QCBs becoming worthless. This is an area where a potential vendor should obtain professional advice.

22

INHERITANCE TAX AND BUSINESS PROPERTY

Inheritance tax (IHT) is a combined gift tax and death duty. It applies to certain gifts and deemed gifts made during a person's lifetime and to the estate on death. For transfers after 5 April 2002 the first £250,000 of chargeable transfers (the nil rate band) is free of IHT. Cumulative transfers in excess of this, which take place either at death or within seven years before death, are taxed at 40% (though the overall impact may be reduced on transfers that take place more than three years before death).

22.1 PERSONS SUBJECT TO IHT

A UK-domiciled individual is subject to IHT on all property owned by him, whether it is located in the UK or overseas. In contrast, a person who has a foreign domicile is in general subject to IHT only on property situated in the UK. Foreign nationals and individuals with family connections overseas should refer to the *Zurich Tax Handbook 2002–03* at 22.1 and 22.15 for further details. This chapter concentrates on the position of individuals domiciled in the UK.

22.2 WHEN A CHARGE ARISES

Inheritance tax can apply in the following circumstances:

- on a gift made by an individual during his lifetime;
- on a lifetime transfer of value which is regarded as a 'chargeable transfer';
- on death.

A person who has an interest in possession under a trust or settlement is normally regarded as entitled to the capital. When the beneficiary dies, the full value of the trust property is treated as part of his estate for IHT purposes (see 22.11.1).

Figure 22.1 opposite indicates the circumstances under which a gift may be a chargeable transfer for IHT purposes.

Figure 22.1 – Chargeable or exempt transfer

22.3 TRANSFERS OF VALUE

22.3.1 Transfers which do not amount to gifts
(IHTA 1984, s 3)

The legislation refers mainly to *transfers* rather than gifts. The reason is that all gifts are transfers of value but not all transfers of value are gifts. For example, where a person deliberately sells an asset at less than market value, he may not be making a gift but he is certainly making a transfer of value. Similarly, deliberately omitting to exercise a right can also be a transfer of value, but this is not a gift in the normal sense of the word. To give a third example, a transfer can feature property which is not even owned by the person making it since the IHT legislation deems that a person has made a gift if his interest in possession under a trust comes to an end (see *Zurich Tax Handbook 2002–03* at 18.4.15).

22.3.2 Gratuitous intent
(IHTA 1984, s 10)

IHT does not normally apply to a transaction unless there is an element of 'bounty' (ie a deliberate intention to make a gift). An unintentional loss of value (eg a loss made on a bad business deal) is not subject to IHT because there was no intention to pass value to another person. On the other hand, it may be difficult to satisfy the Capital Taxes Office (CTO) that there was no gratuitous intent to benefit a relative or connected person if the terms of the transaction seem unusually favourable.

22.3.3 Calculating the value of a transfer
(IHTA 1984, s 3)

The amount of any transfer of value is determined by the reduction in the donor's wealth. This is not necessarily the same as the increase in the recipient's wealth.

This can be illustrated by considering the situation where a person owns 51 out of 100 shares in a company. He has control because he has the majority of the shares. If he were to give two shares to his son, he would relinquish control of the company and his remaining 49 shares might be worth disproportionately less because of this. The two shares given to his son might not be worth particularly much in isolation, and the son may not have acquired a particularly valuable asset, but the father's estate would have gone down in value by the difference between the value of a 51% shareholding and the value of a 49% shareholding. Contrast the way that market value is ascertained for CGT purposes (see 5.5).

22.4 GIFTS WHICH ARE NOT TRANSFERS OF VALUE

Certain gifts and other transactions are not regarded as transfers of value so the issue of whether they are chargeable transfers simply does not arise. These include:

- maintenance of family, dependants etc
- waivers of dividends
- waivers of remuneration

- interest-free loans
- disclaimers of legacies
- deeds of variation.

22.4.1 Maintenance of family, dependants etc
(IHTA 1984, s 11)

The legislation specifically provides that the following lifetime payments are not transfers of value:

(1) Payments for the maintenance of a spouse or former spouse.
(2) Payments for the maintenance, education or training of a child or stepchild under the age of 18.
(3) Payments made to maintain a child over 18 who is in full-time education or training.
(4) Reasonable provision for the care or maintenance of a dependent relative, ie someone who is incapacitated by old age or infirmity from maintaining himself, or a widowed, separated or divorced mother or mother-in-law.

22.4.2 Waivers of dividends
(IHTA 1984, s 15)

A waiver of a dividend is not regarded as a transfer of value provided certain conditions are satisfied:

(1) The dividend must be waived by deed.
(2) The deed must not be executed more than 12 months before the right to the dividend has accrued.
(3) The deed waiving the dividend must be executed before any legal entitlement to the dividend arises.

There is a difference in the treatment of interim and final dividends, as the time at which entitlement may arise can be different.

Interim dividends

A shareholder has no enforceable right to payment before the date on which the board declares that a dividend shall be payable. Therefore, a deed waiving a dividend should be executed before any board resolution is passed.

Final dividends

A company might declare a dividend without stipulating any date for payment. In such circumstances, the declaration creates an immediate debt and it is therefore too late to execute a waiver.

In other cases where a final dividend is declared as being payable at a later date, a shareholder *may* waive his entitlement but must do so before the due date for payment.

In practice, a final dividend requires the shareholders' approval; an individual shareholder may therefore waive a dividend provided that the deed is executed before the company's annual general meeting.

22.4.3 Waivers of remuneration
(IHTA 1984, s 14)

There is a specific provision that a waiver of remuneration does not constitute a transfer of value. The terms of this exemption are based on income tax treatment. In practice, the Revenue normally accepts that remuneration is not subject to income tax under Schedule E if it is waived, and the Schedule E assessment has not become final and conclusive, provided:

(1) the remuneration is formally waived (usually by deed), or, if it has already been paid, it is repaid to the employer; and
(2) the employer's assessable profits are adjusted accordingly.

22.4.4 Interest-free loans
(IHTA 1984, s 29)

The IHT legislation specifically provides that an interest-free loan is not to be treated as a transfer of value provided that the loan is repayable on demand.

This exemption would not cover a situation where a loan was made for a specific period, with the lender having no legal right to call for repayment before that time has expired. The grant of such a loan could be a transfer of value. The Revenue would assess the value of the transfer as the difference between the amount of the loan and the present market value of the loan if it were to be assigned.

22.4.5 Disclaimer of legacies
(IHTA 1984, s 142)

If a person becomes entitled to property under a Will or on an intestacy, or under a trust (for example, a life tenant's death), he may disclaim his entitlement. Where such a disclaimer is made, the legacy or other entitlement is not treated as a transfer of value provided that:

(1) no payment or other consideration is given for the disclaimer, and
(2) the person has not already accepted his entitlement, either expressly or by implication.

22.4.6 Deeds of variation
(IHTA 1984, s 142)

A deed of variation may be entered into where a person has died leaving property to a beneficiary, the effect being to redirect the property. Where the necessary conditions are fulfilled, the revised disposition is treated as having taken place on the deceased person's death. Once again, a person who gives up an entitlement is not treated as making a transfer of value.

The following conditions need to be satisfied:

(1) The deed of variation must be executed within two years of the death.
(2) The deed must be in writing and must specifically refer to the provisions of the Will etc which are to be varied.
(3) It must be signed by the person who would otherwise have benefited, and anyone else who might have benefited.
(4) Only one deed of variation in respect of a particular piece of property can be effective for IHT purposes.
(5) No payment or other consideration may pass between beneficiaries to induce them to enter into the deed of variation (except that a variation which consists of an exchange of inheritances and a cash adjustment is permitted).
(6) The deed must be submitted to the CTO within six months of its being executed.

22.5 EXEMPT TRANSFERS

Even if a transfer takes place, it does not attract IHT if it is an exempt transfer. The following are exempt transfers.

22.5.1 Gifts to spouse
(IHTA 1984, s 18)

There is normally an unlimited exemption for transfers between husband and wife. For this purpose, a couple is regarded as husband and wife until a decree absolute has been made. The exemption covers outright gifts, legacies and transfers of property to a trust under which the spouse has an interest in possession. (The transfer may be either a lifetime transfer or a transfer which takes place on death.)

The exemption is restricted where a UK-domiciled individual makes transfers to a foreign domiciled spouse. In this situation, the exemption is limited to £55,000 (see *Zurich Tax Handbook 2002–03* at 17.5.1).

22.5.2 Normal expenditure out of income
(IHTA 1984, s 21)

A lifetime gift is exempt if it is shown that it was made as part of the donor's normal expenditure and comes out of income. The legislation requires that the gift should be 'normal', ie that the donor had a habit of making such gifts or must have intended to make a series of such gifts. The legislation also requires that by taking one year with another, the pattern of such gifts must have left the donor with sufficient income to maintain his normal standard of living.

Gifts which take the form of payments under deed of covenant or the payment of premiums under life assurance policies written in trust frequently qualify as exempt because of this rule.

22.5.3 Small gifts
(IHTA 1984, s 20)

Any number of individual gifts of up to £250 in any one tax year are exempt. But where gifts to any one individual exceed £250, the exemption is lost completely.

22.5.4 Annual exemption
(IHTA 1984, s 19)

This exemption is available to cover part of a larger gift. The exemption is £3,000 for each tax year. Furthermore, both husband and wife have separate annual exemptions.

If the full £3,000 is not used in a given year, the balance can be carried forward for one year only, and is then allowable only if the exemption for the second year is fully utilised.

22.5.5 Gifts in consideration of marriage
(IHTA 1984, s 22)

Gifts made to a bride or groom in consideration of their marriage are exempt up to the following amounts:

Gifts made by	Maximum exemption
Each parent	£5,000
Grandparents	£2,500
Bride or groom	£2,500
Any other person	£1,000

22.5.6 Gifts to charities
(IHTA 1984, s 23)

Gifts to charities which are established in the UK are exempt regardless of the amount. A charity may be established or registered here even though it carries out its work overseas and the exemption covers gifts to such charities. However, donations made to a foreign charity which is established abroad do not normally qualify.

22.5.7 Gifts for national purposes
(IHTA 1984, s 25)

Gifts to certain national bodies are totally exempt. These bodies include colleges and universities, the National Trust, the National Gallery, the British Museum and other galleries and museums run by local authorities or universities.

22.5.8 Gifts for public benefit
(IHTA 1984, s 26)

This exemption covers gifts of eligible property such as historic buildings, land of outstanding scenic, historic or scientific interest, works of art and collections of national, scientific, historic or artistic interest. It is necessary to clear the position in advance with HM Treasury if the exemption is to be available.

22.5.9 Gifts to political parties
(IHTA 1984, s 24)

Gifts to 'qualifying political parties' are exempt only if certain conditions are satisfied. A political party qualifies if it had at least two MPs returned at the last general election, or if it had at least one member and more than 150,000 votes were cast for its candidates.

22.5.10 Certain transfers to employee trusts
(IHTA 1984, s 28)

Transfers by an individual to an employee trust of shares in a company can be exempt provided all the following conditions are satisfied:

(1) The beneficiaries of the trust must include all or most of the persons employed by or holding office with the company.
(2) Within one year of the transfer:
   (a) the trustees must hold more than 50% of the company's ordinary share capital and have voting control on all questions which affect it as a whole; and
   (b) the trustees' control must not be fettered by some other provision or agreement between the shareholders.

(3) The trust deed must not permit any of the trust property to be applied at any time for the benefit of:

(a) a participator in the company (ie a person who holds a 5% or greater interest);

(b) any person who has been a participator at any time during the ten years prior to the transfer; or

(c) any person connected with a participator or former participator.

A further restriction may apply where a company makes a transfer to an employee trust.

22.6 POTENTIALLY EXEMPT TRANSFERS
(IHTA 1984, s 3A)

22.6.1 Definition

Irrevocable gifts made during an individual's lifetime may, provided certain conditions are satisfied, be 'potentially exempt transfers' (PETs). These gifts become actually exempt only if the donor survives for seven years. If the donor dies during that period, the PET becomes a chargeable transfer. The tax payable depends on the rates of IHT in force at the date of death. The donee is liable to pay the tax.

The main conditions to be satisfied for a gift to be a PET are that the gift is made to:

(1) an individual; or

(2) a trust for a disabled person (see *Zurich Tax Handbook 2002–03* at 18.7);

(3) an accumulation and maintenance trust (see *Zurich Tax Handbook 2002–03* at 18.6).

A gift which is subject to a reservation of benefit (see 22.7) cannot be a PET. Furthermore, a gift to a discretionary trust is a chargeable transfer (see 22.10).

22.6.2 Taper relief
(IHTA 1984, s 7)

Where an individual makes a PET and dies within the seven-year period, taper relief may reduce the amount of tax payable. The tax payable on the transfer which has become a chargeable transfer is subject to the following reduction:

Years between gift and death	Percentage of the full charge
Three to four	80
Four to five	60
Five to six	40
Six to seven	20

22.7 RESERVATION OF BENEFIT
(FA 1986, s 102 & Sch 20)

22.7.1 Introduction

Property which has been gifted may still be deemed to form part of a deceased person's estate unless:

(1) possession and enjoyment of the property was *bona fide* assumed by the donee; and

(2) the property was enjoyed virtually to the entire exclusion of the donor and of any benefit to him by contract or otherwise.

The reference under (2) above means that for all practical purposes this is an 'all or nothing' test. The Revenue view is that the exception is intended to cover only trivial benefits, for example, where the donor of a picture enjoyed the chance to view it when making occasional visits to the donee's home.

The term 'by contract or otherwise' is meant to embrace arrangements which are not legally binding but which amount to an honourable understanding. This might arise where a person gives away a house but remains in occupation. A reservation of benefit would arise even if there is no legal tenancy and the donee could, in law, require the donor to vacate the property at any time.

22.7.2 Two specific exemptions

The legislation specifically states that occupation of property or use of chattels does not count as a benefit provided a market rent is paid by the donor. The legislation also provides for the benefit enjoyed by a donor who occupies property he has given to another where the donor's financial circumstances changed drastically for the worse after the gift was made.

22.7.3 Ending of reservation of benefit

Where a person makes a gift and initially reserves a benefit, but then relinquishes that reservation, the donor is treated as making a PET at the time that he gives up the reserved benefit. The amount of the PET is governed by the market value of the property at that time.

Example – Giving up reservation of benefit

A gives property worth £150,000 in July 1997 but reserves a benefit. The benefit is relinquished in July 2002 when the property is worth £220,000. *A* dies in October 2003.

If no benefit had been reserved, the gift would have been completely exempt by August 2004 (ie seven years after the gift), but because a benefit was retained until July 2002, the seven-year period starts only from that date.

The full £220,000 (ie the value at July 2002 when the reservation of benefit came to an end) would form part of *A*'s estate for IHT purposes.

22.7.4 **Settlements and trusts**

The Revenue has confirmed that a settlor may be a trustee of a settlement created by the settlor without this constituting a reservation of benefit. Also, where the settled property includes shares in a family company, the settlor/trustee may also be a director of the company and may be permitted under the trust deed to retain his remuneration provided it is reasonable in relation to the services rendered.

The position is less clear where a person has sought to reserve the *possibility* of a benefit, eg where an individual has created a settlement and is a potential beneficiary. It is the Revenue's view that a benefit is reserved where the settlor creates a discretionary trust and is a member of a class of potential beneficiaries. This would also apply where the settlor may be added to a class of potential beneficiaries. However, the Revenue has confirmed that no reservation of benefit arises where a person creates a settlement and is a contingent or default beneficiary. This might apply, for example, where property is put into trust for the settlor's children but would revert to the settlor if the children die or become bankrupt.

The legislation does not require that the donor's spouse should be excluded from benefit, and where a discretionary settlement is created it would be possible to include as a potential beneficiary the donor's spouse, any future spouse or widow/widower. However, if property were to be distributed to the donor's spouse from the trust and that property were then to be applied for the benefit of the *settlor,* the Revenue might well take the view that, looked at as a whole, there had been a reservation of benefit.

It is often difficult to distinguish between making a gift with reservation and giving away a part only of what one possesses. In *Munro v Stamp Duty Commrs of NSW* [1934] AC 61 it was held that arrangements made between a donee and a third party to give the donor a benefit were caught, whereas the retention of rights under a contract which was separate from the gift and made before it were not. This gave rise to the 'shearing' or 'carve-out' of the scheme, whereby a gift of land which was already subject to a lease was not a gift with reservation because the lease was not part of the gift. However, a gift of land which was subject to an agreement for a lease back, whether created at the same time or later, was a gift with reservation, the reason being that the gift comprised the grant of the whole, subject to something reserved out of it, as contrasted with a gift of a partial interest leaving something retained in the hands of the grantor (*Nichols v CIR* [1975] STC 278, CA).

The most recent case is *Ingram and Palmer-Tomkinson (Lady Ingram's Executors) v CIR* [1999] STC 37. Lady Ingram transferred a property to the solicitor, who held the property as her nominee. He then executed a lease in favour of Lady Ingram giving her a rent-free lease for 20 years. The land subject to the lease was transferred to a family trust. The executors' appeal was allowed. It was stated: 'Although [FA 1986, s 102] does not allow a donor to have his cake and eat it, there is nothing to stop him from carefully dividing the cake, eating part and having the rest.' It is thus important to define precisely what interests are being given away and those that are being retained. In this case the gift was the capital value of land after deduction of a leasehold interest. Although an owner of property cannot grant a lease to himself (*Rye v Rye* [1962] AC 496), in English law a trustee is not an agent for his beneficiary. The position is different in Scotland where a nominee cannot create an effective lease in favour of his principal, and a person cannot create a lease in favour of himself (*Kidrummy (Jersey) v CIR* [1990] STC 657).

As they apply to gifts of land, the gift with reservation rules are extended where:

(1) the donor retains a right to continue to occupy the land or enjoy a right in relation thereto for less than full consideration; and
(2) the gift is made within seven years after the interest which gives the continued right of occupation, etc is created.

The extended gift with reservation rules do not apply where:

(a) the gift is covered by an exemption from IHT;
(b) the benefit to the donor is negligible from the donee's point of view;
(c) the donor pays full consideration for the benefit; and
(d) the donor's occupation is forced upon him because of an unexpected hardship arising after the gift.

22.8 BUSINESS PROPERTY
(IHTA 1984, ss 103–114)

22.8.1 Basic requirements

A special deduction from liability to IHT is given in respect of value of business property where the following conditions are satisfied:

(1) The property must have been owned during the previous two years; or it must have been inherited from a spouse and, when the spouse's period of ownership is taken into account, the combined period of ownership exceeds two years.
(2) The property must not be subject to a binding contract for sale.

There is no requirement that the business should be carried on in the UK.

22.8.2 Rates of business property relief

Unincorporated businesses

A sole proprietor's interest in his business qualifies for a 100% deduction. A partner's interest in his firm also qualifies for 100% relief. A 50% deduction is available in respect of an asset owned by a partner but used by his firm.

Shares and debentures

Business relief on shares is available only where the company concerned is a trading company or the holding company of a trading group.

The 100% relief is available on shares and debentures in an unquoted company where the transferor had voting control before the transfer. Relief of 100% is also available for a controlling interest in a quoted trading company.

The 100% relief is also available for a transfer of shares in an unquoted trading company provided that the transferor had control of more than 25% of the voting rights before the transfer. Specific legislation on 'related property' means that where a husband and wife's combined shareholding exceeds 25%, the 100% relief is available even though neither spouse has more than 25% when looked at in isolation. A 100% deduction is given for other shareholdings in unquoted trading companies. Shares dealt in on the USM or the AIM are regarded as unquoted shares.

Relief of 50% is available where a controlling shareholder transfers an asset which is used by his company, or where such an asset passes on his death.

22.8.3 Businesses that do not qualify

Business relief is not normally available where the business carried on consists wholly or mainly of dealing in securities, stocks or shares, or land or buildings, or in making investments.

Where the transfer is of shares, business relief may be restricted if the company owns investments. The legislation refers to such investments as 'excepted assets', which are defined as assets which are neither:

(1) used wholly or mainly for the purposes of the business, nor
(2) required for the future use of the business.

Example – Restriction on business property relief

A dies holding shares in X Ltd, and X Ltd's balance sheet shows the following assets:

	£
Investments	750,000
Factory	1,000,000
Stock	300,000
Debtors	200,000
Cash	1,250,000

Only part of the value of the shares qualify for business relief. The part that would not qualify is normally:

Investment	750,000
Total assets	3,500,000

If the cash were excessive in relation to the likely needs and requirements of the business, there could also be a restriction on this count.

22.8.4 Test normally applied on a 'consolidated basis'

Where a company has subsidiaries, it is necessary to look at the group situation (ie shares in subsidiaries may have to be treated as excepted assets if the subsidiaries are investment companies). The CTO has confirmed that business assets held by subsidiaries of subsidiary companies should qualify for business relief.

22.9 AGRICULTURAL PROPERTY
(IHTA 1984, ss 115–124B)

Relief is available on the agricultural value of farmland in the UK, Channel Islands or Isle of Man.

22.9.1 Land occupied by the transferor

Relief is available where the individual had occupied the farmland for the two years prior to the date of the transfer. Where a farm has been sold and another farm acquired, the replacement farm normally qualifies for agricultural property relief provided that the owner occupied the two farms for a combined period of at least two years in the last five years. Agricultural property relief is also available for land owned by an individual but occupied by a firm of which he is a partner, or by a company of which he is the controlling shareholder for the two years preceding the date of the transfer.

22.9.2 Tenanted land

To qualify under this head, the individual must normally have owned the land for at least seven years.

A 100% deduction is available on land which is not occupied by the owner provided he has (or had at the date of his death) the legal right to regain vacant possession within a period not exceeding 12 months.

A 100% deduction is available for tenanted farmland where the owner cannot obtain vacant possession within 12 months. This is generally the case where the land is let under an agricultural tenancy.

22.10 COMPUTATION OF TAX ON LIFETIME TRANSFERS

In practice, IHT is likely to be paid during a person's lifetime only for chargeable transfers made by him to a discretionary trust or on transfers effected through a gift of assets to a company. The IHT is computed as follows:

Table 22.1   IHT payable on lifetime transfers

Initial calculation		
Chargeable transfers made during the preceding seven years		A
Add	Amount of chargeable transfer	B
		C
Deduct	Nil rate band	D
		E
	IHT thereon at 20%	X
Deduct	IHT on a notional transfer of A minus D as if	
	it took place at the same time	Y
	IHT payable in respect of the chargeable transfer	Z
Position if the donor dies within three years		
Chargeable transfers made during the previous seven years		A
Add	Potentially exempt transfers caught by the seven-year rule	B
		C
Add	amount of chargeable transfer	D
		E
Deduct	Nil rate band	F
		G
	IHT thereon at 40%	H
	Deduct IHT at 40% on a notional transfer	
	of A minus F	I
		J

The donee is liable to pay additional IHT of J minus the amount already paid under Z above.

22.11 COMPUTATION OF TAX PAYABLE ON DEATH

22.11.1 Normal basis

The charge on death is normally computed as shown in Fig 22.2. The IHT is the tax on the figure in box 6, minus the tax payable on a normal transfer equal to the amount in box 4 as if the notional transfer took place immediately prior to the death. Some taper relief may be due on the PETs caught by the seven-year rule, see 22.6.2.

A number of special reliefs may be available.

22.11.2 Sales of land at a loss
(IHTA 1984, ss 190–198 as amended by FA 1993, s 199)

Relief is due where land and buildings are sold at a loss within four years of death, provided the loss is at least £1,000 or 5% of probate value (whichever is less). The net proceeds are substituted for the value at the date of death and the IHT is re-computed. However, this relief applies only where the property is sold to an arm's length purchaser rather than to a connected person.

22.11.3 Debts which may be disallowed
(FA 1986, s 103)

As a general rule debts are not deductible where the deceased made a capital transfer to a person who subsequently made a loan-back to the deceased. This rule applies only to loans made after 18 March 1986 but there is no such time limit on the capital transfers. A debt may be disallowed because the deceased had made a capital transfer to the lender even though that capital transfer took place before 18 March 1986. Nor is it of any help that the loan was made on normal commercial terms and a market rate of interest was payable.

22.11.4 Treatment of gifts caught by seven-year rule
(IHTA 1984, s 113A)

Tax on a PET which becomes a chargeable transfer because of the transferor's death is payable by the recipient of the gift.

Business relief is available on a PET that becomes a chargeable transfer only if the conditions in 22.8 are satisfied both at the time of the gift and at the time of death.

Figure 22.2   IHT payable on death

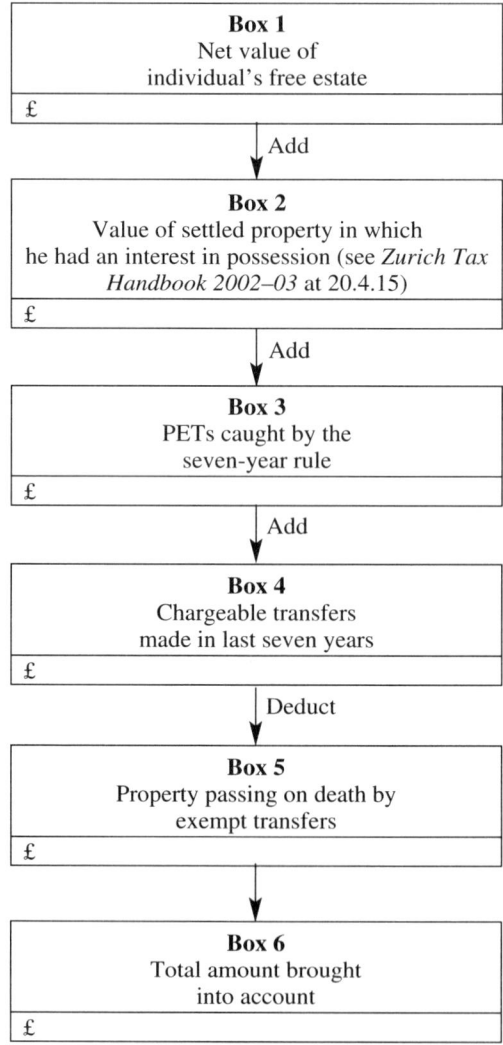

Examples – Business relief on PETs

(1) *A* owns all the shares in a family company. He gives his son a 24% shareholding. Three years later, the company is sold and the son receives cash for his shares. One year after that *A* dies.

Business relief is not normally available as the necessary conditions are not satisfied by the donee at the time of *A*'s death. If the son had reinvested the proceeds in another private company, business relief might have been available after all.

(2) In this case the basic position is as in (1), ie *A* has made a gift to his son of a 24% shareholding. However, this time, the son retains his shares, but by the time *A* dies, the shares are quoted. No relief is due as the son does not control the company and his shares are quoted shares.

(3) The basic position is as in (1) but, in this case, the son retains the shares and they are still unquoted at the time of *A*'s death. The shares attract the 100% relief and this is not lost even if the son disposes of the shares shortly after *A*'s death.

22.11.5 Replacement property

Where a donee has disposed of business property but acquires replacement property, the PET may yet attract business relief. The replacement property must be acquired within three years.

22.12 HANDING ON THE FAMILY BUSINESS/COMPANY WITHOUT ATTRACTING IHT

22.12.1 General strategy

Many proprietors are reluctant to transfer ownership of their businesses or family companies to the next generation. There may be good reasons for this: perhaps the proprietor's children are too young to take on the responsibility or they may not appear to have much aptitude for business. Experience is that most proprietors wish to retain control during their lifetime, but are equally anxious that their work should not go to waste, and often wish to take appropriate steps to avoid heavy death duties on the business.

The best way for a proprietor to plan varies according to the particular circumstances, although the following general strategy suits most situations:

(1) A proprietor should endeavour to provide himself with a guaranteed 'income stream' which is not dependent on the family business/company. Once he has secured this (eg by funding a personal pension plan) he is in a position to contemplate gifts.

(2) Effective use of insurance and pension arrangements can help to cover the position in the short and medium term.

(3) The benefits of business property relief or agricultural relief should be maximised. It is particularly important to make sure that no action is taken which jeopardises these very valuable reliefs.

(4) The proprietor should draw up a Will in the most tax-efficient way.

(5) It usually makes sense for gifts to be made sooner rather than later, especially if the business is growing in value. Ideally, such gifts should be PETs.

(6) Transferring property to a trust may enable the individual to mitigate IHT without relinquishing control of the capital during his lifetime.

22.12.2 Pension arrangements

The tax advantages of funding a pension scheme cannot be overstated. An individual who funds a personal pension plan will secure income tax relief at his marginal rate. Where a company funds a pension scheme for a director, the company normally secures relief against its corporation tax liability.

The pension which results from such contributions confers a degree of financial independence so that the individual relies less on income from his business or family company and is therefore more able to consider giving away part or all of his interest in that business.

Furthermore, most pension arrangements provide death-in-service cover which means that a lump sum may be paid out, free of IHT, if the individual dies before drawing his pension. The existence of such cover (which in the case of company directors may be up to 400% of the individual's salary and other remuneration) means that funds should be available to cover any IHT liability which may arise if the proprietor should die in the short term.

22.12.3 Maximising business relief

It is crucially important that any loans are secured on non-business assets. The reason for this is that business (and agricultural) relief is due only on the net value after deducting any loan secured against the property.

Example – Securing loans

A owns a business worth £500,000. The business assets include a factory which is subject to a £300,000 mortgage. If A should die, business relief is due only on £200,000. In contrast, if A had borrowed against other assets, business relief might have been due on the full £500,000.

It may be possible to secure the best of both worlds. Income tax relief on interest is available where a loan has been raised for a particular purpose, regardless of how the loan is secured. Thus, it seems possible in principle for a person to borrow for a qualifying purpose but secure the loan against another asset (eg his main residence) so that business relief is not restricted on death.

22.12.4 Avoiding buy/sell clauses

In the past, many partnership agreements included a clause intended to protect the widow and family of a deceased partner. Typically, such agreements contained a clause (often called a buy/sell clause) requiring that on the death of a partner the surviving partners purchase the deceased's interest in the firm. Similar arrangements were often contained in shareholder agreements entered into by working shareholder/ directors in private companies. While such arrangements are commercially sensible, there is a problem in that the Revenue regards them as amounting to a binding contract for sale and so not eligible for business property relief at all (see 22.8.1).

This problem can be avoided. It is possible to have a legally enforceable agreement which has almost exactly the same consequences as a buy/sell agreement but which does not jeopardise business relief. The recommended arrangement involves options. Each partner or shareholder/ director grants his colleagues an option and his colleagues grant him an option. The options are exercisable on death and enable the deceased's executors to require the surviving partners/shareholder/directors to buy them out at a fair price.

The Revenue has specifically confirmed that the existence of such options does not preclude availability of business relief or agricultural relief; see SP12/80.

22.12.5 Assets owned by a partner but used by the firm

Where a partner owns an asset (eg a building) which is used by the partnership for its business, business relief is available at the rate of 50%. In some family situations, it may be appropriate for the asset to be brought into the partnership so that on the death of the owner 100% business property relief, rather than 50%, is available.

22.12.6 Assets owned by shareholders

Similarly, a shareholder may own an asset which is used by a private company in which he is a shareholder. Unfortunately, no business property relief is available unless he is a controlling shareholder. It follows that a minority shareholder should carefully consider giving away such an asset (see 22.6 on PETs). Alternatively, it could make sense from this particular point of view to add to his shareholding so that he becomes a controlling shareholder.

22.12.7 Tax-efficient Wills

It is usually desirable for a proprietor to fully utilise the nil rate band rather than leave his entire estate to his spouse. However, this is general advice and the best way of drawing a Will depends upon the individual's particular circumstances.

In some cases, it is likely that property which qualifies for business property relief may be sold after the individual has died. If this property passes in the first instance to the individual's widow, it means that IHT is payable in the long term, when she dies. In a case such as this, it may be appropriate for the individual to draw his Will so that business property passes into a discretionary Will trust. No IHT should be payable if 100% business property relief is available, and the burden of IHT is much reduced in a situation where 50% relief is available. Property held in a discretionary trust will not form part of the widow's estate on her death, even if she is one of the beneficiaries of the Will trust, and in fact receives most of the income. There may be a charge on property held by the trustees once every ten years, but the rate is relatively modest compared with the normal 40% rate which applies where an individual owns non-business property or has an interest in possession.

Example – Planning a Will

> *A* is the managing director and a substantial shareholder in X Ltd. His shares qualify for 100% business property relief on his death. However, his children are not involved in the business and the executors sell the shares for £1m.
>
> If *A* had left the shares to his children, the IHT position would be satisfactory in that no charge would arise on *A*'s death or on Mrs *A*'s death.
>
> If *A* left the whole of his estate to his widow, an IHT charge would eventually arise on capital of £1m, and additional IHT of £400,000 might be payable on Mrs *A*'s death.
>
> If *A* left the shares to a discretionary will trust, Mrs *A* could benefit during her lifetime but there would be no IHT charge on her death. The trustees may be liable for the periodic charge every ten years but the maximum rate at present is 6% (see *Zurich Tax Handbook* 2002–03 at 18.5.12).

22.12.8 Property that cannot attract business property relief on widow's death

An individual may be a partner in a business which the widow cannot take over, eg the individual may be a doctor, dentist or solicitor. If he owns an asset used by the firm (eg the business premises) there is 50% business property relief if the property passes on his death to someone other than his widow. However, there is no business property relief if the property is left to the widow and then forms part of her estate on her death.

22.12.9 Double business property relief

It is sometimes possible to obtain business relief twice. For example, B dies owning non-business assets worth £2m and a 26% shareholding in an unquoted trading company worth £1m; his Will leaves all the non-business assets to his widow and the 26% shareholding to a discretionary Will trust.

INHERITANCE TAX AND BUSINESS PROPERTY

The position is:

	£
Will trust	1m
Less: business relief	1m
Chargeable transfer for IHT purposes	NIL

If the Will trustees then buy £1m of the non-business assets from the widow and sell the 26% shareholding to her, it may qualify for business property relief on her death (provided she survives two years). The position is then:

	£
Will trust	1m
(no charge on widow's death as it does not form part of her estate)	
Widow's free estate	2m
Less: business property relief	1m
IHT payable on	NIL

22.12.10 Deeds of variation

Even if an individual's Will is not drawn up in the most tax-efficient way, it may be possible for the family to reorganise matters during the two years after his death by taking advantage of the provisions on deeds of variation (see 22.4.6).

22.12.11 Family trusts

One advantage for an individual who makes a gift into a settlement is that he may be a trustee and can therefore continue to control the way in which the capital is used.

The Revenue has specifically confirmed that the fact that a settlor is the first named trustee and can therefore exercise voting rights attaching to shares which he has put into trust does not mean that he has reserved a benefit. The Revenue has also confirmed that an individual may include his or her spouse as a potential beneficiary without the trust being caught by the gift with reservation rules. However, this may have adverse income tax consequences in that any income arising to the trustees is taxed as if it were the settlor's income. Accordingly, settlements are usually drawn up so that the spouse cannot benefit during the settlor's lifetime, but can benefit as the settlor's widow. Where the trust deed is worded in this way, the adverse income tax consequences do not arise.

INDEX

Agricultural buildings allowances, 4.22
  introduction, 4.22.1
  provisions applying on ending of lease –
    balancing adjustments, 4.22.5
    qualifying provisions, 4.22.3
    writing-down allowances, 4.22.4
  relevant interest, 4.22.2
  supplementary provisions, 4.22.6
Annuity –
  payable out of profits, 3.4.1

Beneficial loans, 13.6
  beneficial loans used for a qualifying
    purpose, 13.6.2
  de minimis exemption, 13.6.3
  employee loans written off, 13.6.4
  type of loans which are caught, 13.6.1
Benefits-in-kind, 13.3
  accommodation, 13.3.4
  awards under suggestion schemes, 13.3.4
  computer equipment, 13.3.4
  counselling, 13.3.4
  cycles and cycle safety equipment, 13.3.4
  dispensations –
    benefits not taxable for any category of
      employees, 13.3.4
    benefits that may result in a tax charge
      for non-P11D employees, 13.3.2
    tax treatment of specific benefits
      received by non-P11D employee,
      13.3.3
  free use of assets, 13.3.5
  general rules, 13.3.1
  long service awards, 13.3.4
  luncheon vouchers, 13.3.4
  pool cars, 13.3.4
  relocation expenses, 13.3.4
  representative accommodation, 13.3.4
  retirement benefits, 13.3.4
  re-training, 13.3.4
  sandwich courses, 13.3.4
  sports facilities, 13.3.4
  staff canteen and dining facilities, 13.3.4

Benefits-in-kind – *contd*
  workplace nurseries and crèches,13.3.4
  works buses and public transport, 13.3.4
Business premises, 11.0 *et seq.*
  covenant strength, 11.4
    bank guarantees, 11.4.3
    break clause, 11.4.4
    personal guarantees, 11.4.1
    security deposit, 11.4.2
  expiry of the lease, 11.7
    alternative accommodation, 11.7.6
    application to court for new tenancy,
      11.7.5
    breaches of other obligations, 11.7.6
    compensation, 11.7.7
    demolition or reconstruction, 11.7.6
    disrepair, 11.7.6
    landlord's notice, 11.7.2
    opposition to renewal, 11.7.6
    owner occupation, 11.7.6
    request for a new tenancy, 11.7.4
    rent arrears, 11.7.6
    response to landlord's notice, 11.7.3
    right to renew, 11.7.1
    uneconomic subletting, 11.7.6
  privity and continuing liability, 11.3
  protected business tenancy, 11.2
    contracting out of LTA 1954, 11.2.5
    for the purposes of a business, 11.2.4
    occupied by the tenant, 11.2.3
    premises, 11.2.2
    tenancy, 11.2.1
  rent reviews, 11.5
    fixed increases, 11.5.4
    index-linked rents, 11.5.3
    open market, 11.5.1
    turnover rents, 11.5.2
  tenant's notice to determine lease, 11.6
    alienation, 11.6.6
    alterations, 11.6.4
    assignment, 11.6.6
    implied and express covenants, 11.6.1
    payment of rent, 11.6.2

Business premises – *contd*
  repair, 11.6.3
  subletting, 11.6.6
  user, 11.6.5
Business property –
  inheritance tax and, 1.18
Business tenancies, 1.8

Capital –
  employment of, 3.4.1
  revenue, or, 3.6
  withdrawal of, 3.4.1
Capital allowances –
  assets, application to part of, 4.1.13
  basic principles, 4.1
  chargeable period, 4.1.2
  claims for, 4.1.3
  connected persons, 4.1.16
  control, meaning of, 4.1.16
  double relief, exclusion of, 4.1.7
  expenditure –
    meaning of, 4.1.4
    timing of, 4.1.5
  general application, definitions of, 4.1.16
  partnerships, successions and transfers, 4.1.8
  relief, method of granting, 4.1.1
  sale of property and time of sale, 4.1.14
  sale treated as being for alternative amount, 4.1.12
  sales proceeds, apportionment of, 4.1.9
  tax agreements, 4.1.11
  transfers treated as sales, 4.1.15
  two or more persons, 4.1.10
  VAT liabilities and rebates, additional, 4.1.7
Capital gains tax, 1.3, 5.0 *et seq.*
  annual exemption, 5.1.1
  asset destroyed or becoming of negligible value, 5.4.8
  basic outline, 5.1
  business transactions, 6.0 *et seq.*
  loans to –
    companies, 6.1.2
    private businesses, 6.1
    unincorporated businesses, 6.1.1
  losses on unquoted shares –
    nature of relief, 6.2.3
    relief also available for subscriber's spouse, 6.2.2
    similar relief for companies, 6.2.4
    special relief for subscribers, 6.2.1
    payments under loan guarantees, 6.1.3
  chargeable assets, 5.3, 5.3.1
  exemptions, 5.3.2

Capital gains tax – *contd*
  compulsory acquisition, 5.4.5
  computation of capital gains, 5.5
    acquisition values, 5.5.4
    adjustment for amounts charged as income or deducted from income, 5.5.1
    amount to be brought in as disposal value, 5.5.1
    assets acquired via inheritance or from family trust, 5.5.4
    assets held at 31 March 1982, 5.5.3
    contingent consideration, 5.5.1
    contingent liabilities, 5.5.1
    costs allowable, 5.5.2
    indexation, 5.5.5
    market value, 5.5.1
  conditional sale, 5.4.2
  coverage of, 5.2
  disposals by companies with substantial shareholdings, 5.4.9
  gifts, 5.4.7
  hold-over relief: gifts of business property, 6.4
    available on certain gifts, 6.4.3
    business property, definition of, 6.4.1
    chargeable transfers for IHT purposes, 6.4.4
    clawback, 6.4.5
    practical aspects, 6.4.6
    relief on shares, relief on, 6.4.2
  limited liability partnerships, 6.6
  losses, 5.1.3
  option, exercise of an, 5.4.3
  outright sale, 5.4.1
  partners and capital gains, 6.5
    assets held by firm at 31 March 1982, 6.5.2
    limited liability partnerships, 6.6
    partner leaves after roll-over relief secured on purchase of new asset by firm, 6.5.5
    partnership gains divisible among partners, 6.5.3
    partnership's acquisition value, 6.5.1
    revaluations, 6.5.4
  property, exchange of, 5.4.4
  rates of, 5.1.4, 5.1.5
  retirement relief – general provisions, 6.7
    amount available, 6.7.1
    conditions to be satisfied for ten years if full relief to be available, 6.7.4
    date of disposal, 6.7.2
    full-time directors and employees, 6.9
    directors and managers, 6.9.1

Capital gains tax – *contd*
retirement relief – *contd*
full-time directors – *contd*
possible restriction of relief, 6.9.2
sale of premises, etc used by
company, 6.9.3
partners, 6.8.2
retirement through ill health, 6.7.3
sole traders, 6.8.1
trustees, for, 6.7.5
unincorporated traders, 6.8
roll-over relief, 6.3
assets owned by employee or
office-holder, 6.3.10
basic principles, 6.3.1
conditions that need to be satisfied,
6.3.2
freehold, acquisition of, 6.3.7
old assets not used for business
throughout ownership, 6.3.3
partners, for, 6.3.8
personal trading company, use by
individual's, 6.3.9
reinvestment in non-wasting assets,
6.3.5
replacement asset must be brought into
use, 6.3.6
treatment where replacement assets are
wasting assets, 6.3.4
share exchanges, exception for, 5.4.4
spouse transactions, no gain/loss, 5.1.2
sums payable as compensation or
proceeds under insurance policy, 5.4.6
taper relief, 5.6
anti-avoidance measures, 5.6.11
asset used at same time for different
purposes, 5.6.10
basic rule, 5.6.4
business or non-business assets, 5.6.4,
5.6.6
disposals, 5.6.5, 5.6.6
after 5 April 2002, 5.6.13
eligible beneficiaries, 5.6.8
foreign currency, 5.7.4
foreign property, 5.7.3
general application to, 5.6.3
granting of, 5.6.2
land and buildings, 5.7.1
non-qualifying beneficiaries, 5.6.9
overview, 5.6.1
qualifying companies, 5.6.7
shares to qualify as business assets,
conditions for, 5.6.5
special rules, 5.6.12
Cemeteries, 3.4.3

Cessation of a business, 17.20
post-cessation expenses, 17.20.3
redundancy costs, 17.20.2
VAT, 17.20.1
Companies, 14.8
control of, 1.19.2
life assurance, 14.8.1
pensions, 14.8.2
permanent health insurance, 14.8.3
taxation, 1.16
Company cars, 13.5
automatic cars made available to disabled
drivers, 13.5.1
bi-fuel cars, 13.5.1
car benefits, 13.5.1
car parking spaces, 13.5.6
cash alternative, 13.5.7
CO_2 emissions figure, cars with no, 13.5.1
diesel car supplement, 13.5.1
electrically propelled vehicle, 13.5.1
employee contributions, tax treatment of,
13.5.2
private petrol, 13.5.4
related costs, 13.5.5
returns, 13.5.3
Company law, 1.15
administrative documents to be filed at
Companies House, 18.11
annual return, 18.11.5
capital, 18.11.2
charges, mortgages and debentures,
18.11.7
directors or secretary, 18.11.3
formation, 18.11.1
notice of accounting reference date,
18.11.4
registered office, 18.11.6
resolutions, 18.11.8
auditors, 18.10
negligence of, 18.10.1
borrowing, restrictions on –
charges and secured debentures, 18.4.6
debentures, 18.4.4
failure to register a charge, 18.4.8
foreign companies, 18.4.9
mezzanine finance, 18.4.5
registration of charges, 18.4.7
definition of a, 18.1
directors, 18.5
appointment of, 18.5.1
disqualification, 18.5.5
duties, of, 18.5.7
duty of care, 18.5.11
liability of, 18.5.12
loans to, 18.5.10

Company law – *contd*
  directors – *contd*
    meetings, 18.5.3
    non-executive directors, 18.5.2
    removal of director, 18.5.6
    remuneration, of, 18.5.8
    resignation or retirement, 18.5.4
  dividends, 18.8
  incorporation, after, 18.4
    annual return, 18.4.2
    borrowing, 18.4.3
    continuing requirements, 18.4.1
  insurance, 18.5.13
  limited liability, 18.1.1
  meetings, 18.6
    general meetings, 18.6.1
    minutes, 18.6.5
    quorum, 18.6.3
    resolutions, 18.6.6
      filing of, 18.6.7
      written, 18.6.8
    shareholder, 18.6.9
    special notice, 18.6.2
    voting, 18.6.4
  members' rights and duties, 18.6.15
  memorandum of association, 18.2
    articles of association, 18.2.2
    formation requirements, 18.2.3
    name, 18.2.1
    passing off, 18.2.1
  property transactions, 18.5.9
  remedies available to shareholders, 18.6.16
  re-registration, 18.3
    plc to a private company, 18.3.2
    private company to plc, 18.3.1
    stamp duty, 18.3.4
    unlimited companies, 18.3.3
  share capital, 18.7
    bonus issue, 18.6.12
    class rights, 18.6.14
    CREST, 18.6.13
    debenture holder, 18.6.11
    exceptions, 18.7.7
    issued share capital, 18.7.1
    purchase of own shares, 18.7.5, 18.7.6
    redeemable shares, 18.7.4
    reductions of capital, 18.7.2
    types of, 18.6.10
  types of company, 18.1.2
  ultra vires, 18.9
Company proprietor, taxation of, 1.17
  Alternative Investment Market, 21.10.13
  buying a company, 21.1

Company proprietor, taxation of – *contd*
  Alternative Investment Market – *contd*
    checklist of tax points when buying a company, 21.1.3
    income tax relief for capital losses, 21.1.2
    relief for financing costs, 21.1.1
  anti-avoidance legislation, 21.14
    CGT anti-avoidance provisions, 21.14.2
    controlling shareholders, 21.14.3
    section 30 of TCGA 1992, 21.14.4
    share exchanges and take-overs, 21.14.5
    transactions in securities, 21.14.1
  assets, sale or purchase of, by the company, 21.8
    acquisition of property by shareholder, 21.8.4
    capital gains aspects, 21.8.6
    capital gains tax treatment of the director, 21.8.3
    company law aspects, 21.8.9
    purchase by a director, 21.8.1
    purchase by associate of a director, 21.8.2
    retirement relief, interaction with, 21.8.8
    sale at an undervalue, 21.8.7
    sales to the company, 21.8.5
  benefits-in-kind, 21.4
    director's family, 21.4.1
    participators, 21.4.2
  business finance, raising, 21.10
    approved investment funds, 21.10.11
    Enterprise Investment Scheme, 21.10.1
    five-year period, 21.10.9
    individual must not be previously 'connected with the company', 21.10.8
    individuals excluded from EIS relief, 21.10.7
    purchase of own shares, 21.10.10
    qualifying companies, 21.10.2
    qualifying subsidiaries, 21.10.5
    qualifying trades, 21.10.3
    redemption of shares, 21.10.10
    three-year period, 21.10.6
    venture capital trusts, 21.10.12
    wholesale and retail distribution trades, 21.10.4
  capital gains tax planning for longer term, 21.13
    assets owned privately but used by personal company, 21.13.4

Company proprietor, taxation of – *contd*
  capital gains tax planning – *contd*
    forward planning for retirement relief,
      21.13.3
    should investments be held by
      trustees?, 21.13.1
    special rules where settlor or spouse a
      beneficiary, 21.13.2
  checklist of tax considerations for group
    of companies, 21.2.6
  corporation tax planning, 21.2
    commercial considerations, 21.2.2
    companies controlled by associates,
      21.2.3
    disallowable expenditure, 21.2.4
    managing a group's tax affairs, 21.2.5
    maximising benefit of small companies
      rate, 21.2.1
  demergers, 21.12
    advance clearance, 21.12.3
    conditions which must be satisfied,
      21.12.2
    form of, 21.12.1
    informal, 21.12.4
  dividends, 21.5, 21.5.1
  loans by the company, 21.7
  loans to the company, 21.6
    consequences if the company fails,
      21.6.2
    qualifying loans to the company,
      21.6.1
  purchase of own shares, 21.11
    advance clearance procedure, 21.11.6
    benefit to the company's trade,
      21.11.5
    conditions for capital treatment to
      apply, 21.11.1
    definition of unquoted company,
      21.11.2
    ownership of shares for five years,
      21.11.3
    substantial reduction, 21.11.4
  remuneration, treatment of, for PAYE
    and NICs purposes, 21.3
    loans by the employer, 21.3.3
    NIC problem areas, 21.3.2
    receipts basis applies to
      shareholder/directors, 21.3.1
  sale of the company, 21.15
    consideration payable by instalments,
      21.15.4
    contingent liabilities, 21.15.5
    earn-outs, 21.15.6
    pre-sale dividends, 21.15.1
    qualifying corporate bonds, 21.15.7

Company proprietor, taxation of – *contd*
  sale of the company – *contd*
    taking loan notes or other paper from
      the acquirer, 21.15.3
    using CGT hold-over relief, 21.15.2
  self-administered pension schemes, 21.9
    investment in property used by the
      company, 21.9.4
    investment in shares in the company,
      21.9.3
    loans to the company (and associated
      companies), 21.9.2
    overall limit on borrowings by trustees,
      21.9.5
    prohibition on loans to members,
      21.9.1
Company taxation –
  accounting periods, 19.2.1
  corporation tax rates, 19.2.3
  payment of tax, 19.2.7
  profits, apportioning of, 19.2.2
  restriction where there is associated
    company, 19.2.6
  small companies rates and associated
    companies, 19.2.5
  starting rate, 19.2.4
  associated companies, 19.2.5, 19.2.6
  capital allowances, 19.1.3
  capital gains, 19.3
    computation of, 19.3.1
    roll-over relief, 19.3.2
  claims and elections, 19.12.1
  close and investment companies, 19.8
    benefits to participators, 19.8.3
    close companies, 19.8.1
    close investment-holding companies,
      19.8.6
    directors' defalcations, 19.8.4
    investment companies, 19.8.5
    loans to participators, 19.8.2
  company distributions, 19.5
  controlled foreign companies –
    acceptable distribution test, 19.10.5
    anti-avoidance legislation, 19.10
    CGT legislation on non-resident
      companies, 19.10.7
    definition of a CFC, 19.10.2
    exempt activity test, 19.10.4
    legislation on, 19.10.1
    motive test, 19.10.3
    public quotation test, 19.10.6
  corporation tax, liability for, 19.1,
    19.1.1
  double taxation relief on foreign income,
    19.9

Company taxation – *contd*
  double taxation relief – *contd*
    dividends from foreign companies,
      19.9.2
    main reliefs, 19.9.1
    unremittable income, 19.9.3
  Forex transactions, 19.11
    basic rules, 19.11.1
    deferral relief, 19.11.4
    financial instruments, 19.11.6
    local currency election, 19.11.3
    matching, 19.11.2
    tax planning for, 19.11.7
    transitional rules, 19.11.5
  groups of companies, 19.7
    capital gains and transfers within a
      group, 19.7.5
    company leaving a group after an
      intragroup transfer, 19.7.6
    group relationships, 19.7.1
    payment and interest, 19.7.4
    roll-over relief and groups of
      companies, 19.7.7
    transfers of assets between group
      companies, 19.7.3
    use of losses, 19.7.2
  interest and other charges, 19.1.4, 19.4
    annual charges, 19.4.2
    connected parties, 19.4.4
    income tax deduction at source, 19.4.3
    loan relationships, 19.4.1
  losses, 19.6
    arising in the accounting period, 19.1.6
    capital losses, 19.6.3
    charges paid in company's final
      accounting period, 19.6.5
    company ownership, changes in, 19.6.6
    different ways of claiming relief for
      losses, 19.6.2
    surplus charges on income, 19.6.4
  profits, computation of, 19.1.2
Compensation –
  employee, 1.10
  loss of office, 13.19.3
Connected persons, 1.19
  capital gains tax, 1.19.1
  corporation tax and, 1.19.1
  income tax and, 1.19.1
  inheritance tax and, 1.19.2
Consumer protection, 10.14
  cancellation rights, 10.14.1
  Consumer Guarantees Directive, 10.14.4
  discretionary provisions, 10.14.4
  enforcement, 10.14.6
  Enterprise Bill, 10.14.6

Consumer protection – *contd*
  general product safety: the criminal law,
    10.14.3
  OFT –
    approved code of practice, 10.14.6
    co-ordination role of, 10.14.5
    product liability: civil law, 10.14.2
    stop now orders, 10.14.5, 10.14.6
    super-complaints, 10.14.6
Contract law, 1.6, 9.0 *et seq.*
  acceptance, 9.2
    battle of the forms, 9.2.1–9.2.7
    certainty of terms, 9.2.6
    communication of, 9.2.2
    contract to make a contract, 9.2.5
    contractual intention, 9.2.7
    cross offers, 9.2.1
    method of, 9.2.3
    post, by, 9.2.4
  breach of contract, 9.9
    affirming the contract, 9.9.1
    anticipatory breach, 9.9.4
    both parties in breach, 9.9.3
    repudiation must be accepted, 9.9.2
  consideration, 9.3
    agreement not to sue, 9.3.2
    past, 9.3.1
    promising to perform existing
      obligations, 9.3.3
  damages, 9.12
  duress, 9.6.1
  exemption and exclusion clauses, 9.8
    burden of proof, 9.8.2
    consumer –
      dealing as a, 9.8.4
      guarantees, 9.8.4
    liability for negligence, 9.8.1
    reasonableness test, 9.8.4
    sale, supply and hire purchase, 9.8.4
    statutory control, 9.8.4
    third party and, 9.8.3
    Unfair Contract Terms Act 1977, 9.8.4
    Unfair Terms in Consumer Contracts
      Regs 1999, 9.8.4
  frustration, 9.10
    benefit acquired under the contract,
      9.10.4
    consequences of, 9.10.3
    delay, 9.10.1
    excluding the Sale of Goods Act,
      9.10.4
    exclusions from Sale of Goods Act,
      9.10.4
    sale of goods, 9.10.2
    severing part of the contract, 9.10.4

breach of contract – *contd*
  misrepresentation, 9.5
    constructive notice, 9.5.2
    damages for, 9.5.3
    fraudulent, 9.5.3
    innocent, 9.5.3
    negligent, 9.5.3
    non-disclosure, 9.5.1
    other matters, 9.5.4
  mistake, 9.4
    common mistake, 9.4.1
    mutual mistake, 9.4.2
    non est factum, 9.4.4
    unilateral mistake, 9.4.3
  offer, 9.1
    advertisements, 9.1.2
    invitation to treat, 9.1.1
    lapse of time, 9.1.5
    rejection and counter offers, 9.1.4
    termination of, 9.1.3
  privity of contract, 9.11
    Contracts (Rights of Third Parties) Act
      1999, 9.11.1
    defences etc available to promisor,
      9.11.4
    right of third party to enforce,
      9.11.2
    variation and rescission of contract,
      9.11.3
  undue influence, 9.6.2
  terms of contract, 9.7
    battle of the forms, 9.7.2
    collateral contracts, 9.7.6
    conditions and warranties, 9.7.3
    extrinsic evidence, 9.7.5
    implied terms, 9.7.7
    incorporation of terms, 9.7.1
    meaning and construction of term,
      9.7.4
    standard form of contract, 9.7.1
    warranties, 9.7.3
Contributions, 4.30
  allowances under certain rules, 4.30.3
  dredging allowances rules, 4.30.4
  exceptions to general rule, 4.30.2
  rules excluding, 4.30.1
Corporation taxes and CGT, 1.19.1
  associates, taxation of, 1.19.1
  companies, taxation of, 1.19.1
  control, taxation and, 1.19.1

Data subjects' rights, 12.25
Debts, 3.4.1
  proving irrecoverable after event treated
    as discontinuance, 3.4.3

Disbursements or expenses –
  domestic or private purposes, for, 3.4.1
  not wholly and exclusively laid out or
    expended, 3.4.1
Discrimination –
  disability, on grounds of, 12.21
    disability code, 12.21.6
    Disability Commission, 12.21.7
    disability, definition of, 12.21.1
    discrimination, types of, 12.21.2
    exemptions, 12.21.5
    reasonable adjustments, employer's
      duty to make, 12.21.3
    remedies, 12.21.4, 12.21.8
  sex and race, on grounds of, 12.20
    Commission for Racial Equality, role
      of, 12.20.6
    Equal Opportunities Commission, role
      of, 12.20.6
    genuine occupational qualification,
      12.20.3
    liability for discriminatory acts,
      12.20.4
    recruitment, 12.20.1
    remedies, 12.20.5
    types of discrimination, 12.20.2
Dismissal –
  grounds for, 12.10.6
  illegality, contravention of an enactment,
    12.10.9
  procedures, 12.10.7
  redundancy, 12.10.8
  remedies, 12.10.11
  settlement, 12.10.12
  tribunal awards, 12.10.11
Dredging allowances, 4.28
Dwelling houses let on assured tenancies,
  4.29

EEIGs, 16.10
Employment law, 1.9, 12.0 *et seq.*
  continuity of employment, 12.8
    periods where no contract of
      employment exists, 12.8.2
    statutory maternity pay (SMP),
      12.8.4
    weeks that count, 12.8.1
    weeks that do not count, but do not
      break continuity, 12.8.3
  contract of employment, 12.4
    terms of the contract, 12.4.1
  doctrine of restraint of trade, 12.5
    intellectual property rights, 12.5.3
    non-competition covenants, 12.5.1
    non-solicitation covenants, 12.5.2

Employment law – *contd*
employee, 12.3
   directors, 12.3.4
   part-time employees, 12.3.3
   seasonal employees, 12.3.2
   temporary employees, 12.3.1
EU law, impact of, 12.1
   legislation in the form of directives,
      12.1.2
   Treaty of Rome 1957, as amended,
      12.1.1
insolvency of an employer, rights on,
   12.11.7
termination of, 12.12
   accelerated receipt, 12.12.6
   interest, 12.12.7
   lawful methods of, 12.12.1
   mitigation, 12.12.5
   payment in lieu of notice, 12.12.8
   written reasons for dismissal, 12.12.2
   wrongful dismissal, 12.12.3, 12.12.4
worker's status
   contract of service and contract for
      services, distinguishing between,
      12.2.1
   control test, 12.2.1
   integration test, 12.2.1
   multiple test, 12.2.1
   mutuality of obligation, 12.2.1
   overview approach, 12.2.1
written particulars of employment, 12.6
   remedies for failure to provide written
      particulars, 12.6.3
   small employers' exemption, 12.6
   statement of terms and conditions of
      employment, changes to, 12.6.1
   unlawful terms, 12.6.2
wrongful dismissal claims: procedure,
   12.12.9
Enterprise management incentives, 13.18
   capital gains tax treatment, 13.18.7
   company reorganisations, 13.18.8
   eligible employees, 13.18.4
   general requirements, 13.18.2
   income tax treatment, 13.18.6
   introduction, 13.18.1
   qualifying companies, 13.18.3
   requirements as to terms of option etc,
      13.18.5
Entertaining, 3.4.2
Environmental taxes –
   aggregates levy (AL), 20.3
      accounting for AL, 20.3.5
      appeals, 20.3.9
      basic provisions, 20.3.1

Environmental taxes – *contd*
aggregates levy – *contd*
   evasion, misdeclaration and neglect,
      20.3.8
   exempt aggregates, 20.3.3
   information and evidence, 20.3.10
   meaning of aggregates, 20.3.2
   miscellaneous and supplementary
      matters, 20.3.11
   other matters regarding aggregates,
      20.3.4
   recovery and interest, 20.3.7
   registration, 20.3.6
climate change levy (CCL), 20.2
   accounting for CCL, 20.2.6
   appeals, 20.2.10
   basic provisions, 20.2.1
   deemed supplies, 20.2.4
   evasion, misdeclaration and neglect,
      20.2.9
   exempt supplies, 20.2.3
   information and evidence, 20.2.11
   miscellaneous and supplementary
      matters, 20.2.12
   recovery and interest, 20.2.8
   registration, 20.2.7
   taxable supplies, 20.2.2
   time of supply, 20.2.5
landfill tax (LFT), 20.1
   accounting for LFT, 20.1.7
   appeals, 20.1.8
   basic provisions, 20.1.1
   charge to LFT, 20.1.4
   disposal of material as waste, 20.1.2
   exemptions, 20.1.5
   information, powers, penalties,
      secondary liability etc, 20.1.9
   landfill sites, 20.1.3
   registration, 20.1.6
Equal pay, 12.22
   comparator, 12.22.4
   like work, 12.22.1
   material factor defence, 12.22.5
   pension schemes, 12.22.7
   remedies, 12.22.6
   work of equal value, 12.22.3
   work rated as equivalent, 12.22.2
Ex gratia payments, 13.19.2
Expenditure –
   business finance, costs of raising, 3.4.3
   car hire, 3.4.3
   cemeteries, 3.4.3
   charities, gifts in kind to, 3.4.3
   contaminated land, remediation of, 3.4.3
   counselling services for employees, 3.4.3

Expenditure – *contd*
educational establishments, gifts to,
3.4.3
employee share ownership trusts –
contributions to, 3.4.3
costs of establishing, 3.4.3
employees seconded to charities and
educational establishments, 3.4.3
entertaining, 3.4.2
Export Credits Guarantee Department,
payments to, 3.4.3
films, expenditure on, 3.4.3
football ground improvements, pools
payments for, 3.4.3
foreign trades, connected with, 3.4.3
gifts to customers, 3.4.2
illegal payments and fines, 3.4.2
loan relationships, 3.4.3
local enterprise agencies, contributions
to, 3.4.3
medical supplies and equipment, gifts of,
3.4.3
mineral exploration and access, 3.4.3
patent fees, etc and expenses, 3.4.3
payroll giving schemes: contributions to
agent's expenses, 3.4.3
rents payable for electric line, etc
wayleaves, 3.4.3
research and development (R&D), 3.4.3
research associations, universities, etc,
payments to, 3.4.3
restrictive undertakings, consideration for
certain, 3.4.3
schemes for rationalising industry,
3.4.3
security assets and services, 3.4.3
share option or profit-sharing schemes,
costs of establishing, 3.4.3
specifically allowed, 3.4.3
specifically disallowed, 3.4.2
statutory redundancy payments, 3.4.3
taxable lease premiums, 3.4.3
training and enterprise councils and local
enterprise companies, contributions to,
3.4.3
training courses for employees, 3.4.3
trustees of approved profit-sharing
schemes, payments to, 3.4.3
unremittable overseas income, relief for,
3.4.3
war risk premiums, 3.4.2
waste disposal –
preparation expenditure, 3.4.3
restoration payments, 3.4.3
Expense or charge?, 3.8

Flat conversion allowance, 4.23
balancing adjustments, 4.23.7
initial allowances, 4.23.5
introduction, 4.23.1
qualifying buildings and qualifying flats,
4.23.3
qualifying expenditure, 4.23.2
relevant interest in the flat, 4.23.4
supplementary provisions, 4.23.9
writing-down allowances, 4.23.6
writing off qualifying expenditure, 4.23.8

Gifts to customers, 3.4.2

Health and safety, 15.1
compulsory insurance, 15.16
cover, 15.16.2
employers' duties, 15.16.1
issue and display of certificate of
insurance, 15.16.3
penalties under the Act, 15.16.4
consultation with employees, 15.17
Control of Substances Hazardous To
Health (COSHH) Regs 1999, 15.13
assessment of health risks, 15.13.2
defence in proceedings for
contravention of Regulations,
15.13.9
definitions, 15.13.1
health surveillance, 15.13.7
information, instruction and training
etc, 15.13.8
maintenance, examination and test of
control measures etc, 15.13.5
monitoring exposure at the workplace,
15.13.6
prevention or control of exposure,
15.13.3
use of control measures etc, 15.13.4
current trends in health and safety
legislation, 15.3
Fire Precautions (Workplace) Regs 1997,
15.11
amendment to the Management of
Health and Safety at Work Regs
1992, 15.11.2
enforcement, 15.11.3
excepted workplaces, 15.11.5
Fire Precautions Act 1971, 15.11.4
principal requirements, 15.11.1
Health and Safety at Work etc Act 1974
(HSWA), 15.2
articles and substances for use at work,
15.2.3
breach of statutory duty, 15.5.4

Health and safety – *contd*
  Health and Safety at Work – *contd*
    criminal and civil liability, 15.5
      civil liability, 15.5.2
      criminal liability, 15.5.1
      negligence, 15.5.3
      vicarious liability, 15.5.5
    duty not to charge employees, 15.2.6
    duty not to interfere or misuse, 15.2.5
    enforcement procedures, 15.2.7
    general duties of employees at work,
      15.2.4
    general duties of employers to their
      employees, 15.2.1
    general duties other than to employees,
      15.2.2
    improvement notices, 15.2.7
    prohibition notices, 15.2.7
    prosecution and penalties, 15.2.7
  Health and Safety (Consultation with
    Employees) Regs 1996, 15.17.2
  Health and Safety (Display Screen
    Equipment) Regs 1992, 15.10
    employers' duties, 15.10.1
    risk analysis, 15.10.2
  Health and Safety (Information for
    Employees) Regs 1999, 15.14
    abolition of statutory requirements,
      15.14.4
    certificates of exemption, 15.14.2
    modification to the Regulations,
      15.14.3
    posters and leaflets, 15.14.1
  hierarchy of duties under health and
    safety law, 15.2.8
  Lifting Operations and Lifting Equipment
    Regs 1998, 15.12
  Management of Health and Safety at
    Work Regs 1999, 15.4
    risk assessment, 15.4.1
  Manual Handling Operations Regs 1992,
    15.9
    assessment, 15.9.3
    employees' duty, 15.9.2
    employers' duties, 15.9.1
  Personal Protective Equipment at Work
    Regs 1992, 15.8
    employees' duties, 15.8.3
    employers' duties, 15.8.2
    introduction, 15.8.1
  Provision and Use of Work Equipment
    Regs 1998, 15.7
    employers' duties, 15.7.2
    introduction, 15.7.1
    mobile work equipment, 15.7.4

Health and safety – *contd*
  Provision and Use – *contd*
    specific duties of employers, 15.7.3
    reporting injuries, diseases and dangerous
      occurrences, 15.15
    notifiable and reportable major
      injuries, 15.15.2
    principal requirements of RIDDOR,
      15.15.1
    reportable diseases, 15.15.4
    scheduled dangerous occurrences,
      15.15.3
  Safety Representatives and Safety
    Committees Regs 1977, 15.17.1
  Workplace (Health, Safety and Welfare)
    Regs 1992, 15.6
    duty to maintain the workplace, 15.6.2
    introduction, 15.6.1
    structural safety, 15.6.4
    welfare amenity provisions, 15.6.5
    working environment, 15.6.3
Health and safety at work, 1.12
Health insurance –
  permanent, 1.11

Illegal payments and fines, 3.4.2
Income tax, 2.0 *et seq.*
  associates, taxation of, 1.19.1
  companies, taxation of, 1.19.1
  control, taxation and, 1.19.1
  Individuals, taxation of, 1.19.1
  partnerships, taxation of, 1.19.1
  property profits or gains, 2.1, 2.2
  scope of, 1.1
  trustees, taxation of, 1.19.1
Industrial buildings allowance, 4.21
  balancing adjustments, 4.21.7
  commercial buildings (enterprise zones),
    4.21.2
  highway undertakings, 4.21.9, 4.21.10
  initial allowances, 4.21.5
  introduction, 4.21.1
  meaning of 'industrial buildings', 4.21.2
  qualifying expenditure, 4.21.4
  qualifying hotels and sports pavilions,
    4.21.2
  qualifying trade, buildings in use for,
    4.21.2
  relevant interest in the building, 4.21.3
  supplementary provisions, 4.21.2, 4.21.11
  writing-down allowances, 4.21.6
  writing off qualifying expenditure,
    4.21.8
Inheritance tax and business property,
  1.19.2

Inheritance tax – *contd*
  agricultural property, 22.9
    land occupied by the transferor, 22.9.1
    tenanted land, 22.9.2
  associated operations, 1.19.2
  business property, 22.8
    basic requirements, 22.1.8
    businesses that do not qualify, 22.8.3
    rates of business property relief, 22.8.2
    test normally applied on a
      'consolidated basis', 22.8.4
  charge arises, 22.2
  company, control of, 1.19.2
  computation of tax on lifetime transfers,
    22.10
  computation of tax payable on death,
    22.11
    debts which may be disallowed,
      22.11.3
    normal basis, 22.11.1
    replacement property, 22.11.5
    sales of land at a loss, 22.11.2
    treatment of gifts caught by seven-year
      rule, 22.11.4
  deeds of variation, 22.4.6
  exempt transfers, 22.5
    annual exemption, 22.5.4
    certain transfers to employee trusts,
      22.5.10
    gifts –
      charities, to, 22.5.6
      consideration of marriage, in, 22.5.5
      national purposes, for, 22.5.7
      political parties, to, 22.5.9
      public benefit, for, 22.5.8
      spouse, to, 22.5.1
    normal expenditure out of income,
      22.5.2
    small gifts, 22.5.3
  gifts which are not transfers of value,
    22.4
  handing on the family business/company
    without attracting IHT, 22.12
    assets owned by a partner but used by
      the firm, 22.12.5
    assets owned by shareholders,
      22.12.6
    avoiding buy/sell clauses, 22.12.4
    deeds of variation, 22.12.10
    double business property relief,
      22.12.9
    family trusts, 22.12.11
    general strategy, 22.12.1
    maximising business relief, 22.12.3
    pension arrangements, 22.12.2

Inheritance tax – *contd*
  handing on the family – *contd*
    property that cannot attract business
      property relief on widow's death,
      22.12.8
    tax-efficient Wills, 22.12.7
  interest-free loans, 22.4.4
  legacies, disclaimer of, 22.4.5
  maintenance of family, dependants etc,
    22.4.1
  persons subject to IHT, 22.1
  potentially exempt transfers, 22.6
    definition, 22.6.1
    taper relief, 22.6.2
  related property, 1.19.2
  reservation of benefit, 22.7
    ending of reservation of benefit, 22.7.3
    introduction, 22.7.1
    settlements and trusts, 22.7.4
    two specific exemptions, 22.7.2
  transfers of value, 22.3
    calculating, 22.3.3
    gratuitous intent, 22.3.2
    transfers which do not amount to gifts,
      22.3.1
  waivers of dividends, 22.4.2
  waivers of remuneration, 22.4.3
Inland Revenue, compliance and, 13.20
  Collector's audit division, 13.20.1
  role of Schedule E compliance units,
    13.20.2
Insolvency of employer, 12.23
  redundancy payments, 12.23.1
  remedy, 12.23.2
Insurance –
  contract of indemnity, 3.4.1
  health, 1.11
  keyman assurance, loss of profits, 14.6.1
  life assurance, 14.6.1
  redundancy payments, for, 14.6.1
  security for loans, 14.6.1
  sums recoverable under, 3.4.1
Intellectual property, 3.10
  allowances and charges, manner of
    making, 3.10.1
  capital sums, 3.10.1
  creative artists: relief for fluctuating
    profits, 3.10.1
  death, winding-up or partnership change,
    3.10.1
  earned income, treated as, 3.10.1
  know-how, 3.10.1
  patents, 3.10.1
  relief for expenses, 3.10.1
  royalties, taxation of, 3.10.3

Intellectual property – *contd*
sale of, receipts from, 3.10.1
spreading of royalties over several years,
3.10.1
Interest –
business expense, as, 3.4.1
paid to non-UK resident person at more
than reasonable commercial rate, 3.4.1

Know-how allowances, 4.26
allowances and charges, 4.26.3
introduction, 4.26.1
qualifying expenditure, 4.26.2

Life assurance, 1.11, 14.1, 14.2
advantages of qualifying policies, 14.2.4
gain on the happening of a chargeable
event, 14.2.6
qualifying and non-qualifying policies,
14.2.3
tax treatment of policies, 14.2.5
taxing gains on chargeable events, 14.2.7
traditional and unit-linked policies, 14.2.2
types of policy, 14.2.1
Limited company, operating as a –
possible disadvantages, 17.16
admitting future partners, 17.16.4
extra administration, 17.16.1
increased liability for NICs, 17.16.6
loss of privacy, 17.16.2
relief for losses, 17.16.3
tax savings may only be a deferment,
17.16.5
tax considerations, 17.15, 17.15.3, 17.17,
17.18.11
double charge for capital gains,
potential, 17.17.2
lower rate of tax on profits, 17.15.1
possible ways of deferring tax, 17.15.2
work in progress, 17.17.1
transferring a business to a company,
17.18
alternative way of incorporating a
business, 17.18.6
carry forward of past trading losses,
17.18.10
conditions that do not apply, 17.18.4
conditions which must be satisfied,
17.18.2
election to forego roll-over relief on
transfer of business, 17.18.5
income tax consequences, 17.18.7
limitations of s 162 relief, 17.8.3
nature of relief, 17.18.1
stamp duty on the transfer, 17.18.9

VAT consequences of the transfer,
17.18.8
Living accommodation, 13.7
holiday accommodation and foreign
properties, 13.7.4
introduction, 13.7.1
properties owned for more than six years,
13.7.2
reduction in assessable amount, 13.7.3
Loss, relief for, 17.6
anti-avoidance provisions, 17.6.9
capital allowances and loss claims, 17.6.4
carry forward relief against subsequent
assessments, 17.6.1
computation of loss under CY basis,
17.6.8
early years of a trade, 17.6.5
estimated average goes beyond actual
amount, 3.4.1
farming losses, 17.6.9
not connected with or arising out of trade,
3.4.1
relief against general income, 17.6.2
relief by aggregation, 17.6.3
relief for trading losses against capital
gains, 17.6.6
Schedule D Case V losses, 17.6.10
terminal loss relief, 17.6.7

Maternity rights, 12.13
ante-natal care, time off for, 12.13.1
health and safety, 12.13.10
interrelationship with sex discrimination
law, 12.13.11
maternity allowance, 12.13.7
maternity leave, 12.13.2, 12.13.4
notice requirements, 12.13.3
protection from dismissal, 12.13.8
right to return to work, 12.13.5, 12.13.9
simplified framework of maternity pay
and leave, 12.14.4
statutory maternity pay, 12.13.6
Medical reports, access to, 12.26
Mineral extraction allowances, 4.24
Minimum wage, 12.19
Miscellaneous benefits, 13.8
Christmas parties and other annual
functions, 13.8.6
club subscriptions, 13.8.4
council tax, 13.8.1
director's tax paid by employer, 13.8.10
discounted goods and services, 13.8.9
end of year returns, 13.9
in-house tax and financial advice, 13.8.5
legal fees, 13.8.7

Miscellaneous benefits – *contd*
  medical insurance, 13.8.2
  outplacement counselling, 13.8.8
  scholarships, 13.18.11
  telephone rental, 13.8.3

National insurance contributions (NICs),
  13.17
  annual payments, 17.11.2
  Class 1 contributions, 13.17.3
  Class 1A NICs, 13.17.4
  Class 1B NICs, 13.17.5
  Class 4 NICs, 17.11.1
  introduction, 13.17.1
  miscellaneous practical aspects, 17.11
  personal service companies etc, 13.17.2

Parental leave, 12.14
  adoptive leave, framework for, 12.14.4
  amount of, 12.14.1
  framework for, 12.14.4
  review of maternity and parental rights,
    12.14.4
  right to time off to deal with family
    emergencies, 12.14.3
  simplified framework of maternity pay
    and leave, 12.14.4
  workforce agreements and default
    provisions, 12.14.2
Partnership, 14.7
  agreement, 16.8
    existence of, 16.4
  change of partners, 16.8.6
  definition of, 16.1
  disputes, settlement of, 16.8.4
  dissolution and winding-up, 16.9
    appointment of receiver, 16.9.1
    assets valuation on dissolution, 16.9.2
    goodwill, 16.9.3
    insolvency, 16.9.5
    sharing profits after dissolution,
      16.9.4
  financial provisions, 16.8.5
  good faith, 16.81
  liability of partners, 16.7
    inter se, 16.7.2
    third parties, to, 16.7.1
  life assurance, 14.7.1
  limited liability partnerships, 17.12
    carry forward of unrelieved losses,
      17.12.4
    member's contribution to trade,
      17.12.3
    restriction on relief, 17.12.2
    treatment of, 17.12.1

Partnership – *contd*
  Limited Liability Partnership Act 2000,
    16.3
  limited partners, 17.12.5
  limited partnership, 16.2
  management and control, 16.8.2
  meetings, reaching decisions etc, 16.8.3
  partnership law, 1.13
  pensions, 14.7.2
  permanent health insurance, 14.7.3
  salaried partner, 16.5
  taxation of –
    assessment of firm's profits: special
      rules, 17.3
    assessment under CY basis, 17.3.1
    other partnership loans, 17.5.3
    property occupied rent free by
      partnership, 17.5.5
    purchase of plant or machinery, 17.5.4
    qualifying loans, 17.5
    recovery of capital, 17.5.1
    replacement capital, 17.5.2
    treatment of other income, 17.4
    third parties, and, 16.6
Patent allowances, 4.27
  allowances and charges, 4.27.3
  introduction, 4.27.1
  qualifying expenditure, 4.27.2
  supplementary provisions, 4.27.4
PAYE, 13.2
  accounting for, 13.2.10, 13.2.14
  agency workers, 13.2.11
  cash vouchers, 13.2.9
  credit tokens, 13.2.9
  employee of non-UK employer, 13.2.4
  employee non-resident, etc, 13.2.5
  introduction, 13.21
  mobile UK workforce, 13.2.6
  non-cash vouchers, 13.2.9
  payment by intermediary, 13.2.3
  payment for PAYE, meaning of, 13.2.2
  repayments, 13.2.12
  returns –
    end of year, 13.2.15
    expenses and benefits, 13.2.13
  share options, gains from, 13.2.8
  tradable assets, 13.2.7
Pensions, 1.11, 14.3, 14.6.2
  benefits, 14.3.4
  contracting-in and contracting-out, 14.3.3
  contributions, 14.3.4
  introduction, 14.3.1
  moving between different types of
    pension arrangement, 14.3.6
  occupational pension schemes, 14.3.4

Pensions – *contd*
  personal pensions and stakeholder
    pensions, 14.3.5
  retirement annuity contracts, 14.3.5
  state pension scheme, 14.3.2
  top-up occupational schemes, 14.3.4
Permanent health insurance, 14.4, 14.6.3
  introduction, 14.5
  sole traders, 14.6
Personal service companies, 13.10
  agency workers, 13.10.3
  application of the rules, 13.10.1
  deemed Schedule E payment, 13.10.2
  supplementary provisions, 13.10.3
Plant and machinery allowances –
  anti-avoidance provisions, 4.12.5, 4.19
  relevant transactions, 4.19.1
  availability of, 4.3
  available qualifying expenditure (AQE),
    4.7.4
  balancing allowances and balancing
    charges, 4.7.3
  computer software, 4.9
  definition of, 4.2
  disclosure of information between UK
    tax authorities, 4.6.11
  disposal events and disposal values,
    4.7.5
  expensive cars, 4.10
  final chargeable period, 4.7.6
  first year allowances, 4.7.1
  first-year qualifying expenditure, 4.6
    cars with low carbon dioxide
      emissions, 4.6.6
    energy-saving plant or machinery,
      4.6.5
    exclusions, 4.6.8
    gas re-fuelling station, 4.6.7
    general, 4.6.1
    ICT and small enterprises, 4.6.4
    Northern Ireland, 4.6.2
    small or medium-sized enterprises,
      expenditure incurred by, 4.6.3, 4.6.9
    time when expenditure is incurred,
      4.6.10
  fixtures, 4.16
    acquisition of ownership of fixture
      when another ceases to own it,
      4.16.5
    disposal values, 4.16.6
    election to fix apportionment, 4.16.7
    introduction, 4.16.1
    owners of fixtures, persons who are
      treated as, 4.16.2
    ownership of, cessation of, 4.16.4

Plant and machinery allowances – *contd*
  fixtures – *contd*
    restrictions on amount of qualifying
      expenditure, 4.16.3
    hire-purchase etc and plant or machinery
      provided by lessee, 4.8
    plant or machinery provided by lessee,
      4.8.2
    similar contracts, and, 4.8.1
  long-life assets, 4.12
    expenditure, 4.12.1
    expenditure excluded, 4.12.2
    rules applying to, 4.12.4
  mineral and oil industries, provisions
    affecting, 4.15
  miscellaneous, 4.20.1
  monetary limit, 4.12.3
  overseas leasing, 4.13
  partial depreciation subsidies, 4.18
  qualifying activities, 4.4
    asset provided or used only partly for,
      4.17
  qualifying expenditure, 4.5
    buildings, structures and land, 4.5.1
    demolition costs, 4.5.2
    exclusions, 4.5.5
    expenditure on thermal insulation,
      safety measures, etc, 4.5.3
    personal security, 4.5.4
    pooling of, 4.7.2
    writing-down and balancing
      allowances and balancing charges,
      4.7.3
  shares in, 4.20.2
  ships, 4.14
  short-life assets, 4.11
  supplementary provisions. 4.20
Post-cessation receipts and expenses,
  17.7
  expenses, 17.7.2
  receipts, 17.7.1
Premises –
  capital employed in improvement of,
    3.4.1
Profits –
  calculating taxable, 1.2
Property –
  profits and gains, taxation of, 2.1

Receipts, 3.5
  generally, 3.5.1
  items included as trading receipts, 3.5.2
  trading profits, excluded from, 3.5.3
Redundancy, 12.11
  checklist, 12.11.4

Redundancy – *contd*
  consultation and notification
    requirements, 12.11.3
  qualifying conditions, 12.11.1
  redundant employees, additional
    payments to, 3.4.3
  selection process, 12.11.2
  payments, on, 12.11.5, 12.11.6, 13.19.1
Renewals basis, 4.31
Rent –
  domestic offices, 3.4.1
  whole or part of dwelling house, 3.4.1
Repairs –
  alterations of implements, 3.4.1
  premises of, 3.4.1
  utensils or articles, 3.4.1
Research and development (R&D), 3.9
  allowances, 4.25
  allowances and charges, 4.25.3
  introduction, 4.25.1
  qualifying expenditure, 4.25.2
  supplementary provisions, 4.25.4
  allowances for capital expenditure, 3.9.2
  assets ceasing to belong to traders, 3.9.3
  meaning of, 3.9.1
  relief, entitlement to, 3.9.4
  subcontracted –
    extension of tax credit to all
      companies, 3.9.6
  relief, manner of giving effect to, 3.9.5
  vaccine research, tax relief for, 3.9.7
Restrictive covenants, payments for, 13.19.4
Revenue or capital?, 3.6
Royalties –
  similar payments, or, 3.4.1

Sale of goods, 1.7, 10.0 *et seq.*
  acceptance, 10.10.2
  breach of an implied term, 10.6
  buyer, remedies of the, 10.13
    defective quality, damages for, 10.13.3
    delay in delivery, damages for, 10.13.2
    non-delivery, damages for, 10.3.1
    other remedies, 10.13.4
    recovery of money paid to the seller,
      10.13.4
    rejection of goods, 10.13.4
    specific performance, 10.13.4
  Consumer Guarantees Directive, 10.13.5
  consumer protection, *See* Consumer
    protection
  contracts similar to contracts of sale, 10.8
  delivery, 10.10.1
  description, 10.2
  exclusion of implied terms, 10.5

Sale of goods – *contd*
  fitness for purpose, 10.3.1
  implied terms, 10.1
  non-owner, sales by a, 10.11
    exceptions to the rule, 10.11.1
  passing of property and risk, 10.9
    retention of title, 10.9.1
    risk, passing of, 10.9.2
    Romalpa clauses, 10.9.1
  sale by sample, 10.4
  satisfactory quality, 10.3.2
  seller, remedies for the, 10.12
  time, stipulations of, 10.7
Sale of the business, 17.19
  apportionment of sale consideration,
    17.19.1
  transfer of business to company
    immediately before sale, 17.19.2
Schedule D, 2.3–2.7
  annual profits or gains, 2.3
  Case III, 2.5
  Case VI, 2.7
  Cases I and II, 2.4
  Cases IV and V, 2.6
  profession or vocation, 2.4.1
  trade, 2.4.2
Schedule E, 2.8
Self-assessment –
  outline of, 17.8
    alternative to self-assessment, 17.8.3
    amended self-assessments, 17.8.11
    amendments after filing, 17.8.6
    background, 17.8.1
    correction of self-assessments, 17.8.8
    inclusion of estimates, 17.8.4
    liability to make self-assessments,
      17.8.2
    requirement to notify chargeability,
      17.8.9
    revenue enquiries and right to audit,
      17.8.7
    supporting documents, submission of,
      17.8.5
  payment of tax, 17.8.10
  penalties and interest charges, 17.9
    achieving finality, 17.10
    appeals, 17.9.2, 17.9.5
    incorrect returns, 17.9.7
    interest, 17.9.3
    penalties, 17.9.4
    partnerships, 17.9.6
    surcharges, 17.9.1
Self-employed individuals –
  accounting date, moving to later in tax
    year, 17.1.5

Self-employed individuals – *contd*
  accounting periods must not exceed 18
    months, 17.1.7
  business on CY basis, 17.2.1
  capital allowance basis periods, 17.2
  change in accounting date, effect of,
    17.1.4
  current year basis, 17.1
  no accounts for first 12 months, 17.1.2
  opening years, 17.1.1
  overlap relief, 17.1.3
  retirement, 17.1.6
Share option schemes, 13.14
  introduction, 13.14.1
  SAYE option schemes, 13.14.2
Shares –
  dependent subsidiary, in, 13.16.1
  employee share options, 13.12.4
  executive share option schemes, 13.15
    approval, conditions for, 13.15.1
    special employee shares, 13.16
  gifts of, 13.11
  non-approved share options, 13.12.2
    introduction, 13.12.1
    residence status of the employee,
      13.12.3
  profit-sharing schemes, 13.13
  returns by employer, 13.12.5
Stamp duty, 1.5, 8.0 *et seq.*
  avoiding or reducing duty, 8.3
  business assets, sale of, 8.3.6
  business to a company, transfer of a,
    8.3.7
  company reconstructions, 8.3.3
  depositary receipts, 8.3.2
  disadvantaged areas, exemption for,
    8.3.9
  goodwill, exemption for, 8.3.10
  individual pension plans, exemption
    for, 8.3.11
  intra-group transfers, 8.3.8
  loan stock, 8.3.4
  land and buildings, sale of, 8.3.5
  shares or other securities, sale of,
    8.3.1
  development of, 8.5
  documents liable to duty, 8.1
  exempt instruments, 8.1.1–8.1.3
    freehold land and buildings, sale of,
      8.1.2
    lease, sale and grant of, 8.1.3
    shares or other securities, sale of, 8.1.3
  leaflets, explanatory, 8.4
  surrendering leases –
    fixed stamp duty, 8.1.4

Stamp duty – *contd*
  surrendering leases – *contd*
    goodwill and other business assets, sale
      of, 8.1.8
    instruments relating to intellectual
      property, 8.1.10
    partnerships, 8.1.9
    sale of contract, sale of, 8.1.7
    sub-sales, 8.1.6
    VAT and, 8.1.4
  sanctions where duty not paid, 8.2
    interest and penalties, 8.2.1
    late payment, 8.2.1
Statutory payments to employees, 12.16
  guarantee payments, 12.16.2
  medical suspension payment, 12.16.1
Statutory Sick Pay (SSP), 12.15
  amount payable, 12.15.3
  period of payment, 12.15.1
  qualifications for, 12.15.1

Tax and employee compensation –
  amounts deducted in arriving at pay,
    13.1.2
  assessment of employee earnings, 13.1.2
  Schedule E, 13.1
    scope of, 13.1.1
Termination payments, 13.19
Trading profits, computing
  accounting practice, 3.1.2
  anticipated losses, 3.2.5
  change of basis –
    adjustment on, 3.3.1, 3.3.2
    general rules, 3.3.3
    special rules, 3.3.4
    supplementary provisions, 3.3.5
  expenditure –
    general rules, 3.4.1
  expenses, period in which included, 3.2.4
  ownership of goods –
    delivery and passing of, 3.2.6
    pre-trading expenditure, 3.2.7
  receipt –
    period in which assessable, 3.2.2
    timing, 3.2.2
  taxable profits, arriving at, 3.1
Transfer of Undertakings (Protection of
  Employment) Regs 1981 (TUPE), 12.24
  application, 12.24.1
  avoiding the Regulations, 12.24.7
  collective agreements and trade union
    recognition, 12.24.8
  immediately before the transfer, 12.24.3
  provision of information and consultation
    with trade unions, 12.24.9

Transfer of Undertakings – *contd*
redundancy payments, 12.24.6
references, 12.24.10
transfer of employment, 12.24.2
unfair dismissals and business transfers,
12.24.4
what amounts to an ETO reason?, 12.24.5
Transfer pricing, 3.7
Travelling, subsistence and entertaining,
13.4
employees working overseas: family
visits, 13.4.5
entertaining expenses and round-sum
allowances, 13.4.6
general rules, 13.4.1
overseas travelling expenses, 13.4.3
private use of company vans, 13.4.7
spouse's travelling and subsistence
expenses, 13.4.4
subsistence, 13.4.2
TUPE, 12.24

Unfair dismissal, 12.10
assertion of statutory rights, 12.10.5
automatically unfair, 12.10.5
basis of a claim, 12.10.1
constructive dismissal, 12.10.1
dismissal by the employer, 12.10.1
expiry of a fixed term contract, 12.10.1
fairness: has the employer acted
reasonably?, 12.10.4
health and safety related dismissals,
12.10.5
maternity related dismissals, 12.10.5
preconditions, 12.10.1
qualifying period, 12.10.2
reasons for dismissal, 12.10.3
redundancy, 12.10.5
spent convictions, 12.10.5
Sunday working, 12.10.5
termination by the employer, 12.10.1
trade union related dismissals, 12.10.5
transfer of undertaking related dismissals,
12.10.5
whistleblowing, 12.10.5
Unincorporated business, operating as an –
becoming a partner, 17.13
bringing in a partner, 17.13
admitting a partner under CY basis
rules, 17.13.5
capital gains tax considerations,
17.13.3
interest on capital, 17.13.2
keeping certain property assets outside
the firm, 17.13.4

Unincorporated business – *contd*
bringing in a partner – *contd*
relief for loans where new partner
borrows to finance his capital,
17.13.1
buying out a partner, 17.14
annuity arrangements, 17.14.3
borrowing by partners to fund the
buyout, 17.14.5
capital gains tax implications, 17.14.6
change in status to salaried partner,
17.14.1
consultancy arrangement, 17.14.2
demergers, 17.14.8
payment of a capital sum, 17.14.4
splitting the practice, 17.14.7
taxation of, 1.14

Value added tax (VAT), 1.4
accounting for VAT –
business entertainment, 7.14.5
output VAT, ????
motor cars, 7.14.4
partial exemption, 7.14.6
tax invoices, 7.14.2
VAT recovery, 7.14.3
acquisition of goods from member states,
7.6
Act of 1994, 7.2.1
application of, 7.12
agents etc, 7.12.6
annual accounting, 7.16.4
appeals, 7.19
bad debts, 7.11.5
basic principles, 7.3
buildings and land, 7.12.11
co-owners, etc of, 7.12.12
business, 7.5
capital goods, 7.11.3
cash accounting, 7.16.3
change of rate etc –
adjustments on, 7.13.2
supplies spanning, 7.13.1
Crown, application to, 7.12.1
customs notices and leaflets, 7.2.4
departmental reviews, 7.19.2
EC Directives, 7.2.5
enforcement procedures, 7.17
exempt supplies, 7.4.3
export of goods outside EU, 7.15.2
farmers etc, 7.12.15
flat-rate scheme, 7.10.4
fraud, 7.18.1, 7.18.2
fuel for private use, 7.12.17
gaming machines, 7.9.4

Value added tax – *contd*
gold, supplies of, 7.12.6
goods imported for private purposes,
  7.10.5
goods subject to a fiscal warehouse
  regime, 7.8
groups of companies, 7.12.3
imports, 7.15
  goods from outside the member states,
    7.7, 7.15.1
  overseas businesses etc, 7.11.7
input tax, 7.10.1
  credit for, 7.10.2
  disallowance of, 7.10.3
interest, 7.17.9
introduction, 7.1
late registration, 7.17.3
late returns, 7.17.4
legal authorities, 7.2
local authorities, 7.12.2
margin schemes, 7.12.10
misdeclaration penalty, 7.17.5
output tax, 7.10.1
partnerships, 7.12.4
payment of –
  accounting periods, by reference to,
    7.10.2
  on account, 7.10.6
  taxable persons, by, 7.10
penalties, 7.17.2, 7.17.10
personal representatives etc, 7.12.5
place of supply, 7.4.5
place where supplier or recipient of
  services belongs, 7.4.7
reasonable excuse, 7.17.6
reduced rate, 7.4.3
refunds of, 7.11.1
  constructing certain buildings, 7.11.4
  museums and galleries, to, 7.11.2
registration, 7.4.2
reliefs –
  acquisition if importation would attract
    relief, 7.11.6
  exemptions and repayments, 7.11
representatives, 7.12.7
retail schemes, 7.16.1
reverse charge on supplies received from
  abroad, 7.4.6
second-hand schemes, 7.16.2
self-billing, 7.10.7
special schemes, 7.16

Value added tax – *contd*
supplies of goods or services in the UK,
  7.4.3
statutory instruments, 7.2.2
supplementary provisions, 7.13
tax which would have been lost, 7.17.8
taxable persons, 7.4.1
terminal markets, 7.12.9
time of supply, 7.4.4
tour operators, 7.12.14
trading stamp schemes, 7.12.13
transactions within the single market,
  7.15.3
transfers of going concerns, 7.12.8
transport, new means of, 7.13.3
treasury orders, 7.2.3
tribunals, 7.19.1
unincorporated bodies, 7.12.5
value –
  acquisitions from other member states,
    7.9.2
  determination of, 7.9
  imported goods, 7.9.3
  supply of goods and services, 7.9.1
visits by officers, 7.17.1
voluntary disclosure, 7.17.7
zero-rated supplies, 7.4.3

Wages and payment, 12.18
  deductions from wages, 12.18.1
  itemised pay statements, 12.17
  retail workers, 12.18.2
  unlawful deduction, remedy for, 12.18.3
War risk premiums, 3.4.2
Waste disposal –
  preparation expenditure, 3.4.3
  restoration payments, 3.4.3
Work permits, 12.7.2
  applying for, 12.7.3
  immigration matters, 12.7
  introduction, 12.7.1
Working time, 12.9
  daily rest periods, 12.9.3
  exclusions, 12.9.8
  night work, 12.9.2
  paid annual leave, 12.9.6
  qualifications, 12.9.7
  remedies, 12.9.9
  rest breaks, 12.9.5
  weekly limits, 12.9.1
  weekly rest periods, 12.9.4